Homosexuality: An Annotated Bibliography

Homosexuality

AN ANNOTATED BIBLIOGRAPHY

EDITED BY **Martin S. Weinberg**

AND **Alan P. Bell**

of the Institute for Sex Research, Inc.
Founded by Alfred C. Kinsey
Indiana University, Bloomington, Indiana

1817

HARPER & ROW, PUBLISHERS
NEW YORK, EVANSTON
SAN FRANCISCO
LONDON

FIRST EDITION

STANDARD BOOK NUMBER: 06–014541–2

LIBRARY OF CONGRESS CATALOG CARD NUMBER: 70–160653

Contents

Acknowledgments

Although it was the editors who initiated the work which led to the present volume, their efforts were limited to administration and supervision, to the classification of various materials, and to the checking and editing of work which was done originally by many other staff members at the Institute. Almost all of the abstracting was done by the following persons, most of whom were graduate students in the social sciences at Indiana University: Susanna Barrows, Mary Ann Clark, Kim Johnson, Kenneth Bullmer, Charles Logan, Helen Matthews, David Rumple, Mark Sulcov, and Daniel Weinberg. In addition, Sue Miller and Jeffrey Rueble, undergraduates at the University, were extraordinarily dedicated to their work as abstractors and assumed much of the responsibility for the technical preparation of the material for publication. The typing and cross-checking were done, in large part, by Lia Barnes and Elizabeth Ketchen. Colin Williams, at the time a research assistant to the senior editor, directed the work of the abstractors during the first stage of the project. Helen Hofer, a graduate student in library science, helped with the search for the various materials as well as with the final details of the work prior to its submission to the publisher. A special word of thanks is due Rebecca Dixon, Head Librarian, and Mona Anderson, Assistant Librarian, at the Institute. In addition to their regular duties, they spent considerable time and effort in connection with the project especially during its initial stages. Naomi Lawlis and Gail Mathews, staff members of the Inter-Library Loan Department of the Indiana University Library were also helpful in locating materials which the Institute's own library did not possess. Finally, there are two persons to whom the editors are in special debt: Simone Robbins and Jan Shipps. Mrs. Robbins, a specialist in bibliographic matters, was employed during the second year of the project, and it was through her efforts that the work was made to conform to the most stringent of bibliographic standards. She also wrote many of the more difficult abstracts and helped to edit those which others had done. Without her efforts and expertise, the present volume would probably not have been possible. Dr. Shipps, in her role as Project Coordinator, directed the work of the above-named individuals. She herself participated in all of the activities which have already been described in connection with other personnel and was extraordinarily helpful in attending to the many details which inevitably accompany the successful conclusion of a project as vast as this. She worked closely with the editors and was the chief means of communication between them and the other staff members. Because of her willingness to participate in the project in ways which went far beyond the call of duty and because of the quality of work which she demanded of herself and others, it was possible for the editors to fulfill their other research responsibilities during the time that the present work was undertaken.

Preface

In an application made to the National Institute of Mental Health (NIMH) in the summer of 1967 for a research grant to study homosexuality, the Institute for Sex Research proposed that, among other things, "every effort be made to summarize what has been done by ourselves and others with regard to research into homosexuality." It was anticipated that this would involve an extensive examination of the literature and communication with others regarding their conceptualizations, methodologies, and findings. It was pointed out that the Institute's own library, unexcelled in its possession of most of the world's literature on homosexuality, would be of great help in this regard and that, in addition, unpublished dissertations or theses would be sought and studied. In a methodological appendix which accompanied the original proposal the following statements were made:

> During the first year a review of research in homosexuality will be made. Our library contains virtually everything that has been published on the subject of homosexuality, and author cards will be checked during the course of the review. . . . In this way, a sense of the parameters of inquiry will be gained; the kinds of questions which have been asked as well as their usefulness will be known; and the extent to which relationships between homosexuality and other variables have been established or not will be assessed. . . . Further, it is believed that the usual review of research which accompanies the proposals for new research is not sufficient for the task which is presently envisioned. Certainly, given the fact that more and more persons are becoming engaged in homosexual research, the time has come for an attempt to coordinate research activities in this area with a view towards making possible a direct comparison of findings.

The present volume, begun in January, 1969, and made possible through the support given by the National Institute of Mental Health to the Institute for Sex Research for a three-year study of homosexuality (NIMH PHS MH 15527–01), reflects the above intentions. It was published for use by other social scientists with interests in this particular aspect of human sexuality and with other persons in mind as well: physicians, lawyers, clergymen, social workers, teachers, those engaged in various kinds of counseling, legislators, and laymen. We believe that the thoughts and findings of investigators should be made available to persons whose perceptions of a given phenomenon influence their decisions, feelings, and behaviors with regard to it. This, we feel, is especially true with regard to the phenomenon of homosexuality. Despite the fact that millions of Americans and others all over the world have sexual interests and behavioral repertoires which are predominantly, if not exclusively, homosexual, few persons have attempted to come to terms with homosexuality on anything like a rational basis. Somehow it must be made evident to the population at large that there is much that we do not know about homosexuality and that homosexuality must be considered from many different vantage points if more is ever to be learned. It is to this end that the present volume has been published.

In the aforementioned proposal which the Institute for Sex Research made to NIMH in late 1967, the following statement was made:

There is a very large literature on homosexuality, much of which is useless or, even worse, misleading. The subject lends itself to prurient exploitation and to ardent crusading, most of which has been conducted in an atmosphere of biased judgment and misconception. Prior to World War II much of the thinking about homosexuality was confused and remained unverified: such culturally determined traits as masculinity and femininity were thought to be related to psychosexual identity; the concept of genetic intersexes and hermaphroditism confused the issue further; those who identified homosexuality with neuropathic weakness and "tainted" heredity were answered by those who made reference to the golden age of Greece and who offered lists of famous homosexual men. Only a very few publications, based upon relatively objective studies involving a relatively large number of cases, merit attention. Included among these would be the works of Havelock Ellis, Magnus Hirschfeld, Wilhelm Steckel, and the *Jahrbuch für sexuelle Zurschenstufen*—a journal devoted to homosexuality. Other writings were of the "cases I have known" variety—a type of case history compendium popular in Europe and reflected in George Henry's work in the United States.

Since World War II there has been a veritable flood of print concerning homosexuality. The bulk of this consists of bad novels and dubious biographies, although a few insightful and useful exceptions exist. Fortunately, there has also been a marked increase in scientific writings of rather high quality. This is particularly true in the United States; in Europe the clinical emphasis and methodology still predominate, although more recent books by such persons as Freund, Giese, and Schofield indicate that important changes are taking place.

In the United States considerable progress is being made by those of various scientific disciplines. John Money has made a most important contribution to an understanding of the relationship of genetic endowment to homosexuality; the determinism of Kallman has been largely superseded by the concept of morphology as predisposing but not determining one's sexual status. Studies of gender role—how one learns to become a man or woman—are being made by Stoller, Sears, Hampson, and Money. The phenomena of transvestism and transsexualism, so long erroneously regarded as synonymous with homosexuality, are receiving special attention. A newer generation of American anthropologists are beginning to consider homosexuality as a subject worthy of study and not simply as an esoteric footnote; this development is best illustrated by Davenport. Carefully controlled animal experimentation is explicating the phylogenetic bases of homosexual behavior, and the pioneering work of Beach and Young is being carried on by their students.

In the realm of psychiatry and psychology new issues and methodologies are being perceived and used—evident in the publications of Marmor and Hooker—and Bieber has attempted to test empirically hypotheses derived from the psychoanalytic model. Psychometric tests such as the Rorschach and MMPI have been and are being evaluated. Physiological responses to visual stimuli are being tested as diagnostic tools.

Finally, homosexuality has been studied from a sociological perspective. This kind of regard is offered in the work of persons such as Hooker, Reiss, Cory, Achilles, and Leznoff and Westley.

Despite this increasingly encouraging picture of the application of many disciplines to the phenomenon of homosexuality, there are still too few attempts to conjoin the psychological with the sociological in studying the individual homosexual in his social matrix. It is this lacuna that the proposed study hopes to fill in part.

There is little about the books and articles that have been reviewed and annotated in connection with the present bibliography which would lead one to substantially alter the above statement. The uneven quality of the 1,265 items which have been included will be apparent to any reasonably well-informed reader. Although attempts were made to exclude certain kinds of considerations given to homosexuality (see below), what remains still indicates that discussions of homosexuality have consisted primarily of speculations prompted by theoretical models or statements whose constructs have not been tested in any systematic manner. The reader will be introduced to the wide range of emphases and to as many disagreements about how a homosexual orientation develops and is maintained. Some authors are inclined to view a person's genetic endowment as the chief predisposing factor giving rise to homosexuality. Others emphasize the parental relationship—with different assessments of that relationship—as the most crucial variable in the consideration of homosexual development. Studies designed to test these assumptions have been few, while those which have been conducted have usually included small, biased samples as well as measurements which have been subjectively derived. Little attention has been given to the wide range of homosexual orientation and adjustment; most have viewed homosexuality-heterosexuality as a simple dichotomy, while most of their subjects have been those who eschew their homosexual orientation and whose functioning in other areas of their lives has been marginal. Usually there has been no attempt to determine the relationship of etiological factors to subsequent behavior and adjustment. In addition, the focus of these researchers and commentators all too often has precluded any reference to those processes—both sociological and psychological—

which maintain the homosexual's career. The homosexual is most commonly viewed as an inheritor of certain dispositions which were crystallized in the past and which account inevitably for all of his future behavior. He is usually not viewed in his relationship with others whose attitudes and behaviors toward him are crucial determinants of his own. His present concept of himself as this affects his perception of his environment, his view of the future, and a consideration of his behaviors as goal-directed is generally disregarded by those who have sought to understand this phenomenon.

In addition to the narrow emphasis upon factors thought to be relevant in a consideration of homosexuality, opportunities for research which includes different sex and racial memberships in its sample population have been few. Studies have been limited to those of male *or* female homosexuals, white *or* nonwhite homosexuals. No empirical study has attempted to investigate systematically differences in the developmental histories, in the life styles and adjustments, in the sexual attitudes and behaviors, and in the wide range of self- and other-experiencing, which may prove to be functions of such matters as age, sex, education, and race, which transcend whatever important features exist in the homosexual community.

While research pertaining to homosexuality has been conducted by persons who represent a variety of disciplines—those of psychology, sociology, psychiatry, physiology, anthropology—a most apparent characteristic of that research has been its lack of coordination. Individuals with differing conceptualizations and methodologies and unaware of each other's aims or very presence have been found conducting research in the same locale and often using at least a part of the same subject population. It could be maintained that this tendency to work apart from others has resulted in an incredible waste of time, talent, and human resources within the research enterprise. Isolated findings remain unrelated. Important areas of inquiry remain unacknowledged. The fund of knowledge and insight which might serve as a foundation for new and important advances in research is not increased. Differences between the findings of various researchers which may stem from different instrumentation and subject populations remain uninvestigated. And the net effect—that little can be stated with regard to homosexuality which is empirically based, that only a very little of any consequence has been added to the fund of such knowledge—is ubiquitous.

Not unrelated to the above observation is the fact that most researchers are loath to replicate their findings. While limitations of time and personnel, together with financial resources, may account for this failure, this fact remains regrettable. Conclusions are often stated which, given the unreliability of instrumentation and the methods of sample selection, are unwarranted. In addition, these conclusions—uncertainly derived and nowhere replicated—often determine the nature and direction of further inquiry whose parameters of investigation may involve no more than the compounding of error. Scientific inquiry remains such in name only if it is not accompanied by opportunities to measure its phenomena in different times and circumstances.

In reviewing the thinking and research which has been annotated in the present bibliography, the reader is urged to develop a skeptical attitude, to jump to no conclusions on the basis of one book or article, and at the same time to maintain an objectivity which will allow him to consider seriously others' views and findings, especially those with which he may find himself in disagreement. He should consider the ways in which the samples were selected and the nature of the samples that were studied, how the data were collected and analyzed, the basis upon which the author's conclusions were made, and the reliability and validity of the measures that were used. The reader must then ask himself if other conclusions would have been reached or other findings reported if different samples had been used or if other research strategies had been employed. The annotations which are provided were done by a variety of people, are not always of the same style, and do not possess the same degree of comprehensiveness. Thus, the reader will find that he is not always able to review the material as critically as he would like. In this regard, whenever a book or article covered a large number of aspects pertaining to homosexuality, those having to do with etiology and adaptation were especially noted in the annotation, and only passing references were made to the other contents of the work. Given the degree of incompleteness inevitably found in any annotation, the reader is asked to reserve his final judgments about an author's work until he has had an opportunity to review that work in greater detail than the present volume provides.

Bloomington, Indiana M.S.W.
January, 1971 A.P.B.

Homosexuality: An Annotated Bibliography

Introduction

Scope

The present bibliography contains 1,265 items. These include books and articles written with regard to homosexuality and published in the English language (some are translations from foreign journals) during the years 1940–1968. Although many fields are represented in the material which has been chosen for annotation, special emphasis has been given to the fields of psychology, psychiatry, and sociology.

Certain areas have been excluded entirely. These include belles-lettres (i.e., biography, autobiography, literary works) and all popular magazines (excepting *Sexology*) and newspaper articles. However, three bibliographies have been included as a guide to the reader who may be interested in pursuing the subject of homosexuality as it is reflected or portrayed in the field of belles-lettres or imaginative writing: (1) Gene Damon, and Lee Stuart, eds. *The Lesbian in Literature: A Bibliography.* San Francisco: Daughters of Bilitis, 1967, 79 pp., (2) Jeannette Howard Foster. *Sex Variant Women in Literature: A Historical and Quantitative Survey.* New York: Vantage Press, 1956, 412 pp., (3) Noel J. Garde. *The Homosexual in Literature: A Chronological Bibliography circa 700 B.C.–1958.* New York: Village Press, 1959, 32 pp.

Other areas received only a limited coverage. For example, in the area of *law* and *criminology,* no attempt was made to determine the variety of legal sanctions imposed by each state with regard to homosexual practices. Items related to the legal aspects of homosexuality were included only if they had been indexed in the services that were searched (see below). No attempts were made to search the legal indexing services, although representative items in this area do appear. There is a proliferation of works in the areas of *religion, social work,* and *counseling,* but since most have been presented in a popularized fashion, only the most significant items have been included. For every article that has been included from these areas, as many as two or three were excluded. Material involving *medical cases* associated with homosexuality was included only if it was presented chiefly

1

in terms of homosexuality. Because of their ephemeral nature, *federal government employment directives* were usually excluded, even though they may have contained references to homosexuality. On the same basis, only major items which appeared in connection with the controversies generated by the work of Kinsey and his associates will be found in the present bibliography. Most were considered to be of a too general nature, even though many of those who wrote in reaction to this work addressed themselves, at least in part, to Kinsey et al.'s consideration of homosexuality. In the area of *sexual offenses, sexual deviations,* and *sexual perversions,* only those items were included which contained significant material pertaining to homosexuality. Thus, a great deal of material having to do with pedophilia, transvestism, and exhibitionism has been excluded from the present volume. The same is true of the growing amount of literature related to *gender identity.* Most of the books and articles appearing in this area emphasize various aspects of gender role development and make only short, passing references to homosexuality. For this reason, and although there are many who suppose that gender issues are involved in the development of a homosexual orientation, much of the important work which is being done in this area will not be found among the items which appear in this more specialized bibliography. With rare exceptions, most of the material contained in various *homophile publications* (such as *Mattachine Midwest,* the *Ladder,* and *Vector*) has been excluded. Only certain items which have been widely cited in the literature were judged to be of sufficient importance with respect to the purposes of the present work. Most were considered the equivalent of those aforementioned articles appearing in popular magazines (regardless of the level of their discourse) and were omitted in accordance with the same criteria of inclusion.

Finally, general works on human sexuality which may have contained a chapter or section on homosexuality, for the most part, have been omitted since, while there are some exceptions, they tend to be too general, repetitious, and superficial for the purposes of this particular bibliography.

The Search

During the first stage of the present work, a search was made of 112 standard journals from a list compiled from Ulrich's *Guide to Periodicals.* These journals covered such areas as anthropology, criminology, the law, psychology, and sociology. This was followed by a thorough and systematic search of the following services (1940–1968), according to the chronological succession in the titles of these works and with reference to the headings indicated:

1. *Cumulated Index Medicus*
   V.1 (1960)—V.10 (1960)
      Homosexuality
      Sex Deviation
2. *Cumulative Book Index*
   1940–1960
      Sexual Perversion
   1960–1970
      Homosexuality
      Lesbianism
      Sexual Perversion
3. *Current List of Medical Literature*
   V.31 (1957)—V.36 (1959)
      Homosexuality
      Sexual Deviation
4. *Excerpta Medica*
   Section 8, Neurology and Psychiatry
   V.10 (1957)—V.18 (1965)
      Homosexuality
   Section 8B, Psychiatry
   V.19 (1966)—V.22 (1969)
      Homosexuality
      Sexual Deviation
5. *U.S. Library of Congress Catalog.* Books: Subjects
   1950–1954
      Homosexuality
      Lesbianism
      Sexual Perversion
   1955–1959
      Homosexuality
      Bisexuality
      Lesbianism
      Sexual Perversion
      Sodomy
   1960–1964
      Homosexuality
      Lesbianism
      Sexual Perversion
      Sodomy
   1967
      Homosexuality
      Lesbianism

      Sexual Perversion
      Sodomy
    1968
      Homosexuality
      Lesbianism
      Sexual Perversion
6. *Psychological Abstracts*
      V.14 (1940)—V.43 (1969)
      Homosexuality
7. *Quarterly Cumulative Index Medicus*
      V.27 (1940)—V.60 (1956)
      Sex Perversion
8. *Sociological Abstracts*
      V.1 (1953)—V.17 (1969)
      Homosexual
      Homosexuality
      Sex Deviation
9. *Subject Guide to Books in Print 1968*
      Homosexuality
      Lesbianism
      Sexual Perversion
      Sodomy

At the conclusion of this primary search, cross-checks were made of hundreds of reprints contained in the vertical files located in the Institute for Sex Research library, of the shelf list (No. 532: the number assigned to any work pertaining to homosexuality) in the same library, of the subject headings found under "Homosexuality" in the Institute for Sex Research card catalog, of the pamphlet boxes which contain the classification numbers pertaining to homosexuality in the Institute's library, and of the subject headings "Homosexuality" and "Lesbianism" in the Indiana University card catalog.

    Cross-checks were also made of others' bibliographies (those of *Vector* and William J. Parker, in particular), of bibliographies found in several of the major works (such as those of D. J. West, Judd Marmor, etc.), as well as those which the various dissertations and theses contained. In this connection, it must be mentioned that the editors were pleased to find that William J. Parker's extensive and important bibliography on the subject of homosexuality was available prior to the completion of the present work. It was possible to cross-check our own citations with those which were to be found in the following sections of Parker's work: books, theses and dissertations, articles in books, and articles in medical, scientific, and other specialized journals. Every effort was then made to include whatever citations had been omitted inadvertently from our own work. However, it was discovered that although numerous references to certain articles exist, the articles themselves are not always obtainable, even through Inter-Library Loan. In addition, no attempt has been made to include the following topics which can be found in the Parker bibliography: the etiology of alcoholism, transsexualism, transvestism, gender identity, and literary criticism. Parker also included in his bibliography a great many citations of works pertaining to the supposed relationship between homosexuality and paranoia as well as to the association of homosexuality with venereal disease; some but not all of these will be found in the present volume. Thus, although it may be that certain items have been overlooked, the search that was made in connection with the present annotated bibliography is sufficiently exhaustive to allow the reader access to the Medical Literature Analysis and Retrieval System (MEDLARS), a computer bibliography service designed to meet more specialized information needs (i.e., the present bibliography meets the requirements of the "preliminary literature search" which must be made before requesting a MEDLARS demand search).*

The mode of citation and the rules of form used in the body of the abstract itself are those which were recommended by the publisher and can be found in *A Manual of Style,* 12th Edition, Completely Revised for Authors, Editors, and Copywriters, the University of Chicago Press, 1969. Since much of the material in the area of homosexuality is not derived from work done in the natural sciences and because the bibliography is directed to the layman and to professionals whose backgrounds are not necessarily in the sciences, the humanistic style of citation (author, title, etc.) has been used.

It will be apparent to the reader who is familiar with the usual methods employed in the presentation of bibliographic materials that, in certain instances, innovations have been made. While the style manual referred to above has been used as a guide, many problems of form—unique, perhaps, to this field—arose which are not anticipated in the manual. For example, sometimes the title of an article was changed when it appeared as a reprint. Often, when an article appeared in a collection of articles, the editors would fail to note that it was a reprint and not an original contribution to the collection; in such instances, textual comparisons had to be made in order to determine whether or not a publication was actually a reprint.

With regard to authors' names appearing in the citations, the "no conflict" rule employed by the Library of Congress was adapted to our purposes. In general, authors' names were accepted as they appeared in the publication. Where several items were included for a given author, if it was possible to establish beyond the point of reasonable doubt that they were all written by the same person, then the form most commonly employed by

---

*Investigators wishing to make use of those services may submit a MEDLARS Search Request form, which is available through their local medical library or nearest MEDLARS station.

the author was used. If there was reason to doubt that variant forms of an author's name represented the same individual, then names were used as they appeared on the publication. In cases where authors used pseudonyms, however, these were accepted at face value and are not indicated as pseudonyms in the bibliography, even in those instances where the identity of the writer is given on the Library of Congress catalog card.

Articles in journals have been cited in accordance with the aforementioned style manual but with the following modification: issue numbers (number, year) or dates (month, year) were included within the parentheses. This was done for the convenience of the reader. Wherever issue numbers were available, they were used in preference to the date; if the issue number was not available, the abbreviated month was used instead, e.g., 54 (4, 1966): 102–139 versus 54 (Jan., 1966): 102–139. The journal titles themselves were used in the form current at the time of publication rather than the latest form of the title. This was consistent with the policy of using information exactly as it appeared in the publication. In some cases it required a good deal of effort to determine the exact citation. For example, the *Rorschach Research Exchange* went through four title changes until today it is known as the *Journal of Projective Techniques and Personality Assessment;* the *Journal of Social Therapy* is now titled *Corrective Psychiatry and Journal of Social Therapy.* Changes such as these necessitated a search of the *New Serials Titles* which contains the entire history of each journal.

The dissertations, theses, and unpublished material which we believed warranted inclusion have been cited in the usual way except that pagination has been added wherever possible. (This will enable the reader to distinguish the smaller pamphlets from the larger monographs. Pagination was also added, for the same reason, to the citations of books.) The majority of these abstracts were done from the actual dissertations, although a few were taken directly from *Dissertation Abstracts.* Probably the most important of the unpublished material are the NIMH Task Force papers pertaining to homosexuality. The papers were made available by Paul Gebhard, director of the Institute for Sex Research and himself a member of the Task Force, who read and approved each of the annotations. The other unpublished materials were included only if they were considered sufficiently important and also available to the public.

With articles that appear as reprints in collections of works which have not been included in their entirety, the date of their original publication has been entered followed by the full citation of the reprint. However, if the title varied, the full imprint of the original publication was given, followed by the statement, "reprinted as——— in———." Reprints of works published before 1940 and reprinted between 1940–1968 were not included unless they appeared in one of the ten collections whose entire contents were abstracted. For example, the writings of Freud have been excluded with the exception of those that appeared in *The Problem of Homosexuality in Modern Society,* edited by Hendrik M. Ruitenbeek, and *The Homosexuals: As Seen by Themselves and Thirty Authorities,* edited by Aron M. Krich. The other volumes whose entire contents have, with but few exceptions, been abstracted are: *Carol in a Thousand Cities* (Ann Aldrich), *The Homosexual in America: A Subjective Approach* (Donald Webster Cory), *Homosexuality: A Cross Cultural Approach* (Donald Webster Cory, ed.), *Sexual Deviance* (John H. Gagnon, and William Simon, eds.), *Sexual Inversion: The Multiple Roots of Homosexuality* (Judd Marmor, ed.), *They Stand Apart: A Critical Survey of the Problem of Homosexuality* (John Tudor Rees and Harley V. Usill, eds.), *The Pathology and Treatment of Sexual Deviation: A Methodological Approach* (Ismond Rosen, ed.), and *The Third Sex* (Isadore Rubin, ed.).

Classification Procedures

For the convenience of the reader, attempts have been made to classify the materials that have been abstracted in ways that reflect their primary emphases. The bibliography begins with those articles which consider homosexuality from a physiological point of view, followed by those which are psychologically oriented and then by those which offer a sociological perspective. It ends with a list of other bibliographies. These major classifications have been broken down further into various subcategories such as etiology, assessments, and treatments. Works referring to female homosexuality are to be found in a separate subsection within each category; in some cases the work will only be cross-referenced here because it also refers to male homosexuality, and the annotation therefore appears elsewhere. The abstract of a given article or book appears under only one heading, according to its major emphasis. If, in addition, the work deals with aspects of homosexuality which are related to one or more of the other subcategories, then it will be found in the list of cross-references which appears at the conclusion of each section. The number of the main heading placement of the particular citation is noted at the end of the cross-reference so that the annotation can be quickly found without going to the index. Finally, works have been listed in alphabetical (not chronological) order, and each annotation has a unique number for easy cross-reference. Although the reader may disagree with the major category to which a given article has been assigned, he will probably have little difficulty locating an abstract of interest to him if he checks the cross-references which have been provided. In addition, author and subject indexes with which the bibliography concludes should prove to be helpful to the reader who wishes easy access to a given work.

PHYSIOLOGICAL
CONSIDERATIONS

Etiology

GENERAL, MALE

1   BARNOUW, VICTOR, and STERN, JOHN A. "Some Suggestions Concerning Social and Cultural Determinants of Human Sexual Behavior." In *Determinants of Human Sexual Behavior,* edited by George Winokur, pp. 206–209. Springfield, Ill.: Charles C. Thomas, 1963.

There should be additional research concerning homosexuality from both the genetic and the environmental viewpoints. Suggestions for improving the design of future investigations are offered, as are suggestions for kinds of research which could provide means for gauging the comparative significance of biological and environmental determinants involved in the etiology of homosexual tendencies.

2   BAUER, JULIUS. "Homosexuality as an Endocrinological, Psychological, and Genetic Problem." *Journal of Criminal Psychopathology* 2 (2, 1940): 188–197.

Current findings on homosexuality are reviewed. It is concluded that homosexuality is caused by abnormal chromosomal formation, that homosexuals tend to demonstrate morphological characteristics of the opposite sex, and that homosexuality may be hereditary.

3   BEACH, FRANK A. *Hormones and Behavior.* New York: Paul B. Hoeber, 1949, 368 pp.

This is a general treatise on the effects of endocrine secretions on response patterns in all animals from fishes through primates. It contains two pages (70–72) on "Reversals of Mating Relationships, or Bisexual Behavior, in the Human," which conclude a chapter on bisexuality in lower animals. Early studies claimed homosexuality to be mainly or entirely a constitutional, physiological problem. These are described as oversimplified and contrasted with studies that have compared the importance of endocrine influence in man with its importance in lower animals. He concludes that hormonal effects are far less influential in man and are overridden by psychological and social factors.

4   COPPEN, A. J. "Body Build of Male Homosexuals." *British Medical Journal* (5164, 1959): 1443–1445. Also printed in *Advances in Psychosomatic Medicine* 1 (1960): 154–160.

Attempting to determine whether homosexuals have an abnormal discriminant androgyny score (an index of body build) which is related to the sexual development of the individual, a study was made of three groups: 31 male homosexuals who had attended the Maudsley Hospital, a control group of 31 male businessmen, and 22 heterosexual neurotics in the hospital.

It was found that homosexuals have a body build similar to that of patients with other psychiatric disorders, and that it could not be specifically related to their sexual abnormality.

5   CROSS, HAROLD H. U. *The Cross Report on Perversion*. New York: Softcover Library, 1964, 151 pp.

A catalog of sexual "perversions," giving "uncensored" case illustrations, covers a whole spectrum of patterns, homosexuality among them. "True" homosexuality is considered congenital. Male and female homosexuality are discussed mainly through case histories.

6   DARKE, ROY A. "Heredity as an Etiological Factor in Homosexuality." *Journal of Nervous and Mental Disease* 107 (Jan.–June, 1948): 251–268.

In an attempt to determine the etiological role of heredity in homosexuality, 100 male homosexual prisoners at Springfield, Missouri, were administered the Wechsler-Bellevue Test, the Cornell Selectee Index, the Revised Rorschach Multiple Choice Test, and the Goodenough Draw-a-Man Test. Their case histories were also recorded.

No evidence was found of an hereditary etiological determination of homosexuality in human beings. Also there was no indication of a significant statistical difference in the sex ratio at birth of siblings of homosexuals from the normal ratio.

7   ELLIS, ALBERT. "Constitutional Factors in Homosexuality: A Reexamination of the Evidence." In *Advances in Sex Research*, edited by Hugo G. Beigel, pp. 161–186. New York: Harper & Row, 1963.

Evidence from previous etiological studies for the genetic, hormonal, body-build, and brain-damage hypotheses is reviewed, as well as the hypotheses that homosexuality is untreatable and that it is historically and culturally uniform in incidence. These hypotheses are found lacking in objective, confirmatory evidence of a scientific nature. At most, what has been found is that certain genetic, hormonal, and anatomic factors may help indirectly to produce homosexuality in some subjects.

8   "Endocrine Treatment in Homosexual Men." *Therapeutic Notes* (Feb., 1942): 65.

A report of research carried out by C. A. Wright indicates that homosexuality may in part result from a reversal of dominance of the sex hormones in males and females. See. Wright, Clifford A. (no. 86).

9   "Endocrines and Disordered Sexual Behavior." *British Medical Journal* (5018, 1957): 574.

Two studies concerned with the effect of endocrines on sexual behavior are reviewed.

G. I. M. Swyer's work indicates that the levels of sex hormones appear to modify the intensity of sexual activity without affecting the choice of sex object.

G. Garrone and S. Mutrux investigated the excretion of hormones by 50 patients with histories of deviant sexual behavior. A determination of the urinary excretion of total 17-ketosteroids and their different fractions, 3-a-steroids, formaldehydogenic corticoids, "total corticoids," and 17, 21-dihydroxy-20-ketosteroids failed to show evidence of suprarenal or testicular dysfunction. Since the daily excretion of these steroid metabolites did not differ in the 50 patients and 50 normal men of corresponding ages, it was concluded that this study provides no evidence that endocrine disturbance accounts for disordered sexual behavior.

10   FREUND, KURT. "On the Problem of Male Homosexuality." *Review of Czechoslovak Medicine* 11 (1, 1965): 11–17.

The problems of definition of the homosexual and the etiology of homosexuality are discussed. Since it is established that people do have dispositions for homosexual reactions and ties, it is necessary to characterize the homosexual as one who has a preference for erotic partners of the same sex. Although the causes of homosexuality remain unknown, it appears that biological factors are of great importance. Psychotherapy is of only limited use and does not seem to be indicated in the majority of cases.

11   FRIEDMAN, PAUL. "Sexual Deviations." In *American Handbook of Psychiatry*, vol. 1, edited by Silvano Arieti et al., pp. 589–613. New York: Basic Books, 1959.

Among a variety of deviations, homosexuality is briefly discussed, with an outline of constitutional and psychoanalytic theories given.

12   "Genetic Sex of Homosexuals." *British Medical Journal* (5335, 1963): 969–970.

Michael Pritchard tested the Lang hypothesis that some male homosexuals may be sex intergrades with male morphological sex characteristics but with female sex chromosomes. His findings that the nuclear sex of 235 male homosexual subjects was male and that six male homosexuals who were subjected to direct chromosomal investigation all had a normal male sex-chromosome constitution cast doubt on Lang's theory.

The possibility, however, that some homosexuals have a chromosomal anomaly has not been ruled out. Eliot Slater's investigation into the birth order and maternal age of homosexuals is cited as supporting evidence.

13   GENTELE, H.; LAGERHOLM, B.; and LODIN, A. "The Chromosomal Sex of Male Homosexuals." *Acta Dermato-Venereologica* 40 (6, 1960): 470–473.

The proportion of nuclei with sex chromatin in women has been established at 40 to 60 percent. The corresponding figure for normal males is 0 to 6 percent. Previous studies have indicated that sex chromatin in the oral mucosa of male homosexuals may be up to 8 percent—a prevalence on the same order as normal males. The present study, using an experimental population of 50 male homosexuals and 400 to 600 cells from the oral mucosa of each individual, determined that the proportion of cell nuclei with sex bodies was about 8 percent for each male. The same procedures were used to determine the incidence of sex bodies in 15 male and five female heterosexuals. There is no case in which the incidence of sex chromatin for the male homosexuals even approached that for women. No significant "chromosomal sex" difference was found between heterosexual and homosexual males.

14   GLASS S. J.; DEUEL, H. J.; and WRIGHT, CLIFFORD A. "Sex Hormone Studies in Male Homosexuality." *Endocrinology* 26 (Apr., 1940): 590–594.

Homosexuality is based on a hormonal imbalance. To test this theory, assays were made of the urinary androgens and estrogens of 17 male homosexuals and 31 normal males used as controls. The homosexuals had lower androgen: estrogen ratings, suggestive of a definite biologic mechanism in homosexuality.

15   GUYON, RENÉ; HAMBLY, WILFRID D.; HIRSCH, EDWIN W.;
      LORAS, OLIVIER; and WILSON, JOSEPH G. "The Causes of Homo-
      sexuality: A Symposium." *Sexology* 21 (11, 1955): 722–727.

Five noted authorities in various fields present their views of homosexuality.

Guyon recognizes two kinds of homosexuals, the "real" one whose
homosexuality is congenital and unchangeable, and the "accidental" one
who is momentarily deprived of persons of the opposite sex. Since homosexuality is probably caused by a physiological predisposition, homosexuals
should not be considered either diseased or criminal.

Hambly notes that homosexuality appears in many preliterate societies,
an observation supported by the findings of Hambly, Westermarck, Ford
and Beach, Seligman and Devereux.

Hirsch believes that since the homosexual's urge to love the opposite sex
is never developed, the love of one's counterpart consequently predomi-
nates. He states that how homosexual tendencies develop is not yet known
and urges the redefinition of the term "homosexual."

Loras declares that anatomical and glandular diseases are not the sole
cause of homosexuality and rejects the theory that homosexual tendencies
are inherited. Substantiating the neurotic origin (the result of issues related
to the Oedipus complex) of homosexuality which can be treated successfully
through psychotherapy, he makes the observation that although homosexuality without neurosis has been termed perversion, the medical point of view
rejects this moral condemnation.

Granting the fact that there may be many causes of homosexuality,
Wilson considers certain causes to be of prime importance: the lack of
opportunity for a normal or natural outlet of sexual drives; hormonal
disorders; the boarding-school environment, in which crushes may develop
into homosexual affairs when contacts with the opposite sex are restricted;
the seduction of boys by homosexual men; mental illness with psychoses or
feeble-mindedness; an imbalance of determining sex factors (a result of
heredity or environment), which makes it impossible to achieve physical or
sexual gratification; alcoholic indulgence; the Oedipus complex; and, most
important, the public's conciliatory attitude toward homosexuals.

16   HEILBRUN, GERT. "Psychoanalysis of Yesterday, Today, and To-
      morrow." *Archives of General Psychiatry* 4 (4, 1961): 321–330.

Due to the prevalence of a large, conservative contingency among those
who practice it, psychoanalysis is approaching a phase of stagnation. The
impact of this conservatism on nosology and treatment is discussed with
special reference to schizophrenia, overt male homosexuality, juvenile delinquency, and psychosomatic disorders.

It is "more likely than not" that homosexuality can be explained from a physiological as well as—or rather than—a psychogenic viewpoint. Eventually various types of homosexuality will be differentiated using the relative strengths of genetic-biologic and environmental factors in the etiology of the disturbance as a criterion. Therapy which takes such distinctions into account will be more effective than treatment based on accepted theories utilizing traditional therapeutic techniques.

17   HENRY, GEORGE W. "Psychogenic and Constitutional Factors in Homosexuality." *Psychiatric Quarterly* 8 (2, 1934): 243–264. Reprinted as "Psychogenic and Constitutional Factors." In *The Homosexuals: As Seen by Themselves and Thirty Authorities,* edited by Aron M. Krich, pp. 153–174. New York: Citadel Press, 1954.

A psychiatric and medical study of 250 adult male and female patients grouped according to predominance of heterosexual or homosexual tendencies found differences between the two groups with respect to marital adjustment, emotional reactions to parents, sexual trauma in childhood, type of personality disorders, and amount of constitutional deviation from the general average. The psychosexual differences were said to be dependent upon constitutional factors. Constitutional differences, generally being feminine bodily characteristics in the male and masculine in the female, were described.

18   HESTON, L. L., and SHIELDS, JAMES. "Homosexuality in Twins: A Family Study and a Registry Study." *Archives of General Psychiatry* 18 (2, 1968): 149–160.

Previous studies of homosexuality in twins are examined and an unusual family of 14 siblings is considered. Among the siblings were three pair of male monozygotic twins, two pair of which were homosexual, the third being heterosexual. As no environmental factor seemed to differentiate the homosexual from the heterosexual sibs, an etiology based on the interaction of genetic and environmental factors is suggested.

The Maudsley Twin Register (London) is also analyzed and the occurrence of homosexuality in monozygotic and dizygotic twins is discussed.

19   HIRSCHFELD, MAGNUS. "The Homosexual as an Intersex." 1936. Reprinted in *The Homosexuals: As Seen by Themselves and Thirty Authorities,* edited by Aron M. Krich, pp. 119–134. New York: Citadel Press, 1954.

Some of the observations cited to justify the "irrevocable conclusion" that homosexuality is congenital are that homosexuality erupts spontaneously in

children, that children who will become homosexual in later life are differently constituted than those who will grow up to be heterosexual, and that
such children are drawn to persons of the same sex long before puberty.

Other reasons used to prove that the homosexual urge is inborn rather
than acquired are that homosexuals are impotent or merely weakly potent
with the opposite sex, that their first erotic dreams focus on persons of the
same sex, and that they have distinct physical traits and mannerisms which
set them apart as homosexual.

In addition, it is pointed out that homosexuality is linked with the total
personality, that it is clustered in families, that it is extremely tenacious and
is unaffected by extraneous influences, and that it is uniformly distributed
throughout the world and through time.

20   HIRSCHFELD, MAGNUS. *Sexual Anomalies: The Origins, Nature,
      and Treatment of Sexual Disorders.* Rev. ed. New York: Emerson
      Books, 1948, 538 pp.

This general physiological text on sexual and sex-related deviations contains
five chapters on homosexuality. It is argued that sexual hormones exercise
the decisive influence over the entire sexual personality development and
that all sexual anomalies are caused by irregularities in this development.
Varying forms of homosexuality are discussed, and the criteria for their
diagnosis are outlined. These include the absence of normal sexual affinity,
fixation on the same sex, and an intersexual constitution. Aversion to the
opposite sex does not enter the diagnosis, since most homosexuals are
indifferent to, rather than hostile toward, the other sex. Views of homosexuality, including Freudian theory, as an acquired trait are criticized. Attachment to the mother and other factors frequently mentioned in these theories
are suggested to be the results, not the causes of homosexuality. All humans
are bisexual, containing both female and male components. When these
elements are nearly balanced, the individual is intersexual and may go either
way. If the elements of the opposite sex dominate, the person becomes
homosexual. Thus homosexuality is congenital and hereditary and cannot
be eliminated by psychological means.

21   *Homosexuality and Prostitution: A Memorandum of Evidence Pre-
      pared by a Special Committee of the Council of the British Medical
      Association for Submission to the Departmental Committee on Homo-
      sexuality and Prostitution.* London: British Medical Association,
      1955, 94 pp.

A special committee, set up by the British Medical Association to study
homosexuality and prostitution, attempted to construct a realistic approach to these problems by reconciling the many diverse views within the

medical profession on these controversial subjects.

The Committee distinguishes between two groups of homosexuals—"Essential" and "Acquired." Those in the essential group derive their homosexual tendencies from genetic and early environmental factors, while those in the acquired group develop these tendencies later in life. The evidence for the incidence of homosexuality in Great Britain is considered, but no definite conclusions are expressed. In attempting to assess the etiological factors of homosexuality, the Committee surveys evidence supporting genetic, endocrine, and environmental influences. With regard to the law, reforms are called for and the undesirable effects of prison are particularly noted. Sound family life and training of youth is seen as the best preventive measure against homosexuality. Treatment should help the homosexual adjust to his condition and enable him to restrain from overt acts which would bring him in conflict with the law. More facilities for treatment are called for.

22   KALLMANN, FRANZ J. "Comparative Twin Study on the Genetic
      Aspects of Male Homosexuality." *Journal of Nervous and Mental
      Disease* 115 (4, 1952): 283–298.

The case histories of 85 twin male homosexuals (Kinsey rating of 3 to 6) obtained from psychiatric and correctional institutions and by direct contact with the homosexual world were studied. Monozygotic twins were very similar in their sex behavior, even when reared apart. Genes cannot control the choice of a sexual partner, but there may be a genetic imbalance which predisposes men toward homosexuality. Although sexual development should end in heterosexuality, a genetic imbalance, among other things, could prevent this maturation and homosexuality might result. Therefore, genetics has some bearing on homosexuality and most likely operates in disturbing the sexual maturational process, so that the person so afflicted is left more vulnerable to whatever factors lead to homosexuality.

23   KALLMANN, FRANZ J. "Genetic Aspects of Sex Determination and
      Sexual Maturation Potentials in Man." In *Determinants of Human
      Sexual Behavior,* edited by George Winokur, pp. 5–18. Springfield,
      Ill.: Charles C. Thomas, 1963.

Recent cytogenetic techniques have shown that vaguely formulated theories of sexual behavior can be expressed in a biological or biosocial frame in terms of genetically coded sex and maturation potentials.

Females with Turner's syndrome are sterile, having either XO or Xx chromosomes, and are characterized respectively by either a negative or weakly positive nuclear sex. The other extreme is the Superfemale who has three or four X chromosomes, whose nuclear sex is double or triple positive, and who may be either fertile or sexually undeveloped. Males never lack the

X chromosome; in fact, it is thought that its absence is lethal. Males with Klinefelter's syndrome have XXY chromosomes and may have even more than two X chromosomes. Their nuclear sex is positive, double positive, or triple positive, depending on the prevalence of the X chromosomes.

True hermaphroditism is thought to be caused by chromosomal translocations or mosaicism. Pseudohermaphroditism in both males and females is thought to be caused by a mutation at the level of the sex-controlling genes.

Transvestism, isosexual precocity, and overt homosexuality in males is considered to be "beyond the limitations of present cytogenetic techniques." Slater's (1962) and Kallmann's (1952) works are cited as supporting the genetic hypothesis of a predispositional heterogeneity in the formation of a homosexual behavior pattern. It is hypothesized that either chromosomal irregularity, such as might be associated with late maternal age, or some disturbance in a balanced maturation effect of sex-controlling genes may be the genetic cause of disorders in psychosexual maturation.

24   KALLMANN, FRANZ J. "Twin and Sibship Study of Overt Male Homosexuality." *American Journal of Human Genetics* 4 (2, 1952): 136–146.

There is a genetically determined disarrangement in the balance between male and female maturational (hormonal) tendencies in homosexuals. To support this theory, the case histories of 85 twin male homosexuals, obtained from psychiatric and correctional institutions and by direct contacts with the homosexual world, were studied. The twins had Kinsey ratings of 3 to 6, their ages ranged from 18 to over 35, and 40 of them were identical twins.

The majority of identical twins (one-egg pairs) are not only fully concordant as to their overt homosexual practices, but are very similar in both the part taken in their individual sex activities and the visible extent of feminized appearance and behavior displayed. It is significant that the twins developed their sexual tendencies independently and often far apart from each other and that they denied any overt sex play with each other. Thus, this practically complete concordance as to overt homosexuality in monozygotic male twin pairs throws considerable doubt upon the validity of psychodynamic theories and strengthens Kallmann's hypothesis.

25   KINSEY, ALFRED C. "Homosexuality: A Criteria for a Hormonal Explanation of the Homosexual." *Journal of Clinical Endocrinology* 1 (5, 1941): 424–428. Also reprinted as "Criteria for a Hormonal Explanation of the Homosexual." In *Homosexuality: A Cross Cul-*

tural Approach, edited by Donald Webster Cory, pp. 370–383. New York: Julian Press, 1956.

Is there a basis for a hormonal explanation of homosexuality? Over 1,600 males were personally interviewed in search of an answer to this question. The basic error in studies of hormones and homosexual behavior is that homosexuality and heterosexuality are assumed to be two mutually exclusive phenomena emanating from fundamentally and inherently different types of individuals. There are not discrete types of homosexual behavior but gradations of behavior between the two extremes, homosexual and heterosexual. Any hormonal explanation of the homosexual must allow for the fact that between 25 to 50 percent of all males have demonstrated their capacity to respond to homosexual stimuli and that control groups of heterosexuals may very well include people who have had homosexual contacts.

26   KLINTWORTH, GORDON K. "A Pair of Male Monozygotic Twins Discordant for Homosexuality." *Journal of Nervous and Mental Disease* 135 (2, 1962): 113–125.

To determine the relationship between genetic factors and homosexuality, a study was made of a pair of 20-year-old male twins. One of the brothers, a homosexual, was admitted to the Department of Psychological Medicine at the Johannesburg General Hospital, where he mentioned his twin whom he did not believe was a homosexual.

The case histories of the twins were taken, and they were given the Thematic Aperception Test and physical examinations. The latter included photographs, blood tests, ABO (saliva-secretor activity), fingerprints, dental impressions, a test for color blindness, taste threshold to phenylthiocarbamide, skin biopsies (for sex chromatin), and urine tests for follicle-stimulating hormone 17-ketosteroids and 17-hydroxycorticasteroids.

The absence of complete concordance for male homosexuality (only one twin was homosexual) in monozygotic twins can be adequately explained in terms of genetic concepts (the homosexuality in the one twin can also be construed by psychoanalytic theories of a weak father and a dominating mother, et cetera). The fact that discordance for homosexuality in monozygotic twins exists does not in any way invalidate the concept that overt homosexuality is a gene-controlled variant in the intergrative process of psychosexual maturation. Genetic studies in many well-established hereditary diseases have conclusively shown that although a mutant may be present, it does not always produce a recognizable effect. The occurrence of incomplete penetrance can be adequately explained by the fact that other genes and environmental factors modify the expression of the gene under consideration.

27   KOLARSKY, A.; FREUND, KURT; MACHEK, J.; and POLAK, O. "Male Sexual Deviation: Association with Early Temporal Lobe Damage." *Archives of General Psychiatry* 17 (6, 1967): 735–743.

An attempt was made to relate sexual deviancy to early age temporal brain lesions. Eighty-six male epileptic outpatients from an antiepileptic clinic were given psychosexological examinations. The subjects were diagnostically categorized by experts in the field of sexual deviancy on the basis of interviews, femininity questionnaires, the Wechsler-Bellevue I.Q. Test, and neurological examinations.

In two cases homosexuality was associated with brain damage that occurs at the time of delivery or up to the age of three months. An explanation for the association of brain lesions and sexual deviancy was that an early brain lesion destroyed primordial programs which control the selection of stimuli and activities; aberrant sexual programs might have developed as a compensation if the brain lesion was present at a critical period of life.

28   LANG, THEO. "Studies on the Genetic Determination of Homosexuality." *Journal of Nervous and Mental Disease* 92 (1, 1940): 55–64.

To test the genetic determination of homosexuality 1,015 of the homosexuals known to the police departments of Munich, Germany, in 1934 and Hamburg in 1937 were examined. The working hypothesis stated that homosexuals can be, to a certain extent, defined as intersexes. Male homosexuals may be regarded either as more or less feminized males, or as real male sex intergrades who are genetically female but who have lost all morphological sex characteristics except their chromosome formulas. In the cases of those male homosexuals who are transformed females this should result in a significantly greater than normal proportion of male siblings. In dealing with female sex intergrades it was expected that there would be more females among their siblings than males.

Among other things it was found that those under the age of 25 at last police registration had a proportion of males to females of 113.2:100 among their siblings, and those over 25 had a proportion of 128.3:100, lending strong support for this genetic theory, since these ratios deviate clearly from the normal ratio of 106:100.

29   LIEF, HAROLD I.; DINGMAN, J. F.; and BISHOP, M. P. "Psychoendocrinologic Studies in a Male with Cyclic Changes in Sexuality." *Psychosomatic Medicine* 24 (4, 1962): 357–368.

The case of a 23-year-old male graduate student who had a cyclic alternation of feeling and acting male or female for 11 years is reported. The tests and examinations administered included Rorschach, House-Tree-Person Drawings, Rappaport Word Association, Rotter Incomplete Sentences, Minnesota Multiphasic Personality Inventory, neurological examination, electroencephalogram, laboratory examination—17-ketosteroids, follicle-stimulating hormone, sex chromosomes, urinary estrogen, interstitial cell-stimulating hormone, skull X ray, and a testicular biopsy.

Cessation of the patient's cyclic alternation soon after initial therapy was accompanied by a striking increase in excretion of urinary 17-ketoster-oids. The developmental and endocrinological data suggest an association between a derangement in development of androgenic characteristics and the homosexual pattern of adolescence and homoerotic pattern of adult life. The deficiency of adequate levels of male hormones probably served to perpetuate and accentuate pre-existing effeminate childhood patterns.

30   LURIE, LOUIS A. "The Endocrine Factor in Homosexuality: Report of Treatment of 4 Cases with Androgen Hormone." *American Journal of the Medical Sciences* 208 (Aug., 1944): 176–186.

The division of homosexuality into innate and acquired is suggested. The condition of the innate homosexual is explained on the basis of the presence of a somatic factor in the form of an endocrine disorder. The beneficial results of treatment with testosterone propionate in four cases of innate male homosexuality are reported. The need for a somatopsychic approach to an understanding of innate homosexuality is stressed.

31   MAYNE, D. GREGORY. "Homosexuality." *British Journal of Psychiatry* 114 (Jan., 1968): 125.

An etiological theory of homosexuality based on endocrinology is presented. It is suggested that the success of biochemical hormonal control of homosexual behavior is dependent upon the hormone levels of the individual which were established when the sex control center matured (i.e., around birth).

32   MOIR, J. L. "Some Medical Aspects of Crime: Homosexual Offences." *Medico-Legal and Criminological Review* 8 (2, 1940): 121–122.

Many homosexuals may suffer from endocrine disturbances. Descriptions of a series of cases reported in Rio de Janeiro show that 99 percent of the homosexuals suffered from hypotension and indicate that the main cause of this hypotension was endocrine disturbance.

Homosexuality may best be considered a disease rather than a crime. In any case, early detection is necessary so that "the right influence potentials could be guided aright."

More research should be done to help "the sufferers in these cases."

33   MONEY, JOHN. "Factors in the Genesis of Homosexuality." In *Determinants of Human Sexual Behavior*, edited by George Winokur, pp. 19–43. Springfield, Ill.: Charles C. Thomas, 1963.

Factors in the genesis of homosexuality are reviewed. Chromosomes, gonads, hormones, genital morphology and body image, sex assignment, gender identity, psychosexual neutrality and differentiation, imprinting, family and culture patterns are among the factors considered. The conclusion is reached that the final determination of a person's gender identity, and, hence, his erotic arousal pattern, whatever the secondary and antecedent determinants, is a neurocognitional function. It is also concluded that the process takes place primarily after birth, and that the fundamentals are completed before puberty.

34   MONEY, JOHN. "Sexual Dimorphism and Homosexual Gender Identity." [Working Paper] Prepared for Distribution to Members of the National Institute of Mental Health Task Force on Homosexuality. Mimeographed. Bethesda, Md., Nov. 25–26, 1967.

After an initial discussion of the problems of an etiological approach, the current state of knowledge of genetic, endocrinologic, and embryonic factors as they relate to homosexual behavior is reviewed. Foetal and postnatal sex differentiation is discussed. Recent discoveries relating to the influence of foetal hormones upon the hypothalamus are summarized, and the author makes cautious inferences from his own research on girls with endocrinological virilizing conditions.

Although genetically determined physiological traits, such as in Klinefelter's syndrome, can increase the probability of an individual developing a homosexual orientation—particularly during critical developmental periods of early life—the outcome of psychosexual differentiation is independent of genetic and endocrinologic factors. Instead, it is dependent upon the gender assigned the individual by his parents and society. In the vast majority of cases, of course, assigned gender is congruent with genetic gender, but in those few cases of hermaphroditism, pseudohermaphroditism, and other ambiguities the gender identity can be incongruent with gender and consequently result in a technically homosexual orientation.

35   MYERSON, ABRAHAM, and NEUSTADT, RUDOLPH. "Bisexuality and Male Homosexuality: Their Biologic and Medical Aspects." *Clinics* 1 (4, 1942): 932–957.

Sexuality is defined as the "processes which are separable from reproduction and heredity, although at all times intimately linked with them." The character, direction, and intensity of the sexual drives are inherent to begin with, but can be greatly modified by education and training, inhibition and excitation, and by social pressures in general, as well as by metabolic and chemical influences.

Man is bisexual genetically, embryologically, anatomically, and in "the very essence of maleness and femaleness," the sex hormones. For complete physiologic function a certain balance between the "male" and the "female" hormones is necessary. This balance may be destroyed at any one point within a complicated system which is concerned with the formation of sex hormones.

Homosexuality can neither be considered a disease (although it may form the background for neurotic or psychotic symptoms) nor a "normality," i.e., an intermediate sex; therefore it is an "abnormality." The homosexual drive marks one as a psychopathic personality; in addition the homosexual may be neurotic or psychotic.

In studying the urine samples of males it was noted that whenever there was an androgen:estrogen ratio of other than 4–6:1, there was some form of sexual psychopathy; ratios of 3:1 or lower were usually indicative of homosexuality. The amount of androgens in the body is responsible for the strength and vigor of the sex drive of the individual, while the absolute and proportionate amount of estrogens determines its general direction. It was concluded, though, that since bisexuality is a fundamental biologic phenomenon and the biologic aberrations may be small, homosexuality cannot be reliably detected by hormone ratios in the urine.

It is thought that hormone treatment might be an effective form of therapy for homosexuals, since psychotherapy is effective in treating only the neurotic superstructure of homosexuality and not the homosexual drive itself. However, in cases receiving hormone treatment, the effects were temporary, lasting only four to six weeks. The failure is seen as the result of not being able to administer the hormones in a natural manner.

36   MYERSON, ABRAHAM, and NEUSTADT, RUDLOPH. "The Bisexuality of Man." *Journal of the Mount Sinai Hospital* 9 (4, 1942): 668–678.

A preliminary discussion recapitulates the facts of embryology which form the structural basis for bisexuality. On the basis of these facts, there is no question that, although the reproductive apparatus itself usually is sharply unisexual, man is bisexual. Male and female hormones are present in each individual in varied ratios with marked individual fluctuations in the ratio between male and female hormones excreted in the urine. Colorimetric methods were used to determine these ratios as compared with a "rough approximation" of a standard ratio (a normal ratio between male and female hormones in a man is from 4:1 to 6:1).

The subjects were 85 males in whose cases the question of homosexuality had arisen. These cases were: derived from private practice; individuals incarcerated at the Massachusetts State Reformatory in Concord; patients at a university department of hygiene; and individuals suspected of, or showing, some homosexual conduct at the various state or private mental institutions. They were divided into five groups on the basis of the degree or type of their homosexuality. Summaries of typical cases from each group were given, including hormone findings in the urine, expressed as amounts of androgens and estrogens, and the ratios between them.

The chemical tests are relatively crude since essential hormones, such as testosterone and estradiol, are not present as such in the urine, and also because some of the 17-ketosteroids evaluated by the androgen and estrogen tests are not necessarily sexual hormones. "Taking all these errors and difficulties into account, there nevertheless remain important clinical correlations between the sexual constitution of a male and the hormonal values established by the examination of his urine for androgens and estrogens."

37   MYERSON, ABRAHAM, and NEUSTADT, RUDOLPH. "Essential Male Homosexuality and Some Results of Treatment." *Journal of Nervous and Mental Disease* 102 (2, 1945): 194–196.

The hormones in an individual can and do direct his sexual interests and behaviors. To verify this, 15 male homosexuals were orally administered Metandren linguet, a new male hormone preparation. In 13 of the 15 cases, homosexual feelings disappeared or were greatly lessened. A heterosexual drive was established in only five of these 13, and in none of these five was it sufficient to bring about a successful heterosexual life.

It appears that male homosexuality in the adult cannot be completely cured by hormones, but it can be more easily modified by this form of treatment than by any other.

38   MYERSON, ABRAHAM; NEUSTADT, RUDOLPH; and RAK, I. P. "The Male Homosexual: Hormonal and Clinical Studies." *Journal of Nervous and Mental Disease* 93 (2, 1941): 209–212.

Clinical findings made in a hormonic analysis of the urine of a group of 29 male homosexuals are presented. The overt, predominantly active male homosexual without any heterosexual drive could be identified without difficulty and with a small margin of error. Such persons had high female and low male hormonic values. Commentary by Roy Hoskins and Isador

Coriat indicates some disagreement as to the relative etiologic importance of endocrinological and psychological factors.

39   MYERSON, ABRAHAM, and NEUSTADT, RUDOLPH. "Symposium on Social Psychiatry: Bisexuality and Male Homosexuality; Their Biologic and Medical Aspects." *Clinics* 1 (4, 1942): 932–957.

Biochemical studies were made of the urines of 102 males who showed homosexual conduct. The material came from Myerson's own private practice, the Massachusetts State Reformatory in Concord, a university department of hygiene, and various State and private mental institutions. The ages of the subjects ranged from 15 to 65 years, with about 50 percent of all cases between the ages of 27 to 33 years. The subjects were divided into six groups according to degree and nature of their homosexuality.

In 83 percent of all cases examined, including psychotic and endocrine cases, a disproportion between androgens and estrogens in favor of estrogens was found. In no more than 2½ percent of all other cases examined was there a "homosexual" urinary formula present without an existing overt homosexuality. It was concluded that "the amount of androgens in the body is mainly responsible for the strength and vigor of the sex drive of the individual, while the absolute and proportionate amount of estrogens determine its general direction."

Although hormone treatment proved discouraging, progress in the study and understanding of the organic chemistry of sex hormones will lead to real therapeutic progress in the treatment of homosexuality in the future.

40   NEUSTADT, RUDOLPH, and MYERSON, ABRAHAM. "Quantitative Sex Hormone Studies in Homosexuality, Childhood, and Various Neuropsychiatric Disturbances." *American Journal of Psychiatry* 97 (3, 1940): 524–551.

What is the role of the sex hormones in sexual development and sexual constitution? Twenty-nine male homosexuals seen in private practice or in various hospitals by the authors were given hormone tests (androgens and estrogens) and urine tests. In 25 out of the 29 cases there was a uniform or nearly uniform hormone secretion—low male hormone and high female hormone. The most important finding was the reflection of sexual development and sexual constitution in urinary hormone excretion.

41   NEUSTATTER, W. LINDESAY. "Homosexuality: The Medical Aspect." *Practitioner* 172 (Apr., 1954): 364–373.

Two types of homosexuals are distinguished: bisexuals and the complete inverts who have never had any normal impulses. The latter are probably glandularly determined. Treatment comes in one of two forms: attempts at cures, and/or helping the patient to cope with his sexuality and its consequences.

42   NEUSTATTER, W. LINDESAY. "Homosexuality: The Medical Aspects." In *They Stand Apart: A Critical Survey of the Problems of Homosexuality,* edited by John Tudor Rees and Harley V. Usill, pp. 67–139. London: William Heinemann, 1955.

In a critical survey of the etiological role of hormonal, psychological, and constitutional factors, homosexuality is explained as the result of some kind of interplay between psychological and constitutional factors. The psychosis most relevant to the matter of homosexuality is schizophrenia. Various clinical aspects of psychosis, psychoneurosis, and psychopathy are discussed in their connection with homosexuality. The rehabilitative potential of imprisonment of offenders is doubtful, although those who break the law must be reckoned with. The use of prison-hospitals is strongly urged. Treatment may be radical or palliative, i.e., either aimed at total cure or aimed at the elimination of overt homosexual behavior.

43   PARE, C. M. B. "Etiology of Homosexuality: Genetic and Chromosomal Aspects." In *Sexual Inversion: The Multiple Roots of Homosexuality,* edited by Judd Marmor, pp. 70–80. New York: Basic Books, 1965.

Conflicting and inconclusive studies on genetic factors in homosexuality are assessed. Although environment and genetics both seem to play roles, the degree to which genetic and environmental factors are important, in homosexuality as a whole and in any individual, remains uncertain.

44   PARE, C. M. B. "Homosexuality and Chromosomal Sex." *Journal of Psychosomatic Research* 1 (4, 1956): 247–251.

Lang's theory about the etiology of homosexuality was that some male homosexuals were sex intergrades, i.e., genetically female but with no morphological sex characteristics except their chromosome formula. To test this theory, the cells from the mouth scrapings of 50 male homosexuals were examined to determine their chromosomal sex. The subjects, who had been in Maudsley Hospital, ranged in age from 18 to 64 years with a mean age of 35 years. Their average rating on the Kinsey Scale was 4.5. A control group of 25 males and 25 females was used.

The chromosomal sex in all cases was male. This is strong evidence against Lang's theory that many male homosexuals are genotypically female, but this does not exclude a genetic etiology for homosexuality.

45   PARKER, NEVILLE. "Homosexuality in Twins: A Report on Three
      Discordant Pairs." *British Journal of Psychiatry* 110 (467, 1964):
      489–495.

The study sought to determine if the etiology of homosexuality is genetic
or environmental. Three sets of twins were studied: a monozygotic male set;
a dizygotic male pair; and a monozygotic female set. One member of each
pair was diagnosed as a homosexual while being treated for mental disorders at a hospital. Zygosity data for the monozygotic pairs were analyzed.
Case histories and life histories were prepared on all subjects. In each set
of twins, the nonhospitalized twin showed no indication of homosexuality.
Thus, it was concluded that support is shown for an environmental origin
of homosexuality.

46   PARR, DENIS, and SWYER, GERALD ISAAC MCDONALD. "Seminal
      Analysis in 22 Homosexuals." *British Medical Journal* (5209, 1960):
      1359–1361.

To test the notion that homosexuality is correlated with testicular inadequacy 22 homosexual men were studied. Twenty of the men were single, 13
were psychiatric outpatients and nine were referred by Gordon Westwood
from his research on male homosexuality. Their ages ranged from 18 to 56
years, the mean age was 29.8 years, and the median was 28 years. The men
were subjected to seminal analysis (volume, sperm density, and percentage
of abnormal forms) and nuclear sexing (blood smears for cytological appearances).

Eight of the men were highly fertile, four were fertile, five were borderline, three were subfertile, and two were sterile. The distribution of seminal
analysis was similar to that of a control group of 1,000 husbands of married
couples complaining of infertility. However, there was a conspicuous difference between the 13 patients under psychiatric treatment and the nine
subjects referred. Ten of the 13 were fertile or highly fertile, while only two
of the nine referrals were so rated. No hypothesis was formed regarding this
finding, primarily because of the small sample.

47   PERLOFF, WILLIAM H. "The Role of Hormones in Homosexuality."
      Journal of the Albert Einstein Medical Center 11 (3, 1963): 165–178.

Do inadequate hormonal functions cause homosexuality? No correlation
between the choice of sex object and the level of hormone excretion has been
observed. Furthermore, the so-called "sex hormones" are not important in
the determination of "sexual mannerisms" and attitudes. It is concluded
that homosexuality is a purely psychologic phenomenon, neither dependent

on hormonal patterns for its production nor amenable, by endocrine substances, to change.

48   PERLOFF, WILLIAM H. "Role of the Hormones in Human Sexual-
     ity." *Psychosomatic Medicine* 11 (3, 1949): 133–139.

Results of physical examinations of patients which measured precise
amounts of estrogenic and androgenic substances indicate that steroid hormones of the estrogenic and androgenic types have nothing to do with the
choice of sex object. These substances do not determine hetero- or homosexuality. Hormone therapy may affect the sexual urge by increasing or decreasing sexual desire and behavior, but it does not affect object choice.
Therefore, homosexuality is a purely psychologic phenomenon.

49   PRITCHARD, MICHAEL. "Homosexuality and Genetic Sex." *Journal
     of Mental Science: British Journal of Psychiatry* 108 (456, 1962):
     616–623.

Studies of Lang's intersex hypothesis are reviewed in an attempt to reach
a conclusion on its validity. Lang hypothesizes that male homosexuals are
"sex intergrades with male morphological sex characteristics but a female
chromosomal pattern."
     Indirect evidence in support of Lang's hypothesis is provided by surveys
of the sibling sex ratio of homosexuals—that is, there is a higher number
of males. Studies of developmental anomalies do not give credence to the
theory. Nuclear sex has always been found to correspond to phenotypic sex.
One study, indicating that Lang's hypothesis is not tenable, shows that
somatic chromosomes of male homosexuals are definitely male.

50. RABOCH, JAN, and NEDOMA, KAREL. "Sex Chromatin and Sexual
     Behavior: A Study of 36 Men with Female Nuclear Pattern and of
     194 Homosexuals." *Psychosomatic Medicine* 20 (1, 1958): 55–59.

To discover whether there is any connection between "sex chromatin" and
somatosexual development and whether there is a relationship between the
processes resulting in the female nuclear pattern and homosexuality in men,
a study was made of 36 men with a female type of sex chromatin (sexual
glands hypoplastic) and 194 adult homosexual men. The long axis of the
testicles was measured, as well as the amounts and types of ejaculations.
     Two main "upset" periods in the somatosexual development were distin-
guished. The first probably takes place at the early stage of embryonic
development, resulting in the female nuclear pattern type, but the sexual
tendencies are uninfluenced; the second takes place during adolescence
when degenerative processes in the testicles often cause a disturbance

of the hormonal activity of the Leydig cells.

All men with female sex chromatin revealed an obvious hypoplasia of sexual glands. In the adult homosexual group testes of subnormal size were found in only nine of the 194, and in six of the nine the sexual chromatin was masculine. "The authors do not exclude the possibility of finding female sex chromatin in homosexual men, but believe that that would be pure coincidence, and not a causal interrelationship."

51   RADO, SANDOR. "A Critical Examination of the Concept of Bisexuality." 1940. Reprinted in *Sexual Inversion; The Multiple Roots of Homosexuality,* edited by Judd Marmor, pp. 175–189. New York: Basic Books, 1965.

The views of Krafft-Ebing on bisexuality were introduced into psychoanalysis by Freud in 1905 and subsequently accepted as fact by many researchers. The assumption that the peripheral part of the sexual apparatus contains a bisexual predisposition (this must be true of the central part as well) led Hirschfeld to his view of homosexuality as an inborn characteristic brought about by a specific proportion of male and female substances in the brain. If the term bisexuality is used in a biologically legitimate sense, "there is no such thing as bisexuality either in man or in any other of the higher vertebrates." Rather than assuming that homosexuality results from a homosexual component in the constitution, its chief causal factor is the "affect of anxiety, which inhibits standard stimulation and compels the 'ego action system in the individual' to bring forth an altered scheme of stimulation as a 'reparative adjustment.' " It is imperative to replace the false concept of bisexuality with a psychological theory based upon firmer biological foundations.

52   ROSANOFF, WILLIAM R., and MURPHY, FRANCIS E. "The Basal Metabolic Rate, Fasting Blood Sugar, Glucose Tolerance, and Size of the Sella Turcica in Homosexuals." *American Journal of Psychiatry* 101 (Jul., 1944): 97–99.

Basal metabolic rate determinations, fast blood sugar determinations, glucose tolerance tests, and measurements of X-ray films of the pituitary fossae were made on a group of male homosexual inmates at the Medical Center for Federal Prisoners at Springfield, Missouri. The homosexual patients selected were those who played the feminine role in the homosexual relationship. They were generally effeminate in manner and interests, had experienced "strong emotional attachments to men," and had had repeated overt homosexual encounters. A control group of nonhomosexual patients were given the same series of tests. No significant differences were found between the two groups.

53   RUBIN, ISADORE. "Homosexuality: Conflicting Theories." 1960.
       Reprinted in *The Third Sex,* edited by Isadore Rubin, pp. 13–22.
       New York: New Book Co., 1961.

It is noted that "sharp differences exist concerning the nature and causes
of homosexuality," and brief discussions of a number of theories are presented. Etiological theories based on environmental concepts, utilizing psychological and sociological data, are contrasted with theories based on
constitutional factors such as genetic abnormality, hormonal imbalance, or
inheritance.

With regard to the incidence of homosexuality, the estimates of Havelock
Ellis and Magnus Hirschfeld are compared with statistics taken from the
Kinsey Reports, which are said to be the "most reliable and authoritative
figures available."

Works by English and Pearson, Curran and Parr, Liddicoat, Westwood,
and Freud are mentioned in the discussion about whether homosexuality
is a symptom of pathology.

It is concluded that "no one has all the answers" when it comes to a
knowledge about homosexuality.

54   RUDOLF, G. de M. "The Experimental Effect of Sex-Hormone
       Therapy upon Anxiety in Homosexual Types." *British Journal of
       Medical Psychology* 18 (3–4, 1941): 317–322.

Many homosexuals suffer from physiological as well as psychological abnormalities. Two male and two female homosexuals suffering from anxiety
were treated by the administration of Antuitrin S (an extract of pregnancy
urine containing the anterior-pituitary-like sex hormone) and by psychotherapy. All four cases improved (i.e., their anxiety diminished), thus suggesting that anxiety in predominantly homosexual cases can be directly
dependent upon a deficient stimulation of the gonads.

55   SAVITSCH, EUGENE de. *Homosexuality, Transvestism, and Change
       of Sex.* Springfield, Ill.: Charles C. Thomas, 1958, 120 pp.

A surgeon attempts to answer questions about change-of-sex operations,
discussing transvestism and homosexuality as they underlie the desire to
change sex. "Genuine homosexuality" is portrayed as an inherent, unaltera-
ble biological condition, with environmental factors contributing little. The
recommended treatment is castration or change of sex. Punitive legal reactions are denounced in view of the nature of homosexuality.

56   SECOR, H. W. "Can Hormones Cure Homosexuals?" *Sexology* 16
       (11, 1950): 721–727.

Findings by Lurie, Neustadt and Myerson, Young and Rundlett, and
Wright are cited to show correlations between hormonal imbalance and
homosexuality. Every homosexual should be examined not only by a psychologist, but by an endocrine specialist as well, since so many homosexuals
have endocrinological imbalances and can therefore be treated.

57   SEVRINGHAUS, E. L., and CHORNYAK, JOHN. "Hormones of Homo-
      sexuals." *Sexology* 12 (12, 1946): 740–741.

Homosexual behavior was investigated with reference to the differential
possession of abnormal sex hormones. The subjects were 21 male homosexual soldiers. A control group was composed of seven heterosexual soldiers
(under psychiatric treatment).

Three 24-hour urine samples were taken from each man, controlling for
time, age, and diet. Ten of the 21 homosexual subjects had no discoverable
sex-stimulating hormone, 10 had some (four of them possessed an excess
of the hormone). The controls had some sex-stimulating hormone. There
seemed to be no relation between the amount of sex-stimulating hormone
and the physical characteristics of the men.

Although the results do not lead to any explanation of homosexual
behavior, they do indicate that an endocrine disturbance may accompany
homosexual behavior in many cases.

58   SEVRINGHAUS, E. L., and CHORNYAK, JOHN. "A Study of Homo-
      sexual Adult Males." *Psychosomatic Medicine* 7 (5, 1945): 302–305.

Is an endocrine disturbance related to homosexuality? A study was made
of 21 male homosexual soldiers (19 to 31 years old, average age 23) who
were under the observation of the authors for diagnosis, and seven heterosexual male soldiers (23 to 33 years old, average age 26) who served as
controls. A collection of three 24-hour urine specimens was made for
bio-assay to determine 17-ketosteroids and pituitary gonadotrophins. The
homosexual group had a slightly lower average of ketosteroid excretion, but
it was not a significant difference. The striking finding was the lack of
gonadotrophic hormone in 10 of the homosexuals. This suggests that there
is an endocrine disturbance in some cases of homosexuality.

59   SILVERMAN, DANIEL, and ROSANOFF, WILLIAM R. "Electroen-
      cephalographic and Neurologic Studies of Homosexuals." *Journal
      of Nervous and Mental Disease* 101 (4, 1945): 311–321.

Homosexuality may be related to disorders of the central nervous system.
The case histories of 55 male homosexuals from the psychopathic unit of
the Medical Center for Federal Prisoners in Springfield, Missouri, were
taken, and their electroencephalograms were studied. The subjects were

from 17 to 43 years old, with an average age of 25.9 years.

A high incidence of histories and neurological signs suggestive of cerebral lesions was found, as well as neuropathic taint in the family histories. Pathological or borderline variant EEG's were present in 75 percent of the cases. In conclusion, an inherited or early acquired abnormality of the central nervous system played a contributory role in the development of homosexuality in the 55 cases studied.

60   SLATER, ELIOT. "Birth Order and Maternal Age of Homosexuals."
      Lancet 1 (7220, 1962): 69–71.

In a study of 401 male homosexuals, it was found that they were generally born later in sibship than was theoretically expected. Three hundred and thirty-eight epileptic controls did not differ significantly from the expected norm. The mean of the maternal ages of these male homosexuals also was significantly higher than those of other groups, although the variation of maternal age was even more striking. These findings supported a hypothesis of heterogeneity in the etiology of homosexuality and suggested that a chromosomal anomaly, such as might be associated with late maternal age, may be a contributing factor.

61   STAFFORD-CLARK, D. "Essentials of the Clinical Approach." In
      *The Pathology and Treatment of Sexual Deviation: A Methodological
      Approach,* edited by Ismond Rosen, pp. 57–86. London: Oxford
      University Press, 1964.

A psychiatric discussion of etiological factors in various sorts of deviation, including homosexuality, cites evidence pointing to constitutional and endocrine factors, while environmental factors are regarded as less important. Despite these considerations, individual psychotherapy, rather than drug therapy, is the recommended form of treatment.

62   SWYER, G. I. M. "Homosexuality: The Endocrinological Aspects."
      Practitioner 172 (1030, 1954): 374–377.

Does an imbalance of hormones cause homosexuality? The capacity for sexual response is not primarily dependent upon the sex hormones, and the directon of sexual development is influenced mainly by psychological and environmental conditioning. The levels of sex hormones appear to do little more than modify the intensity of sexual activity. There is no convincing evidence that homosexuality is dependent upon hormonal aberrations. Their use in treatment is also disappointing.

63   WHALEN, RICHARD E. "Homosexuality in Non-Human Animals."
      Mimeographed. Irvine, Calif.: University of California, n.d., 10 pp.

Recent studies of animals lead to the conclusion that "male-female differences in the probability of cross-gender behavior are the result of a differential development of masculine and feminine control systems, development which is critically influenced by the presence or absence of gonadal hormones during a sensitive period of development."

These and other recent findings are important to our understanding of cross-gender behavior in animals, although since unique postural responses are not characteristic of coital responses in humans, in this sense they may be of little use to our understanding of human homosexuality.

Studies of cross-gender response performance, and especially studies of stimulus selection in animals, may lead to further understanding of the apparently anomalous stimulus selection aspects of human homosexuality, although an early resolution of the problems in these research areas is not expected.

Since "homosexual" behavior occurs in genetic and endocrinologically normal males and females of most species, simple hormonal causes of masculine and feminine gender are not likely to be found.

64   WILLIAMS, EDWIN G. "Homosexuality: A Biological Anomaly."
       Journal of Nervous and Mental Disease 99 (1, 1944): 65–70.

To verify that there is a biological basis for those male homosexuals who assume the feminine role in homosexual intercourse, prostigmine was administered to two control groups and two groups of homosexuals. The control groups were 19 sexually normal male hospital employees and 13 sexually normal post-addict males. The homosexual groups were 12 masculine male post-addict homosexuals and 12 feminine male post-addict homosexuals. All the post-addicts had been hospitalized for drug addiction.

There was a definite biological difference between the "feminine" male homosexuals and all others studied. This group showed an absence of the usual reduction in serum cholinesterase following the subcutaneous administration of prostigmine. It should be noted that women normally show such a reduction themselves.

65   WINOKUR, GEORGE, ed. *Determinants of Human Sexual Behavior.*
       Springfield, Ill.: Charles C. Thomas, 1963, 230 pp.

Human sexuality was the topic of the Fourth Annual Conference of the Social Science Institute of Washington University in St. Louis. This volume reproduces some of the papers presented at the conference and also includes five papers as commentaries on the general subject which are original works arising from the research reported and the questions which arose during the meeting. See Barnouw, Victor, and Stern, John A. (no. 1). Gildea, Edwin F., and Robins, Lee N. (no. 416). Kallmann, Franz J. (no. 23). Money, John (no. 33). Sines, Jacob O., and Pittman, David J. (no. 1019). Winokur, George (no. 603).

66   WITSCHI, EMIL, and MENGERT, WILLIAM F. "Endocrine Studies on Human Hermaphrodites and Their Bearing on the Interpretation of Homosexuality." *Journal of Clinical Endocrinology* 2 (5, 1942): 279–286.

Two hermaphrodite sisters, 26 and 24 years old, were seen and treated by the authors. The sisters were chromosomally male. Surgical removal of the penis and gonads, treatment with hormones, and the manufacture of a vagina for one were accomplished. Their hermaphroditism was genetically determined, but the possibility of hormonal interference through the placenta cannot be ruled out. If these two sex-reversed females had been legally declared male at birth, their inclinations and instincts would have marked them as homosexuals. Therefore, a certain number of homosexuals may arise by sex reversal. The fathers of some homosexual men are carriers of a gene which, if transmitted to daughters, causes female-to-male sex reversal, creating potential homosexuals. Some homosexuals are men partially feminized through maternal hormonal influences.

CROSS-REFERENCES

Allen, Clifford. "Homosexuality: The Psychological Factor." *Medical Press* 217 (1947): 222–223. No. 651.

Allen, Clifford. "The Meaning of Homosexuality." *Medical World* 80 (1, 1954): 9–16. Reprinted in *International Journal of Sexology* 7 (4, 1954): 207–212. No. 90.

Allen, Clifford. *The Sexual Perversions and Abnormalities: A Study in the Psychology of Paraphilia.* 2d ed. London: Oxford University Press, 1949, 346 pp. No. 93.

Armstrong, C. N. "Diversities of Sex." *British Medical Journal* (4923, 1955): 1173–1177. No. 292.

Beggs, Keith Siddons. "Some Legal, Social and Psychiatric Aspects of Homosexual Behavior: A Guide for the Social Worker in the Sex Clinic." Master's thesis, University of Wisconsin, 1950, 298 pp. No. 955.

Berg, Charles. "The Problem of Homosexuality." *American Journal of Psychotherapy* 10 (4, 1956): 696–708; 11 (1, 1957): 65–79. No. 305.

Boss, Medard. *Meaning and Content of Sexual Perversions: A Daseinsanalytic Approach to the Psychopathology of the Phenomenon of Love.* Translated by Liese Lewis Abell. 2d ed. New York: Grune & Stratton, 1949, 153 pp. No. 108.

Caprio, Frank S.; Dalven, Joseph; Benjamin, Harry; and Lanval, Marc. "The Causes of Homosexuality: A Symposium." *Sexology* 21 (10, 1955): 633–637. No. 119.

Cavanagh, John R. *Counseling the Invert.* Milwaukee, Wisc.: Bruce Publishing Co., 1966, 306 pp. No. 668.

DeRiver, J. Paul. *Crime and the Sexual Psychopath.* Springfield, Ill.: Charles C. Thomas, 1958, 346 pp. No. 129.

East, W. Norwood. "Homosexuality." *Medical Press* 217 (Sept. 3, 1947): 215–217. No. 130.

East, W. Norwood. "Sexual Offenders." *Journal of Nervous and Mental Disease* 103 (6, 1946): 626–666. No. 131.

Ellis, Albert. *Homosexuality: Its Causes and Cure.* New York: Lyle Stuart, 1965, 288 pp. No. 680.

Gershman, Harry. "Considerations of Some Aspects of Homosexuality." *American Journal of Psychoanalysis* 13 (1953): 82–83. No. 409.

Gillespie, W. H.; Pasche, Francis; and Wicdeman, George H. "Symposium on Homosexuality." *International Journal of Psycho-Analysis* 45 (2–3, 1964): 203–216. No. 151.

Glover, Benjamin. "Observations on Homosexuality among University Students." *Journal of Nervous and Mental Disease* 113 (5, 1951): 377–387. Reprinted as "Homosexuality among University Students." In *The Homosexuals: As Seen by Themselves and Thirty Authorities,* edited by Aron M. Krich, pp. 141–153. New York: Citadel Press, 1954. No. 698.

Green, Eugene W., and Johnson, L. G. "Homosexuality." *Journal of Criminal Psychopathology* 5 (3, 1944): 467–480. No. 155.

Greenspan, Herbert, and Campbell, John D. "The Homosexual as a Personality Type." *American Journal of Psychiatry* 101 (5, 1945): 682–689. No. 428.

Herman, Morris, and Wortis, S. B. "Aberrant Sex-Behavior in Humans." *Annals of the New York Academy of Science* 47 (art. 5, 1947): 639–645. No. 444.

Holeman, R. Eugene, and Winokur, George. "Effeminate Homosexuality: A Disease of Childhood." *American Journal of Orthopsychiatry* 35 (1, 1965): 48–56. No. 449.

Hooker, Evelyn. "Homosexuality: Summary of Studies." In *Sex Ways in Fact and Faith: Bases for Christian Family Policy,* edited by Evelyn M. Duvall and Sylvanus M. Duvall, pp. 166–183. New York: Association Press, 1961. No. 1260.

Kinsey, Alfred C.; Pomeroy, Wardell B.; and Martin, Clyde E. *Sexual Behavior in the Human Male.* Philadelphia: W. B. Saunders Co., 1948, 804 pp. No. 869.

Kinsey, Alfred C.; Reichert, Philip; Cauldwell, David O.; and Mozes, Eugene B. "The Causes of Homosexuality: A Symposium." *Sexology* 21 (9, 1955): 558–562. No. 185.

Lambert, Carl. "Homosexuals." *Medical Press* 232 (1954): 523–526. No. 722.

M., M. "A Sociologist Looks at Homosexuality: A Criticism of the Current Sociological Text, *Sociology of Deviant Behavior* by Marshall B. Clinard." *Homophile Studies* 1 (2, 1958): 48–49, 64. No. 1096.

"Male Homosexuality." *Lancet* 2 (7111, 1959): 1077–1080. No. 879.

Marmor, Judd. "Homosexuality." *Student Personnel Newsletter, State University College, Buffalo* 1 (3, 1967): 15–34. No. 205.

Marmor, Judd, ed. *Sexual Inversion: The Multiple Roots of Homosexuality.* New York: Basic Books, 1965, 358 pp. No. 206.

Moore, Thomas V. "The Pathogenesis and Treatment of Homosexual Disorders: A Digest of Some Pertinent Evidence." *Journal of Personality* 14 (1945): 47–83. No. 213.

Mesnikoff, Alvin M.; Rainer, John D.; Kolb, Lawrence C.; and Carr, Arthur C.

"Intrafamilial Determinants of Divergent Sexual Behavior in Twins." *American Journal of Psychiatry* 119 (8, 1963): 732–738. No. 210.

Myerson, Abraham, and Neustadt, Rudolph. "Essential Male Homosexuality and Results of Treatment." *Archives of Neurology and Psychiatry* 55 (3, 1946): 291–293. No. 79.

Nash, John, and Hayes, Frank. "The Parental Relationships of Male Homosexuals: Some Theoretical Issues and a Pilot Study." *Australian Journal of Psychology* 17 (1, 1965): 35–43. No. 217.

Nielson, Nils. "The Riddle of Homosexuality." *International Journal of Sexology* 6 (1, 1952): 51–53. No. 218.

"Origins of Homosexuality." *British Medical Journal* (5470, 1965): 1077–1078. No. 220.

Perloff, William H. "Hormones and Homosexuality." In *Sexual Inversion: The Multiple Roots of Homosexuality,* edited by Judd Marmor, pp. 44–69. New York: Basic Books, 1965. No. 226.

Rasmussen, E. Wulff. "Experimental Homosexual Behavior in Male Albino Rats." *Acta Psychologica* 11 (1955): 303–334. No. 230.

Ross, Mathew, and Mendelsohn, Fred. "Homosexuality in College: A Preliminary Report of Data Obtained from One Hundred Thirty-three Students Seen in a University Student Health Service and a Review of Pertinent Literature." *Archives of Neurology and Psychiatry* 80 (2, 1958): 253–263. No. 898.

Roth, Martin, and Ball, J. R. B. "Psychiatric Aspects of Intersexuality." In *Intersexuality in Vertebrates Including Man,* edited by C. N. Armstrong and A. J. Marshall, pp. 395–443. London: Academic Press, 1964. No. 235.

Simon, Carleton. "Homosexualists and Sex Crimes." Presented before the International Association of Chiefs of Police at Duluth, Minnesota, September 21–25, 1947, 8 pp. No. 1238.

Ullerstam, Lars. *The Erotic Minorities.* New York: Grove Press, 1966, 172 pp. No. 1249.

West, D. J. *Homosexuality.* Chicago: Aldine Publishing Co., 1968, 304 pp. No. 922.

West, D. J. *The Other Man: A Study of the Social, Legal and Clinical Aspects of Homosexuality.* New York: Whiteside and William Morrow & Co., 1955, 224 pp. No. 924.

Wortis, Joseph. "Intersexuality and Effeminacy in the Male Homosexual." *American Journal of Orthopsychiatry* 10 (3, 1940): 567–570. No. 610.

Wright, Clifford A. "Results of Endocrine Treatment in a Controlled Group of Homosexual Men." *Medical Record* 154 (2, 1941): 60–61. No. 85.

Yankowski, John S., and Wolff, Hermann K. *The Tortured Sex.* Los Angeles: Holloway House Publishing Co., 1965, 224 pp. No. 927.

FEMALE

67 DEUTSCH, HELENE. "Homosexuality." In *The Psychology of Women: A Psychoanalytic Interpretation,* vol. 1, pp. 325–353. New York: Grune & Stratton, 1944.

A chapter in a study of feminine psychology divides female homosexuals into two types—physiological and psychogenic. Females who become homosexual for physiological reasons include not only those women with abnormal genitalia, but also those who have only superficial masculine characteristics such as deep voice, facial hair, or absence of breast development. Homosexuality develops in this latter group as a result of psychologic as well as biologic influences. Experiences during puberty are especially important in the development of homosexuality in girls with superficial masculine characteristics. To some extent psychogenic homosexuality is likewise a "continuation of puberty experiences." Girls choosing other girls as sexual objects during this developmental stage, and finding the relationship satisfactory, sometimes continue to make homosexual object choices in adulthood. Hostility toward the mother, fear of the father, and deprivation of oral gratification are other factors which help to explain female homosexuality.

Several abbreviated case histories are included.

CROSS-REFERENCES

Cory, Donald Webster. *The Lesbian in America.* New York: Citadel Press, 1964, 288 pp. No. 934.

Kinsey, Alfred C.; Pomeroy, Wardell B.; Martin, Clyde E.; and Gebhard, Paul H. *Sexual Behavior in the Human Female.* Philadelphia: W. B. Saunders & Co., 1953, 842 pp. No. 940.

Querlin, Marise. *Women Without Men.* Translated by Malcolm McGraw. New York: Dell Publishing Co., 1965, 174 pp. No. 943.

Ross, Mathew, and Mendelsohn, Fred. "Homosexuality in College: A Preliminary Report of Data Obtained from One Hundred Thirty-three Students Seen in a University Student Health Service and a Review of Pertinent Literature." *Archives of Neurology and Psychiatry* 80 (2, 1958): 253–263. No. 898.

Treatments

GENERAL, MALE

68   BALL, J. R., and ARMSTRONG, JEAN J. "The Use of LSD-25 (D-Lysergic Acid Diethylamide) in the Treatment of the Sexual Perversions." *Canadian Psychiatric Association Journal* 6 (Aug., 1961): 231–235.

A method of using LSD-25 in the treatment of sexual perversions is described. A single large dose was administered, and the patient was hospitalized for three days. The case histories of a frotteur and a pedophile, in which success was obtained, are presented. The technique was used with a total of 10 patients, including one female and five male homosexuals, but was unsuccessful with all except the above-mentioned cases. The conclusion was that success is possible only if the patient is of above average intelligence and genuinely wishes to get rid of the perversion. While it is not claimed that this method is preferable to others using LSD-25, it is occasionally very effective, is economical, and so far has not resulted in any unfortunate developments. A bibliography of papers reporting the use of LSD-25 in psychotherapy is also included.

69   BARAHAL, HYMAN S. "Testosterone in Psychotic Male Homosexuals." *Psychiatric Quarterly* 14 (2, 1940): 319–330.

A study was undertaken to determine the changes which could be produced by the administration of an active testicular hormone to psychotic male homosexuals displaying some physical signs of deficiency in the secondary sexual characteristics. The subjects were seven white male psychotics aged 25 to 31, with gonadal insufficiency. As observed by hospital staff, all had engaged in homosexual activity. For 18 weeks, each of the subjects received injections of 25 mgm. testosterone propionate three times a week. Brief case histories were given, with two sets of before-after photographs included.

Although all the subjects demonstrated an increase in secondary sex characteristics, an increase in homosexual activity resulted and the mental condition of the patients did not change. These results seem to give support to the theory of a learned rather than a genetic or endocrinological cause of homosexuality.

70   BARTHOLOMEW, A. A. "A Long-Acting Phenothiazine as a Possible Agent to Control Deviant Sexual Behavior." *American Journal of Psychiatry* 124 (Jul., 1968): 917–923.

A test to determine the extent to which phenothiazine controls sex drive was carried out with 26 sexually deviant patients (11 were homosexuals and the remainder either pedophiles or persons with histories which included indecent exposure or indecent assault on adults) and a control group of 26 nonsexually deviant patients. Each group was given an injection of phenothiazine intramuscularly every two weeks for approximately 24 weeks. Of the 26 nonsexually deviant patients, 17 reported a reduction in sex drive. Likewise, 17 of the sexually deviant patients, including seven of the 11 adult homosexuals, reported a reduction in sex drive.

"The result in both sexually normal and deviant groups suggests that the drug is of value in reducing sexual drive and performance, with no undue side effects observed provided antiparkinsonian drugs are given."

71   BUKI, RUDOLPH A. "The Use of Psychotropic Drugs in the
      Rehabilitation of Sex-Deviated Criminals." *American Journal of
      Psychiatry* 120 (12, 1964): 1170–1175.

Combinations of amitriptyline and perphenazine were administered on an
experimental basis to 40 hospitalized male patients, 15 of whom were
diagnosed as having primarily homosexual deviations. During the testing
period of one to five months the patients were also in group therapy. Six
of the homosexual patients improved satisfactorily, four improved but required longer treatment, and five showed no change.

   With regard to all of the patients, the combination of a tranquilizer and
an antidepressant were of considerable value in helping them overcome
their anxiety to the degree that they could undergo psychotherapy, which
offers the only hope of a permanent cure.

72   "Castration of a Male Homosexual." *British Medical Journal* (4894,
      1954): 1001.

An answer to a question about whether a 52-year-old male homosexual
should be castrated suggests that castration is not necessary. Instead the
patient should be put on stilboestrol or some equivalent hormone to suppress sexual desire.

73   DINERSTEIN, RUSSELL H., and GLUECK, BERNARD C., Jr. "Sub-
      Coma Insulin Therapy in the Treatment of Homosexual Panic
      States." *Journal of Social Therapy* 1 (4, 1955): 182–186.

The problem of homosexuality in prison and the ways of handling it are
described. Acute panic states, mostly due to homosexual conflict, can be
handled in a prison hospital. Guards, nurses, and other inmates can be
educated with regard to these problems and the methods of handling them.
The patients described in this report were given small doses of insulin,
phenobarbital, and sodium Amytal in order to reduce their anxiety and to
prepare them for future psychotherapy.

74   GLASS, S. J., and JOHNSON, ROSWELL H. "Limitations and Com-
      plications of Organotherapy in Male Homosexuality." *Journal of
      Clinical Endocrinology* 4 (11, 1944): 540–544.

To determine whether homosexuals can be effectively treated by hormone
therapy, testosterone propionate, chorionic gonadotropin, and methyl testosterone were administered to 11 male homosexuals, aged 16 to 34. Or-

ganotherapy failed to influence the psychosexual behavior in eight of the 11 patients but did seem to benefit three of them. Five reported an intensification of the homosexual drive.

75   LITKEY, L. J., and FENICZY, PONGRAC. "An Approach to the Control of Homosexual Practices." *International Journal of Neuropsychiatry* 3 (1, 1967): 20–23.

A study conducted at the New Jersey State Hospital with 12 of the most troublesome patients utilized thioridazine in an effort to curb their sexual preoccupation and homosexual practices. All the subjects had been placed under maximum security detention because of their troublesome behavior. A marked alteration in behavior occurred within one week after the drug had been administered, and within three weeks the condition of eight patients was so improved that it was possible to return them to the institutions from which they had been transferred. During interviews, all patients commented spontaneously on a diminished sexual preoccupation. Seven brief representative case histories are presented. The study suggests important consequences for the control of abnormal sexual behavior in prisons and mental institutions.

76   MACDONALD, JOHN M. "Homosexuality." *Journal of the American Medical Association* 180 (8, 1962): 707.

In answer to a question about whether a 40-year-old homosexual male should (at his own request) be castrated so that he would not have to fear being accused of raping an adolescent male, it is stated that castration is not recommended. Instead, estrogenic treatment in conjunction with psychotherapy is suggested.

77   MARTIN, AGNES JOYCE. "A Case of Homosexuality and Personality Disorder in a Man of 36 Treated by LSD and Resolved within Two Months." *Psychotherapy and Psychosomatics* 15 (1, 1967): 44.

The abstract of a paper presented at the Seventh International Congress of Psychotherapy in 1967 reports the case of a 36-year-old male suffering from homosexuality and a character disorder. Although two years of individual and group therapy and aversion therapy were unsuccessful, when the patient was treated by LSD he was able to resolve his problem and achieve a strong heterosexual relationship with a woman.

78   MARTIN, AGNES JOYCE. "The Treatment of 12 Male Homosexuals with L.S.D." *Acta Psychotherapeutica et Psychosomatica* 10 (5, 1962): 394–402.

Homosexuals were treated with lysergic acid diethylamide because of the drug's ability to enhance the recall and re-experience of early memories, and because it creates a dynamic transference situation. The therapist had to be present at all times in order to collect this unconscious material.

The subjects were 12 male homosexuals chosen from 100 chronic neurotic outpatients. None had had previous psychotic episodes. All had a desire to get well, were intelligent, and possessed insight. Their homosexuality was thought to be due to an arrested emotional development. Started on a dose of 50 gamma of LSD given on an empty stomach, the dosage was increased 20 gamma each time until a maximum reaction, useful in the therapeutic transference situation, was obtained.

Seven of the 12 became heterosexually oriented. Varying amounts of individual or group treatment were required following the LSD treatment. A follow-up of three to six years indicated that only one patient had a slight relapse.

79 MYERSON, ABRAHAM, and NEUSTADT, RUDOLPH. "Essential Male Homosexuality and Results of Treatment." *Archives of Neurology and Psychiatry* 55 (3, 1946): 291–293.

Although it had been reported that "essential male homosexuality" is characterized by a low excretion of male hormones and a relatively high excretion of female hormones, further evidence indicates that the chemical tests were not sufficiently discriminating. Although most male homosexuals have a lack of androgens and an excess of estrogens, there are nonhomosexuals who present similar hormonal patterns.

Fifteen patients with essential male homosexuality were treated with methyl testosterone, the male hormone, with the following results: two patients reported no effect, and 13 reported a lessened or no longer existent homosexual drive; only five of the 13 established a direct heterosexual drive, and in none of them was it sufficient to bring about a successful heterosexual life. The preparation was administered for two months with a two-month resting period. It does not seem likely that adult male homosexuality can be cured by the use of prepared hormones. The treatment of homosexuality with endocrine preparations encounters difficulties common to all endocrine therapy—the commercial products are not identical with the bodily substances and do not act in the same manner.

80 OWENSBY, NEWDIGATE M. "Homosexuality and Lesbianism Treated with Metrazol." *Journal of Nervous and Mental Disease* 92 (1, 1940): 65–66.

Homosexuality and lesbianism are symptoms of an underdeveloped schizophrenia which was arrested at the particular phase in its psychosexual development when the libido became fixated. Metrazol liberates this fixation. To prove these theories, therapy using only Metrazol was given to five males and one female. Ranging in age from 19 to 44 years, all the subjects were white, some of them were in prison, and others were seen in private practice. All six subjects ceased their homosexual behavior and desires, and were able to become completely heterosexual in their orientation.

81   ROSENZWEIG, SAUL. "An Hypothesis Regarding Cycles of Behavior in a Schizophrenic Patient." *Psychiatric Quarterly* 16 (1, 1942): 463–468.

While studying the therapeutic effects of sex hormone medication in a schizophrenic patient over a period of three years, well-defined recurrent cycles of behavior were noted. They were characterized by phases in which heterosexual tension competed with homosexual tendencies for dominance. These cyclical phases can be interpreted as miniature recapitulations of the ontogenetic development of the patient in his early life. The sex hormone medication appeared to intensify these cycles.

82   ROSENZWEIG, SAUL, and HOSKINS, R. G. "A Note on the Ineffectualness of Sex-Hormone Medication in a Case of Pronounced Homosexuality." *Psychosomatic Medicine* 3 (1, 1941): 87–89.

The case of a mental institution patient (a Negro male, 46 years old), described as a "marked homosexual," is discussed. A variety of estrogenic, androgenic, and gonadotrophic preparations were administered to him over a seven-month period. "No influence upon the behavior or the personality of the patient could be detected." It is concluded that endocrine medication cannot alter personality.

83   WHITAKER, L. HOWARD. "Lysergic Acid Diethylamide in Psychotherapy." *Medical Journal of Australia* 1 (1, 1964): 5–8; 1 (2, 1964): 36–41.

The use of lysergic acid diethylamide (LSD-25) in psychotherapy was tested on 100 patients, nine of whom were classified as male homosexuals. Initial interviews were conducted to discover those patients who would be most likely to benefit from the experience. The patients who were hospitalized for this were given injections of LSD together with nicotinic acid by mouth in order to reduce perceptive disturbance. After the treatment one homosexual "recovered," three were "much improved," three were "unchanged," and two "evaded" treatment. The failure of treatment in these homosexuals was due to an inadequate conscious motivation to "recover."

84   WHITAKER, L. HOWARD. "Oestrogen and Psychosexual Disorders." *Medical Journal of Australia* 46 (16, 1959): 547–549.

The treatment of 26 males for psychosexual disorders by the administration of stilboestrol is described. Seven of the group were overt homosexuals, and nine had homosexual fantasies and low heterosexual drives. None of the overt homosexuals developed an interest in heterosexuality after treatment, and their homosexual drive reappeared when the stilboestrol was withdrawn. Most of the nine males without overt homosexual experience appeared to be heterosexual in orientation after two years of treatment. The use of stilboestrol is seen as an effective control, but not as a cure for homosexuality.

85   WRIGHT, CLIFFORD A. "Results of Endocrine Treatment in a Controlled Group of Homosexual Men." *Medical Record* 154 (2, 1941): 60–61.

Endocrine treatment for a group of homosexual men is described in an attempt to show that hormone imbalance is etiologically important in homosexuality. First, hormone assays were done on 17 homosexual and 31 normal men. The androgens (in international units) were divided by total gamma estrogens to form ratios, and it was concluded that any androgen-estrogen ratios of less than 10 indicated homosexuality. Then endocrine treatment with Antuitrin S and follutein was instituted and continued on 14 homosexual men for approximately one year. Periodic hormone assays were made. In all but one case an increase in androgen-estrogen ratio resulted. Most of the group reported improvement in general health.

Although subjective evidence regarding homosexual desire and activity is of questionable value, it should be noted that nine men reported that homosexuality had become less of a problem to them. Three men claimed to be cured of homosexuality and four reported improvement in that their desire for homosexual activity was less intense.

86   ZLOTLOW, MOSES, and PAGANINI, ALBERT E. "Autoerotic and Homoerotic Manifestations in Hospitalized Male Postlobotomy Patients." *Psychiatric Quarterly* 33 (3, 1959): 490–497.

Lobotomies performed on patients increase their sexual behavior. One hundred unselected cases of male postlobotomy patients, institutionalized for at least 10 years at Pilgrim State Hospital in New York, were studied by observations of their institutional life and case history reports regarding their sexual behavior. Sixty of the 100 patients showed homoerotic or autoerotic manifestations at the time of the study. Forty of these had shown the same signs before the operation; thus 20 had apparently developed them after their lobotomy operations. Eight patients had had homoerotic and autoerotic manifestations before the operation but not after it. Whereas prior to the operation, management problems were those of assaultiveness and aggressiveness, after the operation problems arose which had to do with the patients' sexual behaviors. It does not seem that lobotomies precipitate the release of sexual behavior, but that the preoperative characteristics of assaultiveness and aggressiveness had masked sexual impulses prior to the operation.

CROSS-REFERENCES

Bowman, Karl M., and Engle, Bernice. "Sex Offenses: The Medical and Legal Implications of Sex Variations." *Law and Contemporary Problems* 25 (2, 1960): 292–308. No. 1135.

Buki, Rudolph A. "A Treatment Program for Homosexuals." *Diseases of the Nervous System* 25 (5, 1964): 304–307. No. 663.

Freed, Louis F. "Medico-Sociological Data in the Therapy of Homosexuality." *South African Medical Journal* 28 (48, 1954): 1022–1023. No. 143.

Freund, Kurt. "Some Problems in the Treatment of Homosexuality." In *Behavior Therapy and the Neuroses,* edited by H. J. Eysenck, pp. 312–326. New York: Pergamon Press, 1960. No. 697.

Glueck, Bernard C., Jr. "Psychodynamic Patterns in the Homosexual Sex Offender." *American Journal of Psychiatry* 112 (8, 1956): 584–590. No. 421.

Heilbrun, Gert. "Psychoanalysis of Yesterday, Today, and Tomorrow." *Archives of General Psychiatry* 4 (4, 1961): 321–330. No. 16.

Hemphill, R. E.; Leitch, A.; and Stuart, J. R. "A Factual Study of Male Homosexuality." *British Medical Journal* (5083, 1958): 1317–1323. No. 442.

Lurie, Louis A. "The Endocrine Factor in Homosexuality: Report of Treatment of 4 Cases with Androgen Hormone."*American Journal of the Medical Sciences* 208 (Aug., 1944): 176–186. No. 30.

Mayne, D. Gregory. "Homosexuality." *British Journal of Psychiatry* 114 (Jan., 1968): 125. No. 31.

Myerson, Araham, and Neustadt, Rudolph. "Bisexuality and Male Homosexuality: Their Biologic and Medical Aspects." *Clinics* 1 (4, 1942): 932–957. No. 35.

Myerson, Abraham, and Neustadt, Rudolph. "Essential Male Homosexuality and Some Results of Treatment." *Journal of Nervous and Mental Disease* 102 (2, 1945): 194–196. No. 37.

Myerson, Abraham, and Neustadt, Rudolph. "Symposium on Social Psychiatry: Bisexuality and Male Homosexuality; Their Biologic and Medical Aspects." *Clinics* 1 (4, 1942): 932–957. No. 39.

Perloff, William H. "The Role of Hormones in Homosexuality." *Journal of the Albert Einstein Medical Center* 11 (3, 1963): 165–178. No. 47.

Perloff, William H. "Role of the Hormones in Human Sexuality." *Psychosomatic Medicine* 11 (3, 1949): 133–139. No. 48.

Rowe, William S. "The Treatment of Homosexuality and Associated Perversions by Psychotherapy and Aversion Therapy." *Medical Journal of Australia* 2 (14, 1967): 637–639. No. 764.

Rudolf, G. de M. "The Experimental Effect of Sex-Hormone Therapy upon Anxiety in Homosexual Types." *British Journal of Medical Psychology* 18 (3–4, 1941): 317–322. No. 54.

Savitsch, Eugene de. *Homosexuality, Transvestism, and Change of Sex.* Springfield, Ill.: Charles C. Thomas, 1958, 120 pp. No. 55.

Secor, H. W. "Can Hormones Cure Homosexuals?" *Sexology* 16 (11, 1950): 721–727. No. 56.

Stafford-Clark, D. "Essentials of the Clinical Approach." In *The Pathology and Treatment of Sexual Deviation: A Methodological Approach,* edited by Ismond Rosen, pp. 57–86. London: Oxford University Press, 1964. No. 61.

Swyer, G. I. M. "Homosexuality: The Endocrinological Aspects." *Practitioner* 172 (Apr., 1954): 374–377. No. 62.

"Treatment of Homosexuality." *British Medical Journal* (5083, 1958): 1347. No. 788.

Ullerstam, Lars. *The Erotic Minorities.* New York: Grove Press, 1966, 172 pp. No. 1249.

FEMALE

87   ABRAMSON, HAROLD A. "Lysergic Acid Diethylamide (LSD-25), III. As an Adjunct to Psychotherapy with Elimination of Fear of Homosexuality." *Journal of Psychology* 39(Jan., 1955): 127–155.

The use of LSD-25 in psychotherapy is reported, and directions are given for the preparation of patients for four-hour interviews while under the influence of the drug. A verbatim recording of such an interview with a woman 40 years old is presented. Under LSD-25, the patient's fear of being homosexual was reconstructed in connection with her masturbation behavior. The integrative processes of her ego became more manifest, and she was able to lose her fear of being homosexual. It was indicated that a process termed "ego-enhancement" occurred in which the processes of ego reconstruction resulted in reinforcement of the integrative functions of the ego. The solution of the psychodynamic problem of the individual must be a part of any realistic evaluation of the meaning of masturbation by the female in our culture.

CROSS-REFERENCES

Owensby, Newdigate M. "Homosexuality and Lesbianism Treated with Metrazol." *Journal of Nervous and Mental Disease* 92 (1, 1940): 65–66. No. 80.

PSYCHOLOGICAL
CONSIDERATIONS

Etiology

GENERAL, MALE

88   ALLEN, CLIFFORD. "The Homosexual." *Medical World* 78 (2, 1953): 144–148.

Of the possible causes of homosexuality, only the psychological hypothesis is valid. Any disturbance in family relationships can affect the development of the child and cause homosexuality. Treatment which consists of intensive psychotherapy is most likely to succeed with a young patient who wishes to be cured, who has not had widespread homosexual experience, and who has a painful concomitant neurosis. Even when a cure is impossible, individuals may be helped to sublimate their emotions.

89   ALLEN, CLIFFORD. *Homosexuality: Its Nature, Causation and Treatment.* London: Staples Press, 1958, 143 pp.

Although there are chapters on the incidence, social significance, and treatment of homosexuality, including a chapter on the Wolfenden Report, most of the book consists of a psychiatric evaluation of homosexuality and its causes. Homosexuality is considered a form of vice, a genetic aberration, a glandular disease, a psychological disorder, or a combination of these. None of these factors can have an effect without the additional presence of a psychological disorder, stemming from a hostility toward the mother or father, excessive affection for the mother, or affection for an insufficiently heterosexual father.

Homosexuality may be primarily avoided by an intact and happy home atmosphere and the avoidance of environments where homosexuality prevails. Its treatment and cure are possible through psychotherapy. Cases are presented which illustrate the author's point of view.

44

90   ALLEN, CLIFFORD. "The Meaning of Homosexuality." *Medical World* 80 (1, 1954): 9–16. Reprinted in *International Journal of Sexology* 7 (4, 1954): 207–212.

A general discussion of homosexuality emphasizes etiology and treatment. Theories about physiological causes are discounted, and psychological theories are stressed. Homosexual behavior results when the child does not successfully pass through the normal homosexual phase at puberty. Children who mold their personality on the parent of the opposite sex often become homosexual. Much homosexual behavior can be explained by a lack of opportunity to develop heterosexual relationships, as in prison or in boarding schools.

While treatment is sometimes difficult and usually expensive, homosexuals can be cured.

91   ALLEN, CLIFFORD. "Perversions, Sexual." In *The Encyclopedia of Sexual Behavior,* edited by Albert Ellis and Albert Abarbanel, pp. 802–811. 2d rev. ed. New York: Hawthorn Books, 1967.

Although in the past homosexuality has been traced to sin, degeneracy, inherited disease, and endocrine disorders, all the available evidence indicates that homosexuality is a psychological disease. Homosexuals come from broken homes characterized by hostility toward the mother, excessive affection for the mother, hostility toward the father, the Oedipus complex, and affection for an insufficiently masculine father.

92   ALLEN, CLIFFORD. "The Problems of Homosexuality." *International Journal of Sexology* 6 (1, 1952): 40–42.

In the light of his treatment of homosexual cases, a psychoanalyst discusses the causes and treatment of homosexuality. Homosexuality is a psychological condition rather than a physical one. Homosexuality is an orientation toward an abnormal object, and the sexual aim itself may also be abnormal.

Homosexuality occurs because of a broken home, an absent father, or a father who is antipathetic when present. Common ways in which it is produced include hostility toward or excessive affection for the mother, hostility toward the father, and affection for the father when the father himself does not show sufficient heterosexual traits.

93   ALLEN, CLIFFORD. *The Sexual Perversions and Abnormalities: A Study in the Psychology of Paraphilia.* 2d ed. London: Oxford University Press, 1949, 346 pp.

A psychiatric analysis of the entire range of sexual abnormalities contains 29 pages on homosexuality, which discuss its causation and social problems. The four etiological possibilities considered are genetic aberration, endocrine disorder, psychological disease, and a combination of these. The evidence for genetic and endocrine factors is examined and found insufficient. As to psychological disease, Allen asserts "there is no doubt of the importance of this factor." He believes that homosexuality can be produced by the persistence of excessive emotion, either negative or positive, which has been aroused by the parents in the past. Hostility toward the mother or father, or excessive affection for the mother, leads to the Oedipal complex, the unsuccessful resolution of which results in homosexuality. Affection for an insufficiently heterosexual father may also lead to homosexuality. The special social problem of homosexuality, as compared to other forms of sexual deviance, is that homosexuals band together in communities. Allen indicates the futility of imprisonment for homosexual offenses.

94   ALLEN, CLIFFORD. "When Homosexuals Marry." 1957. Reprinted in *The Third Sex*, edited by Isadore Rubin, pp. 58–62. New York: New Book Co., 1961.

Homosexuality is a biological stage of development; children pass through homosexual stages before the age of seven and later at puberty. For various reasons they may be fixated at this immature stage. Probably the most powerful causes of the child's failure to develop are unsatisfactory parental relationships, unhappy or broken homes, and unfortunate early sex experiences. Psychotherapy can help many homosexuals overcome their sexual immaturity. A homosexual-heterosexual marriage usually ends tragically because there are too many points of strain to be adjusted. No homosexual should ever marry to rid himself of homosexuality.

95   APPERSON, LOUISE BEHRENS, and MCADOO, W. GEORGE, JR. "Parental Factors in the Childhood of Homosexuals." *Journal of Abnormal Psychology* 73 (3, Part 1, 1968): 201–206.

The relationship between adult homosexuality and parental attitudes during the subjects' childhoods is explored. A group of adequately functioning homosexuals and nonhomosexual controls were administered the Perception of Parent Behavior Scale. Anonymously gathered data were factor-analyzed, resulting in patterns of reactions which indicated highly significant differences between homosexuals and controls.

On a pattern of "socialization," or emphasizing respect for certain other people, controls scored much higher than did homosexuals, especially for fathers. Hospitalized schizophrenics, compared in the same manner, described their parents as more restrictive than did the homosexual subjects.

96 AUERBACK, A. "Understanding Sexual Deviations, 2. Homosexuality." *Postgraduate Medicine* 43 (Mar., 1968): 169–173.

The studies of Kinsey and others suggest that homosexuality is one of the most common known psychologic disorders. No biological basis for homosexuality has been determined—hormonal and physical characteristics have not shown measurable differences. Psychological studies indicate that homosexuality arises from distorted psychosexual development. Male and female homosexuality are intimately connected with the developing child's relationship to his parents. Female homosexuality is not recognized as criminal; no laws pertain to lesbians. Recently, laws regarding male homosexuality as criminal have begun to come under scrutiny.

97 BAKWIN, HARRY, and BAKWIN, RUTH M. "Homosexual Behavior in Children." *Journal of Pediatrics* 43 (1, 1953): 108–111.

The home situation is very important in the etiology of homosexuality. Special attention to the attitudes of the parents toward one another and toward the child is needed, and any homosexual trends in adolescence should not be punished but should be freely discussed with attempts at understanding.

Various studies on the subject are cited with brief reports of the findings.

98 BANIS, VICTOR J. *Men & Their Boys: The Homosexual Relationship Between Adult and Adolescent.* Los Angeles: Medco Books, 1966, 144 pp.

Pederasty, here used to denote the relationship between a young or adolescent male and an older male, with a sexual connotation—either overt or implied—is discussed through numerous dramatized and somewhat fictionalized case histories. The great variety of factors involved and the impossibility of categorizing such cases are stressed, and it is concluded that overt sex acts in an adult-youth relationship do not necessarily lead to homosexuality whereas, conversely, the "corruption of youth" can occur without a sexual involvement. Often the boy with a special need for a father image seeks a father or brother surrogate although sexual or financial needs may be additional causative factors. The presence or absence of sexual acts is of less importance to the sexual development of the youth than the over-all relationship between the boy and the older man.

A brief historical review of pederasty and a discussion of the over-all aspects of the problem are included. The severity of legal penalties in the

United States is indicated. The cycle or repeat factor which induces an adult, who was initiated into homosexuality in his youth by an adult to similarly introduce youngsters to these practices, is regarded as of prime importance. Banis urges more intensive and far-reaching research with regard to pederasty.

99   BAUMEYER, FRANZ. "The Schreber Case." *International Journal of Psychoanalysis* 37 (1, 1956): 61–74.

Extracts from the case history of Paul Schreber and a brief review of Freud's interpretation of the Schreber case are presented. There is an emphasis on the clarification of the causes of the homosexual tendencies which Freud was unable to trace from Schreber's life history.

The genesis of homosexual impulses in males is a highly complex process in which both an innate factor—i.e., innate bisexuality—and specific childhood experiences, especially those affecting pregenital impulses, are significant. Other writers have advanced the opinion that the homosexual is characterized by tendencies toward softness and surrender which develop as a result of the early suppression of active fighting impulses. Schreber can be regarded as an illustration of this conception.

100   BENDA, CLEMENS E. "Existential Psychotherapy of Homosexuality." *Review of Existential Psychology and Psychiatry* 3 (1963): 133–152.

Existential therapy does not focus on concepts like homosexuality, but upon "human beings whose distorted imagery of the world and mankind prevents full acceptance of their natural role as man." Aberrant sexual behavior is not caused by the attitude of one parent. It can only develop when both parents fail the child and he lacks a "true loving relationship" with both mother and father. For instance, hatred and fear of the father is not likely to result in homosexuality if a boy has a loving and not a seductive relationship with his mother. Existential therapy's goal is to enable the homosexual to form loving, "normal" sexual attachments by correcting the distorted view of existence he possesses by providing strong emotional experiences.

101   BENDER, LAURETTA, and PASTER, SAMUEL. "Homosexual Trends in Children." *American Journal of Orthopsychiatry* 11 (1941): 730–743.

Various theories concerning the origins of homosexuality, especially those which emphasize the importance of childhood experiences in determining future patterns of behavior, are reviewed. In this connection, the cases of 22 prepubescent children of four to 12 years of age are discussed. Revealing homosexual trends in their activities, they had been admitted for observation at the psychiatric division of Bellevue Hospital. They were found to fall mainly into three groups. First, some of the children identified with a domineering homosexual parent or parent-surrogate of the same sex when the parent of the opposite sex was inadequate. These children showed neurotic features. Second, some identified with the parent of the opposite sex when the parent of the same sex was hated or was considered ineffectual or else was absent. These children also revealed neurotic difficulties. Third, there were those who, after a period during infancy in which both parents were absent, underwent a delayed identification with a parent-substitute of the opposite sex. These children tended to become psychopathic personalities. The experiences of these children are compared with those who participate in group sexual experimentation during the latent stage or who, in the "homosexual" stage of psychosexual development, engage in transient homosexual activity. Finally, the case of a pubescent boy who expressed homosexual trends by setting fires in the company of another boy is described.

The conclusions which are drawn from the cases which are considered include the notion that early social and sexual freedom may reduce the likelihood of a homosexual orientation, that inadequate family life enhances it, and that early social deprivations within and outside the family also have serious psychic consequences which go beyond the matter of homosexual development.

102   BENE, EVA. "On the Genesis of Male Homosexuality: An Attempt at Clarifying the Role of the Parents." *British Journal of Psychiatry* 111 (478, 1965): 803–813.

A short questionnaire and the Bene-Anthony Family Relations Test for recall of early family relationships were administered to 85 male homosexuals and 84 married men. The homosexual males were selected through homophile clubs and organizations; the married men were from a hospital staff.

The following hypotheses were confirmed: homosexual men more often have poor relationships with their fathers than heterosexual men; homosexual men more often consider their fathers ineffectual; and homosexual men take their fathers as models less often than heterosexual men. The following hypotheses were not confirmed: homosexual men are more attached to their mothers and they are overprotected and overindulged; they see their mothers as more competent and they more often take them as models than heterosexual men do. It was concluded that homosexual males appear to be more attached to their mothers because their relations with their fathers are so poor. It is suggested that more attention be given to the role of the father for its influence upon homosexual development.

103 BERG, CHARLES, and ALLEN, CLIFFORD. *The Problem of Homosexuality.* New York: Citadel Press, 1958, 221 pp.

A three-part psychiatric examination of the problem of homosexuality includes its nature, causation, and treatment; the psychological foundations of the phenomenon; and the text of the British Parliamentary Committee on Homosexuality (the Wolfenden Report) with a discussion and criticism of it. It is emphasized that since homosexuality is essentially just a particular form which the sexual drive has taken to express itself, it should therefore be subject to modification and alteration. The social implications of homosexuality and its relation to crime, suicide, alcoholism, insanity, and prostitution are explained. Finally, the prevention and treatment of homosexuality are discussed, accompanied with illustrations from case histories which support the claims that it is a curable condition.

104 BEUKENKAMP, CORNELIUS. "Phantom Patricide." *Archives of General Psychiatry* 3 (3, 1960): 282–288.

Cultural changes in the past 50 years have required psychologists, psychiatrists, and psychoanalysts to revise their thinking about the universality of the patricidal struggle. Freud, who saw the drive to murder the primal father and replace him with a more benevolent father-surrogate as a deeply imbedded archaic process present in all males, was familiar with a typical nineteenth-century European family constellation in which the mother was often little more than a secondary appendage in the struggle between the son and his authoritarian father. In Western society today the status of the mother has increased so much that the family leadership role is often reversed, and often instead of finding himself in a struggle with a "strong" father, a son finds himself in combat with a father who is little more than a sibling rival.

If the father proves inadequate in the competition which is essential for his son's natural development into manliness, confusion in the normal process of masculine identification may occur. In this case the patricidal drive produces even more guilt in the son than if he had found his adversary to be a more capable opponent. In addition, this situation sometimes leads the son to single out his father as his love object when choosing an incest partner, causing a severe conflict which may further reinforce the symbiotic relationship between the son and the mother and lead ultimately to actual patricide or to homosexuality.

A case history of an overt homosexual with a background of this nature is given as illustration. After individual treatment, he entered into group therapy where he was able to compose a substitute family group and act out a "phantom" patricide. Soon after he was able to leave psychotherapy and make a heterosexual adjustment which led to marriage.

105   BIEBER, IRVING. "Advising the Homosexual." *Medical Aspects of Human Sexuality* 2 (3, 1968): 34–39.

A psychiatric discussion of homosexuality, including its etiology and treatment, is presented. Constitutional factors are not involved in the etiology of homosexuality; rather, it is a condition patterned within the family. Most male homosexuals are characterized by one particular type of parent-child relationship, a mother who has an inappropriately intimate relationship with the son. There are psychotherapeutic techniques which can lead many homosexuals and bisexuals to exclusive heterosexuality.

106   BIEBER, IRVING. "Clinical Aspects of Male Homosexuality." In *Sexual Inversion: The Multiple Roots of Homosexuality,* edited by Judd Marmor, pp. 248–267. New York: Basic Books, 1965.

In a discussion of the experiential hypothesis of the origins of homosexuality, the typical parental relationships of homosexuals are summarized. Homosexuality is an adaptation resulting from immobilizing fears surrounding heterosexual activity. In psychoanalytic therapy the central problem is the delineation of the many irrational beliefs underlying these fears.

In contrast with a widely held psychoanalytic view that the female is the centrally feared and hated figure, the view given of the basic psychodynamics of homosexuality is that the male is feared and hated and that the woman is loved but avoided.

107   BLACKMAN, NATHAN J. "The Genesis of Homosexuality." *Journal of the Missouri Medical Association* 47 (11, 1950): 814–817.

A homosexual identification, developed primarily to avoid castration and Oedipal fears in relationship to sexual gratification, may be reinforced by a keenly perceived "feeling tone" of being isolated, which is a product of early family dynamics. If a meaningful parent withholds emotional warmth, the child feels insecure, alone, misunderstood, and out of place. Homosexual liaisons may be deliberately sought out because, although such relationships recreate these feelings of insecurity, the person feels more secure since there is a partner who shares these feelings of isolation and loneliness with him.

Four case studies illustrate how the feeling tone of isolation relates to homosexuality.

108 BOSS, MEDARD. *Meaning and Content of Sexual Perversions: A Daseinsanalytic Approach to the Psychopathology of the Phenomenon of Love.* Translated by Liese Lewis Abell. 2d ed. New York: Grune & Stratton, 1949, 153 pp.

Anthropological interpretations of homosexuality which stress biological explanations are wrong. Even if some bases for hereditary and endocrinological theories are found in the future, they can only give evidence as to how homosexuality can manifest itself anatomically and physiologically. They can offer no explanation as to the very meaning and essence of homosexuality. Psychoanalysis, the other approach to sexual perversions, also fails to encompass the entire truth about sexual perversions. Both these theories fail because they do not adequately take into consideration the phenomenon of love.

109 BOWMAN, KARL M., and ENGLE, BERNICE. "The Problem of Homosexuality." *Journal of Social Hygiene* 39 (1, 1953): 2–16.

The incidence of overt homosexuality, its causes, its treatment, and possible ways of prevention are discussed. There are two types of homosexuals, overt and latent (conscious homosexual drives which are controlled and unconscious homosexual drives). Although homosexual relationships are common in many cultures at all periods, they are more common among males than among females in both human beings and animals. For prevention "the father should take an important part in training the boy and restraining his instinctual drives, while the mother should offer warm care and affection. The boy thus has a man to identify with and a beloved mother-figure to possess as an ideal. Boys and girls should have many opportunities to mix with each other and to form early attachments, but sexual interests should not be stimulated until adolescence has begun."

110 BRILL, A. A. "Sexual Manifestations in Neurotic and Psychotic Symptoms." *Psychiatric Quarterly* 14 (1, 1940): 9–16.

The psychoanalytical case histories of two patients are presented, both of whom demonstrated paranoia and homosexual tendencies in their sexual behavior. One was age 23, and the other was age 46. Both were male, unmarried, and of normal intelligence.

Paranoia is considered to be a distorted homosexuality. In these particular cases there is a strong mother fixation, precluding any erotic relations with other women. The homosexual focuses on same-sex relations while the paranoid expresses hatred toward those of the same sex.

The cases demonstrate the functioning of the libido in the formation and functioning of neuroses and psychoneuroses. Freud's libido theory provides a useful model for viewing the phenomena.

111   BROWN, DANIEL G. "Childhood Development and Sexual Devia-
       tions." *Sexology* 28 (7, 1962): 476–480.

Factors in childhood development which appear to be functionally related to the development of homosexuality in adults are prolonged segregation of the sexes, certain intensely exciting and gratifying homosexual experiences in childhood, seduction by adult homosexuals, threatening and painful experiences in connection with sex play or relationships with the opposite sex, and the development of a sex role typical of the other sex. Male children who become predominantly or exclusively homosexual in adulthood often have childhoods in which there was an excessively close and abnormally strong mother-son relationship, and a father who is either a physical or psychological nonentity as far as the son is concerned.

Recommendations for the prevention of homosexuality include the maintenance of warm and close ties between father and son, and the respect and love of parents for their child as a boy or as a girl. The child should never be terrified by being threatened in connection with sexual play with opposite-sex children.

112   BROWN, DANIEL G. "Homosexuality and Family Dynamics."
       Bulletin of the Menninger Clinic 27 (5, 1963): 227–232.

The term homosexuality is properly applied only to the specific deviation in which sexual desire and activity is directed toward the same sex. There is sufficient evidence to warrant the conclusion that adult male homosexuals often have a childhood in which there is an excessively close and abnormally strong mother-son relationship. The father is usually either passive, weak, and ineffective or is abusive, hostile, rejecting, and indifferent to the son. Works by Terman and Miles, Freud, Schilder, Fenichel, Hamilton, West, and Bieber, et al., are cited to support these findings about homosexuals.

Although this family background is common to male homosexuals, not everyone with these types of parents is homosexual. It is suggested that more research be carried out concerning the over-all variable of timing and continuity or discontinuity of the family pattern.

113   BROWN, JAMES H. "Homosexuality as an Adaptation in Handling
       Aggression." *Journal of the Louisiana State Medical Society* 115 (9,
       1963): 304–311.

Literature pertaining to varying psychoanalytic views on the origins of homosexuality and methods of treating it is reviewed. A detailed case history demonstrates some of the nonsexual strivings which can be observed in male homosexuality: a dependency versus aggressive masculine image, an inability to identify with a punitive father, and an ensuing power struggle. It is suggested that these nonsexual strivings satisfy an unconscious need and are the underlying causes of homosexuality.

114   BYCHOWSKI, GUSTAV. "The Ego and the Introjects." *Psycho-analytic Quarterly* 25 (1, 1956): 11–36.

In an article treating various aspects of ego-splitting, the second section entitled "Construction of Male Homosexuality" contains a highly theoretical application of Freudian psychoanalysis to problems of the origin and maintenance of homosexuality. Two case histories taken from private practice are used for illustrative purposes.

   Male homosexuals usually come from families with aggressive mothers and passive fathers, creating a situation not conducive to adequate ego formation or to proper control of libidinal energy. The homosexual is similar to the schizophrenic in that he rapidly shifts role behavior, from passive to active or vice versa.

115   BYCHOWSKI, GUSTAV. "The Ego of Homosexuals." *International Journal of Psycho-Analysis* 26 (3–4, 1945): 114–127.

In an investigation of the extent to which the choice of perversion is determined by the characteristics of the ego, the following observations are made: "The homosexual ego is directed by an attempt to overcome its pre-natal and post-natal narcissism, and to restore or rebuild its highly imperfect power to love . . . it is an attempt to prevent the constantly impending danger of depression and depersonalization."

116   CAMPBELL, ROBERT J. "Homosexuality." In *The Adolescent: His Search for Understanding,* edited by William Christian Bier, pp. 58–61. New York: Fordham University Press, 1961.

Homosexuality is probably much more prevalent than is commonly believed, since most research statistics omit latent homosexuals and those who do not reach orgasm. Homosexuality, excluding accidental homosexuality, may result from several causes: fixation at pregenital levels, fear of castration, intense Oedipal attachment to the mother, narcissism and narcissistic object choice, and a readiness to substitute identification for object relationships. Occasional overt homosexual relationships in adolescence are best ignored, but some danger signals indicating that the activity may be more than a passing stage include: rejection of the individual from the peer group because of his homosexual activities, continuation of homosexual behavior into late adolescence, frequent episodes of fellatio or anal intercourse, and homosexual contacts with adult males.

117   CAPRIO, FRANK S. "The Homosexual Problem." *Sexology* 20 (8, 1954): 510–517.

Homosexuality is a symptom of some deep-seated nervous disorder that can be traced to the development of a neurotic relationship with certain members of the family who are likely to be neurotic. Homosexual tendencies develop as the result of a number of contributory factors: influence of parents, religious training, sexual experience in childhood, feelings of inferiority associated with specific handicaps, personal reactions to the home environment, susceptibility to influences within the community, and exposure to situations which tend to threaten one's sense of security (death of a parent, divorce, poverty, et cetera). Proper sex education in our schools and universities can do much to prevent homosexuality. Since homosexuality is psychological in origin, psychoanalysis offers the greatest hope for correction.

118   CAPRIO, FRANK S. *Variations in Sexual Behavior: A Psychodynamic Study of Deviations in Various Expressions of Sexual Behavior.* New York: Citadel Press, 1955, 344 pp.

A psychodynamic study of sexual deviations deals in part with homosexuality, male and female. Homosexuality is described as a symptom of neurosis resulting when sexual development is arrested at a preheterosexual stage. The homosexual is essentially narcissistic. Male homosexuals seek fellatio only because of their inability to perform autofellatio. Female homosexuality is also an extension of autoeroticism, a form of mutual masturbation.

   Detailed case histories are presented for both male and female homosexuality.

119   CAPRIO, FRANK S.; DALVEN, JOSEPH; BENJAMIN, HARRY; and LANVAL, MARC. "The Causes of Homosexuality: A Symposium." *Sexology* 21 (10, 1955): 633–637.

Four professionals discuss the etiology of homosexuality. According to Caprio, homosexuality is a projection of self-love, a form of cooperative or mutual self-gratification. Secondary or contributory causes include feelings of inferiority, loneliness, fear of marriage, unpleasant sexual experiences in childhood and adolescence, instability of parents, a neurotic home environment, various cultural influences, alcohol, personality deficiencies, and seduction by an experienced invert.

Dalven finds the main underlying causes of homosexuality to be a faulty environment and conditioning during the early years of childhood, faulty sex education, military camps, penal institutions, horror stories surrounding the normal sex act, successful introduction to homosexual activities during puberty and adolescence, and any prolonged unbalanced relationship between one's parents, or one of the parents and the child, or the absence of one parent.

Benjamin and Lanval, on the other hand, believe that homosexual behavior is not only psychologically acquired but that it can be determined by one's genetic endowment as well.

120 CAULDWELL, DAVID O. "Homosexual Patterns." *Sexology* 17 (2, 1950): 88–93.

A person is basically endowed with the potential to develop any pattern of sexuality. If one's more pleasant social contacts are with members of his own sex, he tends to develop the sex variant pattern which leads to adult exclusive homosexuality. Latent homosexuality develops as a result of environment. Parents are responsible for the prevention or the development of the homosexual character, and society, or the state, must assume responsibility for the education of parents that is needed to prevent poor social and psychosexual adjustment.

121 CHESSER, EUSTACE. *Sexual Behavior: Normal and Abnormal.* New York: Medical Publications, 1949, 221 pp.

An abbreviated and general summary of the condition of homosexuality is presented. Homosexuality is compared to various forms of autoeroticism in that both result from emotional experiences which have produced arrested development and have their basis in unconscious mechanisms. As a result, the homosexual is not held responsible for his condition. A case study involving homosexuality in conjunction with masochism is presented.

122 CHURCHILL, WAINWRIGHT. *Homosexual Behavior Among Males: A Cross-Cultural and Cross-Species Investigation.* New York: Hawthorn Books, 1967, 340 pp.

A psychological investigation of homosexual behavior among males includes the history of laws against homosexual behavior, the moral concerns and implications of such legislation, and the theories pertaining to the cause of homosexuality. Homosexual responsiveness is a component of mammalian sexuality, increasing as the evolutionary scale is ascended. Homosexual preferences are based on experiences (conscious and/or unconscious stimulation) which are acquired, learned, and conditioned in the individual.

The general sex-negativity ("erotophobia" and "homoerotophobia") of our culture is illustrated in its attempt to dictate moral legislation.

123   CORY, DONALD WEBSTER. "Homosexuality." In *The Encyclopedia of Sexual Behavior,* edited by Albert Ellis and Albert Abarbanel, pp. 485–493. 2d rev. ed. New York: Hawthorn Books, 1967.

Such words as "homosexual," "bisexual," "lesbian," and various slang terms are defined. Many early and some contemporary writers believe in inborn or congenital homosexuality, although this has been strongly challenged. Freudian theory holds that homosexuality is a flight from incest, involving the Oedipus or Electra complexes. With a variety of backgrounds leading to homosexuality an eclectic, pluralistic approach is recommended. Statistics on incidence are cited from the Kinsey studies, and lesbianism is found to be less common than male homosexuality. Suggested reasons for this are that female sexual demands are less imperious than male, females can more easily find sex mates, and females who repress heterosexuality are more likely to retreat into asexuality. While therapy for homosexuals who often suffer from anxiety and neuroses was formerly discouraged and adjustment to homosexuality encouraged, this is now being questioned.

124   CRANE, HARRY W. "The Environmental Factor in Sexual Inversion." *Journal of the Elisha Mitchell Scientific Society* 61 (Aug., 1945): 243–248.

The case of a 25-year-old single male who underwent psychotherapy is cited as evidence that environmental factors constitute the basis of homosexuality.

The patient's homosexuality resulted from environmental influences active during his youth. His parents treated him as if he were a girl and taught him to fear sexual interest in members of the opposite sex. He also experienced a traumatic circumcision.

125   DANK, BARRY M. "A Social Psychological Theory of Homosexuality and Sex-Role Learning." Master's thesis, University of Wisconsin, 1966, 211 pp.

This thesis is an attempt to integrate research and theory on sex-role learning (i.e., the development of masculinity and femininity) developed by scholars with respect to the early family relations of male homosexuals.

It was found that research findings available on the development of masculinity and femininity in children show that young boys with a higher degree of feminine identification came from family backgrounds similar to those of adult male homosexuals. There is one significant exception: male homosexuals, compared to young boys with a higher degree of feminine identification, do not come as frequently from families in which an older adjacent sister is present.

Given the similarity of family backgrounds of adult male homosexuals and young boys with a high degree of feminine identification, it was argued that a theoretical explanation developed by Orville Brim was available ("Family Structure and Sex-Role Learning By Children," *Sociometry,* 1958).

Brim's theory, originally proposed to explain culturally inappropriate sex-role identification, has been extended in this thesis to explain the development of a homosexual preference. The central concept employed by Brim was that of sex-role assimilation. It was argued that boys with a high degree of femininity as well as adult male homosexuals had both experienced childhood situations in which "behavior learned through role-taking and appropriate to the other [sex] is confused with and undifferentiated from behavior learned as part of one's own role. The latter becomes tinged or diluted with characteristics belonging to someone else's role." It was therefore argued that inappropriate sex-role identification and homosexual preference are both the result of the same underlying social psychological process—culturally inappropriate role-taking during childhood.

126 DAVIS, KINGSLEY. "Sexual Behavior." In *Contemporary Social Problems,* edited by Robert K. Merton and Robert A. Nisbet, pp. 322–372. 2d ed. New York: Harcourt, Brace & World, 1966.

Sexual norms and types and the causes of sexual problems are discussed and a detailed examination is made of two forms of violation—homosexuality and prostitution. The violations are used as examples which illustrate the sociological principle that to understand a type of deviancy one must understand the norms that define it as deviancy. The family seems to hold the key to the norms which are part of the system of sexual control. There are degrees of legitimacy and illegitimacy in any society, and violations as well as conformity have their rules and rewards. The persistence of these forms of deviancy can be seen as due to the counterforces set in motion by the very control of sex itself.

127 DENFORD, J. D. "The Psychodynamics of Homosexuality." *New Zealand Medical Journal* 66 (Nov., 1967): 743–744.

The condensation of a paper read at a conference on psychiatry at the University of Otago Medical School in August, 1967, presents a review of recent modifications of psychoanalytic theory concerning the development of homosexuality. Parental behaviors and characteristics which are not anticipated by conventional appraisals of the Oedipal situation are discussed with regard to their impact upon psychosexual development. Boys with hostile, frightening, ineffectual, or absent fathers often become negative about men and, in turn, value and thus identify with women. The narcissistic element in homosexual object choice can often be observed when neither parent serves as a satisfactory model for a love object. Heterosexuality is often discouraged and homosexual relationships—perhaps unconsciously—are encouraged when a possessive and/or seductive mother is part of the pattern of family dynamics. For boys, in such a situation incestuous associations may be the primary origin of guilt, anxiety, and conscious disgust that heterosexual contacts provoke. For girls, a lack of ability to develop an identity apart from the mother leads to relationships with other women which repeat the same features.

Unsolved problems of personal power, poor tolerance of anxiety, and fears of inadequacy are among the nonparental factors mentioned in connection with a homosexual adaptation. When homosexual activity occurs only episodically, it may be due to a temporarily unstable mental change and can usually be interpreted as a symptom of a depressive reaction or its equivalent.

128   DENNISTON, R. H. "Ambisexuality in Animals." In *Sexual Inversion: The Multiple Roots of Homosexuality,* edited by Judd Marmor, pp. 27–43. New York: Basic Books, 1965.

In surveying the animal world it becomes clear that there is a universality of socially conditioned homosexual behavior among animals. Homosexuality occurs in every type of animal studied. Conditioning, rather than hormones or structure, is of primary importance.

129   DERIVER, J. PAUL. *Crime and the Sexual Psychopath.* Springfield, Ill.: Charles C. Thomas, 1958, 346 pp.

A forensic psychiatrist presents a wide variety of criminal cases involving sexual deviance, including male and female homosexuality, voyeurism, pedophilia, rape, exhibitionism, and numerous other forms. Pictures of the offenders and sometimes their victims are displayed along with descriptions of their crimes. Although an unresolved Oedipus complex is seen as the basic cause of homosexuality, some homosexuality may be classified as hereditary.

130   EAST, W. NORWOOD. "Homosexuality." *Medical Press* 217 (Sept. 3, 1947): 215–217.

Both genetic and environmental factors play a part in the etiology of homosexuality. Homosexuality can be overcome through psychotherapy, and the courts should make such therapy a condition of probation for those charged with it.

131   EAST, W. NORWOOD. "Sexual Offenders." *Journal of Nervous and Mental Disease* 103 (6, 1946): 626–666.

Homosexuality, among other types of sexual offenses, is discussed in this survey article. A general introduction includes some statistics on all varieties of sex offenders in England during the 1930's. The predisposition toward homosexuality is believed to be a function of four factors: a general tendency among all humans toward varied sexual outlets; for some people, a specific inherited tendency toward homosexuality; a physical appearance which encourages early homosexual seduction; and early sexual conditioning toward homosexual behavior. Homosexuality is also discussed in relation to other forms of sexual behavior. While fetishism is rarely observed among homosexuals, the combination of homosexuality and sado-masochism is rather common. In general, there is a higher incidence of psychological abnormality among homosexuals than among heterosexuals. While simplistic equations of alcoholism with homosexuality are denied, a causal connection is made between homosexuality and paranoia.

132   EDWARDS, HAROLD EUGENE. "The Relationship Between Reported Early Life Experiences with Parents and Adult Male Homosexuality." Ph.D. dissertation, University of Tennessee, 1963, 97 pp.

A pilot study was made with the subjects and their matched controls drawn from a population of neuropsychiatric patients. This was followed by a larger study which drew both subjects and matched controls from prison. It was hypothesized that homosexual males tend to identify with their mothers when the mothers are nurturant, rewarding, and punitive and their fathers are low in nurturance and not active in discipline. It was also predicted that parents would be low in compatibility and the mothers would be dominant.

Information gathered from the subjects and the controls about the behavior of their parents indicated that fathers were low in nurturance, but not nonpunishing. Mothers were excessively controlling, but not strongly nurturant or punitive. Mothers were dominant for the neuropsychiatric homosexuals, but not for the prisoner population. The homosexuals were not distinguished from the heterosexuals on parental compatibility.

133   EHRENWALD, JAN. "The Symbiotic Matrix of Paranoid Delusions and the Homosexual Alternative." *American Journal of Psychoanalysis* 20 (1960): 49–65.

The background history of a patient suffering from paranoia often includes a description of a pathologically symbiotic parent-child relationship—one in which the child is unable to define personal ego boundaries because his or her personality is fused with that of the parent. Clinicians most often find such relationships between a son and his mother, but mother-daughter, father-daughter, and father-son relationships can also be of this type.

When an obsessive, compulsive parent assumes total control and forces the child to serve as an extension of the parental personality, the normal struggle for individuation, self-expression, and self-realization is drastically distorted. The delusions of grandeur, of persecution, and/or of being controlled by some "magic" power so often seen in the paranoid patient may very well be reflections of actual suffocating parental control which obtained during the patient's childhood.

There are only two alternatives in such cases, both of which are self-defeating. The patient can give up the struggle and comply with the wishes of the omnipotent parent figure or some psychically satisfactory surrogate figure, which leads to the development of a passive homosexual pattern; or frantic resistance and rebellion can be employed as a defense against such compliance, leading to a regressive disorganization of the ego.

Clinical observations from four cases in which early symbiotic parent-child relationships played a part in paranoid psychodynamics as well as references to Freud's analysis of the Schreber case are used as illustrations.

The author's ideas are commented on and expanded in discussions by Gustav Bychowski and Harold Kelman.

134   ELLIS, ALBERT. "The Sexual Psychology of Human Hermaphrodites." *Psychosomatic Medicine* 7 (2, 1945): 108–125.

Studying the sexual psychology of human hermaphrodites may help determine why some individuals become overtly homosexual while others do not. The case histories of 84 hermaphrodites (39 raised as males and 45 as females) reported by other investigators were reviewed. The variables of these investigations included body build, the sex of which they were raised, sex role, physiological factors, and sexual interests. Six percent of these cases were homosexual in relation to their upbringing as a member of one sex, and another 4 percent were bisexual. The latter were all raised as females.

Homosexuality and heterosexuality in hermaphrodites were primarily caused by environmental factors. The purely physiological characteristics of hermaphrodites actually had little to do with their object choices.

135   ERICKSON, RALPH J. "Male Homosexuality and Society." *Bulletin of the National Association of Secondary-School Principals* 45 (Nov., 1961): 128–134.

Homosexuality is one type of adjustment to sexual problems. Between 2 and 5 percent of all males are homosexuals, yet very little data is available for a scientific study of the problem.

There are two kinds of homosexuals, those who take the passive-feminine role and those who take the active-masculine role in intercourse. The PMH (passive male homosexual) is treated and dressed as a girl in infancy and adolescence. An overprotective mother and an absent, missing, or passive father result in a strong identification with the mother. The Terman-Miles Test of Masculinity-Femininity rates PMH as the "Intermediate Sex"; few PMH ever marry. On the other hand, AMH (active male homosexuals), as children, prefer typical "boyish" games. Identification with the father is strong, and there is an almost complete separation from anything feminine. A desire to dominate and to be aggressive characterizes this "third sex." It was found that AMH did not differ from college males in masculinity.

Homosexuality is primarily a learned behavior which begins at home. Parents are in a good position to help prevent their sons from developing into homosexuals. Early signs of extreme active or passive behavior should be modified by parents or by a professional in the field of psychology.

136   ERNST, JOHN R. "Homosexuality and Crime." *Journal of Clinical Psychopathology* 8 (5, 1947): 763–769.

Through reports given during the course of psychotherapy it was found that the homosexuality of a male patient was related to his family situation. As a result of what had occurred the patient acquired an immature, unstable, and inadequate personality which increased his susceptibility to sex deviation.

The basic source of effeminacy and homosexuality in boys is the mother of the family. Sublimation should be taught to the latent homosexual by means of occupations which require originality and creative ability.

137   FAIN, MICHEL, and MARTY, PIERRE. "The Synthetic Function of Homosexual Cathexis in the Treatment of Adults." *International Journal of Psycho-Analysis* 41 (4–5, 1960): 401–406.

Relying primarily on French research, the development over the last 10 years of psychoanalytic theories of adult homosexuality is described. This development is seen as a synthesis of conflicting clinical data leading to a pregenital interpretation of homosexuality along the lines indicated by Freud. The theories converge on the concept of the desire of the homosexual to be approached by an omnipotent phallic personage. The classic manifestations of homosexual cathexis in transference are schematically discussed.

The theoretical bases stemming chiefly from Freud's work for this conceptualization of the issues involved are presented.

138   FAIRBAIRN, W. RONALD. "A Note on the Origin of Male Homosexuality." *British Journal of Medical Psychology* 37 (1, 1964): 31–32.

Substitution of the penis for the breast as the principal cause of male homosexuality was demonstrated in the case of a patient in analysis. During the analytic process it became clear that the patient believed or valued his penis as a breast substitute and that he thought of his mother as a castrator.

139   FELDMAN, SANDOR S. "On Homosexuality." In *Perversions: Psychodynamics and Therapy,* edited by Sandor Lorand and Michael Balint, pp. 71–96. New York: Random House, 1956.

Case studies of males and females are presented to demonstrate that homosexuals in both sexes have started out as heterosexuals but that some traumatic situation changed their heterosexual orientation toward homosexuality. Whenever, during childhood or adulthood, the individual's life-love-position became insecure, a perversion developed; whenever guilt became prevalent, a neurosis developed; when both threats were present, neurosis and perversion developed. Whenever, in the Freudian pregenital phase of sexual development a contact with a heterosexual object was not permitted, a homosexual neurosis developed.

140   FENICHEL, OTTO. *The Psychoanalytic Theory of Neurosis.* New York: W. W. Norton, 1945, 703 pp.

In a summary of psychoanalytic doctrines, male and female homosexuality is discussed in relation to perversions and impulse neuroses. In males, it is often the reaction to castration-anxiety that causes homosexuality; the anxiety is provoked by the sight of female genitals and the reaction is one of fear and avoidance. Some homosexuality is a regression to an early state of father-fixation. However, most homosexuality involves an inability to resolve the Oedipal complex. Failure to obtain the love object (mother) tends to make the individual regress from the level of object love to that of identification; he becomes the object which he cannot possess. In females, homosexuality can result from regression to an attachment to the mother. A secondary etiological factor may be a castration complex caused by first sight of the penis.

141   FODOR, NANDOR. "Homosexuality of an Identical Twin: A Study in Retrojection, Parts 1–2." *Psychoanalysis and the Psychoanalytic Review* 45 (4, 1958): 105–124; 46 (1, 1959): 111–121.

The psychoanalytic case history of a 25-year-old homosexual male whose twin brother died at birth is presented. Traumatized by the thought of his brother's decomposing body, the patient began to experience fratricidal fantasies which are described as retrojection designed to keep his feelings of guilt repressed. The patient came to develop mechanisms (including homosexuality) which served as an escape from responsibility for the present. Feeling that he had no legitimate place in life because he felt it was his brother who should have lived, he acted out a number of roles. The twin was his father and mother; he was father and mother to the twin. He was identified on each level with one or the other and with both. Playing the homosexual role was just another acting-out mechanism.

The weakness of the patient's ego boundaries developed from a strong ambivalence toward his parents. He was constantly merging, flowing into another personality or drawing that personality into himself as if to find or to replace the missing twin. He was able to identify with the analyst, as a new father image and to overcome his unconscious identification with his mother, thereby beginning to lead an exclusively heterosexual life.

142   FORKNER, CLAUDE E., et al. "Homosexuality." *New York Medicine* 10 (11, 1954): 455–473.

A panel discussion on various aspects of homosexuality is summarized. Homosexual behavior occurs among most animal species and in many societies of the world. Homosexual behavior may variously mean intense affectionate feelings, or libidinal strivings, or actual physical consummation, alone or in combination. Homosexual activity does not provide evidence of psychopathic personality. The etiology of homosexual behavior is the outcome of biologic, psychologic, and sociologic factors operating simultaneously. Long-term psychotherapy of a psychoanalytic variety may bring cure. Adult homosexuality is a failure of development or a fixation of the pattern (normal personality growth) at the preadolescent level. It is the result of overidentification with the parent of the opposite sex, and failure of identification with the parent-model of the same sex.

143   FREED, LOUIS F. "Medico-Sociological Data in the Therapy of Homosexuality." *South African Medical Journal* 28 (48, 1954): 1022–1023.

Medico-sociological data may be utilized in the therapy of homosexuality, which is largely a sociological problem and an index of social disorganization. Although homosexuality may be associated with intersexuality, the latter alone is not sufficient for its development. From the standpoint of integral medicine, the adequate treatment of homosexuality requires a physical examination to determine the degree of biological predisposition or intersexuality, a psychological examination to determine the degree of psychic regression and of psychic repression, and an examination of the socioeconomic background of the patient to determine the degree of frustration present. The success of the integralistic approach to the problem depends on the harmonic coordination of medical, judicial, and social-welfare agencies.

144   FREEMAN, LUCY, and THEODORES, MARTIN, eds. *The Why Report.*
       New York: Arthur Bernhard, 1964, 602 pp.

Two interviews on homosexuality appear in a collection of 45 interviews with psychiatrists, psychoanalysts, and psychologists on the topics of love, hate, sexual problems, family, work, and treatment. Dr. Lewis L. Robbins, Medical Director of Hillside Hospital, Queens, N.Y., is asked "What are the causes of homosexuality?" His answer includes references to the Oedipal conflict, the fear of castration by the mother, and the repression of father-rivalry. Dr. Edmund Bergler, a psychoanalyst, is asked "What would you say to a man who complains, 'Lately, I've had the strangest thoughts about other men . . . I think I'm homosexual'? " He replies that one must be sexually attracted to the same sex to be homosexual. Homosexuality is a "self-damaging" behavior, a masochistic revival of early fears, and a seeking after frustration, jealousy, misery, and punishment.

145   FREUND, KURT, and PINKAVA, V. "Homosexuality in Man and Its
       Association with Parental Relationships." *Review of Czechoslovak
       Medicine* 7 (1, 1961): 32 40.

There is an association between homosexuality and a deficiency in family relationships in the patient's childhood. To verify this, a study was made of 154 homosexual men and 154 neurotics who were hospitalized in the University of Prague psychiatric hospital, and of 128 homosexual men and 128 nonpsychiatric patients. Each homosexual man was compared with a neurotic or nonpsychiatric patient of the same educational level and age. A questionnaire was administered, and McNemar's test for matched pairs and chi square were used.

The homosexuals described their fathers more often as intolerant, unconcerned, or rude; they said that their mothers were sad, and more often wanted a daughter at the time of their birth. The homosexual patients stated more frequently that they preferred the mother to the father, that the mother was very much appreciated by the family, that their parents had often quarreled, and that their fathers were habitual drinkers. It was impossible to demonstrate any association between parental deprivation (i.e., absence of a parent, an unfavorable parent-child or interparental relationship, et cetera) and homosexuality.

146 "Genesis of Homosexuality." *Canadian Medical Association Journal* 93 (Nov. 6, 1965): 1041.

Eve Bene's research using the Bene-Anthony Family Relations Test indicates that a significant cause of homosexuality is the lack of normal childhood relations with parents. The quality of the child's relationship to the mother is important, but more emphasis must be accorded to the place and importance of the father in the family constellation in theories of homosexual etiology.

147 GERSHMAN, HARRY. "The Evolution of Gender Identity." *American Journal of Psychoanalysis* 28 (1, 1968): 80–90.

Gender identity refers to the social and psychological aspects of being masculine or feminine. The core of gender identity is fixed by age three and is the result of early infant-mother interaction. The infant-mother relationship is the initial object relationship of the child, and a distorted self-image may occur if the mother does not provide sufficient emotional stimulation. A homosexual has doubts about his assigned sexual role, and his sexual activities are reparative, calculated to restore the gender image by fusion with a person of the same sex. A case study of a homosexual patient is given.

148 GERSHMAN, HARRY. "Psychopathology of Compulsive Homosexuality." *American Journal of Psychoanalysis* 17 (1, 1957): 58–77.

Observations are based upon experiences gained over a period of years through the psychoanalytic treatment of about 20 patients.

A distinction needs to be made between "homosexual behavior" and "compulsive homosexuality." "Homosexual behavior" is a reflection of the fact that man and animals can be stimulated by a variety of means and are thus capable of homosexual activity. "Compulsive homosexuality," on the other hand, is not normal because it indicates a persistent emotional and physical attraction to members of the same sex. It reflects a personality distortion initiated by the earliest experiences of the individual and is perpetuated by the compulsive strategies which evolve during the course of his life (the neurotic aspects of his character structure). "Compulsive homosexuality" is an outgrowth of an acquired conflict relating to the whole person, the symbolic expression (in sexual language) of a person's inner conflict. The basic problem is one of alienation, compartmentalization, externalization, massive resignation, and emptiness.

149 GERSHMAN, HARRY. "Reflections on the Nature of Homosexuality." *American Journal of Psychoanalysis* 26 (1, 1966): 46–59.

The "compulsive homosexual" is one who indicates persistent emotional and physical attraction to one's own sex (a reflection of personality development). "Compulsive homosexuality" is an illness which in only a minor degree disturbs one's personality. It must be distinguished from homosexual behaviors which are not compulsive and which may have quite different meanings depending upon the culture in which they occur.

The compulsive-homosexual-to-be has much more anxiety in his early years, which results in the blocking of the maturational process. The narcissistic features of his personality stem from an inability to separate from his mother. The parents, by presenting a faulty polarization of mature masculinity and femininity, deform the child's sexual identity. Homosexuality is a reparative maneuver for healing a flaw in sexual identity. In perversion there is a drive toward meaningful love relationships, but this drive often assumes "grotesque and bizarre forms."

150   GILLESPIE, W. H. "The General Theory of Sexual Perversion."
       International Journal of Psycho-Analysis 37 (4–5, 1956): 396–403.

Observations which came from work with patients in psychoanalytic treatment are made on sexual perversions and their causes. Perversion constitutes a defense against the castration anxiety and guilt feelings associated with the Oedipus complex. The raw materials of perversion are supplied by the constituent elements of infantile sexuality. Libidinization of anxiety, guilt, and pain is the method of defense. The ego's behavior and defensive maneuvers are also important—the ego adopts the least threatening aspects of infantile sexuality and is thus able to deny those which are more threatening.

151   GILLESPIE, W. H.; PASCHE, FRANCIS; and WIEDEMAN, GEORGE
       H. "Symposium on Homosexuality." *International Journal of Psycho-Analysis* 45 (2–3, 1964): 203–216.

Three papers were read as a unit at the 23rd International Psycho-Analytic Congress, Stockholm, July–August, 1963. All were theoretical, psychoanalytic discussions of the etiology of homosexuality. They were based on surveys of the literature and personal observations by the authors, all practicing psychoanalysts.

Gillespie (London): Homosexuality is not like other perversions for it has been practiced in certain societies openly and ideally. Also there may be genetic factors at work. Although psychoanalytic theory has focused primarily on the Oedipal triangle, there may be a second type of homosexuality arising out of pre-Oedipal fixations.

Pasche (Paris): Male homosexuality is defined as the "sum of behavior which expresses a feminine attitude toward father." Homosexuality can take four forms: repressed, fantasied, manifest, and sublimated. The family of the homosexual possesses three characteristics: mother is the model for identification, a tender father prematurely terminates the relationship he has with his child, and mother treats son as the penis she lacks. Oedipal and pre-Oedipal homosexuality are not distinguished.

Wiedeman (New York): The theories which stress single causes of male homosexuality are discounted. Although the total life experience may be causative from early childhood through adolescence, one of the strongest influences is a lack of sexual identity in the first two to three years of life.

152   GLAUBER, I. Peter. "The Rebirth Motif in Homosexuality and Its Teleological Significance." *International Journal of Psycho-Analysis* 37 (4–5, 1956): 416–421.

Observations are presented of a syndrome involved in homosexuality which Glauber noted in the psychoanalytic treatment of his patients. "Important determinants in homosexuality include fixation in the pleasure-ego phase of development, wherein the image of the self in the form of a phallus represents a part-object cathexis of the self-image mainly with destructive aggression and a similar feeling about the cathexis of the object interferes with the process of identification. Homosexuality is a substitutive process, an acting-out, and serves purposes of relieving intropsychic [*sic*] tension and of restitutive wishes."

153   GLOVER, EDWARD. "Sexual Disorders and Offences, I. The Social and Legal Aspects of Sexual Abnormality. [1956. Reprinted.] II. The Problem of Male Homosexuality." In his *The Roots of Crime*, pp. 173–243. New York: International Universities Press, 1960.

It is emphasized that sexual perversions are derived from infantile sexual components and are regressions to such earlier systems. Manifestations of abnormal sexual conduct require psychological observation and treatment. Every sexual offender, without exception, should be psychologically examined and treated, preferably by medical psychologists not officially connected with the court.

The danger of conflict over unconscious homosexuality (the inverted Oedipus phase) is due to a lack of success in mastering the sadistic, sadomasochistic, or masochistic impulses that are released when the positive Oedipus situation is abandoned in favor of the negative or homosexual phase. However, unconscious homosexuality is responsible for many important and constructive developments both individually and socially, and also contributes to a mutual understanding between the sexes by the development of bisexual character traits.

Treatment success depends upon the extent to which the purely psychological disposition to homosexual object choice can be uncovered, the degree in which current ego difficulties and frustrations can be offset, and the degree of transference rapport that can be established or analyzed. In the treatment of unselected cases of male homosexuality or the treatment of homosexuality as a whole, efforts "should be directed as much at the 'diseased' prejudices of society as at the diseased propensities of the individual homosexual."

154   GRECO, MARSHALL C. "Social Psychological Differentials in the Initiation and Retention of Chronic Homosexuality." *American Psychologist* 1 (7, 1946): 240.

A paper read at a meeting of the American Psychological Association in July, 1946, summarizes a series of studies undertaken to determine the nature of the social-psychological situations which contribute to the initiation and continued practice of homosexuality. The case history, the "own story" technique and projective methods were used to study a number of homosexuals contacted in a reformatory, a penitentiary, and in private practice. The following tentative postulates were abstracted: homosexuality is adopted only when it contributes to one's social adjustment; mere contiguous association is not significant to its initiation; only those needs arising from an attempt to adjust to individuals who are current sources of reward are significant in the adoption and retention of homosexual practices.

155   GREEN, EUGENE W., and JOHNSON, L. G. "Homosexuality." *Journal of Criminal Psychopathology* 5 (3, 1944): 467–480.

A review of the literature on homosexuality covers the following areas. Historical: Homosexuality is referred to in almost all historical periods, suggesting that it may be an inherent, universal aspect of man. Classification: Both legal and psychiatric classifications are briefly listed. Structural development: It is noted that sex characteristics are not limited to gonadal forms but exist in all parts of the physique and temperament. Environment: Freud and Ferenczi are given credit for pointing out the importance of preadolescent environmental influences. Culture: Calling on such persons as Mead and Malinowski, it is shown that sexual characteristics are culturally determined. Hormones: A correlation exists between hormonal characteristics and sexual behavior, but it is probably not causal. Dynamics: A homosexual must be studied within the context of his total social and cultural milieu. Therapy: Psychotherapy should be primarily aimed at adjustment rather than at a change to heterosexual behavior.

Following the review of the literature, several case studies are presented.

156   GREENBLATT, DAVID ROBERT. "Semantic Differential Analysis of the 'Triangular System' Hypothesis in 'Adjusted' Overt Male

Homosexuals." Ph.D. dissertation, University of California, 1966, 273 pp.

A test was made of the Bieber hypothesis of a "triangular system" in the etiology of homosexuality, where the mother is close-binding-intimate and the father is detached or hostile-detached. Subjects rated "person concepts" (e.g., Mother) and "interaction concepts" (e.g., Son-Mother) on various scales (e.g., friendly-hostile). Thirty homosexuals were matched with 30 married males and both were given the test.

The "triangular system" hypothesis was not confirmed by factor analysis of the Semantic Differential "person concepts." Homosexuals rated their fathers as good, generous, pleasant, dominant, and underprotective; and their mothers as good, generous, pleasant, neither dominant nor subordinate, and neither overprotective nor underprotective. The "interaction concepts" data for homosexuals suggest that if the father-son relationship is an important determinant of homosexual object choice, the critical period of influence is from age 10 to 15, during which time the relationship between the two grows steadily colder. Comparable data are not available for heterosexuals inasmuch as the two groups used different frames of reference in making their judgments.

157   GREENSTEIN, JULES M. "Father Characteristics and Sex Typing." *Journal of Personality and Social Psychology* 3 (3, 1966): 271–277.

Three approaches to sex-role identification theory, Mowrer (1950), Broffenbrenner (1960), and Parsons (1955), were tested by assessing the effects of prolonged father absence on male adolescents. Ratings of father characteristics and measures of sex-typing (i.e., homosexual tendencies, fantasy identification, masculinity-femininity) were used.

Seventy-five boys between the ages of 13 and 18 were involved, 25 without fathers and 50 with fathers. There were no significant differences between father-present and father-absent boys in any of the dimensions usually related to sex-typing; sex-typing was not related to power distribution within the family; and father-closeness is positively associated with overt homosexuality. Reinforcement may be a possible mechanism of sex-typing, but this needs further study.

158   GROUP FOR THE ADVANCEMENT OF PSYCHIATRY. Committee on Cooperation with Governmental Agencies. "Report on Homosexuality with Particular Emphasis on This Problem in Governmental Agencies." *Report of the Group for the Advancement of Psychiatry* 30 (1955): 1–7.

A general discussion of homosexuality from a social and psychiatric point of view is presented. Homosexuality reflects either an arrest at or a regression to an immature level of psychosexual development. Psychotherapy offers the best chance for success in treating homosexuals. Since homosexuals can and have functioned with distinction in the government setting, each individual should be considered on his own merit according to the place and circumstances.

159   HACKER, HELEN MAYER. "The Ishmael Complex." *American Journal of Psychotherapy* 6 (3, 1952): 494–512.

The Ishmael complex is an unconscious myth particularly prevalent in the American middle class. This myth is based upon a common theme, found in a number of juvenile classics (e.g., *Moby Dick; Huckleberry Finn*), of an "isolated, aim-inhibited, homosexual relationship between a declassed American lad and a colored outcast. . . ." The Ishmael complex manifests itself in the form of masculine fellowship, but it is carefully sublimated in order not to violate cultural normative standards. Overt homosexuality represents a fixation on the prepubertal Ishmael level. Such an arrested development may occur when the young male's wish for tender solicitude from his father is frustrated and/or when his mother exhibits little or no qualities of companionship. In such circumstances, an individual, in adulthood, can be driven by an extraordinary compulsion to fulfill the idyllic relationship expressed in the Ishmael complex.

160   HACKER, HELEN MAYER. "The New Burdens of Masculinity." *Marriage and Family Living* 19 (3, 1957): 227–233.

Studies of the sociology of dominant groups have not focused on the study of men as a dominant group. In the discussion of "new burdens" faced by men in a changing society, homosexuality is seen as an indication of role conflicts. The "flight from masculinity" may reflect the confusion of social and sexual roles. It also may be a "rerouting of aggression and hostility perhaps in response to heightened social demands—from women and competitors."

161   HADDEN, SAMUEL B. "Etiologic Factors in Male Homosexuality." In *Proceedings of the IV World Congress of Psychiatry,* Madrid, Sept. 5–11, 1966, pp. 3067–3069. International Congress Series no. 150. New York: Excerpta Medica, 1967–68.

Homosexuality is an experientially determined pattern of maladaptation which is amenable to treatment. Etiologic factors include disturbed child-parent relationships, interparental conflict, and lack of effective scrambling peer play relationships in the toddler and preschool age. Effective rough-and-tumble peer play relationships may compensate for defective family relationships. Group psychotherapy is superior to individual therapy as a method of treatment. A better understanding of etiologic factors and dissemination of this knowledge should aid in prevention.

162 HADDEN, SAMUEL B. "Male Homosexuality." *Pennsylvania Medicine* 70 (Feb., 1967): 78–80.

Homosexuality is an experientially determined pattern of maladaptation and, hence, amenable to treatment. Disturbed child-parent relationships and interparental conflict contribute to the development of various patterns of maladjustment. Lack of effective scrambling peer relationships in the toddler and preschool period is a most important factor in creating the loneliness and aloofness that predisposes to homosexuality. These peer play relationships may compensate for defective child-parent and interparental relationships. Homosexuality may be altered by individual treatment but group psychotherapy is a superior method. The experiences leading to the development of a homosexual adaptation are more easily brought out through group interaction.

163 HADFIELD, J. A. "Origins of Homosexuality." *British Medical Journal* (5486, 1966): 678.

Reports of two cases of male homosexuality are presented to show that homosexuality is not necessarily a constitutional disorder but can be caused by experiences that happen very early in a child's life. The essential feature in each of these cases was an extreme fear of women caused by a specific terrifying experience in early childhood. The therapeutic outcome in both cases was a complete change to heterosexuality.

164 HAMILTON, GILBERT VAN TASSEL. "Homosexuals and Their Mothers." 1936. Reprinted in *On the Causes of Homosexuality: Two Essays, the Second in Reply to the First,* by Gilbert Van Tassel Hamilton and Gershon Legman, pp. 5–15. New York: Breaking Point, 1950. Also reprinted as "Incest and Homosexuality." In *The Homosexuals: As Seen by Themselves and Thirty Authorities,* edited by Aron M. Krich, pp. 214–226. New York: Citadel Press, 1954. Also reprinted as "Defensive Homosexuality: Homosexuality as a Defense Against Incest." In *Homosexuality: A Cross Cultural Approach,* edited by Donald Webster Cory, pp. 354–369. New York: Julian Press, 1956.

It is observed "that fear of incest is the most important of the factors involved in the overdevelopment of the homosexual tendency." It is tentatively concluded that overt homosexuality in both males and females is a defensive "flight from incest," although female homosexuality has a more complex determination in which post-infantile factors play an important role.

165   HAMMER, EMANUEL F. "Symptoms of Sexual Deviation: Dynamics and Etiology." *Psychoanalytic Review* 55 (1, 1968): 5–27.

How to understand the etiology and dynamics of sexual perversion is discussed with reference to the findings from a study of 286 males in which projective techniques, interviews, and/or therapy experience were used. In addition to several incest cases, the subject population included heterosexual and homosexual pedophiles, exhibitionists, and rapists. These were either men incarcerated at Sing Sing Prison for sexual felonies, men seen at the New York City Criminal Court Psychiatric Clinic for more minor sex offenses, or men in private therapy or psychoanalytic treatment for similar symptoms; their ages ranged from 18 to 63 years with a mean age of 32 years.

Men incarcerated at Sing Sing for nonsex offenses, men seen at the Criminal Court Psychiatric Clinic in connection with nonsex offenses, and private psychiatric patients without perversions were used—sometimes formally, sometimes informally—as control groups for purposes of comparison with various subgroups in the subject population.

Sexual offenders (in contrast with the controls) experienced extreme castration anxiety and had mothers who were seductive and fathers who were indifferent and distant, or harsh, cruel, and physically primitive. They were also found to possess a concrete orientation with less capacity to fantasize or to obtain sublimatory outlets for their sexual impulses.

Much of the discussion pertains to factors associated with acting-out behaviors, on the one hand, and sublimation on the other. Consideration is also given to the question of why certain people operate on a concrete level while others tend to develop neuroses rather than perversions when they become threatened by Oedipal conflicts and castration anxiety. Several cases are discussed in order to illustrate the points that are made.

166   HAMPSON, JOHN L. "Deviant Sexual Behavior: Homosexuality, Transvestism." In *Human Reproduction and Sexual Behavior,* edited by Charles W. Lloyd, pp. 498–510. Philadelphia: Lea & Febiger, 1964.

The use of, or preference for, a sexual partner of the same sex is the only common denominator in homosexuality; it is not a single entity or condition. Homosexual behavior which is situational, incidental, or neurotic in nature may be entirely unrelated to a person's self-perception of gender role. Effeminate "passive" homosexuality in males, masculine "aggressive" homosexuality in females, and transvestism, however, are all directly related to gender role inversion.

Gender role, which is primarily determined by social learning during the earliest years of a child's life, is not automatically set by "instinct" nor by the body's anatomy and physiology. Instead "an individual's gender role, including erotic orientation, becomes established during the process of growing up as the result of a myriad of life experiences subtly imposed and governed by the culture of which he or she is a member." Role rehearsal in childhood play and fantasy facilitate this aspect of personality development.

The possibility of successful psychiatric treatment is much greater when homosexual acting-out is the result of neurotic and sociopathic disorders, than it is when homosexuality is based on faulty gender identification. Although psychotherapy may be useful in alleviating guilt and fear and in assisting in satisfactory life adjustment, there seems little reason for therapeutic optimism with regard to changing sexual orientation in cases where homosexuality is based on sex-role inversion.

Early detection of faulty gender-role learning during the first few years of a child's life is necessary if remedial intervention is to take place with any hope of success.

167 HAYWARD, SUMNER C. "Modification of Sexual Behavior of the Male Albino Rat." *Journal of Comparative and Physiological Psychology* 50 (1, 1957): 70–73.

Controlled investigations of the behavior modification of a nonprimate animal may throw light on research in the sexual behavior modification of primates. Twenty male albino rats (10 treatment and 10 controls) 21 days of age were trained to make discriminatory responses to the female-in-heat but not to a mature male. This was done by shocking them in the presence of a female-in-heat and not shocking them in the presence of a male. The controls received no shock. It was found that "a discriminative avoidance response to a compartment containing a female-in-heat can be learned early in life by the young male albino rat and lasts almost unabated . . . into full maturity." The treatment group spent a significantly greater amount of time in the compartment with the stimulus male than the controls and were greatly inhibited sexually with the female-in-heat. No homosexual behavior of any significance for either group was observed.

168 HENNESSEY, MAURICE A. R. "Homosexual Charges Against Children." *Journal of Criminal Psychopathology* 2 (4, 1941): 524–532.

A psychiatric and social work follow-up of 66 boys and 14 girls charged in Cuyahoga County Juvenile Court, Ohio, with homosexual behavior is reported.

Homosexual charges against children are very infrequent. Conditioning factors are multiple and often polyvalent in each case. Since sex is one aspect of the personality and homosexuality is a phase in development, conditioning factors determine the utilization of such regressive childish behavior. Amoral and immoral homes, the lack of religious training, and the lack of ethical precept or example are potent and frequent factors in the easy acceptance of sex delinquency.

169   HENRY, GEORGE W. *Sex Variants: A Study of Homosexual Patterns.* New York: Paul B. Hoeber, 1948, 1130 pp.

A psychiatric study of male and female homosexuality was conducted through the intensive analysis of 80 case histories. The data included medical examination results, family background, and personal history (in autobiographical style), and the results of masculinity-femininity tests. The following impressions are suggested: sex variance is in part a by-product of civilization, constitutional deficiencies are less evident than psychological ones but are more evident in sex variants than in normal heterosexuals, and sex variance is likely to result from a family background of high masculinity in the female members of the family and high femininity in the male members.

170   HENRY, GEORGE W., and GROSS, ALFRED A. "The Homosexual Delinquent." *Mental Hygiene* 25 (3, 1941): 420–442.

The characteristics of the homosexual delinquent were studied through the case histories and psychotherapy of 100 male prison inmates (78 white and 22 Negro). The delinquent homosexual (as opposed to the economically well-adjusted homosexual) is handicapped by a poor biological start, inferior housing, limited education, and little if any vocational training. Since prisons cannot deal effectively with homosexuals, they should be placed in penal hospitals and given psychiatric treatment.

171   HIGLEY, H. E. "One Hundred Males Arrested for Homosexuality." *Journal of the American Osteopathic Association* 54 (3, 1954): 194–197.

The cases of 100 adult males arrested for homosexuality in Los Angeles County were chosen at random from the case history files of the Meyers Clinic. They were statistically evaluated according to their status at the time of arrest, the circumstances of their arrest, and certain aspects of their childhood environments. The childhood sexual experiences of part of the group were also tabulated.

The most significant factor in the childhood environment of the group was the relationship of the child to his parents. The incidence of broken homes was relatively low (18 percent), but only 19 percent of the men reported a good relationship with a father figure. Although 28 percent reported a good relationship with their mothers, another 28 percent complained of overprotection and domination by the mother.

Only 17 percent received any information about sex from their parents. Seventy-three men reported a total of 120 different childhood sexual experiences of various types, and 40 percent reported experiencing genital handling by men in their prepubertal years.

172   HOOKER, EVELYN. "Homosexuality." In *International Encyclopedia of the Social Sciences,* pp. 222–233. New York: Macmillan Co., 1968.

Four major theoretical issues concerning the etiology and determinants of homosexuality are indicated. Is the human organism psychosexually neutral at birth, or are there inherent sexual predispositions? What is the nature and content of the learning processes by which homosexual object choice develops? Are particular periods in the developmental process, such as early childhood or adolescence, critical for homosexual object choice? Are parent-child relationships in the nuclear family crucial in determining whether an individual becomes homosexual, or are peer relationships in childhood and adolescence, and deviant subcultures in adolescence and early adult life, of equal or possibly greater importance? These controversial issues cannot be resolved by the research evidence currently available.

A brief historical review of major studies illustrates differences in theoretical assumptions, methodological approaches, findings, and conclusions, and indicates important areas for continued research. Topics discussed include etiology, personality psychodynamics and correlates in adult homosexuality, role differentiation and typology, demographic and cultural variation, and subcultures and social organizations.

The diversity of forms of adult homosexuality is stressed, as well as the many combinations of variables which produce them. "No single class of determinants, whether psychodynamic, cultural, or biological, accounts for all or even one of these diverse forms."

173   HORNSTRA, L. "Homosexuality." *International Journal of Psycho-Analysis* 48 (3, 1967): 394–402.

Both analytical and nonanalytical materials are taken as a basis for discussing the schematic defensive structure of some forms of homosexuality. Lesbianism and fetishism are discussed, and a limited consideration of therapy is presented.

It is observed that there is no question of a "bisexual disposition" which can develop in one direction or another under the pressure of influences and circumstances. Homosexuality is seen primarily as a defense against anxiety and not as a search for sexual satisfaction. Rather than seeing it as the result of the Oedipal conflict, the disturbance is held to be one which originates much earlier in the "primeval situation."

As a fetish the homosexual's penis is viewed as a concentration of his own identity. It is stated also that a child's fear is not caused by the simple sight of a female figure without a penis, but by the threat of retaliation provoked by his own wishes. Finally, it is suggested that "splitting of the ego," to which Freud refers, develops not from the denial of the female's lack of a penis, but from the threat of theft of the male homosexual's own penis, which is a part of his ego.

174   HULBECK, CHARLES R. "Emotional Conflicts in Homosexuality."
       American Journal of Psychoanalysis 8 (1, 1948): 72–73.

Homosexuality develops from character neurosis. The homosexual shows the characteristics of a neurotic personality, which results from basic anxiety brought about by special adverse environmental circumstances existing during early formative years, especially by neurotic attitudes toward the child. Homosexuals externalize their inner problems, believing that the environment is responsible for their failures and disappointments. With an overemphasis upon love as the solution of all difficulties, the homosexual seeks some substitute for real love and affection which, to him, seem unobtainable.

175   JAMES, B. "Learning Theory and Homosexuality." *New Zealand
       Medical Journal* 66 (Nov., 1967): 748–751.

The application of learning theory to the study of the etiology of homosexuality can extend and clarify existing psychological and sociological theoretical concepts. Applying the conceptualization of learning theory to homosexuality, sex drive and fear of heterosexual relationships are defined as primary drives, the need for self-esteem and acceptance as secondary drives. Homosexual behavior is then seen as a response reinforced by reduction of the sex drive and avoidance of fear, as well as by the feeling of being important and accepted.

Learning theorists do not view homosexuality as a complex psychiatric syndrome, but instead interpret homosexual behavior as a biologically and socially maladaptive response reinforced by reduction of the impelling drives of sexual desire and fear of opposite sex object choices.

176   JERSILD, JENS. *Boy Prostitution.* Translated by Oscar Bojesen.
       Copenhagen: G. E. C. Gad, 1956, 101 pp.

A documentary and statistical study of male homosexual prostitution in Denmark presents short cases and reports statistics of the incidence of male prostitution in Denmark. Legislation on male prostitution in Denmark and abroad is discussed. Statistics on boy prostitutes are presented which are said to "speak clearly of bad homes, police records, child welfare boards, reformatories, excessive drinking, unemployment, laziness and insufficient training or education." Clients of boy prostitutes are described in terms of their social class, intelligence, physique, and other characteristics.

177 JONAS, CARL H. "An Objective Approach to the Personality and Environment in Homosexuality." *Psychiatric Quarterly* 18 (4, 1944): 626–641.

Interviews were conducted with 60 male overt homosexuals (53 white and seven Negro, from 18 to 45 years old) and 60 controls (54 white and six Negro, from 18 to 44 years old), chosen at random from among convalescent surgical patients.

Of the 60 homosexuals, 43 favored their mothers as contrasted to 18 of the control cases. Twenty-eight homosexuals were either only children or youngest children in contrast to 16 cases among the controls. Disruptive domestic situations occurred in 24 cases of the homosexuals as compared to 17 cases in the controls.

Homosexuality is not a disease entity. It is a manifestation of poor personality integration, such behavior being precipitated by the accumulated effects of adverse environmental and emotional influences.

178 KAGAN, JEROME. "Acquisition and Significance of Sex Typing and Sex Role Identity." In *Review of Child Development Research,* edited by Martin L. Hoffman and Lois Wladis Hoffman, vol. 1, pp. 137–167. New York: Russell Sage Foundation, 1964.

The adolescent's acquisition of the concepts of maleness and femaleness, his acquisition of a male or female identity, and the learning of sex-appropriate responses, or sex role, are discussed. Since disturbances in sex-role identification are associated with disturbances in sexual behavior, homosexual behavior may be related to anxiety over not attaining the masculine ideal. This anxiety may lead to self-identification as a homosexual and to the avoidance of girls. This self-labeling and response to the label can become a vicious circle culminating in a homosexual commitment.

179 KAPLAN, DONALD M. "Homosexuality and American Theatre: A Psychoanalytic Comment." *Tulane Drama Review* 9 (3, 1965): 25–55.

In a discussion of the increasing effect of homosexuals in the theater it is suggested that psychoanalytic theory possesses a vocabulary that can deal with it regardless of its various manifestations. By relating and comparing the homosexual to the actor, it is concluded that there are a number of similarities within the context of psychoanalytic theory. Homosexuality is characterized by "the content of immature defiance, the form of decadent realism and the failure of sentimentality." Without the dependency originating in some typically doubtful identificatory experience one cannot be either a homosexual or an actor. "Homosexuality and acting are perverse solutions to anxieties about identification"; thus "overt and covert homosexuality and its constellation of infantile perversity are part of the actor's basic resources."

180   KAPLAN, EUGENE A. "Homosexuality: A Search for the Ego-Ideal." *Archives of General Psychiatry* 16 (3, 1967): 355–358.

Homosexuality stems from a number of factors. One of these may be "the search for an ego-ideal by individuals whose self-images are devalued or impaired." The search for this ego-ideal through homosexual relations may often be a substitute for the more usual ascription of this role to the father.

Three cases are outlined, each having in common a person who is dissatisfied with his self-image, sees others who resemble the image, and has sexual relations with them. These people are identification objects, and the feeling or fantasy of identification is enhanced through sexuality. Hence, the homosexual is much like the narcissist, except that the homosexual is so dissatisfied with himself that he acts out his self-image with another.

In therapy, the explanation should include the origin of the person's negative self-image and of the ego-ideal. There may be other ways than homosexuality for the person to become the kind of person he would like to be; these should also be explored.

181   KARDINER, ABRAM. "The Flight from Masculinity." 1954. Reprinted in *The Problem of Homosexuality in Modern Society*, edited by Hendrik M. Ruitenbeek, pp. 17–39. New York: E. P. Dutton & Co., 1963.

Homosexuality in our culture is a social disease brought on by the pressures of Western civilization. The difficulties of meeting the demands of "masculinity" lead some men to seek relief in homosexuality. A homosexual relationship is based on give and take between partners, in which the male escapes the great demands made by the female. Some of the characteristics of the social milieu which have contributed to an increase in homosexuality are examined in detail.

182   KARPMAN, BENJAMIN. *The Sexual Offender and His Offenses: Etiology, Pathology, Psychodynamics and Treatment.* New York: Julian Press, 1954, 744 pp.

An extensive review of the literature and of the psychodynamic formulation of the problem of sex offenses is given. Part I, the review of the literature, classifies articles from 1912 to 1951 under subject headings with abstracts of the essentials from each. Summaries of these abstracts are presented at the end of each chapter. Most of the material pertaining to homosexuality is found in Chapter 10, which covers etiology, the homosexual as a personality type, latent homosexuality, homosexuality and delinquency, the homosexual in the Army, and the treatment of homosexuality. The review of the literature on the etiology of homosexuality concludes with the following statement: "The causes of homosexuality are believed psychosexual; homosexuality usually is considered a sign of retarded emotional development."

Part II discusses the psychodynamics of sexual offenses, including homosexuality. Homosexuality is classified as a biological paraphilia, the paraphilias being a branch of the neuroses. Virtually all other paraphilias, such as fellatio, cunnilingus, pederasty, et cetera—even in a heterosexual framework—relate to unconscious, unresolved homosexuality. Paraphilias are forms of sexual activity which run counter to accepted social behavior and which are characterized by the absence of a biological aim.

183   KENDLER, HOWARD H. "S. F., A Case of Homosexual Panic." *Journal of Abnormal and Social Psychology* 42 (1, 1947): 112–119.

The homosexual panic experienced by a married 19-year-old male in the Army is described. The patient was given the Army-Wechsler Intelligence Test and treated with psychotherapy. The development of this case of homosexuality paralleled Freud's theories regarding the etiology of homosexuality.

184   KINSEY, ALFRED C.; POMEROY, WARDELL B.; MARTIN, CLYDE E.; and GEBHARD, PAUL H. "Concepts of Normality and Abnormality in Sexual Behavior." In *Psychosexual Development in Health and Disease,* edited by Paul H. Hoch and Joseph Zubin, pp. 11–32. New York: Grune & Stratton, 1949.

The historical origins of Anglo-American written laws incorporating social customs which condemn certain kinds of sexual behavior as "unnatural acts" are reviewed. Human sexual behavior patterns are also reviewed and data taken from *Sexual Behavior in the Human Male,* by Kinsey et al., are used as a basis for concluding that the sexual behavior of the human being originates in varied indiscriminate sexual responses which, as a result of conditioning and social pressures, generally become limited to what has traditionally been interpreted as normal. Therefore, present concepts of normality and abnormality in human sexual behavior are simply moral evaluations.

185   KINSEY, ALFRED C.; REICHERT, PHILIP; CAULDWELL, DAVID O.; and MOZES, EUGENE B. "The Causes of Homosexuality: A Symposium." *Sexology* 21 (9, 1955): 558–562.

Discussion by various professionals on the etiology of homosexuality is presented.

Kinsey indicates the following factors leading to homosexual behavior: ". . . the basic physiologic capacity of every mammal to respond to any sufficient stimulus; the accident which leads an individual into his or her first sexual experience with a person of the same sex; the conditioning effects of such experience; and the indirect but powerful conditioning which the opinions of other persons and the social codes may have on an individual's decision to accept or reject this type of sexual contact."

Reichert says that an interplay of causes—hormonal imbalance, influence of surroundings, fear of pregnancy, doing what is forbidden, and sexual curiosities of children—may establish homosexual patterns throughout one's life.

Cauldwell believes that homosexuality is a personality trait resulting from the wrong kind of early environmental conditioning; a male child may have been overpampered by female relatives; the child tends to be like those who have responsibility for its early training, hence the male desires to take a female role or vice versa.

Mozes holds that homosexuality is an arrest in sexual development. This fixation is caused by excessive emotion in the parent-child relationship (either positive or negative) and by being subjected to highly adverse parental influences. Inborn traits may render some persons more susceptible to this form of maladjustment.

186   KNIGHT, EDWARD H. "Overt Male Homosexuality." In *Sexual Behavior and the Law,* edited by Ralph Slovenko, pp. 434–461. Springfield, Ill.: Charles C. Thomas, 1965.

Overt male homosexuality is an abnormal form of personality growth which results mainly from environmentally induced disturbances of early psychological development. Some undetermined physiologic predisposition may also be present.

Sexual differentiation into male identity is disturbed or hampered in the early infantile period by conflicts involving separation from the mother or by fears and prohibitions involved in patterning oneself after the image of the father. As a result of this failure to develop an acceptable masculine identity, three types of overt male homosexuality may develop: the passive feminine types, the aggressive masculine types, and the boyish types. Society must try to understand the psychology of male homosexuality, design social legislation to protect the rights of individuals, and assist the homosexual in securing early diagnosis and treatment.

187 KOLB, LAWRENCE C., and JOHNSON, ADELAIDE M. "Etiology and Therapy of Overt Homosexuality." *Psychoanalytic Quarterly* 24 (4, 1955): 506–515.

Latent homosexuality may become overt homosexuality if encouraged by a parent or surrogate parent, consciously or unconsciously. Three adult male patients are reported on. Two were single, one married. All sought treatment voluntarily with two of the three cases seeking help for their homosexual tendencies. They were given psychoanalytic treatment by the authors in regular sessions of private practice.

In two cases a parent—the mother—had dominated the subject as a boy, had acted out seductive impulses toward the subject, and had encouraged friendships with male friends which resulted in homosexual experiences. In the third case the therapist was too permissive and allowed latent homosexuality to become overt. This was later reversed after 30 months of treatment.

188 KRICH, ARON M., ed. *The Homosexuals: As Seen by Themselves and Thirty Authorities.* New York: Citadel Press, 1954, 346 pp. Also published as *Homosexuality: A Subjective and Objective Investigation,* edited by Charles Berg. London: Allen & Unwin, 1958, 416 pp.

This collection of articles is divided into two parts. Part One consists of individual case histories of homosexuals and autobiographical essays written by homosexuals. Part Two presents an "overview of major trends in treatment." The psychobiological approach and the psychoanalytic approach to the cause and cure of homosexuality are both represented.

See Bergler, Edmund (no. 310). Brody, Morris Wolf (no. 802). Ferenczi, Sandor (no. 384). Flournoy, Henri (no. 691). Freud, Sigmund (no. 273). Glover, Benjamin (no. 698). Hamburger, Christian (no. 432). Hamilton, Gilbert Van Tassel (no. 164). Hirschfeld, Magnus (no. 19). Jung, Carl Gustav (no. 463). Schilder, Paul (no. 551). Schwarz, Oswald (no. 241). Sprague, George S. (no. 774). Thompson, Clara (no. 584). Wulff, Moshe (no. 264).

189   LANGSLEY, DONALD G.; SCHWARTZ, MICHAEL N.; and FAIR-
      BAIRN, ROBERT H. "Father-Son Incest." *Comprehensive Psychiatry*
      9 (3, 1968): 218–226.

A case of father-son incest is reported. The phenomenon was studied
through investigations of both parents, the son, and the family group as a
unit. Whereas father-daughter incest depends on the family setting as well
as the psychological problems of the father and daughter, this case of
father-son incest appeared to be more closely linked to the father's psychosexual problems than to family interaction. The homosexual incest
which occurred was a living-out by the father of his own adolescent conflicts. He had had homosexual experiences before he was married. His
marriage served the purpose of getting a son to replace the boy he had loved
in his teens.

190   LAWTON, SHAILER UPTON, AND ARCHER, JULES. *Sexual Conduct
      of the Teenager.* New York: Spectrolux Corp., 1951, 180 pp.

A journalistic study of the variety and incidence of sexual behaviors among
teen-agers gives advice to parents, teachers, and teen-agers. The short section on homosexuality reports the Kinsey findings on incidence and theo-
rizes that heterosexual promiscuity may be a mask for homosexual
tendencies. Suggested principal causes of lesbianism are the advantage of
orgasm without fear of pregnancy, penis envy, a family background with
a negative father-influence, and seduction.

191   LAYCOCK, S. R. "Homosexuality—A Mental Hygiene Problem."
      Canadian Medical Association Journal 63 (Sept., 1950): 245–250.

Homosexuality is a matter of degree in many people, so that the only true
test of degree of homosexuality is the degree to which the psychic and/or
overt sex interests and activities are directed toward the opposite sex. The
causes of homosexuality are multiple; it is well to think of it as sexual and
emotional immaturity. Homosexuals should be helped to live in a social
rather than an antisocial way and aided in living as full and rich a life as
possible.

192   LEGMAN, GERSHON. "Fathers and Sons." In *On the Cause of Homo-
      sexuality: Two Essays, the Second in Reply to the First,* by G. V.
      Hamilton and G. Legman, pp. 17–31. New York: Breaking Point,
      1950.

Special attention is given to the father-son relationship for its contribution
to a homosexual orientation. The male homosexual is seen as avoiding "the

dangerous competition with his father for his mother's love" and competing, instead, with his mother for his father's love. This competition involves a denigration of the mother and of women generally, which results in a disinclination to consider them suitable sexual objects. At the same time the male homosexual "becomes" his mother in order to win the favor of his father whom he fears. His sexual behaviors, expressive of what is termed a "defensive homosexuality," represent a re-enactment of this original theme.

193   LEWINSKY, HILDE. "Features from a Case of Homosexuality." *Psychoanalytic Quarterly* 21 (3, 1952): 344–354.

The case history of a 36-year-old male homosexual is presented. His homosexuality seemed, through analysis, to be a method of reaction to a severe prohibition against masturbation. It was also an eroticized fixation to that part of the Oedipal conflict in which he was unable to cope in rivalry both with his father and his brothers. His castration complex derived from heterosexual incestuous strivings. Heterosexuality became a double threat of direct punishment from the vagina and punishment by the father and the eldest brother. Thus, he turned toward homosexuality.

194   LIDDICOAT, RENÉE. "Homosexuality: Results of a Survey as Related to Various Theories." Ph.D. dissertation, University of the Witwatersrand, Johannesburg, South Africa, 1956.

A review of the literature reveals that many of the theories regarding homosexuality are based on studies of subjects who were either institutionalized or were undergoing psychiatric treatment.

A study of 100 noninstitutionalized homosexuals was made in order to investigate how the results would compare with the findings from research involving homosexuals who were either institutionalized or in psychiatric treatment.

Biographical material about the 100 subjects was summarized, and they were given the Wechsler-Bellevue Adult Intelligence Test. A control group of heterosexuals matched with regard to age, education, and type of occupation was similarly studied and results of the comparisons between the two groups are given. Some of the findings are: No single environmental factor was common to all individual cases, and no single theory applied to all subjects. Etiological factors appeared to be multiple and individual. Although the homosexual males showed a tendency toward a schizoid adjustment, and the females toward a mild anxiety state, they were not, as a group, found to be more neurotic than the heterosexuals.

In accordance with prevailing theories, it was found that a large propor-

tion of the homosexual subjects showed some psychosomatic and/or psychoneurotic symptoms, that 60 percent came from disrupted or unhappy
homes, and that the homosexuals were more interested in artistic activities
than were the controls.

Contrary to prevailing theories, it was found that instability in the family
was pronounced in only a few instances; that the subjects' indifference to
parents on the conscious level was more pronounced than cross-parent
fixation; that seduction was not a prominent factor in the subjects' histories;
and that with regard to employment, the homosexuals were as stable as the
controls. There was little support for the general contention that homosexuals tend to be emotionally unreliable and generally promiscuous.

195 LIDDICOAT, RENÉE. "Homosexuality: Results of a Survey as
Related to Various Theories." *British Medical Journal* (5053, 1957):
1110–1111.

Various etiological theories of homosexuality were tested, using case histories of 50 male and 50 female noninstitutionalized homosexuals. None of
the subjects had police records nor had they sought psychiatric help. Their
ages ranged from 22 to 60 years, with the mean for the males 35 and for
the females 37. A control group of 100 was used, matched for relevant
variables, although the mean I.Q.'s of the homosexuals were significantly
higher than those of the controls.

Some psychosomatic and/or psychoneurotic symptoms were present in
the homosexuals. Sixty percent came from disrupted or unhappy homes,
and indifference to parents was more prevalent than cross-parent fixation.
The homosexuals were more inclined to activities in the arts, and were not
emotionally unreliable or sexually promiscuous.

196 LITIN, EDWARD M.; GIFFIN, MARY E.; and JOHNSON, ADELAIDE
M. "Parental Influence in Unusual Sexual Behavior in Children."
Psychoanalytic Quarterly 25 (1, 1956): 37–55.

Perversion and antisocial sexual behavior in children and adolescents result
from the adaptation of the child's ego to subtle parental attitudes which
distort the development of the child. Parents of these children unwittingly
seduce them and encourage their aberrant behavior. Initial therapy for such
patients may involve temporarily separating the child from his parent, and
the parents as well as the child must undergo analysis. Of the 11 case
histories reported, two involved problems of homosexuality.

197 LONDON, LOUIS S., and CAPRIO, FRANK S. *Sexual Deviations.*
Washington, D. C.: Linacre Press, 1950, 702 pp.

This is a general psychiatric and psychoanalytic text on sexual deviations. Part One consists of a brief historical survey and short discussions of the development of the sexual impulse in the child and its deviation in the adult. Part Two, which comprises the bulk of the text, consists of cases drawn from clinical practice to illustrate numerous types of deviation. Part Three is on the therapeutic and sociological aspects of deviation.

Four male and four female homosexual cases are presented in Part Two. It is concluded that homosexuality is an acquired disorder of psychogenic origin which is amenable to treatment. It is the result of a fixation at the pregenital or Oedipal level.

198 LORAND, SANDOR, AND BALINT, MICHAEL, eds. *Perversions: Psychodynamics and Therapy.* New York: Random House, 1956, 307 pp.

A summary of current views on perversion is presented in this collection of articles. All the contributors accept Freud's formulations on perversions, although many point out additional factors which play major roles in the etiology of perversions. Part Two contains four articles on homosexuality and Part Five contains two articles on the therapy of perversions, especially male homosexuality. See Bacon, Catherine Lillie (no. 267). Bychowski, Gustav (no. 338). Eidelberg, Ludwig (no. 676). Feldman, Sandor S. (no. 139). Lorand, Sandor (no. 728). Miller, Milton L. (no. 510).

199 LURIE, LOUIS A., and JONAS, CARL H. "Causes of Homosexuality." *Sexology* 11 (12, 1945): 743–746.

Homosexuality is a manifestation of poor personality integration and should be considered in a category similar to excessive masturbation and chronic alcoholism. Homosexuality becomes desirable or necessary as an outlet for libidinous drives in certain individuals, largely because of a combination of adverse psychogenic and environmental forces. These forces have varying interrelationships.

200 McCORD, WILLIAM; McCORD, JOAN; AND VERDEN, PAUL. "Family Relationships and Sexual Deviance in Lower-Class Adolescents." *International Journal of Social Psychiatry* 8 (3, 1962): 165–179.

A sociological study was made of 115 sexually deviant boys and 74 nonsexually deviant boys in the Cambridge-Somerville Youth Study, many of whom were actively homosexual. The study employed both direct and indirect observation.

Adolescent sexual deviation results from a familial environment characterized by authoritarian punishment of heterosexual behavior and certain experiences which weaken the child's desire to adopt the masculine role. Other variables in the child's environment which direct the unique form of sexual deviation are a feminine identification resulting from a poor or totally lacking father-son relationship, sexual perversion (nonhomosexual) resulting from parental behavior intensifying the child's sexual conflicts, and total sexual repression from parental reprimands.

201 McLEISH, JOHN. "The Homosexual." *Medical World* 93 (8, 1960): 237–239.

Taking issue with the literary view that homosexuality represents a higher state of humanity, it is here claimed that homosexuality is indicative of immaturity. It is recognized that many people indulging in homosexual activity are not true homosexuals but rather have various other motives such as the expense of dating or unavailability of women. The true homosexual regards heterosexual relations with distaste. In general his behavior is characterized by a failure to develop emotionally and by infantile attitudes. The true homosexual may have inherited a weakened psychosexual constitution which, combined with certain home conditions, can cause it to be impossible for him to have a heterosexual relationship. The homosexual, however, is not the only type of person with immature sexual relations, as evidenced by the number of marriages that are mere domestic conveniences, et cetera. In addition to inheriting a weakened psychosexual constitution, the true homosexual undergoes a long learning process in which the natural human sexual reactions are systematically diverted and trained in unnatural ways. Often neurotic mothers are responsible for inhibiting the development of heterosexual friendships.

The problem of treating the homosexual is essentially that of re-educating him. Psychotherapy is the method most used, but the results have not been encouraging because few homosexuals want to be "cured." At a clinic specializing in treatment of homosexuals half of those referred refused treatment, one-quarter showed no improvement, and one-quarter lost their homosexual urges entirely. The last group consisted of men under 30 who had not been practicing homosexuals very long. They were also interested in the opposite sex. A large number of these men had been before the courts, and this form of treatment may have set them on the right road with the psychotherapy being irrelevant to their "cure."

202 McPARTLAND, JOHN. *Sex in Our Changing World.* New York: Rinehart & Co., 1947, 280 pp.

The generally adverse effects of two world wars and a major depression on manners, morals, and sexual behavior in the United States are described.

It is argued that homosexuality is increasing as a result of urbanization, the increasing complexity of economic life, and the cultivation of "infantilism" in young boys through exaggerated mother-son relationships. Brief case histories of several male and female homosexuals are included.

203   "Male Homosexuality." *Lancet* 269 (6884, 1955): 291–293.

A homosexual expresses his views on homosexuality. Considering the prevalence of homosexuality and citing the Kinsey Report, he notes that there is a continuous gradation among adults from a completely heterosexual through a bisexual to a completely homosexual orientation.

   Homosexuality is determined primarily by early psychological environment. There is little evidence for genetic influence, although it may play a role, and endocrines appear to have no bearing on the development of homosexuality. Contrary to popular belief, most homosexuals are indistinguishable from heterosexuals. The author feels his own state can be accounted for by his early environment. His mother never loved him and he felt her oversolicitude was a sham. As a result of this early experience, he still believes that no woman can ever love him and that any show of affection by a woman is a pretense.

   Sixteen years of psychoanalysis produced few positive results. Although homosexuality has become increasingly unsatisfactory for him, heterosexual relations remain as difficult as ever. Psychoanalytic treatment might be effective for a younger person in altering the balance between homosexuality and heterosexuality, but the cost and time for analysis prohibit its effective use for more than a tiny fraction of the 650,000 estimated homosexuals in England.

   Most homosexuals think the laws making private consensual homosexual acts a crime are an invasion of their private lives. The most important argument for a change in the law, however, is that it is a necessary preliminary for any real study of the subject. As long as laws making homosexuality a crime are in effect, the majority of homosexuals will continue to guard their secret closely.

204   · MARKS, BEN. "Homosexuality." *Harper Hospital Bulletin* 26 (5, 1968): 242–247.

The etiology, classification, behavior characteristics, and legal status of homosexuality are discussed. Although there are several theories regarding its etiology, the most significant is that which views it as involving an arrested psychosexual development. There are four main types of homosexuals: the accidental, the latent, the overt, and the paranoid. Homosexuality should be considered an illness, and homosexual acts between adults in private should be legal.

205   MARMOR, JUDD. "Homosexuality." *Student Personnel Newsletter,*
       State University College, Buffalo 1 (3, 1967): 15–34.

A lecture on homosexuality discusses its causation, laws pertaining to it,
and its treatment. Homosexuality develops as an adaptational response to
certain kinds of environmental circumstances including psychodynamic
factors, sociocultural factors, biological factors, and specific situational
factors. However, the subtle influence of temporal quantitative and qualitative factors must also be considered. For homosexuality to result, the three
major factors needed are impaired gender identity, fear of sexual activity
with the opposite sex, and some experience with homosexuality. Our laws
should be changed to permit homosexual behavior between consenting
adults. Homosexuals can be helped through psychiatric treatment.

206   MARMOR, JUDD, ed. *Sexual Inversion: The Multiple Roots of Homo-*
       sexuality. New York: Basic Books, 1965, 358 pp.

The basic orientation in assembling this collection of papers was that causality in the area of homosexuality "cannot be sought in any single factor but
is multifactorial." Consequently information has been gathered from all
pertinent fields, including history, comparative zoology, genetics, endocrinology, sociology, anthropology, law, psychology, and psychoanalytic
psychiatry. In the introduction, this definition is offered: "I prefer . . . to
define the clinical homosexual as one who is motivated, in adult life, by a
definite preferential erotic attraction to members of the same sex and who
usually (but not necessarily) engages in overt sexual relations with them."
Other topics included in the introductory discussion are the biological
factor, psychological bisexuality, the etiology of the homosexual pattern,
social and cultural determinants, homosexuality as an illness, the homosexual personality, social discrimination against homosexuals, and the treatment of homosexuality.

   See Bieber, Irving (no. 106). Denniston, R. H. (no. 128). Fisher, Saul H.
(no. 977). Hooker, Evelyn (no. 861). Mayerson, Peter, and Lief, Harold I.
(no. 736). Opler, Marvin K. (no. 1013). Ovesey, Lionel (no. 222). Pare, C.
M. B. (no. 43). Perloff, William H. (no. 226). Rado, Sandor (no.51). Romm,
May E. (no. 282). Salzman, Leon (no. 546). Szasz, Thomas S. (no. 1249).
Taylor, Gordon Rattray (no. 1027). Wilbur, Cornelia B. (no. 285).

207   MARTENSEN-LARSEN, O. "The Family Constellation and Homo-
       sexualism." *Acta Genetica et Statistica Medica* 7 (1957): 445–446.

The family constellations of 63 homosexual men and 44 homosexual women
are analyzed. Homosexual men were often found in dependent sibling situa-

tions (only child or youngest child) where there was little opportunity for dominating other children; homosexual women, on the other hand, tended to come from either the upper or lower part of their sibships.

The study does not explain why unisexual sibships are found in some families, but the results of the investigation suggest that some relation between an "unhealthy unisexual atmosphere" and homosexuality does exist.

208   MATHES, IRMA DELORIS BENDEL. "Adult Male Homosexuality and Perception of Instrumentality, Expressiveness, and Coalition in Parental Role Structure." Ph.D. dissertation, University of Missouri, 1966, 256 pp.

This social-psychological study tested the association between adult male homosexuality and parental role structure in the nuclear family of orientation. Homosexuality was hypothesized to occur when family role patterns prevent identification with the father and encourage strong identification with the mother. Following Parsonian theory it was hypothesized that internalization and identification will weaken when there is a reversal of the instrumental-expressive division of labor by sex or a weakening of the parental coalition.

A questionnaire was given to 100 homosexual males and 100 matched presumed heterosexuals.

The first and second hypotheses, predicting that the homosexual group would perceive the mother as higher and the father as lower in instrumentality, were supported. The third and fourth hypotheses, predicting that the homosexual group would perceive the mother as higher and the father as lower in expressiveness, were rejected. The fifth, sixth, and seventh hypotheses, predicting that homosexuals would perceive the parental coalition as weaker, the mother-son coalition as stronger, and the father-son coalition as weaker (compared to heterosexuals) were strongly supported.

209   MAYER, EDWARD E. "The Sex Deviate." *Pennsylvania Medical Journal* 53 (1, 1950): 32–38.

This general discussion of the medical, legal, religious, and psychiatric aspects of the sex deviate gives the homosexual the most consideration. The drama of sex begins in childhood and in any psychologic and biologic situation may produce deviations in sex development. The basis for narcissistic displacements, for guilt feelings, and for defensive sadistic impulses can be laid bare to an adolescent so that he can adjust to and control his tendencies even if they cannot be eradicated.

210   MESNIKOFF, ALVIN M.; RAINER, JOHN D.; KOLB, LAWRENCE C.; and CARR, ARTHUR C. "Intrafamilial Determinants of Divergent

Sexual Behavior in Twins." *American Journal of Psychiatry* 119 (8, 1963): 732–738.

An investigation of five sets of twins attempted to identify the significant factors in determining a homosexual or a heterosexual orientation. Tests for zygosity and chromosomal sex revealed no significant biological basis to explain atypical sexual role determination. Instead only intrafamilial forces were found to influence psychosexual role definition.

The interplay of forces which leads to the preference of one twin by one parent and the other twin by the other parent affects the intensity of the Oedipal conflict and its outcome, and this in turn is important in choice of sexual role.

In addition, the following forces, either alone or in combination, were identified as important: prenatal fantasies and wishes of each parent as to the sex of the expected child; prenatal attitudes to twins' birth; the family significance of the names given the twins; parental efforts at differentiating the twins; physical distinguishing features in the twins and the emotional significance of such features to the family; the differing object relations of the twins from birth; attitude of the individual twin to his body (as perceived and seen ideally); fantasy life, particularly in the sexual area; and superego growth of the twins, especially in relation to allowed and prohibited forms of sexual activity.

211   MILLER, PAUL R. "The Effeminate Passive Obligatory Homosexual." *Archives of Neurology and Psychiatry* 80 (5, 1958): 612–618.

The cause of effeminate obligatory homosexuality was sought by interviewing 50 male homosexuals, 33 of whom were white and 17 Negro. They had a mean I.Q. of 103 and a mean age of 25 years.

The predisposing cause is rejection by one or both parents with or without overindulgent seductive approval of aberrant behavior by one parent. The precipitating cause is the accidental or opportunistic homosexual seduction, usually in late childhood, by an irresponsible adolescent. The perpetuating causes are the satisfaction of general security needs by homosexual means and the blocking of heterosexual development by rigid feminine identification and by effeminate behavior necessary to find homosexual partners.

212   MONCHY, RENÉ de. "A Clinical Type of Male Homosexuality." *International Journal of Psycho-Analysis* 46 (2, 1965): 218–225.

The case history of a 29-year-old homosexual male who underwent psychoanalysis is presented. The patient's homosexuality was due to experiences in childhood rather than to constitutional factors. There was no inferior ego structure. Psychoanalysis should be the method of treatment in cases involving homosexuality.

213 MOORE, THOMAS V. "The Pathogenesis and Treatment of Homosexual Disorders: A Digest of Some Pertinent Evidence." *Journal of Personality* 14 (1945): 47–83.

The relation between inborn and psychological factors in the etiology of homosexuality is discussed. There is no adequate evidence that homosexuality is an organic trait transmitted by heredity, nor is there any conclusive evidence that homosexuals constitute a specific biological type. The principal factors operating in homosexuality are: an overprotecting mother, an inadequate and unhappy home, the experience of rejection and consequent seeking of affection from an adult in a homosexual relationship, being treated as a child of the opposite sex, and such environmental factors as easy access to homosexuals and the homosexual society which is provided by an urban environment.

"The existence of a society of homosexuals is a detriment to the commonweal, and therefore laws against homosexuality should not be repealed absolutely but modified so as to insure the treatment rather than the criminal prosecution of homosexuals." Psychotherapeutic treatment of homosexuals can effect changes in their behavior.

214 MORROW, JOSEPH E.; CUPP, MARION E.; and SACHS, LEWIS B. "A Possible Explanation of the Excessive Brother-to-Sister Ratios Reported in Siblings of Male Homosexuals." *Journal of Nervous and Mental Disease* 140 (4, 1965): 305–306.

It is noted that previous studies have reported sibling sex ratios for male homosexuals in excess of 121:100 and that this ratio is significantly different from the 106:100 ratio of males to females in the society. Three hundred and thirty-five male college students were polled regarding their siblings in order to provide information on sibling ratios for male groups other than homosexuals. The student ratio was 125:100. It is suggested that 106:100 may not be the sibling sex ratio to expect when sampling from an all-male population. It is also pointed out that larger ratios would be expected if the proportion of near or entirely unisexual families exceeds the proportion expected in a random or binomial distribution.

215 MURRAY, JOHN B. "Learning in Homosexuality." *Psychological Reports* 23 (2, 1968): 659–662.

Sex-role identity is a product of learning. Cues for role identity come from parents, a child's own body, and external genitalia. The necessary distinction of sex in the biological sense and sex role as a reflection of culture are discussed in relation to the influences of learning in homosexuality. Homosexuality as the result of deficient learning or absent models offered to the developing child is considered.

216 MUSAPH, H. "On Homosexuality." *Psychiatria, Neurologia, Neurochirurgia* 63 (3, 1960): 203–211.

A significant fact in the psychology of homosexuality is the pathological character of the relation to the mother figure. There is also a constitutionally determined, or congenital, inability to cope adequately with certain conflict situations produced by the environment during a number of sensitive phases which probably occur in the first two years of life. This results in an insufficient degree of frustration tolerance, excessive perseverance of the pleasure principle, and too weak an ego, which is opposed by an unduly strong and sadistic superego.

217 NASH, JOHN, and HAYES, FRANK. "The Parental Relationships of Male Homosexuals: Some Theoretical Issues and a Pilot Study." *Australian Journal of Psychology* 17 (1, 1965): 35–43.

A questionnaire was administered to 118 male subjects—about two-thirds were convicted prisoners and the other third volunteers—in order to determine if early experiences rather than biological factors are important to the origins of homosexuality and whether the relationship with the father is critical.

Three categories of homosexuals are distinguished—"actives," "passives," and "active-passives." Homosexuality may have a dominance hierarchy, and the position of the three groups is discussed. "Passives" differ from "actives" in having a closer relationship with the mother; "passives" also tend to have worse relationships with the father than "actives." No findings with regard to the "active-passives" are reported.

Homosexuality is a learned behavior, but for some individuals their physiological make-up renders this learning easier than for others.

218 NIELSON, NILS. "The Riddle of Homosexuality." *International Journal of Sexology* 6 (1, 1952): 51–53.

It is suggested that other authors should use factual rather than subjective arguments in discussing homosexuality. On this basis the following theories are rejected: that homosexuality is an inborn quality, that it is a conditioned reflex, and that it can be fully explained by a psychoanalytic approach.

219 ORGEL, SAMUEL ZACHARY. "The Development of a Perversion: Homosexuality and Associated Transvestitism." *Journal of the Hillside Hospital* 17 (4, 1968): 405–409.

A brief report of the essential factors in a case of homosexuality and associated transvestitism described the analysis of the 23-year-old son of a neuropsychiatrist. Although the patient hated his father, he had at one time been the father's favorite. As a sickly child, the son had been allowed to sleep with his father, whose erect penis the boy found fascinating. When he was six, the patient was frightened by a dream in which he was attacked by an unattached penis. Upon awakening he sought comfort by going to his parents' bedroom; instead he saw his father and mother engaged in sexual intercourse.

Soon thereafter he began to spend all his time with his mother, his aunt, and a maid. For almost a decade, these three females overfed and over-protected the patient and erotically stimulated him. During these years the patient enjoyed secretly dressing in his mother's clothes. Due to his mother's severe prohibition, there was no masturbatory activity.

In an attempt to overcome the anxiety caused by an intense incestuous drive toward his mother, the patient turned to homosexuality.

Treatment was difficult because the patient's father was usually identified with the psychoanalyst and expressed in a negative transference. Analysis was finally completed with the fifth analyst who worked with the patient.

220 "Origins of Homosexuality." *British Medical Journal* (5470, 1965): 1077–1078.

In this general discussion of various etiological theories of homosexuality, no conclusions are reached. No matter what means of treatment and pre-vention are employed, homosexuality will remain. Changes in the law, public education, and public attitudes may help remove some of the disabili-ties affecting the lives of homosexuals.

221 OVESEY, LIONEL. "The Homosexual Conflict: An Adaptational Analysis." 1954. Reprinted in *The Problem of Homosexuality in Modern Society,* edited by Hendrik M. Ruitenbeek, pp. 127–140. New York: E. P. Dutton & Co., 1963.

Societal forces play a crucial role in the psychodynamics of homosexuality. In an adaptational frame of reference psychological behavior is the result of two forces, needs of the individual and societal demands. Oral, anal, and sexual needs seek gratification through end goals, but the particular adapta-tions through which these goals are achieved vary with the social environ-ment. The culturally-determined psychosocial needs are not innate; they develop from exposure to society, and their nature is determined by the demands of that society. Therefore, in an adaptational context in contrast to the instinctual view, the behavior of the individual will vary as his social environment varies. The taking-off point for a homosexual adaptation is a sexual inhibition, or fear of normal sexual functioning. Failing in heterosexual performance, the person diverts his sexual need to a safer, homosexual object. Anxieties about homosexuality can be broken down into three motivational components: sexuality, dependency, and power.

222   OVESEY, LIONEL. "Pseudohomosexuality and Homosexuality in Men: Psychodynamics as a Guide to Treatment." In *Sexual Inversion: The Multiple Roots of Homosexuality,* edited by Judd Marmor, pp. 211–233. New York: Basic Books, 1965.

Typical dreams experienced by homosexuals and pseudohomosexuals are analyzed in order to psychoanalytically distinguish between the groups.

Pseudohomosexuality results from a masculinity crisis and feelings of inadequacy, while true homosexuality is a sexual deviation that results when fear interferes with heterosexual relations.

223   OVESEY, LIONEL; GAYLIN, WILLARD M.; and HENDIN, HERBERT. "Psychotherapy of Male Homosexuality: Psychodynamic Formulation." *Archives of General Psychiatry* 9 (1, 1963): 19–31.

A theoretical approach to the treatment of male homosexuality is described. Three case histories are reported—all treated some years previously by psychotherapy. Therapists must understand the different unconscious motivations—homosexuality, dependency, and power—that impel men to flee from women and to seek contact with other men. Only homosexual motivation seeks sexual gratification as an end goal; the other two, termed "pseudohomosexual" motivations, make use of the genital organs for non-sexual goals.

224   PAITICH, DANIEL. "Attitudes Toward Parents in Male Homosexuals and Exhibitionists." Ph.D. dissertation, University of Toronto, 1964, 110 pp.

This is a test of the hypothesis, derived from various psychoanalytic theories, that exhibitionists, bisexuals, and exclusive homosexuals differ from normal individuals in attitudes toward their parents' general competence, amount of affection received from parents, amount of strictness and aggression of parents, and amount of aggression of parents toward each other. An attitude scale was constructed through a scalogram analysis of responses to a questionnaire given to 164 normals (teachers, firemen, and friends of members of a community action group) and 162 male sex deviates (from the Forensic Clinic, Toronto). Differences in attitude scale scores were evaluated by a one-way analysis of variance.

Hypotheses regarding attitudes toward the mother, attitudes about the father's strictness and aggression (toward the subject), and about the father's aggression toward the mother were not supported. However, the normal individuals tested consistently showed stronger favorable attitudes about the father's affection than all three sexually deviant groups, and stronger favorable attitudes about the father's general competence than two of the deviant groups. It can be said, therefore, that some support was found for the hypothesis with respect to attitudes toward the father's affection and general competence.

225   PAITICH, DANIEL. "Parent-Child Relations and Sexual Deviation."
       Forensic Clinic Seminar, no. 47. Toronto: Toronto Psychiatric Hos-
       pital, 1960. Mimeographed, 27 pp.

A study designed to determine whether parent-child relationships are related to the development of sexual deviation was carried out by asking 160 subjects to answer a questionnaire about their parents' behavior and their own attitudes toward their parents. The subjects were divided into a control group of 115 "normal" men who were either university students, city firemen, or members of a civic organization, and a group of 45 sexual deviates, including 15 male exhibitionists, 15 men whose sexual experience was exclusively homosexual, and 15 men with a history of both homosexual and heterosexual activity.

Parent-child relationships, relations between the subjects' parents, and subjects' judgment of parental competence were examined. When the data were subjected to factor analysis, the mother's strictness and aggression, the mother's aggression toward the father, the mother's general competence, the father's general competence, the father's affection, and the subject's negative attitude toward the father emerged as significant categories.

The most important results of the analysis of mean factor estimates for the sex deviate group and the control group were that sexual deviation in the offspring is significantly related to the mother's aggression toward the father and to the father's lack of general competence. Other results indicate that the mothers of nonexclusive homosexuals scored highest on general competence, followed in descending order by the mothers of those in the control group, the mothers of exhibitionists, and the mothers of exclusive homosexuals. The mothers of exclusive homosexuals were judged to be stricter and more aggressive than the mothers of nonexclusive homosexuals. Exhibitionists and exclusive homosexuals had a more negative attitude toward their fathers than those in the control group.

It was concluded that "parent-child relationships are significantly related to the development of sexual deviation."

226   PERLOFF, WILLIAM H. "Hormones and Homosexuality." In *Sexual Inversion: The Multiple Roots of Homosexuality*, edited by Judd Marmor, pp. 44–69. New York: Basic Books, 1965.

Genetic, hormonal, and psychological factors all influence human sexual behavior. The maturation of the sex organs is dependent on androgenic and estrogenic hormones. However, the most important factors are the psychological ones. These factors largely control the choice of sex object and the intensity of sexual emotion. Homosexuality is a psychological condition. It is not produced by a hormonal deficiency and it cannot be cured by endocrine treatment.

This article is essentially the same as one entitled "Role of the Hormones in Human Sexuality" which was published in *Psychosomatic Medicine* 11 (3, 1949): 133–139.

227   PIOTROWSKI, ZYGMUNT A. "Inadequate Heterosexuality." *Psychiatric Quarterly* 41 (2, 1967): 360–365.

Certain attitudes of the parents toward the child are more important in the development of homosexuality than biological and congenital factors. Although homosexuality is severely neurotic behavior which frustrated, unhappy heterosexuals adopt, it should not be assumed that inadequate heterosexuality will result in homosexuality. The author presents his own classification of deviation ranging from 1 (adequate heterosexuality) to 3 (homosexual adaptation). He warns the reader against labeling all inadequate heterosexuality as latent homosexuality.

228   POMEROY, WARDELL B. "Parents and Homosexuality." *Sexology* 32 (8, 1966): 508–511; (9, 1966): 588–590.

Some of the myths regarding homosexuality are reviewed and the ways in which homosexuality develops are discussed. The Kinsey 7-point scale, adolescent homosexual play, and latent homosexuality are mentioned to show that homosexuality is not a distinct entity. The causes of homosexuality are rooted in the failure to develop heterosexually. Parents must encourage heterosexuality while not overly emulating male roles. Both father and mother should be open and affectionate toward their sons.

229   RAINER, JOHN D.; MESNIKOFF, ALVIN M.; KOLB, LAWRENCE C.; and CARR, ARTHUR C. "Homosexuality and Heterosexuality in Identical Twins." *Psychosomatic Medicine* 22 (4, 1960): 251–259.

In an effort to hold the genetic factor constant, the relationship of life experiences to divergent psychosexual roles was examined in two sets of identical twins, one set male and the other female. One of each set of twins was homosexual.

The method of investigation included the use of free association, family and social studies, and physiological data based partly upon blood tests. The determining life experiences for the differentiation of the sexual role were found in the prenatal fantasies of the parents of one pair for a child different in sex from that of the twins at birth, and an anatomical differentiation in the twins which determined for the mother a special attachment for one or the other. The parental attitude toward the role of the individual child disclosed through its naming was also significant.

230   RASMUSSEN, E. WULFF. "Experimental Homosexual Behavior in Male Albino Rats." *Acta Psychologica* 11 (1955): 303–334.

Research conducted with animals was carried out in an attempt to uncover certain aspects of the etiology of human homosexuality. The study was designed to determine whether there is a biological foundation for the theory that punishment, prohibition, or social disapproval gradually create an inhibition toward the opposite sex which results in the individual's desire to seek an outlet with the same sex, even if an opportunity for immediate contact with the opposite sex exists. Male rats were given an electric shock every time they tried to mate with a female in order to see if this would lead them to attempt to copulate with an introduced male. Of 62 animals tested, 27 showed unmistakable homosexual behavior; 11 displayed behavior not regarded as unmistakably homosexual, but nonetheless homosexual in character; and 24 displayed behavior determined as not being homosexual in nature.

Although drawing conclusions concerning man from experiments with rats is difficult, it is hypothesized that human homosexual behavior seems to be the result of the interaction between at least two of the following factors: strength of the sexual drive, inhibitions with regard to the opposite sex established by the environment, lack of opportunity for sexual relationships with members of the opposite sex, and hormonal imbalance.

231   REGARDIE, FRANCIS I. "Analysis of a Homosexual." *Psychiatric Quarterly* 23 (3, 1949): 548–566.

The analysis of a case of homosexuality is presented with an emphasis upon the patient's dreams. A 38-year-old married male underwent psychoanalysis with the additional use of hypnosis. The cause of his homosexuality was functional maldevelopment. As a child he had been very dependent upon his mother, and his homosexuality is viewed as a reaction-formation built up to repress his Oedipal desires. The therapy was successful and the patient was able to return to a complete heterosexual relationship with his wife.

232 ROBERTIELLO, RICHARD C. "Clinical Notes: Results of Separation from Iposexual Parents During the Oedipal Period, [and] A Female Homosexual Panic." *Psychoanalytic Review* 51 (4, 1964–65): 670–672.

Suppression of hostile and sexual feelings in children and female homosexual panic are discussed. The notion is advanced that during the Oedipal period, there are strong sexual attractions to the parent of the opposite sex and hostile feelings toward the parent of the same sex who is seen as a rival to be eliminated. When the same-sex parent leaves home (due to divorce, death, severe illness) the child feels that his unconscious wish has caused the separation. Guilt feelings and anticipation of punishment are "defended against" by the suppression of both hostile and sexual feelings. The child will often become passive, unassertive, and inadequate. It is suggested that the reconstruction of these feelings in therapy will lead to an understanding of these particular defensive adaptations.

The case study of a female patient who experienced a panic reaction is described. The patient had developed fears of inadequacy in her doctoral program. After failing a class given by a female professor, the patient was afraid she would be found lacking a mind since she equated mind and intelligence with penis and masculinity. Her defense involved a fantasy of homosexual involvement with the female professor. Counseling therapy uncovered the cause of the anxiety, and the panic was subsequently diminished.

233 ROFF, MERRILL. "Some Childhood and Adolescent Characteristics of Adult Homosexuals." U.S. Army Medical Research and Development Command, Report no. 66–5. n.p.: May, 1966, 28 pp.

The thesis of this study is that knowledge of peer-group relations during childhood can be predictive of maladjusted, in this case homosexual, behavior in adulthood. The subjects were 172 child guidance clinic cases, 86 of whom were diagnosed as homosexual while in the Army or at the time of separation from active duty, the other 86 having made a successful adjustment to Army life at the noncommissioned officer level. An analysis of school records was undertaken and each case was identified as having "poor," "undecided," or "good" peer-group adjustment. These were then compared with the adult outcome—labeled "good" or "homosexual."

The homosexual group was found to have poorer early peer relations. These findings "tend to agree with those obtained retrospectively by Bieber, et al., *Homosexuality: A Psychoanalytic Study,* and to disagree with the retrospective findings of Gebhard, Gagnon, Pomeroy and Christenson, *Sex Offenders: An Analysis of Types.* "

234   ROM, PAUL. "The Problem of 'Distance' in Sex Behavior." *International Journal of Social Psychiatry* 3 (2, 1957): 145–151.

Sexual perversions and aberrations are forms of neurotic distance-creating. Homosexuality is a technique for avoiding the full responsibilities of a sexual partnership. Therapy should aim at helping these people to understand their creation of distance from "normal" patterns.

235   ROTH, MARTIN, and BALL, J. R. B. "Psychiatric Aspects of Intersexuality." In *Intersexuality in Vertebrates Including Man,* edited by C. N. Armstrong and A. J. Marshall, pp. 395–443. London: Academic Press, 1964.

A discussion of male and female homosexuality considers its incidence, genetical and constitutional factors, early developmental origins, psychological and psychiatric aspects. Genetic and constitutional studies of homosexuality are reviewed, with the conclusion that heredity may provide a partial but not an adequate explanation. Although castration fear and other specific reactions included in Freudian theory are questioned, the importance of parent-child bonds is accepted, particularly an intense relationship with the mother and an unsatisfactory one with the father. Exclusive homosexuality, appearing only among humans, is the result of social learning.

Although neurotics are found among homosexuals, so are normal personalities. In 1957 Scott proposed a classification of homosexuality which included the following types: adolescents and mentally immature adults, severely damaged personalities, relatively intact personalities, latent and well-compensated homosexuals, and individuals with serious mental disablement.

Lesbianism is far more rare than male homosexuality, and knowledge about it is superficial. Much more research into its psychological and social origins is needed.

236   RUBIN, ISADORE, ed. *The Third Sex.* New York: New Book Co., 1961, 112 pp. Also printed as his *Homosexuals Today.* New York: Health Publications, 1965, 112 pp.

A series of articles on male and female homosexuality is reprinted from *Sexology* magazine. A wide range of topics is covered, including theories of causality, the history of homosexuality, recent research, problems of treatment, the social life and problems of homosexuals, myths about homosexuality, and the need for law reform. Ten "additional notes" that appear here and there in the text consist of quotations or brief abstracts of articles on these topics.

See Allen, Clifford (no. 94), (no. 810). Benjamin, Harry (no. 1132). Dengrove, Edward (no. 272). Dingwall, Eric J. (no. 971). Ellis, Albert (no. 681). Harper, Robert A. (no. 434). Kirkendall, Lester A. (no. 717). "New Light on Homosexuality" (no. 517). Rubin, Isadore (no. 53), (no. 765), (no. 901), (no. 902), (no. 1230). Stiller, Richard (no. 1023). Tarail, Mark (no. 780). Walker, Kenneth (no. 1253). Wood, Robert (no. 263), (no. 1036). Woodward, L. T. (no. 797).

237 RUBINSTEIN, L. H. "The Role of Identifications in Homosexuality and Transvestitism in Men and Women." In *The Pathology and Treatment of Sexual Deviation: A Methodological Approach,* edited by Ismond Rosen, pp. 163–195. London: Oxford University Press, 1964.

"Dual identification" or cross-identification is discussed as a major factor in the etiology of homosexuality. Case histories are used to illustrate these dual identifications—for example, identification with both father, brother, and mother in the case of an apparently active male homosexual with marked underlying passivity. Although the complexity and importance of this mechanism is not commonly recognized, successful analysis of homosexuality depends upon the disentanglement of these combined Oedipal and narcissistic attachments. Female homosexuality and transvestitism are often the result of an identification with both the father and the mother which is accompanied by an envy of the male sibling.

238 RUITENBEEK, HENDRIK M. "Men Alone: The Male Homosexual and the Disintegrated Family." Reprinted in *The Problem of Homosexuality in Modern Society,* edited by Hendrik M. Ruitenbeek, pp. 80–93. New York: E. P. Dutton & Co., 1963.

The alienation and loneliness of contemporary life and the disintegration of the family in our society are cited as causes for an increase in homosexuality. The contemporary family does not provide the male model necessary for a boy to develop an ideal for the accepted masculine role. Greater social mobility makes it easier for the homosexual to function and for the homosexual subculture to exist.

239 RUITENBEEK, HENDRIK M., ed. *The Problem of Homosexuality in Modern Society.* New York: E. P. Dutton & Co., 1963, 304 pp.

A collection of 16 articles reprinted from other sources was assembled to provide information not easily accessible to the lay reader, and also to stimulate thinking which may lead to further research on homosexuality as a sociological phenomenon. The selections are justified in the introduction and it is explained that the preponderance of psychoanalytical material is due to the scarcity of sociological studies in this area.

See Beauvoir, Simone de (no. 268). Devereux, George (no. 969). Ellis, Albert (no. 678). Ferenczi, Sandor (no. 384). Freud, Sigmund (no. 394). Hooker, Evelyn (no. 453). Kardiner, Abram (no. 181). Leznoff, Maurice, and Westley, William A. (no. 874). Lindner, Robert (no. 875). Ovesey, Lionel (no. 221). Rado, Sandor (no. 536). Raven, Simon (no. 893). Reiss, Albert J., Jr. (no. 895). Ruitenbeek, Hendrik M. (no. 238). Thompson, Clara (no. 584). Van den Haag, Ernest (no. 1119).

240   SCHMIDEBERG, MELITTA. "A Note on Homosexuality and Circumcision." *Psychoanalytic Review* 35 (2, 1948): 183–184.

Brief case histories of two non-Jewish schizoid patients, both of whom had grown up without a father and both of whom had been circumcised, are described. In the homosexual patient, resentment and fear of his mother associated with the circumcision was an important factor in the development of his homosexuality. One motive for his homosexuality was a desire to be reunited with his foreskin.

241   SCHWARZ, OSWALD. "Sexuality of the Pubescent, Part b. Homosexuality of Youth." In *The Psychology of Sex,* by Oswald Schwarz, pp. 45–52. Harmondsworth, Middlesex: Penguin Books, 1949. Reprinted as "Homosexuality of Youth." In *The Homosexuals: As Seen by Themselves and Thirty Authorities,* edited by Aron M. Krich, pp. 134–141. New York: Citadel Press, 1954.

Like masturbation, homosexuality in youth may be considered a step in sexual development; but unlike the former, it is always definitely abnormal, largely induced by the environment, and practiced by only a small number of boys. Its cause lies in an abnormality of the whole personality, stemming mainly from a desire for support and security.

242   SECOR, H. W. "What Causes Homosexuality?" *Sexology* 16 (4, 1949): 226–232.

The etiology of homosexuality is discussed with special reference to the work of Clara Thompson. Homosexuality may indicate a fear of the opposite sex, a fear of adult responsibility, a need to defy authority, or a mental

flight from reality into absorption in body stimulation. The family constellation is an important influence in the development of homosexuality. Which
parent loves a child more, which wields more power, which is more depend-
able, and whether the child was aware that his sex was a disappointment
to one or both of his parents are all relevant to this problem. Tendencies
toward homosexuality may be brought about by a lack of self-esteem,
personal intimidation, a fear of intimacy, or loneliness.

243   "Sex Today and Tomorrow." *Medical Press* 241 (21, 1959): 459–
       460.

Homosexuality is frequently seen in the early sexual development of children. Their heterosexuality usually soon dominates, however, and the
homosexuality disappears. Those who remain homosexual are seen as failing to reach sexual maturity because of unfortunate experiences during
puberty, and in the vast majority of cases this misfortune is accidental. If
the homosexual really wants to become heterosexual, which is seldom the
case, he can do so "provided he has the necessary patience, persistence and
resolution."

244   SHEARER, MARSHALL. "Homosexuality and the Pediatrician: Early
       Recognition and Preventive Counselling." *Clinical Pediatrics* 5
       (Aug., 1966): 514–518.

Early recognition of homosexual traits by the pediatrician can help in
correcting this trend. Abnormal parental attitudes and behavior are the
major causes of deviation. These may include a harsh and unloving father
(especially when harsh on sons but permissive with daughters), a domineering mother, a weak father who presents an inadequate masculine model, or
a mother who must find a relationship with the son because she has little
or no relationship with the father.
     Both boys and girls with homosexual tendencies exhibit a pseudo-
maturity. Boys perceive themselves as frail and clumsy; girls are generally
competitive and aggressive. In childhood, the most reliable sign of future
adult homosexual orientation is an excessive fear of illness or bodily injury.

245   SIMPSON, GEORGE. *People in Families.* New York: Thomas Y. Cro-
       well Co., 1960, 554 pp.

A general sociological text on the family, mating, marriage, child development, and family-related deviant behavior, includes a chapter on homosexuality, prostitution, and incest. The Freudian theory of choice of love-object
and development of homosexuality is presented, and Kinsey data on the
incidence of homosexuality and social attitudes toward it are reported.

246   SLATER, ELIOT. "Sibs and Children of Homosexuals." In *Symposium on Nuclear Sex*, edited by D. Robertson Smith and William H. Davidson, pp. 79–83. New York: Interscience Publishers, 1958.

Previous work has indicated that the intersexual theory of homosexuality should be discarded. However, the higher ratio of male to female sibs noted among homosexuals by several studies remains to be explained. Further confirmation of this relationship (of male to female sibs) was sought in this study. The case records of 286 homosexual patients in the Maudsley-Bethlem Joint Hospital were examined. A slight, but statistically insignificant higher ratio of male to female sibs was found.

247   SMITT, JARL WAGNER. "Homosexuality in a New Light." *International Journal of Sexology* 6 (1, 1952): 36–39.

A new theory regarding the causes of homosexuality is presented. None of four previous theories of the cause of homosexuality (Hirschfeld's "intersex-theory," Krafft-Ebing's "psychopathy-theory," Freud's "neurosis-theory," and Kinsey's "learning-theory") is able to explain the inner nature of the development of homosexuality. Only the "instinct imprinting theory" (based upon the work of Lorenz-Tinbergen's theory of instincts) is able to point out those factors which are common to the four points of view. The central point in this theory is that "the individual's instinctive life is to a considerable degree determined during the actual functioning of the instincts in the periods when the instincts concerned, one after another, become 'mature' in a biological sense; the individual's final instinctive attitude is thus formed on the groundwork of his own personal experiences. The formative process is called 'instinct imprinting.' " There are two characteristics of this process: the instinct becomes mature enough to allow imprinting to occur at a definite age; and the irreversibility of the process —that is, the imprint is not weakened when it has once appeared.

A program designed to prevent the development of homosexuality and based upon imprinting theory includes: a warmer upbringing to reduce the severity of the Western civilization's masculine way of life, the elimination of the many single-sex school environments, the provision of natural and realistic sex information, and a greater tolerance toward the various manifestations of sexuality, including homosexuality.

248   SOCARIDES, CHARLES W. "A Provisional Theory of Aetiology in Male Homosexuality: A Case of Preoedipal Origin." *International Journal of Psycho-Analysis* 49 (1, 1968): 27–37.

Male homosexuality is based upon a pre-Oedipal nuclear conflict. The case of a 30-year-old single man suffering from depression, who underwent

psychoanalysis, is used to illustrate this contention. The obligatory homosexual is unable to progress from the mother-child unity of earliest infancy
to individuation. As a result there exists a fixation, with a concomitant
tendency to regress to the earliest mother-child relationship. Thus, it would
appear that homosexuality is a transitional condition somewhere between
the psychoses, the borderline psychoses and/or the neuroses.

249   SPRINCE, MARJORIE P. "A Contribution to the Study of Homosexu-
       ality in Adolescence." *Journal of Child Psychology and Psychiatry
       and Allied Disciplines* 5 (2, 1964): 103–117.

The analytical material of an overt adolescent homosexual is examined in
order to distinguish transitory adolescent homosexual features from the
permanent character traits of homosexual pathology. Factors decisive to
homosexual development are discussed. While the extent of ego regression
appears decisive, the final outcome is difficult to predict because qualitative
and quantitative factors, together with the unknown influence of the adolescent process, may finally tip the balance in one direction or the other.

250   STANLEY -JONES, D. "Sexual Inversion: An Ethical Study." *Lancet*
       252 (6447, 1947): 366–369.

Sexual inversion, also called homosexuality, is an attitude of mind in which
the affections are turned toward members of the same sex. All children pass
through a homosexual phase of development, and if a fixation arises at that
time the person will not pass on to heterosexuality. It is the moral duty of
the medical profession to deal with cases of sexual psychopaths, and they
must be blamed for the present lack of treatment facilities.

251   STORR, ANTHONY. *Sexual Deviation.* Baltimore: Penguin Books,
       1964, 139 pp.

In a survey treatment of the most common sexual deviations the introductory chapters discuss the hypothesis that "sexual deviations are chiefly the
result of the persistence of childhood feelings of guilt and inferiority." These
chapters are followed by fairly general discussions of sado-masochism,
fetishism, transvestism, female homosexuality, male homosexuality, exhibitionism, frotteurism, voyeurism, buggery, and pedophilia. Two final chapters cover methods of treatment.

252   ULLMAN, PAUL S. "Parental Participation in Childrearing as Evalu-
       ated by Male Social Deviates." *Pacific Sociological Review* 3 (2,
       1960): 89–95.

At a California prison-hospital questionnaires were administered to 325
inmates with histories of deviant sexual behavior and 311 inmates with no

records of deviant sexual behavior. The case records of each subject were also utilized in the data collecting process.

The findings supported the hypothesis that with the exception of homosexuals, sexually deviant males do not differ from other inmates with respect to the childrearing practices of their parents. Sexual psychopaths, pedophiliacs, and rapists appear to have been subjected to childrearing practices similar to the childrearing practices of parents of prisoners with no history of sexual deviation.

Homosexuals, however, do not appear to have had similar childrearing experiences. Instead they exhibit a pattern of childrearing characterized by maternal overparticipation in training (i.e., bossing, punishing, scolding, etc.) and paternal underparticipation in maintenance behavior (i.e., love, attention, praise, etc.).

253   WEISSMAN, PHILIP. "Structural Considerations in Overt Male Bisexuality." *International Journal of Psycho-Analysis* 43 (2–3, 1962): 159–168.

Two structural considerations are discussed: the stage of development of the love object relationship (whether narcissistic or real); and the role of the superego. The relationship between normal and overt male homosexuality is also discussed. In the former, both the unconscious heterosexual behavior and the unconscious homosexuality are derived mainly from the Oedipal conflict. In overt male homosexuality, if it is derived from pre-Oedipal identification with the mother and with object relations on a narcissistic level, then the overt bisexuality is basically a homosexual perversion. If the overt bisexuality is Oedipal in nature, the superego demands a regressive object choice along with the heterosexual object choice. The homosexuality in the one case is derived from acting out of the homosexual component as part of the repetition of the entire Oedipal conflict; in the other case the overt homosexuality represents a defense against heterosexual Oedipal wishes.

In normal male bisexuality overt sexual behavior is mainly heterosexual, but the unconscious wish is to be in the mother's feminine role in the sexual relationship with the father. Through overt male bisexuality the person gratifies both his heterosexual and homosexual wishes.

254   WELLMAN, MARVIN. "Overt Homosexuality with Spontaneous Remission." *Canadian Medical Association Journal* 75 (Aug., 1956): 273–279.

The case of a 22-year-old male with a history of homosexual interests and overt behavior is reported. During the patient's psychotherapy it was found that his homosexuality occurred as part of his struggle to either escape from the control of his mother or to adjust himself to it. The homosexuality was but one among several neurotic symptoms. When the mother finally relegated herself to an emotionally supporting role, the patient recovered spontaneously from the homosexual manifestations and from the other neurotic symptoms which had developed.

255   WEST, D. J. "Parental Figures in the Genesis of Male Homosexuality." *International Journal of Social Psychiatry* 5 (2, 1959): 85–97.

Many writers have suggested that a great number of homosexuals have a family history which includes a dominating mother and a weak, unsatisfactory, or absent father. In this study the case records of 50 homosexual male neurotic patients and 50 heterosexual male neurotic patients, matched for age and primary or secondary diagnosis, all inpatients of Maudsley-Bethlem Joint Hospital, were compared in an effort to find out if a higher incidence of unsatisfactory father-son and overintense mother-son relationships would be found among the homosexuals. Abstracts of the hospital case histories of each patient were prepared. Information about the relationships of the patient to his parents was included, but all information about the patients' sexual habits was deleted. Two psychiatrists rated the parental relationships according to their deviation from the ideal of a competent parent on a 4-point scale. The results showed a significant difference between the groups, with the presence of an overintense and unsatisfactory father relationship found more frequently among the members of the homosexual group.

256   WESTWOOD, GORDON. *Society and the Homosexual.* New York: E. P. Dutton & Co., 1952, 191 pp.

Homosexuality should be brought out into the open where it can be discussed and reconsidered. It is viewed as being largely ignored by the general public and clouded in ignorance as a result. The British attitude toward homosexuality is viewed as one of ridicule and disgust which manifests itself in the laws which attempt to stamp out homosexuality. Homosexuality is set in the perspective of a social as well as a sexual manifestation, and its chief cause is maladjustment during early childhood. The only known antidote appears to be lengthy psychotherapy. The habits, social setting, hopes and fears, conflicts, and aspirations of the homosexual are described.

257   WHALEN, RICHARD E. "Sexual Motivation." *Psychological Review* 73 (2, 1966): 151–163.

Current theories of sexual motivation emphasize the hormonal determinants of animal motivation and the experiential determinants of human and animal sexual motivation which has two components: sexual arousal and sexual arousability, which are a function of both biological and experiential factors. The difference between the state of sexual motivation and the expression of sexual behavior is stressed. Since homosexual relationships vary in different cultures it is concluded that a homosexual behavior pattern is part of one's sexual motivation.

258   "What Makes a Sexual Deviate?" *Sexology* 17 (7, 1951): 412–419.

The editorial staff of *Sexology* presents a discussion of the development of sexual deviations. Sexual deviates never grow up sexually and remain mentally and sexually at some early stage of their childhood. Homosexual tendencies are of purely mental or psychological origin.

259   WINTERSTEIN, ALFRED. "On the Oral Basis of a Case of Male Homosexuality." *International Journal of Psycho-Analysis* 37 (4–5, 1956): 298–302.

The case study of a married man in his early thirties, who was seen in therapy complaining of inhibitions, feelings of inferiority, guilt, and premature ejaculation, is reported.

The patient was diagnosed as homosexual although his homosexuality had, up to then, only found expression in his fantasies. "Vacillating between the phallic sister and the father, he adopted in his negative Oedipus complex a position half-way between the two, and thus made a compromise. The desire to be anally pierced by his father's penis is not only the result of fear of castration by the father, but also a periodic avoiding of the oral conflict, which is secondarily projected onto the father."

260   WITTELS, FRITZ. "Struggles of a Homosexual in Pre-Hitler Germany." *Journal of Criminal Psychopathology* 4 (3, 1943): 408–423.

A 27-year-old German homosexual male employed what are described as typically German defense mechanisms (i.e., supermasculinity, et cetera) during his psychosexual development. Many attempts were made by him to relieve his fixation on his mother and his older brother, but these resulted in overt homosexuality. Analysis, although incomplete, enabled him to return to a normal heterosexual life.

261   WOHL, R. RICHARD, and TROSMAN, HARRY. "A Retrospect of Freud's 'Leonardo,' An Assessment of a Psychoanalytic Case." *Psychiatry* 18 (1, 1955): 27–39.

A critique of Freud's *Leonardo da Vinci* contends that Freud forced documented evidence of Leonardo's life into his own preconceived notion of homosexuality. Particularly erroneous was Freud's treatment of the allegedly close mother-son nexus. At the time Freud wrote on Leonardo, only scanty evidence on homosexuality was available. Oversimplifying and overgeneralizing the inconclusive theories of homosexual psychogenesis, Freud transformed Leonardo's rejecting and depriving mother into a loving and highly protective one.

262   WOLFSON, WILLIAM, and GROSS, ALFRED. "A Footnote to the Etiological Study of the Homosexual Syndrome." *International Journal of Sexology* 6 (3, 1953): 178–179.

Interviews were conducted with 1,500 male homosexuals from all social classes. These men were contacted through either the New York City courts or the George W. Henry Foundation. Their social histories were taken in the interviews, and each subject was specifically questioned about his age at his first homosexual experience.

The great majority of men reported they became acquainted with homosexual activity near the onset of puberty and were introduced to overt practice either by somewhat older boys or by an adult, usually by the older boys. Very rarely is group sex play mentioned. However, it seems evident that there are youths who are peculiarly prone to submission to homosexual advances. This might be referred to as a "readiness for seduction." Professionals should devise tests to recognize the factors which make boys susceptible to homosexuality.

263   WOOD, ROBERT. "New Report on Homosexuality." 1961. Reprinted in *The Third Sex,* edited by Isadore Rubin, pp. 48–52. New York: New Book Co., 1961.

A British research study of 127 male homosexuals prepared for the British Social Biology Council by Gordon Westwood is reported. Noninstitutionalized homosexuals were interviewed for information on family backgrounds, social behavior, and sex activities. More than half reported their homes had been happy and unbroken. No evidence was found that seduction was important in the development of their homosexuality. The respondents did not appear effeminate and most did not work in artistic or nonmanual occupations, although there is a tendency for homosexuals to enter these occupations.

264   WULFF, MOSHE. "A Case of Male Homosexuality." 1942. Reprinted in *The Homosexuals: As Seen by Themselves and Thirty Authorities,* edited by Aron M. Krich, pp. 324–342. New York: Citadel Press, 1954.

The case study of a 27-year-old man seen in psychoanalytic therapy because of psychical impotence is reported. The problem was found to be related to "a peculiar situation in the constellation of the Oedipus complex." At the time at which object choice occurred, only the parent of the subject's own sex was present. From the very first, this parent had taken the place of the parent of the opposite sex. As a result of this constellation, the only object choice which could be brought out by rivalry was a homosexual one. A complete cure was effected, and four years later the patient was a married man with a second child on the way, felt quite normal, happy, and free from disturbance of any kind.

265 WYDEN, PETER, and WYDEN, BARBARA. *Growing Up Straight: What Every Thoughtful Parent Should Know About Homosexuality.* New York: Stein & Day, 1968, 256 pp.

Based on the most recent scientific studies and research, false notions and needless worries about homosexuality are explored. Factors which may lead to homosexuality—divorce, boarding school, summer camp, military service, death in the family, and the "mother-father-child interactive system" —are considered. The ways in which parents may cause homosexuality in their children are carefully detailed and the usually neglected importance of the father's role is emphasized.

While the emotional relationship between the child and the parent may not be the exclusive cause of homosexuality, the influence of other factors is only slight and contributory. Peer relationships and certain of today's cultural trends, (i.e., war, living conditions in slum neighborhoods, and racial persecution and treatment), are seen as being encouraging to homosexuality.

While the focus is primarily upon means of prevention, an optimistic view for the cure of homosexuality is presented. Rearing children in a "sexually sound" home is the most effective means of preventing homosexuality.

266 YOUNG, WILLIAM C., ed. *Sex and Internal Secretions.* 3d ed. 2 vols. Baltimore: Williams & Wilkins Co., 1961, 1609 pp.

Research is cited to support the importance of gonadal hormones in the development of sexual responsiveness in man, but the conclusion is reached that homosexuality and other behavioral disorders of sex are "fundamentally disorders of eroticism." The relationship of these disorders to other sex variables is believed to be peripheral. The concept of a psychological sexual neutrality in humans at birth is advanced. The critical period for the imprinting of gender role and orientation is thought to be between 18 months and three years.

CROSS-REFERENCES

Allen, Clifford. "Homosexuality: The Psychological Factor." *Medical Press* 217 (1947): 222–223. No. 651.

Allen, Clifford. "The Heterosexual and Homosexual Perversions." In *A Textbook of Psychosexual Disorders*, pp. 165–204. New York: Oxford University Press, 1962. No. 288.

Austin, Sean Harlan. "Analysis and Prediction of Male Homosexual Case History Material: A Replication and Extension." Master's thesis, San Francisco State College, 1967, 125 pp. No. 295.

Barahal, Hyman S. "Testosterone in Psychotic Male Homosexuals." *Psychiatric Quarterly* 14 (2, 1940): 319–330. No. 69.

Barnouw, Victor, and Stern, John A. "Some Suggestions Concerning Social and Cultural Determinants of Human Sexual Behavior." In *Determinants of Human Sexual Behavior*, edited by George Winokur, pp. 206–209. Springfield, Ill.: Charles C. Thomas, 1963. No. 1.

Beach, Frank A. *Hormones and Behavior.* New York: Paul B. Hoeber, 1949, 368 pp. No. 3.

Beggs, Keith Siddons. "Some Legal, Social and Psychiatric Aspects of Homosexual Behavior: A Guide for the Social Worker in the Sex Clinic." Master's thesis, University of Wisconsin, 1950, 298 pp. No. 955.

Berg, Charles. "The Problem of Homosexuality." *American Journal of Psychotherapy* 10 (4, 1956): 696–708; 11 (1, 1957): 65–79. No. 305.

Bergler, Edmund. *Counterfeit-Sex: Homosexuality, Impotence, Frigidity.* 2d rev. ed. New York: Grune & Stratton, 1958, 380 pp. No. 307.

Bieber, Irving. "Changing Concepts of the Genesis and Therapy of Male Homosexuality." Paper read at American Orthopsychiatric Association Meeting, 18 March 1965, in New York. Mimeographed, 9 pp. No. 657. Reported in *American Journal of Orthopsychiatry* 35 (Mar., 1965): No. 203.

Bieber, Irving, et al. *Homosexuality: A Psychoanalytic Study.* New York: Basic Books, 1962, 358 pp. No. 314.

Branham, Vernon C. "Behavior Disorders in Prison." *Journal of Criminal Psychopathology* 1 (3, 1940): 234–246. No. 959.

Brown, Daniel G. "Inversion and Homosexuality." *American Journal of Orthopsychiatry* 28 (2, 1958): 424–429. No. 331.

Brown, Daniel G. "The Development of Sex-Role Inversion and Homosexuality." *Journal of Pediatrics* 50 (5, 1957): 613–619. No. 330.

Brown, Daniel G., and Lynn, David B. "Human Sexual Development: An Outline of Components and Concepts." *Journal of Marriage and the Family* 28 (2, 1966): 155–162. No. 332.

Buki, Rudolph A. "A Treatment Program for Homosexuals." *Diseases of the Nervous System* 25 (5, 1964): 304–307. No. 663.

Caprio, Frank S., and Brenner, Donald R. *Sexual Behavior: Psycho-Legal Aspects.* New York: Citadel Press, 1961, 384 pp. No. 1141.

Carson, Laura E. "Are We Hiding Behind a Word?" *Mental Hygiene* 42 (3, 1958): 558–561. No. 1063.

Carstairs, G. Morris. "Cultural Differences in Sexual Deviation." In *The Pathology and Treatment of Sexual Deviation: A Methodological Approach,* edited by Ismond Rosen, pp. 419–434. London: Oxford University Press, 1964. No. 962.

Carstairs, G. Morris, and Grygier, Tadeusz G. "Anthropological, Psychometric, and Psychotherapeutic Aspects of Homosexuality." *Bulletin of the British Psychological Society* 32 (1957): 46–47. No. 964.

Cavanagh, John R. *Counseling the Invert.* Milwaukee, Wisc.: Bruce Publishing Co., 1966, 306 pp. No. 668.

Chang, Judy, and Block, Jack. "A Study of Identification in Male Homosexuals." *Journal of Consulting Psychology* 24 (4, 1960): 307–310. No. 347.

Chesser, Eustace. *Odd Man Out: Homosexuality in Men and Women.* London: Victor Gollancz, 1959, 192 pp. No. 1065.

Cornsweet, A. C., and Hayes, M. F. "Conditioned Response to Fellatio." *American Journal of Psychiatry* 103 (Jul., 1946): 76–78. No. 351.

Cory, Donald Webster. *The Homosexual in America: A Subjective Approach.* New York: Greenberg, 1951, 326 pp. No. 826.

Ellis, Albert. "A Homosexual Treated with Rational Psychotherapy." *Journal of Clinical Psychology* 15 (3, 1959): 338–343. No. 679.

Ellis, Albert. *Homosexuality: Its Causes and Cure.* New York: Lyle Stuart, 1965, 288 pp. No. 680.

Fischoff, Joseph. "Preoedipal Influences in a Boy's Determination to be 'Feminine' during the Oedipal Period." *Journal of the American Academy of Child Psychiatry* 3 (2, 1964): 273–286. No. 389.

Fisher, Saul H. "A Note on Male Homosexuality and the Role of Women in Ancient Greece." In *Sexual Inversion: The Multiple Roots of Homosexuality,* edited by Judd Marmor, pp. 165–172. New York: Basic Books, 1965. No. 977.

Freud, Anna. "Clinical Observations on the Treatment of Manifest Male Homosexuality." Paper read at meeting of the New York Psychoanalytic Society, 17 April 1950. Reported by Herbert F. Waldhorn. *Psychoanalytic Quarterly* 20 (2, 1951): 337–338. No. 695.

Friedman, Paul. "Sexual Deviations." In *American Handbook of Psychiatry,* vol. 1, edited by Silvano Arieti et al., pp. 589–613. New York: Basic Books, 1959. No. 11.

Gadpaille, Warren J. "Homosexual Experience in Adolescence." *Medical Aspects of Human Sexuality* 2 (10, 1968): 29–38. No. 404.

Gebhard, Paul H.; Gagnon, John H.; Pomeroy, Wardell B.; and Christensen, Cornelia V. *Sex Offenders: An Analysis of Types.* New York: Harper & Row, 1965, 923 pp. No. 846.

Gerber, Israel Joshua. *Man on a Pendulum: A Case History of an Invert.* New York: American Press, 1955, 320 pp. No. 847.

Gershman, Harry. "Considerations of Some Aspects of Homosexuality." *American Journal of Psychoanalysis* 13 (1953): 82–83. No. 409.

Gilbert, S. F. "Homosexuality and Hypnotherapy." *British Journal of Medical Hypnotism* 5 (3, 1954): 2–7. No. 415.

Ginsburg, Kenneth N. "The 'Meat-Rack': A Study of the Male Homosexual Prostitute." *American Journal of Psychotherapy* 21 (2, 1967): 170–185. No. 848.

Glover, Edward. "The Social and Legal Aspects of Sexual Abnormality." *Medico-Legal and Criminological Review* 13 (3, 1945): 133–148. No. 419.

Greco, Marshall C., and Wright, James C. "The Correctional Institution in the Etiology of Chronic Homosexuality." *American Journal of Orthopsychiatry* 14 (2, 1944): 295–307. No. 984.

Guyon, René; Hambly, Wilfrid D.; Hirsch, Edwin W.; Loras, Olivier; and Wilson, Joseph G. "The Causes of Homosexuality: A Symposium." *Sexology* 21 (11, 1955): 722–727. No. 15.

Heilbrun, Gert. "Psychoanalysis of Yesterday, Today, and Tomorrow." *Archives of General Psychiatry* 4 (4, 1961): 321–330. No. 16.

Henry, George W. *All the Sexes: A Study of Masculinity and Femininity.* Toronto and New York: Rinehart, 1955, 599 pp. No. 443.

Henry, George W. "Psychogenic and Constitutional Factors in Homosexuality." *Psychiatric Quarterly* 8 (2, 1934): 243–264. Reprinted as "Psychogenic and Constitutional Factors." In *The Homosexuals: As Seen by Themselves and Thirty Authorities,* edited by Aron M. Krich, pp. 153–174. New York: Citadel Press, 1954. No. 17.

Herman, Morris, and Wortis, S. B. "Aberrant Sex-Behavior in Humans." *Annals of the New York Academy of Science* 47 (art. 5, 1947): 639–645. No. 444.

Heston, L. L., and Shields, James. "Homosexuality in Twins: A Family Study and a Registry Study." *Archives of General Psychiatry* 18 (2, 1968): 149–160. No. 18.

Hewitt, Charles C. "On the Meaning of Effeminacy in Homosexual Men." *American Journal of Psychotherapy* 15 (4, 1961): 592–602. No. 446.

Hoffman, Martin. *The Gay World: Male Homosexuality and the Social Creation of Evil.* New York: Basic Books, 1968, 212 pp. No. 855.

"Homosexuality and Moral Welfare." *Lancet* 266 (6810, 1954): 505–506. No. 1084.

Homosexuality and Prostitution: A Memorandum of Evidence Prepared by a Special Committee of the Council of the British Medical Association for Submission to the Departmental Committee on Homosexuality and Prostitution. London: British Medical Association, 1955, 94 pp. No. 21.

Hooker, Evelyn. "Homosexuality: Summary of Studies." In *Sex Ways in Fact and Faith: Bases for Christian Family Policy,* edited by Evelyn M. Duvall and Sylvanus M. Duvall, pp. 166–183. New York: Association Press, 1961. No. 1260.

Ivimey, Muriel. "Homosexuality." Summary of a lecture for Auxiliary Council to the Association for the Advancement of Psychoanalysis, 1947. Mimeographed, 4 pp. No. 460.

Jones, H. Kimball. *Toward a Christian Understanding of the Homosexual.* New York: Association Press, 1966, 160 pp. No. 1086.

Juzwiak, Marijo. "Understanding the Homosexual Patient." *RN* [Registered Nurse] 27 (4, 1964): 53–59, 118. No. 1087.

Kinsey, Alfred C.; Pomeroy, Wardell B.; and Martin, Clyde E. *Sexual Behavior in the Human Male.* Philadelphia: W. B. Saunders Co., 1948, 804 pp. No. 869.

Koegler, Ronald R., and Kline, Lawrence Y. "Psychotherapy Research: An Approach Utilizing Autonomic Response Measurements." *American Journal of Psychotherapy* 19 (2, 1965): 268–279. No. 477.

Kolb, Lawrence C. "Therapy of Homosexuality." *Current Psychiatric Therapies* 3 (1963): 131–137. No. 719.

Laidlaw, Robert W. "A Clinical Approach to Homosexuality." *Marriage and Family Living* 14 (1, 1952): 39–45. No. 721.

Lambert, Carl. "Homosexuals." *Medical Press* 232 (1954): 523–526. No. 722.

Lindner, Robert. "Homosexuality and the Contemporary Scene." 1956. Reprinted in *The Problem of Homosexuality in Modern Society,* edited by Hendrik M. Ruitenbeek, pp. 52–79. New York: E. P. Dutton & Co., 1963. No. 875.

Lipkowitz, Marvin H. "Homosexuality as a Defense Against Feminine Strivings: A Case Report." *Journal of Nervous and Mental Disease* 138 (Apr., 1964): 394–398. No. 494.

McCreary, John K. "Psychopathia Homosexualis." *Canadian Journal of Psychology* 4 (1950): 63–74. No. 500.

Maclay, D. T. "Boys Who Commit Sexual Misdemeanors." *British Medical Journal* (5167, 1960): 186–190. No. 503.

Magee, Bryan. *One in Twenty: A Study of Homosexuality in Men and Women.* London: Secker & Warburg, 1966, 192 pp. No. 878.

"Male Homosexuality." *Lancet* 2 (7111, 1959): 1077–1080. No. 879.

Marlowe, Kenneth. "The Life of the Homosexual Prostitute." *Sexology* 31 (1, 1964): 24–26. No. 880.

Mead, Margaret. *Male and Female: A Study of the Sexes in a Changing World.* New York: William Morrow & Co., 1949, 477 pp. No. 1009.

Mercer, Jessie Decamarron. *They Walk in Shadow: A Study of Sexual Variations with Emphasis on the Ambisexual and Homosexual Components and Our Contemporary Sex Laws.* New York: Comet Press Books, 1959, 573 pp. No. 1207.

Money, John. "Sexual Dimorphism and Homosexual Gender Identity." [Working Paper] Prepared for Distribution to Members of the National Institute of Mental Health Task Force on Homosexuality. Mimeographed. Bethesda, Md., Nov. 25–26, 1967. No. 34.

Monsour, Karem J. "Migraine: Dynamics and Choice of Symptom." *Psychoanalytic Quarterly* 26 (4, 1957): 479–493. No. 511.

Myerson, Abraham; Neustadt, Rudolph; and Rak, I. P. "The Male Homosexual: Hormonal and Clinical Studies." *Journal of Nervous and Mental Disease* 93 (2, 1941): 209–212. No. 38.

Neustatter, W. Lindesay. "Homosexuality: The Medical Aspects." In *They Stand Apart: A Critical Survey of the Problems of Homosexuality,* edited by John Tudor Rees and Harley V. Usill, pp. 67–139. London: William Heinemann, 1955. No. 42.

O'Connor, P. J. "Aetiological Factors in Homosexuality as Seen in Royal Air Force Psychiatric Practice." *British Journal of Psychiatry* 110 (466, 1964): 381–391. No. 522.

Ollendorff, Robert H. V. *The Juvenile Homosexual Experience and Its Effect on Adult Sexuality.* New York: Julian Press, 1966, 245 pp. No. 750.

"The Other Side: Living with Homosexuality." *Canadian Medical Association Journal* 86 (May 12, 1962): 875–878. No. 888.

Parker, Neville. "Homosexuality in Twins: A Report on Three Discordant Pairs." *British Journal of Psychiatry* 110 (467, 1964): 489–495. No. 45.

Pascoe, Herbert. "Deviant Sexual Behavior and the Sex Criminal." *Canadian Medical Association Journal* 84 (Jan. 28, 1961): 206–211. No. 1210.

Perloff, William H. "The Role of Hormones in Homosexuality." *Journal of the Albert Einstein Medical Center* 11 (3, 1963): 165–178. No. 47.

Rado, Sandor. "An Adaptational View of Sexual Behavior." 1949, rev. 1955. Reprinted in *The Problem of Homosexuality in Modern Society,* edited by Hendrik M. Ruitenbeek, pp. 94–126. New York: E. P. Dutton & Co., 1963. No. 536.

Rado, Sandor. "A Critical Examination of the Concept of Bisexuality." 1940. Reprinted in *Sexual Inversion: The Multiple Roots of Homosexuality,* edited by Judd Marmor, pp. 175–189. New York: Basic Books, 1965. No. 51.

Ramsey, Glenn V. "The Sexual Development of Boys." *American Journal of Psychology* 56 (2, 1943): 217–233. No. 892.

Roche, Philip Q. "Sexual Deviations." *Federal Probation* 14 (3, 1950): 3–11. No. 1111.

Ross, Mathew, and Mendelsohn, Fred. "Homosexuality in College: A Preliminary Report of Data Obtained from One Hundred Thirty-three Students Seen in a University Student Health Service and a Review of Pertinent Literature." *Archives of Neurology and Psychiatry* 80 (2, 1958): 253–263. No. 898.

Rubin, Isadore. "A Homosexual Doctor's Story." 1960. Reprinted in *The Third Sex,* edited by Isadore Rubin, pp. 44–47. New York: New Book Co., 1961. No. 901.

Rubin, Isadore. "Homosexuality: Conflicting Theories." 1960. Reprinted in *The Third Sex,* edited by Isadore Rubin, pp. 13–22. New York: New Book Co., 1961. No. 53.

Schur, Edwin M. *Crimes without Victims—Deviant Behavior and Public Policy: Abortion, Homosexuality, and Drug Addiction.* Englewood Cliffs, N. J.: Prentice-Hall, 1965, 180 pp. No. 907.

Simon, Carleton. "Homosexualists and Sex Crimes." Presented before the International Association of Chiefs of Police at Duluth, Minnesota, September 21–25, 1947, 8 pp. No. 1238.

Socarides, Charles W. *The Overt Homosexual.* New York: Grune & Stratton, 1968, 245 pp. No. 571.

Socarides, Charles W. "Theoretical and Clinical Aspects of Overt Male Homosexuality." *Journal of the American Psychoanalytic Association* 8 (3, 1960): 552–566. No. 572.

Stafford-Clark, D. "Essentials of the Clinical Approach." In *The Pathology and Treatment of Sexual Deviation: A Methodological Approach,* edited by Ismond Rosen, pp. 57–86. London: Oxford University Press, 1964. No. 61.

Swyer, Gerald Isaac McDonald. "Homosexuality: The Endocrinological Aspects." *Practitioner* 172 (1030, 1954): 374–377. No. 62.

Thomson, Peter G. "Vicissitudes of the Transference in a Male Homosexual." *International Journal of Psycho-Analysis* 49 (4, 1968): 629–639. No. 585.

Tripp, C. A. "Who Is a Homosexual?" *Social Progress: A Journal of Church and Society* 58 (2, 1967): 13–21. No. 789.

Ullerstam, Lars. *The Erotic Minorities.* New York: Grove Press, 1966, 172 pp. No. 1249.

Van den Haag, Ernest. "Notes on Homosexuality and Its Cultural Setting." Reprinted in *The Problem of Homosexuality in Modern Society,* edited by Hendrik M. Ruitenbeek, pp. 291–302. New York: E. P. Dutton & Co., 1963. No. 1119.

West, D. J. *Homosexuality.* Chicago: Aldine Publishing Co., 1968, 304 pp. No. 922.

West, D. J. *The Other Man: A Study of the Social, Legal and Clinical Aspects of Homosexuality.* New York: Whiteside and William Morrow & Co., 1955, 224 pp. No. 924.

Yankowski, John S., and Wolff, Hermann K. *The Tortured Sex.* Los Angeles: Holloway House Publishing Co., 1965, 224 pp. No. 927.

Willis, Stanley E. *Understanding and Counseling the Male Homosexual.* Boston: Little, Brown & Co., 1967, 225 pp. No. 602.

Winokur, George, ed. *Determinants of Human Sexual Behavior.* Springfield, Ill.; Charles C. Thomas, 1963, 230 pp. No. 65.

Wittels, Fritz. "Homosexuality." In *Encyclopedia of Criminology,* edited by Vernon C. Branham and Samuel B. Kutash, pp. 190–194. New York: Philosophical Library, 1949. No. 605.

FEMALE

267   BACON, CATHERINE LILLIE. "A Developmental Theory of Female Homosexuality." In *Perversions: Psychodynamics and Therapy,* edited by Sandor Lorand and Michael Balint, pp. 131–159. New York: Random House, 1956.

It is suggested that homosexuality and masculine identification in females "may serve as a protection against anxiety," and by using case histories and accounts of the dreams of psychiatric patients as illustrations, the early sources of this process are shown. Homosexuality reduces triangular relationships to two-way relationships, when the girl gives up her father-attachment. The Oedipal relationship is another attempt to reduce triangular relationships to two-way ones. When the relationship is broken, usually by the father, the patient is unable to go on to another man because of fear of retaliation from the father, and this forces her into homosexuality.

268   Beauvoir, Simone de. "The Lesbian." 1952. Reprinted in *Carol in a Thousand Cities,* edited by Ann Aldrich, pp. 181–205. Greenwich, Conn.: Fawcett Publications, 1960. Also reprinted in *The Problem of Homosexuality in Modern America,* edited by Hendrik M. Ruitenbeek, pp. 279–290. New York: E. P. Dutton & Co., 1963.

Homosexuality "is an attitude chosen in a certain situation—that is, at once motivated and freely adopted." Although physiological conditions, psychological history, and social circumstances all contribute to an explanation of homosexuality, no one factor is determinative. Neither narcissism nor the mother fixation always leads to homosexuality. Resenting her role as object in opposition to man as subject, the lesbian refuses to accept the conditions of passivity and docility inherent in her feminine role. It is foolish to make sharp distinctions between heterosexual and homosexual women, just as it is a mistake to distinguish between masculine and feminine roles in the latter. There is much in common between normal and homosexual women, and lesbian sexuality is ambiguous. A woman feels inferior because the requirements of femininity actually belittle her. Resentment, spite, fear of pregnancy, the trauma of a previous abortion, are common reasons for lesbianism as well as for frigidity. "It is one way, among others, in which woman solves the problems posed by her condition in general, by her erotic situation in particular."

269   BENE, EVA. "On the Genesis of Female Homosexuality." *British Journal of Psychiatry* 111 (478, 1965): 815–821.

The Bene-Anthony Family Relations Tests and a questionnaire for the recall of early family relationships were given to 37 lesbians and 80 married females. The lesbians were selected through a homophile group in London and the married females from a market research study.

It was found lesbians tended to have weaker fathers, but to be more afraid of and hostile toward them, and they were less likely to want to model themselves after either of their parents. There was some indication (the differences were not significant) that lesbians tended to have more domineering and less affectionate mothers, to be more hostile toward their mothers, and to see their parents as having desired a son.

270   BERGLER, EDMUND. "The Respective Importance of Reality and Phantasy in the Genesis of Female Homosexuality." *Journal of Criminal Psychopathology* 5 (1, 1943): 27–48.

Five case histories of female homosexuality from private practice were selected for study. These cases had two points in common: the subjects experienced traumatic events in childhood, and all attributed their homosexuality to these events. In each case the events were of a different type.

After analysis of the cases, it was decided that the traumatic events, although seen as causative by the patients, were not so in reality. The traumatic events were among many contributing factors, the more important being unconscious fantasies centering upon the pre-Oedipal mother relationship.

271   BETTELHEIM, BRUNO. "Growing Up Female." In *Psychoanalysis and Contemporary American Culture,* edited by Hendrik M. Ruitenbeek, pp. 168–184. New York: Dell Publishing Co., 1964.

For modern woman, the conflict between her education and the feminine role she is expected to play in the family and in the home may leave her unsatisfied and frustrated. The 19th century idea that woman's place is in the home is incompatible with today's modern technological society, and may result in a poor marriage and/or homosexuality. Men also find it difficult to take their male place in the home, and to find fulfillment in women, after being dominated by their mothers and female teachers throughout their early years. They may ultimately seek the company of their own sex in which they can be on a truly equal basis, freed from feelings of anxiety, disappointment, or inferiority.

272   DENGROVE, EDWARD. "Homosexuality in Women." 1957. Reprinted in *The Third Sex,* edited by Isadore Rubin, pp. 23–27. New York: New Book Co., 1961.

In a general sketch of lesbianism, it is noted that female homosexuals are seldom masculine and may be very feminine, with feminine sexual drives. Women turn to homosexuality from loneliness or sexual frustration or from fear of men and feelings of inferiority. Hereditary and hormonal factors are discounted.

273   Freud, Sigmund. "The Psychogenesis of a Case of Homosexuality in a Woman." In his *Collected Papers,* translated by Joan Riviere, vol. 2, pp. 202–231. London: Leonard and V. Woolf at the Hogarth Press and the Institute of Psycho-Analysis, 1924. Reprinted as "A Case of Homsexuality in a Woman." In *The Homosexuals: As Seen by Themselves and Thirty Authorities,* edited by Aron M. Krich, pp. 262–285. New York: Citadel Press, 1954. Also reprinted as "A Case of Homosexuality in a Woman." in *Carol in a Thousand Cities,* edited by Ann Aldrich, pp. 123–152. Greenwich, Conn.: Fawcett Publications, 1960.

Commitment to homosexuality is traced in the report of the psychoanalysis of a woman patient. The patient had a normal feminine Oedipal crisis as a child, and during the latency period she was strongly impressed by her brother's genitals. At puberty, she experienced a revival of the Oedipal crisis, wishing to have a male child by her father. When, instead, her mother got pregnant, she was "furiously resentful" and "forswore her womanhood and sought another goal for her libido." The woman with whom she fell in love was a substitute for her mother and her brother, thus corresponding to both her feminine and her masculine ideals. Freud did not see any psychoanalytic solution to her homosexuality.

274   GUNDLACH, RALPH H., and RIESS, BERNARD F. "Birth Order and Sex of Siblings in a Sample of Lesbians and Non-Lesbians." *Psychological Reports* 20 (1, 1967): 61–62.

Data are presented which indicate that a number of variables may have an effect upon the sex life of an individual. A nationwide survey was taken of middle-class lesbians and "comparable" nonlesbians; the sample included 217 lesbians and 231 nonlesbians.

Among other things, the respondents were asked to indicate the birth order and sex of their siblings. It was found that more lesbians than nonlesbians were "only" children (45 versus 31). Nonlesbians tended to have brothers and lesbians did not (136 versus 109). Lesbians were likely to be first-born and less likely to be last-born in families of two, three, or four children. Three factors emerge from the data as significant in their contribution to female homosexuality: the desire of parents for a boy which tends to make the female child seek a male role; the experience of parental antipathy; and the experience of rape at an early age.

275   HAMMER MAX. "Homosexuality and the Reversed Oedipus Complex." *Corrective Psychiatry and Journal of Social Therapy* 14 (1, 1968): 45–47.

A consistent set of psychodynamics appears repeatedly in the history of female homosexuals who play the "butch" role. In early life there was invariably a period when the father was absent due to death, divorce, or a tour of duty in the armed forces. During this time the daughter lives alone with her mother, typically an immature, dependent woman, who turned to the daughter for the gratification of her unmet dependency and affectional needs. The result is a reversal of roles which the daughter learns to accept and enjoy.

Upon the father's return or when the mother remarries, the daughter sees this male figure as an intruder and does everything in her power to alienate the mother from him. In her competition with the father, the daughter assumes a masculine, aggressive air and solidifies identification. Since she is in competition with males, she becomes extremely hostile toward them and since she is angry about being female she is also hostile toward most females. This situation often leads to some kind of acting-out and eventual incarceration in a reformatory.

276   KAYE, HARVEY E., et al. "Homosexuality in Women." *Archives of General Psychiatry* 17 (Nov., 1967): 626–634.

An attempt was made to acquire basic clinical data within the psychoanalytic framework by asking the analysts of 24 female homosexual and 24 female heterosexual patients to fill out questionnaires about these patients. Analysis of the resulting data indicates that homosexuality in women is a massive adaptational response to a crippling inhibition of normal heterosexual development.

There is a basic and fundamental drive in female homosexuals toward heterosexuality, which is blocked by anxiety, inhibition, or threat. Questionnaire responses about the homosexual subjects revealed a history of threats and punishments for sex play with boys, fear of and/or aversion to the male penis, scrotum, and ejaculation, as well as a fear of pregnancy.

The parents of these subjects had discouraged the development of feminine attributes which resulted in an interfered-with feminine identification. A developmental constellation of traits or activities was found which these girls used to avoid the female role and move toward a homosexual adaptation.

Noteworthy characteristics among their fathers were found: they tended to be puritanical, exploitative, feared by their daughters, overly possessive, physically interested in their daughters, yet tending to discourage their development as adults. The mothers of both groups had pathological relationships with their daughters: they were dominant, somewhat puritanical, women, who were perceived as being rather contemptuous of their daughters, whose developing femininity they tended not to encourage.

Indications are that psychoanalytic treatment of homosexual women can be effective, since there seems to be at least a 50 percent probability of improvement for those who present themselves for treatment and remain in it.

277   KEISER, SYLVAN, and SCHAFFER, DORA. "Environmental Factors in Homosexuality in Adolescent Girls." *Psychoanalytic Review* 36 (3, 1949): 283–295.

To determine some of the defects in a child's environment which, along with unconscious dynamic pathology, cause homosexuality, a study was made of adolescent girls who were in a Bellevue Hospital ward for psychiatric observation. Through these observations and from the case histories of the girls, three types were determined: aggressive, fighting, masculine girls (in this case usually Negro girls) who carried knives; outwardly passive girls; and completely maladjusted girls who have refused the feminine role from infancy.

The histories of aggressive-masculine girls disclosed mothers who were very promiscuous or who were often physically assaulted by men. Sadistic fathers (often men who beat their wives) were found in the backgrounds of the outwardly passive girls. The maladjusted girls often came from homes in which the father had been absent. These girls exhibited penis envy from childhood.

In summary, gross pathological environmental factors contributed to defective ego developments in these adolescent girls. Homosexual behavior was the result.

278   KENYON, F. E. "Studies in Female Homosexuality, IV. Social and Psychiatric Aspects. V. Sexual Development, Attitudes and Experiences." *British Journal of Psychiatry* 114 (Nov., 1968): 1337–1350.

One hundred and twenty-three subjects were selected from a lesbian organization interested in social research. They were matched with a group of 123 heterosexual women who belonged to a woman's organization also interested in social research.

The results of a questionnaire study indicated that more of the lesbians had a university education, but that their work record was poorer than that of the controls. There was a greater rejection of religion among the lesbians. Fewer were members of a Women's Institute, but more had been in the Armed Forces or police. More of the lesbians had had a poor relationship with their mothers, and more of their mothers had died by the time of the study. More had also had a poor relationship with their fathers, fewer rated their parents' marriage as having been happy, and there was a higher incidence of separation and divorce among their parents. More of their mothers had had a positive psychiatric history (but not their fathers). Ordinal position in the family was not significant, but fewer lesbians reported a happy childhood. More lesbians had a positive psychiatric history (the most common syndrome being depression), but only 5 percent required inpatient treatment.

Other results indicated that fewer lesbians received sexual instruction from their mothers, and the general family attitude toward sex was more rejecting. More lesbians showed a family history of homosexuality, and believed their parents would have preferred a boy.

The projected scheme for this series of reports includes a review of the literature on female homosexuality (I); the results of psychological tests (II); and physical characteristics and medical history (III)—all to be published separately elsewhere. See also Kenyon, F. E. (no. 635); (no. 636); (no. 637).

279   KHAN, M. MASUD R. "The Role of Infantile Sexuality and Early Object Relations in Female Homosexuality." In *The Pathology and*

Treatment of Sexual Deviation: A Methodological Approach, edited by Ismond Rosen, pp. 221–292. London: Oxford University Press, 1964.

In a psychoanalytic investigation of Freud's theory of the role of early family sexual experiences in the development of female homosexuality, clinical material on a young female homosexual patient is used to illustrate the importance of infantile sexuality and the mother-child relationship in female homosexuality. Homosexuality is an attempt to repeat and elaborate the conflicts arising from the mother-daughter relation. The roles of castration anxiety, penis awe, and other aspects of the Oedipus complex are explored. Conflictual early object-relations with mother, father, and brother had detrimental effects on body-ego and identity formation in the patient. Superego development was distorted through a regressive idealization of early body-care experience from the mother (ego-ideal).

280   KREMER, MALVINA W., and RIFKIN, ALFRED H. "The Early Development of Homosexuality: A Study of Adolescent Lesbians." Paper read at meeting of the American Psychiatric Association, Boston, Mass., 13–17 May 1968. Printed in *American Journal of Psychiatry* 126 (1, 1969): 91–96.

A test for the presence of a reversed Oedipal formulation with a close-binding father and a dominant, puritanical mother took the form of diagnostic, open-ended interviews, with questions referring particularly to family structure and relationships. The subjects were 25 lesbian girls, aged 12 to 17 years, drawn from schools serving predominantly lower-class populations. They had not sought treatment.

The reversed Oedipal formulation was not found. The girls' fathers were not close-binding, but hostile, exploitative, detached, and absent. The mothers were not dominant, but mainly overburdened and ill-equipped for their responsibilities. The findings suggested that homosexuality may be a final common behavioral pathway rather than a single entity with a single etiology.

281   MOZES, EUGENE B. "The Lesbian." *Sexology* 18 (5, 1951): 294–299; 18 (6, 1952): 384–389.

The causes and treatment of lesbianism and the general nature of the lesbian are discussed.

There is no hormonal difference or difference in physical make-up, including secondary sex characteristics, between homosexuals and heterosexuals. Lesbianism represents an arrest in sexual development; the sex instinct is inborn but the direction of the instinct is not. There is no clear-cut distinction between lesbians and nonlesbians because there are all degrees of lesbianism, or varying degrees of sexual attraction and relations with members of the same sex. It seems there are about as many lesbians as male homosexuals, and that 4 percent, or one out of 25 women, are exclusively lesbian. Overattachment to the mother and fear and hatred of the father, or a complete identification with the father and jealousy of the mother can lead to lesbianism.

Lesbianism is also a sexual neurosis which requires psychiatric treatment. However, much more can be done by preventing homosexuality than by treating an already confirmed lesbian. "Proper knowledge of all aspects of sex life" is necessary for prevention. Agreeing with R. P. Knight of the Menninger Clinic on ways to prevent frigidity in women, it is suggested that the same method can also be applied to lesbianism. Parents should not influence the child to behave as though it belonged to the other sex (cross-dressing). Mothers should never talk to little girls about difficulties in childbirth. Parental indignation, intimidation, and severe punishment for childhood sexual manifestations do much more harm than the experiences themselves. Children of both sexes should be allowed to play or bathe naked in front of each other during the first eight or 10 years of life. However, observation of the parent of the opposite sex in the nude is harmful. Repeated warnings against boys and men as nasty, cruel beasts constantly seeking to seduce little girls are much worse than no education at all.

282   ROMM, MAY E. "Sexuality and Homosexuality in Women." In *Sexual Inversion: The Multiple Roots of Homosexuality*, edited by Judd Marmor, pp. 282–301. New York: Basic Books, 1965.

Homosexuality is not an illness but a deviation from normal psychosexual development. The theories of different psychoanalytic thinkers are presented as partial explanations of female homosexuality. Unresolved Oedipal problems, castration fears, penis envy, early traumatic experience involving the genitalia, regression to the fetal tie with the mother, and cultural factors causing feelings of inferiority about one's own sex are among the etiological factors considered.

283   SOCARIDES, CHARLES W. "The Historical Development of Theoretical and Clinical Concepts of Overt Female Homosexuality." *Journal of the American Psychoanalytic Association* 11 (Apr., 1963): 385–414.

A review of the literature on female homosexuality is divided into sections on constitutional versus acquired factors, the concept of bisexuality, Freud's contributions, developmental factors, contributions from ego psychology, the relationship of female homosexuality to other perversions and psychoses including nosological considerations, and therapy.

Under each of these headings the relevant literature is usually discussed in chronological order. Each section begins with a brief general discussion of its subject matter.

284 WARREN, JEAN A. "The Etiology of Female Homosexuality." Paper read at Journal Club meeting 1 May 1963, Department of Psychiatry, School of Medicine, Indiana University. Mimeographed. 12 pp.

The etiology of female homosexuality is not yet clear. Probably multiple causations converge and this symptom like other neurotic ones is overdetermined. In most cases psychological determinants are the most potent.

The theories of Freud and his later followers and critics are presented. It is concluded that "we must continue to search for explanations" of how female homosexuality comes about.

285 WILBUR, CORNELIA B. "Clinical Aspects of Female Homosexuality." In *Sexual Inversion: The Multiple Roots of Homosexuality*, edited by Judd Marmor, pp. 268–281. New York: Basic Books, 1965.

Female homosexuality is "associated with specific types of family constellation, the commonest of which probably includes a domineering, hostile, antiheterosexual mother and a weak, unassertive, detached, and pallid father." The daughter has intense Oedipal problems with the father, and adopts homosexuality as a defense against her incestuous wishes. Her homosexual adaptation is intensified by lack of peer-group acceptance. Female homosexual relationships are characterized by great ambivalence, longing for love, intense elements of hostility, and chronic anxiety. Successful psychotherapy is possible with adequate motivation and cooperation.

CROSS-REFERENCES

Aldrich, Ann. *We Walk Alone.* New York: Fawcett Publications, 1955, 143 pp. No. 931.

Atia, Isaad Mohammed, and Muftic, Mahmoud Kamal. "Hypnosis in the Psychosomatic Investigation of Female Homosexuality." *British Journal of Medical Hypnotism* 9 (1, 1957): 41–46. No. 1039.

Caprio, Frank S. *Female Homosexuality: A Psychodynamic Study of Lesbianism.* New York: Citadel Press, 1954, 334 pp. Chapter 16. "Therapeutic Management: Preventive Measures," pp. 285–298. Reprinted as "Preventive Measures." In *Carol in a Thousand Cities,* edited by Ann Aldrich, pp. 153–166.

Greenwich, Conn.: Fawcett Publications, 1960. No. 626.

Caprio, Frank S. *Variations in Sexual Behavior: A Psychodynamic Study of Deviations in Various Expressions of Sexual Behavior.* New York: Citadel Press,
1955, 344 pp. No. 118.

Chesser, Eustace. *Odd Man Out: Homosexuality in Men and Women.* London:
Victor Gollancz, 1959, 192 pp. No. 1065.

Cory, Donald Webster. "Homosexuality." In *The Encyclopedia of Sexual Behavior,*
edited by Albert Ellis and Albert Abarbanel, pp. 485–493. 2d rev. ed. New
York: Hawthorn Books, 1967. No. 123.

Cory, Donald Webster. *The Lesbian in America.* New York: Citadel Press, 1964,
288 pp. No. 934.

Deutsch, Helene. "Homosexuality." In *The Psychology of Women: A Psychoanalytic
Interpretation,* vol. 1, pp. 325–353. New York: Grune & Stratton, 1944. No.
67.

"DOB Questionnaire Reveals Some Facts about Lesbians." *Ladder* 3 (12, 1959):
4–26. No. 935.

Ellis, Albert. "The Truth about Lesbians." *Sexology* 30 (10, 1964): 652–655. No.
937.

Fenichel, Otto. *The Psychoanalytic Theory of Neurosis.* New York: W. W. Norton,
1945, 703 pp. No. 140.

Hamilton, Gilbert Van Tassel. "Homosexuals and their Mothers." 1936. Reprinted
in *On the Causes of Homosexuality: Two Essays, the Second in Reply to the First,*
by Gilbert Van Tassel Hamilton and Gershon Legman, pp. 5–15. New York:
Breaking Point, 1950. Also reprinted as "Incest and Homosexuality." In *The
Homosexuals: As Seen by Themselves and Thirty Authorities,* edited by Aron
M. Krich, pp. 214–226. New York: Citadel Press, 1954. Also reprinted as
"Defensive Homosexuality: Homosexuality as a Defense Against Incest." In
Homosexuality: A Cross Cultural Approach, edited by Donald Webster Cory,
pp. 354–369. New York: Julian Press, 1956. No. 164.

"Homosexuality." *Lancet* 257 (6568, 1949): 128–129. No. 939.

Hornstra, L. "Homosexuality." *International Journal of Psycho-Analysis* 48 (3,
1967): 394–402. No. 173.

Kinsey, Alfred C.; Pomeroy, Wardell B.; Martin, Clyde E.; and Gebhard, Paul H.
Sexual Behavior in the Human Female. Philadelphia: W. B. Saunders & Co.,
1953, 842 pp. No. 940.

Laidlaw, Robert W. "A Clinical Approach to Homosexuality." *Marriage and
Family Living* 14 (1, 1952): 39–45. No. 721.

Lawton, Shailer Upton, and Archer, Jules. *Sexual Conduct of the Teenager.* New
York: Spectrolux Corp., 1951, 180 pp. No. 190.

Liddicoat, Renée. "Homosexuality: Results of a Survey as Related to Various
Theories." Ph. D. dissertation, University of the Witwatersrand, Johannesburg,
South Africa, 1956. No. 194.

Magee, Bryan. *One in Twenty: A Study of Homosexuality in Men and Women.*
London: Secker & Warburg, 1966, 192 pp. No. 878.

Martensen-Larsen, O. "The Family Constellation and Homosexualism." *Acta
Genetica et Statistica Medica* 7 (1957): 445–446. No. 207.

Monsour, Karem J. "Migraine: Dynamics and Choice of Symptom." *Psychoanalytic Quarterly* 26 (4, 1957): 479–493. No. 511.

Querlin, Marise. *Women without Men.* Translated by Malcolm McGraw. New York: Dell Publishing Co., 1965, 174 pp. No. 943.

Rancourt, Réjane, and Limoges, Thérèse. "Homosexuality among Women." *Canadian Nurse* 63 (12, 1967): 42–44. No. 944.

Roche, Philip Q. "Sexual Deviations." *Federal Probation* 14 (3, 1950); 3–11. No. 1111.

Ross, Mathew, and Mendelsohn, Fred. "Homosexuality in College: A Preliminary Report of Data Obtained from One Hundred Thirty-three Students Seen in a University Student Health Service and a Review of Pertinent Literature." *Archives of Neurology and Psychiatry* 80 (2, 1958): 253–263. No. 898.

Roth, Martin, and Ball, J. R. B. "Psychiatric Aspects of Intersexuality." In *Intersexuality in Vertebrates Including Man,* edited by C. N. Armstrong and A. J. Marshall, pp. 395–443. London: Academic Press, 1964. No. 235.

Schur, Edwin M. *Crimes without Victims—Deviant Behavior and Public Policy: Abortion, Homosexuality, and Drug Addiction.* Englewood Cliffs, N. J.: Prentice-Hall, 1965, 180 pp. No. 907.

Simon, William, and Gagnon, John H. "The Lesbians: A Preliminary Overview." In *Sexual Deviance,* edited by John H. Gagnon and William Simon, pp. 247–282. New York: Harper & Row, 1967. No. 947.

Sprague, W. D. *The Lesbian in Our Society.* New York: Tower Publications, 1962, 189 pp. No. 948.

Storr, Anthony. *Sexual Deviation.* Baltimore: Penguin Books, 1964, 139 pp. No. 251.

Assessments

GENERAL, MALE

286 AARONSON, BERNARD S., and GRUMPELT, HOWARD R. "Homosexuality and Some MMPI Measures of Masculinity-Femininity." *Journal of Clinical Psychology* 17 (3, 1961): 245–247.

An attempt was made to determine if male homosexuals exhibit feminine personality characteristics. Profiles obtained on the Minnesota Multiphasic Personality Inventory (MMPI) for 25 homosexual patients were matched with those obtained for 25 non-homosexual patients. The three MMPI measures [which were: the T Score on the M-F Scale (MFS); the rank of the MFS in the profile (MFR), consisting of 10 clinical scales set forth in the test manual; and the score on the Masculinity-Femininity Index (MFI) based on a relationship among the Hy, Pa, Hs, and P+ (T) scales] used differentiated homosexuals from heterosexuals, although a subset of masculine oriented homosexuals was discovered. It was concluded that while a feminine orientation is related to homosexuality, it does not seem equally relevant in all cases. The relationship between male homosexuality and feminine orientation may be more correlative than causal.

287   ADLER, KURT A. "Life Style, Gender Role, and the Symptom of Homosexuality." *Journal of Individual Psychology* 23 (1, 1967): 67–78.

It is not sexuality which determines the personality, but rather the total personality and style of life which determine the form of sexual as well as other behavior. How human beings use the sexual organs and functions with which they are endowed depends upon the individuals' goals. People's thoughts and feelings about themselves, others, and their relationships with others determine how they will use their sexual organs.

"What is specific about the homosexual symptom, aside from a prolonged uncertainty as to gender identity in childhood, is fear of the opposite sex, or fear of inadequacy in one's proper sex role, or both. . . . The type of excuse homosexuals use to establish their distance from the opposite sex and to deny their own sex depends not on their homosexuality as such, but on the type of neurosis, psychosis or personality disorder from which they are suffering."

288   ALLEN, CLIFFORD. "The Heterosexual and Homosexual Perversions." In *A Textbook of Psychosexual Disorders,* pp. 165–204. New York: Oxford University Press, 1962.

The conclusion that homosexuality must be principally caused by psychological rather than by endocrine or genetic factors is supported by the work of Kinsey and others. The persistence of excessive emotion, either negative or positive, which has been aroused in the past by the parents, has a strong influence on the development of homosexuality. Specifically, hostility to the mother, excessive affection for the mother, hostility to the father, and affection for the father when the father does not demonstrate sufficient heterosexual traits are the four ways in which it can be caused.

Homosexuals are not a single homogeneous group; instead there are a large number of different types, some of which are more responsive to therapy than others. Twelve types of homosexuals are described, and the possibility that other types exist is noted.

Homosexuals cause social problems because they join together and form a community within the structure of society. The fear of blackmail and the often less than desirable behavior by police are problems about which the homosexual must be wary. Since prisons with their sexual deprivation are ideal places to produce homosexuality, it is useless to sentence homosexuals to prison.

A number of homosexuals contribute a great deal to the community, but the contributions are not necessarily artistic in nature as is usually believed. The homosexual is neither a fiend nor a genius. He is a sick man whose illness creates special social problems. Frequently, he responds to the opposite sex with extremely negative feelings, a repulsion that seems to be linked with the fear of intercourse. Four detailed case histories of homosexuality in men and women are presented.

289   ALLEN, FREDERICK H. "Homosexuality in Relation to the Problem of Human Differences." *American Journal of Orthopsychiatry* 10 (1, 1940): 129–135.

Homosexuality is an individual reaction to the experience of difference from others, while nationalism is a cultural response which has its roots in past racial differences. "Nationalism in its narrower and more intense manifestations might well be described as cultural homosexuality." The two phenomena spring from a feeling of insecurity, representing attempts to find safer ways of living. Paranoid sequences often follow in both cases.

290   ANOMALY. *The Invert and His Social Adjustment: To Which Is Added a Sequel by the Same Author.* 2d rev. ed. Baltimore: Williams & Wilkins Co., 1948, 290 pp.

A practical discussion of male homosexuality in the light of personal experience is presented. It is maintained that inversion is an involuntary, abnormal condition that ought to be cured, if possible, rather than defended as a way of life. The condition is either congenital or developed very early and persists until it is cured. Early diagnosis, avoidance of homosexual environments, and medical help are recommended for cure.

There is "almost an exact parallel between the psychological and physiological life and development of the normal man and that of the invert." Except for their inversion, homosexuals as a group are like heterosexuals in every way: their physical traits, abilities, moral and ethical conduct or lack thereof, need for stable love relations, and sexual awakening, and adolescent problems.

291   ARIETI, SILVANO. "Sexual Conflict in Psychotic Disorders." In *Sexual Problems: Diagnosis and Treatment in Medical Practice,* edited by Charles William Wahl, pp. 228–237. New York: Free Press, 1967.

Homosexuality in the preschizophrenic and schizophrenic is dealt with as a cause of psychosis. Homosexuality may lead to psychosis only when it engenders a great deal of anxiety in the patient. Psychosis and homosexuality reinforce one another. Cases of schizophrenia complicated by overt homosexuality are the most difficult to treat.

292   ARMSTRONG, C. N. "Diversities of Sex." *British Medical Journal* (4923, 1955): 1173–1177.

There are two types of homosexuals in both sexes—passive and active. Certain female characteristics are recognized in several passive male homosexuals. In discussing these characteristics with reference to two cases which are described in detail, it is stated: "There is no doubt that active male homosexuals recognize passive male homosexuals by some means unknown. Is there a sixth sense?" Although recognizing that it is yet unclear whether homosexuality is genetically or environmentally determined, it is concluded that it is extremely likely that homosexual characteristics are inborn and of genetic determination.

293   ARONSON, GERALD J. "Delusion of Pregnancy in a Male Homosexual with an Abdominal Cancer." *Bulletin of the Menninger Clinic* 16 (5, 1952): 159–166.

This is the case report of a 60-year-old homosexual male suffering from delusions of pregnancy. Treatment consisted of surgery and psychotherapy. The patient's sensation of abdominal pressure (a cancerous tumor) led him to believe that he was pregnant. This belief was brought about by: the need to maintain the experience of somatic health (via denial); the instinctual wishes nuclear to homosexuality presumably stimulating, and being stimulated by, a regressive misinterpretation of the abdominal sensation; and an oversynthesis of the ego.

294   ARTHUR, GAVIN. *The Circle of Sex.* San Francisco: Pan-Graphic Press, 1962, 86 pp.

The face of a clock is used as a symbol to portray a single sexual continuum encompassing the entire range of sexual make-up. Half the dial is for males and half for females. Emotional and psychosexual orientations are distributed around the dial without rigid boundaries. Each of the 12 types, ranging from exclusively heterosexual to exclusively homosexual for both men and women, is described. Examples taken from history and literature are used for illustrations.

295   AUSTIN, SEAN HARLAN. "Analysis and Prediction of Male Homosexual Case History Material: A Replication and Extension." Master's thesis, San Francisco State College, 1967, 125 pp.

Forty-nine nonincarcerated, nonpatient, overt, male adult homosexual volunteers from the San Francisco homosexual community were interviewed. Data from the interview protocols were evaluated in an attempt to replicate earlier research which had "strongly suggested that the homosexual symptom in adult males could be delineated into specific sub-symptoms of personality traits and characteristic homosexual behavior patterns . . . [and that] certain early personality variables and life history events could be shown to be discriminative and predictive of these specific sub-symptoms."

Chi square was used to measure the degree of nonrandomness of association between 89 criteria and 64 predictor variables which had been identified in the earlier study. Multivariate analysis utilizing the predictor variables was also carried out.

This statistical analysis indicated that it is practical to view homosexuality as a set of discrete subsymptoms. The over-all success of prediction was slightly less than 70 percent, and many of the predictor variables failed to show a discriminative effect in this replication attempt.

296 AUSTIN, SEAN HARLAN. "Analysis and Prediction of the Male Homosexual Symptomatology from Case History Information." Honors Thesis, Lawrence University, 1965, 75 pp.

Attempting to predict homosexual behavior patterns on the basis of life histories which covered early experiences and early personality structure, homosexual behavior patterns (criterion variables) are related to symptoms found in case histories (predictor variables).

The criterion variables were broken into five item clusters which included present ego-alien motives, present ego-alien motive combinations, present ego structure, psychiatric symptoms, and current homosexual behavior.

The item clusters used for the predictor variables were childhood and adolescent ego-alien motives, childhood and adolescent ego-alien motive combinations, childhood and adolescent ego structure, family structure, masturbation history, sex training history, heterosexual experience, and general life events and constructs.

Fifty-four adult males for whom full case histories had been compiled by trained clinicians and published in journals or texts were studied.

Thirty-five criterion variables related to 65 predictor variables at or above the .10 level of confidence. Discriminant analysis on the best of these variables yielded a median accuracy of slightly more than 80 percent. It was concluded that certain specific symptoms of adult male homosexuality can be predicted from life history information.

297 AUSTIN, SEAN HARLAN. "An Experimental Multivariate Analysis of Male Homosexual Case History Material." Paper read at meeting

of Western Psychological Association, May 1967, in San Francisco. Mimeographed. 9 pp.

The internal consistency of case history material was tested by determining whether specific adult personality constructs and behavior patterns of overt male homosexuals could be predicted from case history information. Variables were selected and arbitrarily divided into two categories for statistical analyses—64 dependent variables and 89 predictor variables. Fifty-four cases of homosexuality drawn from the psychological literature were measured for the presence or absence of adult and early personality constructs and behavioral patterns.

It was tentatively concluded that certain specific symptoms of male homosexuality can be predicted from life history information.

298 BARKER, ALMAN J.; MATHIS, JERRY K.; and POWERS, CLAIR A. "Drawing Characteristics of Male Homosexuals." *Journal of Clinical Psychology* 9 (2, 1953): 185–188.

An attempt was made to determine if the drawings of a male and a female figure by a group of male homosexual soldiers would be significantly different from those drawn by a group of male nonhomosexual soldiers. Drawings were obtained from 50 male homosexuals and 35 male nonhomosexuals. The Machover Human Figure Drawing Test was used, and the drawings were evaluated using Machover's "Outline of Interpretive Features" as a guide. Two areas where significant differences occurred were a delay in the identification of the self-sex figure and a distortion of the female figure. No propensity to draw the opposite sex first was found, as earlier work had suggested; in the present study 46 of the 50 homosexuals drew male figures first. Also, the homosexual group did not give female characteristics to their male figures as had been reported in the literature. The authors recognized three main problems that imposed limitations on their conclusions: the small number of subjects, an inadequate control group, and the effects of an Army environment.

299 BARNETTE, W. LESLIE. "Study of an Adult Male Homosexual and Terman-Miles M-F Scores." *American Journal of Orthopsychiatry* 12 (April, 1942): 346–352.

A case study is reported of a well-adjusted and cultured homosexual whose responses to the Terman-Miles Masculinity-Femininity test were studied. The subject was a 44-year-old male homosexual who was a resident of New York City, unmarried, and a professional musician. Biographical data were compiled while the subject underwent psychoanalytic treatment with the author. The Terman-Miles Masculinity-Femininity test and the Kwalwasser Music Information and Appreciation Test were administered.

On the Terman-Miles test the subject's emotional responses were rated masculine while in all other areas of the test he was rated feminine. His highest feminine score was in "interests, likes." The tests showed the patient to be a superior adult intellectually, to have a strong vocational interest and superior musical talent, and to be high in musical achievements. Although neurotic, he was "socially and emotionally well-adjusted." In sum, he was judged to be the kind of homosexual who is well-behaved and does not generate problems for society, and who is intellectually and socially a valuable individual.

300 BARR, RICHARD H., and HILL, GERALD. "Acquired Spasmodic Torticollis in a Male Homosexual." *Journal of Nervous and Mental Disease* 130 (4, 1960): 325–330.

The case history of a 37-year-old single male homosexual suffering from muscular spasms in his neck is given. The patient's spasmodic torticollis is believed to be symptomatic of emotional conflicts. It appears there is a continuum from the primary emotional origin to neurologic etiology. The patient received medical treatment and psychotherapy.

301 BECKER, A. L. "A Third Sex? Some Speculations on a Sexuality Spectrum." *Medical Proceedings* 13 (4, 1967): 67–74.

A spectrum of sexuality developed on anatomical, physiological, and psychological bases, as well as on overt behavior, is proposed. It would allow the classification of individuals along a masculinity-femininity continuum having at one extreme men whose masculinity is so intense that they can relate only to other males, and at the other extreme women whose femininity is so intense that they can relate only to other females.

Moving from the masculine to the feminine end of the spectrum, gradations in between would include: men whose biological and psychological constitutions are normal and whose sexual relationships are heterosexual; men who are biologically male but psychologically female, whose sexual relationships are homosexual; male transvestites; male transsexuals; female transsexuals; female transvestites; women who are biologically female but psychologically male, whose sexual relationships are homosexual; and women whose biological and psychological constitutions are normal and whose sexual relationships are heterosexual.

The discussion includes comments on unusual features in cases of transsexual males, a review of psychodynamic determinants of sexual identification, a description of how hyperheterosexuality often masks the type of homosexuality which can fall at the extremes of the sexuality spectrum, and some suggestions for the treatment of homosexuality.

302   BENDEL, R. "The Modified Szondi Test in Male Homosexuality, I."
       International Journal of Sexology 8 (4, 1955): 226–227.

The usefulness of Laszlo's modification of the Szondi Test (L-Test) for
diagnostic purposes in homosexual cases is assessed by administering it to
seven manifest homosexuals and three borderline cases.

Of the 10 cases the L-Test showed nine in which there were traits of
homosexuality, and six in which there was a great probability of it. Since
the syndromes of Szondi can be entirely demonstrated in none of the 10
cases, it is impossible to establish a diagnosis solely with the test. However,
it can still be very useful for diagnostic purposes.

Part II of this article, written by E. Stumper, concerns the use of the
Thematic Apperception Test to diagnose other sexual perversions such as
exhibitionism.

303   BENDER, LAURETTA, AND GRUGETT, ALVIN E., JR. "A Follow-Up
       Report on Children Who Had Atypical Sexual Experience." *Ameri-*
       can Journal of Orthopsychiatry 22 (Oct., 1952): 825–837.

This is a follow-up of an earlier report. The first series in this report
pertained to children who had been sexually involved with adults (group
1); the second series concerned those children who had a deep confusion
over their sexual identity (group 2). Two tentative conclusions were
reached. Overt sexual behavior of the several kinds described did not necessarily forecast either their retention into adult life or maladjustments specifically rooted in such experience. "The more striking successful outcome of
the first group suggested that overt sex activity in childhood with adult
partners was in one way a deflection of the normally developing sexual
impulses and that such a deflection was responsive to social and clinical
treatment. The other group's predominantly negative outcome, with its
emphasis on serious psychopathology, contrastingly suggested that a child
who in prepubescent years presented problems in sexual identification
. . . would continue to have serious distortions in his personality development." However, good institutional care during adolescence could still yield
positive results in some instances.

304   BERDIE, RALPH F. "A Femininity Adjective Check List." *Journal*
       of Applied Psychology 43 (5, 1959): 327–333.

An adjective check list was developed to provide an easily obtainable index
of psychological masculinity-femininity. As subjects, the project used 400
male and 200 female freshman college students and 43 noninstitutionalized
male homosexuals. Taking only a few minutes to complete, the adjective

scale was based upon 61 items included in a list of 148 adjectives.

The index "substantially" distinguishes between groups of male and female college freshmen, and between a group of homosexual men and male college freshmen. Although the instrument's test-retest reliability and inter-scale correlations are reasonably high, it is not meant to be used for individual diagnosis.

305 BERG, CHARLES. "The Problem of Homosexuality." *American Journal of Psychotherapy* 10 (4, 1956): 696–708; 11 (1, 1957): 65–79.

Homosexuality is neither a disease, nor a clinical entity, but is rather "nothing more than a particular form of expression of a psychic state which is common to all living creatures." Assessing the progress of knowledge concerning homosexuality since Freud's time, findings are excerpted from such authorities as Jenkins, Allen, Mead, Kinsey, Thompson, Jones, Fenichel, and Stekel. Neither of the two etiological theories (the congenital or biological theory and the acquired or psychologic theory) provides a complete answer to the problems of homosexuality. Since human behavior, compulsions, and beliefs emanate from unconscious fantasies and emotional problems, an understanding of homosexuality can come "only through knowledge of the unconscious fantasies, revealed through deep personal analysis." Manifest homosexuality may be an unconsciously determined denial of heterosexuality.

From a legislative point of view, two psychological conditions should be recognized—homosexuality and a reaction of horror against it. The latter, which has resulted in senseless prohibitions and penalties, may be combated only through a knowledge of the facts and an understanding of nature's ways.

The antithesis between the hypotheses of congenital and acquired factors in the etiology of homosexuality is illusionary and based upon the old dogma of the immutability of species. All behavioral reactions and instincts result from a continuing evolutionary process of reactive adaptation to environment. Hence, "homosexuality like everything else, is both congenital and acquired, with relative quantitative variations of each of the etiologic factors."

306 BERGLER, EDMUND. "Contribution to the Psychology of Homosexuals." *Samiksa* 8 (4, 1954): 205–209.

Somerset Maugham's general remarks on the psychology of homosexuals are concentrated upon in a discussion of an essay on El Greco by Maugham. What Maugham designates as emotional coldness on the part of homosexuals is due not to a lack of heterosexual experience, but to greater inner conflict which absorbs all inner energy. The "inane flippancy" and "sardonic humour" of homosexuals to which he refers conceal psychopathic trends and the defense mechanism of injustice-collecting. Maugham's main contribution to an evaluation of the homosexual lies in cutting down the myth that every homosexual is automatically special and a superartistic advance on the norm when he declares that the homosexual excels in "decoration, embroidery, [and] ornament."

Bergler disagrees with what he calls the two extremes of attitudes toward homosexuality—the advocates of police prosecution, and the adherents of the approach sponsored by Kinsey which would accord full partnership to those who "slightly deviate" from the "hetero-homosexual balance."

307   BERGLER, EDMUND. *Counterfeit-Sex: Homosexuality, Impotence, Frigidity.* 2d rev. ed. New York: Grune & Stratton, 1958, 380 pp.

Neurotic sex, designated as "counterfeit sex," indicates the caricature neurotics create out of sex. Homosexuality is viewed as the unconscious misuse of sex for the expression of completely unrelated inner conflicts. Using the psychiatric-psychoanalytic method, homosexuality in both sexes is investigated according to genetic principles. Extensive case material is presented to demonstrate the complexity of the problem and to substantiate the theory that the genetic basis for homosexuality is one of many pathological elaborations of the unsolved masochistic attachment to the pre-Oedipal mother.

308   BERGLER, EDMUND. "Differential Diagnosis Between Spurious Homosexuality and Perversion Homosexuality." *Psychiatric Quarterly* 21 (3, 1947): 399–409.

A distinction is made between the two forms of male homosexuality, "perversion homosexuality" and "unconscious feminine identification." Perversion homosexuality is characterized by conscious acceptance of sexual gratification derived from a relation with an object of the same sex. These people are "orally regressed." The spurious homosexual is a completely different type of neurotic, the "passive-feminine" man. The effeminate man is not a homosexual whereas the markedly effeminate homosexual shows a camouflage hiding his real conflict.

309   BERGLER, EDMUND. *Homosexuality: Disease or Way of Life?* New York: Hill & Wang, 1956, 302 pp.

In a psychiatric report based upon treatment of male and female homosexuals, it is indicated that homosexuality is not a variant way of life, but a neurotic disease which stems from the homosexual's striving for defeat, humiliation, and rejection. The homosexual is an "injustice collector" or a psychic masochist, taking flight to a male partner as an antidote for the woman he fears. The types of homosexuals, the myth of bisexuality, and artistic creativity are discussed. It is claimed homosexuality is increasing because of persons such as Kinsey whose assertions have exaggerated the number of homosexuals. These are called "statistically induced homosexuals." In conclusion, it is asserted that homosexuals can be cured by psychiatric-psychoanalysis.

310   BERGLER, EDMUND. "The Myth of a New National Disease: Homosexuality and the Kinsey Report." *Psychiatric Quarterly* 22 (1, 1948): 66–88. Reprinted as "Homosexuality and the Kinsey Report." In *The Homosexuals: As Seen by Themselves and Thirty Authorities,* edited by Aron M. Krich, pp. 226–250. New York: Citadel Press, 1954.

The section on homosexuality in *Sexual Behavior in the Human Male* (Kinsey, et al.) is criticized on several points. First, Kinsey is criticized for ignoring the unconscious aspects of homosexuality and for making unkind comments about Freudian psychoanalysis. Second, the types of subjects used and the interview process is questioned. Most of the subjects are highly neurotic. The interview schedule is criticized because it seeks to obtain information in a matter of minutes while psychiatrists have found that months are necessary to obtain the same "facts." Third, the Kinsey Scale is criticized for attempting to rigidly quantify a "multitude of completely different genetic problems." Fourth, the Kinsey study is berated for ignoring "tender love" in its discussion of the relative stability of homosexual and heterosexual marriages. Fifth, quoting Kinsey on the need for accepting homosexuality as a fact devoid of psychopathology, it is felt that Kinsey acts as an apologist for the "perversion." Kinsey is seen as taking the position that homosexuality may only be changed through endocrinology though no passages are quoted in support of this belief about Kinsey's position. Sixth, and last, the Kinsey study is accused of damaging any real scientific attempts which might be made to cure the "disease."

311   BERGLER, EDMUND. *One Thousand Homosexuals: Conspiracy of Silence, or Curing and Deglamorizing Homosexuals?* Paterson, N. J.: Pageant Books, 1959, 249 pp.

Homosexuality is a disease and is curable, particularly when detected at an early age. A conspiracy of silence which surrounds homosexuality only serves to glamorize it, thus increasing the problem. The work of Kinsey is also criticized as adding to this glamorization.

312   BERGLER, EDMUND. "Spurious Homosexuality." *Psychiatric Quarterly Supplement* 128 (1, 1954): 68–77.

The cases of 12 pseudo-homosexual patients treated by psychoanalysis are presented to support the contention that there is a form of spurious homosexuality which is not true homosexuality. The genuine or real homosexual is characterized by an unconscious defense mechanism of man-to-man relationships which he uses to escape his repressed masochistic attachment to the image of the pre-Oedipal mother, and by an injustice-collector personality based upon oral-masochistic regression.

313   BERGMANN, MARTIN S. "Homosexuality on the Rorschach Test." *Bulletin of the Menninger Clinic* 9 (3, 1945): 78–83.

To validate the supposition that homosexuality can be detected through the use of the Rorschach, the test was administered to 20 homosexual soldiers, 19 of whom were white and one Negro, ranging in age from 18 to 36, with 24 as the average age. The homosexuals gave a high percentage of sexual responses, reflecting their specific anxiety. Other responses revealed heterosexual revulsion, homosexual arousal, and a reluctance to distinguish positively between male and female figures.

The conclusion is that although the Rorschach cannot be used as an infallible instrument for the detection of homosexuality, it could be of practical value to military psychiatrists.

314   BIEBER, IRVING, et al. *Homosexuality: A Psychoanalytic Study.* New York: Basic Books, 1962, 358 pp.

The results of research conducted through the administration of questionnaires to 77 psychoanalysts, who filled out information on 106 of their homosexual patients and 100 contrast patients, are reported. Various theoretical viewpoints on homosexuality are surveyed with an emphasis upon psychoanalytic theories. Developmental data from the questionnaires present eight childhood traits which distinguished the homosexuals from the contrast patients. These included an excessive fear of physical injury and the avoidance of physical fights. The homosexuals had played predominantly with girls or were lone wolves. They did not play competitive group games. They were considered "clinging" as children and were reluctant to start school.

The data on early family experiences are interpreted as showing a pattern of a close-binding mother who is dominant over the father, and a detached or hostile detached father. Homosexuality is believed to arise from fears of the opposite sex developed in early family relations. The outcome of psychoanalytic therapy is evaluated. Prolonged treatment yields a more favorable prognosis.

315 BIEBER, IRVING; GERSHMAN, HARRY; OVESEY, LIONEL; and WEISS, FREDERICK A. "The Meaning of Homosexual Trends in Therapy: A Round Table Discussion." *American Journal of Psychoanalysis* 24 (1, 1964): 60–76.

The ideas of Irving Bieber, Harry Gershman, Lionel Ovesey and Frederick A. Weiss on the meaning of homosexual trends in therapy are presented separately. No consensus about the definition of the term "homosexual trends in therapy" is reached.

[Bieber] "Homosexual trends" are phenomena observed in heterosexuals such as preoccupation with homosexuality, unreasonable hostility toward homosexuals, anxiety about becoming homosexual, et cetera. More commonly observed in men than in women, and in men, associated with a much higher level of anxiety, these trends do not preclude an active heterosexual life. They are not evidence of latent homosexuality, but instead seem to indicate an "intense fear of complete heterosexual fulfillment."

[Gershman] Homosexual trends reflect one's doubt about one's sexual identity as it conflicts with one's biological endowment. Anxiety emanates from this discrepancy. The separation between overt and latent homosexuality is a matter of the degree of the underlying anxiety.

[Ovesey] There are three distinct motivations which produce homosexual trends during psychotherapy: homosexuality, dependency, and power. The first, a true homosexual motivation, is a symptom of a neurosis; the homosexual trends are the way the patient attempts to allay castration anxiety by a phobic avoidance of the female genital. The other two motivations, dependency and power, are pseudo-homosexual motivations indicating patients' efforts to deal with dependency needs or with problems relating to power.

[Weiss] Homosexual trends are unconscious attempts to overcome self-alienation, self-hate, lack of identity, emptiness, loneliness, emotional deadness, or the fear of destruction.

316 BILLS, NORMAN GEORGE. "The Personality Structure of Alcoholics, Homosexuals, and Paranoids as Revealed by Their Responses to the Thematic Apperception Test." Ph.D. dissertation, Western Reserve University, 1953, 228 pp.

Variables from three areas of study (conceptions of self and other; the psychoanalytic theory of psychosexual development; and the psychoanalytic theory of the id, ego, and superego) were included in a study of some of the differences and similarities in the personality structure of 20 chronic alcoholics, 12 overt homosexuals, 20 paranoid schizophrenics, and 20 "normals." All were white males between the ages of 19 and 40.

On the basis of their responses to the Thematic Apperception Test (TAT), the normal group was found to be significantly differentiated from the clinical groups in having more positive self-conceptions; the homosexual group was more varied and less consistent than the alcoholic and paranoid groups. The homosexual group had more positive conceptions of the father than the paranoid group and more positive conceptions of themselves than the alcoholic group. The homosexuals' self-conceptions were characterized as "good," "successful," "happy," "rebellious," "independent," and "decisive" in comparison with the other two clinical groups (but not to the extent that this was true of the normal group).

Of the 194 hypotheses that were constructed, 55 of them were upheld at the 5 percent level of confidence or better. It is stated that this is important evidence for the predictive value (and therefore the validity) of psychoanalytic theory.

317   BIRD, M. S. "Some Emotional Problems Dealt with in the Special Clinic." *British Journal of Venereal Diseases* 41 (Sept., 1965): 217–220.

In a general discussion of homosexual cases, including male and female teen-agers and young adults, some of their characteristics are indicated. Many of the male homosexuals were promiscuous, subject to fluctuating moods and intense loneliness, and given to worry over having to lead a double life and the need to excel at work. The female homosexuals were less promiscuous, had been petted by their fathers in childhood, but were subsequently rejected in adolescence because they had become "difficult."

318   BLACKMAN, NATHAN J. "The Culpability of the Homosexual." *Missouri Medicine* 50 (1, 1953): 27–29.

A general discussion on the psychiatric aspects of homosexuality is presented. Homosexuality is a symptom, a part of a need within a person to challenge, taunt, and deny his relation and obligation to mature responsiveness. Homosexual persons need treatment rather than punitive, repressive measures.

319   BLAINE, GRAHAM B., JR., and MCARTHUR, CHARLES C. "Basic Character Disorders and Homosexuality." In their *Emotional Problems of the Student,* pp. 107–115. New York: Appleton-Century-Crofts, 1961.

The incidence of homosexuality is difficult to determine because of the vagueness of the concept. Kinsey's definition of a relationship leading to orgasm is not always appropriate; homosexuality is present in everyone to some extent, though the degree varies considerably.

College students, usually still in adolescence, may experience homosexual desires which result in fear, confusion, depression, or panic. However, childhood experiences, rather than immediate decisions, determine whether or not a person will become a homosexual.

Psychotherapy is useful for helping students who are worried about their homosexual feelings. Homosexual college students are usually inoffensive and discreet, providing little or no threat to others.

320 BLEDSOE, ROBERT J. *Male Sexual Deviations and Bizarre Practices.* Los Angeles: Sherbourne Press, 1964, 157 pp.

A psychological study of male sexual deviations is based on numerous case histories. Such practices as masturbation, oral genital acts, anal intercourse, sadistic activities, bestiality, et cetera, are discussed. Sexual perversions have been with us since the beginning of time and no one can be termed 100 percent "normal."

321 BOTWINICK, JACK, and MACHOVER, SOLOMON. "A Psychometric Examination of Latent Homosexuality in Alcoholism." *Quarterly Journal of Studies on Alcohol* 12 (Jun., 1951): 268–272.

The theory that alcoholism is a condition involving some homosexual components was tested using the M-F and I Scales of the Terman and Miles Attitude Interest Analysis and the M-F Scale of the Minnesota Multiphasic Personality Inventory (MMPI). The tests were administered to 39 literate male patients between 30 and 49 years of age who had been diagnosed as alcoholics at the Kings County Hospital in Brooklyn, N.Y.

No statistically significant difference between the mean M-F scores of the alcoholics and the mean M-F scores of the normative population was found. There was, however, a significant difference between the mean I scores of the two groups. These differences point to the "normality" of the experimental alcoholic population in regard to the sexual interest pattern. The conclusion is that "insofar as the tests used in this study measure homosexuality, latent or otherwise, homosexuality cannot be an essential factor in alcoholism, although it may play a dynamic role in individual cases."

322 BOZARTH, RENÉ, and GROSS, ALFRED A. "Homosexuality: Sin or Sickness? A Dialogue." *Pastoral Psychology* 13 (129, 1962): 35–42.

Whether or not homosexuality is a sin, a sickness, or a crime is considered in a dialogue between the two authors. Bozarth concludes that homosexuality is a symptom of a deep-seated personality problem, rather than a disease. Gross believes that homosexuality is morally neutral, but that when the state of homosexuality is translated into an act it becomes criminal in the eyes of the law and sinful in the eyes of the Church.

Bozarth outlines some of the advice he would give to a pastor counseling a homosexual: the homosexual must be shown his own worth as a person; he must be helped to free himself from the effects of neurotic behavior; and he must be educated as to the nature of his problem. Beyond these guides, the "whole armor of the Church's teaching" must be brought to bear upon the problem. The homosexual and the counselor should be engaged in a process of discovering the most acceptable mode of conduct for the homosexual himself, the community, and the Church.

323   BRAATEN, LEIF JOHAN, and DARLING, C. DOUGLAS. "Overt and Covert Homosexual Problems among Male College Students." *Genetic Psychology Monographs* 71 (2, 1965): 269–310.

The Minnesota Multiphasic Personality Inventory, the Mooney Problem Check List, student health records, clinical folders of the Mental Health Division at Cornell University, and a rating form developed by the principal investigator for assessing overt and covert homosexual tendencies, were employed in a study of homosexuality in a college setting. The sample, based upon all of the students who had used the Mental Health Division over a three-year period, included 42 male students (3 percent of the students using the mental health facility) who were coded as overt homosexuals, 34 male students (2 percent) who were coded as covert homosexuals, and 50 control students.

The research compared overt homosexuals with covert homosexuals, and both groups with the controls. The findings showed that in relation to covert homosexuals, the overt homosexuals were referred more frequently by the University Proctor, were overrepresented in the agriculture and hotel schools, scored higher on the Psychopathic Deviation Scale and lower on the Social Introversion Scale of the MMPI, and more often admitted having indulged in unusual sex practices, whereas the coverts tended to complain about excessive daydreaming and shyness. With reference to the controls, the homosexuals tended to come from different colleges of the University; to have higher academic achievement although equal in aptitude level; to show more of a liking for participation in the fine arts, drama, and literature; to contain proportionally fewer Jewish students; to score higher on the M-F Scale of the MMPI; to have proportionally more "close-binding-intimate" mothers; and to have proportionally more detached, hostile, or indifferent fathers. Less than one-third of the homosexuals displayed signs of being effeminate. It was found that of all the overt homosexuals, one-half showed significant heterosexual strivings, one-third showed some significant movement toward heterosexuality as a result of therapy, and two-thirds engaged in promiscuous sexual patterns rather than in love affairs.

324   BRADY, JOHN PAUL, and LEVITT, EUGENE E. "Precedent and Preference in Sexual Practice." *Psychiatric Spectator* 1 (11, 1964): 5–6.

A questionnaire designed to determine sexual experience was given to 68 male graduate students. The subjects were then asked to score sexual excitability on a 6-point scale to three different sets of 19 thematically different photographs representing a wide range of potentially arousing stimuli.

Those with more sexual experience reported a greater degree of responsiveness to the photographic materials. Positive correlations were noted between those with past homosexual experience and photographs of a partially clad male, but not with photographs depicting frank homosexual activity. A positive correlation was also found between experience involving anal intercourse and the stimulating effect of a photograph depicting the masochistic experience of a male.

325   BRADY, JOHN PAUL, and LEVITT, EUGENE E. "The Relation of Sexual Preferences to Sexual Experiences." *Psychological Record* 15 (3, 1965): 377–384.

A questionnaire relating to past sexual activity was used to assess sexual experience. Sexual preference was determined by showing subjects three sets of 19 thematic photographs. The subjects were 68 male graduate students, 21 to 32 years old with a mean age of 23.9; 56 percent were single, 44 percent were married.

Having had a particular sexual experience was not correlated positively or negatively with arousal by the photographs showing the same experience. Homosexual experiences correlated with responses to pictures of partially clad males rather than to those scenes showing overt homosexual activity.

326   BRADY, JOHN PAUL, and LEVITT, EUGENE E. "The Scalability of Sexual Experiences." *Psychological Record* 15 (2, 1965): 275–279.

To determine if the sexual experience of an individual increases in a fixed pattern, a questionnaire was administered to 68 male graduate students. The students were between 21 and 32 years of age, with the mean age 23.9; 56 percent were single and 44 percent married. Items of the questionnaire relating to past heterosexual and homosexual activity were subjected to a scalogram analysis.

It was found that sexual history follows a fixed cumulative pattern, conforming to a Guttman Scale. This held true for both married and single subjects. Respondents who had experienced homosexual activity "sometime in life" had also experienced most or all types of heterosexual activity. It appeared that the homosexual experiences of the subjects probably took place at or near puberty and thus did not have the same significance as homosexual experiences occurring at a later time.

327 BRANDT, LEWIS W. "Castration: Fantasy and Reality." *Psychotherapy: Theory, Research and Practice* 3 (2, 1966): 85–87.

The relationship between the reality of castration and fantasies concerning castration is of great importance for psychotherapeutic theory and practice. Certain conclusions are drawn from a survey of the literature. The psychoanalysis of a 21-year-old patient, who initially sought treatment for a speech impediment, is also considered.

The loss of an erection after ejaculation is an actual or real castration, i.e., the man is temporarily impotent. Thus, fellatio represents both actual castration and a fancied, permanent castration (of the father) to the fellator. The analyst should know the real aspects of castration in order to better understand the fantasy of the patient.

328 BRODY, EUGENE B. "From Schizophrenic to Homosexual: A Crisis in Role and Relating." *American Journal of Psychotherapy* 17 (4, 1963): 579–595.

The case of an adult schizophrenic male who was hospitalized and treated through psychoanalysis is discussed. An attempt is made to understand his schizophrenic behavior with particular reference to his homosexual and masochistic ways of relating to other people and to his efforts to move from one role position to another. After two years of intensive psychotherapy, the patient became overtly homosexual. The homosexual role offered him a new way of achieving an identity outside of the web of his family and of permitting significant relationships with people other than his parents for the first time in his life.

329 BROMBERG, WALTER. "Sex Offense as a Disguise." *Corrective Psychiatry and Journal of Social Therapy* 11 (6, 1965): 293–298.

While sexual gratification is unquestionably the mainspring of many sexual offenses, sexual crimes may also express aggression, hostility, and/or fear. With regard to homosexuality, offenses such as sodomy with minors, and assault or homicide by homosexuals are often disguises for other than sexual aims.

Because society places such great social value on sexuality, young persons sometimes equate genitality with self-esteem, making orgasm a necessary concomitant to success as a person. Homosexual behavior, thus, can be an aggressive defense for the special values given genitality. In addition, it may be a defense against deeper, unperceived castration anxieties and may indicate an unconscious fear of the female.

Sex crimes can also be an expression of aggression and hostility toward society. In a series of murders of youths by homosexuals, most of the guilty men were "unconsciously uneasy with the accepted social values of orgiastic freedom." They could accept the ease with which they could find homosexual partners for their orgasms, but unconsciously they could not accept a society which permitted such freedom.

330   BROWN, DANIEL G. "The Development of Sex-Role Inversion and Homosexuality." *Journal of Pediatrics* 50 (5, 1957): 613–619.

Sex-role inversion and homosexuality must be differentiated. Inversion refers to the adoption of the sex role and introjection of the psychological identity of the opposite sex. Homosexuality refers to sexual desire and activity between two members of the same sex. Thus, while certain forms of homosexuality (passive male and active female) are expressions of personality inversion, other forms of homosexuality have nothing to do with inversion. Inversion has its roots in the earliest years of life when the child forms, at first involuntarily and later consciously, an identification-attachment to the parent of the opposite sex and thereby introjects the sex role of the opposite sex.

331   BROWN, DANIEL G. "Inversion and Homosexuality." *American Journal of Orthopsychiatry* 28 (2, 1958): 424–429.

Too often homosexuality and sexual inversion are equated by professionals. Homosexuality refers to sexual activity or the desire for such activity with members of the same sex. Sexual inversion, on the other hand, refers to the "total personality structure" of an individual whose sex-role is that of the opposite sex.

It is hypothesized that sexual inversion is a result of early and prolonged identification with the parent of the opposite sex, and that it is more often found among males than among females.

332   BROWN, DANIEL G., and LYNN, DAVID B. "Human Sexual Development: An Outline of Components and Concepts." *Journal of Marriage and the Family* 28 (2, 1966): 155–162.

In the context of a general discussion of human sexual development, homosexuality is described as "the phenomenon in which an individual predominantly or exclusively desires and/or obtains genital sexual stimulation and gratification with a person of the same biological sex." Sex-role inversion (the individual adopts the sex role of the other sex) must be differentiated from homosexuality. Many homosexuals are not inverted in their sex or gender roles. Imprinting with homosexual stimuli may account for a person becoming a chronic homosexual. However, this does not explain the differences between homosexuals who are inverted and those who are not.

333 BROWN, PAUL T. "On the Differentiation of Homo- or Heteroerotic Interest in the Male: An Operant Technique Illustrated in a Case of a Motor-cycle Fetishist." *Behaviour Research and Therapy* 2 (1, 1964): 31–35.

A 32-year-old man, who obtained sexual satisfaction by stealing and riding motorcycles, was tested by viewing three sets of pictures (three homoerotic pictures of males, three heteroerotic pictures of females, and three non-erotic pictures of inanimate objects). He was permitted to open the shutter to view any specific picture as many times as he wanted. The hypothesis that homoerotic stimuli would produce more shutter openings than heteroerotic and neutral stimuli was confirmed.

334 BRUCE, EARLE WESLEY. "Comparison of Traits of the Homosexual from Tests and from Life History Materials." Master's thesis, University of Chicago, 1942, 124 pp.

Research designed to determine the difference between personality characteristics of homosexuals and the general population was conducted by administering the Bernreuter Personality Inventory and the Humm-Wadsworth Temperament Scale to 53 males active in the Chicago homosexual community. The test results were compared with the results of the same tests derived from groups from the general population and with the information contained in the life histories of 39 of the men. (These life histories were obtained by the investigator during informal interviews conducted in a social setting.)

The homosexuals were found to score higher than the general population on the standardized test indicators of neuroticism, introversion, and self-consciousness, and lower on self-sufficiency, dominance, self-confidence, and sociability. The homosexuals also scored higher on five of the seven components measured on the Humm-Wadsworth Temperament Scale—hysteroid, manic, depressive, autistic, and paranoid. In general, these same characteristics were found in the life history material (much of which is given verbatim in the text).

335 Brussel, JAMES A. "The Tchaikowsky Troika." *Psychiatric Quarterly Supplement* 36 (2, 1962): 304–322.

Peter Ilyich Tchaikowsky was involved in a relationship which might be described as a homosexual troika which was founded on the needs of the participants who seem to have had complementary schizoid personalities. In addition to the composer, the members of the troika included Tchaikowsky's brother, Modeste, and Nadejda Philaretovna von Meck, the musician's benefactress. The troika collapsed when Nadejda withdrew support, and the two men found cultural outlets for their bizarre attitudes.

The homosexual nature of Tchaikowsky's personality was shown through his relationships with his brother (a case of incestuous homosexuality) and his benefactress, his disastrous marriage, the styles in his music, and his suicidal death.

336   BURTON, ARTHUR. "The Use of the Masculinity-Femininity Scale of the MMPI as an Aid in the Diagnosis of Sexual Inversion." *Journal of Psychology* 24 (1947): 161–164.

To see if the Masculinity-Femininity Scale of the Minnesota Multiphasic Personality Inventory (MMPI) would aid in the identification of inverts or homosexuals, a study was made of 20 rapists, 34 sexual inverts, and 84 other delinquents charged with a variety of criminal offenses. All were males aged 14 to 21 who had been committed to the California Youth Authority. The M-F Scale was given at the time of admission. Because of its verbal nature, it was given only to those who tested dull-normal or higher on the Wechsler-Bellevue.

Inverts were found to score significantly higher on the scale than either rapists or delinquents who were sexually normal. However, the reliability coefficient based on the retest of 34 cases was .70 + .09. It was concluded that the reliability of the M-F Scale is too low for individual clinical use.

337   BYCHOWSKI, GUSTAV. "The Ego and the Object of the Homosexual." *International Journal of Psycho-Analysis* 42 (3, 1961): 255–259.

The problem of object choice and object relations in homosexuals is closely related to the ego characteristics of the person. The homosexual's ego has much in common with the ego of the schizophrenic group, and there are also some striking analogies between the homosexual and the adolescent. The homosexual's ego boundaries lack fixity. His immature ego is fetishistic, narcissistic and prenarcissistic, and has oral-sadistic features.

338   BYCHOWSKI, GUSTAV. "Homosexuality and Psychosis." In *Perversions: Psychodynamics and Therapy,* edited by Sandor Lorand and Michael Balint, pp. 97–130. New York: Random House, 1956.

An outline of the relationship of homosexuality to various forms of psychoses is presented. Noting that confusion over sexual identity is a part of schizophrenic symptomatology, it is suggested that latent homosexuality is an element in latent schizophrenia. Ego weakness, too, is characteristic of both homosexuals and schizophrenics. Elements of homosexuality may also appear in various forms of depression, drug addiction, and alcoholism.

339 BYCHOWSKI, GUSTAV. "The Structure of Homosexual Acting Out." *Psychoanalytic Quarterly* 23 (1, 1954): 48–61.

The basic prerequisite of homosexual acting out seems to be a weak ego structure based upon a narcissistic and prenarcissistic disposition. This accounts for the fact that narcissistic projection plays an outstanding part in the choice of homosexual partners, who owe their high, though transient, value to their function as substitutes for the ego and the archaic parental images which were introjected early in life.

340 BYRNE, THOMAS R., JR., and MULLIGAN, FRANCIS M. " 'Psychopathic Personality' and 'Sexual Deviation': Medical Terms or Legal Catch-Alls—Analysis of the Status of the Homosexual Alien." *Temple Law Quarterly* 40 (4, 1967): 328–347.

A psychiatric and legalistic discussion of the homosexual as a psychopathic personality and a sexual deviate is presented. Homosexuals, unlike psychopaths, are not mentally ill, nor do they universally exhibit antisocial behavior.

The authors recommend that aliens be given specific notice that homosexual behavior on their part is adequate cause for deportation.

341 CAIN, ARTHUR H. "Homosexuality and Alcohol." *Sexology* 30 (5, 1963): 296–298.

To decide if alcoholics are repressed homosexuals, a study of 40 cases of alcoholism was conducted over a period of 15 years. The subjects were men and women of all socioeconomic levels, and from all religious and ethnic groups. They ranged in age from 21 to 65. Interviews were conducted and the Rorschach was given. It was found that homosexuality occurs no more frequently among alcoholics than among nonalcoholics; most homosexuals do not drink at all.

342 CANDIDUS. *The Nature of Man: The Problem of Homosexuality.* Cambridge: Deighton, Bell, 1954, 7 pp.

Man is not completely heterosexual by nature. In fact, the intersexual or the bisexual is as common and normal as the completely heterosexual person. Homosexuality is not necessarily a perversion, but perversions may be an extension of homosexuality and should be classified in the category of paraphilias. The laws which rely on the principle that homosexual behavior is a criminal act should be re-examined and amended for the good of society and in accordance with the principles on which society has been founded.

343   CASADY, RICHARD R. "Sexual Problems of Children: Their Detection and Management." In *Sexual Problems: Diagnosis and Treatment in Medical Practice,* edited by Charles William Wahl, pp. 115–132. New York: Free Press, 1967.

It is very difficult to determine a homosexual orientation in children. Although in preadolescence and adolescence, homosexual episodes occur with frequency, homosexuality should not be considered a psychological abnormality until the teens or later.

344   CASON, HULSEY. "A Case of Sexual Psychopathy." *Journal of Clinical Psychopathology* 8 (5, 1947): 785–800.

The case history is reported of a 31-year-old male prison inmate who is a homosexual and has a psychopathic personality. The information was gathered through psychotherapy and a review of the case files. Much of this man's behavior (his homosexual acts and the robberies he had performed) was designed to compensate for feelings of inferiority which had been experienced due to his physical defects at an early age and his homosexual make-up.

345   CASTELNUOVO-TEDESCO, PIETRO. "Ulcerative Colitis in an Adolescent Boy Subjected to a Homosexual Assault: Report of a Case." *Psychosomatic Medicine* 24 (2, 1962): 148–156.

The case of a 14-year-old boy who was afflicted with ulcerative colitis following a homosexual attack and who had experienced a series of events in which he had been inflexibly disciplined is presented. The patient's condition is discussed in terms of the dynamics of his obsessive-compulsive character structure and the problem of the boy's rebellious versus compliant behavior in the relationships he had with his parents.

It is suggested that rebellion versus compliance may be of more significance in patients with ulcerative colitis than is commonly realized. An attempt is made to account for the clinical observation that ulcerative colitis is rarely found among overt homosexuals.

346   CATTELL, RAYMOND B., and MORONY, JOHN H. "The Use of the 16 PF in Distinguishing Homosexuals, Normals, and General Criminals." *Journal of Consulting Psychology* 26 (6, 1962): 531–540.

The Sixteen Personality Factor Questionnaire (PF) was used with reference to a number of methodological and theoretical questions concerning the diagnosis of homosexuality and the development of a homosexual personality profile. The profiles of 100 adult male prisoners convicted of one or more homosexual acts proved to be different from those of a sample of adult Australians who were at an unskilled occupational level and of about the same age as the prisoners. Differences were also found between the homosexuals' profiles and those of 67 prisoners imprisoned for crimes other than homosexuality. The imprisoned homosexuals were also compared to a sample of 33 uncharged homosexuals who differed from the prisoners in the direction of higher social status. The profiles of those two samples had a pattern similarity coefficient (r_p) of 0.92, which was significant. The profile of homosexuals was found to be similar to the profile of neurotics ($r_p = 0.81$).

It was concluded that homosexuality is a particular choice of symptoms made by a primarily neurotic individual characterized by a weak ego, an unusual degree of extroversion, a low degree of superego development, and a radicalism of social outlook.

347   CHANG, JUDY, and BLOCK, JACK. "A Study of Identification in Male Homosexuals." *Journal of Consulting Psychology* 24 (4, 1960): 307–310.

A study was designed to test the Freudian notion that homosexuality in the male is based upon overidentification with the mother as well as an underidentification with the father. Two groups of subjects from the same community were tested; one group was made up of 20 apparently well-adjusted (only one had ever had psychotherapy) homosexual males and the other consisted of 20 non-homosexual males. The mean age of the homosexual group was slightly higher than that of the control group, but otherwise the two groups were evenly matched according to age and education.

Each subject was given a list of 79 adjectives and instructed to indicate 30 adjectives which were characteristic of his ideal self, and 30 which were particularly uncharacteristic. This procedure was repeated for the subject's mother, father, and perceived self. Scores of identification were then derived from this data.

The results showed that the distance between mother and father was significantly greater for the homosexuals than for the nonhomosexuals. The homosexuals showed a significantly greater degree of identification with their mother than the nonhomosexuals, and a nonsignificant trend of less identification with father. The distance between mother and father was a joint result of both constituent scores. The group did not differ significantly in self-acceptance (correspondence between ideal self and perceived self).

Only two of the 79 adjectives discriminated between the ideal-self descriptions for the two groups, "sympathetic" was used more frequently as a characteristic by the nonhomosexual group, and a denial of being "dependent" was used more by the homosexual group.

348 CHAPMAN, A. H., and REESE, D. G. "Homosexual Signs in Rorschachs of Early Schizophrenics." *Journal of Clinical Psychology* 9 (1, 1953): 30–32.

An effort to determine whether patients undergoing early schizophrenic psychoses show definite evidence of homosexuality in their Rorschachs was made through the study of two groups. Six males who were developing schizophrenic psychoses were compared with a control group of six males who fell within normal limits in a psychiatric diagnostic study. All the men were between the ages of 17 and 24, and none had conscious homosexual urges or preoccupations or any history of overt homosexual practices.

The Rorschach responses were scored for the various homosexual signs listed by Ulett: sexual and anatomical responses, castration and phallic symbols, confusion of sexual identification, derealization and mythical distortion, feminine identification, dislike of female genital symbols, and esoteric and artistic languages and references.

The schizophrenic's Rorschachs showed 40 homosexual signs, an average of 6.7 signs per Rorschach. The controls showed 11 signs, an average of 1.8 per Rorschach. The most striking differences occurred in the castration and phallic symbols, feminine identification, derealization and mythical distortion. The evidence tends to support the concept that in the process of a schizophrenic breakdown, the patient passes through a period when homosexual drives are significant and prominent.

349 CLARKE, R. V. G. "The Slater Selective Vocabulary Test and Male Homosexuality." *British Journal of Medical Psychology* 38 (4, 1965): 339–340.

To test the hypothesis that homosexual men are characterized by feminine interests, the Slater Selective Vocabulary Test (1944) was administered to a group of 20 male psychiatric patients with symptoms of homosexuality and a group of 20 nonpatient males with heterosexual orientations. The two groups were individually matched for age, I.Q., and socioeconomic class. The heterosexual group knew more masculine words than did the homosexual group, and both groups knew the same amount of feminine words.

350 CLECKLEY, HERVEY MILTON. *The Caricature of Love: A Discussion of Social, Psychiatric, and Literary Manifestations of Pathologic Sexuality.* New York: Ronald Press, 1957, 319 pp.

The image of homosexuality that emerges from the work of psychiatrists, other authorities in the field, and through works of literature is examined. These sources generally portray homosexuality as essentially "normal" and in some ways beneficial to society. In an attempt to combat this idea and the impression that homosexuals can be fulfilled and happy if only they are left alone, it is insisted that homosexuality is a psychiatric disorder, an illness that causes a great deal of misery.

351   CORNSWEET, A. C., and HAYES, M. F. "Conditioned Response to Fellatio." *American Journal of Psychiatry* 103 (Jul., 1946): 76–78.

A study to determine the identifying features in the homosexual personality structure was conducted through psychiatric and psychological interviews. The Wechsler-Bellevue Intelligence Scale was also administered. The study involved approximately 200 males from 18 to 20 years of age.

The homosexual trend began in infantile sexual patterns and masturbation during puberty. This was later supplemented by mutual masturbation and advanced to both active and passive fellatio. The subjects felt disgust with women as sexual partners and had experienced strong childhood attachments to their mothers or mother surrogates. With the exception of two mental deficients, their I.Q.'s were 90 or above.

As the homosexual ages, his desire and ability to be fellated diminishes and he becomes the fellator. This seems to occur when the physical sensations derived during the act become localized in the mouth, lips and throat. This pattern seems to be characteristic of overt homosexuals only; latent homosexuals have a more generalized physical reaction.

352   CORY, DONALD WEBSTER. "Homosexuality: Active and Passive." *Journal of Sex Education* 5 (1, 1952): 19–22.

Various male homosexual relationships and sexual acts are reviewed to demonstrate that categorizing homosexuals as "active" and "passive," and then attributing personality and character traits on this basis, makes very little sense. Terms which describe more adequately the nature of the sex acts are offered: oral-insertor, anal-insertor, oral-receptor, anal-receptor, and simultaneous oral-receptor and oral-insertor.

353   CORY, DONALD WEBSTER, and LEROY, JOHN P. "Are Homosexuals Creative?" *Sexology* 29 (3, 1962): 162–165.

This is a reply to a study done by Albert Ellis ("Are Homosexuals Really Creative," *Sexology,* Sept., 1962) in which it was found that homosexuals are less creative as a group than heterosexuals.

Ellis's use of subjective judgments rather than objective methods of testing as well as the kinds of groups which he studied (therapy patients) are criticized. It is argued that subjects under therapy are not typical of the American population and that therefore the results of the Ellis study should not be generalized to the general population.

The argument is made that since the homosexual stands outside the mainstream of life, he sees humanity differently, originally, and hence "stands closer to the wellsprings from which true creativity flows."

354   CURRAN, DESMOND. "Sexual Perversions and Their Treatment." *Practitioner* 158 (946, 1947): 343–348.

Sexual perversions, including homosexuality, are intertwined with normal manifestations of sex. Homosexuality, which is often reinforced or maintained by special circumstances, should therefore be regarded as a normal phase of development. The fact that homosexuality is associated with pleasure, as are other sexual activities, necessarily makes its treatment difficult.

355   CURRAN, DESMOND, and PARR, DENIS. "Homosexuality: An Analysis of 100 Male Cases Seen in Private Practice." *British Medical Journal* (5022, 1957): 797–801.

Detailed results of an analysis of data taken from the case records of 100 male patients with homosexual problems are presented. How the subjects had been referred for treatment, their age, education, occupational status, marital status, and whether they had been in difficulty with the law as a result of their homosexuality are reported.

It was found that in addition to their homosexual problems, 43 of the patients had either an associated psychiatric syndrome or a neurotic, inadequate, or sociopathic personality, or a combination of both. Eighty-nine of the patients had had one or more homosexual relationships since adolescence. Although sufficient information was only available on 60 patients, these persons had committed 600–700 homosexual acts a year. The 17 pedophiliacs were older than the others, were more often married, were in therapy more often because of the charges made against them, and were more socially isolated from other homosexuals.

The recommendations for treatment were: inpatient care for 11 cases, psychotherapy for 23 cases, and discussion, simple counseling, prescription of medicine or environmental adjustments for the remaining 66 cases.

Of the 59 patients about whom follow-up information was available from letters sent to relatives, psychiatrists, et cetera, as well as to the patients themselves, nine reported less intense homosexual feelings or increased capacity for heterosexual arousal after treatment; three became more homosexual in preference; and no change was found in the other 47. Eleven showed improved discretion in or control of their homosexual behaviors.

Twenty-three showed improved subjective adjustment, and one had committed suicide.

356   DAEN, PHYLLIS. "The Body Image and Sexual Preferences of Al-
       coholic, Homosexual and Heterosexual Males." Ph.D. dissertation,
       Adelphi College, 1960, 78 pp.

Three tests, designed to determine whether elements of latent homosexuality were present in alcholics, were given to 30 overt male homosexuals, 30
male alcoholics, and 30 married male heterosexuals. As far as possible the
three groups of subjects were matched for age, education, intelligence, and
ethnic background.

One test (the McElroy Symbol Test) failed to discriminate between
homosexuals and heterosexuals and so could not be applied to the study of
alcoholics.

A Slide Presentation Test, similar to the one developed by Zamansky,
involved comparisons of paired pictures of men and women. The differences
in responses between the homosexual group and the heterosexual group
were used as a basis for devising a homosexuality-heterosexuality scale. The
responses of the alcoholics were then compared with the scores of the
reference groups. Since their scores lay between the responses of the homosexual and heterosexual groups in a statistically significant pattern, if was
concluded that alcoholic subjects alternated in their choice of sex object.

The Machover Draw-a-Person Test was used to study the subjects' body
image. When the data were compared by the application of a rating scale
based on indicators of homosexuality in drawings and by a panel of expert
judges, it was found that on this test, too, the alcoholics' responses fell
between the responses of the reference groups, indicating that alcoholics
have an ambiguous body image.

The results on both the Slide Presentation Test and the Draw-a-Person
Test supported the possibility of latent homosexuality in alcoholics.

357   DARKE, ROY A., and GEIL, GEORGE A. "Homosexual Activity:
       Relation of Degree and Role to the Goodenough Test and to the
       Cornell Selectee Index." *Journal of Nervous and Mental Disease* 108
       (3, 1948): 217–240.

The case histories of 100 male homosexuals from the Medical Center for
Federal Prisoners at Springfield, Missouri, were obtained, and the prisoners
were administered the Goodenough Draw-a-Man Test, the Cornell Selectee
Index, and the Wechsler-Bellevue Scale. Both the Goodenough test and the
Cornell Selectee Index proved valuable in the study of male homosexuality
and are recommended for use in future studies. Several factors (feminism,
absurd distortion, et cetera) proved statistically significant in comparisons

made on the basis of the degree of or the role assumed in homosexual activity.

358 DASTON, PAUL GEORGE. "Perception of Homosexual Words in Paranoid Schizophrenia." Ph.D. dissertation, Michigan State College, 1952, 102 pp.

During an investigation of the relation between homosexuality and schizophrenia, it was postulated that if homosexuality is an area of concern to paranoid individuals, greater recognition of tachistoscopically-presented words reflecting homosexuality would be shown by these individuals than by the control subjects. Three groups were studied: paranoid schizophrenics, unclassified schizophrenics, and normals. Paranoids showed a quicker recognition of homosexual words than the other two groups, which did not differ statistically from each other.

It was concluded that the psychoanalytic postulate is supported and that the relation is due more to paranoid than to schizophrenic components.

359 DAVID, HENRY P., and RABINOWITZ, WILLIAM. "Szondi Patterns in Epileptic and Homosexual Males." *Journal of Consulting Psychology* 16 (4, 1952): 247–250.

An attempt was made to determine the extent to which signs and patterns described by Szondi and Deri as characteristic of idiopathic epileptics and overt homosexuals actually differentiate these two groups. One hundred idiopathic epileptics and 100 overt homosexuals, all single white males between the ages of 18 and 49, were administered 31 diagnostic signs or patterns from Szondi's and Deri's volumes. Of 16 different signs for epilepsy, five were statistically significant. In two cases, however, frequencies were greater in the homosexual than in the epileptic group—the direction opposite to that predicted. Of nine different signs for homosexuality, three were statistically significant. The failure of most of the signs to differentiate the groups would seem to argue against the routine administration of the Szondi Test for these purposes in clinical practice.

360 DAVIDS, ANTHONY; JOELSON, MARK; and MCARTHUR, CHARLES C. "Rorschach and TAT Indices of Homosexuality in Overt Homosexuals, Neurotics, and Normal Males." *Journal of Abnormal and Social Psychology* 53 (2, 1956): 161–172.

In examining the ways in which projective techniques can be used for the diagnosis and analysis of homosexuality, the Rorschach and the Thematic Apperception Test (TAT) were administered to a group of overt homosexuals, a group of neurotics, and a control group. Each group numbered 20, and all participants were male students at large Eastern universities.

It was found that the homosexual group gave a greater mean number of proposed homosexual Rorschach and TAT signs than either of the non-homosexual groups. On the Rorschach, four individual signs and four Rorschach cards were found to be useful in differentiating the homosexual and non-homosexual groups. An additional Rorschach sign (termed the "rear view") was found, and it was proposed that it be submitted to further testing. Two individual signs and five cards from the TAT were found to be useful, and five new signs appeared to differentiate the two groups. Correlations between the number of homosexual Roschach signs and homosexual TAT signs, within the homosexual group, proved significant. Within the nonhomosexual groups these correlations were not significant, possibly indicating that these tests are too crude to use as instruments for the detection of latent homosexuality. Limitations on the uses of these tests in predicting homosexuality were discussed, noting that there are dangers in expecting them to serve as the sole indicators of homosexuality.

361   DEAN, ROBERT B. "Some MMPI and Biographical Questionnaire Correlates of Non-Institutionalized Male Homosexuals." Master's thesis, San Jose State College, 1967, 113 pp.

The Minnesota Multiphasic Personality Inventory (MMPI) and a biographical questionnaire were administered to a diversified group of 113 nonincarcerated and nonhospitalized male homosexuals. The responses were used to develop a biographical questionnaire which could be used nearly as well as a personal interview for eliciting information from male homosexuals. In addition, the results were studied to assess the general psychological adjustment of homosexual males.

In order to test the relationship between MMPI data and certain background factors, paired categories reflecting the information gained from the biographical questionnaire were developed, and the MMPI profiles of the subjects classified in one category were compared with the profiles of those in the other. Homosexuals who had been arrested for their homosexual activity, for example, were compared with those who had been arrested for other reasons; homosexuals who had also had heterosexual experience were compared with those who had had no heterosexual experience; homosexuals who belonged to homophile organizations were compared with those who did not, et cetera.

362   DEAN, ROBERT B., and RICHARDSON, HAROLD. "Analysis of MMPI Profiles of Forty College-Educated Overt Male Homosexuals." *Journal of Consulting Psychology* 28 (6, 1964): 483–486.

A study was made to prove that "the MMPI [Minnesota Multiphasic Personality Inventory] profile of a group of highly educated, socially functioning, male homosexuals, not presently in legal difficulties because of homosexual behavior, would not show definite indications of neurotic, psychotic, or other pathological personality deviations." The subjects, 40 overt male homosexuals (two were in psychotherapy), were matched with a control group, taken from Barron's 1963 sample of graduate students, which was similar to the experimental group in age, education, and heterogeneity of background.

Subjected to a two-tailed t test, the Pd and M-F scales and the Sc and Ma scales of the two groups were significantly different. In general, the profiles of the two groups were alike in regard to shape and elevation. Both were within the defined normal range of T scores, less than 70, with the homosexual group only slightly higher than the control group. Only the M-F scale exceeded $T \leq 70$ for both groups, with the homosexuals higher than the controls, but this was probably due to the education level of the groups. It was concluded that at least highly educated, socially functioning, male homosexuals do not show signs of severe personality disturbances.

363   DEAN, ROBERT B., and RICHARDSON, HAROLD. "On MMPI High-Point Codes of Homosexual Versus Heterosexual Males." *Journal of Consulting Psychology* 30 (6, 1966): 558–560.

The criticisms that Zucker and Manosevitz (1966) directed at the analysis of the Minnesota Multiphasic Personality Inventory scores, in "Analysis of MMPI Profiles of Forty College-Educated Overt Male Homosexuals," are answered. With the exception of the comments on the M-F scale, the points regarding individual scale differences are well taken. The implication that a high M-F was not indicative of sexual inversion had not been intended; instead the suggestion should have been that it was not an indication of psychopathology in and of itself.

There is concern that a new approach suggested by Zucker and Manosevitz would link high-point codes for the homosexual group without considering the appearance of similar pairings in the control group. A new experiment was devised as follows: The sample was the same as Dean and Richardson (1964) with the addition of an H_2 group differing from the H_1 group in that it had a lower education level and was obtained from an urban rather than a suburban area. As in the first sample, there was no random selection, and the MMPI code scores were again subjected to an x^2 test for significance.

Combining code types as suggested by Zucker and Manosevitz (Mf-Ma, Mf-Sc, Mf-O), a nonsignificant difference was obtained. When compared, H_1 and H_2 also produced a nonsignificant difference. It was explained that feminine interests apparently override differences in education. When H_1 was compared with C, an insignificant x^2 was obtained, but when H_2 was compared with C, the outcome was a highly significant x^2 (p < .001). In comparing H_1, H_2, and C with code-types not combined, a significant x^2 resulted; which was explained by the difference in education level between H_2 and C.

It was concluded that comparing homosexuals and nonhomosexuals on individual scale differences tends to hide differences within the group and that larger samples than those reported here or than those which had been previously reported are needed.

364   DE LUCA, JOSEPH N. "Performance of Overt Male Homosexuals and Controls on the Blacky Test." *Journal of Clinical Psychology* 23 (4, 1967): 497.

To investigate whether homosexuals and controls score differently on the Blacky Pictures, a study was made of 20 homosexuals and 40 controls. The subjects were all Army inductees in their third to fifth week of basic training. They were matched for age (21 years), education (11 years), and I.Q. (99). The Blacky Pictures were individually administered in accordance with Gerald S. Blum's procedure.

The homosexuals showed significantly greater disturbance than the controls on only one of the 30 factors measured, and this, it was concluded, could have been due to chance.

The conclusion was that the Blacky Pictures do not differentiate overt male homosexuals from a matched group of nonhomosexuals.

365   DE LUCA, JOSEPH N. "The Structure of Homosexuality." *Journal of Projective Techniques and Personality Assessment* 30 (2, 1966): 187–191.

Forty-two overt homosexual males with no history of psychiatric treatment or shame about their homosexuality, and 25 heterosexual male controls were given a questionnaire as well as a Rorschach using the Klopfer method (Klopfer, 1954). The Rorschach signs were measured by the standards established by Wheeler (1949).

The results of the Rorschach were analyzed to determine whether differences in personality can be shown to exist among homosexual males in relation to their preferences for sodomy versus fellatio and the active versus the passive role, and whether the differences in Rorschach results are caused by the type of homosexuality as well as by the existence of homosexuality alone. The data was also used to see if homosexual males are more creative than heterosexual males, and if the type of homosexuality preferred will vary with the type of anxiety present.

The findings indicated that subgroups of homosexuals (Passive, Active,

Fellatio, Sodomy, Active and Passive, Active and Passive Fellatio and Active and Passive Sodomy, Passive Fellatio, Passive Sodomy, Active Fellatio) showed significant differences in Rorschach interpretations, $p < .05$ on 28 of 75 Rorschach signs. Differences were found for the tests taken as a whole, but individual signs were not significant in revealing the presence or absence of homosexuality or the type of homosexual activity. Creativity signs were not significant. And heterosexuals and homosexuals were not discovered to differ to any significant degree for psychological inadequacies.

366   DEMARIA, LAURA ACHARD de. "Homosexual Acting Out." *International Journal of Psycho-Analysis* 49 (2-3, 1968): 219–220.

Several traits of homosexual acting out are described, including repetition-compulsion, primary oral anxieties, choice of homosexual objects, transference factors in acting out, and the homosexual ritual. In the course of treatment, some homosexual subjects tend to act out a repressed memory of a former homosexual act. This serves as self-inflicted vengeance or "secondary masochism."

Primary oral anxieties are expressed by regression to pregenital levels and are dramatized in certain facets of homosexual intercourse. This regression springs from a splitting of the maternal image into one which is "sick." Therapy brings out a desire for improved relations with the mother.

Objects chosen by homosexuals are of two kinds: narcissistic and worthless. In the former, aspects of the self which were "lost" are projected. In the latter, the homosexual identifies with worthlessness and anonymity.

Homosexuals generally find it difficult to experience negative transference in analysis. Their desire to destroy the analyst (and thus suffer destruction) is avoided by an irrational belief in the magic of the homosexual ritual which functions to exorcise the primal scene and dramatize the way it was experienced by the patient. The need for further systematic interpretations of acting-out behavior during treatment is discussed.

367   DE MARTINO, MANFRED F. "Human Figure Drawings by Mentally Retarded Males." *Journal of Clinical Psychology* 10 (3, 1954): 241–244.

Human figure drawings, found useful in psychodiagnostic work with the mentally retarded, were used in a study conducted to investigate the male figure drawings produced by 100 mentally retarded nonhomosexual males. The drawings by 37 mentally retarded homosexual males were also compared with those of an equivalent group of nonhomosexuals. Most of the homosexuals drew their own sex first, and high heels and eyelashes appeared in their drawings more frequently than in those of nonhomosexuals.

368 DENGROVE, EDWARD. "When a 'Homosexual' Is Not a Homosexual." *Sexology* 32 (1, 1965): 4–6.

The belief that not all "homosexuals" are homosexuals was sustained in the case of a young male patient who expressed anxiety about homosexual urges. A survey was made of the various definitions of homosexuality found in the works of Alfred C. Kinsey, John Hampson, Irving Bieber, and John Money. According to their definitions, the patient could not be considered homosexual because he did not present the following characteristics of confirmed homosexuals: in the Draw-a-Picture Test he drew a man (homosexual males will usually draw a woman); his childhood experiences did not conform to the usual homosexual sequence (homosexuals generally came from an emotionally sick family environment); and latent homosexuals are more prone to seek treatment, as the young male patient, and be cured.

369 DeRiver, J. PAUL. *The Sexual Criminal: A Psychoanalytic Study.* Springfield, Ill.: Charles C. Thomas, 1949, 281 pp.

Sadism, masochism, and the psychological aspects of criminal investigation are examined in their relation to the pathological aspects of sexual offenders. The sadistic features sometimes present in homosexuality are discussed. Sadistic homosexual murder is considered a symbolic expression of twisted sexual impulses that cannot find normal outlets. Cases describing the offenders and their victims are presented.

370 DEVEREUX, GEORGE. "Retaliatory Homosexual Triumph Over the Father." *International Journal of Psycho-Analysis* 41 (2-3, 1960): 157–161.

Clinical material is cited which indicates that the Oedipal fantasy involves not only the slaying of the father and cohabitation with the mother, but also a homosexual triumph over the feminized father. The subject, a young unmarried male whose problem was impotence, had undergone psychoanalysis twice weekly for some months.

The Oedipal fantasy may be interpreted as an attack which could be justified by the earlier homosexual aggressions of the father against the son.

371 DICKEY, BRENDA A. "Attitudes Toward Sex Roles and Feelings of Adequacy in Homosexual Males." *Journal of Consulting Psychology* 25 (2, 1961): 116–122.

A study was made to test the hypothesis that greater feelings of adequacy are found among homosexual males who have homosexual contacts and associations, who have less pressure toward heterosexual associations, who

identify with the typical homosexual male, who see less desirable characteristics in the heterosexual male, and who see a smaller difference between
themselves and the typical homosexual than between themselves and the
typical heterosexual.

Forty-seven subjects were selected through the Mattachine Society by
contacts within the Society who were told to sample as diverse a group as
possible in Denver and San Francisco. A paper-and-pencil questionnaire
was administered by the Mattachine contacts. Adequacy feeling was measured by a list of 46 ideal-self-concepts and self-concept discrepancies and
by 20 Minnesota Multiphasic Personality Inventory statements on
adequacy in roles.

The results of the study did not support the hypothesis. In general, it was
found that homosexual males who thought of themselves as adequate,
tended to hold to the masculine norms of the dominant culture. Specific
results were: homosexually "married" males feel more adequate than those
who are homosexually unmarried; if a homosexual is "satisfied" with his
job, he will tend to feel adequate; those who indicate a preference for
leisure-time contact with heterosexuals tend to feel more adequate than
those who prefer such contact with homosexuals; those who feel that the
role of the heterosexual male is more desirable are more adequate than those
who prefer homosexual role characteristics; and adequacy feelings are present in those who see themselves as more like the typical heterosexual male
than like the typical homosexual male.

372 DOIDGE, WILLIAM THOMAS. "Perceptual Differences in Male
Homosexuals." Ph.D. dissertation, University of Texas, 1956, 98 pp.

Eighty males of the United States Air Force were assigned to four groups
on the basis of the degree of their homosexuality. Their orientations ranged
from exclusive homosexuality to exclusive heterosexuality. When perceptual differences were studied by means of a battery of 10 psychological tests,
the following conclusions were reached: individuals who engage in homosexual activities but who remain mostly heterosexual do not demonstrate
the perceptual distortions nor pathological indications of the markedly
homosexual individual; male homosexuals possess a feminine identification
which can be demonstrated by tests designed to measure interests, preferences, and attitudes; male homosexuals demonstrate a greater preference for
narcissistic object choice than heterosexuals; and male homosexuality, in
the American culture at least, is accompanied by high levels of anxiety.

373 DOIDGE, WILLIAM THOMAS, and HOLTZMAN, WAYNE H. "Implications of Homosexuality Among Air Force Trainees." *Journal
of Consulting Psychology* 24 (1, 1960): 9–13.

A study was made of two homosexual groups and two heterosexual groups to determine whether homosexuality is symptomatic of a more general personality disturbance or whether it may be regarded as confined to the sexual sector alone. Each group of subjects contained 20 individuals who were in the psychiatric clinic at Lackland Air Force Base. The following tests were administered: the Sexual Identification Survey, Homosexual Homonyms, Edwards Personal Preference Schedule, Heineman's Forced-Choice Anxiety Scale, Worchel's Self-Activities Inventory, Food Preference and Aversion Scale, Rorschach, the Blacky Pictures, Minnesota Multiphasic Personality Inventory, and six subtests of the Wechsler Adult Intelligence Scale (Vocabulary, Information, Similarities, Picture Completion, Block Design and Digit Symbol).

The results of the study indicated that homosexuality was symptomatic of a more general personality disturbance. The homosexuals appeared to suffer from an emotional disorder which was relatively pervasive and severe.

374   DOSHAY, LEWIS J. *The Boy Sex Offender and His Later Career.*
       New York: Grune & Stratton, 1943, 206 pp.

In a psychiatric and statistical study of background factors in juvenile sexual delinquency in males the following are considered: the home environment, personalities of the parents, community factors, and personalities of the delinquents. Homosexuality per se is infrequently mentioned, although the sex offense of greatest frequency involved sodomy (buggery). These acts are not to be taken as evidence of homosexuality. Court-treated juvenile sex offenders rarely become homosexuals in later life.

375   DUE, FLOYD O., and WRIGHT, M. ERIK. "The Use of Content
       Analysis in Rorschach Interpretation, 1. Differential Characteristics
       of Male Homosexuals." *Rorschach Research Exchange and Journal
       of Projective Techniques* 9 (4, 1945): 169–177.

Forty-two male homosexuals were administered a Rorschach which was modified so that subjects could write down their spontaneous projections and/or select responses from a list of suggestions. Content analysis not only identified certain types of overt homosexuals, but it also indicated the importance of homosexual conflict in other diagnostic groups. The characteristic responses of male homosexuals were: derealization (mythical distortion, qualifications toward the abnormal, and dehumanization), confusion of sexual identification, feminine identification, castration and phallic symbolism, sexual and anatomical responses, esoteric language and artistic references, and paranoid reactions.

376   DUFFY, CLINTON T., and HIRSHBERG, AL. *Sex and Crime.* New York: Doubleday & Co., 1965, 203 pp.

Sex is seen as the cause of nearly all crime, and as the dominant force driving nearly all criminals. Although not all homosexuals are criminals, any crime a homosexual does commit can be directly attributed to his sexual abnormality.

377   ELLIS, ALBERT. "Are Homosexuals Necessarily Neurotic?" 1955. Reprinted in *Homosexuality: A Cross Cultural Approach,* edited by Donald Webster Cory, pp. 407–414. New York: Julian Press, 1956.

Although all homosexuals are not necessarily neurotic, the great majority of them indubitably are. Only those homosexuals who are incapable of enjoying sex participation except with a member of their own sex are necessarily neurotic. On the one hand, a neurotic is an individual who acts in a childish, irrational, effectively stupid manner. A pervert, on the other hand, is physiologically or theoretically able to obtain sex satisfaction in several different ways, but is limited to one or two major forms of sex outlet because he is irrationally, fearfully fixated or fetishistically restricted by certain ideas or behavioral habits which he learned at some earlier time in his life. Thus, a neurotic and a pervert are exactly the same thing.

378   ELLIS, ALBERT. "Are Homosexuals Really Creative?" *Sexology* 29 (2, 1962): 88–93.

Homosexuals are not unusually creative, i.e., they do not include in their ranks an unusually high proportion of great writers, composers, and performing artists. To verify this hypothesis, a study was made of 66 homosexual patients who had been in intensive psychotherapy for some time and 150 "highly heterosexual" patients. The homosexual patients were divided into three subgroups: 19 bisexuals, 33 confirmed homosexuals who maintained their own sex roles, and 14 "inverts" (those who were exclusively homosexual, but who had adopted the role of the opposite sex). These three groups were compared with a control group of 150 heterosexual patients who had been rated on a clinical basis and classified as high, moderate, or very low in creativity.

There was a distinct decline in creativity from the most heterosexual to the most homosexual patients studied. The percentage of heterosexual patients who showed little or no creativity was significantly lower than that of confirmed homosexuals and "inverted" patients. It was also found that a higher percentage of the heterosexuals (61 percent) and bisexuals (63 percent) than of the homosexuals (54 percent) and the "inverts" (53 percent) became more creative during the course of treatment.

379   ELLIS, ALBERT. "Homosexuality and Creativity." *Journal of Clinical Psychology* 15 (4, 1959): 376–379.

Since some persons had supposed that homosexuals are more artistic or creative than heterosexuals, a study was designed to determine group differences in clinical diagnosis, creativity, and clinical improvement during therapy. The subjects, 36 males with severe homosexual problems and 150 males who were exceptionally heterosexual, were all patients who had undergone psychotherapy. The homosexual patients were divided into: bisexuals (overtly homosexual with a reasonably strong heterosexual component), fixed homosexuals (exclusively or predominantly homosexual but maintaining their own sex role), and inverts (exclusively homosexual accompanied by sex role inversion).

The patients were rated by the therapist as: neurotic, borderline psychotic, or psychotic; highly, moderately, or noncreative; distinctly or a little more creative after therapy; clinically improved or not after therapy; changed or not toward heterosexuality after therapy. In creativity ratings, the criteria of "sensitivity to problems, ideational fluency, flexibility of set, ideational novelty, synthesizing ability, analyzing ability," and an ability "to find new solutions to a problem or new modes of artistic expression" were employed.

Compared to the homosexual patients, the exceptionally heterosexual patients were significantly less emotionally disturbed, more creative, and more clinically improved during therapy. Compared to the fixed homosexual and inverted patients, the bisexual patients were significantly more creative, more clinically improved, and made greater gains in heterosexuality. Compared to the homosexual inverts, the fixed homosexuals without sex-role inversion were significantly more creative and more clinically improved. A good part of the relationship between degree of homosexuality and lesser creativity and clinical improvement is attributed to the greater severity of emotional disturbance found among homosexual patients.

380   ELLIS, ALBERT. "Homosexuality: The Right To Be Wrong." *Journal of Sex Research* 4 (2, 1968): 96–107.

The contention is made that to be only homosexual, only heterosexual, or to be fixated on any one sexual object is "wrong." However, it is believed that anyone has the right to his fixations, right or wrong, as long as they involve no harm to other persons.

There are seven reasons why fixated homosexuality is wrong: cultural restrictions create difficulties; people should expose themselves to a "great deal" of heterosexual behavior before choosing homosexuality exclusively (a "great deal" means with several members of the opposite sex); irrational fears are present in all fixated homosexuals; fixated homosexuals are "short-range hedonists," who fail to live responsibly; fixated homosexuals are psychotic; it is not true, as has been reported, that some fixated homosexuals are as well adjusted as nondeviants; and they usually have other types of emotional disturbances. It is pointed out that although these persons may be seen as wrong or foolish, there should be no blame or sense of sin associated with their behaviors. Humans are fallible and should always be forgiven. It is their "inalienable right."

381   ELLIS, ALBERT, and ALLEN, CLIFFORD. "On the Cure of Homosexuality." *International Journal of Sexology* 5 (3, 1952): 135–142.

The two authors disagree on the nature of homosexuality. Ellis asserts that exclusive homosexuals are necessarily neurotic and have at least one of four distinct neurotic symptoms (a sexual fixation, a specific phobia, an obsession, or a distinct compulsion). Exclusive homosexuals who undergo therapy should try to cure their neurosis, and not merely lose their homosexual desires. This cure need have little to do with the complete substitution of the female for the male as the desired love object. The psychotherapist should help the homosexual to become unneurotically bisexual in his desires. Allen agrees with Ellis that homosexuality is the result of a fixation, but he does not believe that exclusive homosexuals are necessarily neurotic.

382   FEIN, LEAH GOLD. "Rorschach Signs of Homosexuality in Male College Students." *Journal of Clinical Psychology* 6 (3, 1950): 248–253.

In an effort to determine homosexual indicators in response to the Rorschach, 43 male college students (nine homosexuals, 10 neurotics, and 24 normals) were tested individually. Responses identified as homosexual indicators were those about feminine apparel and behavior, men with feminine attributes, men with sex connotations, men with sex aversion, and references to males and females in symmetrical blot areas.

Esoteric language and art references were suggestive of homosexual tendencies. Sex organ, anatomy and X-ray responses, qualifications toward the abnormal, castration and phallic symbolism became indicators of homosexuality only when there was an accumulation of such responses. Feminine gender responses were not indicators of homosexuality. Paranoid reactions and confusion of sex identification were more indicative of insecurity and uncertainty than of homosexuality in male college students.

383   FENICHEL, OTTO. "The Psychology of Transvestitism." In *The Collected Papers of Otto Fenichel: First Series,* by Otto Fenichel, pp. 167–180. New York: W. W. Norton & Co., 1953.

The behavior of the transvestite has "points of contact with various other perverse practices." The transvestite has in common with the fetishist the overestimation of feminine clothes and body linen. He has the same feminine psychic attitude as the passive homosexual (and the feminine masochist). However, his narcissistic regression in identification with a woman goes far beyond that of the homosexual. The primary object tendency for the transvestite, as for the passive homosexual, is the father. On a more superficial level the mother is also a sexual object. The transvestite has not given up belief in the phallic nature of women, however, and he has identified himself with the woman with a penis.

A case history of a 40-year-old male, whose principal childhood sex object was his sister, whom he desired to be, is given to illustrate the point of view discussed herein.

The dread of castration is what conditions the disappearance of infantile sexuality. Those with perverse sexual behavior are trying to master their anxiety by denying its cause. The transvestite tries to refute the fact of castration, while the homosexual has no regard for anyone who lacks the penis.

384   FERENCZI, SANDOR. "The Nosology of Male Homosexuality (Homo-Erotism)." In his *Contributions to Psycho-Analysis,* pp. 250–268. Translated by Ernest Jones. Boston: Richard G. Badger, 1916. Reprinted in *The Problem of Homosexuality in Modern Society,* edited by Hendrik M. Ruitenbeek, pp. 3–16. New York: E. P. Dutton & Co., 1963. Also reprinted as "Types of Male Homosexuality." In *The Homosexuals: As Seen by Themselves and Thirty Authorities,* edited by Aron M. Krich, pp. 188–201. New York: Citadel Press, 1954.

A psychoanalytic discussion presents some facts and viewpoints which may make it easier to devise a correct nosological classification of homosexual clinical pictures. A distinction is made between passive homosexuality (termed "subject-homoerotism" and in which a man feels that he is a woman and is "inverted with respect to his own ego") and active homosexuality (termed "object-homoerotism" and in which a man is a man in every respect except that the object of his inclination is exchanged). According to Magnus Hirschfeld, the former is a true "sexual intermediate stage," and the latter is an obsessional neurosis.

385   FINE, REUBEN. "The Case of El: The MAPS Test." *Journal of Projective Techniques and Personality Assessment* 25 (4, 1961): 383–389.

The Make A Picture Story test responses given by El, a male homosexual, indicate El's anxieties about the loss of love, his inability to find peace, and his preoccupation with nudity and exhibitionism. Other sources of ego strength, however, tend to counterbalance the psychopathological aspects, and El's scores fall within the "normal," and not the schizophrenic range.

See Forer (no. 390); Hooker (no. 454); Meyer (no. 509); Murray (no. 513); and Shneidman (no. 562 and no. 563).

386　FINE, REUBEN. "A Transference Manifestation of Male Homosexuals." *Psychoanalysis and the Psychoanalytic Review* 48 (2, 1961): 116–120.

It is observed that male homosexuals in therapy rarely express any homosexual feelings about the analyst. This observation is based on experience with seven overt homosexual patients treated over a period of 10 years. Five of the patients were minimally bisexual, six were in analysis, and one was in psychotherapy. Although it is noted that the case material is small and perhaps atypical, other male therapists were consulted who related similar experiences.

The split in the homosexual love object and the heterosexual love object are similar, but the homosexual pushes the split farther, manifesting it in an analytic situation as a splitting off of the analyst from the world of accessible homosexual objects. This is interpreted as meaning that the patient is afraid of his homosexuality, bypassing or minimizing his homosexual acting-out, which is a serious stumbling block to analytic progress.

387　FINE, ROSWELL H. "Apparent Homosexuality in the Adolescent Girl." *Diseases of the Nervous System* 21 (11, 1960): 634–637.

Homosexuality and homosexual symptomatology are differentiated by using as an example the case history of a 15-year-old girl who underwent individual and group psychotherapy in Los Guilucos, a state correctional school for girls in California. Homosexual symptomatology should not be confused with homosexuality, as the former will be found to exist in transient situational personality disorders. There is a vast difference between "playing at it"—homosexual play, et cetera, a behaviorial manifestation—and "overt homosexuality" as a definite specific clinical entity.

388　FINK, MAXIMILIAN. "Clinical Conference: Homosexuality with Panic and Paranoid States." *Journal of the Hillside Hospital* 2 (3, 1953): 164–190.

The psychoanalytic case history of a 26-year-old married patient, whose homosexuality formed the basis of his panic state, is reported. The presenting problem of panic was based on homosexual fears which were, in turn, based upon fears of castration. This castration anxiety came from a confused identification with a biparental imago.

389   FISCHOFF, JOSEPH. "Preoedipal Influences in a Boy's Determination To Be 'Feminine' During the Oedipal Period." *Journal of the American Academy of Child Psychiatry* 3 (2, 1964): 273–286.

A relationship exists between feminine behavior in young boys and adolescent and adult homosexuality. It is therefore useful to treat young boys who, during the Oedipal period, demonstrate a conscious desire to be feminine. Two case histories are given as illustrations.

The first patient entered therapy at the age of four. During the previous year he had manifested a conscious desire to be a girl and had exhibited feminine mannerisms. The second patient was six when referred for treatment. He desired to be a pretty girl and felt he could be like his mother, a commercial artist, by pursuing activities such as painting and drawing.

In these and in other cases the father is seen as being passive or weak, but behind him is the all-powerful mother. The boy turns to the mother as a source of protection and becomes totally submissive to her. The desire to be a girl is both an expression of being powerful like the mother and an expression of anger toward her.

390   FORER, BERTRAM R. "The Case of El: Vocational Choice." *Journal of Projective Techniques and Personality Assessment* 25 (4, 1961): 371–374.

A psychoanalytic approach to vocational choice focuses upon the clerical and teaching occupations of a 30-year-old male homosexual. The article concludes that since El's vocational choices are "autonomous" from his homosexuality, his positions as bank teller, accountant, and teacher represent an attempt to establish adaptation on a nonhomosexual basis and are congruent with his strong interest in compulsive activities, his desire for order and control, and his high clerical and computational scores.

See Fine (no. 385); Hooker (no. 454); Meyer (no. 509); Murray (no. 513); and Shneidman (no. 562 and no. 563).

391   FRAIBERG, SELMA H. "Homosexual Conflicts." In *Adolescents: Psychoanalytic Approach to Problems and Therapy,* edited by Sandor Lorand and Henry I. Schneer, pp. 78–112. New York: Paul B. Hoeber, 1961.

The amount of "allowable" homosexuality during male puberty does not include sexual contact with an adult, which represents a dangerous regression to the original homosexual object, the father. This is illustrated by the detailed case history of a boy who underwent analysis from age 11 to 14. The case afforded the opportunity for a detailed study of the homosexual conflicts in the prepubertal and pubertal phases. Symptoms of the conflict took the form of tics—eye-blinking and nose-twitching—and a lack of aggressive masculinity. During therapy, the patient made an apparent shift from passive timidity to aggressive masculinity, although passive tendencies persisted. He was tormented by fears of genital damage and castration. The absence of conflict between the adolescent boy and his original love object, the father, was an ominous sign of a predisposition toward homosexuality. A homosexual experience with an adult, a camp counselor, and a later threatening relationship with a football coach came at a crucial time in his development and might easily have led, without the intervention of therapy, to a homosexual orientation in adolescence. In later adolescence, at age 17, the patient was inhibited in his relationships with both sexes and, although he did not develop a neurosis, sought further help in analysis.

392   FRANK, GEORGE H. "A Test of the Use of a Figure Drawing Test as an Indicator of Sexual Inversion." *Psychological Reports* 1 (3, 1955): 137–138.

A test of Machover's hypothesis concerning the use of the figure drawing test as an indicator of sexual inversion was made by observing the performance of "normals." Of the 18 males and 56 females, none of whom showed any observable problem of homosexuality, who were used, 90 percent of the males and 68 percent of the females drew their own sex first.

The results supported Machover's hypothesis, since if people without observable problems in sexual identification draw their own sex first, then people who draw the opposite sex first are deviating from the norm. The large percentage of females who drew figures of the opposite sex first indicates that females may often identify with males in our culture.

393   FREEMAN, THOMAS. "Clinical and Theoretical Observations on Male Homosexuality." *International Journal of Psycho-Analysis* 36 (4–5, 1955): 335–347.

Observations based on clinical material drawn from two sets of patients, three suffering primarily from inhibitions of genital potency and three from overt homosexuality, are presented. The patients' ages were from 22 to 39 years and all were under treatment from seven months to two years. Freud's views are confirmed, in that there is nothing specific about the psychological factors to be found in cases of male homosexuality (that is, similar constitutional, environmental, and psychological forces are found in "normals" also). It is suggested that the "masculine protest" of homosexual patients has a defensive function protecting them from an underlying passive femininity of which they are afraid. It is also unlikely that there is a specific "homosexual ego." The more disturbed the early childhood experiences the more abnormal the ego will be, and this need not be accompanied by a manifest masculinity. It is also possible for homosexuality to occur in the presence of a relatively intact ego.

394   FREUD, SIGMUND. "A Letter from Freud." 1951. Reprinted as "Letter to an American Mother." In *The Problem of Homosexuality in Modern Society,* edited by Hendrik M. Ruitenbeck, pp. 1–2. New York: E. P. Dutton & Co., 1963.

In a letter from Freud to a woman who had written him concerning her son's homosexuality, he explains that homosexuality is "a variation of the sexual function produced by a certain arrest of sexual development" and not a vice, an illness, or a degradation.

The result of treatment cannot be predicted. In some cases it is possible to develop "the blighted germs of heterosexual tendencies, which are present in every homosexual," but analysis is more likely to relieve neurotic conflicts whether the patient remains homosexual or becomes heterosexual.

395   FREUND, KURT. "Diagnosing Homo- or Heterosexuality and Erotic Age-Preference by Means of a Psychophysiological Test." *Behaviour Research and Therapy* 5 (3, 1967): 209–228.

Further evidence was presented for the theory that erotic preference can be diagnosed by measuring penis changes in subjects exposed to erotic stimuli, e.g., color photographs of nude men, women, and children. The subjects were 27 heterosexual and 20 homosexual pedophiliacs, 23 homosexuals who preferred adolescents, 25 homosexuals who preferred adults, and 35 heterosexual controls. The patients were shown photographs of nude men, women, and children in a fixed, randomly selected order. Penile volumetry was recorded. Prior to the tests the patients were given injections of testosterone. The report concentrated on the diagnostic interpretations of the testing procedures, establishing standards for homo-heterosexual distinctions and age preferences. Individual cases where results were ambiguous were described in some detail. No conclusions were reached since the samples were considered an inaccurate representation of any wide-based population.

396   FREUND, KURT. "Erotic Preference in Pedophilia." *Behaviour Research and Therapy* 5 (4, 1967): 339–348.

How can the erotic object preference of male pedophiliacs, ephebophiliacs, androphiliacs, and normals be ascertained? This study sought to distinguish the relative importance of sex-specific versus sexually neutral signs in the determination of erotic age preference. Three hypotheses were tested. Pedophiliacs show reactions to sexually neutral features of somatic maturity which are different from those of men who have an erotic preference for adults. Pedophilia is based upon a preference for sex-specific signs of an attenuated character. Pedophilia is based upon an aversion to certain sex-specific signs found in adults but not in children.

The subjects were 27 heterosexual and 20 homosexual pedophiliacs, 23 ephebophiliacs, 25 androphiliacs, and 35 men in whom there was no reason to suspect any abnormality of erotic preference. Measurement was made of penis volume changes in response to 60 color photographs of nude men, women, and children of both sexes.

In homosexual pedophiliacs, the child of the nonpreferred sex was preferred, in contrast to the findings with androphiliacs where female children were least preferred. A similar trend was found in the comparison of heterosexual pedophiliacs and normals. In each subject group, except that of the normals, the age group in the nonpreferred sex attaining the highest rank corresponded to the age group of the most preferred object. The results argued against the validity of any hypothesis which attempts to explain pedophilia solely on the basis of preference for or aversion to particular sex-specific signs. The desirability of exploring further the role of sexually neutral signs is indicated.

397   FREUND, KURT. "Laboratory Differential Diagnosis of Homo- and Heterosexuality: An Experiment with Faking." *Review of Czechoslovak Medicine* 7 (1, 1961): 20–31.

Attempts were made to verify the usefulness of previously reported methods for diagnosing male homosexuality by the measurement of penis changes related to visual stimulation.

In the first experiment 39 homosexuals and 31 neurotics were used. The homosexuals either had been under medical observation for some time or had admitted their homosexuality. The neurotic men were patients in the university hospital with no record of homosexuality. The second experiment involved a test of induced faking, using 40 heterosexual and 24 homosexual men.

The visual stimuli consisted of a series of erotic photographs of male or female subjects of varying ages. Part of the test was aimed at determining if the technique could discriminate the age of the desired partner for the subject.

The tests did discriminate between homosexuals and heterosexuals (p < .01). However, the tests failed to show any significant results with respect to the preferred age of sex partners. In the second experiment, the experimenters were able to develop a set of diagnostic criteria for determining faked responses. The usefulness of these procedures for diagnosing cases of suspected faked homosexuality on the part of military draftees is discussed.

398   FREUND, KURT. "A Laboratory Method for Diagnosing Predominance of Homo- or Hetero-erotic Interests in the Male." *Behaviour Research and Therapy* 1 (1, 1963): 85–93.

A study was conducted to determine if volume changes of the male genital while the patient viewed potentially erotic objects could be useful in diagnosing sexual deviations. The subjects were 123 patients at the Charles University Psychiatric Hospital in Prague. Fifty-eight of the patients were exclusively homosexual, and 65 were exclusively heterosexual. Of the homosexuals 26 had erotic preference for adults, 25 for adolescents, and seven for children. Of the heterosexuals 24 were normal, five had erotic preference for adolescents, and five for children. The patients' ages ranged from 16 to 60. A second group of subjects consisted of 31 neurotic patients who were normal heterosexuals, 25 homosexual men who were interested in adults, and 14 homosexual men who desired adolescents or children.

In testing both groups, the method consisted of showing the patients photographs of nude men, women, and children, and then measuring changes in penile volume. The photos shown to the second group included more photos of women and children. The patients were given injections of testosterone and were made to ingest wine and caffeine.

For the first group only one of 77 usable "tracings" (the graph of penile volume change) differed from the case history diagnosis. Some tracings were described as obvious attempts to fake homosexuality by young men facing military service. The differentiation of erotic preference for men, women, and children was also significant with certain categories of homosexuals and heterosexuals (p < .05). The results were substantiated by the second group, and some improvement in testing was accomplished.

399   FREUND, KURT; DIAMANT, J.; and PINKAVA, V. "On the Validity and Reliability of the Phalloplethysmographic (Php) Diagnosis of Some Sexual Deviations." *Review of Czechoslovak Medicine* 4 (2, 1958): 145–151.

To determine if sexual deviations can be diagnosed through measuring the genitals of male subjects viewing certain types of pictures, a sample of 123 hospitalized male patients was used. Fifty-eight of the patients were exclusively or almost exclusively homosexual, and 65 were exclusively or almost exclusively heterosexual. The ages of the group ranged from 16 to 60 years.

Phalloplethysmographic (Php) measurements of the patients' sexual organs were obtained while they viewed 40 colored photographs of nude male and female figures varying in age from children to adults. The statistical tests used were the binomial and the Mann-Whitney. It was found that 76 out of 77 subjects showing marked increases in Php measurements were correctly predicted from a knowledge of their sexual status; i.e., knowing the Php results from viewing the pictures almost perfectly predicted the sexual inclination of each person.

400   FREY, EGON C. "Dreams of Male Homosexuals and the Attitude of Society." *Journal of Individual Psychology* 18 (1, 1962): 26–34.

Characteristic dreams of homosexuals are interpreted, and the hidden anxiety caused by social discrimination is revealed. The dreams are also viewed as confirming "certain findings by Adler: the tendency of the homosexual to degrade the other sex, the harmful influence of discouraging childhood experiences, and of an effeminating environment." The progress or ineffectiveness of therapy could also be seen in the dreams. A closing plea is made to change the laws which make the "androphile" homosexual, or one who has only adult love partners, a criminal.

401   FRIBERG, RICHARD ROY. "Measures of Homosexuality: Cross-Validation of Two MMPI Scales and Implications for Usage." *Journal of Consulting Psychology* 31 (1, 1967): 88–91.

A cross-validation study was made of the work of J. H. Panton who had used the Minnesota Multiphasic Personality Inventory M-F Scale for evaluating homosexuality in groups within a psychiatric population. The potential usefulness of the MMPI Scale HSX as a measure of general sexual deviancy in such populations was also explored.

The subjects were 19 homosexuals from a psychiatric hospital, 16 nonhomosexual sexual deviates from a psychiatric hospital, 67 general abnormals, and 50 normals.

Although Panton's work was supported, the use of the scales as an aid in individual description and classification did not appear to be justified. Of interest was the finding that neither a high educational level appeared to be a significant factor in raising M-F and HSX scores within a homosexual group of patients, nor did educational level or intelligence appear to lead to elevated scores on those scales among hospitalized male schizophrenics.

402   FRIBERG, RICHARD ROY. "A Study of Homosexuality and Related Characteristics in Paranoid Schizophrenia." Ph.D. dissertation, University of Minnesota, 1964, 143 pp.

In a test of the hypothesized link between homosexuality and paranoid disorders, the frequency of homosexuality and related variables in paranoid schizophrenia is compared to their frequency in other types of schizophrenia. Data were gathered through hospital records and Minnesota Multiphasic Personality Inventory records on paranoid and nonparanoid schizophrenics in a single hospital. The hypothesis was not upheld, and it was concluded that the psychoanalytic formulation of the relation between homosexuality and paranoia is without foundation.

403　FRIEND, MAURICE R.; SCHIDDEL, LOUISE; KLEIN, BETTY; and DUNAEFF, DOROTHY. "Observations on the Development of Transvestitism in Boys." *American Journal of Orthopsychiatry* 24 (3, 1954): 563–575.

Clinical observations of three cases of transvestitism in boys are reported. "Special stress is placed upon the pathological mother-child relationship with marked evidence of separation anxiety and primitive identification processes, occurring before the onset of the phallic period." From the clinical material transvestite play in children appeared to be the result of an identification with a phallic mother as a means of handling a severe castration threat. Special importance is placed upon the traumatic significance of early object identification with both mother and father figures. The idea that transvestitism in children is a transitional symptom in homosexual development is also discussed.

404　GADPAILLE, WARREN J. "Homosexual Experience in Adolescence." *Medical Aspects of Human Sexuality* 2 (10, 1968): 29–38.

The number of homosexuals in the population has been overestimated because of a failure to recognize a distinction between casual and sporadic homosexual experience during adolescence and such activity which comes about when an individual is motivated exclusively or preferentially to seek active sexual gratification with a member of the same sex.

Casual and sporadic homosexual activity is common among adolescents of both sexes. Generally it is not clinically significant and should be seen rather as a temporary defense against the fears associated with the move toward full heterosexual relationships. In many instances, homosexual activity is merely a safe form of sexual experimentation and exploration, and even though partners are involved, the experience itself is self-centered in that what is really important is what the adolescents are learning about their own feelings and sensations.

When homosexual activity occurs right after puberty it may be viewed as age-specific, even age-appropriate. Sometimes, however, adolescents will continue such activity into adulthood, and instead of finding heterosexual outlets, will develop a homosexual orientation. It is difficult to predict which adolescents will settle into a homosexual pattern, but factors which aid in making such a determination are age and frequency of occurrence and the nature of the homosexual experience, specific situational influences, developmental evidence of sex identity and sex-appropriate behavior, the "in love" phenomenon, and the nature of the family interactions. "Age alone is not a very helpful differential criterion. . . . [But] the later in adolescence homosexual activity occurs or continues, the more likely it is to have prognostic significance."

405   GARMA, ANGEL. "The Psychosomatic Shift through Obesity, Migraine, Peptic Ulcer, and Myocardial Infarction in a Homosexual." *International Journal of Psycho-Analysis* 49 (2-3, 1968): 241–245.

The case of an obese 39-year-old homosexual and his regressive level of sexuality, which was expressed by migraine attacks, a peptic ulcer, and a myocardial infarction, is reported. The patient's symptoms are discussed in relation to his homosexual behavior. His obesity developed as the result of an unconscious desire to be stuffed by a mother or by a persecutory maternal breast to keep him immobile and imprisoned, as though in the womb.

The migraine attacks began during puberty when the patient first initiated his practice of homosexuality. His headache was the organic expression of thoughts of impotence and of homosexuality, to which he was fixated. His ulcer became manifest at age 30 after practicing fellatio for some time. He felt that his penis was a knife retained in his stomach which cut him and made his mouth bleed. He attempted to calm the oral sensations by consuming highly indigestible food and by spitting.

The patient's shift from an ulcer to infarction was effected by the death of a brother-in-law caused by a myocardial infarction which, in turn, revived childhood memories of the death of a grandmother from the same cause. He became more independent of his parents and more adventurous in his genitality. In situations of conflict, he no longer ate harmful food, but instead undertook exhausting, muscular activity, finally suffering an infarction of the cardiac muscle.

The organic lesions, the patient's ulcer and infarction, held the meaning of genital castration which, owing to his regression from an oral-digestive to anal-sadistic level, took place in organs which had acquired secondary genital significance.

406   GAYLIN, WILLARD M. "The Homosexual Act as a Symptom." *Psychiatry Digest* 25 (Dec., 1964): 25–30.

The great number of purposes for which the homosexual act may be exploited indicates that it is a symptom and not a disease in itself. The homosexual act can be compared to compulsive hand-washing, eating, and other ritualistic behavior which allays unconscious anxiety. This view allows us to apply the knowledge psychiatry and psychoanalysis have about the nature of symptoms and their formation and dissipation to homosexuality.

407   GEIL, GEORGE A. "The Goodenough Test as Applied to Adult Delinquents." *Journal of Clinical Psychopathology* 9 (1, 1948): 62–82.

The drawings of male figures made by 1,000 subjects at the Medical Center for Federal Prisoners in Springfield, Missouri, were evaluated. Evaluations were made on variables such as primitivity and maturity, clothing, posturing, and femininity. This study indicated that nearly half of the known homosexuals projected feminine characteristics onto their male figure drawings. The homosexual groups' tendencies on the other variables are reported and briefly discussed.

408   GEIL, GEORGE A. "The Use of the Goodenough Test for Revealing Male Homosexuality." *Journal of Clinical Psychopathology and Psychotherapy* 6 (1944): 307–321.

The Goodenough Draw-a-Man Test was used in this attempt to determine whether drawing a man with feminine characteristics would prove significant in the detection of homosexuality. Slight body size and the presence of breasts were the criteria for judging whether the drawing had feminine characteristics.

Observers who did not know the subjects selected the 16 most feminine and 16 most masculine figures from a collection of 801 drawings. Case histories of the persons who had drawn these extremely feminine and extremely masculine figures were examined for evidence of homosexual behavior. Among those who drew the feminine figures, 13 of the 16 were confirmed as homosexuals; among those who drew the masculine figures, only one was confirmed as a homosexual, another was suspected to be homosexual and the case histories of the rest provided no evidence of homosexuality.

The findings reveal that many sex deviants will project their homosexual tendencies in a pictoral representation of a male adult figure. Not all known homosexuals will depict a male with female features, but in those who do, it is a significant indication that there is a female component present in the personality structure of that individual.

409   GERSHMAN, HARRY. "Considerations of Some Aspects of Homosexuality." *American Journal of Psychoanalysis* 13 (1953): 82–83.

Homosexuality is an experiential phenomenon rather than the expression of an underlying biological or physiological need. It is a symptom of underlying psychological pathology rather than the expression of an independent impulse. Homosexuality is an expression of faulty inter- and intra-psychic processes which originate in the person's early life and are perpetuated by unresolved inner conflicts. Homosexuals are alienated people who are sadistic and masochistic, have feelings of emptiness and boredom, repress much emotion, and are marked by massive resignation. The main determinants, which can be influenced by constitutional factors (a temperamental quality), of the choice of these symptoms are the experiences the individual has had.

410   GERSHMAN, HARRY. "Homosexuality and Some Aspects of Creativity." *American Journal of Psychoanalysis* 24 (1, 1964): 29–38.

Are homosexuals more creative than heterosexuals? Creativity is an attribute of man and all men are creative. It is not rooted in psychopathology, but emerges from man's need to relate to the world around him. Creativity can be restricted and inhibited by these psychopathological processes. Since psychopathology is integrated into personality structure it therefore influences creativity. Sexuality and creativity are causally unrelated and represent and express differing aspects of personality and behavior. Homosexuality is psychopathologic and hence there is no association between it and creativity, although in some instances it may favor or channelize creativity.

411   GIBBENS, T. C. N. "The Sexual Behaviour of Young Criminals." *Journal of Mental Science* 103 (432, 1957): 527–540.

The past and present sexual behavior of 200 young Borstal prison inmates (ages 16 to 21) is described and related to their previous criminal behavior. Case histories taken during routine psychiatric interviews were studied, and the behavior of the inmates during commitment was observed. Total sex drive, masturbation, heterosexual behavior, and homosexual behavior were considered. Wherever possible, tentative comparisons were made with nondelinquents.

A general difference which was noted between the delinquent and nondelinquent groups is that sexual behavior of all kinds begins earlier and is more vigorous among the delinquents, but that after this early and active start much of the physical and sociosexual activity is given up and the nondelinquent group catches up and often passes the delinquent group in total sexual activity.

Although it was felt that the inmates probably suppressed mention of their homosexual experiences, it was determined that 50 of the 200 had homosexual problems of varying intensity. When this group of 50 was compared with the remainder of the cases, it was found that boys with homosexual problems were more likely to have had histories of neurotic symptoms and psychiatric treatment; their verbal intelligence measured higher than their performance intelligence; and fewer had major physical disabilities. No significant connection was found between homosexual experience and disturbed relationships to siblings, truancy, convictions for violent offense, or having a broken home.

412   GIBBINS, R. J., and WALTERS, R. H. "Three Preliminary Studies of a Psychoanalytic Theory of Alcohol Addiction." *Quarterly Journal of Studies on Alcohol* 21 (4, 1960): 618–641.

Three experiments which attempted to discover whether a link exists between alcoholism and repressed homosexuality were carried out using alcoholic patients, homosexuals, and a control group. The subjects, instrumentation, and procedures of each experiment are described in some detail. All of the experiments involved measuring subjects' visual recognition thresholds in response to masculine-feminine pictures or in response to homosexual, neutral, or male anatomy words. In two of the three experiments the responses of the alcoholics fell between those of the homosexual and the normal subjects. While the experiments did not provide strong evidence for a psychoanalytic theory linking alcoholism and homosexuality, the results from this limited study suggest that further investigations should be made.

413   GIDE, ANDRÉ. *Corydon*. New York: Farrar, Straus, 1950, 220 pp.

In the form of four Socratic dialogues, a philosophical inquiry is formulated into the nature and moral character of homosexuality. Theorizing that homosexuality is not biologically abnormal, unnatural, or wrong, evidence of homosexuality in many animal species is cited. Since the sexual drive of males greatly exceeds that of females, males are naturally attracted to each other. A commentary by Frank Beach on the second dialogue brings the reader up to date on some of the biological and anthropological information which is presented.

414   GIESE, HANS. "Differences in the Homosexual Relations of Man and Woman." *International Journal of Sexology* 7 (4, 1954): 225–227.

Differences in sex are products of cultural differentiation, so there must be a distinction between primary and secondary differences in sex. Primary differences are those which present themselves in a distinct sexual situation only. Secondary differences are those giving rise to a changing adaptation and way of life. These differences in sex manifest themselves in homosexuality with regard to bodily sexual practice (anatomical possibilities in sexual intercourse are different and so are psychological considerations—tenderness is important in relations between females and sexual satisfaction is more important in relations between men). With regard to the legal aspects of homosexuality, it is stated that if both the sexes are formally and legally given equality regarding their rights and duties, then, since the woman has a right to participate in lesbian practices, the man must be given the same right. Or, if the man is legally bound to abstain from homosexual practices, the woman should be similarly restricted. It is concluded that the only right way to check homosexual conduct is to give homosexuality the benefit of legal protection.

415   GILBERT, S. F. "Homosexuality and Hypnotherapy." *British Journal of Medical Hypnotism* 5 (3, 1954): 2–7.

Homosexuals can be classified as "pure," heterosexual, or latent types, or as "male partners." The "pure" type is found to be related to parental domination to an extreme degree and to an unusual dependency upon the mother long after the conclusion of childhood. This type of homosexual displays more feminine than masculine characteristics which are reflected in his dependent and passive behaviors. Another etiological factor associated with this type is an overstimulation during infancy of the analerotic zone. The heterosexual type is more masculine in his behaviors, and yet even his sexual identity is not very firmly established. Although he may be married, it is not unusual for such a person to engage in extramarital homosexual behaviors. The latent type is often found in males who cannot accept whatever feminine characteristics they possess and whose uncertainty is often reflected in a strong aversion toward those who engage in homosexual acts. The "male partner" is one whose sexual drive is so strong that the sex of his partner is of no consequence. Sometimes his sexual behaviors involve the search for new thrills and with little regard for their social consequence.

In a discussion of the use of hypnotherapy with each of the above types, it is believed that the "pure" homosexual is most amenable to hypnotherapy and that the "male partners" are least likely to respond to such treatment. It is argued that "pure" homosexuals should not be punished for activities which are symptomatic of a more general personality disturbance but that the "male partner" should be treated as a criminal and penalized to the full extent of the law.

416   GILDEA, EDWIN F., and ROBINS, LEE N. "Suggestions for Research in Sexual Behavior." In *Determinants of Human Sexual Behavior,* edited by George Winokur, pp. 193–194. Springfield, Ill.: Charles C. Thomas, 1963.

Since research findings concerning the determination of sexual identification are sometimes contradictory, it is suggested that certain of these studies be repeated. Before this is done, specific criteria for determining sexual identification, psychiatric health or illness, and the degree of homosexual interest should be established.

417   GILLESPIE, W. H. "Notes on the Analysis of Sexual Perversions." *International Journal of Psycho-Analysis* 33 (4, 1952): 397–402.

"What characterizes perversion and makes it different from neurosis or psychosis is a special technique of exploiting the mechanism of splitting of the ego, by which the pervert avoids psychosis, since a part of his ego continues to accept reality and to behave fairly normally in the nonsexual sphere. The split allows his mind to function on two levels at once: the pregenital, oral-sadistic level corresponding to psychosis, and the phallic level, where his conscious mental content bears so much resemblance to the repressed content of the neurotic."

418   GLICK, BURTON S. "Homosexual Panic: Clinical and Theoretical Considerations." *Journal of Nervous and Mental Disease* 129 (1, 1959): 20–28.

An attempt is made to define and understand the concept "homosexual panic." "Acute homosexual panic is an acute schizophrenic reaction, usually temporary in duration, displaying the full panoply of schizophrenic symptoms accompanied by sensations of intense terror manifesting themselves in wild excitement or catatonic paralysis. It is based upon the patient's fear of loss of control of unconscious wishes to offer himself as a homosexual object which he feels will result in the most dire consequences."

419   GLOVER, EDWARD. "The Social and Legal Aspects of Sexual Abnormality." *Medico-Legal and Criminological Review* 13 (3, 1945): 133–148.

Roles played by medicine and law in dealing with sexual offenders are discussed. Although both are concerned with the diagnosis, prevention, and treatment of disorders, medical science is primarily concerned with the individual's health, while law is concerned with the community's well-being.

With regard to problems concerning sexual behavior, it is important to recognize that unconscious fantasies arise from the child's frustrated impulses during early sexual development (autoerotic impulses and the Oedipus situation, for example), and that sexual and psychoneurotic disorders can form if these fantasies are reactivated in later life. Adult neuroses are built on infantile neuroses, and adolescent and adult sexual disorders "serve the function of attempting to cure earlier disordered functions." Since sexual disorders are forms of mental illness, sexual offenders should be given psychological examinations and have the option of receiving treatment. These examinations should not be performed by a psychologist officially connected with the court.

Treatment and prevention of sexual offenses must be approached from "the point of view of sexual pathology and social expediency." Society must protect itself from acts of public indecency but it does not have the right to "punish" psychological disorders. Society is intolerant and "regressive" in its attitudes toward aberrant sexual behavior.

A discussion of the paper by doctors present at its presentation is appended. Comments include a discussion of sexual offenders in prison, success of treatment, and aggressive impulses.

420   GLUECK, BERNARD C., JR. "An Evaluation of the Homosexual Offender." *Minnesota Law Review* 41 (2, 1957): 187–210.

An evaluation of legal concepts about homosexual offenses and current psychiatric attitudes regarding them is given.

Although no state specifies homosexuality as a crime by that name, homosexual acts are usually prohibited under the name of sodomy or crimes against nature. Also, although the criminal statutes and special sex legislation apply in theory to both male and female homosexuals, several states have statutes which do not apply to female homosexuals. As Kinsey found, not one female had been convicted in the United States for homosexual activity up to 1952. Sodomy laws are complicated by the fact that they also apply to heterosexual relations even between married couples. The New York State Sex Delinquency Research Committee (1955), studying sex offenders, found in its study that the parents of offenders had failed to reward their children for obedience, but instead had punished them continuously or used the threat of punishment to control their behavior. Thus the children failed to internalize processes of conformity and consequently lacked feelings of self-esteem and pride, which resulted in very low self-appraisals as adults. Defects in the operation of conscience result, so that any control over their behavior must be external to them. In this study it was found that 79 percent of the homosexual offenders were diagnosed as having some type of schizophrenic illness.

421 GLUECK, BERNARD C., JR. "Psychodynamic Patterns in the Homosexual Sex Offender." *American Journal of Psychiatry* 112 (8, 1956): 584–590.

In order to describe some of the psychodynamic factors in the homosexual pedophile, 30 homosexual pedophiles and 30 rapists at Sing Sing Prison were studied. Fifty prisoners convicted of nonsexual offenses were used as controls. Psychiatric evaluations were made, and the Blacky Pictures, the Wechsler-Bellevue Intelligence Scale, the Rorschach, the Thematic Apperception Test, and the House-Tree-Person Test were administered.

The following characteristics were noted among the sex offenders: 76 percent of the homosexual pedophiles used a schizophrenic adaptation; there was a marked fear of approaching an adult female sex object, with corresponding genital elimination factors; there was a serious impairment of the capacity for abstract thinking, with impaired ability to utilize fantasy, et cetera, as an outlet for sexual conflicts and tensions; and there was a serious impairment of conscience formation, and resultant impairment of the restraining effects of conscience on overt behavior.

Organic therapies, especially electroshock, are described.

422 GOLDFRIED, MARVIN R. "On the Diagnosis of Homosexuality from the Rorschach." *Journal of Consulting Psychology* 30 (4, 1966): 338–349.

The validity of H. M. Wheeler's approach to diagnosing male homosexuality by means of the Rorschach is considered. The literature on research findings related to the topic is reviewed. Six of the 20 Wheeler signs (1, 3, 4, 5, 6, 14) have very low validity; only six are unquestionably useful (7, 8, 10, 16, 17, 20); and the remaining eight (2, 6, 11, 12, 13, 15, 18, 19) are of uncertain validity. Therefore, although the findings based on Wheeler's indices are questionable, it is believed that the test is generally valid and that it can be used to distinguish overt homosexual males from those not indicating any sign of homosexuality. He suggests that a restructuring of the indices is needed along with reliable tests of statistical significance to firmly establish the validity for the Rorschach when used for these purposes. The main value of the Rorschach is in revealing those individuals who are troubled by homosexuality.

423 GRAMS, ARMIN, and RINDER, LAWRENCE. "Signs of Homosexuality in Human-Figure Drawings." *Journal of Consulting Psychology* 22 (5, 1958): 394.

To test the validity of the 15 signs in human figure drawing which Karen Machover lists as predictive of homosexuality, a study using the drawing tests was made with 50 adolescent subjects. The subjects, inmates of a state training school, were divided into two groups which were matched for age, I.Q., race, and education.

Each subject drew a person and then drew another person of the sex opposite that of the first figure drawn. Three psychologists then rated the drawings for the purported homosexual signs. None of the signs proved to have either individual or collective validity.

424 GRAUER, DAVID. "Homosexuality and the Paranoid Psychoses as Related to the Concept of Narcissism." *Psychoanalytic Quarterly* 24 (4, 1955): 516–526.

Freud's theory that latent homosexuality is closely related to paranoia was examined and found to be unconfirmed in the literature. Freud's entire theory of the etiology of paranoia rests upon his concept of narcissism, in which the libido is withdrawn from objects and turned on one's self. In paranoia the person supposedly tries to free himself from this state, but is not able to go beyond his homosexual fixations. The delusions of paranoids are expressions of homosexual impulses or of defensive mechanisms.

A challenge of this view could result in seeing no logical necessity for regarding paranoia as primarily an expression of latent homosexuality. Using the conceptualization of ego psychology, it is possible to interpret the eruption of homosexual impulses in paranoids as the consequence of a breakdown in ego integration and ego identity.

425 GRAUER, DAVID. "Homosexuality in Paranoid Schizophrenia as Revealed by the Rorschach Test." *Journal of Consulting Psychology* 18 (6, 1954): 459–462.

In "A Study of the Freudian Theory of Paranoia by Means of the Rorschach Test" published in the *Journal of Projective Techniques* in 1952, M. L. Aronson reported that the Rorschach records of paranoid psychotics contain evidence of a higher degree of a homosexual tendency than those of nonparanoid psychotics. To test these findings a study was made of 31 paranoid schizophrenics in a psychiatric ward of a Veterans Administration hospital. The average age of the subjects was 28; their average I.Q. was 100; and their average educational level was the completion of 10 grades. Their Rorschach records were scored for homosexual content by means of Wheeler's signs.

A comparison of the records of this study's paranoid schizophrenics and Aronson's nonparanoid psychotics revealed no statistically reliable difference. Homosexual tendencies, as measured by Wheeler's signs, had no prognostic significance for the group in the more recent study. The results of this study were related instead to certain clinical findings.

426   GREEN, RICHARD, and MONEY, JOHN. "Stage-Acting, Role-Taking, and Effeminate Impersonation during Boyhood." *Archives of General Psychiatry* 15 (5, 1966): 535–538.

The primacy between acting and homosexuality exists from an early age, because acting tendencies can be found in early childhood in boys who also display effeminate behavior to a considerable degree. The subjects were 20 prepubertal boys (aged three to 13 years), referred by physicians, educators, or clinics at Johns Hopkins because of symptoms of effeminacy. Homosexual genital behavior was not a requirement. Six- to 10-hour interviews were conducted with follow-up interviews given at yearly intervals for a period of one to eight years.

In nine of the boys, prior to puberty there was seen a striking capacity for role-taking and stage-acting. This is significant because of the alleged high incidence of homosexuality among actors. The data indicate that this is not due solely to the theater offering such persons a social haven in later years. "The path toward acting begins at a time in life when social acceptance and safety of the theater would not yet be apparent to the boy concerned."

427   GREENSON, RALPH R. "On Homosexuality and Gender Identity." *International Journal of Psycho-Analysis* 45 (2–3, 1964): 217–219.

It is proposed that a study of gender identity will offer valuable insights into some of the special problems concerning the fate of homosexuality in various types of patients. For most psychiatric patients the appearance of homosexuality in their treatment stirs up a peculiar kind of dread—a threat to their gender identity (it seems that only bisexuals and overt homosexuals have no anxiety about their gender identity). The neurotic adult reacts as though the gender of his sexual object determines his own gender.

The development of gender identity begins when the child becomes aware of the differences between the sexes. It is brought about by his own awareness of the anatomical and physiological structures in himself, by the manner in which the parental and social figures label him in accordance with his sexual structures and others in accordance with theirs, and by a biological force which seems to be present from birth and which can be decisive in pushing a child in the direction of a particular gender. Thus, there are three different phases: "I am me, John"; "I am me, John, a boy"; and, "I am me, John, a boy, which means that I like to do sexual things with girls." The only adults who seem to be able to dispense with this diversity in gender between self and the love object are the homosexual inverts. Some of them remain fixated at phase two and thus their sense of gender identity is independent of the sex of the love object.

428 GREENSPAN, HERBERT, and CAMPBELL, JOHN D. "The Homosexual as a Personality Type." *American Journal of Psychiatry* 101 (5, 1945): 682–689.

The homosexual personality is a psychopathological type. The true homosexual possesses certain identifying and consistent traits which clearly differentiate him from other personalities with which he has been classified. He is average or above average in intelligence; he frequently has aesthetic interests; he likes dealing in the abstract, probably on an emotional level; he enjoys music and is fond of the arts. Emotionally like the average woman, the homosexual develops an egocentric, subtle, and satirical attitude.

429 GRYGIER, TADEUSZ G. "Homosexuality, Neurosis and 'Normality': A Pilot Study in Psychological Measurement." *British Journal of Delinquency* 9 (1, 1958): 59–61.

In order to determine the personality attributes of neurotic homosexuals as compared with nonhomosexual neurotics, the Dynamic Personality Inventory (DPI) was administered to 20 male neurotics with known homosexual histories, 22 male neurotics with no evidence of homosexuality, and 33 men and 42 women who were considered "normal."

The DPI is a useful research tool for the study of homosexuality and neurosis. The relationship between them is complex, and more research is needed to confirm the tentative findings of this study (especially a study of nonneurotic homosexuals).

In many respects the neurotic homosexuals are similar to other neurotics; some of these characteristics are similar to those of the normal feminine personality. The homosexual group differed significantly from other neurotics with respect to passivity, narcissism, and a need for warmth, comfort, and support, and they showed a typically feminine pattern of behavior. The homosexuals also showed a typically feminine pattern of interests and attitudes and had a normal capacity for social role-taking; but tended to take feminine rather than masculine roles.

430 GRYGIER, TADEUSZ G. "Psychometric Aspects of Homosexuality." *Journal of Mental Science* 103 (432, 1957): 514–525.

Some attempts at measuring the psychological characteristics of the homosexual and the direction and intensity of his impulses are described. These include personality inventories, semantic tests, perceptual projective tests, and tests of interpersonal relations (sentence-completion, drawing-completion, et cetera).

It appears that no exact measures of the direction of sexual attraction are available at the present time. Projective techniques, especially the Draw-a-Person Test, Rorschach, and thematic tests give some indication of homosexual attraction, but the validity of the indicators is uncertain.

The concepts of masculinity and femininity are not always understood. The usual technique used to measure masculinity and femininity is the questionnaire, but more comprehensive tests, such as the Terman-Miles or those measuring personality in development terms, may be more promising.

431   HADER, MARVIN. "Homosexuality as Part of Our Aging Process."
       Psychiatric Quarterly 40 (3, 1966): 515–524.

The amount of homosexuality among male inmates of an old-age home is reported. Twenty-three Jewish males, 73 to 94 years old, served as subjects. The controls were 23 elderly Jewish women, also residents of the institution. The amount of heterosexual and homosexual activity of the subjects was recorded through psychiatric interviews, medical examinations, and interviews with neighbors, relatives, and rabbis in addition to the personnel of the institution.

Homosexuality appears to increase in old age among men. Dreams, friendships, and themes expressed during interviews with the male subjects all tended to be homosexually oriented. For the women controls, their friends were also women, but their dreams and expressed themes in interviews tended to be heterosexual. Male homosexuality is seen as possibly supporting the theory that a second adolescence occurs which is accompanied by homosexual interest and activity.

432   HAMBURGER, CHRISTIAN; STÜRUP, GEORG K.; and DAHL-
       IVERSEN, E. "Transvestism: Hormonal, Psychiatric and Surgical
       Treatment." *Journal of the American Medical Association* 152 (5,
       1953): 391–396. Reprinted as "Transvestism." In *The Homosexuals:
       As Seen by Themselves and Thirty Authorities,* edited by Aron M.
       Krich, pp. 293–308. New York: Citadel Press, 1954.

The symptoms, course, and possible origin of true transvestism in males are discussed. True transvestism, or eonism, is considered to be of a psychic and possibly a constitutional origin rather than of a sexual origin. It is very rare in its extreme form and is considered as completely separate from homosexuality. The true male transvestite finds homosexuality repellent and is disturbed whenever he is mistaken as a homosexual. The medical profession, moreover, knows so little about this disease that it is often confused or identified with homosexuality. Disagreement is also expressed with the many psychoanalysts who hold that latent homosexuality is apparent in all cases of transvestism.

433   HAMMER, EMANUEL F. "Relationship between Diagnosis of Psychosexual Pathology and the Sex of the First Drawn Person." *Journal of Clinical Psychology* 10 (2, 1954): 168–170.

The hypothesis that the sex of the first drawn person may be used as an index of sexual identification has been tested a number of times. Results of these studies are conflicting, indicating a need for further testing of the hypothesis. Eighty-four sex offenders imprisoned at Sing Sing Prison served as subjects of a new study. The group consisted of 31 rapists, 33 heterosexual pedophiles, and 20 homosexual pedophiles. The variable of opposite-sex-person-drawn-first was compared by means of Fischer's test across all three groups. The rapist group was used as a control group and no significant difference was found between the rapist and pedophile groups. In conclusion it was noted that "considerable doubt is cast on the projective drawing postulate that the sex of the first figure drawn may serve as an index of the subject's sexual identification or as evidence of psychosexual conflicts of sexual inversion."

434   HARPER, ROBERT ALLAN. "Can Homosexuals Be Changed?" 1960. Reprinted in *The Third Sex*, edited by Isadore Rubin, pp. 67–72. New York: New Book Co., 1961.

Three major psychological components of homosexuality are pointed out: a basic antisexuality or puritanism, a low self-esteem and self-confidence, and a compulsive adherence to a continually reinforced homosexual mode of orgastic satisfaction. Therapy must expose the irrational base of the fears of the opposite sex and their self-defeating nature. "Getting the patient to increase his heterosexuality, rather than focusing attention on his homosexuality, is of primary importance in therapy."

435   HARPER, ROBERT ALLAN. "Psychological Aspects of Homosexuality." In *Advances in Sex Research*, edited by Hugo C. Beigel, pp. 187–197. New York: Harper & Row, 1963.

Three major psychological components of homosexuality are identified as a basic antisexuality in general and heterosexuality in particular, a low personal self-esteem, and a compulsive reinforcement of a homosexual mode of orgastic satisfaction. These three factors are analyzed with frequent reference to actual cases.

436   HART, HENRY HARPER. "Fear of Homosexuality in College Students." In *Psychosocial Problems of College Men*, edited by Bryant

M. Wedge, pp. 200–213. New Haven, Conn.: Yale University Press, 1958.

Comparative methods involving six cases are used to show that a major common factor in students' fears of homosexuality is a relative failure of integrative mechanisms. This ego weakness results from growing up in an atmosphere of parental discord. Only one of the six persons described became a homosexual. The fact that homosexuality is used as a defense against castration anxiety, as well as a stimulus to it, does not differentiate it from other ego defensive mechanisms such as identification, projection, repression, et cetera. When it breaks down as a defense against anxiety, homosexuals often seek cure through psychoanalysis.

437   HARTMAN, BERNARD J. "Comparison of Selected Experimental MMPI Profiles of Sexual Deviates and Sociopaths without Sexual Deviation." *Psychological Reports* 20 (1, 1967): 234.

To obtain findings regarding personality traits which differentiate sexual deviates from sociopaths without sexual deviance, a study was made of 36 state mental hospital patients, 18 of whom were diagnosed as sexual deviates, and 18 as sociopaths without sexual deviance. Experimental scales based upon responses made to the MMPI were used as a basis of comparison. They were as follows: sexual deviation, amorality, social alienation, impulsivity, hostility, personal and emotional sensitivity, ego-strength, control, responsibility, manifest anxiety, and emotional immaturity.

All the patients had scores of 70 *T* or above on the Psychopathic Deviate Scale. Multiple t-tests for related scores yielded no significant values.

438   HASELKORN, HARRY. "The Vocational Interests of a Group of Homosexuals." Ph.D. dissertation, New York University, 1953, 119 pp.

In order to study the relation between personality variables and vocational interests, male homosexuals were chosen as subjects because they were believed to have personalities which were relatively homogeneous. Administering the Strong Vocational Interest Blank and the Kuder Preference Record, it was found that vocational interests of the homosexual group tended to be, like those of females, highest in the cultural, aesthetic, or expressive fields. This tendency held true for both latent and overt homosexuals, although in comparison to the overt group, the latent group tended to have traditional male interests. However, both groups were more inclined toward traditional male interests than the "women in general" group on which the female norms were based.

439   HASELKORN, HARRY. "The Vocational Interests of a Group of Male Homosexuals." *Journal of Counseling Psychology* 3 (1, 1956): 8–11.

Three groups of patients from the Bronx Veterans Administration Hospital were given the Kuder Preference Record and the Strong Vocational Interest Blank. The groups of 20 men each were matched for age, education, and broad areas of employment. The first group was made up of homosexuals; the second group was composed of neuropsychiatric patients (with no evidence of homosexuality in their hospital records); the third group was made up of other patients (nonneuropsychiatric and nonhomosexual). The scores of the groups were compared to see whether homosexuality would affect vocational preference. There were significant differences in only eight of the 75 scales used between the homosexual group and the other two groups. Vocational interests among the homosexuals were high in the cultural, aesthetic, and expressive fields. However, this same trend was found in the control groups. Differences among the three groups were most apparent in the mechanical, scientific, and technical fields.

440   HASTINGS, DONALD W. "A Paranoid Reaction with Manifest Homosexuality." *Archives of Neurology and Psychiatry* 45 (2, 1941): 379–381.

Freud and others indicate that if homosexuality is repressed it may appear in paranoid delusions associated with a schizophrenic syndrome. A case is briefly reported in which homosexuality was not repressed but was simply blocked in its overt expression. It was postulated that when the expression of homosexuality is consciously blocked from its goal and not repressed, the same type of paranoid delusions may be formed, although less intense symptoms may be produced.

441   HEERSEMA, PHILIP H. "Homosexuality and the Physician." *Journal of the American Medical Association* 193 (10, 1965): 815–817.

The physician's responsibility with regard to the problem of homosexuality is discussed. Homosexuality is an illness, not a way of life. It is a medical problem in that it represents an obstructed personality growth engendered by a more or less chronic anxiety state. The homosexual needs psychiatric treatment, and the effectiveness of the treatment depends primarily upon a realistic and an understanding attitude on the part of the physician.

442   HEMPHILL, R. E.; LEITCH, A.; and STUART, J. R. "A Factual Study of Male Homosexuality." *British Medical Journal* (5083, 1958): 1317–1323.

An investigation of 64 male prisoners in England, aged 20 to 61, with an average age of 40.5 years is reported. The prisoners were given physical examinations as well as intelligence and other personality tests. Only minor differences were found between the homosexuals and the normal population. No physical characteristics set them apart, nor did any psychological factors, although the homosexuals did show a stronger interest in art and culture. Estrogen treatment had the effect of diminishing sex drive and relieving the patient of anxiety but did not alter his sexual orientation.

443   HENRY, GEORGE W. *All the Sexes: A Study of Masculinity and Femininity.* Toronto and New York: Rinehart, 1955, 599 pp.

In a psychiatric study of sexual development and adjustment the major argument is that there is no hard and fast division between masculinity and femininity, but that there are many gradations and elements of both in every person. As contributing elements in adjustment, constitutional predisposition, physiological and endocrine factors, anatomical factors, and environmental and psychological factors are considered. Types of adjustment, including homosexuality, are discussed with case examples. Factors influencing the personality development of males and females are indicated, one of the major ones being dominance of the mother or father. Homosexuality is included in the discussion, primarily through case histories of sex offenders and their treatment by the law, social workers, clergymen, and psychiatrists.

444   HERMAN, MORRIS, and WORTIS, S. B. "Aberrant Sex-Behavior in Humans." *Annals of the New York Academy of Science* 47 (art. 5, 1947): 639–645.

Aberrant sex behavior is defined as "sex activity utilized by preference as an end-point in gratification, despite the opportunity and ready availability of heterosexual genital contact." This kind of behavior may be divided into three types—inhibition, augmentation, and deflection of sexual impulses. Homosexuality is described as a deflection of sexual impulses.

Three distinct groups of homosexuals are distinguished: those who have shown manifestations of homosexuality since early childhood, those who developed homosexual tendencies after adolescence, and those who have been able to repress strong homosexual tendencies. Individuals in the first group are almost exclusively homosexual, and it is suggested that the predominant causative factor is constitutional or biological. The second group is usually characterized by individuals showing various admixtures of homosexuality and heterosexuality. The third group, those who have repressed their homosexual tendencies, is characterized by individuals exhibiting certain personality traits such as extreme shyness with members of the same sex, et cetera.

445 HESS, ECKHARD H.; SELTZER, ALLAN, L.; and SHLIEN, JOHN M. "Pupil Response of Hetero- and Homo-sexual Males to Pictures of Men and Women: A Pilot Study." *Journal of Abnormal and Social Psychology* 70 (3, 1965): 165–168.

To see if change in the size of the pupil of the human eye varies with a subject's interest in various pictorial stimuli, a study was made of five heterosexual males and five known homosexual males. Their ages were from 24 to 34 years, and all were of the same educational and social levels. None was in therapy. The subjects were shown 15 slides of nude males and females (paintings and photographs), and their pupil responses were photographed simultaneously.

Each heterosexual male had a greater pupil response (i.e., a greater dilation) when looking at pictures of women than when looking at pictures of men. The homosexual male subjects responded in the opposite direction. Measurement of changes in pupil size permitted clear-cut discrimination between the two groups.

446 HEWITT, CHARLES C. "On the Meaning of Effeminacy in Homosexual Men." *American Journal of Psychotherapy* 15 (4, 1961): 592–602.

The most significant factor specific to homosexuality is effeminacy. The feminine component in homosexual men is usually unconscious, but is essential to union with other males and provides the heterosexual element without which homosexual acts would be revolting or at least unappetizing. Homosexuality should be considered as an impulse which serves a variety of psychologic needs and conflicts. The feminine orientation of homosexual men is first adopted in childhood as a defense against fears and anxieties engendered by an environment which presents masculine activities and attitudes as threatening or unrewarding. The homosexual impulse is usually fostered by a neurosis which is characterized by passivity, compliance, and compulsive self-effacement.

447 HOCH, PAUL H., and ZUBIN, JOSEPH, eds. *Psychosexual Development in Health and Disease.* Proceedings of the 38th Annual Meeting of the American Psychopathological Association, June 1948, in New York City. New York: Grune & Stratton, 1949, 283 pp.

A collection of articles on psychosexual development is presented from the perspectives of zoology and biology, anthropology, clinical psychology and psychoanalysis, and sociology. The articles are on psychosexual development in general, and contain only brief or passing references to homosexuality itself. Kinsey et al. note in preadolescent children a roughly normal distribution of behavior on a heterosexual-homosexual continuum, which then shifts toward heterosexuality during adolescence for both physiological and social reasons. Frank Beach notes the frequency and the apparently satisfactory nature of homosexuality between males in several animal species, particularly primates, and suggests that bisexuality may be the natural pattern. C. S. Ford reports the wide incidence and acceptance cross-culturally of homosexuality. Sandor Rado argues against Freud that there is no inborn desire for members of the same sex. Instead, same-sex activity is an acting-out of male-female activity, seeking to fulfill the male-female design. Gustav Bychowski insists that, despite Kinsey's data which suggests the statistical normality of homosexuality, it is clinically abnormal and is often either evidence of, or in itself, a pathological condition. E. W. Burgess examines homosexuality in terms of attitude and role, instead of erotic attachment and orgasm. The process of sex identification and early experiences affect the development of one's sexual self-concept, which in turn affects behavior.

448   HOLDEN, H. M. "Psychotherapy of a Shared Syndrome in Identical Twins." *British Journal of Psychiatry* 111 (478, 1965): 859–864.

"To demonstrate the remarkable dynamic interaction between one particular set of twins against the background of their own family and in particular, their mother," a case study is presented. The subjects were twin brothers, 32 years old, both practicing homosexuals with a penchant for elderly men.

Both presented themselves for treatment complaining of deep feelings of inferiority. They were taken on for psychotherapy as a joint pair in weekly interviews.

Part of the alleged "identity" of this pair was due to a process of "identification" which kept them shackled together. Each needed to internalize the other so that in this way he could also maintain his close link with their mother. No fresh light has been thrown on the etiology of homosexuality, but it is suggested that similar bonds may exist in other twins, not homosexual in nature, and it is also suggested that an exploration of these ties may be of value in understanding the nature of the "identification" that exists between so many twins.

449   HOLEMAN, R. EUGENE, and WINOKUR, GEORGE. "Effeminate Homosexuality: A Disease of Childhood." *American Journal of Orthopsychiatry* 35 (1, 1965): 48–56.

A controlled study was conducted to ascertain the childhood behavior of effeminate homosexuals. Drawn from a prison population, the subjects were 36 homosexuals (24 of whom were effeminate and 12 noneffeminate) and

25 controls (five facultative—while in prison only—homosexuals and 20 nonhomosexuals). All the subjects were first evaluated on the basis of previous psychiatric diagnoses and with regard to their sexual adjustment. Then all were given a two-and-one-half-hour standardized interview which included sections on family history, sex education, social experience, hetero- and homosexual experience, antisocial behavior, et cetera.

This "systematic study" indicated that effeminate homosexuals exhibited effeminacy before puberty. The effeminate homosexuals reported more effeminate behavior and earlier homosexual episodes as children than did either the noneffeminate homosexuals or the controls. Birth order and age of mother did not differentiate the homosexuals from the controls. Family history revealed two homosexual siblings for the effeminate homosexuals. On the basis of these findings, studies are needed which would ascertain whether or not a genetic etiology is reasonable and, if so, to investigate the mode of transmission.

450   "Homosexuality." *GP* [*General Practitioner*] 16 (4, 1957): 132.

A summary of Norman Reider's address to the California Academy of General Practice, October, 1956, emphasizes the prevalence of homosexuality in America and the symptomatic nature of homosexuality (or fear of it) in some emotional illnesses. Reider's plea for the dispassionate psychological understanding of homosexuals by physicians is also reiterated. See Reider, Norman (no. 759).

451   "Homosexuality and Left-Handedness." *British Medical Journal* (5479, 1966): 91.

It is suggested that although the attempt to train a left-handed child to become right-handed sometimes produces emotional strain or stammering, there is no evidence to indicate that efforts to change inborn left-handedness can cause homosexuality.

452   "Homosexuality and Prostitution." *British Medical Journal* (4954, 1955): 1492–1493, and *British Medical Journal Supplement* (2656, 1955): 165–170.

The main points in a memorandum of evidence on homosexuality and prostitution prepared by a special committee of the Council of the British Medical Association for submission to the Departmental Committee are summarized.

Regarding homosexuality, a distinction is made between "essential homosexuals" whose abnormality is caused either by genetic or by early environmental factors, and persons whose homosexual activity is fairly casual or incidental. The difficulty of estimating the number of homosexuals in Britain is cited, and the present state of the law and the necessity for protecting young people from homosexual assaults is discussed.

See *Homosexuality and Prostitution: A Memorandum of Evidence Prepared by a Special Committee of the Council of the British Medical Association for Submission to the Departmental Committee on Homosexuality and Prostitution.* London: British Medical Association, 1955, 94 pp.

453 HOOKER, EVELYN. "The Adjustment of the Male Overt Homosexual." 1957. Reprinted in *The Problem of Homosexuality in Modern America,* edited by Hendrik M. Ruitenbeek, pp. 141–161. New York: E. P. Dutton & Co., 1963.

A comparative study of personality structure and psychological adjustment was conducted with 30 male homosexuals and 30 male heterosexuals who were matched for age, education, and I.Q. The mean age for the homosexuals was 34.5 and for the heterosexuals was 36.6, with the age for both groups ranging from 25 to 50. The mean I.Q. (Otis) for the homosexuals was 115.4 and for the heterosexuals 116.2, with both groups ranging from 90 to 135. The mean education for the homosexuals was 13.9 years and for the heterosexuals 14.3 years. None of the subjects were in therapy; all but three of the homosexuals had had no heterosexual experience; all but three of the heterosexuals had been exclusively heterosexual beyond adolescence; and there were none with extensive homosexual experience. The subjects were rated a relatively pure 0 or 6 on the Kinsey homosexual-heterosexual scale.

Two judges independently reviewed Rorschach protocols, Thematic Apperception Tests and Make A Picture Story responses. They judged the subjects' adjustment on a 5-point rating scale, and in addition, attempted to distinguish the homosexuals from the heterosexuals with the Rorschach protocols. The percentage of agreement between the judges was reported. The two groups did not differ significantly in ratings received and the homosexuals could not be distinguished from the heterosexuals.

The tentative conclusions are: homosexuality is not a single clinical entity; homosexuality is a deviation in sexual pattern which is still within the normal range psychologically; there is no necessary relation between heterosexual sexual orientation and other aspects of a person's intrapsychic or interpersonal functioning.

454 HOOKER, EVELYN. "The Case of El: A Biography." *Journal of Projective Techniques and Personality Assessment* 25 (3, 1961): 252–267.

El, chosen as a case study for a symposium of the American Psychological Association, was a 30-year-old white male homosexual. An alcoholic, El had attempted suicide six times and had been a patient at mental hospitals three times during the preceding five years. His familial background included a dependent, seductive, and ambivalent mother who had been married three times, a father whom he had never known, and a half-brother with whom he unsuccessfully competed. Since both his stepfathers had served in the Navy, his childhood relationships were repeatedly severed by annual moves. Most of these relationships had involved homosexual activity. When he matured, El worked as a teacher, a bank teller, and an accountant—"straight" and conscientious by day and an alcoholic and homosexual by night. More recently, the trauma of his stormy homosexual relationships had precipitated job losses, depressions, suicide attempts, and increased drinking. According to the article, El's psychological route appeared to be "inevitable."

See Fine (no. 385); Forer (no. 390); Meyer (no. 509); Murray (no. 513); and Shneidman (no. 562 and no. 563).

455   HOOKER, EVELYN. "Male Homosexuality in the Rorschach." *Journal of Projective Techniques* 22 (1, 1958): 33–54.

The assumption that male overt homosexuality can be diagnosed with some confidence by the Rorschach was examined in a study of 30 males. All of the subjects identified themselves as having been exclusively homosexual; they were not currently in psychotherapy; and they gave surface evidence of "normal" adjustment. Wheeler signs (using the Rorschach), clinical judgments, Schafer's content themes of homosexuality, and life history interviews were employed.

Some kinds of homosexual records (anal orientation and feminine emphasis) could be distinguished with certainty, but most could not. The exploration of new signs did not show definite results, although "language quality" warranted further investigation. Without other substantiating evidence the Rorschach failed in a large number of instances.

456   HOOKER, EVELYN. "What Is a Criterion?" *Journal of Projective Techniques* 23 (3, 1959): 278–281.

A commentary in the Symposium on "Current Aspects of the Problem of Validity" emphasizes "validity" in the context of homosexuality. A review of published studies of homosexual and heterosexual responses to the Rorschach and the TAT reiterates the minor clinical differences between the two groups. Rather than trying to ascertain who is a homosexual, it is proposed that more studies be directed toward a definition of the character and range of homosexuality. Homosexuality is a "multi-manifested phenomenon"; the oversimplified concept of a homosexual needs to be reexamined and revised.

457   HOROWITZ, MARDI J. "The Homosexual's Image of Himself."
       Mental Hygiene 48 (2, 1964): 197–201.

Two surveys conducted by the Daughters of Bilitis, a lesbian organization, to obtain data on male and female homosexuality, are reported. Homosexuality referred to self-concepts as well as to sexual practices. In general, overt homosexuals were found to have less conflict about their self-image, whereas latent homosexuals appeared more likely to be subject to conflict and neurosis. It was concluded that homosexuality may be used as an antisocial, antiparental form of acting out, or as a defense against identity diffusion.

458   HOUSTON, LAWRENCE NATHANIEL. "An Investigation of the Relationship between the Vocational Interests and Homosexual Behavior of Institutionalized Youthful Offenders." Ed.D. dissertation, Temple University, 1964, 97 pp.

With the purpose of developing another tool that will aid in the diagnosis of homosexuality, a psychological study of youthful offenders attempts to determine patterns of occupational choice that differentiate between inmates who have been involved in homosexual behavior and those who have not. One hundred and ninety male inmates between the ages of 15 and 21, 80 of whom had been involved in a homosexual act during or prior to commitment, were administered the Draw-a-Person Test, the California Capacity Questionnaire, and the Picture Interest Inventory. Although a significantly greater proportion of those with homosexual experience drew a female as their first figure on the DAP Test, no other differences were noted on this test. The nonhomosexuals scored significantly higher on the CCQ Non-Language scale and were significantly higher on the total I.Q. scale. The homosexuals were different on all of the PII scales except the Esthetic scale. They were high (70th percentile or higher) on the Interpersonal Service, Business, and Verbal scales and low (30th percentile or lower) on the Natural, Mechanical, and Scientific scales.

459   HOUSTON, LAWRENCE NATHANIEL. "Vocational Interest Patterns of Institutionalized Youthful Offenders as Measured by a Nonverbal Inventory." *Journal of Clinical Psychology* 21 (2, 1965): 213–214.

As verbal techniques have been unsuccessful in determining homosexuality, a nonverbal technique was tested on a group of 80 incarcerated young offenders, who had given overt indications of passive homosexual behavior, and on a control group of 110 offenders with no indication of homosexual behavior. Results were: homosexuals drew female figures before drawing male figures, had significantly lower I.Q.'s, and had a characteristic pattern of vocational interests.

460 IVIMEY, MURIEL. "Homosexuality." Summary of a lecture for Auxiliary Council to the Association for the Advancement of Psychoanalysis, 1947. Mimeographed, 4 pp.

A discussion of the etiology of homosexuality and the personality characteristics of homosexuals is presented. Homosexuality is based upon neurotic character disturbances acquired in a person's formative years. The neurotic character traits formed (exaggerated, distorted, highly intensified, and compulsive ways of dealing with people in order to insure safety) become part of the personality, determining character, and resulting in disturbances in human relations. Thus, homosexuality is one type of such disturbance in human relations. The homosexual has basic anxiety and, as a consequence, has compulsive needs for human intimacy. Along with these needs and at variance with them, he has compulsive aggressive tendencies to control, master, and exploit others. These tendencies are compliant, aggressive, and detachment trends. The homosexual's disturbance in sex life is not specifically sexual in origin, but is a symptom, or one of the manifestations of neurosis affecting his personality as a whole.

461 JAMES, ROBERT E. "Precipitating Factors in Acute Homosexual Panic with a Case Presentation." *Quarterly Review of Psychiatry and Neurology* 2 (4, 1947): 530–533.

Acute homosexual panic is briefly described as a state "produced by the inability to repress perverse sexual cravings which are predominantly of a homosexual nature." The homosexuality, however, is not overt but latent, and the panic state comes about as the homosexual feelings press to the surface for expression. Feelings of guilt, and the inability to win group approval in spite of efforts to do so, result in panic. Attacks of panic may be precipitated by anything which impairs the integrity of the ego. The case history of a 22-year-old married, white male musician, whose acute homosexual panic was precipitated by the absence of the love object (an older brother), is presented.

462 JERSILD, JENS. *The Normal Homosexual Male Versus the Boy Molester.* Translated by Eva Nissen. Cophenhagen: Arnold Busck, 1967, 112 pp.

A statistical study based upon police records and files contrasted normal homosexual males with pedophiliacs. The homosexual offenders were divided into four groups. Group A included the "sexually bungled" neurotics, only about 18 percent of whom were exclusively or predominantly homosexual. Group B consisted of offenders who were exclusively or largely homosexual, and who had also had relations with a large number of boys. Group C included those who were exclusively or largely homosexual, but only occasionally interested in boys. In Group D were those exclusively or largely homosexual, but not interested in boys.

These groups were contrasted with each other and with the general population on such factors as residence, age, social level, marriage, medical reports on mental status, prevailing psychic state, and I.Q. Differences in most factors were found between the groups, with the nonpedophiliacs being closest to the general population.

463   JUNG, CARL GUSTAV. "The Significance of the Unconscious in Individual Education." In *Contributions to Analytical Psychology*, translated by H. G. and Cary F. Baynes, pp. 391–400. London: K. Paul, Trench, Trubner, 1928. Reprinted as "Analysis of Two Homosexual Dreams." In *The Homosexuals: As Seen by Themselves and Thirty Authorities*, edited by Aron M. Krich, pp. 286–293. New York: Citadel Press, 1954.

Two homosexual dreams about cathedrals receive various psychoanalytical interpretations. In one, the beautiful building symbolized maternal ties, with the beauty of the scene a compensatory reaction to the ugliness of the patient's real life. The second dream, although also of a cathedral, included a complex ceremony which was interpreted as representing the patient's hopefulness that therapy would transform him from a homosexual into a heterosexual.

464   KARON, BERTRAM P., and ROSBERG, JACK. "The Homosexual Urges in Schizophrenia." *Psychoanalysis and Psychoanalytic Review* 45 (4, 1958): 50–56.

Homosexual urges and the defenses they engender play a significant part in the pathology of schizophrenic patients. The fear of being "drained" is the most significant underlying factor in the development of homosexual urges in schizophrenic patients. Such a fear of being drained through the penis leads the patient to view homosexual relations as the only kind of relations which are reciprocal and hence not draining. It is from these deepest roots of the fantasy of draining, the wish for the vagina, and the wish for a resolution of the original mother-child relationship that the homosexual urge originates.

465   KARPMAN, BENJAMIN. "Dream Life in a Case of Transvestism: With Particular Attention to the Problem of Latent Homosexual-

ity." *Journal of Nervous and Mental Disease* 106 (Jul.–Dec., 1947): 292–337.

The problem of unconscious, or latent, homosexuality has an interlocking relationship with other paraphilias, including transvestism. A partially studied case (the patient disappeared after 50 sessions of analysis) of transvestism is presented in detail. The subject was a 37-year-old male, married but separated, and the father of two little girls. His 53 formally recorded dreams are considered and accompanied by analytical commentary.

Where does homosexuality stop and transvestism begin or vice versa? Although the patient was homosexual in every way he refused to recognize his homosexuality. His transvestism was interpreted as a mechanism of flight, a compromise with reality, designed to defend him from the realization that he was homosexual. Eighty percent of his dreams were concerned with transvestism and homosexuality, and many included masculine women who possessed male sex organs. These women were a combination of an unconsciously desired homosexual partner and a forbidden sister for whom he had unconscious incestuous desires. He also had frequent dreams of men making love to him. Besides incest, homosexuality, and masturbation, the patient was fetishistic and performed cunnilingus.

466   KARPMAN, BENJAMIN. "The Structure of Neuroses: With Special Differentials Between Neurosis, Psychosis, Homosexuality, Alcoholism, Psychopathy, and Criminality." *Archives of Criminal Psychodynamics* 4 (4, 1961): 599–646.

Homosexuality is classified as a neurosis, not as a psychosis and not as a symptom of psychopathy. It is "definitely curable."

467   KATAN, MAURITS. "Schreber's Delusion of the End of the World." *Psychoanalytic Quarterly* 18 (1, 1949): 60–66.

Freud used Schreber's autobiography for the elucidation of two theories: delusion is a defense against homosexuality, and delusion is an attempt at restitution. From the autobiography another function of delusion could be distinguished: the warding off of a danger.

The patient, Schreber, went through stages in the development of his psychosis. Toward the end he was able to feel that the world would not end, because he was able to control his masturbation, which was stimulated by the homosexual nature of his attachments to God and to his first therapist.

468   KAYY, W. H. *The Gay Geniuses: Psychiatric and Literary Studies of Famous Homosexuals.* Glendale, Calif.: Marvin Miller, 1965, 223 pp.

It is contended that homosexuality, overt and latent, is commonly associated with genius. The personal histories of more than 70 famous historical figures including intellectuals, artists and musicians, military men, rulers, religious leaders, and other types are presented, as well as those of several famous women.

469   KENDRICK, D. C., and CLARKE, R. V. G. "Attitudinal Differences Between Heterosexually and Homosexually Oriented Males." *British Journal of Psychiatry* 113 (494, 1967): 95–99.

A study was conducted to determine if homosexuals who are in a state of cognitive dissonance (accepting their homosexuality and then entering therapy) are more apt to derogate the familial and social aspects of their world. The subjects were 20 males referred to the Maudsley Hospital with a presenting symptom of homosexuality and 20 normal males matched for age, intelligence, and socioeconomic class. Eighteen of the 20 homosexuals had ratings of 5 or 6 on the Kinsey Scale, and the other two had ratings of 3 and 4.

Attitudinal differences were assessed by means of the Semantic Differential technique. Twenty concepts ("Myself as I am," "Myself as I'd like to be," "My mother," "Sex," "Being queer," et cetera) were fitted into the framework proposed by Kelly to cover family, intimates, valencies, authorities, and values. The Slater Selective Vocabulary Scale and t-tests were used. The 20 concepts were rated on 20 scales: 12 evaluative, five potency and three activity bipolar adjectives.

The groups differed on the Evaluative and Potency Scales, but not on the Activity Scales. On the Evaluative Scales the homosexuals had higher scores than the normal males, that is, less favorable attitudes. On the Potency Scales, the homosexuals had lower scores, that is, the concepts were regarded as stronger and more severe. That homosexuality would produce a derogation of certain models or aspects of the family and society was supported at a relative level; on certain concepts the homosexuals had less favorable attitudes than the normal males, but in no way could they be considered to have "paranoid" attitudes.

470   KHAN, M. Masud R. "Foreskin Fetishism and Its Relation to Ego Pathology in a Male Homosexual." *International Journal of Psycho-Analysis* 46 (1, 1965): 64–80.

The case of a male homosexual with a foreskin fetish is presented. The subject was an unmarried 40-year-old man who underwent psychoanalysis. The case material suggested that the phallic mother-image upon which the fetishist fixated was composed from sensations derived from the self-phallus in the excited states and the maternal object toward whom these were directed. Also involved were passive longings for the father's penis.

471   KIRKENDALL, Lester A. "Adolescent Homosexual Fears." *Sexology* 27 (12, 1961): 818–821.

Observations based on clinical experience are made. Some adolescent boys are overly concerned about homosexuality. They do not realize that during early and middle adolescence sex play between boys is a common and natural occurrence. Once they are made aware of this fact, they are relieved of a great deal of worry and anxiety.

472   KLAF, FRANKLIN S. "Evidence of Paranoid Ideation in Overt Homosexuals." *Journal of Social Therapy* 7 (1, 1961): 48–51.

Freud's paranoia hypothesis was expanded to find if paranoid ideation would be prominent among overt homosexuals. The case records of 100 randomly selected overt homosexuals at Maudsley Hospital in London were analyzed. The sample included 78 males, with an average age of 33.5 years, and 22 females, with an average age of 31.5 years. Among the male patients, 19.3 percent were married; among the female patients, 18.2 were married. It was decided not to include a control group of nonhomosexuals in the study. It was found that the association between paranoia and homosexuality is not limited to repressed homosexuality, and that opportunities to satisfy homosexual desires do not protect persons from developing paranoid defenses.

473   KLAF, FRANKLIN S., and DAVIS, CHARLES A. "Homosexuality and Paranoid Schizophrenia: A Survey of 150 Cases and Controls." *American Journal of Psychiatry* 116 (12, 1960): 1070–1075.

According to Freud, paranoid psychotic symptoms develop as a defense against emerging unconscious homosexual wishes. To verify this, the case histories and medical charts of 150 male paranoid schizophrenics and a control group of 150 male nonpsychotic cases were studied. All the subjects were at the United States Public Health Service Hospital in Fort Worth, Texas. It was found that acutely ill psychotic patients were preoccupied with homosexual thoughts and wishes. Of the paranoid schizophrenics, 41.8 percent had such homosexual preoccupations. Only 6 percent of the control group had such preoccupations. Although Freud's theory seems to have been substantiated, more studies are necessary to verify it. The two trends, paranoia and homosexuality, may exist together and yet not necessarily be related.

474 KLEIN, HENRIETTE R., and HORWITZ, WILLIAM A. "Psychosexual Factors in the Paranoid Phenomena." *American Journal of Psychiatry* 105 (9, 1949): 697–701.

To discover what common denominators are to be found in a group of patients with paranoid thinking and feeling, 40 male and 40 female patients at the New York State Psychiatric Institute were studied. All had been previously diagnosed as paranoid or schizophrenic paranoid types. Their cases were studied in terms of their psychosexual development. Later, this was correlated with behavior, preoccupation, and delusions as expressed in action or through symbols.

The character structures of the patients varied considerably. Most came from distrust-provoking backgrounds and showed histories of preoccupation with competitive and social strivings with failures or unsuccessful attempts to maintain ego stature. Failures in love or sex situations were conspicuous. Guilt associated with sexuality, particularly masturbation, was prevalent. Among the chief sexual preoccupations during their illness was the fear of being considered perverted. In many the fear of being or becoming homosexual was an expression of failure, a blow to their pride, or a general distrust of acceptance from others. These fears did not, of necessity, represent homosexual strivings.

The paranoid mechanism cannot be explained solely by homosexual conflict, although it is pertinent. Alternative theories deserve further investigation.

475 KNIGHT, JAMES A. "False Pregnancy in a Male." *Psychosomatic Medicine* 22 (4, 1960): 266.

A 33-year-old merchant marine seaman entered therapy because he felt he was pregnant. He had transvestic tendencies, but homosexuality was seen as the nuclear conflict. Of the three motivational components of homosexuality—sex, power, and dependency—the sexual component was the weakest in him. The patient's struggle for power, coupled with his socially unacceptable sexual interests, pushed him into a delusion of grandeur as a specific self-reparative effort, i.e., the patient saw his pregnancy as an act of God.

476 KNIGHT, ROBERT P. "The Relationship of Latent Homosexuality to the Mechanism of Paranoid Delusions." *Bulletin of the Menninger Clinic* 4 (5, 1940): 149–159.

Although homosexual conflicts are the basis of all paranoia, paranoiacs are compelled to deny their homosexual wish fantasies. This denial is not due to a fear of the social disapproval of homosexuality, but to an intense concern about the safety of both subject and object because of the destructive anal-sadistic wishes which are present. These wishes accompany the attempt to love and to obtain passive anal gratification from the object.

477 KOEGLER, RONALD R., and KLINE, LAWRENCE Y. "Psychotherapy Research: An Approach Utilizing Autonomic Response Measurements." *American Journal of Psychotherapy* 19 (2, 1965): 268–279.

The relationship between homosexuality and paranoid schizophrenia was the original aim of the investigation. However, basic problems concerning the responses of the autonomic nervous system (ANS) and the level of psychologic stress first had to be solved.

The 50 subjects, including 30 males, were medical school students, college students, and medical secretaries. Galvanic skin resistance (GSR), galvanic skin resistance lability, cardiotachiometric heart rate, peripheral (finger pulse) blood volume, and respiration were measured. Movies were used as stimuli.

There was a general tendency for peripheral blood volume and respiration rate to be least sensitive. It was concluded that noting simultaneous responses is the best method for determining the degree of psychologic stress, although only the magnitude and not the nature of the stress can be determined.

On the basis of preliminary findings, using the above method with three male homosexuals and three male paranoid schizophrenics, it is speculated that heterosexual, rather than homosexual, panic is a prevalent factor in paranoid schizophrenia, and that heterosexual panic might be an important precipitating factor in homosexuality. This is in keeping with contemporary ideas which regard homosexuality as a flight from heterosexuality.

478 KOENIG, KARL P. "The Differentiation of Hetero- or Homoerotic Interests in the Male: Some Comments on Articles by Brown and Freund." *Behaviour Research and Therapy* 2 (Apr., 1965): 305–311.

The works of P. T. Brown and Kurt Freund are discussed and criticized. Freund's study is found to be "comprehensive and painstakingly performed," but hard to understand, especially the tables which were not adequately explained or labeled. Brown's study is criticized because of his use of only one subject, because the description of his methodology was unclear, and because the statistical treatment of the data was "inappropriate." Beyond the diagnostic uses of the techniques employed by Freund and Brown, these techniques could be used in various aspects of treatment or for measuring progress during treatment of homosexuals or impotent heterosexual males.

A reply to Koenig's remarks by P. T. Brown is also included.

479 KOPP, SISTER MARY AUDREY. "A Study of Anomia and Homosexuality in Delinquent Adolescent Girls." Ph.D. dissertation, University of St. Louis, 1960, 185 pp.

The hypothesis that homosexuality is associated with a high rate of anomic pressure (normlessness, goallessness, psychological isolation, and anxiety) was tested using an "Anomic Pressure Rating Schedule" which included inventories on reference group conflicts, attitudes toward social authorities, self-concept, role identification, and anxiety. In pretests the schedule successfully differentiated between delinquent and nondelinquent girls.

One hundred delinquent girls in a Minnesota institution were divided into groups that reflected the extent of their homosexual experience and behavior. When the Anomic Pressure Rating Schedule was administered, the results showed significantly higher ratings of anomia for the homosexual girls.

Anomia refers to the sociopsychological state of the individual characterized by tenuous self-to-other and self-to-group relations, intense affectional deprivation and feelings of isolation which make the norms structured in the roles of the dominant culture or subculture meaningless. It should be distinguished from *anomie,* which refers to the condition of normlessness in the group or social subsystem.

480 KRIEGER, MARGERY H., and WORCHEL, PHILIP. "A Test of the Psychoanalytic Theory of Identification." *Journal of Individual Psychology* 16 (1, 1960): 56–63.

Freud perceived identification as having effects on the superego, the ego, and character. Inasmuch as a person should become like the parent with whom he identifies, there should be a significant degree of similarity between the kind of person he perceives himself to be and the kind of person he perceives that parent to be. The three major directions of identification were seen in the development of the normal person, the neurotic individual, and the homosexual individual. Following this line of reasoning, three hypotheses were tested. These were that the normal individual identifies more with the parent of the same sex than with the parent of the opposite sex, that the neurotic individual identifies with both parents, and that the homosexual identifies more with the parent of the opposite sex. Thirty subjects, including 10 from each of the three categories (six men, four women), made Q-sorts of statements describing themselves, their ideal selves, their fathers, and their mothers. Degree of identification was derived from correlating self- and ideal-sorts with sorts for father and for mother.

The results did not support any of the hypotheses. Instead, it was found that normals identified equally with both parents, and that neurotics identified significantly more with the parent of the opposite sex. When the data were examined separately for men and women, they showed that men identified significantly more with either parent than women did (the normal subjects even more so than the total group); and that while homosexual men identified significantly more with their fathers, homosexual women did not identify more with their mothers.

481   KRIPPNER, STANLEY. "The Identification of Male Homosexuality
      With the MMPI." *Journal of Clinical Psychology* 20 (1, 1964): 159–
      161.

To determine how well homosexuals could be identified through the use of the M-F Scale of the Minnesota Multiphasic Personality Inventory and Panton's Scale, a group of 72 male upperclassmen was tested. Twenty-two items which differentiated between homosexuals and nonhomosexuals were used from the MMPI. The subjects, all of whom were self-referrals for vocational, educational, and personal counseling, were divided into two groups: those who discussed homosexual problems (20) and those who did not discuss these problems (52) in their personal interviews.

The M-F Scale identified 75 percent of the subjects reporting homosexual problems; the Panton Scale identified 80 percent. All subjects who reported homosexual problems had high scores on either the M-F or the Panton Scale.

482   KUBIE, LAWRENCE S. "Psychiatric Implications of the Kinsey Re-
      port." *Psychosomatic Medicine* 10 (2, 1948): 95–106.

The work of Kinsey et al. is praised for its contributions, but is criticized from a psychiatric viewpoint for some of the interpretations which are made about sexual behavior. The findings concerning homosexual behavior are used as examples throughout the article. The criticisms cover statistical handling of the material and theoretical preconceptions.

The emphasis on the mean and the cumulative frequency give false impressions. Use of the mean does not accurately represent the tendency of the majority because most of the distributions are skewed. The cumulative frequency does not distinguish between past and present behavior, i.e., the significance of reaching orgasm is different in preadolescence than in middle age.

Theoretical preconceptions are criticized on the basis of the concept of normality, the significance of conscious and unconscious psychological factors in the interpretation of variations, and the concept of sexuality. The implication that homosexuality must be accepted as "normal" because it is prevalent is wholly unwarranted. It is suggested that there be an emphasis on unconscious goals and motivations, rather than on orgasm.

Two basic implications of Kinsey et al. must be rejected. One is that overt manifestations of sexual patterns are all that one needs to know about human sexuality. The other is that where any behavior pattern is widespread it is superfluous to explain it.

483   KUETHE, JAMES L., and WEINGARTNER, HERBERT. "Male-Female Schemata of Homosexual and Non-Homosexual Penitentiary Inmates." *Journal of Personality* 32 (1, 1964): 23–31.

Social schemata are aroused when an individual is confronted with social objects, with the specific content of the social objects determining which schemata are aroused. To compare the social schemata used by homosexuals with those used by heterosexuals, a study was made of 100 inmates of the Maryland Penitentiary, including 50 overt homosexuals. The subjects were asked to perform experimental tasks which included placing cut-out figures on a felt field (free-placement technique), using figures of men, women, and rectangles, and replacing the observed figures on the display.

The nonhomosexual inmates employed man-woman schemata that were comparable to the schemata used by normal populations. The schemata used by the homosexuals differed from other populations and were consistent with their sexual orientation. The nonhomosexuals did not usually permit men and women figures to be separated while the homosexuals did. The homosexuals replaced two men figures closer together than they did the men and women figures; the nonhomosexuals usually placed the men and women figures much closer together.

484   LAGACHE, DANIEL. "From Homosexuality to Jealousy." *International Journal of Psycho-Analysis* 30 (3, 1949): 195.

An author's abstract of a paper presented at the 16th International Psycho-Analytic Congress describes the case history of a male homosexual whose analysis was terminated when he turned toward heterosexuality and became engaged to be married. The patient's homosexual activities—fellatio, swallowing of semen, fantasies of cutting off the penis of his partner—had signified attempts to attain masculinity. Passive homosexual behavior (which might threaten castration) had not been present. Prior to his marriage, the patient went through an episode of a short-lived but violent jealousy in which he saw the analyst as a rival for the affections of his fiancée. Clinically this particular episode was seen as evidence of a heterosexual attitude which implied a reduction of castration anxiety, and it was therefore considered a therapeutically important attempt at rejecting homosexuality.

485   LAGACHE, DANIEL. "Homosexuality and Jealousy." *International
       Journal of Psycho-Analysis* 31 (1–2, 1950): 24–31.

The notion that jealousy and homosexuality may function as defenses
against each other is illustrated by the case of a 32-year-old male homosexual who was in psychoanalysis with the author. During the patient's treatment when efforts were made at heterosexuality, violent jealousy broke out.
It was determined that his jealousy was a defense directed principally
against a passive homosexual fixation on the father, which itself had been
determined in part by paternal neglect in the education of the patient.

486   LASZLO, CARL. "Notes on Various Phenomena in Male Homosexu-
       ality." *International Journal of Sexology* 8 (4, 1955): 220–225.

A list of 24 symptoms of homosexuality based upon a review of the scientific
literature is presented. The different symptoms of homosexuality, what is
known about homosexuality, and other classification schemes are considered and a classification of male homosexuality is developed which involves
six categories—the normal "bisexual" forms, the inverts, the narcissistic
estranged types, the neurotic forms, the perverted forms, and the onanistic-
infantile forms.

   The active and passive roles of male homosexuality are discussed at
length, much of the literature on the subject is reviewed, and it is concluded
that apparently complementary and contradictory active and passive attitudes are implied throughout the literature.

487   LEVINE, JACOB. "The Sexual Adjustment of Alcoholics: A Clinical
       Study of a Selected Sample." *Quarterly Journal of Studies on Alcohol*
       16 (4, 1955): 675–680.

A study of 79 alcoholics (16 women and 63 men) was made by utilizing the
records of psychotherapeutic interviews from an outpatient clinic. Two of
the men were overt homosexuals and 44 expressed indifference to heterosexual intercourse. Three males expressed strong heterosexual desires. Quotations from three of the females showed a lack of interest in sex; one other
expressed fears of the opposite sex.

   The family dynamics of the alcoholics, as revealed through the records,
showed a strong dependency on the mother and an absence of a healthy
male figure for identification. These findings were consistent with the psychoanalytic hypothesis that the alcoholic has a basic homosexual problem.

488   LEWINSKY, HILDE. "Notes on Two Special Features in a Homosex-
       ual Patient." *International Journal of Psycho-Analysis* 30 (1, 1949):
       56.

A patient, who had a homosexual masturbation fantasy of playing with the buttocks and anus of a policeman and who felt masturbation was worse than homosexuality, is described. Castration anxiety was the cause of his preoccupations, which illustrated the devices employed by the unconscious to overcome the threat of castration without giving up forbidden pleasures. Because of castration anxiety the patient tried in his fantasies to corrupt authority figures (i.e., the policeman) and to rob them of their power. He circumvented a strict masturbation prohibition by playing with someone else's penis and letting someone else play with his.

489   LIDDICOAT, RENÉE. "A Study of Non-Institutionalized Homosexuals." *Journal of the National Institute of Personnel Research* 8 (1961): 217–249.

Noninstitutionalized homosexuals were compared with a control group of homosexuals in order to discover differences in personality and intelligence, as well as to locate factors leading to the cause of homosexuality. The subjects were 50 male and 50 female volunteers, all acknowledged homosexuals living in South Africa and contacted through mutual friends. The mean age for the males was 35.8 years, and for the females 37.1 years. The controls were selected from the files of the National Institute to match the homosexual group as closely as possible. The criterion for sexual normality was marriage. Biographical material was obtained from the subjects through interviews, and the Wechsler-Bellevue Adult Intelligence Test was administered.

"Mother-fixation" on a conscious level was not discernible in a majority of the subjects. The first homosexual experience of the subjects was rarely a result of seduction (13 cases). The first homosexual experience had come at an earlier age for the men than for the women. Occupations were widely varied, but more homosexuals were self-employed than were members of the control group. The male control group tended to prefer more masculine activities (science, mechanics, sports, et cetera) than did the male homosexuals. No difference in preference of activities was seen between the female homosexuals and the female controls. Forty-three cases of permanent relationships of five or more years were found among the homosexuals. Of these, the mean duration was 8.9 years for the male homosexuals and 11.2 years for the female homosexuals. For the over-all group the mean duration was 4.0 years for the men and 6.15 years for the women. The mean verbal I.Q. on the Wechsler-Bellevue Test of the male and female homosexuals was higher than that of the control group (p < .04). No evidence of psychopathology was discovered among the homosexuals.

490 LINDNER, HAROLD. "Sexual Responsiveness to Perceptual Tests in a Group of Sexual Offenders." *Journal of Personality* 21 (1, 1952): 364–374.

A group of 67 male sex offenders from Maryland's House of Correction and State Reformatory was studied to determine if sexual offenders are perceptually sensitized to sexual stimuli. A control group consisted of 67 male prisoners who were not sex offenders. The Serial Drawing Test and the Incomplete Picture Test were used. The sexual offender group showed a sexually oriented perceptual sensitization to the test variables that was significantly different from that of the control group. The sexual offenders demonstrated their sexually oriented perceptual sensitizations, and their oriented responses were not limited to sexually suggestive stimuli but extended as well to test stimuli which were not intended to be essentially sexual in character. The controls did not show any clear-cut indications of a sexually oriented perceptual sensitization.

491 LINDNER, ROBERT. *Must You Conform?* New York: Rinehart & Co., 1956, 210 pp.

A psychoanalytic attempt is made to formulate and answer the problem of conformity from the personal and intimate to the sociopolitical and universal. A chapter on homosexuality is included. Homosexuality is considered to be a pattern of sex orientation adopted as a solution to the conflict between the sexual instincts and the repressive effects of the prevailing sex morality on sexual expression. It is, then, a reaction of nonconformity or rebellion. Since the conformance pressure in society is becoming more intense, so is homosexuality. New arguments for legalizing homosexual behavior between adults in private are stated.

492 LINDZEY, GARDNER. "Seer Versus Sign." *Journal of Experimental Research in Personality* 1 (1, 1965): 17–26.

Two consecutive studies concerned with clinical and actuarial prediction were discussed. Thematic Apperception Test (TAT) protocols were obtained from 20 male homosexual and 20 male nonhomosexual students in the first study and from 14 homosexual and 16 nonhomosexual prisoners in the second study. In the first study a clinician was able to classify the protocols according to sexual orientation with 95 percent accuracy. Twenty objective TAT indices were nearly as accurate when they were combined using actuarial methods. However, when applied to the prison population, the actuarial method was totally ineffective. The clinicians proved to be more accurate. The implications for the clinical-actuarial prediction controversy and the utility of objective "signs" derived from projective technique protocols was discussed.

493 LINDZEY, GARDNER; TEJESSY, CHARLOTTE; and ZAMANSKY, HAROLD S. "Thematic Apperception Test: An Empirical Examination of Some Indices of Homosexuality." *Journal of Abnormal and Social Psychology* 57 (1, 1958): 67–75.

To test the theory that Thematic Apperception Test indices can be used as indicators of homosexuality, the test was administered to two groups: 20 Harvard undergraduate homosexual males and 20 undergraduate heterosexual males. Of the 20 indices used, 16 differentiated between the two groups in the predicted direction, while three reversed the prediction and one showed no difference. Of the 16 predicted differences the nine which were significant at the .05 level were feminine identification, attitude toward marriage, man killing woman, unstable identification, shallow heterosexual relations, symbolism or allegory, derogatory sexual terms applied to women, homosexual content, and positive introduction of female. A judge was able to sort the protocols into homosexual and normal groups with 95 percent success.

494 LIPKOWITZ, MARVIN H. "Homosexuality as a Defense against Feminine Strivings: A Case Report." *Journal of Nervous and Mental Disease* 138 (Apr., 1964): 394–398.

The case of a 37-year-old male who adopted active homosexuality as a defense against feminine instincts is reported. The subject was hospitalized for attempting suicide and subsequently underwent psychotherapy. His homosexual acts served as compromise formations between opposing ego forces. This points to the impracticality of classifying homosexuals according to the acts performed at any given time, or even in terms of the consciously held sense of identity at any given time, as the system proposed by Ferenczi suggests.

495 LONDON, LOUIS S. *Abnormal Sexual Behavior.* New York: Julian Press, 1957, 427 pp.

A psychoanalytic discussion of 23 cases of neuroses and paraphiliac neuroses includes a description of the analysis of a person with a homosexual neurosis. Hysterical manifestations were present in this patient, because, according to Freudian theory, he did not satisfy his libidinous urge. The patient showed conflict between his "acquired instinctive cravings" and his religious training and developed impotence as a compromise.

496 LONDON, LOUIS S. "Homosexual Panic with Hallucinations: A Case
     Study." *Medical Times* 92 (Feb., 1964): 175–189.

The treatment of a 20-year-old male suffering from panic and auditory
hallucinations associated with his overt homosexuality is described. The
patient engaged in both heterosexual and homosexual practices, although
he found men more attractive. Contents of 22 dreams and their interpretation, together with parts of conversations which took place while the patient
was under the influence of sodium amytal, are included. After treatment the
patient's sexual proclivities remained the same, but he no longer experienced the hallucinations. After 10 years the situation apparently remained the same.

497 McCAGHY, CHARLES H. "Child Molesters: A Study of Their Ca-
     reers as Deviants." In *Criminal Behavior Systems: A Typology,* ed-
     ited by Marshall B. Clinard and Richard Quinney, pp. 75–88. New
     York: Holt, Rinehart and Winston, 1967.

One of the goals of a sociological study of 181 persons convicted for child
molesting was to test hypotheses concerning relationships between societal
reaction against this form of sexual deviance and the ways in which molesters verbally cope with that reaction. The particular hypothesis bearing on
homosexuality has to do with the verbal motives which the subject expressed to explain or to justify the incident of child molesting for which he
was convicted.

Because homosexual contacts represent a departure from usual sexual
role expectations, it had been assumed that subjects involved in homosexual
activity with children would be likely to employ motives of either complete
denial ("it didn't happen") or denial of responsibility ("too drunk to know
what I was doing," "everything went blank," et cetera). Contrary to this
expectation, however, only 25 percent of the subjects who had molested
males used denial motives, compared with 53 percent of those who had
molested females. In addition, homosexual offenders were much more likely
than heterosexual offenders to admit other undetected instances of similar
sexual encounters with children.

The explanation given for this phenomenon is that since many homosexuals have already internalized images of themselves as sexual deviants, their
self-concepts are not seriously threatened by accusations of child molesting.
They already accept their deviant sexual role and so have less need to deny
the molesting accusation or to justify their behavior as molesters. It is
suggested that "the homosexual molester might be more likely to recidivate,
since societal reaction against his sexual practices does not threaten his
established self-concept."

498   McCONAGHY, N. "Penile Volume Change to Moving Pictures of
       Male and Female Nudes in Heterosexual and Homosexual Males."
       Behaviour Research and Therapy 5 (1, 1967): 43–48.

A method of determining sexual orientation by measuring changes in penile
volume is described. Eleven heterosexual males with no report of homosexual feeling, and 22 males who had reported significant homosexual feeling,
were shown moving pictures of nude males and females for 10 seconds at
one minute intervals during the showing of a travelogue-type movie. The
movies of the female were preceded by a red circle, those of the male by
a green triangle. The sexual orientation of all heterosexual subjects was
determined correctly by the measurements used in the study, and 14 of the
22 males who had indicated strong homosexual feelings were correctly
identified. Freund's claim (1963) that penile volume changes in response to
male and female nude pictures provide a valid measure of sexual orientation
in males appeared to be confirmed.i

499   McCORD, WILLIAM, and McCORD, JOAN. *Psychopathy and Delin-
       quency.* New York: Grune & Stratton, 1956, 230 pp.

A neurological and sociopsychological study of the relation between psychopathy and delinquency briefly mentions homosexuality as a frequent
characteristic of psychopaths.

500   McCREARY, JOHN K. "Psychopathia Homosexualis." *Canadian
       Journal of Psychology* 4 (1950): 63–74.

Homosexuality may be a phase of normal development, "forming an easy,
or at least a convenient transition from autoerotic practices, which require
only the self, to genuine heterosexuality, which requires a person of the
opposite sex." If one fails to make the transition, homosexual "deviation"
may be used as a coping mechanism toward dominance or submission.
Kinsey's work indicates that cultural mores must be considered more extensively in order to determine how the individual uses homosexuality as a
coping mechanism. It is probable that there are three main types of homosexuality: active homosexuals who play the male role, passive homosexuals
who play a passive role, and still other homosexuals who play a mixed role.
    There are three prevailing theories about the etiology of homosexuality:
inherent inclinations, faulty conditioning through "unsatisfactory" childhood adjustments, and imbalanced sex hormone distributions. Multicausal-
ity, with perhaps a single dominant cause, seems to be the most plausible
explanation. Henry's data (1941) is cited as providing "evidence in support
of the view that homosexual deviations are due primarily to stresses in the

individual's environmental milieu, and in most cases those of his early home life."

Due to legal punishment and moral disapproval, homosexuality in the United States seems to be related to neuroses and psychoses. Further scientific and objective treatment of the problem is needed.

501 McGUIRE, RUTH MARJORIE. "An Inquiry into Attitudes and Value Systems of a Minority Group: A Comparative Study of Attitudes and Value Systems of Adult Male Homosexuals with Adult Male Heterosexuals." Ph.D. dissertation, New York University, 1966, 180 pp.

The attitudes and value systems of overt male homosexuals are assessed by testing a series of hypotheses which link the independent variables of sexual object choice and psychiatric treatment status to certain dependent variables, including attitudes toward the self, basic social institutions, and the mentally ill.

A questionnaire was given to 217 adult males, and they were divided into homosexual and heterosexual groups on the basis of their responses. They were also distinguished on the basis of whether they were currently undergoing or had never received psychological treatment. Differences between these groups were measured with respect to several dependent variables. Homosexuals and men never in treatment were found to be more authoritarian than their counterparts. Neither sexual object choice nor treatment status were related to feelings of alienation. Sexual object choice was not related to attitudes toward institutionalized religion, but men never treated had more favorable attitudes in this regard than men having treatment. Sexual object choice was not related to attitudes toward government policies, but men never treated were more conservative. Heterosexuals had self-images of being more conventionally masculine, but men in or never in treatment did not differ with regard to this variable. Neither sexual object choice nor treatment status was related to extroversion, and object choice was not related to introversion, but men never in treatment saw themselves as less introverted than men in treatment. Men in treatment saw themselves as more neurotic, but sexual object choice was not related to this. Homosexuals held stronger convictions of being intellectually and aesthetically superior, but men in or never in treatment were not different in this regard. Men in treatment favored less social restriction of the mentally ill; sexual object choice was not related to this. Differences pertaining to other background variables were also discussed.

502 MACHOVER, SOLOMON; PUZZO, FRANK S.; MACHOVER, KAREN; and PLUMEAU, FRANCIS. "Clinical and Objective Studies of Person-

ality Variables in Alcoholism, III. An Objective Study of Homosexuality in Alcoholism." *Quarterly Journal of Studies on Alcohol* 20 (3, 1959): 528–542.

Two hypotheses were tested: homosexual trends are more prevalent among male alcoholics than among nonalcoholics, and homosexual trends are more evident in remitted than in unremitted alcoholics. The Masculinity-Femininity Scale of the Minnesota Multiphasic Personality Inventory (MMPI:M-F) and scales derived from the Rorschach and the Machover Figure Drawing Test (MFDT) were administered to a group of 23 alcoholics in a state of remission, a group of 23 alcoholics who still had a drinking problem, and a control group of 23 subjects. A criterion group of 23 practicing male homosexuals was used in the development of the scales.

The first hypothesis was not confirmed. The alcoholics' scores for homosexual trends, when compared with those of the control group, showed no significant difference.

The second hypothesis was confirmed. The remitted alcoholics scored higher with regard to homosexuality than the unremitted alcoholics on all three tests. It was suggested that the unremitted alcoholics may have manifested lower homosexual scores because of a more rigid, global defensiveness, or a lower level of differentiation in psychosexual development.

503   MACLAY, D. T. "Boys Who Commit Sexual Misdemeanors." *British Medical Journal* (5167, 1960): 186–190.

Abbreviated case studies of 29 boys who committed some form of sexual misdemeanor are presented; five of the boys were guilty of homosexual offenses. Poor emotional adjustment and homes that fail to provide an adequate measure of emotional support are factors that have a positive correlation with the tendency to commit such acts.

504   MAINORD, FLORENCE R. "A Note on the Use of Figure Drawings in the Diagnosis of Sexual Inversion." *Journal of Clinical Psychology* 9 (2, 1953): 188–189.

An attempt to test the hypothesis that drawing a figure of the opposite sex first is a possible sign of sexual inversion was made by obtaining drawings from 307 elementary psychology students in a college class and 269 patients in a hospital. Of the students, 94.7 percent of the males drew a male figure first and 82.3 percent of the male hospital patients also drew a male figure first. Only 56.6 percent of the female students drew a female figure first and 60.9 percent of the female patients drew a female first. On the basis of these results, it is suggested that this sign might be a valid one when considering the drawings of males.

It appears, however, that a large number of females draw males first because of the androcentric nature of the society, thereby reducing the value of this sign in detecting female homosexuality.

505   MARGETTS, E. L. "Sex Deviations." *McGill Medical Journal* 19 (1, 1950): 49–63.

The basic syndromes of sexual deviations, including homosexuality, are discussed. Treatment is briefly reviewed with emphasis on a new visual association technique which can be used to investigate cases of sex abnormalities.

506   MARMOR, JUDD. "Notes on Some Psychodynamic Aspects of Homosexuality." Preliminary Draft of Working Paper Prepared for the National Institute of Mental Health Task Force on Homosexuality. Mimeographed. Los Angeles: Cedars Sinai Medical Center, Nov., 1967.

The problem of mental health and homosexuality centers on the problem of defining mental health. Since mental health is a relative concept, both qualitatively and quantitatively, probably no one is absolutely healthy. There is no evidence that the majority of homosexuals have any physiological differences from heterosexuals, nor, except for their deviant sexual object preference, that they are uniquely different from heterosexuals at the psychological level. Further research is needed to determine if there are any significant differences in mental health between male and female homosexuals.

On the basis of present research it is impossible to delineate any psychodynamic pattern that would fit most homosexuals, since there is as wide a personality variation among homosexuals as among heterosexuals. An important research question is "whether it may be possible to find any primary psychodynamic features that are etiologically relevant or uniquely inherent in homosexual object choice, as distinguished from secondary psychodynamic features that are the consequences of such an object choice (in our society)." More research is also needed on female homosexuals. The conflicting reports of the psychological testing of homosexuals need to be resolved by more studies of large numbers of nonpatient homosexual populations.

507   MARONE, SILVIO. "Homosexuality and Art." *International Journal of Sexology* 7 (4, 1954): 175–190.

In a general introduction, homosexuality is defined (the author considers the term "missexuality" more accurate), theories and classifications of homosexuality are discussed, and some homosexual characteristics are considered. With this as a background, Da Vinci, Michelangelo, and Raphael are described from a sexological and psychoanalytic point of view. The early childhood environment of each artist is presented and the "homosexuality" in their subsequent works is described. It is concluded that each man possessed an intuitive intelligence, an intense sensibility, an inconstant will, a passive and sublimated libido, a physical and intellectual narcissism, and an exhibitionistic tendency as part of his homosexual make-up. Homosexual behavior is not rare among artists, and homosexuality has a great influence on art.

Comments by Clifford Allen are included.

508   MEKETON, BETTY W.; GRIFFITH, RICHARD M.; TAYLOR, VIVIAN H.; and WIEDEMAN, JANE S. "Rorschach Homosexual Signs in Paranoid Schizophrenics." *Journal of Abnormal and Social Psychology* 65 (4, 1962): 280–284.

Wheeler's list (1949) of Rorschach homosexual indices, developed to detect nonovert homosexuality, was used to test the Freudian hypothesis of the dynamic importance of latent homosexuality in the paranoia syndrome. The test was administered to hospitalized paranoid schizophrenics who were in a Veterans Administration Hospital and whose responses were compared with those of neurotics and alcoholics.

The Rorschach protocols were scored by both a psychology trainee and a hospital staff member. In addition they were screened by two assistants (inexperienced with the test) whose lists of possible signs served as an insurance against omissions. The four judges worked independently and without knowledge of diagnoses.

Support of the Freudian hypothesis of the relationship between paranoia and homosexuality and of previously validated results based upon Wheeler's list appeared questionable. However, when figures reported in the literature were collated, it was found that "in general, widely different groups from widely separated settings have given strikingly consistent results which support the validity both of content analysis of the Rorschach and of Wheeler's indices for overt homosexuality."

509   MEYER, MORTIMER M. "The Case of El: Blind Analysis of the Tests of an Unknown Patient." *Journal of Projective Techniques and Personality Assessment* 25 (4, 1961): 375–382.

El, a homosexual case study, is analyzed on the basis of the Rorschach protocol and other test materials. Especially stressed are his dependency conflicts and his problems of psychosexual identification.

See Fine (no. 385); Forer (no. 390); Hooker (no. 454); Murray (no. 513); and Shneidman (no. 562 and no. 563).

510   MILLER, MILTON L. "The Relation Between Submission and Aggression in Male Homosexuality." In *Perversions: Psychodynamics and Therapy,* edited by Sandor Lorand and Michael Balint, pp. 160–179. New York: Random House, 1956.

Psychoanalytic experience suggests that male homosexuals react with both aggression and submission in the presence of an aggression-provoking stimulus. Resulting from the inability to identify with a powerful father, this pattern is both a reaction to frustration and an expression of castration fear. Illustrative case histories are presented. In therapy, insight into the aggressive-submissive pattern is helpful in reducing anxiety as well as some of the general symptomatology of male homosexuality.

511   MONSOUR, KAREM J. "Migraine: Dynamics and Choice of Symptom." *Psychoanalytic Quarterly* 26 (4, 1957): 479–493.

In women, conflict over sexual desires that revive competition and anger toward other women can stimulate migraine attacks. The anger is repressed, and anxiety and guilt about the competitive feelings lead to a masochistic attitude. The migraine reflects this masochistic attitude; the head serves as a substitute for the female reproductive and sexual organs.

These same dynamic factors appear to operate in men with migraine attacks. Their repressed passive homosexual desires are an identification with a masochistic mother. The migraines can be considered to be a substitute for an unacceptable passive response to another man. As in women, there is a wish to produce a baby in the desired relationship with the father.

512   MOORE, ROBERT A., and SELZER, MELVIN L. "Male Homosexuality, Paranoia, and the Schizophrenias." *American Journal of Psychiatry* 119 (8, 1963): 743–747.

Freud's theory that paranoid psychotic symptoms develop as a defense against emerging unconscious homosexual wishes was tested in a study of 128 male paranoid schizophrenics and a control group of 77 nonparanoid schizophrenics. All of the subjects were hospitalized at the University of Michigan Medical Center. Their case histories were studied, and psychotherapy and psychological tests were administered.

Some form of homosexuality was found in 78 percent of the paranoids, while it appeared in only 47 percent of the nonparanoids. However, since a considerable number of nonparanoid schizophrenics are also troubled by homosexual desires, either latent or overt, other factors must be sought if we are to understand the motivations of paranoia.

513 MURRAY, HENRY A. "Commentary on the Case of El." *Journal of Projective Techniques and Personality Assessment* 25 (4, 1961): 404–411.

The commentary summarizes much of the material on a male homosexual case study. El, a "straight" accountant by day and an alcoholic homosexual by night, is described as possessing two contrasting conscious overt personalities, rather than one overt conscious personality and one covert unconscious personality. The article hypothesizes that El's great attachment to his mother (which is revealed in symbols of incest and matricide) leads to "an absence of any other attachments to persons as persons." The maternal bond may be the factor which makes El unable to trust and love others and incapable of establishing goals and programs.

See Fine (no. 385); Forer (no. 390); Hooker (no. 454); Meyer (no. 509); and Shneidman (no. 562 and no. 563).

514 NACHT, S.; DIATKINE, R.; and FAVREAU, J. "The Ego in Perverse Relationships." *International Journal of Psycho-Analysis* 37 (4, 1956): 404–413.

Taking into account their polymorphous nature and the complexity of the elaborations which underlie them, three groups of sexual perversions may be enumerated: sado-masochistic perversions, overt homosexuality, and other clinical forms which may be considered as flights from object relationships which are felt to be too dangerous.

Clinical observations show that not all homosexuals can be grouped together under a single heading. Brief descriptions are given of satisfied inverts, anxious homosexuals who seek treatment, those characterized by the existence of depressing and frankly revengeful elements, and those feeling such sexual inhibitions that even their homosexuality does not go beyond masturbation fantasies. It is generally concluded that satisfactory therapeutic results can only be obtained when the perversion is accompanied by a neurosis.

515 NAGLER, SIMON H. Fetishism: A Review and a Case Study." *Psychiatric Quarterly* 31 (4, 1957): 713–741.

A detailed case history of a homosexual foot fetishist is presented. Fear of the male social role in the face of an overwhelming sense of inadequacy and low self-esteem, rather than fear of castration or a desire to escape from women, is seen as a factor common to homosexuality, fetishism, and transvestism.

516   NEUSTATTER, W. LINDESAY. "Sex and Its Problems, XI. The Medi-
       cal Aspects of Homosexuality." *Practitioner* 199 (1193, 1967): 704–
       710.

In a summary of the etiological theories and clinical aspects of homosexuality, homosexuals are divided into two groups: those interested in other
adults or adolescents and those who interfere with children. Although
homosexuality may be associated with psychosis, the majority of homosexuals are not psychopathic, but are stable, respectable, and useful members
of society. Psychoanalytic psychotherapy which attempts to remove patients' inhibitions is more successful than glandular or aversion therapy;
however, the word "cured" should always be used with extreme caution.
Punishment by imprisonment is of no avail. Palliative treatment by an
understanding doctor may help the homosexual to accept his lot and overcome his depressions and anxieties. Adolescent homosexuality is a difficult
problem varying with the predisposition of the boys involved, and should
be handled in a matter-of-fact way, rather than by severe moralistic reactions. Changes in the legal aspects of homosexuality resulting from the
change in British law are also discussed.

517   "New Light on Homosexuality." 1957. Reprinted in *The Third Sex,*
       edited by Isadore Rubin, pp. 40–43. New York: New Book Co.,
       1961.

The research staff of *Sexology* magazine summarizes a report of a British
survey of 100 male homosexuals chosen from a large sample of psychiatric
cases. The major conclusion of that survey was that they were "on the whole
successful and valuable members of society. . . ." Only half of the patients
showed psychiatric abnormalities other than homosexuality, and many of
those were reactions to the difficulties of being homosexual. Patients who
had some kind of psychotherapy were compared with a matched group who
had had none. In a five-year follow-up no significant difference was found
between the two groups with regard to change of sexual orientation, discretion, or control.

518   NIELSON, NILS. "What Is Homosexuality?" *International Journal
       of Sexology* 6 (3, 1953): 188.

"A man, a woman, or an animal is homosexual when it prefers intercourse
with individuals of the same sex and abhors sexual contact with the opposite
sex. It follows then, that an individual may have homosexual intercourse
without being a homosexual." Many cases treated and cured are not homosexuals at all; they are, rather, frustrated heterosexuals. A real homosexual

with a pronounced "horror feminae" is exceedingly difficult to treat. Homosexuality is often dangerous to society because most homosexuals prefer youngsters, whose mental health and social adaptation may be endangered when these preferences are acted out.

519   NITSCHE, CARL J.; ROBINSON, J. FRANKLIN; and PARSONS, EDWARD T. "Homosexuality and the Rorschach." *Journal of Consulting Psychology* 20 (3, 1956): 196.

To determine whether certain Rorschach content categories occur more frequently in protocols of homosexuals than in those of nonhomosexuals, a study was made of 38 white males referred to an adult mental health clinic. The men were divided into two groups: 19 recently convicted homosexuals and 19 patients with no known homosexual activity. Twelve content categories of the Rorschach were selected: mythical, distortion, qualifications toward the abnormal, dehumanization, double identification, uncertainty, evasiveness, projection of feminized behavior, preoccupation with feminine apparel, castration and phallic symbolism, sexual and anatomical responses, esoteric language and artistic references, and dislike of female genital symbols.

The homosexuals had more responses in nine of the 12 categories, but the differences were not statistically significant at the .05 level. The mean for the homosexual group was 4.2 responses within the selected categories, while the mean for the non-homosexual group was 2.7.

520   NORMAN, JACOB P. "Evidence and Clinical Significance of Homosexuality in 100 Unanalyzed Cases of Dementia Praecox." *Journal of Nervous and Mental Disease* 107 (5, 1948): 484–489.

There is a causal psychodynamic relationship between sexual perversion and psychoneurosis. Delusions of persecution in paranoia and schizophrenia have their origin in unsuccessfully repressed homosexual tendencies. To verify these theories, a study was made of 125 hospitalized male patients. Seventy-five of the patients were dementia praecox, paranoid; 25 were dementia praecox, catatonic; and 25 were psychoneurotic, anxiety types. Their hospital case records were studied, and sodium Amytal was administered.

Strong conscious and unconscious homosexual tendencies were found in dementia praecox, paranoid patients. There was also evidence that the majority of cases showed a strong Oedipus complex fixation. However, this cannot be considered proof that homosexual tendencies were an etiologic factor in the schizophrenic process. It may be merely parallel or concomitant to other constitutional bodily dysfunction.

521   "Notes on Homosexuality: Excerpts from a Consultation." *Social Progress: A Journal of Church and Society* 58 (2, 1967): 26–30.

Excerpts from a consultation on law and homosexuality held by the United Presbyterian Church of America cover four areas of discussion: definition of homosexuality, change versus acceptance, dangers in homosexuality, and modification of legal sanctions. Whether homosexuality is a normal condition which is often accompanied by psychological problems caused by social pressures, or whether it is an illness which should be eliminated is also considered.

522   O'CONNOR, P. J. "Aetiological Factors in Homosexuality as Seen in Royal Air Force Psychiatric Practice." *British Journal of Psychiatry* 110 (466, 1964): 381–391.

In a study undertaken to learn the etiology of homosexuality and to find out what percentage of the homosexuals referred to the researcher (a psychiatrist) were mentally ill, 50 homosexual males and 50 neurotic males were picked at random from the investigator's patients. All were serving in the Royal Air Forces during the same time (1958–1959). Their ages ranged from 16 to 51 years. The case histories of the 100 subjects were compiled while the patients were under treatment, and these histories were then subjected to content analysis in order to determine the degree of their neuroticism, the types of relationships they had experienced in family life, and the level of their anxiety.

The homosexuals were found to be highly neurotic. It is believed that a poor relationship between the homosexual and his father retards the proper development of the reproductive instinct. Most of the homosexuals were artistic, extremely fond of the female parent, and nonaggressive.

523   O'CONNOR, WILLIAM A. "Some Notes on Suicide." *British Journal of Medical Psychology* 21 (3, 1948): 222–228.

An attempt is made to explain the phenomenon of self-destruction on the basis of experience with an unspecified number of cases. In more than 50 percent of the cases studied, homosexual tendencies were uncovered. It is pointed out that this may be accidental and no general conclusions are drawn. The case material "helps to strengthen the theory that the two factors, suicide and malfunction of the erotic instinct, are coincident, and that Freud's dichotomy of the total cognitive organization of the psyche into erotic and death urges is a fundamental one."

524   OLIVER, WAYNE A., and MOSHER, DONALD L. "Psychopathology and Guilt in Heterosexual and Subgroups of Homosexual Reforma-

tory Inmates." *Journal of Abnormal Psychology* 73 (4, 1968): 323–329.

An attempt was made to identify differences in patterns of psychopathology between incarcerated male heterosexuals and homosexual insertees and insertors. The subjects, inmates in a Federal reformatory, included 25 heterosexuals, 25 homosexual insertees, and 25 homosexual insertors. All were white with no previous history of psychiatric care and homogeneous in socioeconomic characteristics. The subjects were given the Minnesota Multiphasic Personality Inventory and the Mosher Forced-Choice Guilt Inventory.

All three groups were found to be impulsive and antisocial. The insertees demonstrated confusion about their personal and sexual identity and possessed a generally nonaggressive manner. The insertors, appearing highly psychotic, showed the greatest degree of psychopathology.

525   OVESEY, LIONEL. "The Pseudohomosexual Anxiety." *Psychiatry* 18 (1, 1955): 17–25.

Homosexual anxiety about dependency and power motives should be called "pseudo-homosexual" anxiety because, unlike the homosexual motive, these motives do not seek sexual goals. This observation is based on the case of a 30-year-old married male who underwent psychoanalysis. The patient was suffering from pseudo-homosexual anxieties of dependency and power. He was a very weak, dependent, and submissive person who was able to overcome his anxieties by using a homosexual adaptational frame of reference. Although true homosexuality and pseudo homosexuality are separate, they are in no way mutually exclusive.

526   OVESEY, LIONEL. "Pseudohomosexuality, the Paranoid Mechanism, and Paranoia." *Psychiatry* 18 (2, 1955): 163–173.

Paranoid phenomena can stem from nonsexual adaptations to societal stimuli, and motivationally do not necessarily have anything to do with homosexuality. Anxieties about homosexuality need not be made up only of sexual motives, but also of dependency and power motives. These latter two motives make up the pseudo-homosexual conflict. It can develop only in those men who fail to meet successfully the societal standards for masculine performance. The cause is either never having learned how to meet these standards; or learning how, but suffering from an inhibition of assertion and the inability to put their knowledge to effective use. It is the power motivation which is the constant feature in paranoid phenomena, not the homosexual motivation, although they, along with dependency motivation, can occur together.

527   PANTON, JAMES H. "A New MMPI Scale for the Identification of
Homosexuality." *Journal of Clinical Psychology* 16 (1, 1960): 17–21.

A new Minnesota Multiphasic Personality Inventory scale was developed
in an attempt to identify homosexuality. The new scale was based on the
idea that a propensity for homosexual behavior is derived from various
personality factors, which are scorable on the MMPI but independent of the
M-F scale. The subjects were 58 male prison inmates with confirmed homosexuality and a control group of 174 nonhomosexuals from the same
prison. The mean age of the subjects was 26.2 years, and the mean I.Q. was
96.9.

Twenty-two items successfully differentiated between the homosexual
and the nonhomosexual inmates, irrespective of I.Q. These items were
designated as the HSX scale. The use of the HSX scale at Washington State
Penitentiary resulted in much the same findings. Although the HSX scale
helps diagnose and classify incoming inmates, other clinical indices of
evaluation must also be used.

528   PARR, DENIS. "Homosexuality in Clinical Practice." *Proceedings of
the Royal Society of Medicine* 50 (1957): 651–654.

Male psychiatric patients were studied in regard to incidence of homosexuality, specific forms of homosexual relations, and psychological disturbances. Data on incidence were secured from several groups: mental
hospitals' returns of primary diagnosis for 24,412 patients; 1,329 hospital
inpatients; 500 hospital outpatients; and 2,550 patients seen in private practice. A more detailed study was made of 150 outpatient and 50 inpatient
cases selected on the basis of adequacy of documentation and homosexual
classification.

Incidence of homosexuality was less than 0.27 percent for the mental
hospitals' returns group, 5.3 percent for the hospital inpatient group, 6.8
percent for the hospital outpatient group, and 5.0 percent for the group seen
in private practice. The maximum incidence was in the 25 to 35 age group,
and the highest incidence of homosexual crime was in the 31 to 40 age
group.

From the group selected for detailed study it was found that most subjects
practiced both active and passive homosexual roles; 68 of the 150 outpatients were free from gross personality disorder, neurosis, or psychosis; 29
of the 200 subjects had pedophiliac impulses at one time or another; significantly more of the pedophiliacs than the nonpedophiliacs were bisexual;
and there was not a significant relationship between a history of seduction
and a tendency to pedophilia in adult life.

529   PASCAL, G. R., and HERZBERG, F. C. "The Detection of Deviant
       Sexual Practice from Performance on the Rorschach Test." *Journal
       of Projective Techniques* 16 (3, 1952): 366–373.

The Rorschach, followed by the "Testing the Limits for Sex" test, was
administered to 78 inmates of the Western State Penitentiary. The sample
included 19 controls, 19 rapists, 20 pedophiliacs, and 20 homosexuals. The
groups were matched for age, intelligence, and length of imprisonment. The
results of the test revealed that the controls were undifferentiated from the
rapists, and that both these groups differed significantly from the pedophiliac and homosexual groups. Homosexuals and pedophiliacs gave more
deviant responses than the controls and rapists.

530   PHILLIPS, J. P. N. "A Note on the Scoring of the Sexual Orientation
       Method." *Behaviour Research and Therapy* 6 (1968): 121–123.

The Sexual Orientation Method (S.O.M.) of determining homo- and
heteroerotic orientation is based on the assumption that the adjectival
statement scale positions are equally spaced. It is believed that this is an
unjustified assumption which may cause the system to regard consistent
patterns as inconsistent. The S.O.M. uses five statements which are paired
with each other in all possible combinations. The subject is asked to select
between paired statements. It is suggested that certain modifications (i.e.,
omitting certain pairs of statements) will make the assumption of symmetry
unnecessary.

531   PLANANSKY, KAREL, and JOHNSTON, ROY. "The Incidence and
       Relationship of Homosexual and Paranoid Features in Schizophre-
       nia." *Journal of Mental Science: British Journal of Psychiatry* 108
       (456, 1962): 604–615.

A study was made of 150 male psychotic patients in the suicide and violent
ward of a Veterans' Hospital to test the hypothesis that there is a relationship between homosexuality and paranoid schizophrenia. Using clinical and
service records, the researchers recorded symptoms of paranoia, assessed
them, and differentiated four degrees of paranoia. The relationships between
degrees of paranoia and sexual experiences were analyzed. Knowledge of
the subjects' homosexual experience was obtained from service and clinical
records and from the normal therapeutic routine of the hospital. Symbolic
signs of homosexuality were ignored.

    In accordance with what would be expected in a psychotic population,
a high incidence of sexual problems was found. However, the amount of
habitual homosexuality in the sample was less than Kinsey's findings (2

percent compared to 4 percent). No significant relationships were found between sexual experience (either heterosexual or homosexual) and degree of paranoia. It was concluded that in schizophrenia, homosexuality and paranoia are not related.

532 PRADOS, MIGUEL. "Personality Studies of Homosexuals." *Revue de Psychologie* 1 (1, 1946): 103–119.

The Rorschach technique was examined to determine its usefulness for diagnosing homosexuality. The sample consisted of 12 male homosexuals between the ages of 18 and 48 years, who came of their own accord for psychiatric consultations. The methods used to interpret the results of the Rorschach included the orthodox criteria, content analysis, and sequence analysis. Using ordinary criteria all patients showed many signs of maladjustment and inhibition, and all were diagnosed as having neurotic personalities. However, this approach failed to differentiate homosexuals from other neurotic personalities. Using content analysis, some homosexual signs of a high practical value were found—derealization, confusion of sexual identification, feminine identification, castration and phallic symbolism, sexual and anatomical responses, esoteric connotations, and obvious pregenital responses. The presence of a single sign could be sufficient for diagnosis, provided it was accompanied by other minor signs. The sequence analysis showed that additional answers during the Rorschach inquiry were of high diagnostic value.

533 PRINCE, C. V. "Homosexuality, Transvestism and Transsexualism: Reflections on Their Etiology and Differentiation." *American Journal of Psychotherapy* 11 (1, 1957): 80–85.

It is suggested that there are three different aspects of womanliness with which a young male may identify: the sexual, the psychological and emotional, and the social. The outcome is respectively homosexuality, transsexualism, and transvestism. There are no sharp delineations between these outcomes. Which choice a young male makes depends upon his own early life circumstances.

Harry Benjamin states in a preamble that "This article neither proves nor disproves the existence of a predisposing constitutional factor in the deviations he [Prince] discusses."

534 PRITCHARD, MICHAEL, and GRAHAM, PHILIP. "An Investigation of a Group of Patients Who Have Attended Both the Child and Adult Department of the Same Psychiatric Hospital." *British Journal of Psychiatry* 112 (487, 1966): 603–612.

A study designed to compare the clinical profiles of persons who had been seen by the psychiatric clinics both as children and as adults was carried out at the Bethlem Royal and Maudsley hospitals. The records of 75 patients were assembled and examined in order to investigate the relationship of childhood experiences to adult psychiatric illness occurring in the same person.

Significant associations were found between delinquency in childhood and antisocial personality in adult life and between neurotic disorder in childhood and in adult life.

Although the number of cases was very small there was a "striking incidence" of the combination of neurotic symptoms and temper in childhood and homosexuality during adulthood. In addition, three of the five adult homosexuals in the study had originally been referred to the Children's Department because of educational backwardness combined with mild behavioral problems.

535   "Psychopathology and Treatment of Sexual Deviation: The Male Homosexual." *British Medical Journal* (5208, 1960): 304.

At a conference on sexual deviation one speaker, L. H. Rubinstein, made reference to the problem of identification in male homosexuals. The active homosexual must maintain a precarious balance between the father-mother image and the passive child image, whereas the passive homosexual need only identify with the latter. The active homosexual needs to be more closely identified with the parental image than with that of the passive child if his strength within the homosexual relationship is to be maintained. The passive homosexual will see his partner as the stronger man and thus perpetuate his conception of himself as a child. Another speaker, W. Patterson Brown, observed that in the clinical treatment of male homosexuals by psychotherapy, the best results were obtained with young intelligent patients, preferably with no serious defect of appearance, health, or education.

536   RADO, SANDOR. "An Adaptational View of Sexual Behavior." 1949, rev. 1955. Reprinted in *The Problem of Homosexuality in Modern Society,* edited by Hendrik M. Ruitenbeek, pp. 94–126. New York: E. P. Dutton & Co., 1963.

The physical and psychodynamic patterns of "standard" heterosexual behavior which may be modified by fear or feelings of guilt are discussed. Homosexuality, "homogeneous pairs," is one form of modified sexual behavior. These pairs imitate the heterosexual male-female sexual patterns, but eliminate the threatening presence of the opposite sex. Evidence is not found for a common causation of homosexuality, but it is noted that "Different types of homogenous pairs have different developmental histories."

537   RAMSAY, R. W., and VELZEN, V. VAN. "Behaviour Therapy for Sexual Perversions." *Behaviour Research and Therapy* 6 (2, 1968): 233.

In an investigation of the attitudes of homosexuals and heterosexuals to the same and opposite sexes, 24 male heterosexual students in a fraternity house, 25 homosexuals known to the experimenters, and seven bisexuals were studied. The subjects were asked to indicate, in a questionnaire which was mailed to them, the degree of their emotional reactions to 10 homosexual situations and to 10 heterosexual situations. The homosexuals disliked intimate heterosexual situations and the heterosexuals disliked intimate homosexual situations. It was thought that an effective form of treatment for homosexuals might be systematic desensitization, during or prior to aversion therapy.

538   REITZELL, JEANNE MANNHEIM. "A Comparative Study of Hysterics, Homosexuals and Alcoholics Using Content Analysis of Rorschach Responses." *Rorschach Research Exchange and Journal of Projective Techniques* 13 (2, 1949): 127–141.

The Rorschach can be used to discriminate between personality organizations underlying observable behavior. The hypothesis was tested that the earlier in life the underlying organization is established, the more definitely it will express itself in observable behavior. Since alcoholics develop later than either hysterics or homosexuals it was expected that the Rorschach patterns would be clearer in the case of the latter two.

The homosexual subjects were 24 males and two females, most of whom had been referred as probation cases. Of 22 items previously found as indicative of homosexual Rorschach patterns only three were able to distinguish homosexual patterns from the other two patterns examined. The findings were not statistically significant, but it was felt that the samples were too small.

539   ROBBINS, BERNARD S. "Psychological Implications of the Male Homosexual 'Marriage.'" *Psychoanalytic Review* 30 (4, 1943): 428–437.

Homosexual "marriage" was studied through the psychoanalysis of two single male homosexuals, 28 and 23 years old. The homosexual is a neurotic personality in whom the major manifest symptom is a passionate sexual craving for a member of the same sex. The "marriages" nurture the greatest opportunity for mutual sadistic exploitation. The homosexual's dominant neurotic drive is sadism, and it is this which determines the distinguishing symptom—homoerotism.

540   ROSENFELD, HERBERT. "Remarks on the Relation of Male Homo-sexuality to Paranoia, Paranoid Anxiety and Narcissism." *International Journal of Psycho-Analysis* 30 (1, 1949): 36–47.

Psychoanalysis was undertaken with three patients, a 41-year-old single man, a 38-year-old man, and a married man who was latently homosexual. It was found that increased paranoid anxieties encourage the development of strong manifest or latent homosexual tendencies as a defense. That is, paranoia develops when the defensive function of the patients' homosexuality fails. Narcissistic homosexual attraction is caused by the projection of parts of the self, particularly the penis, onto another man.

541   R[UBIN], I[SADORE], ed. "Sex Society Forum on Homosexuality." *Sexology* 26 (3, 1959): 169.

A discussion of the problem of homosexuality by Donald Webster Cory, Robert A. Harper, and Robert Veit Sherwin is summarized. According to Cory, homosexuality is a sickness or neurotic disturbance which society should not persecute or ridicule. Harper believes that most homosexual patients are insecure, have low personal esteem, are unusually sensitive to the repressive aspects of our antisexual society, and had parents who were extremely puritanical in their attitudes toward sex. According to Sherwin, the legal treatment of homosexuals is just short of barbaric; the chief method of arresting homosexuals (i.e., entrapment) is unconstitutional.

542   RUBINS, JACK L. "The Neurotic Personality and Certain Sexual Perversions." *Contemporary Psychoanalysis* 4 (1967): 53–72.

An account of the treatment of eight persons who practice transvestism, fetishism, exhibitionism, or voyeurism includes a short discussion of the clinical features usually present in either latent or dormant homosexuality. These clinical features include the active rejection of one's own sex, repeated and/or satisfactory adolescent homosexual contacts, a distorted sexual self-concept and identity, and an inability to enjoy heterosexual intercourse.

The histories of the eight patients discussed in this article include no evidence of the presence of these clinical features. Although their perversions—transvestism, fetishism, exhibitionism, and voyeurism—served as a means of mechanizing, impersonalizing, and distancing sexual relationships, these particular perversions did not preclude the desire for heterosexual relationships. Transvestism, fetishism, exhibitionism, and voyeurism, therefore, may be seen as limited perversions, and their presence does not necessarily indicate the presence of either latent or dormant homosexuality.

543   RUITENBEEK, HENDRIK M., ed. *Homosexuality and Creative Genius.* New York: Astor-Honor, 1967, 330 pp.

The lives and works of several writers, whose overt or latent homosexuality is believed to have been intricately related to their artistic output, were examined to determine the relationship between homosexuality and literary creativity. In the introduction homosexuality and creativity are briefly discussed as two separate phenomena about which contemporary psychoanalysts are still divided. Homosexuality today is considered not only a problem of sexual expression, but also one of identity. Creativity is considered by some experts as resulting from neurosis and by others as the resolution of more realistic conflicts such as illness, loss of loved ones, and death. Still others regard creativity in terms of health or as the result of "peak experience." Even the definition of the term "creative" is subject to dispute. The problem of the relationship between homosexuality and creativity is pinpointed as a question of whether creativity is a "function of neurosis or neurosis a mere troubler of the creative waters."

Two general essays which preface the studies on individual writers are "Eroticism as Portrayed in Literature," by Frederic J. Farnell, and "The Mother Complex in Literature," by Claude D. Daly. One or more studies are presented on each of the following writers: Oscar Wilde, John Addington Symonds, Walt Whitman, Radclyffe Hall, Denis de Saint-Pavin, Arthur Rimbaud, André Gide, Marcel Proust, Percy Bysshe Shelley, and Emile Zola. Each essay is prefaced with a brief introduction by the editor.

544   RUSKIN, SAMUEL H. "Analysis of Sex Offenders Among Male Psychiatric Patients." *American Journal of Psychiatry* 97 (4, 1941): 955–968.

An investigation of the relationship between sex delinquency and mental disease and whether it occurred before or after the onset of psychotic symptoms is described. Individual psychotherapy was given to 130 male patients (123 were white and seven were Negro) who were sex offenders being treated at the Eloise Hospital in Eloise, Michigan. Fourteen of the 130 (or 10.8 percent) were sex offenders before the recognizable onset of their psychosis; 116 (or 89.2 percent) became sexually deviate afterwards. Certain types of psychotics showed a predominance toward certain types of delinquencies: schizophrenics showed a predominance toward homosexuality, molesting of women and physical assault; mentally deficient patients (8.5 percent of 130) tended toward homosexuality.

545   SALZMAN, LEON. "The Concept of Latent Homosexuality." *American Journal of Psychoanalysis* 17 (2, 1957): 161–169.

The concept of latency as used in psychological theory is discussed with particular reference to the concept of latent homosexuality. The concept of latent homosexuality has played a vital role in the theory of personality development. Latency implies dormancy (the presence of fully developed and matured functions in an inactive state) and potentiality (the presence of possible, but undeveloped, functions). Freud used latency almost exclusively in the sense of dormancy, and as such, it required an acceptance of the bisexual theory of sexual development as the explanation for the development of homosexuality. Since homosexuality is a potentiality in all human beings under certain developmental conditions, a special concept is needed. That is, either notions about latent homosexuality must be revised, or else it must be defined more precisely if it is to be a useful, meaningful concept in personality theory.

546   SALZMAN, LEON. " 'Latent' Homosexuality." In *Sexual Inversion: The Multiple Roots of Homosexuality,* edited by Judd Marmor, pp. 234–247. New York: Basic Books, 1965.

The concept of latent homosexuality can be given up only when it is accepted that sexual behavior, although of biologic origin, plays many roles in a person's life. The term "latent homosexuality" has been loosely used and abused by professionals as well as by laymen. Since it carries derogatory connotations, its validity should be definitely demonstrated or else the term should be completely abandoned.

547   SALZMAN, LEON. "Paranoid State-Theory and Therapy." *Archives of General Psychiatry* 2 (6, 1960): 679–693.

Two extensive case histories which include reports of treatment are used to demonstrate that the Freudian notion of paranoid development based on latent or repressed homosexuality is mistaken. It is suggested, instead, that paranoia occurs when a patient feels himself to be a figure of special prominence or importance and realistic rejections and failures frustrate these grandiose claims.

    This thesis is the reverse of the traditional Freudian idea which holds that paranoid development is based on latent or repressed homosexuality and that the grandiosity is a secondary development used to rationalize the delusion and to explain the attention of the world on the patient.

548   SAPPENFIELD, BERT R. "A Proposed Heterosexual Theory of Delusions." *Psychological Reports* 16 (1, 1965): 84–86.

Freud's theory that paranoid delusions might be based on a homosexual conflict, Ovesey's theory basing paranoid delusions on "pseudo homosexuality," and the biosocial theory of Norman Cameron are all reviewed and criticized. An alternative hypothesis is suggested—that paranoid delusions may arise from incestuous sexuality. The possibility that all paranoid delusions derive from incestuous conflict, or that some delusions have their source in homosexuality while others arise from incestuous sexuality is discussed. It is also conjectured that earlier incestuous conflicts are a major source of homosexuality.

549   SAUL, LEON J. "Feminine Significance of the Nose." *Psychoanalytic Quarterly* 17 (1, 1948): 51–57.

Symbols can be bisexual in nature. The feminine significance of the nose is discussed in the case of a male latent homosexual in analysis. The patient had a terrifying father and a seductive, dominating mother who prevented him from any interaction with girls. Though not an overt homosexual, the patient had passive feminine wishes and desires, expressed in three dreams in which the nose served as a feminine symbol representing the vagina and the anus.

550   SAUL, LEON J., and BECK, AARON T. "Psychodynamics of Male Homosexuality." *International Journal of Psycho-Analysis* 42 (1–2, 1961): 43–48.

The relationships between homosexuality and other mechanisms and motivations operating in the individual are described. Homosexuality is seen as a reflection of deeper needs and drives. This study is based on a survey of the literature and examples from patients' case histories. The interpretations are based on psychoanalytic theory.

There are two functions of homosexuality in males: a method for gratifying infantile needs for love, omnipotence, masochism, power, and adequacy; and a defense against incestuous drives and against hostility toward other men. Psychoanalysis can reveal to the patient the operation of these factors and lead to a decrease in homosexual urges.

551   SCHILDER, PAUL. "On Homosexuality." 1929. Reprinted in *The Homosexuals: As Seen by Themselves and Thirty Authorities*, edited by Aron M. Krich, pp. 201–214. New York: Citadel Press, 1954.

A psychoanalyst discusses several cases of homosexuality from his practice. From these cases is derived the general theory that "bisexuality is somehow. characteristic of the basal constitution of every human being. . . ." Male and female, passive and active impulses are present in everyone. Homosexuality is "not something completely new but something which exaggerates only what can also be found in the sex life of the normal male and female."

552 SCHMIDT, ELSA, and BROWN, PAUL T. "Experimental Testing of Two Psychoanalytic Hypotheses." *British Journal of Medical Psychology* 38 (2, 1965): 177–180.

Two experiments are described. One involved a 32-year-old male who had a long history of motorcycle thefts and who was diagnosed as a motorcycle fetishist and latent homosexual. The object of the experiment was to determine if an interdependence existed between homosexuality and fetishism. A series of words were recorded. The words were preceded by taps and were recorded at a lower intensity than the taps. The patient adjusted the volume so that he could just hear the taps. The subject was instructed to listen for the taps and write down the first word that came into his mind after he heard a tap. The method of the experiment and the results are fully described. The hypothesized relation between the fetish object and homosexuality was not demonstrated.

553 SCHNECK, JEROME M. "Sleep Paralysis: Psychodynamics." *Psychiatric Quarterly* 22, (3, 1948): 462–469.

Sleep paralysis in the absence of narcolepsy or cataplexy is believed to be more common than heretofore realized. The paralysis occurs upon awakening and before going to sleep, times when sexual desires may be most intense but least controllable. Studies of cases lead to the formulation of a theory that the psychodynamics of sleep paralysis is related to a conflict about the expression or repression of unconscious homosexual drives, with the paralysis representing an unsatisfactory compromise with regard to homosexual desires.

554 SCHNECK, JEROME M. "Some Aspects of Homosexuality in Relation to Hypnosis." *Psychoanalytic Review* 37 (4, 1950): 351–357.

The sexual aspects and meanings of hypnosis are discussed in the case report of a 21-year-old single male referred for hypnotherapy because of a hearing disability. The patient had engaged in homosexual behavior, and he had equated the meaning of hypnosis with homosexuality. Therefore, it is advised that investigations of certain aspects of hypnosis (reactivation of the

Oedipal situation, elements of castration anxiety, and masochistic components) be made.

555 SCHWARTZ, BERNARD J. "An Empirical Test of Two Freudian Hypotheses Concerning Castration Anxiety." *Journal of Personality* 24 (3, 1956): 318–327.

Two hypotheses from psychoanalytic theory were tested: overt homosexual males show more intense castration anxieties than normal males and males show more intense castration anxiety than females. Thematic Apperception Test (TAT) scores were obtained from subjects and control groups. The hypotheses were supported by the data.

556 SCHWARZ, HEDWIG. "A Case of Character Disorder." *Bulletin of the Menninger Clinic* 16 (1, 1952): 20–30.

The case of a single homosexual male who underwent psychoanalysis is presented as an example of one type of character disorder. The patient's problems, mainly concerning job instability, did not manifest themselves in a circumscribed set of symptoms, but in the form of a typical behavior pattern which was clearly a deviation from the normal.

557 SCOTT, PETER D. "Definition, Classification, Prognosis and Treatment." In *The Pathology and Treatment of Sexual Deviation: A Methodological Approach,* edited by Ismond Rosen, pp. 87–119. London: Oxford University Press, 1964.

A psychiatric discussion of sexual perversions, including homosexuality, focuses on problems of classification. Homosexuality is classified clinically into "facultative homosexual behavior" and "homosexuality due to 'constitutional' or early experiential psychogenic factors, or both." Other classificatory dimensions include arrested development versus regression—the former being more difficult to treat—and pathologic versus nonpathologic or subcultural deviance. Studies of aversion therapy, hormone treatment, and castration are reviewed.

558 SCOTT, PETER D. "Homosexuality, with Special Reference to Classification." *Proceedings of the Royal Society of Medicine* 50 (9, 1957): 659–660.

Since the quality of the personality of individuals seems to be of major importance in matters of prognosis and treatment, it is suggested that this should serve as the basis for classifying male homosexuals. The broad classifications are as follows: adolescents and mentally immature adults; severely damaged personalities, including very effeminate individuals, inadequate, downtrodden, and dull individuals, and resentful, antisocially inclined individuals; relatively intact, well-socialized personalities with a homosexual orientation; latent and well-compensated homosexuals; and individuals in which homosexuality coexists with a serious mental disability.

559   SCOTT, THOMAS R.; WELLS, WILLIAM H.; WOOD, DOROTHY Z.; and MORGAN, DAVID I. "Pupillary Response and Sexual Interest Reexamined." *Journal of Clinical Psychology* 23 (4, 1967): 433–438.

To determine whether pupillary response to pictures is a reliable indicator of sexual orientation and other interest patterns, three experiments were made. The subjects for the first experiment were 10 male and 10 female college students, and for the second 30 male and 30 female college students, for the third five heterosexual and five homosexual male prison inmates. The subjects were shown pictures of seminude males and females.

The researchers failed to find any difference in pupillary response for males and females, or between heterosexuals and homosexuals. In addition there was no evidence that nonpreferred stimuli elicit pupillary constriction, whereas preferred stimuli did appear to elicit dilation. The experiments were conducted in response to E. H. Hess's opposite observations reported in *Scientific American,* 1965, vol. 212, no. 4, pp. 46–54. See Hess (no. 445).

560   SEGAL, MOREY, M. "Transvestitism as an Impulse and as a Defence." *International Journal of Psycho-Analysis* 46 (2, 1965): 209–217.

The relationship of separation anxiety and multiple identifications in transvestitism, the interrelation between transvestitism and homosexuality, the role which the symbiotic process plays in the evolution of transvestitism are considered. Clinical material from three cases is used as a basis for the conclusions which are reached.

Masculine transvestitism in a woman serves as a compromise solution which enables her to identify and maintain contact with the father, while at the same time in her sexual pursuit of women, she preserves the symbiotic bond to the mother. Masculine transvestitism in women is always alloplastic and the homosexuality is not "disguided."

Contrary to female homosexual wishes, overt passive homosexual wishes in male transvestites are often intolerable. The resolutions available are denial by a reactive heterosexual promiscuity; marked projection which becomes clinically manifested as a paranoid state; development of a predominantly obsessive-compulsive character disorder with mild paranoid trends; evasive perversion (transvestitism or fetishism) by regression, splitting of the ego, and the emergence of a more primitive ego component; and schizophrenic psychosis.

Transvestitism is more closely related to homosexuality than fetishism.

In children, transvestitism is considered as a transitional symptom toward an ultimate homosexual adaptation. In adults, transvestitism may be transitory or may interchange with homosexuality. Nonetheless, the nuclear symbiotic relationship to the mother remains the most basic connection, of which homosexuality is a later development. Transvestitism can be considered as a compromise formation for those males who perceive homosexuality as incompatible with their own mental masculine conceptions and a challenge to their ideal of a man.

561 SEIDENBERG, ROBERT. "A Note on the Theory of Homosexuality: The Body as Object." *Journal of Nervous and Mental Disease* 128 (2, 1959): 179–181.

The ideas of Freud, Fairbairn, and Szasz on object relatedness and object loss are briefly reviewed. The case of a 32-year-old male in therapy for homosexual feelings, who related to his own body as an object, is presented. His attempts to transfer his preoccupation with his own body to an external object through homosexual fantasies are described.

562 SHNEIDMAN, EDWIN S. "The Case of El: Psychological Test Data." *Journal of Projective Techniques and Personality Assessment* 25 (2, 1961): 131–154.

El, a 30-year-old Caucasian male homosexual, was selected as a case study for a symposium of the American Psychological Association in September 1961. He agreed to take 16 tests, namely, the Rorschach, the Thematic Apperception Test, the Make A Picture Story test, the Forer Sentence Completion Test, the Shneidman Interest-Completion Test, the Strong Vocational Interest Blank, the Kuder Preference Record (Vocational), The Guilford-Shneidman-Zimmerman Interest Survey, the Allport-Vernon-Lindzey Study of Values, the Hildreth Feeling and Attitude Scale, the Cornell Selectee Index, the Minnesota Multiphasic Personality Inventory, the Hartford Retreat Scale, the Wechsler Adult Intelligence Scale, the Watson-Glaser Test of Critical Thinking, and the Tsedek Test of Moral Judgment. The entire texts of these tests are reproduced in the article. El's biography, together with discussions and interpretations of the various tests by several clinicians, are included in the two subsequent issues of the *Journal.*
See Fine (no. 385); Forer (no. 390); Hooker (no. 454); Meyer (no. 509); Murray (no. 513); and Shneidman (no. 563).

563 SHNEIDMAN, EDWIN S. "The Logic of El: A Psycho-Logical Approach to the Analysis of Test Data." *Journal of Projective Techniques and Personality Assessment* 25 (4, 1961): 390–403.

As part of a symposium on El, a male homosexual, the article focuses upon the "intellective" or cognitive aspects of El's mind and the personality correlates of these logical aspects. It demonstrates El's anxieties about involvements and his capacity to lead a dual life.

See Fine (no. 385); Forer (no. 390); Hooker (no. 454); Meyer (no. 509); Murray (no. 513); and Shneidman (no. 562).

564   SIEGAL, LEWIS J. "Homosexuality: Psychotherapeutic Approach and Its Criminogenic Challenge." *Group Psychotherapy* 8 (1, 1955): 321–326.

Very little can be done for men who "continue to carry over their homosexual 'perversity' into adolescence and adulthood." The case history of a 19-year-old boy is presented to support this contention. Unfortunately, this youth's homosexuality was combined with psychopathy, which "is absent in a goodly number of cases of apparent homosexuality."

565   SILBER, AUSTIN. "Object Choice in a Case of Male Homosexuality." *Psychoanalytic Quarterly* 30 (4, 1961): 497–503.

The report is given of a case history illustrating an observation made by Freud about male sibling rivalry. The younger brother's jealousy and sense of rivalry toward an older brother can be changed into a relationship in which the older brother becomes a love object.

During psychoanalysis a middle-aged man who compulsively sought homosexuals to perform fellatio on him reported feelings of *déjà vu* upon his brother's death, thus revealing prior death wishes. The anxiety created by this rivalry and subsequent victory led to the patient's attempt to take back his wish by bringing his brother back to life in the form of an erect, red penis. (His brother had red hair.)

566   SJOSTEDT, ELSIE MARIE, and HURWITZ, IRVING. "A Developmental Study of Sexual Functioning by Means of a Cognitive Analysis." *Journal of Projective Techniques* 23 (2, 1959): 237–246.

A study was made of 74 male white sexual deviants from the Wisconsin Division of Corrections, including 36 exhibitionists and 38 homosexuals (15 were married, and 23 were unmarried). Eighty white married males, who had been used in previous research at Worcester State Hospital, were used as a control group. The Roschach and I.Q. tests (Stanford-Binet, Wechsler-Bellevue, Otis, and Corsini) were administered.

Deviant sexual activity was not found to be associated with a lower order of cognitive development. The combined group of deviants produced significantly more FC (form dominates over color—associated with relatively mature perceptual-cognitive functioning) responses, the married homosexuals being the highest in this regard, than did the normal controls. The unmarried homosexuals showed a wide variation in development.

567 SLATER, ELIOT, and SLATER, PATRICK. "A Study in the Assessment of Homosexual Traits." *British Journal of Medical Psychology* 21 (1, 1947): 61–74.

It was proposed, on the basis of a genetic theory, that psychological traits which differentiate men from women would also differentiate constitutionally different types of men from one another. Fifty "normal" men and 37 homosexual men who were referred to the neurological wing of Sutton E. M. S. Hospital for treatment were given a selective vocabulary test. Their ages ranged from 19 to 57 years. The test was also given in high schools to 74 boys and 78 girls, all 15 years old.

The test differentiated effectively between boys and girls of the same age, education, and home background. It also differentiated the homosexuals from normal men. The homosexuals formed a heterogeneous group in terms of their test scores.

568 SLOVENKO, RALPH. "Sexual Deviation: Response to an Adaptational Crisis." *University of Colorado Law Review* 40 (1967–1968): 222–241.

Sexual deviation, a means of adaptation, is seen as an attempt at overcoming a psychological, sexual, or physical imbalance in life. Homosexuality is used as an illustration of sexual deviancy to show that the sexual deviant is not only sexually different from others, but is also angry because he feels he has been cheated and because he lacks confidence. The sexual confusion of the sex pervert, considered a borderline psychotic, often results in aggressive behavior against society.

569 SMITH, CHARLES E. "The Homosexual Federal Offender: A Study of 100 Cases." *Journal of Criminal Law, Criminology and Police Science* 44 (5, 1954): 582–592.

Some observations on the problem of the incarceration of homosexuals in an all-male environment were made. They were based on a study of 100 homosexuals in federal prisons. Fifteen of the homosexuals had been committed for offenses directly related to their sexual deviation (nine on sodomy charges and six for postal law violations—letters of solicitation).

Statistical compilations of case histories were made, and arrest reports, et cetera, were studied. Offenses of car theft, mail theft, robbery, and forgery occurred much more frequently among the homosexual than among the general prison population. By way of explanation, it was noted that the crimes were committed on an impulse, that poor judgment was exercised, and that these persons often fitted into the diagnostic category of the sociopathic or psychopathic personality type. A high incidence of diagnosed mental disorder existed in this group.

570   SOCARIDES, CHARLES W. "The Development of a Fetishistic Perversion: The Contribution of Preoedipal Phase Conflict." *Journal of the American Psychoanalytic Association* 8 (2, 1960): 281–311.

The unresolved wish in the male to have a child may antedate the Oedipal childhood conflict. A case history of a young, artistic, intelligent male transvestite in analysis is presented. His homosexual tendencies, which reveal themselves through his dreams, are shown.

571   SOCARIDES, CHARLES W. *The Overt Homosexual.* New York: Grune & Stratton, 1968, 245 pp.

A compendium of the accumulated psychoanalytic perspectives on homosexuality are discussed in the light of the author's clinical experience and observations as a psychoanalyst. His own theoretical emphasis is summarized as follows: "The homosexual is fixated on the wish for the mother-child unity. This, however, signals an attempt to regress to the undifferentiated phase and a total destruction of the self in a union with the mother. It is to be avoided at any cost. All further activities of his life are designed to ward off the realization of his situation. Homosexual behavior appears to be the solution for forestalling a powerful affective state which threatens to destroy the individual both by anxiety and loss of personal identity with a return to the amorphous, undifferentiated state of the ego. The choice of partner of the same sex, a phenomenon of the polymorphous-perverseness of infantile sexuality, is pressed into service for repression of the basic conflict: the mother-child unity accompanied by dire fear of loss of self."

The volume contains a review of the literature, an account of Freud's contributions to the research problems of homosexuality, and a section on theory providing a discussion of theoretical concepts concerning the development of both male and female homosexuality, the role of aggression, projection, and identification, the adolescent phase of development, and the relationship of homosexuality to other clinical states. A section on therapy with suggested procedures for treatment, which are related to the author's conceptualization of the issues involved, is also included.

572   SOCARIDES, CHARLES W. "Theoretical and Clinical Aspects of Overt Male Homosexuality." *Journal of the American Psychoanalytic Association* 8 (3, 1960): 552–566.

An American Psychoanalytic Association panel discussion is reported. The following topics are included: a historical survey of the literature on overt male homosexuality; the structure and meaning of the homosexual love object, characteristics of the homosexual ego, the clinical appearance of the pathology of homosexuality, and the meaning of the fantasies that are acted out in this entity; the genetic psychic determinants for overt homosexuality; and therapeutic problems in the psychoanalysis of overt male homosexuals.

573 SOLYOM, LESLIE, and BECK, PHILIP R. "GSR Assessment of Aberrant Sexual Behavior." *International Journal of Neuropsychiatry* 3 (1, 1967): 52–59.

Four male subjects with sexually aberrant behavior (one homosexual and three fetishists) were shown photographs of objects sexually stimulating to them—in the case of the homosexual the photograph was that of a seminude male—and their Galvanic Skin Responses were measured. The responses were compared with responses to photographs of a geometric pattern and of seminude females. The responses to the subjects' particular sexually stimulating object were stronger and more prolonged than the responses to neutral and heterosexual stimuli. The significance of this method for diagnosis and treatment was discussed.

574 SPENCER, J. C. "Contributions to the Symposium on Sexual Deviation." *Canadian Journal of Corrections* 3 (1961): 481–484.

A number of statistics based on a study of 132 sexual offenders seen at the Toronto Forensic Clinic are presented in the course of a general discussion of sexual deviation in Canada. Whereas exhibitionist activity is carried out mainly by persons who are between puberty and their middle thirties and pedophiliac activity is more often engaged in by persons still in adolescence or in their late thirties or late fifties, homosexuals reach the peak of their activities in their late twenties, which decline during their thirties and increase again in their forties.

In addition, a comparison of intelligence test scores indicated that while exhibitionists and pedophiles had essentially normal I.Q.'s, the average intelligence of the homosexual offender was considerably above normal (I.Q. = 114). Homosexuals also had a higher level of educational achievement and were predominantly employed in white-collar occupations. The value of incarceration for sex offenses, except in the case of rape, is questioned.

575 SPENCER, S. J. G. "Homosexuality among Oxford Undergraduates." *Journal of Mental Science* 105 (439, 1959): 393–405.

To collect data on the incidence and persistence of homosexual trends and practices at Oxford University, a study was made of 51 of 100 Oxford undergraduate psychiatric patients (all complaining of homosexuality) and 35 of 100 freshmen controls. Lack of heterosexual interest corresponded with homosexual interest in the patients but not in the controls. The Minnesota Multiphasic Personality Inventory masculinity-femininity scale was administered.

Ten patients and 27 controls showed a homosexuality in which an adolescent phase of interest in a practice with coevals occurred in subjects having more brothers than average or going to boarding schools. Their stability was relatively high. The patients were relatively mesomorphic but in severe conflict with their mothers. The controls were mesopenic and in less maternal conflict. They may be "facultative homosexuals."

Forty-one patients and eight controls showed a homosexuality "wherein the greater the muscle lack, the worse the prognosis. . . . The group consisted mainly of day pupils. The controls tended to be in the lower social grades." Among the patients, at least 24 (or 47 percent) of all homosexuals were estimated to come into Kinsey's gradings of four or more. In 14 the prognosis for a "swing over" was considered dubious, and in a further 10 definitely poor. Homosexuality was associated among the patients with suicidal attempts, gestures, or urges. Psychotherapy was considered helpful for five patients.

The importance of mesopenia and conflict with the mother in these subjects was stressed.

576   STOLLER, ROBERT J. "Identity, Homosexuality, and Paranoidness."
       In his *Sex and Gender: On the Development of Masculinity and Femininity,* pp. 154–162. New York: Science House, 1968.

The explanation that it is the awareness of social disapproval of homosexuality in our society that produces the paranoid reaction on the part of homosexuals is not satisfactory. In persons whose gender identity is not firmly fixed homosexuality is a threat. Perhaps the reason most homosexuals do not become psychotic is that they have relatively "comfortable" identities as homosexuals; thus, homosexuality does not pose a great threat.

The unusual case history of a patient who became disturbed because heterosexuality threatened his identity as a homosexual is presented. "Paranoidness" thus may result from the threat to the sense of identity from either direction, homosexuality or heterosexuality.

577   STOLLER, ROBERT J. "The Transsexual's Denial of Homosexuality." In his *Sex and Gender: On the Development of Masculinity and Femininity,* pp. 141–153. New York: Science House, 1968.

Emphasizing, as Greenson does, the difference between the desire to possess another person and the desire to be that person ("I want to have" versus "I want to be"), it is stated that the same word, "homosexual," should not be used for the man who wants other men and for the man who is effeminate. If part of a man's effeminacy is the result of his having identified with the woman's sexual role, he will desire men sexually; the gender and sexual aspects would be inextricably related. If he identifies with the nonsexual aspects of a female, they will not be so related. The answer to why transsexuals and many transvestites insist that they are not homosexual may lie in an understanding of the formation of, and the later struggle to maintain, a gender identity.

578 SULZBERGER, CARL FULTON. "An Undiscovered Source of Heterosexual Disturbance." *Psychoanalytic Review* 42 (4, 1955): 435–437.

The relationship between the attitude of one sex to the other is discussed. Every frustration of sublimated homosexual strivings can result in an unconscious antagonism to the opposite sex; the opposite sex is unconsciously sensed as being the cause of the frustration. The person seeks to restore the balance by hostility toward the opposite sex. This explains many conflicts between the sexes. Sublimated homosexual strivings must be gratified through social success or achievements before heterosexual needs can be fulfilled.

579 "Symposium on 'Reinterpretations of the Schreber Case: Freud's Theory of Paranoia.'" Introduction and Summary by Philip M. Kitay; and four papers by Arthur C. Carr, William G. Niederland, Jules Nydes, and Robert B. White. *International Journal of Psycho-Analysis* 44 (2, 1963): 191–223.

In these papers the panelists reexamine the famous Schreber case 50 years after the publication of Freud's paper in which he used the case to affirm his theory of paranoia as a defense against homosexuality. Although much criticism has been directed against Freud's interpretation of the case, the panelists' main criticism is that Freud "did not push his own formulation far enough and broadly enough." The classical Freudian interpretation gives insufficient recognition to the importance of hostile destructive drives and neglects the influence of Schreber's conflicts with his mother in the etiology of his illness. Each panelist emphasizes specific etiological factors in the case, and new documentary evidence in support of Freud is summarized.

Carr examines evidence opposing the Freudian theory that paranoid delusions are always a defense against homosexuality, evidence based on the fact that many cases of paranoid symptomatology do not appear to reflect any homosexual problem, and case reports that demonstrate a coexistence of paranoid delusions and overt homosexuality, sometimes without apparent conflict. These arguments are found unconvincing upon close examination and several modifications, necessary to any reinterpretation of the Schreber case in the light of developments in ego psychology since 1911, are suggested.

Certain specific hypotheses, which are suggested by a review of cases with paranoid symptomatology, are examined in terms of their relevance to the Schreber case.

580   SYMPOSIUM ON THE PREDICTION OF OVERT BEHAVIOR THROUGH THE USE OF PROJECTIVE TECHNIQUES. *The Prediction of Overt Behavior Through the Use of Projective Techniques,* by Arthur C. Carr, et al., Springfield, Ill.: Charles C. Thomas, 1960, 177 pp.

The reports presented constituted the proceedings of a symposium presented at the Annual Convention of the American Psychological Association in September, 1959. Arthur C. Carr, who organized the symposium, gave a brief introduction. The findings of Evelyn Hooker regarding the impossibility of distinguishing Rorschach protocols of homosexuals from those of a matched heterosexual control group make a more precise formulation of the underlying principles for inferring overt behavior from projective test responses imperative.

Test protocols on a pair of identical twins, one of whom was homosexual, were made available to each symposium participant, who was free to use the data in any way he chose. Forer considered the Sentence Completions, Henry the Thematic Apperception Test, Hutt the Revised Bender-Gestalt Visual Motor Test, and Piotrowski the Rorschach. Carr discussed the developmental histories of the twins, and Hooker presented a detailed discussion of the varying interpretations given by these experts. Because of the "remarkably varied and idiosyncratic patterns of handling the data," the validity of prediction of either overt or covert behavior from projective tests is doubtful. The critical question is how to predict overt behavior from the covert. It was stated that discrepancies in interpretation of the data by the participants could be due as much to different theoretical conceptions of homosexuality as to differences in test data.

An appendix includes the full test protocols.

581   TAYLOR, A. J. W., and MCLACHLAN, D. G. "MMPI Profiles of Six Transvestites." *Journal of Clinical Psychology* 19 (3, 1963): 330–332.

The Minnesota Multiphasic Personality Inventory was administered to six male transvestites. Four of the transvestites were practicing homosexuals and none of the six had biological deviations toward femininity. Scale five differentiated the practicing homosexuals from the practicing heterosexuals with no homosexual experience.

582   TAYLOR, CHUCK. "The Successful Homosexual." *One* 7 (5, 1959): 5–9.

An interview with a male homosexual who is a teacher in the elementary schools is presented. From the interview it was found that a homosexual may or may not be a successful member in society and may make an outstanding teacher because of certain qualities a homosexual tends to have: understanding, insight, patience, neatness, parental yearnings, and a wide range of interests. These successful homosexuals are usually very covert and very careful in their dealings with children. The admirable, successful homosexuals are not usually known to be homosexuals by the general public, and the less admirable and obvious ones make for sweeping condemnations of all of them.

583   THOMAS, RICHARD WALLACE. "An Investigation of the Psychoanalytic Theory of Homosexuality." Ph.D. dissertation, University of Kentucky, 1951, 167 pp.

In order to test psychoanalytic theory regarding homosexuality, a group of 40 overtly homosexual male veterans of World War II and a control group of 20 hospitalized male veterans of World War II, whose Rorschachs showed no homosexual content, were given the Minnesota Multiphasic Personality Inventory (short form) and the Blacky Pictures test.

   No support was found for theories that all homosexuals have regressed to the early oral stage of psychosexual development; that active homosexuals would show masturbation guilt; that castration anxiety is very important in the etiology of homosexuality; and that active—as opposed to passive—homosexuals have nothing effeminate about them. The results of the tests also indicated that active homosexuals show a marked disturbance at the oral-sadistic level; that passive homosexuals are fixated at the anal stage; that homosexuals are characterized by persistent Oedipal intensity; and that they have a feminine identification. In addition homosexuals show disturbance in the area of positive ego ideal, choose narcissistic love objects, and also choose anaclitic love objects, and passive homosexuals act and feel like women. No significant results were found regarding the theory that a special type of homosexuality is caused by intense sibling rivalry or regarding the concept of anal expulsiveness.

584   THOMPSON, CLARA. "Changing Concepts of Homosexuality in Psychoanalysis." *Psychiatry* 10 (2, 1947): 183–189. Reprinted in *The*

Problem of Homosexuality in Modern Society, edited by Hendrik M. Ruitenbeek, pp. 40–51. New York: E. P. Dutton, 1963. Also reprinted as "Changing Concepts in Psychoanalysis." In *The Homosexuals: As Seen by Themselves and Thirty Authorities,* edited by Aron M. Krich, pp. 251–261. New York: Citadel Press, 1954. Also reprinted as "Changing Concepts of Homosexuality." In *Carol in a Thousand Cities,* edited by Ann Aldrich, pp. 167–179. Greenwich, Conn.: Fawcett Publications, 1960.

Since "homosexuality" includes so many different types of behavior, the whole subject is reviewed tracing various psychoanalytic ideas about homosexuality and describing the status of the concept today. Although the specific cause of homosexuality cannot be found, it may be said that it gives sexual satisfaction, copes with the problem of isolation and loneliness, and brings freedom from responsibility as well as, at times, financial support.

Homosexuality will never be found to be the cause of the rest of the neurotic structure, although it may contribute to whatever other problems exist. Psychoanalysis must deal primarily with the personality structure, realizing that the symptom is a secondary development from that.

585 THOMSON, PETER G. "Vicissitudes of the Transference in a Male Homosexual." *International Journal of Psycho-Analysis* 49 (4, 1968): 629–639.

The cause, development, and fluctuation of male homosexual transference are considered through a case study. Transference is viewed in relation to fusion with an archaic maternal image, and how this image is used to ward off violent, sadistic sexual desires. The patient, a 30-year-old Jewish professional man, sought help through psychoanalysis for problems of homosexuality. The patient's early years are discussed in relation to his present problem. The outstanding feature of his history was the premature and traumatic disruption of the primary union, when the patient's father "snatched" him from his mother's arms. Much of the patient's behavior reflects his attempts to reclaim the established object of the mother by introjection and by the development of an intense, destructive aggression. The parental introjects and their function are described as well as issues pertaining to the patient's sexual identity.

586 THORNER, H. A. "Notes on a Case of Male Homosexuality." *International Journal of Psycho-Analysis* 30 (1, 1949): 31–35.

The psychological factors which influence or determine the mixture of the sexual characteristics in an individual and the sex of the love object were sought in the psychoanalysis of a male homosexual.

The patient's manifest homosexuality took the place of another symptom and was a defense against anxiety; his constant change of partners was of a compulsive nature. His homosexuality was a symptom of a general neurosis rather than an illness or a perversion. Homosexuality, manifest or latent, receives its significance not from the choice of a love object of the same sex, but from the unconscious fantasy material which breaks through in the homosexual activity.

587   THORNTON, NATHANIEL. "Some Mechanisms of Paranoia." *Psychoanalytic Review* 35 (3, 1948): 290–294.

Freud has said that paranoia represents the individual's striving toward the repression of homosexual tendencies which the ego is unprepared to acknowledge or entertain. However, while many cases of paranoia have manifested a homosexual component, it is probably not justified to attribute it to all cases.

588   TONG, J. E. "Galvanic Skin Response Studies of Sex Responsiveness in Sex Offenders and Others." *Journal of Mental Science* 106 (445, 1960): 1475–1485.

The Galvanic Skin Response/Word Association technique is presented as a useful method of determining sexual responsiveness in offenders. A word list, consisting of three sex and/or homosexual words, two homosexual words, two sex words, five sadistic/aggressive words, five arson words, 20 neutral words, and one miscellaneous word, was presented on different occasions to 140 disordered mentally defective male patients. The patients were classified as homosexual, sexual, violent, or miscellaneous. The patients' recorded Galvanic Skin Responses and eye blinks were assessed and the primary response was found to differentiate the classified patients at a high level of confidence. Following the repetition of "table," "sex," "jacket," "strangle," and "floor," other variations indicated habituation for the word "sex," and the fear stimulus. A dual index of habituation rate and GSR was present in 50 percent of the sex offenders but in none of the other groups, and it was found to be somewhat associated with the nature of the sex disorder. Other differences which were observed included responsiveness to Rorschach colors and primary GSR in the sex group, a varying association of primary sex response with pain-resistance rating, and variations in GSR to homosexual words such as "intercourse," "kiss," "bottle," and "bottom." Usage of ambiguous stimuli, "bottle," "bottom," is deserving of further study. A greater number of responses to sexual cues by sex offenders than by other offenders was indicated by the data. Increased physiological (GSR) activity (eye-blink) when sex words are repeated to a patient may be contraindicative of interview therapy because of tension experienced by the patient.

589   TUFO, GUSTAVE F. "The Genesis of Homosexuality." *Journal of American Institute of Homeopathy* 57 (3–4, 1964): 33–34.

The isolation felt by homosexuals, their subsequent needs to continually recreate this feeling of aloneness, and the common theory that homosexuality arises from a felt need to achieve sexual fulfillment without suffering anxiety from Oedipal complexes are discussed briefly. "Successful" treatment in psychotherapy can result from patient and sympathetic understanding of the needs which homosexual relationships satisfy.

590   VILHOTTI, ANTHONY J. "An Investigation of the Use of the D.A.P. in the Diagnosis of Homosexuality in Mentally Deficient Males." *American Journal of Mental Deficiency* 62 (4, 1958): 708–711.

To determine whether the drawing of the female figure, in response to the instructions to "draw a person," would occur to a significantly greater degree among mentally deficient male homosexuals as compared to non-homosexual mentally deficient males, the Draw-a-Person Test was given to 50 male homosexuals and 50 male nonhomosexuals of the Rainier State School. The I.Q. was 30–79 for the homosexuals, and 20–99 for the non-homosexuals.

The results indicated that the sign of drawing the female figure as diagnostic of male homosexuality was not useful in differentiating between homosexual and nonhomosexual groups of institutionalized mental deficients.

591   WAHL, CHARLES WILLIAM. "Psychiatric Techniques in the Taking of a Sexual History." In *Sexual Problems: Diagnosis and Treatment in Medical Practice,* edited by Charles William Wahl, pp. 13–21. New York: Free Press, 1967.

The techniques involved in obtaining a patient's detailed sexual history, including homosexuality, are explained. Either direct or indirect interviews may be conducted, with a progression from the general medical to the sexual history, and in the latter, from the least to the most embarrassing areas of sexual experience.

Questions concerning homosexuality should begin with inquiries about when the patient first acquired information about the subject, just what was learned, and whether this information was upsetting to the patient. These initial queries should be followed by a question concerning any experiences of being approached by homosexual persons and the degree of emotional distress any such experience may have caused. At this point, most patients can be asked directly if they have ever had a homosexual experience. An affirmative answer should be probed for the frequency of subsequent same-sex encounters, the number and nature of the sexual partners, the character of the sex acts, and, most important, any conflict resulting from homosexual experiences.

592   WALKER, EDWARD L. "The Terman-Miles 'M-F' Test and the Prison Classification Program." *Journal of Genetic Psychology* 59 (1941): 27–40.

To determine if the Terman-Miles Attitude-Interest Analysis Test of masculinity-femininity could detect homosexuals among adult males, 250 male prisoners (of which 20 were homosexuals) at the Indiana State Prison, were given the test. The homosexuals were classified according to "active" and "passive" behavior patterns. It was found that passive homosexuals were just as likely to make a high masculine score as a high feminine score, and active or aggressive homosexuals made scores almost as widely scattered. No aspect of test performance could be found which would point out members of either group. Therefore, the Terman-Miles Attitude-Interest Analysis Test is of little practical value as a diagnostic tool in detecting homosexuals in a prison.

593   WALTERS, ORVILLE S. "A Methodological Critique of Freud's Schreber Analysis." *Psychoanalytic Review* 42 (4, 1955): 321–342.

The widely accepted concept that paranoid symptoms are due to unconscious homosexual conflict is challenged. Because Freud's analysis of Dr. Schreber's autobiography formed the basis for this concept, this analysis and Freud's methodological approach are examined in detail from the statement of the problem to the final "clarification of the initial problem in the light of the tested hypothesis." The application of the theory to account for all paranoia is not warranted by empirical findings, although evidence of homosexual conflict was found in a limited number of the patients studied. Numerous authorities and studies are cited to indicate the inadequacy of the theory; the tendency of ideas to become frozen through continued uncritical acceptance is also emphasized. The acceptance of Freud's theory tends to prevent the exploration of other possible etiologic factors in the individual and obstructs progress toward a clearer understanding of paranoia as a symptom complex with a diverse etiology.

594   WATSON, CHARLES G. "A Test of the Relationship Between Repressed Homosexuality and Paranoid Mechanisms." *Journal of Clinical Psychology* 21 (4, 1965): 380–384.

In an attempt to test Freud's hypothesis that the etiology of paranoia begins with repressed homosexuality, it was hypothesized that paranoid schizophrenics will score lower than nonparanoid schizophrenic controls on a true-false test of homosexual aversions, that paranoids with homosexual tendencies will take longer to respond to homosexual themes in the Thematic Apperception Test pictures than nonparanoids, and that paranoids will have a higher mean raw score on the Minnesota Multiphasic Personality Inventory M-F Test than nonparanoid schizophrenics.

The 46 subjects, all under 50 years old, included 23 paranoid schizophrenics and 23 nonparanoid schizophrenic males from a Veterans Administration Hospital. There was no difference between the groups with respect to age, education, length of hospitalization, or I.Q.

A true-false Homosexuality Awareness Scale (reproduced in the text) was used with 23 items overtly judging homosexual thought (for example, "I like to be with handsome men"). In addition, the homosexual awareness test included the M-F Scale from the MMPI and 23 filler items. The TAT pictures consisted of two cards, one with high homosexual content and the other with a neutral content. (The pictures are reproduced in the text.)

The first and second hypotheses were supported. The first was significant at $p < .01$, and the second at $p < .05$. The third hypothesis was rejected. Repression of homosexual tendencies and thought were more typical of paranoid schizophrenics than of nonparanoid schizophrenics.

595   WAYNE, DAVID M.; ADAMS, M.; and ROWE, LILLIAN A. "A Study of Military Prisoners at a Disciplinary Barracks Suspected of Homosexual Activities." *Military Surgeon* 101 (6, 1947): 499–504.

A military study was made of 50 male prisoners suspected of homosexuality and 50 known homosexual male prisoners. The control group consisted of an equal number of men selected at random from the prison population. A modified group Rorschach, the Thematic Apperception Test, and the Bender-Gestalt Test were administered, and case records were anlayzed. In the majority of background and personality characteristics, the known and suspected homosexuals did not differ essentially from the control group. The TAT was not able to identify the homosexuals. The Rorschach did not reveal sexual deviation as a single personality characteristic; sexual deviation could be found in connection with almost any personality structure.

596   Weisman, Avery D. "Self-Destruction and Sexual Perversion." In *Essays in Self-Destruction,* edited by Edwin S. Shneidman, pp. 419–434, New York: Science House, Inc., 1967.

One of three case studies of sexual deviants with suicidal tendencies was a male homosexual executive. Unable to resolve the conflict between a growing heterosexual desire and a pattern of homosexual behavior, he made several attempts at suicide, the final one being successful.

Homosexual "inclinations" are also found in the two other case studies —notably in the case of a 35-year-old machinist. Having been paid for sexual activity with both males and females, he identified with female prostitutes and believed he was becoming a lesbian.

597 WEISS, EDOARDO. "Bisexuality and Ego Structure." *International Journal of Psycho-Analysis* 39 (1958): 91–97.

The dynamic processes of "internalization," "externalization," and "resonance identification" are discussed in connection with a certain type of male homosexuality. In such a case, a "male, who does not dare to assert his phallic masculine drives or feels a phallic deficiency, may externalize his penis and its function into an object representation of another man who possesses an efficient penis." Since such a man cannot egotize his own penis, he substitutes another male's penis for his own and through the process of "resonance identification" with the love object feels restored to a sexual entireness. These processes are compared with those which are involved in the penis-envy of a girl and the experience of feminine mutilation. Finally, the longing for a woman by a man and vice versa are discussed with reference to the above dynamic processes and are understood as an attempt on the part of the man or the woman to re-establish a bisexual unity.

598 WHEELER, WILLIAM MARSHALL. "An Analysis of Rorschach Indices of Male Homosexuality." *Rorschach Research Exchange and Journal of Projective Techniques* 13 (2, 1949): 97–126.

To determine the relationship between estimates of homosexuality based upon selected Rorschach content signs and clinical judgments derived from therapeutic contacts, a study was made of 100 male patients at the Los Angeles Veterans Administration Mental Hygiene Clinic. The subjects ranged in age from 19 to 47 years. Twenty signs of the Rorschach, the "Wheeler content signs test," were used.

"A combined picture of the male homosexual would be: a somewhat paranoid individual with derogatory attitudes toward people, especially women, which is accompanied by a feminine identification. There are indications of anal interests and interest in physical relationships between like beings. There is apparently some preoccupation with sex in general and some autoerotic concern." There is a need to develop objective signs and determinations of the Rorschach, since therapists' clinical judgments, subject to the influences of training, tend to be unreliable.

599 WHEELER, WILLIAM MARSHALL. "An Analysis of Rorschach Indices of Male Homosexuality as Compared with Clinical Data." Ph.D. dissertation, University of California, 1948, 60 pp.

An estimate of homosexuality based upon the Rorschach and another based upon therapeutic contacts was obtained and analyzed in terms of the items contributing to each estimate and in terms of the relationship between the two estimates. Four factors—a concern over homosexual and autosexual experiences, a lack of "warmth" in heterosexual relations, a tendency to identify with the mother, and a history of being restricted to an all-male environment—were associated with a "homosexual" score on the Rorschach and with a homosexual designation made from a therapeutic evaluation. Effeminate appearance or manner was indicative of homosexuality in the therapeutic ratings but was not associated with a "homosexual" score on the Rorschach. Fourteen items on the Rorschach seemed to be of sufficient consistency to enable their use in clinical practice. Four items could not be judged as to consistency because they appeared too infrequently. Two items were deemed inconsistent.

600 WHITAKER, LEIGHTON, JR. "The Use of an Extended Draw-a-Person Test to Identify Homosexual and Effeminate Men." *Journal of Consulting Psychology* 25 (6, 1961): 482–485.

The subjects of study were 236 men aged 16 to 65 years (28 years as the average) referred through a court clinic. A psychologist classified each man as either heterosexual or homosexual (criterion for being judged homosexual was the subject's admission of one or more impulses toward or overt action of homosexuality) and not effeminate or effeminate (criteria for being judged effeminate were effeminate actions, speech, et cetera, or the subject's admission of feminine feelings or of playing a feminine role). After the classification procedure the DAP was administered, with requests first to "draw a person," then "draw a person of the opposite sex," and finally to draw a person whose sex was of the subject's own choosing.

The results supported the theoretical expectation that psychosexual identity is projected into free choice drawings, the psychometric signs were not more efficient overall than the clinical ratings of the psychologists in predicting homosexual or effeminacy characteristics.

601 WIEDEMAN, GEORGE H. "Survey of Psychoanalytic Literature on Overt Male Homosexuality." *Journal of the American Psychoanalytic Association* 10 (2, 1962): 386–409.

The psychoanalytic investigation of homosexuality was initiated by Sigmund Freud in 1905 in "Three Essays on the Theory of Sexuality." Until then homosexuality was mainly considered a constitutional variant. Further study of homosexuality from the point of view of structural theory, the consideration of early phases of libidinal and ego development, and examination of transference problems would bring a greater understanding of the problem.

602 WILLIS, STANLEY E. *Understanding and Counseling the Male Homosexual.* Boston: Little, Brown & Co., 1967, 225 pp.

The lack of success in explaining the psychodynamics of homosexuality is due to the fact that it has been considered a static condition with a single underlying cause and that its complex and highly fluid transactional aspects have been ignored. Even in the same individual, homosexual behavior may represent a wide variety of complex adaptive or defensive coping transactions which vary from one set of circumstances to another.

Repeatedly stressing that a new theory and a new technique of treatment is needed for each patient and for each occasion, the therapist is warned not to resort to a generalized or stereotyped concept of the dynamics of homosexuality. It is also pointed out that the therapist errs if he confuses the benign forms represented by a homosexual interest or an occasional homosexual act with the more significant problems of the various forms of invariable homosexual identification which are more likely to be symptomatic of psychopathology. Case material representing the wide variety of dynamic features present in homosexual patterns is included. Some of this material illustrates the presence of the residuals of a childhood fear of being rejected or abandoned, which is viewed as a significant feature of the dynamics of most homosexual behavior, and as a more prevalent phenomenon than castration anxiety. Other cases indicate that many homosexual acts are principally motivated by the wish to pair with, attach to, and to achieve identification with a powerful figure in an attempt to achieve a sense of security.

603 WINOKUR, GEORGE. "Sexual Behavior: Its Relationship to Certain Affects and Psychiatric Diseases." In *Determinants of Human Sexual Behavior,* edited by George Winokur, pp. 76–100. Springfield, Ill.: Charles C. Thomas, 1963.

The literature is reviewed and data are presented on the interaction between sexuality and other affects and on the interaction between sexuality and psychiatric illness. It is concluded that a relationship may exist between sexual factors and pain, response to stress, and anger. However, it is felt that these situations are quite complex and relationships are not invariable.

It is also concluded that sexuality has little or no effect in the etiology of manic-depressive disease and chronic brain syndromes and that any causal relationship between homosexuality and paranoid schizophrenia must be considered quite tenuous.

604 Winterstein-Lambert, E. "Observations on Homosexuals." *Bulletin de la Faculté de Médecine de Istanbul* 12 (3, 1949): 216–220.

For the purpose of this paper male homosexuals are defined as "those who admit finding, actively or passively, physical and emotional expression of their sexuality in contact with their own sex." Data about 100 neurotic homosexual soldiers and 100 neurotic nonhomosexual soldiers were compared and it was found that the homosexuals had significantly higher intelligence scores and educational backgrounds, higher unsuccessful work records, and more neurotic symptoms. The necessity of help in finding satisfactory occupations is stressed as an important step in treatment of homosexual neurotics. Attention is drawn to the existence of a stable successful homosexual community not in need of psychological treatment.

605 WITTELS, FRITZ. "Homosexuality." In *Encyclopedia of Criminology,* edited by Vernon C. Branham and Samuel B. Kutash, pp. 190–194. New York: Philosophical Library, 1949.

This presentation is divided into two sections. The first presents a description of the present state of knowledge about homosexuality. The second is a discussion of the mechanisms which are used as defenses against latent homosexuality. The first part stresses that homosexuality appears to arise from sociopsychological causes imbedded in early childhood experience, and heredity plays little or no part. It is also pointed out that homosexuality is not a disease and that it does not prevent adjustment to society, nor does it preclude living an "efficient" life. A brief description of homosexual panic concludes the first section.

The second part states that all men have a feminine component and that a high percentage of men have some degree of homosexuality which is defended against in four ways. First, there are the "morbid defenses" which are cruel, destructive, possessive, and tend to be pathological. A second type of defense mechanism is narcissism. Sublimation is a third means of defense, while a fourth may involve addiction to alcohol or to habit-forming drugs.

606 WOLFSON, WILLIAM. "Factors Associated with the Adjustment on Probation of One Hundred Sex Deviates." Master's Thesis, College of the City of New York, 1948, 105 pp.

The subsequent adjustment of a sample of 100 male homosexuals placed on probation after being adjudged guilty of committing a homosexual act by New York City Magistrates' Court is studied. The data were obtained from court records; in not every case are the data complete. In addition, the factors which could be studied were limited by the records which the New York probation officers kept; many pertinent factors were therefore inaccessible. An appendix includes a "Pre-Sentence Investigation Guide" of the New York City Magistrates' Courts, a sample case study, copies of the forms to be filled out by probation officers, and a typical preliminary investigation report.

607   WOLMAN, BENJAMIN B. "Interactional Treatment of Homosexuality." *Psychotherapy and Psychosomatics* 15 (1, 1967): 70.

The abstract of a paper read at the Seventh International Congress of Psychotherapy in 1967 reports that homosexuality is not a clinical entity, but may be found in all three types of mental disorders (hypervectorials, hyperinstrumentals, and paramutuals). Homosexuality must be understood as a human search for identity and affection and may be successfully treated by interactional methods.

608   WOLOWITZ, HOWARD MARTIN. "Attraction and Aversion to Power: A Conflict Theory of Homosexuality in Male Paranoids." Ph.D. dissertation, University of Michigan, 1961, 85 pp.

The traditional psychoanalytic conceptualization of the attraction of the male paranoid to other males was tested. Photographs of men and women which had been rated on Osgood's Semantic Differential on the potency factor, or "power value," were shown to subjects who then manipulated the distance between themselves and the photographs. This made it possible to measure the subjects' resultant attraction to the photographs.

The results of the study did not support the hypothesis. However, a supplementary hypothesis which specified the power value of the other male as a factor responsible for the male paranoid's attraction or revulsion regarding other males was supported by the data.

609   WOLOWITZ, HOWARD MARTIN. "Attraction and Aversion to Power: A Psychoanalytic Conflict Theory of Homosexuality in Male Paranoids." *Journal of Abnormal Psychology* 70 (5, 1965): 360–370.

In a study designed to test the supposition that male paranoids possess strong "approach-avoidance conflict," typified by a need for power and a fear of being destroyed by the more powerful arousing male, 67 male schizophrenics (eight of whom were ultimately rejected), all hospitalized, were selected as subjects. Thirty-five of the patients were paranoid (one psychiatrist, at least, claiming paranoia) and 24 were nonparanoid. Five separate psychiatric diagnoses were available to the experimenter. No other significant difference appeared between the two groups, except that the paranoids had slightly more education.

To measure attraction toward the potent male, an apparatus was designed which allowed the subject to alter the distance between himself and selected photographs. Tendencies of approach and avoidance were measured by the subject's placement of the photographs. A total of 48 photographs were used, including 24 male faces, 19 female faces, and five inanimate. Sixty-four volunteer college students, male and female, rated the photographs on a Semantic Differential Scale (Osgood, 1957), which allowed the experimenter to rate the "perceival power" of the photographs. The placement of a photograph by each schizophrenic patient was rated relative to the distance for all the photographs he placed.

The operational hypothesis was that as the potency value of male pictures (as ranked by the college students) increased, the male paranoid would place them farther away than the female photos. This hypothesis was supported as follows: potency affected placement by paranoids ($r = 0.408$) but did not affect nonparanoids ($r = 0.107$). The paranoid males were not affected by the potency value of female photos ($r = 0.019$).

This study tends to negate the value of the older homosexual attraction theory of paranoia (Freud, 1911), since both the paranoid and the nonparanoid subjects tended to place the male photographs farther away than those of the females.

610 WORTIS, JOSEPH. "Intersexuality and Effeminacy in the Male Homosexual." *American Journal of Orthopsychiatry* 10 (3, 1940): 567–570.

Many male homosexuals are unmistakably effeminate, but there is no indication from comparable available data that the male homosexual tends to have an intersexual body build. Using a small number of cases, effeminacy is found to be attributable to a more or less articulated wish to be a woman. This effeminacy involves tastes and manners rather than body build and is psychologically rather than constitutionally determined. Thus, the homosexual male is often the end result of a boy's unfortunate identification with a woman. It is concluded that the actual evidence for any constant or typical intersexual traits, among male homosexuals at least, is still wanting.

611 YAMAHIRO, ROY S., and GRIFFITH, RICHARD M. "Validity of Two Indices of Sexual Deviancy." *Journal of Clinical Psychology* 16 (1, 1960): 21–24.

The ability of Wheeler's Rorschach content indices and the Marsh-Hilliard-Liechti Minnesota Multiphasic Personality Inventory sexual deviation scale to detect the sexual deviancy of "normal" homosexuals was tested. The subjects were 23 involuntary patients, aged 16 to 58 years, with a mean I.Q. of 110.0. The MMPI was administered to a comparison group of 110 narcotic addicts.

Wheeler's test holds up well for homosexuality if one allows for the length of a record by using the percentage of total responses rather than the raw number of signs.

The subjects scored high on the MMPI sexual deviation scale. And since in the original study neurotics and psychotics also scored high, and in this study narcotic addicts scored high, the conclusion is strengthened that the scale measures not only sexual deviance but personality deviancy as well.

612   ZAMANSKY, HAROLD S. "An Investigation of the Psychoanalytic Theory of Paranoid Delusions." *Journal of Personality* 26 (3, 1958): 410–425.

To investigate the theory that paranoid delusions are developed in an attempt to cope with powerful but unconscious homosexual urges, a measure of object choice (determined by the difference in time spent looking at pictures of different kinds of humans) was made. The subjects were 20 hospitalized psychotic male patients in whom paranoid delusions were dominant, and 20 hospitalized schizophrenic males in whom paranoid symptoms were absent. The ages of the subjects ranged from 23 to 45, with an average of 30. They had been hospitalized from one month to two years with an average of 13 months.

It was found that men with paranoid delusions tend to avoid explicit or direct manifestations of homosexual object preference; their homosexuality tends to be characterized by a primary attraction toward men as subjects, and not necessarily by an avoidance of women. It is suggested that the homosexuality of the male paranoid appears to be an intermediary process in the development of his delusions, rather than being the primary etiological agent. Also, one of the defensive functions which the homosexuality of the male paranoid serves is to help neutralize and eroticize powerful aggressive wishes directed toward male figures.

613   ZAMANSKY, HAROLD S. "A Technique for Assessing Homosexual Tendencies." *Journal of Personality* 24 (4, 1956): 436–448.

The theory that homosexual males, when compared to normal males, will look at pictures of men longer than at pictures of women, will be attracted more to pictures of men than to neutral or nonhuman pictures, and will manifest a greater avoidance of women than will normal males was studied.

The subjects included 20 overt male homosexuals with no gross psycho-pathology, most of whom were not in therapy (five or six were from counseling bureaus of several Eastern colleges and the rest were referred from these subjects), and 20 male controls, all of whom were juniors in an Eastern college. All 40 were of superior intelligence and education, and came from an above average socioeconomic background. None was married, and all but one in each group were white. The mean age of the experimental group was 23 years, and 21 years for the controls.

Twenty-four pairs of cards (pictures of men, women, and neutral objects) were viewed through a tachistoscopic apparatus. The experimenter recorded the subjects' eye movements and the viewing time for each picture. Five judges rated the pictures (threatening male-female pairs) and obtained scores for each subject.

The homosexuals spent 3.55 seconds looking at the pictures of men, and 2.37 seconds looking at the female pictures. They viewed male pictures longer than neutral pictures (p < .01), and had a greater avoidance of female pictures (p < .05). Thus, the picture-pairs technique seems to be a valid indicator of the presence of strong homosexual tendencies. It was concluded that the homosexuality of the male homosexual is probably characterized by an attraction to males and by a rejection of females.

614   ZEFF, LEO J. "Self Acceptance Vs. Rejection." *Mattachine Review* 4 (3, 1958): 4–9.

The subject for a panel discussion was the homosexual's experience of rejection and the factors which contribute to it. One of the most outstanding problems of the neurotic homosexual is that he carries his homosexuality as if it were a sore thumb. He measures everything and defines all or most of his experiences in terms of his homosexuality. It is this kind of reaction, not his homosexuality, that makes him neurotic. Membership in a minority group is not neurotic per se; it is rather a certain kind of reaction to being in a minority group that makes an individual neurotic. The individual's negative reaction to his minority status causes him at least as much trouble as the attitude of the majority group, and it is this negative reaction which results in the "self-fulfilling prophecy" of rejection by society.

615   ZUCKER, ROBERT A., and MANOSEVITZ, MARTIN. "MMPI Patterns of Overt Male Homosexuals: Reinterpretation and Comment on Dean and Richardson's Study." *Journal of Consulting Psychology* 30 (6, 1966): 555–557.

Dean and Richardson (1966) are criticized for using a unidimensional rather than a multidimensional framework for differentiating homosexuals from nonhomosexuals. It is felt that homosexuals are different from normals in more ways than just their choice of sexual outlet. Using the data presented in the Dean and Richardson paper, it is pointed out that certain statistically significant correlations had been explained away. Dean and Richardson based their analysis on the lack of T scores higher than 70, even though certain workers have claimed that lower scores can have validity for diagnostic purposes. As for the individual scales, M-F was the highest for both H (homosexual group) and C (control). The difference between H and C for the M-F scores was also greatest. This cannot be explained away by claiming high education for both since this does not explain the difference that was found between the two groups. The two groups had been matched for education. M-F is considered a "good diagnostic indicator" of "sexual inversion," since a high score indicates preference for feminine occupation. That Pd scores were higher for the H group is explained by the need for "antisocial acting out" for homosexuals. The higher Ma score showed that a sufficiently high degree of nonconformity exists in the H group to permit adjustment and the maintenance of a successful career. It is pointed out that these attributes exist in the sample only and would be incompatible in an individual. Pairing codes in an attempt to give a multidimensional approach to the analysis, they find M-F/Ma, M-F/Sc, and M-F/D to represent types within the H group.

616   ZUGER, BERNARD. "Effeminate Behavior Present in Boys from Early Childhood, I. The Clinical Syndrome and Follow-Up Studies." *Journal of Pediatrics* 69 (6, 1966): 1098–1107.

A report is given on the long-range study and follow-up of the consequences of effeminate behavior in young boys. The subjects were 20 boys undergoing psychotherapy who had first been referred to hospitals or to private therapists at ages four to 16 years. Four of the boys were not seeking help for problems related to effeminate behavior.

Of the 10 children who were 13 years old or older at the time of the follow-up study, four were homosexuals, three were probably homosexuals, two were apparently heterosexual, and for one the outcome was uncertain. Most of the boys had given up transvestite activities after therapy, but their effeminate behavior often came out in other more covert and devious ways. It was concluded that effeminate symptoms constitute a clinical entity and that the outcome involves the sexual identification of the child.

CROSS-REFERENCES

Allen, Clifford. "Homosexuality: The Psychological Factor." *Medical Press* 217 (1947): 222–223. No. 651.
Allen, Clifford. "Perversions, Sexual." In *The Encyclopedia of Sexual Behavior,* edited by Albert Ellis and Albert Abarbanel, pp. 802–811. 2d rev. ed. New York: Hawthorn Books, 1967. No. 91.
Alexander, Leo. "Psychotherapy of Sexual Deviation with the Aid of Hypnosis."

American Journal of Clinical Hypnosis 9 (3, 1967): 181–183. No. 650.

Berg, Charles, and Allen, Clifford. *The Problem of Homosexuality.* New York: Citadel Press, 1958, 221 pp. No. 103.

Bieber, Irving. "Clinical Aspects of Male Homosexuality." In *Sexual Inversion: The Multiple Roots of Homosexuality,* edited by Judd Marmor, pp. 248–267. New York: Basic Books, 1965. No. 106.

Brancale, Ralph; Ellis, Albert; and Doorbar, Ruth R. "Psychiatric and Psychological Investigations of Convicted Sex Offenders: A Summary Report." *American Journal of Psychiatry* 109 (Jul., 1952): 17–21. No. 1137.

Coburn, Vincent P. "Homosexuality and the Invalidation of Marriage." *Jurist* 20 (4, 1960): 441–459. No. 821.

Cory, Donald Webster. *The Homosexual in America: A Subjective Approach.* New York: Greenberg, 1951, 326 pp. No. 826.

Cory, Donald Webster, and LeRoy, John P. *The Homosexual and His Society: A View from Within.* New York: Citadel Press, 1963, 276 pp. No. 828.

"Criminal Factors in Homosexuality." *Corrective Psychiatry and Journal of Social Therapy* 13 (4, 1967): 181–183. No. 1153.

Dean, Robert B. "Some Considerations on Promiscuity in Male Homosexuals." Mimeographed. N.p., Apr., 1967. No. 833.

East, W. Norwood. "Sexual Offenders." *Journal of Nervous and Mental Disease* 103 (6, 1946): 626–666. No. 131.

Ehrenwald, Jan. "The Symbiotic Matrix of Paranoid Delusions and the Homosexual Alternative." *American Journal of Psychoanalysis* 20 (1960): 49–65. No. 133.

Ellis, Albert. *Homosexuality: Its Causes and Cure.* New York: Lyle Stuart, 1965, 288 pp. No. 680.

Farina, Amerigo; Allen, Jon G.; and Saul, B. Brigid B. "The Role of the Stigmatized Person in Affecting Social Relationships." *Journal of Personality* 36 (2, 1968): 169–182. No. 1073.

Fitzgerald, Thomas K. "A Theoretical Typology of Homosexuality in the United States." *Corrective Psychiatry and Journal of Social Therapy* 9 (1, 1963): 28–35. No. 838.

Forkner, Claude E., et al. "Homosexuality." *New York Medicine* 10 (11, 1954): 455–473. No. 142.

Freeman, Lucy, and Theodores, Martin, eds. *The Why Report.* New York: Arthur Bernhard, 1964, 602 pp. No. 144.

Freyhan, F. A. "Homosexual Prostitution: A Case Report." *Delaware State Medical Journal* 19 (5, 1947): 92–94. No. 840.

Freud, Anna. "Some Clinical Remarks Concerning the Treatment of Cases of Male Homosexuality." *International Journal of Psycho-Analysis* 30 (3, 1949): 195. No. 696.

Gershman, Harry. "Psychopathology of Compulsive Homosexuality." *American Journal of Psychoanalysis* 17 (1, 1957): 58–77. No. 148.

Glover, Edward. "Sexual Disorders and Offences, I. The Social and Legal Aspects of Sexual Abnormality. [1956. Reprinted.] II. The Problem of Male Homosexuality." In his *The Roots of Crime,* pp. 173–243. New York: International Universities Press, 1960. No. 153.

Hadden, Samuel B. "The Psychotherapy of Homosexuality, 2. Group Psychotherapy in Homosexuality." *Psychiatric Opinion* 4 (2, 1967): 9–12. No. 703.

Hampson, John L. "Deviant Sexual Behavior: Homosexuality, Transvestism." In *Human Reproduction and Sexual Behavior,* edited by Charles W. Lloyd, pp. 498–510. Philadelphia: Lea & Febiger, 1964. No. 166.

Hoffman, Martin. *The Gay World: Male Homosexuality and the Social Creation of Evil.* New York: Basic Books, 1968, 212 pp. No. 855.

"Homosexuality and Prostitution." *British Journal of Delinquency* 6 (4, 1956): 315–317. No. 1085.

Hooker, Evelyn. "An Empirical Study of Some Relations between Sexual Patterns and Gender Identity in Male Homosexuals." In *Sex Research: New Developments,* edited by John Money, pp. 24–52. New York: Holt, Rinehart and Winston, 1965. No. 858.

Hooker, Evelyn. "Homosexuality." In *International Encyclopedia of the Social Sciences,* pp. 222–233. New York: Macmillan Co., 1968. No. 172.

Hooker, Evelyn. "Homosexuality: Summary of Studies." In *Sex Ways in Fact and Faith: Bases for Christian Family Policy,* edited by Evelyn M. Duvall and Sylvanus M. Duvall, pp. 166–183. New York: Association Press, 1961. No. 1260.

Hooker, Evelyn. "A Preliminary Analysis of Group Behavior of Homosexuals." *Journal of Psychology* 42 (1956): 217–225. No. 862.

Hulbeck, Charles R. "Emotional Conflicts in Homosexuality." *American Journal of Psychoanalysis* 8 (1, 1948): 72–73. No. 174.

Jones, H. Kimball. *Toward a Christian Understanding of the Homosexual.* New York: Association Press, 1966, 160 pp. No. 1086.

Karpman, Benjamin. "Considerations Bearing on the Problems of Sexual Offenses." *Journal of Criminal Law, Criminology, and Police Science* 43 (1, 1952): 13–28. No. 1192.

Karpman, Benjamin. *The Sexual Offender and His Offenses: Etiology, Pathology, Psychodynamics and Treatment.* New York: Julian Press, 1954, 744 pp. No. 182.

Kempe, G. Th. "The Homosexual in Society." *British Journal of Delinquency* 5 (1, 1954): 4–20. Also printed in abridged form as "The Homophiles in Society." *International Journal of Sexology* 7 (4, 1954): 217–219. No. 868.

Laidlaw, Robert W. "A Clinical Approach to Homosexuality." *Marriage and Family Living* 14 (1, 1952): 39–45. No. 721.

Laycock, S. R. "Homosexuality—A Mental Hygiene Problem." *Canadian Medical Association Journal* 63 (Sept., 1950): 245–250. No. 191.

Learoyd, C. G. "The Problem of Homosexuality." *Practitioner* 172 (1030, 1954): 355–363. No. 1092.

Lorand, Sandor, and Balint, Michael, eds. *Perversions: Psychodynamics and Therapy.* New York: Random House, 1956, 307 pp. No. 198.

Liddicoat, Renée. "Homosexuality: Results of a Survey as Related to Various Theories." Ph.D. dissertation, University of the Witwatersrand, Johannesburg, South Africa, 1956. No. 194.

McLeish, John. "The Homosexual." *Medical World* 93 (8, 1960): 237–239. No. 201.

Marks, Ben. "Homosexuality." *Harper Hospital Bulletin* 26 (5, 1968): 242–247. No. 204.

Marlowe, Kenneth. "The Life of the Homosexual Prostitute." *Sexology* 31 (1, 1964): 24–26. No. 880.

Marmor, Judd, ed. *Sexual Inversion: The Multiple Roots of Homosexuality.* New York: Basic Books, 1965, 358 pp. No. 206.

Mathews, Arthur Guy. *Is Homosexuality a Menace?* New York: Robert M. McBride Co., 1957, 302 pp. No. 1100.

Mercer, Jessie Decamarron. *They Walk in Shadow: A Study of Sexual Variations with Emphasis on the Ambisexual and Homosexual Components and Our Contemporary Sex Laws.* New York: Comet Press Books, 1959, 573 pp. No. 1207.

Money, John, and Hosta, Geoffrey. "Negro Folklore of Male Pregnancy." *Journal of Sex Research* 4 (1, 1968): 34–50. No. 883.

Morse, Benjamin. *The Homosexual: A Frank Study of Abnormal Sex Life among Males.* Derby, Conn.: Monarch Press, 1962, 158 pp. No. 884.

Myerson, Abraham, and Neustadt, Rudolph. "Bisexuality and Male Homosexuality: Their Biologic and Medical Aspects." *Clinics* 1 (4, 1942): 932–957. No. 35.

Ollendorff, Robert H. V. *The Juvenile Homosexual Experience and Its Effect on Adult Sexuality.* New York: Julian Press, 1966, 245 pp. No. 750.

Ovesey, Lionel. "Pseudohomosexuality and Homosexuality in Men: Psychodynamics as a Guide to Treatment." In *Sexual Inversion: The Multiple Roots of Homosexuality,* edited by Judd Marmor, pp. 211–233. New York: Basic Books, 1965. No. 222.

Owensby, Newdigate M. "Homosexuality and Lesbianism Treated with Metrazol." *Journal of Nervous and Mental Disease* 92 (1, 1940): 65–66. No. 80.

Pascoe, Herbert. "Deviant Sexual Behavior and the Sex Criminal." *Canadian Medical Association Journal* 84 (Jan. 28, 1961): 206–211. No. 1210.

"Report of the Departmental Committee on Homosexual Offences and Prostitution." *British Medical Journal* (5045, 1957): 639–640. No. 896.

Roth, Martin, and Ball, J. R. B. "Psychiatric Aspects of Intersexuality." In *Intersexuality in Vertebrates Including Man,* edited by C. N. Armstrong and A. J. Marshall, pp. 395–443. London: Academic Press, 1964. No. 235.

Royal Society of Medicine. "Discussion on the Social Aspects of Homosexuality [Summary]." *Proceedings* 40 (10, 1947): 585–592. Also reported in *British Medical Journal* (4506, 1947): 691–692. No. 900.

Rubin, Isadore. "Homosexuality: Conflicting Theories." 1960. Reprinted in *The Third Sex,* edited by Isadore Rubin, pp. 13–22. New York: New Book Co., 1961. No. 53.

Schofield, Michael George. *Sociological Aspects of Homosexuality: A Comparative Study of Three Types of Homosexuals.* Boston: Little, Brown & Co., 1965, 244 pp. No. 906.

Schur, Edwin M. *Crimes Without Victims—Deviant Behavior and Public Policy: Abortion, Homosexuality, and Drug Addiction.* Englewood Cliffs, N. J.: Prentice-Hall, 1965, 180 pp. No. 907.

Shearer, Marshall. "Homosexuality and the Pediatrician: Early Recognition and Preventive Counselling." *Clinical Pediatrics* 5 (Aug., 1966): 514–518. No. 244.

Storr, Anthony. *Sexual Deviation.* Baltimore: Penguin Books, 1964, 139 pp. No. 251.

Tappan, Paul W. "Some Myths about the Sex Offender." *Federal Probation* 19 (2, 1955): 7–12. No. 1248.

Van den Haag, Ernest. "Notes on Homosexuality and Its Cultural Setting." Reprinted in *The Problem of Homosexuality in Modern Society,* edited by Hendrik M. Ruitenbeek, pp. 291–302. New York: E. P. Dutton & Co., 1963. No. 1119.

West, D. J. *Homosexuality.* Chicago: Aldine Publishing Co., 1968, 304 pp. No. 922.

Westwood, Gordon. *Society and the Homosexual.* New York: E. P. Dutton & Co., 1952, 191 pp. No. 256.

Winokur, George, ed. *Determinants of Human Sexual Behavior.* Springfield, Ill.: Charles C. Thomas, 1963, 230 pp. No. 65.

Wood, Robert. "New Report on Homosexuality." 1961. Reprinted in *The Third Sex,* edited by Isadore Rubin, pp. 48–52. New York: New Book Co., 1961. No. 263.

Zucker, Luise J. "Mental Health and Homosexuality." *Journal of Sex Research* 2 (2, 1966): 111–125. No. 647.

FEMALE

617   ARMON, VIRGINIA. "Some Personality Variables in Overt Female Homosexuality." Ph.D. dissertation, University of Southern California, 1958, 213 pp.

A psychoanalytic clinical study tested the following hypotheses about homosexual women: they will show a stronger dependency orientation than heterosexuals; they will perceive women and feminine relationships with a hostile-aggressive cathexis which should not be as pronounced in heterosexual women; they will show a more rejecting attitude toward men than heterosexual women; they will stress the aggressive features of the masculine role; they will reject feminine identification and show more conflict over sexual role; and they will be more limited in personal social adjustment.

The subjects were 30 female homosexuals provided through the Mattachine Society in Los Angeles and heterosexual controls chosen from Parent Observation Classes of the Los Angeles Board of Education. The controls were selected on the basis of age and commitment to normal marriage. Content ratings were made of Rorschachs administered to both groups.

The first, fourth, and fifth hypotheses were not confirmed. The second and third hypotheses were supported at the .01 and .05 levels of significance, and (because homosexual women were more prone than heterosexual women to be restricted in Rorschach color responses, to use human-animal combinations in Rorschach content, and to obtain low Goodenough scores in figure drawing) the sixth hypothesis was tentatively accepted.

A review of the literature which emphasizes the development of psycho-analytic theories and prior studies of this nature is included.

618   ARMON, VIRGINIA. "Some Personality Variables in Overt Female Homosexuality." *Journal of Projective Techniques* 24 (3, 1960): 292–309.

In order to test a number of hypotheses about female homosexuality which were drawn from the general body of psychoanalytic literature, 30 overt homosexual women (reached through the Mattachine Society or One, Inc.) and 30 heterosexual women (drawn from a group of married women whose children were participating in a different research program) were given the Rorschach and the Figure-Drawing Test.

The over-all results of the experiment tended to show that projective techniques were of little value in differentiating females with a homosexual orientation from females whose orientation is heterosexual. The results of psychologists' judgments about homosexuality were not statistically significant with reference to whether homosexual women show stronger dependency; whether they are more hostile and rejecting toward men; whether they are more fearful of the hostile-aggressive masculine role; whether they show more confusion, conflict about, and rejection of the female role; and whether they are more limited in personal-social adjustment than their heterosexual counterparts. Strong support was found for the hypothesis that lesbian perceptions of women are shaped by a hostile-aggressive cathexis. The data suggest that female homosexuality is not a single "clinical entity."

619   BARAHAL, HYMAN S. "Female Transvestism and Homosexuality." *Psychiatric Quarterly* 27 (3, 1953): 390–438.

The homosexuality of a 22-year-old lesbian, labeled a transvestite and undergoing psychoanalytic treatment, appeared to consist more of the need for domination, possession, and sadism than of love for women. Homosexuality is a symptom in a neurotic structure and cannot exist without neurosis. It has no meaning except as a multidetermined manifestation of neurosis. Female transvestism is not a manifestation of homosexuality but of a drive for masculinity.

620   BARNES, JOSEPHINE. "The Unmarried Woman." *Practitioner* 172 (1030, 1954): 405–410.

Homosexuality receives some attention in this survey of sexual factors affecting the health of single women. Jealousy or dominance within adult homosexual relationships often engenders tension or guilt. Emotional or

sexual problems encountered by female homosexuals are sometimes referred to a physician, most frequently in the form of unrelated physical
complaints or nervous disorders.

621   BENEDEK, THERESE. *Psychosexual Functions in Women.* Studies in
      Psychosomatic Medicine, vol. 2. New York: Ronald Press, 1952, 435
      pp.

Three case histories of homosexual women are presented. There is, however, no emphasis upon homosexuality. The book is primarily concerned
with the psychosomatic features of female sexuality, especially those involving the endocrinological aspects of the interaction of body and mind.

622   BERGLER, EDMUND. "D. H. Lawrence's 'The Fox' and the Psycho-
      analytic Theory of Lesbianism." *Journal of Nervous and Mental
      Disease* 126 (5, 1958): 488–491.

A psychoanalytic explanation of Lawrence's "The Fox" and an elaboration
on the theory of lesbianism are presented. Lesbianism is based on oral-
masochism working on a five-layer structure: stabilization on the oral-
masochistic, hence pre-Oedipal, level; first superego veto, objecting to the
pleasure-in-displeasure pattern; first defense of pseudo-aggression; second
superego veto, objecting to this hatred; and second defense of pseudo love,
with Oedipal camouflage.

623   BERGLER, EDMUND. "Lesbianism, Facts and Fiction." *Marriage
      Hygiene* 1 (4, 1948): 197–202.

The "romantic aura" myth regarding homosexuality must be debunked.
Lesbianism, like male homosexuality, should be recognized as a mental
disease which can be cured through psychoanalysis.
    Although lesbians consciously act out a husband-wife relationship, they
are in reality unconsciously acting out a complicated variation of a child-
mother relationship. As a "psychic masochist," a lesbian regresses to the
oral stage of development, leaving her dependent on a mother figure for
psychic security, while she retains strivings for independence and need
fulfillment. This causes a complicated conflict which may be described
clinically as the "masochistically 'mistreated' child" versus the "cruel,
refusing mother."
    That female homosexuality is a mother-child type of relationship is in-
dicated further by the fact that the chief sexual practices employed by
lesbians are cunnilingus and breast-sucking, or mutual masturbation in
which the clitoris is unconsciously identified with the nipple.
    Masculine women are not necessarily homosexual; indeed, if a woman

who is markedly masculine is likewise a lesbian, then her masculinity is merely a camouflage hiding the need to play a role in a mother-child homosexual relationship.

624   BLANTON, SMILEY. "Phallic Women." *Psychoanalytic Quarterly* 16 (2, 1947): 214–224.

Using clinical material, a description is given of a type of phallic woman who is feminine in appearance and attitude, and desirous of appearing to respond in heterosexual relationships. If she is not too old or rigid, such a woman usually will respond to analysis. With a resolution of her penis envy and castration anxiety, she is likely to achieve an ideal psychosexual adaptation.

625   CAPRIO, FRANK S. "Female Homosexuality." *Sexology* 21 (8, 1955): 494–499.

The term homosexual, as derived from the Greek and Latin, refers to sexual relations in one form or another with one's own sex. The word lesbian originated from the name of the island Lesbos, near the mainland of Greece, where Sappho and her disciples engaged in mutual sex practices. In dealing with homosexuality, psychiatrists make a distinction between the overt (one conscious and active about her homosexual cravings) and the latent (one who may or may not be aware of her homosexual tendencies but represses the urge). Homosexuals can be seen as exclusively homosexual, bisexual, or occasionally homosexual. Those with single or isolated homosexual experiences cannot be regarded as lesbians. The word "homosexual" is an unfortunate term which conveys different connotations to different people, causing much confusion.

Homosexuality is acquired and represents the behavior symptom of a deep-seated and unresolved neurosis. If the invert wants to be cured and cooperates, psychoanalysis and psychotherapy can usually bring favorable results. Lesbians are capable of carrying out satisfactory sex relations with the opposite sex. Self-gratification does not cause homosexuality. Not all lesbians manifest a definite preference for their own sex early in life and not all are mannish in appearance. Since lesbianism is a personality disorder, psychiatry should treat the personality structure rather than treat homosexuality as a disease.

626   CAPRIO, FRANK S. *Female Homosexuality: A Psychodynamic Study of Lesbianism.* New York: Citadel Press, 1954, 334 pp. Chapter 16. "Therapeutic Management: Preventive Measures," pp. 285–298. Reprinted as "Preventive Measures." In *Carol in a Thousand Cities,*

edited by Ann Aldrich, pp. 153–166. Greenwich, Conn.: Fawcett Publications, 1960.

Topics which are related to lesbianism and considered from the psychoanalytic viewpoint include the meaning of homosexuality, its methods of gratification, the history of lesbianism, lesbianism in literature, its contemporary incidence, lesbianism and crime, the psychogenesis and psychopathology of lesbianism, and its prevention and treatment. Three complete and detailed case histories are presented.

Lesbianism, of which the multiple causal factors include parental influence, psychic traumas, and seduction, is not a disease entity, but rather a symptom of neurosis. Its narcissistic features are given special emphasis.

In a chapter on therapeutic management, particular attention is given to preventive measures which include a fuller dissemination of sex knowledge; sex education for children, parents, and society in general; better legislation in the handling of sex offenders; more research and facilities for sex guidance and treatment. The harmful effects of derogatory social attitudes toward lesbianism are illustrated with case examples.

627 CAPRIO, FRANK S. "Homosexual Women." *Sexology* 22 (9, 1956): 560–565.

Homosexual patterns are acquired; they are the behavior-symptoms of a deep-seated and unresolved neurosis. Because of their socially disapproved mode of living, lesbians suffer from a pervading sense of loneliness and unhappiness. There is seldom any permanence to a female homosexual alliance. There is some degree of homosexuality, latent or overt, in many women. In the usual course of sexual development, the homosexual inclination becomes sublimated in the form of friendships and nonsexual activities. As a person grows to maturity, heterosexuality finds expression in the form of an attraction to the opposite sex, and as it does, the homosexual component becomes repressed. However, in some instances this repression of the homosexual element is not successful, and the individual finds herself a victim of bisexual conflicts. Frigidity is often the symptom-consequence of this bisexual struggle. As long as human beings are innately polysexual—obtaining sex gratification in every possible manner—there will be inverts. As Dr. Kinsey pointed out: "The homosexual has been a significant part of human sexual activity since the dawn of history, primarily because it is an expression of capacities that are basic in the human animal."

628 FREEDMAN, MARK J. "Homosexuality Among Women and Psychological Adjustment." Ph.D. dissertation, Case Western Reserve University, 1967, 113 pp.

The relationship between homosexuality and psychological functioning was studied by exploring the psychological adjustment and personality characteristics of 62 members of the Daughters of Bilitis organization, whose sexual orientation was presumed to be primarily homosexual, and a control group of 67 members of the women's volunteer division of a national service organization whose sexual orientation was presumed to be heterosexual. A test battery was developed; it was made up of two personal data sheets covering general personal history, history of individual or group psychotherapy, measures of job satisfaction and mental health, and two personality inventories—the Personal Orientation Inventory (similar to MMPI) and the Eysenck Personality Inventory.

This test battery was administered to both groups of subjects and the scores were used to develop ratings of personality adjustment, scores of variability and measures of neuroticism, self-acceptance, independence and inner-direction, acceptance of aggression, work satisfaction, and ability to develop warm interpersonal relationships. The relative dominance of interpersonal factors over sexual factors in the subjects' lives and the sources of life satisfactions and dissatisfactions with reference to the relative frequencies of interpersonal factors were also investigated.

Significant differences between the two groups were found only in three areas: the homosexual group had more independence and inner-direction, had greater acceptance of aggression, and found greater satisfaction in work than the control group. It was expected that the heterosexual group would have greater self-acceptance and that the homosexual group would have a greater capacity for warm interpersonal relationships, but differences between the two groups were not found in these areas.

Possible flaws in sampling procedures and testing instruments were discussed.

629   FROMM, ERIKA O., and ELONEN, ANNA S. "The Use of Projective Techniques in the Study of a Case of Female Homosexuality." *Journal of Projective Techniques* 15 (2, 1951): 185–230.

A report of projective testing techniques used with a 22-year-old homosexual woman at the University of Chicago Clinic indicates that such testing techniques can uncover emotional disturbances and aid in their diagnosis. The patient, a former WAC who had entered the clinic because of anxiety, was given the Rorschach, the Thematic Apperception Test, the Szondi, the Stanford-Binet, and the Kuhlmann tests. Two possible new signs for detecting homosexuality on the Rorschach were found: the deprecation of human beings in general, and of figures of the opposite sex in particular.

630 GIANNELL, A. STEVEN. "Giannell's Criminosynthesis Theory Applied to Female Homosexuality." *Journal of Psychology* 64 (2, 1966): 213–222.

A study was made of 103 white female homosexuals recruited from gay bars in Ohio and Michigan. Their mean age was 22 years, and their average educational level was 12 years. The subjects, classified as "butch," "femme," or "neutral," were interviewed according to Giannell's Criminosynthesis Theory which uses an index of criminality based upon the following factors: need frustration, internal inhibitions, external inhibitions, contact with reality, situational crime potential, potential satisfaction. Only "need frustration" was subjected to comparison with a heterosexual control group consisting of Edward's College Normative Sample. The Edwards Personal Preference Schedule was used to rate "need frustration" on the basis of such factors as succorance, nurturance, autonomy, aggression, deference, and heterosexuality. The homosexuals showed the same need for succorance as the heterosexuals, were higher on the need for nurturance, autonomy and aggression, and had lower needs for deference and heterosexuality. No differences were found between the three types of homosexuals. The qualitative data of the interviews indicated that the homosexuals showed low internal inhibition, low external inhibition, low contact with reality, high situational deviant potential, and a high potential satisfaction from homosexual behavior. It was concluded from the study that criminosynthesis is a useful method for studying crime and deviance.

631 GOLDBERG, PHILIP A., and MILSTEIN, JUDITH T. "Perceptual Investigation of Psychoanalytic Theory Concerning Latent Homosexuality in Women." *Perceptual and Motor Skills* 21 (12, 1965): 645–646.

Testing the hypotheses that stimuli with a high degree of homosexual threat will evoke ego defensive operations, and that stimuli in the same continuum of psychosexual relevance but low in homosexual threat will evoke perceptual vigilance, twenty-five female college students were divided into two groups on the basis of Minnesota Multiphasic Personality Inventory M-F scores: 15 high-latent homosexuals and 10 low-latent homosexuals. The M-F score was the highest in the first group and lowest in the second group.

The subjects viewed six pictures: a clothed male, a clothed female, a figure whose sex was ambiguous, a nude male, a nude female, and two nude females. It was predicted that the first three pictures would threaten neither group, but that the last three would threaten the high-latent group. The pictures were shown using a tachistoscope, starting with a .01 second exposure and increasing in steps of .01 seconds. The experience of threat was indicated by a retarded identification of the subject matter of the picture.

The high-latent homosexual group took longer to identify the high-threat pictures and less time to identify the low-threat pictures than the low-latent group (p < .02). Group differences on any one picture were not significant. The findings are viewed as supporting the general psychoanalytic theory which states that an individual seeks devious ways not to perceive psychosexual cues which confront him with a homosexual threat.

632   GREENBERG, HARVEY R.; BLANK, H. ROBERT; and GREENSON, DANIEL P. "The Jelly Baby: Conception, Immaculate and Non-Immaculate." *Psychiatric Quarterly* 42 (2, 1968): 211–216.

The formation of an undetermined jellylike mass, or "baby," during menses is discussed. Finger manipulation and oral intercourse between a "butch" and a "fem," two female sexual partners, is suggested as the cause for this mass which is discharged by the "fem" within two or three weeks after contact.

Described as "a bizarre birth fantasy, not previously reported in the literature," this obscure group of fantasies seems to "have arisen spontaneously from a street society of delinquent girls," some of whom were later admitted to the Bronx Youth House.

633   GUNDLACH, RALPH H., and RIESS, BERNARD F. "Lesbianism." *International Mental Health Research Newsletter* 5 (3–4, 1963): 14–15.

A research project, to be conducted on the basis that female homosexuality will not show the same dynamics as male homosexuality, is described. A pretested questionnaire is to be used in comparing four adult female groups: nonpatient, overt homosexuals; overt homosexuals in treatment; nonpatient nonhomosexuals; and nonhomosexuals in treatment. The questionnaire concerns early family life and parental relationships, self concepts, interests, and patterns of heterosexual and homosexual experience.

634   HOWARD, STEPHEN JAMES. "Determinants of Sex-Role Identification of Homosexual Female Delinquents." Ph.D. dissertation, University of Southern California, 1962, 76 pp.

Institutionalized female homosexuals were studied to determine why some lesbians identify with the masculine role and some with the feminine role. Personality variables of subjects and their parents were examined to determine if psychologists, on the basis of subjects' responses to the Rorschach, the Thematic Apperception Test, and the Draw-a-Person Test, would: perceive the subjects as having been rejected by their mothers, with those assuming masculine roles feeling more strongly rejected than those assuming feminine roles; see those assuming feminine roles as possessing a feminine identification and those assuming a masculine role as possessing a masculine identification; evaluate those assuming a feminine role as predominantly passive-masochistic and those assuming masculine roles as aggressive-sadistic; perceive the fathers of those assuming feminine roles as weak and inadequate and the fathers of those assuming masculine roles as aggressive and domineering; and evaluate the aggression of those assuming feminine roles as being predominantly directed toward mothers and women and to fathers and men for those assuming masculine roles. Hypotheses one, two, and four were supported on most measures, while hypotheses three and five were not.

635   KENYON, F. E. "Physique and Physical Health of Female Homosexuals." *Journal of Neurology, Neurosurgery and Psychiatry* 31 (5, 1968): 487–489.

A sample of 123 lesbians selected from the Minorities Research Group and a control group of 123 heterosexual women selected from branches of the National Association of Ladies' Circles were investigated by means of a questionnaire, the Maudsley Personality Inventory (M.P.I.) and the Cornell Medical Index Health Questionnaire (C.M.I.). This report includes those findings pertaining to the subjects' physical characteristics and medical histories.

The lesbians were significantly heavier, had bigger busts and waists and slightly bigger hips, but were less tall than the heterosexual control group. The general medical and surgical histories of the two groups were similar. Although fewer lesbians experienced premenstrual tension, significantly more resented menstruation than those in the control group. Significantly more lesbians preferred having a female doctor. See also Kenyon, F. E. (no. 278); (no. 636); (no. 637).

636   KENYON, F. E. "Studies in Female Homosexuality: Psychological Test Results." *Journal of Consulting and Clinical Psychology* 32 (5, 1968): 510–513.

As part of a study which compared 123 lesbians (nonpatient and noninstitutionalized) with 123 normal heterosexual women, the Maudsley Personality Inventory (M.P.I.) and the Cornell Medical Index Health Questionnaire (C.M.I.) were administered to both groups. On M.P.I. scores, the lesbians showed a significantly higher mean Neuroticism Score, but their mean Extraversion Score differences were not significant. The lesbians also scored significantly higher on the M-R scores (indicating that they were more severely disturbed in their moods and feelings) than the controls on the

C.M.I. Three tables summarize the M.P.I. and C.M.I. scores, and give a detailed sectional analysis of the C.M.I. scores. It was concluded that although the lesbians were higher in neuroticism, the exact nature of this association needs further study to determine whether lesbianism is a facet of a general emotional instability or a secondary emotional reaction. See also Kenyon, F. E. (no. 278); (no. 635); (no. 637).

637   KENYON, F. E. "Studies in Female Homosexuality, VI. The Exclusively Homosexual Group." *Acta Psychiatrica Scandinavica* 44 (3, 1968): 224–237.

Continuing the report of a study of 123 lesbians and a heterosexual control group, comparisons were made between the exclusively homosexual group (EHG), the predominantly homosexual group (PHG), and the controls. Twelve tables summarize the data, with the last table giving the statistically significant differences between the EHG and the PHG. In many respects the EHG was found to be more stable than the PHG. For example, the EHG appeared to be less neurotic, to be in better physical health, to have had more happy childhoods and better relationships with their mothers, and to experience fewer guilt feelings and religious conflicts than the other group. It was as if their homosexuality were so firmly fixed that they had accepted and made a better adjustment to it. Even when differences between the two subgroups were not significant, those between the homosexual group as a whole and the heterosexual controls frequently were.

The main results are presented in the paper under the following headings: psychological test results; physical characteristics, and medical history; social and psychiatric aspects; and sexual development, attitudes, and experiences. See also Kenyon, F. E. (no. 278); (no. 635); (no. 636).

638   KLAF, FRANKLIN S. "Female Homosexuality and Paranoid Schizophrenia: A Survey of 75 Cases and Controls." *Archives of General Psychiatry* 4 (1, 1961): 84–86.

Freud's hypothesis on male paranoid schizophrenia and unconscious homosexuality (i.e., "psychotic symptoms develop as a defense against emerging unconscious homosexual wishes") is applied to females. The subjects were 75 paranoid schizophrenic females (the average age was 35.2 years; 49.3 percent were married) and 100 nonpsychotic female patients (the average age was 32.9 years; 53 percent were married). The groups were matched for religion and previous homosexual experience. The subjects' case histories were reviewed, using the criteria of the American Psychiatric Association.

No significant difference was found between the schizophrenics and the controls in the degree of their preoccupation with homosexuality. Fifty-three percent of the paranoid schizophrenic group had delusions or hallucinatons of a sexual content, both homosexual and heterosexual. The persecutor of the paranoid was not significantly of the same sex. Significant differences were found between the paranoid schizophrenics and the controls in that the former had many more religious preoccupations.

639 LANDIS, CARNEY, et al. *Sex in Development.* New York: Paul B. Hoeber, 1940, 329 pp.

The growth and development of the emotional and sexual aspects of personality are examined from a psychiatric viewpoint. Physiological, anatomical, and medical information is also collected on a group of 153 normal women and 142 female psychiatric patients.

A chapter entitled "The Homoerotic Woman" discusses the attitudes, beliefs, incidents, and practices reported by homoerotic women. A representative case history is presented for each of the three types of homoerotic women: "temporary" homoerotic, "consistent" homoerotic, and "sporadic" homosexual.

640 MACVICAR, JOAN A. "Homosexual Delinquent Girls: Identification with Mother and Perception of Parents." Ph.D. dissertation, Boston University, 1967, 147 pp.

This psychological study was designed to test the hypotheses that homosexual delinquent girls, compared to heterosexual delinquent girls, would perceive their mothers as less rewarding and would identify less strongly with them. Perceptions of the mother were measured by the Roe-Siegelman Parent-Child Relationship Questionnaire. Identification was measured by the degree of similarity with which subjects rated themselves and their mothers on evaluative and potency dimensions of the Semantic Differential. Sixteen homosexual and 16 heterosexual inmates of a correctional institution were studied. They were matched on age, I.Q., level of education, length of institutionalization, race, and father absence-presence. The first hypothesis was confirmed on one of the measures, but not on the others. The second hypothesis was not confirmed.

641 MILLER, WILLIAM G., and HANNUM, THOMAS E. "Characteristics of Homosexually Involved Incarcerated Females." *Journal of Consulting Psychology* 27 (3, 1963): 277.

A study was made to examine differences between a group of homosexually involved female prisoners and another group of female prisoners who were not homosexually involved. The tests used in the study were the Minnesota Multiphasic Personality Inventory, the Kuder Preference Record, the Wide Range Achievement Test, and the Otis Quick-Scoring Mental Ability Test. Case history data were studied and counseling interviews were conducted.

The study failed to find any evidence of factors common to either group; in fact, many similarities between the groups were ascertained.

642 PARDES, HERBERT; STEINBERG, JORGE; and SIMONS, RICHARD C. "A Rare Case of Overt and Mutual Homosexuality in Female Identical Twins." *Psychiatric Quarterly* 41 (1, 1967): 108–133.

Material obtained from identical female twins is presented.

The subjects were 36-year-old identical female twins. They were both overt homosexuals, and they had had sexual relationships with each other as well as with others. Initial diagnostic interviews were conducted in which case histories were elicited. Staff diagnostic conferences were held, and the Wechsler-Bellevue Intelligence tests and the Rorschach were administered.

The case histories of the twins are described, but no analysis as to etiology is given. The girls did not show signs of psychosis. One twin did show more "ego strength" than the other. It was discovered that certain technical problems arise when identical twins are treated in the same clinic.

643 POMEROY, WARDELL B. "Question of the Month: Unconscious Lesbianism." *Sexology* 32 (4, 1965): 226–227.

Pomeroy discusses the use of the term "latent homosexuality" and goes on to state that being unfeminine need have no relation to homosexuality.

644 SIMON, ROBERT I. "A Case of Female Transsexualism." *American Journal of Psychiatry* 123 (12, 1967): 1598–1601.

The case of a 37-year-old woman manifesting successive stages of homosexuality, transvestism, and transsexualism is reported. Considering herself heterosexual, a man in a woman's body, the patient was antipathetic to lesbians and resisted others' efforts to make her dress as a woman. She attempted to make a heterosexual adjustment to marriage and underwent intensive psychotherapy, but each attempt was followed by anxiety, suicidal ideation, and a deeper commitment to "phallic position." She made no attempt to undergo reconstructive surgery. It is suggested that she was not a "true" transsexual, since a desire to alter sexual organs to that of the opposite sex distinguishes transsexualism from homosexuality and transvestism. Several dynamic mechanisms of transsexualism are discussed.

645 SOCARIDES, CHARLES W. "Theoretical and Clinical Aspects of Overt Female Homosexuality." *Journal of the American Psychoanalytic Association* 10 (3, 1962): 579–592.

This is the report of an American Psychoanalytic Association panel. Issues which appear through the discussions were: object loss; the frequent suicide attempts apparently provoked by the threat of the materialization of female object loss; the mechanism of turning of aggression against the self; the strong proclivity for regression toward the early maternal relationships; the relationship of bisexuality to female homosexuality; Oedipal development in homosexual women; and the dynamics of gradual shift during therapy from the pregenital homosexual aim of binding aggressive and libidinal drives to that of actual heterosexual object relations.

646   WITTENBERG, RUDOLPH. "Lesbianism as a Transitory Solution of the Ego." *Psychoanalytic Review* 43 (3, 1956): 348–357.

The case report of a 20-year-old married lesbian with intense guilt over her homosexual feelings is reported as an example of lesbianism as one of the transitory solutions of the partially split ego. The Rorschach was used; and psychoanalysis was undertaken.

The homosexual syndrome represented an unsuccessful partial repression leading to a partial split in the ego and a bisexual conflict. This transitory solution "maintained the megalomanic wishes by pseudo sublimation, partial regression and acting out with substitutes, which increased the pathological aspects of narcissism."

647   ZUCKER, LUISE J. "Mental Health and Homosexuality." *Journal of Sex Research* 2 (2, 1966): 111–125.

Are we justified in making the assumption that male and female homosexuality are the same disease and can be treated the same in therapy? Three cases of female homosexuality were studied. The subjects were 25, 28, and 29 years old, and had or were just completing Ph.D. degrees. They were treated by psychotherapy.

Different factors are operating in male and female homosexuality and differences also appear in its causes. There is a deeper and more complex feeling of rejection in the female homosexual. The sexual development of women is blocked by traditions and customs not present for men. For women, homosexuality is a means of escape. Among women one rarely finds the type of homosexual with weak inner conflicts, centering chiefly around social considerations and outward appearances, that one finds among men. The conflict itself is not the same in both sexes and therefore motivation for treatment varies. The female is better motivated for treatment and better able to maintain her interest in therapy than the male.

CROSS-REFERENCES

Aldrich, Ann. *Carol in a Thousand Cities.* Greenwich, Conn.: Fawcett Publications, 1960, 256 pp. No. 928.
Aldrich, Ann. *We Walk Alone.* New York: Fawcett Publications, 1955, 143 pp. No. 931.

Allison, Ruth. *Lesbianism: Its Secrets and Practices.* Los Angeles: Medico Books, 1967, 167 pp. No. 932.

Armstrong, C. N. "Diversities of Sex." *British Medical Journal* (4923, 1955): 1173–1177. No. 292.

Giese, Hans. "Differences in the Homosexual Relations of Man and Woman." *International Journal of Sexology* 7 (4, 1954): 225–227. No. 414.

Bird, M.S. "Some Emotional Problems Dealt with in the Special Clinic." *British Journal of Venereal Diseases* 41 (Sept., 1965): 217–220. No. 317.

Horowitz, Mardi J. "The Homosexual's Image of Himself." *Mental Hygiene* 48 (2, 1964): 197–201. No. 457.

Klaf, Franklin S. "Evidence of Paranoid Ideation in Overt Homosexuals." *Journal of Social Therapy* 7 (1, 1961): 48–51. No. 472.

Levine, Jacob. "The Sexual Adjustment of Alcoholics: A Clinical Study of a Selected Sample." *Quarterly Journal of Studies on Alcohol* 16 (4, 1955): 675–680. No. 487.

Liddicoat, Renée. "Homosexuality: Results of a Survey as Related to Various Theories." Ph.D. dissertation, University of the Witwatersrand, Johannesburg, South Africa, 1956. No. 194.

Liddicoat, Renée. "A Study of Non-Institutionalized Homosexuals." *Journal of the National Institute of Personnel Research* 8 (1961): 217–249. No. 489.

Monsour, Karem J. "Migraine: Dynamics and Choice of Symptom." *Psychoanalytic Quarterly* 26 (4, 1957): 479–493. No. 511.

Owensby, Newdigate M. "Homosexuality and Lesbianism Treated with Metrazol." *Journal of Nervous and Mental Disease* 92 (1, 1940): 65–66. No. 80.

Schur, Edwin M. *Crimes without Victims—Deviant Behavior and Public Policy: Abortion, Homosexuality, and Drug Addiction.* Englewood Cliffs, N. J.: Prentice-Hall, 1965, 180 pp. No. 907.

Segal, Morey M. "Transvestitism as an Impulse and as a Defence." *International Journal of Psycho-Analysis* 46 (2, 1965): 209–217. No. 560.

Sprague, W. D. *The Lesbian in Our Society.* New York: Tower Publications, 1962, 189 pp. No. 948.

Storr, Anthony. *Sexual Deviation.* Baltimore: Penguin Books, 1964, 139 pp. No. 251.

Wade, Carlson. *The Troubled Sex.* New York: Universal Publishing and Distribution Corps., 1961, 192 pp. No. 950.

Wilbur, Cornelia B. "Clinical Aspects of Female Homosexuality." In *Sexual Inversion: The Multiple Roots of Homosexuality,* edited by Judd Marmor, pp. 268–281. New York: Basic Books, 1965. No. 285.

Treatments

GENERAL, MALE

648   ALEXANDER, LEO. "Clinical Experiences with Hypnosis in Psychiatric Treatment." *International Journal of Neuropsychiatry* 3 (2, 1967): 118–124.

Hypnosis may be decisively helpful in the treatment of sexually deviant behavior. It often provides prompt clarification of the dynamic meanings of the need that originally initiated the behavior.

649 ALEXANDER, LEO. "Conditional Reflexes as Related to Hypnosis and Hypnotic Techniques." *American Journal of Clinical Hypnosis* 10 (3, 1968): 157–159.

"[The] technique of associating a new conditional signal to an unconditional need or to extinguish an old and noxious conditional signal, thus freeing the unconditional need to new, more desirable associations, is particularly important and feasible in the treatment of sexual deviations, such as homosexuality because in sexual behavior a sharper distinction between its conditional and unconditional determinants is possible than in other aspects of human behavior."

650 ALEXANDER, LEO. "Psychotherapy of Sexual Deviation with the Aid of Hypnosis." *American Journal of Clinical Hypnosis* 9 (3, 1967): 181–183.

Hypnosis is a useful technique to employ in the treatment of patients with sexual deviations because it can be used not only to extinguish conditional associations which make the deviant behavior satisfying, but also to establish more appropriate conditional associations. Moreover, the positive conditional determinants of homosexuality (loneliness, fear, passivity strivings, and/or illusions of genital inferiority) and the negative conditional determinants (identification of all women with the mother, the idea that heterosexual sexuality is always immoral, and that women are fundamentally different from men in their desire to enjoy sexual relations) can readily be identified under hypnosis.

Suggestions aimed at strengthening those conditional dynamic determinants which are positive and eliminating those which are negative can be effective in treatments which use hypnosis as a technique.

651 ALLEN, CLIFFORD. "Homosexuality: The Psychological Factor." *Medical Press* 217 (1947): 222–223.

There is no evidence that homosexuality is congenital or endocrinological in origin. The evidence which does exist indicates psychological causes for this condition. Some forms of homosexuality may be cured by psychotherapy. Treatable homosexuals vary from simple cases of sexual deprivation to those cases which are much more complicated. The castration of homosexual males is unwarrantable, since it does not destroy the sexual impulse. Its only effect may be to make the active homosexual more passive.

652   ANANT, SANTOKH. "Former Alcoholics and Social Drinking: An
       Unexpected Finding." *Canadian Psychologist* 9 (1, 1968): 35.

The successful use of verbal aversion treatment for a 55-year-old male with
a history of alcoholism and homosexuality since age 17 is discussed. While
under the influence of alcohol, the patient seduced young boys. Following
therapy, he remained sober for two years and was able to begin and stop
drinking at will.

   It is suggested that a further examination of the use of verbal aversion
therapy with alcoholics may be fruitful.

653   BAKWIN, HARRY. "Deviant Gender-Role Behavior in Children:
       Relation to Homosexuality." *Pediatrics* 41 (3, 1968): 620–629.

Since deviant gender-role behavior does not always result in homosexuality,
preventive measures taken in childhood offer some hope of being effective.
To support this theory a report is given on observations which were made
of 14 boys and three girls during childhood, with follow-up observation into
adulthood. Cases from other researchers are also reported. Gender-role
behavior is inborn, but greatly influenced by learning processes. Effeminate
behavior in boys is most striking during the years three to seven. Thereafter,
possibly owing to social disapproval, it tends to abate and in most instances
only minor residua remain during adolescence. In girls, the masculine-like
behavior is more likely to persist in a fully developed form until adolescence.
Thereafter, it too tends to become attenuated, some residua usually persist-
ing. As in the case of the male, the behavior sometimes persists in a fully
developed form in adult life. Deviant gender-role behavior merits the interest of the pediatrician since the risk of homosexuality in adult life is high.

654   BENTLER, P. M. "A Note on the Treatment of Adolescent Sex
       Problems." *Journal of Child Psychology and Psychiatry and Allied
       Disciplines* 9 (2, 1968): 125–129.

A social learning approach to the psychotherapeutic treatment of adolescent sexual problems, especially homosexuality and transvestism, is considered. Case studies, in which this approach was used, of three homosexual
boys aged 14, 16, and 20 years, and three transvestite boys aged 11, 13, and
16 years are reported. Treatment included interviews and verbal reinforce-
ments of heterosexual behavior. It was suggested that verbal reinforcement
of heterosexual dating patterns during an experimentally controlled interview would generalize to uncontrolled social situations and allow for later
self-reinforcement or reward by masturbatory orgasm. The goals of therapy

included increasing relevant masculine, sex-typed behavior, and increasing "appropriate" sexual behavior.

655   BERGLER, EDMUND. "Eight Prerequisites for the Psychoanalytic Treatment of Homosexuality." *Psychoanalytic Review* 31 (1944): 253–286.

Many authorities claim that Freud believed homosexuals to be incurable. A careful study of Freud's writings, however, indicates that this is not necessarily true. Several psychoanalytic authorities are found who agree on this point.

Male homosexuality is seen as the result of the "wrecking of the breast complex."

Several practical points should be kept in mind when selecting and treating patients for homosexuality: the patient must want to get well; treatment must be voluntary; the patient should not display many self-destructive tendencies; it is easier to treat those who have engaged in or are engaged in homosexual relations than those who merely fantasize them; the existence of extreme dependence on the mother is not very helpful to the therapy; the patient should not be using his homosexuality as a "weapon" against his family; and the possibility of being cured should be admitted by the patient. Analysts would do better to stress the oral nature of homosexuality if their therapy is to be successful.

656   BERGLER, EDMUND. "What Every Physician Should Know about Homosexuality." *International Record of Medicine* 171 (11, 1958): 685–690.

Early medical and psychological approaches toward homosexuality are discussed, and it is noted that for decades psychiatric-psychoanalytic treatment could offer the homosexual little more than a reduction of guilt and reconciliation to his fate. It is contended that a recent upsurge in homosexuality has been partly the result of the Kinsey Report, and Kinsey is given the responsibility for a new homosexual factor, the "statistically induced homosexual"—the borderline case who has been swayed to homosexuality by the argument that homosexuals make up one-third of the population. Kinsey's methodology and his figure of 37 percent incidence are severely criticized.

Homosexuality is defined as "a subdivision of neurosis, characterized by the fact that deep unconscious fear of women pushes the male homosexual to 'another continent'—man." The implications of this definition are discussed with special reference made to the psychic masochism prevalent among homosexuals. It is concluded that under certain conditions the chances for therapeutic success are excellent. Suggestions are given to the general practitioner for dealing with cases of homosexuality, and a 6-point program for the dissemination of information about the problem is offered.

657 BIEBER, IRVING. "Changing Concepts of the Genesis and Therapy of Male Homosexuality." Paper read at American Orthopsychiatric Association Meeting, 18 March 1965, in New York. Mimeographed, 9 pp. Reported in *American Journal of Orthopsychiatry* 35 (Mar., 1965): 203.

A report on the psychoanalytic treatment of 106 male homosexuals is given. Twenty-nine of these homosexuals terminated therapy as exclusively heterosexual individuals. Prophylactic therapy should be directed toward detecting and treating the prehomosexual child and toward treating both parents whenever possible. The father is the central and more decisive figure in the development of homosexuality in a son. The changing concepts in the genesis and treatment of male homosexuality can be summarized by two statements. Homosexuality is homemade, and homosexuals are latent heterosexuals who can successfully revert.

658 BIEBER, TOBY. "On Treating Male Homosexuals." *Archives of General Psychiatry* 16 (1, 1967): 60–63.

"This report has emphasized the view that inversion is a pathologic adaptation of submission and heterosexual renunciation which arises out of early fears established in family life. The perception of threat from women is a nuclear paranoid mechanism. Homosexuals displace their fear of men to the less frightening, feminine object." Fear of aggressive men is the greatest single determinant of homosexuality, although not the only one, and is the most potent force maintaining this adaptation.

"Therapy is oriented toward the working through of irrational fears of reprisal from feared men for heterosexual activity."

659 BIEBER, TOBY. "The Psychotherapy of Homosexuality, 3. A Female Therapist's View." *Psychiatric Opinion* 4 (2, 1967): 12–15.

There are many advantages in using a combination of individual and group therapy in treating certain homosexual patients. The female therapist can function effectively in both a group situation and in working individually with patients. The therapist must be careful not to assume a mother role in the group, however. In order to avoid the rivalry and competition for the therapist's favor and protection which would result if the group were entirely composed of homosexuals, it is necessary for the groups to be mixed, with both male and female, heterosexual and homosexual members.

Male homosexuals whose mothers were controlling and seductive, yet sexually repressive, and whose fathers were either absent or hostile, detached and sexually competitive, often develop overriding fears of men. When such a person is in individual treatment with a female therapist, positive and erotic feelings toward the therapist appear, while the "deeply entrenched hostilities, presumably rooted in long-standing resentments to a castrating mother do not." Group therapy allows the transfer of these positive feelings toward the female therapist to other women in the group, thereby encouraging a movement in the direction of heterosexuality.

660   BOUCHAL, M., and BÁRTOVÁ, D. "The Attitude of Homosexuals after the Change in the Criminal Code." *Activitas Nervosa Superior* 6 (1964): 100–101.

A change in the law effected in 1962 in Czechoslovakia on sexual intercourse between persons of the same sex enabled members of the psychiatric clinic staff at Brünn to follow up the attitudes of homosexuals toward their deviation, toward society, and toward the change in the criminal code.

Examining 10 homosexuals who came for treatment at the sexological center of the clinic in 1962, the researchers used Giese's modified questionnaire which was expanded by questions aimed at the subject's external and internal motive and at the attitude of the patient toward his deviation and the change in the law. The assumption that the amendment would bring the homosexuals absolute psychic relief was only partially fulfilled, because only four of the 10 persons examined regarded the amendment as a relief. Of these four, only one was characterized as highly sensitive, while four of the remaining six were hypersensitive or emotionally unstable. Thus, the need for psychiatric care still existed. If there is no therapeutic possibility of eliminating the deviation, psychiatrists must consider therapy aimed at the strengthening of the homosexual's consciousness, and the removal of the feeling of exclusiveness, guilt, and inferiority.

661   BROMBERG, WALTER, and FRANKLIN, GIRARD H. "The Treatment of Sexual Deviates with Group Psychodrama." *Group Psychotherapy* 4 (4, 1952): 274–289.

The sample in the present study consisted of 75 patients convicted of sexual offenses, ranging from incest to lewd and lascivious conduct, who were regularly committed under the sex psychopath law to the Mendocino State Hospital, California. Psychodrama sessions were conducted in a setting resembling the one prescribed by Moreno.

The group appeared to go through four phases characterized by: warming up and the emergence of anxieties, emerging dependence reactions, acting out (the portrayal of individual problems), and ambivalence (reality appreciation). A number of the illustrations of each phase involved the participation of the homosexual patients. It was found that the psychodrama, viewed as a permissive group experience, promises with further technical refinement to be an effective means of treating sexual offenders.

662 BROWN, W. PATERSON. "The Homosexual Male: Treatment in an Out-Patient Clinic." In *The Pathology and Treatment of Sexual Deviation: A Methodological Approach*, edited by Ismond Rosen, pp. 196–220. London: Oxford University Press, 1964.

This is a guide to psychiatric outpatient treatment of male homosexuality. Criteria for selection for psychotherapy are discussed and suggestions are made of the general attitudes which should be conveyed, such as speaking simply and not exaggerating the difference between normal and abnormal. A single case is used to illustrate the treatment process in which the therapist presents a new father-image to the boy patient.

663 BUKI, RUDOLPH A. "A Treatment Program for Homosexuals." *Diseases of the Nervous System* 25 (5, 1964): 304–307.

Homosexuality is seen as a sexual impulse which, because of developmental defects, has remained immature or has undergone deviation in the course of maturation. Possible treatment methods are discussed, and the results of a program combining drugs (trifluoperazine and tranylcypromine), group psychotherapy, and educational therapy are presented. Fifty-six patients participated in this program, and after nine months of treatment a total of 24 had been released. With the exception of four cases, no homosexual activity had been reported. It was concluded that "this treatment program appears to be useful in rehabilitating such patients."

664 CABEEN, CHARLES W., and COLEMAN, JAMES C. "The Selection of Sex-Offender Patients for Group Psychotherapy." *International Journal of Group Psychotherapy* 12 (3, 1962): 326–334.

In a study of 120 male sex offenders adjudged to be "sexual psychopaths" and committed by the courts to Metropolitan State Hospital, Norwalk, California, subjects were divided into groups of six to eight, with each group so structured that it contained a range of intelligence levels. The following were found: the age or intelligence of the subjects did not necessarily have consequences for the outcome of therapy; patients diagnosed as neurotic tended to show improvement more often than those diagnosed as psychopathic; the homosexual offenders improved as often as the heterosexual offenders; repeaters, or those with a previous arrest record for sex offenses, were not necessarily poorer risks for therapy than first offenders.

665   CAPPON, DANIEL. *Toward an Understanding of Homosexuality.*
       Englewood Cliffs, N. J., Prentice-Hall, 1965, 302 pp.

A clinical and phenomenological approach to the treatment of homosexuality is presented in the progression of a hypothetical, composite patient. The clinical manifestations and sources of homosexuality are discussed, and the "natural history" of a homosexual is recounted. The goals and results of psychotherapy are noted.

666   CAPPON, DANIEL. "Understanding Homosexuality." *Postgraduate Medicine* 42 (4, 1967): A131–A136.

The diagnosis, psychopathology, history, prognosis and treatment of homosexual problems is covered in a general discussion of homosexuality.

667   CAUTELA, JOSEPH R. "Covert Sensitization." *Psychological Reports* 20 (2, 1967): 459–468.

"Covert sensitization," a new treatment for a maladaptive approach behavior, is described. The patient is instructed by the therapist to imagine himself approaching a desired object (liquor, food, a homosexual). A covert image (vomiting) is then suggested. The patient mentally retreats from the unpleasant thought, is then asked to imagine a pleasant situation (fresh air, an invigorating shower), and experiences relief because the noxious experience has been terminated. Covert sensitization has been effectively applied to problems of alcoholism, obesity, homosexuality, and juvenile delinquency. Its success is based upon the sense of control the patient comes to feel over his own behavior.

668   CAVANAGH, JOHN R. *Counseling the Invert.* Milwaukee, Wisc.: Bruce Publishing Co., 1966, 306 pp.

In a guide for clerical, medical, and psychiatric counselors, homosexuality is treated as a medico-psychologic problem and not a disease. A wide variety of etiological factors and theories is reviewed, including organic, genetic, and psychologic factors. Abstracts of the theories of a number of influential thinkers are presented. Proximate factors are found in family relations, sexual immaturity, and other experiences.

Chapters are divided into "clinics" (orientations that can be used by the pastor, psychiatrist, doctor, government agencies, and the law). Moral responsibility of the homosexual is also treated at length. Although homosexuality is "objectively immoral," the invert is not responsible for his condition, though he may be responsible for individual acts, except under certain conditions of diminished responsibility.

A broad survey of treatment methods includes imprisonment, castration, behavior therapy, hypnosis, shock therapy, drug therapy, and psychotherapy.

669   CAVANAGH, JOHN R. "The Psychotherapy of Homosexuality, 1. Some Thoughts on Individual Therapy." *Psychiatric Opinion* 4 (2, 1967): 4–8.

Provided the subject is sufficiently motivated, homosexuals can be treated on an individual basis with intensive psychotherapy or psychoanalysis. The type of therapy will depend upon whether the aim is to develop a completely heterosexual attitude in the patient, to develop an attitude which would include an acceptance of heterosexual relationships without entirely eliminating homosexual behavior, or whether the patient should accept his condition as essentially unchangeable and decide to remain abstinent.

When the intensity of the patient's sex drive is low (a factor independent of sexual orientation) the outcome of treatment is more likely to be successful. A homosexual with a chronically established behavior pattern, who is not concerned about the problem or is not motivated to change, is unlikely to persist in therapy. A bad treatment prognosis can be anticipated when therapy is undertaken because of pressure from relatives or when a threat of punitive measures is present. A favorable prognosis is more likely for those who desire a normal marriage and children, for those who have had heterosexual experience, and for those whose homosexual symptoms appeared only under the influence of alcohol. Women are more likely than men to continue in treatment, and those with more than a high school education are also more likely to do so.

670   CLARK, D. F. "A Note on Avoidance Conditioning Techniques in Sexual Disorder." *Behaviour Research and Therapy* 3 (3, 1965): 203–206.

A modification of the aversion-relief therapy first described by Thorpe, et al. (1964), and its application to a transvestite patient and a homosexual patient are discussed.

In association with the patients' difficulties, Thorpe presented negative verbal stimuli accompanied with an electrical shock. At the end of a series of negative stimuli, a positive stimulus with no shock was presented, producing relief. Modifications described here include increasing the number of positive stimuli and arranging the positive and negative stimuli in a random order.

At the time of writing, the homosexual patient had begun to have heterosexual masturbation fantasies, and the transvestite had begun to have intercourse with his wife and his cross-dressing had ceased.

671   COATES, STEPHEN. "Clinical Psychology in Sexual Deviation." In *The Pathology and Treatment of Sexual Deviation: A Methodological Approach,* edited by Ismond Rosen, pp. 381–415. London: Oxford University Press, 1964.

The use of psychological tests in research and diagnosis of sexual deviation (including homosexuality) is reviewed. It is concluded that almost all tests prove to be of little clinical value. Criticism of the application of reciprocal inhibition techniques and aversion therapy by behavior therapists to the treatment of sexual deviation is based on humanitarian grounds, theoretical grounds, and on the fact that a detailed reassessment of these methods indicates that behavior therapy differs less from psychotherapy than theory would indicate.

672   COATES, STEPHEN. "Homosexuality and the Rorschach Test." *British Journal of Medical Psychology* 35 (2, 1962): 177–190.

Not only can some homosexual patients be helped by weekly psychotherapy, but also success can sometimes be predicted from the Rorschach. This was determined through a study using psychotherapy and the Rorschach with 45 male homosexuals who were patients in the Portman Clinic. The patients had either been referred by the courts or were self-referrals. After treatment they were divided into categories of much worse homosexual behavior, worse, same, stopped, or better.

Fifty-seven percent of the treated adults either stopped or were better; only 10 percent of the untreated did so. No relationship was found between the Kinsey rating and the degree of success of treatment. The younger patients, under 21, had a much better prognosis than the older ones, unless they had completely identified with their form of life. Patients who had had some heterosexual experience also tended to do better in therapy. There was a highly significant relationship between a "catastrophic" response (castration anxiety) to Card 2 of the Rorschach and success in treatment—if the response was present there was a greater chance of success in treatment.

673   CORY, DONALD WEBSTER, and LEROY, JOHN P. "Why Homosexuals Resist Cure." *Sexology* 30 (7, 1964): 480–482.

Some reasons for the difficulty of changing or "curing" homosexuals are given in an essay. Some homosexuals do not want to change and some "feed" on their guilt. Rebellious young homosexuals do not seek change.

674   DI SCIPIO, WILLIAM J. "Modified Progressive Desensitization and Homosexuality." *British Journal of Medical Psychology* 41 (3, 1968): 267–272.

A form of behavior therapy was used in an attempt to help a 34-year-old male homosexual patient overcome his phobic fear of female genitalia.

On the assumption that the removal of his phobic anxiety about the vagina would make heterosexual intercourse possible for the patient, thus decreasing his homosexual activity, a program of modified desensitization therapy was designed. In early sessions the patient considered such anxiety-producing images as caressing female breasts and genitalia; in later sessions he was shown pictures of seminude females; and in the final three sessions, photographs of heterosexual intercourse.

Only minimal success was achieved. The patient was apparently able to overcome his fear of female genitalia, but after several unsuccessful attempts to accomplish intercourse with his wife, he reverted to his former homosexual behavior. Because he felt that the therapist had done everything possible to change him and had been unable to do so, he decided to live as a passive homosexual.

Although the use of progressive desensitization therapy did not change the undesirable behavior pattern in this particular instance, it did eliminate the specific anxiety syndrome from which the patient had been suffering. With a more precise method of therapist-patient interaction, as well as a more suitable way of manipulating the social environment, the further application of this method could prove useful in the treatment of homosexuality.

675   DOYLE, THOMAS L. "Homosexuality and Its Treatment." *Nursing Outlook* 15 (8, 1967): 38–40.

The dynamics of homosexuality and methods of treatment are reviewed and discussed. The homosexual is defined as one who has an interest in and sexual attraction to a member of the same sex. Contact between men includes kissing, caressing, mutual masturbation, fellatio, and anal intercourse. Women homosexuals practice similar behavior with more frequent oral-genital contact.

There are four phases in the growth and development of "normal" individuals. During the "oral period," from birth to age three, all satisfaction is gained through feeding via the breast, spoon, or bottle. Ages three to 10 are characterized by an interest in the same sex. A "normal" or "homosexual" stage begins at age 11 or 12 with an emphasis upon hero worship. A strong heterosexual interest begins in late adolescence.

A child will sometimes relieve stress by utilizing the predominant characteristic of the adolescent phase (same-sex interest) as an outlet. A fixation at this immature sexual level may develop, and regression to that level later in life can occur accompanied by homosexual activities under certain stress situations.

Treatment for homosexuality is "psychoanalytically-oriented psycho-therapy"; it is available in a hospital's psychiatric clinic, a treatment center, or from a private analyst. Treatment may take as long as two years, the length of time depending upon the patient's disposition. Good results can be obtained if the patient does not resist change and if he willingly works with the analyst for a sufficient period of time.

676   EIDELBERG, LUDWIG. "Analysis of a Case of a Male Homosexual."
       In *Perversions: Psychodynamics and Therapy,* edited by Sandor Lo-
       rand and Michael Balint, pp. 279–289. New York: Random House,
       1956.

The final months of the successful psychoanalytic treatment of a homosex-ual are recounted, presenting facts of interest to the advanced student of psychoanalysis. The patient's unconscious infantile omnipotence, until it was resolved, prevented a successful adjustment. The handling of this prob-lem is of special significance in the case of perversion. In manifest homosex-uality, identification with and fixation on the pre-Oedipal mother is especially important. The phallic and the anal material present in such cases should not be regarded as trivial or bypassed, nor should prior knowledge from other cases blind the analyst to new discoveries in treating a particular patient.

677   ELIASBERG, W. G. "Group Treatment of Homosexuals on Proba-
       tion." *Group Psychotherapy* 7 (3–4, 1954): 218–226.

An account of the group therapy treatment of 12 homosexuals on probation suggests that, like any other analytic treatment, such treatment must begin with the "imposition of voluntariness." The patient must be guaranteed the right of privacy, even when such treatment is a condition of probation, and he must be reassured that what he says within the group will be considered privileged communication.

The technique used in the two therapy groups reported here was Group-Dream-Analysis, whereby the group, with the help of a therapist-modera-tor, analyzed the dreams of each member. In this way the group member was permitted to act out both the analyst and analysand roles, which allowed the group participants to overcome the rigid character roles which had been obtained in their lives.

Since a number of the group members were able to substitute heterosexu-ality for homosexuality, the treatment technique was considered successful.

Several cases are described in some detail.

678   ELLIS, ALBERT. "The Effectiveness of Psychotherapy with In-
       dividuals Who Have Severe Homosexual Problems." 1956. Re-

printed in *The Problem of Homosexuality in Modern Society,* edited by Hendrik M. Ruitenbeek, pp. 175–182. New York: E. P. Dutton & Co., 1963.

The effectiveness of treating homosexuality with an active form of psychoanalytically oriented psychotherapy is assessed by reviewing the cases of 40 patients (28 males, 12 females). Eighteen of the patients were under 25 years of age, 19 were between 26 and 35, and three were over 36. One had a grade school education, 10 had a high school education, 23 had some college training, and six had done graduate work. Thirty-one of them were single, five were married, and four were divorced or separated.

In comparison to the males, the female patients were more improved as a result of treatment, were more often married or divorced, and were more often evaluated as severely emotionally disturbed (chi square p < .05). Those who desired heterosexual adjustment were found to benefit more from treatment (p < .01). The majority of homosexuals who are seriously concerned about their condition and willing to work to improve it may, in the course of active psychoanalytically oriented psychotherapy, be helped to achieve a more satisfactory heterosexual orientation.

679 ELLIS, ALBERT. "A Homosexual Treated with Rational Psychotherapy." *Journal of Clinical Psychology* 15 (3, 1959): 338–343.

The treatment of a 35-year-old male severely troubled by a fixed pattern of homosexuality is discussed. "Rational psychotherapy," a special therapeutic approach, was used. The therapy dealt with the client's severe feelings of inadequacy and fear of rejection by first unmasking, and then inducing the client himself to contradict and act against his irrational beliefs. Specifically, the client was shown that failure with girls was not a crime but could be viewed as a learning experience; that it was not overly important if others did not love him; and that perfect achievement is a humanly impossible goal. He was encouraged to date girls so that he could overcome his fears concerning them. His dates and sexual experiences with girls were discussed objectively and criticized. The therapist made suggestions as to what kinds of sexual overtures to make and when to make them, et cetera. The client's symptoms began to disappear rapidly as he changed the fundamental beliefs that motivated his homosexual behavior, and he was ultimately able to change from an exclusive homosexual orientation to a nearly 100 percent heterosexual orientation. The main cause of his homosexuality was not seen as an Oedipal attachment to his mother, but rather as his feelings of inferiority and fear of rejection.

680 ELLIS, ALBERT. *Homosexuality: Its Causes and Cure.* New York: Lyle Stuart, 1965, 288 pp.

The evidence on constitutional factors as a cause of homosexuality is re-examined and rejected. Psychological factors which are etiologically important are general conditioning and learning, parental and familial conditioning, desire to adopt the role of the other sex, difficulties and dangers of heterosexuality, need to be loved, anti-sexuality and puritanism, fixation and fetishism, inadequacy feelings, hostility and rebelliousness, and severe emotional difficulties. Exclusive homosexuality is regarded as self-defeating behavior; it is the result of emotional disturbance.

The treatment recommended for homosexuality is a special technique called "rational-emotive psychotherapy." It is based on the hypothesis that neurotic and psychotic emotions and actions stem from irrational basic assumptions, beliefs, or philosophies. The goal of therapy is to bring these beliefs to light and to show the patient how he is maintaining and reinforcing them with his neurotic symptoms. They are then countered and replaced by more rational, less self-defeating beliefs and actions. Cases are presented in full detail, with verbatim transcripts illustrating the technique.

A terminal essay entitled "Homosexuality and the Mystique of the Gigantic Penis," by Donald Webster Cory commends Ellis for calling attention to a previously uninvestigated area of homosexual behavior, the fact that male homosexuals are attracted by and aroused by other males who have big penises, but discounts various psychoanalytic interpretations of this phenomenon. A simpler explanation, "If the penis is so good, then more of it should be even better," is proposed.

681   ELLIS, ALBERT. "New Hope for Homosexuals." 1958. Reprinted in
       The Third Sex, edited by Isadore Rubin, pp. 53–57. New York: New
       Book Co., 1961.

In a study of 28 male and 12 female homosexuals seen for intensive psychotherapy, 64 percent of the males and all of the females were distinctly or considerably oriented toward heterosexuality after treatment, even though the therapy focused upon the underlying neurosis rather than upon the homosexual behavior itself. Another study, by Milton H. Gurwitz, is also reported, showing the successful treatment of 16 out of 18 exhibitionists and voyeurs.

682   ELLIS, ALBERT. "The Use of Psychotherapy with Homosexuals."
       Mattachine Review 2 (1, 1956): 14–16.

The results of psychoanalytically-oriented psychotherapy of 53 homosexual individuals (41 males and 12 females) are given. The female patients improved more than the males, were more often married or divorced, and were more seriously emotionally disturbed. Those who entered therapy with little or moderate desire to overcome their homosexual problems made some progress toward heterosexuality in 50 percent of the cases and 15 percent made considerable progress. Those who came to therapy with a considerable desire to overcome their homosexual problems become somewhat more heterosexual in 100 percent of the cases and considerably more heterosexual in 80 percent of the cases. Statistically, these findings were highly significant.

Virtually every homosexual who wants to achieve satisfactory heterosexual relations may be enabled to do so if he works persistently with a competent psychotherapist toward his goal.

683   ENGLISH, O. SPURGEON. "A Primer on Homosexuality." *GP* [*General Practice*] 7 (4, 1953): 55–60.

Kinsey's findings on homosexuality as presented in his 1948 report are summarized and advice is given to family physicians who are called in as consultants in cases of homosexuality. Kinsey's Scale is briefly described and the prevalence of homosexuality in this country is noted. Homosexuality is not an easily defined phenomenon. Claims by other authorities that homosexuality is either hereditary or capable of cure are denied. The best type of treatment is some form of directive therapy aimed at sublimating the homosexual urge. Incarceration of the individual is contraindicated.

684   "Fatal Emetine Poisoning from Aversion Treatment." Re W. T. (Westminster Inquest, February 7, 1964.) *Medico-Legal Journal* 32 (2, 1964): 95.

Aversion therapy was conducted with a male homosexual who had a heart condition. The particular form of aversion therapy involved creation of nausea, by means of an emetic, accompanied by talking about his homosexuality. The second part of the therapy involved recovery from the nausea and talking about pleasant ideas and heterosexual fantasies, which was sometimes aided by lysergic acid. In this case, the patient died as a result of a heart attack brought on by the use of the emetic.

685   FELDMAN, M. P. "Aversion Therapy for Sexual Deviations: A Critical Review." *Psychological Bulletin* 65 (2, 1966): 65–79.

The poor record of success in treating sexual deviations with various psychotherapeutic methods suggests that further investigation of learning theory techniques is in order. A description is given of the methods which a variety of researchers have employed in using aversion therapy in the treatment of homosexuality and other sex deviations. These methods are assessed critically, problems which exist with the use of aversion therapy are noted, and suggestions for improvements are made.

The works surveyed seem to indicate that instrumental rather than classical conditioning and electric shock rather than chemical aversion are most effective. The record of aversion therapy thus far is encouraging but not conclusive.

686   FELDMAN, M. P. "The Treatment of Homosexuality by Aversion Therapy." In *Progress in Behaviour Therapy: Proceedings of a Symposium,* edited by Hugh Freeman, pp. 59–72. Bristol: John Wright & Sons Ltd., 1968.

An anticipatory avoidance method incorporated procedures designed to reduce the possibility of extinguishing avoidance responses that patients learned whenever an attractive male was encountered.

Of 43 patients presented for treatment, 36 completed the full course of treatment. Twenty-five patients were rated as "improved" one year after completion of treatment. Fourteen of these were rated 0 on the Kinsey Scale, nine at 1 and two at 2.

It was noted that a pretreatment history of heterosexual interest at some stage in the patient's life appears to be a critical variable in determining a successful response to aversion treatment.

It is suggested that the most practical research need for the present is the development of techniques to create heterosexual approach behavior for individuals who have never displayed this and who wish to alter their pattern of sexual expression.

687   FELDMAN, M. P., and MacCULLOCH, M. J. "The Application of Anticipatory Avoidance Learning to the Treatment of Homosexuality, I. Theory, Technique and Preliminary Results." *Behaviour Research and Therapy* 2 (3, 1965): 165–183.

The purpose of the study was to develop a method, known as the "Sexual Orientation Method," to assess the relative levels of homo- and heteroerotic orientation in patients known to display homosexual behavior. Clinical interviews and the questionnaire technique were used, the latter borrowing from the semantic differential and personal questionnaire techniques. The subjects were 32 homosexual patients whose treatment had been completed and for whom at least a three-month follow-up was available.

This method provides results which are internally consistent, exhibit unidimensionality, and have a satisfactorily high reliability and validity. It provides a wide range of scores, and hence is a means of picking up relatively small changes in orientation. It is intended only for the purpose of plotting changes or the absence of changes in the relative levels of erotic interest as treatment proceeds.

See also MacCulloch, M. J.; Feldman, M. P.; and Pinshoff, J. M. (no. 729). See also Feldman, M. P.; MacCulloch, M. J.; Mellor, Valerie; and Pinschof, J. M. (no. 688).

688   FELDMAN, M. P.; MACCULLOCH, M. J.; MELLOR, VALERIE; and PINSCHOF, J. M. "The Application of Anticipatory Avoidance Learning to the Treatment of Homosexuality, III. The Sexual Orientation Method." *Behaviour Research and Therapy* 4 (4, 1966): 289–299.

A method for finding the relative levels of homo- and heteroerotic orientation at the outset of a therapy, designed to treat homosexuality (termed the "Sexual Orientation Method") and to show any changes in these relative levels as treatment proceeds, was tested. The last of a three-part progress report summarizes the results of the study.

See also Feldman, M. P., and MacCulloch, M. J. (no. 687). See also MacCulloch, M. J.; Feldman, M. P.; and Pinschof, J. M. (no. 729).

689   FELDMAN, M. P., and MACCULLOCH, M. J. "A Systematic Approach to the Treatment of Homosexuality by Conditioned Aversion: Preliminary Report." *American Journal of Psychiatry* 121 (2, 1964): 167–171.

A technique enabling the clinical application of anticipatory avoidance learning to the treatment of homosexuals was devised. A photograph of a male, attractive to the patient, was presented on a screen. The patient was able to continue to look at the photograph, but if he did not remove it within eight seconds he received an electric shock determined to be unpleasant, which lasted until he removed the picture. As soon as it was removed, the shock ceased, and a photograph of a female replaced that of the male. The sessions lasted 20 minutes, and an average of 20 of these sessions was required before a change of sexual interest can be said to have occurred or to have failed to occur. Clinical data were presented on the first of a series of patients who underwent this treatment, along with a progress report after a nine-month follow-up. The treatment was successful for this particular individual, but no conclusions were drawn on the basis of this one successful outcome.

690   FINNEY, JOSEPH CLAUDE. "Homosexuality Treated by Combined Psychotherapy." *Journal of Social Therapy* 6 (1, 1960): 27–34.

The combined use of individual and group psychotherapy is more beneficial than either alone. This was demonstrated in the cases of three homosexual men (two were married and aged 26 and 29 years, the other was divorced and 40 years old).

The 29-year-old married man dropped out of therapy, but the other two men were able to abandon their homosexual behavior. Although they were only partly cured of their underlying psychoneuroses, the combination of both individual and group therapy showed great promise.

691   FLOURNOY, HENRI. "An Analytic Session in a Case of Male Homosexuality." Translated by Vera Damman. In *Drives, Affects, Behavior,* edited by Rudolf M. Loewenstein, pp. 229–240. New York: International Universities Press, 1953. Reprinted as "An Analytic Session." In *The Homosexuals: As Seen by Themselves and Thirty Authorities,* edited by Aron M. Krich, pp. 308–312. New York: Citadel Press, 1954.

A psychoanalytic session with a patient who is oscillating between homosexuality and heterosexuality is described. Dream analysis and the transference to the analyst are discussed.

692   FOX, BEATRICE, and DI SCIPIO, WILLIAM J. "An Exploratory Study in the Treatment of Homosexuality by Combining Principles from Psychoanalytical Theory and Conditioning: Theoretical and Methodological Considerations." *British Journal of Medical Psychology* 41 (Sept., 1968): 273–282.

A case history describing an attempt to use conditioning techniques along with psychotherapy to reduce the homosexual desires of a patient and to stimulate his heterosexual desires is given.

The patient, a 34-year-old male, was originally referred to the psychologist for confirmation of a diagnosis of manic-depressive psychosis, rather than for treatment in connection with his sexual problems. Although he had been married for nine years, the patient's marriage had never been consummated because the act of penetration, both of female and male sexual partners, was repugnant to him.

Treatment was designed to determine the degree to which heterosexual activity was inadequate in the patient, to try to eliminate his "phobic" response to heterosexual activity, and to try by positive retraining to reestablish an "unconditioned" heterosexual response. In this way it was hoped that homosexual liaisons would become less attractive and that the patient's marriage relationship could be improved.

The experiment was not fully completed since the patient stopped treatment after six months. It was established, however, that the patient had discontinued daily masturbation to homosexual fantasies, and that while he felt neutral about the vagina, he had begun to feel a positive attraction to other parts of the nude female body. He appeared to have made a satisfactory adjustment to everyday life.

In spite of the incomplete nature of the experiment, it was suggested that such a combination of analytic and behavioral techniques may be more emotionally satisfying for a patient than when behavior therapy is used by itself.

693 FOXE, ARTHUR N. "Psychoanalysis of a Sodomist." *American Journal of Orthopsychiatry* 11 (1, 1941): 133–142.

A 37-year-old male underwent two and a half years of intensive psychoanalysis while imprisoned for committing sodomy. During childhood he had viewed relations with females as being punishable and relations with males as evoking only secrecy and evasion. In later years, his homosexual attempts were characterized by immature methods and sources of gratification. After he and an 11-year-old boy both developed a skin rash, parents and police were notified. He pled guilty to sodomy and was imprisoned.

During treatment, the patient showed much improvement: he lost his fear of men, became more confident around women, learned two new trades, became more spontaneous and less depressed, and in general developed a more mature approach to life.

It is suggested that the government does more harm than service to society by imprisoning such people, and that incarceration involves considerable damage to the individual.

694 FRANK, JEROME D. "Treatment of Homosexuals." Working Paper Prepared for the National Institute of Mental Health Task Force on Homosexuality. Mimeographed. Baltimore: Johns Hopkins University, Nov. 20, 1967, 13 pp.

A representative sampling of the literature is reviewed in order to summarize the current status of the treatment of homosexuality.

Most methods of psychotherapy use an interview approach. All the therapies based on the analytical model assume the same basic etiological theory that childhood experiences are the main contributory factor. Variations on this theory lead to variations in therapy, which may include group therapy or classical or instrumental aversion therapy. This varying methodology is exemplified by the work of Cappon, Ellis, Hatterer, Hadden, and Feldman. Regardless of the approach a high degree of motivation and cooperativeness, as well as a great deal of time and money, is required on the part of the patient. A strong positive relationship between patient and therapist is also necessary. Such therapy is usually aimed at the discouragement of homosexual behavior and the encouragement of heterosexual activity. Although the adjunctive use of hormones is contra-indicated, it is sometimes useful to encourage heterosexual activity whenever a heterosexual relationship is eminent.

It is difficult, if not impossible, to compare the results of these various methods of treatment because the samples differ and are not adequately defined, controls are usually lacking, follow-ups are irregular or nonexistent, and criteria for improvement vary. Probably some homosexuals can be appreciably helped by any of these psychotherapeutic techniques; about one-fifth of the exclusive homosexuals may achieve some heterosexual interests and competence if they wish to do so. Group approaches and instrumental aversion therapies seem to hold the most promise for future research and progress.

695 FREUD, ANNA. "Clinical Observations on the Treatment of Manifest Male Homosexuality." Paper read at meeting of the New York Psychoanalytic Society, 17 April 1950. Reported by Herbert F. Waldhorn. *Psychoanalytic Quarterly* 20 (2, 1951): 337–338.

A paper read at a meeting of the New York Psychoanalytic Society is reported. First, the psychoanalytic literature on manifest homosexuality is surveyed and it is noted that a general attitude of therapeutic pessimism prevails. Next, four cases of homosexuality in which each patient did well in analysis are reported. It is noted that accurate prognostic information cannot be obtained by evaluating the patient's apparent motivation for cure or his classification based upon overt behavior. Therapeutically helpful information can be obtained only by recognizing the homosexual's unconscious desire to play both the active and passive roles in a relationship. When this condition is recognized and the childhood phase of phallic narcissism is reenacted, heterosexual potency is restored. However, fantasies originating from passive desires prevent the full ability to possess and love a woman. A fantasy of the penis dissolving during intercourse represents the conflict between masculinity and femininity in each of these patients. Full heterosexuality can be achieved only after a resolution of this fantasy.

In a discussion of the paper, Edmund Bergler noted that the penis-dissolving fantasy was not a castration fear, but a fear of complete annihilation resulting from deep oral regression. Anna Freud felt that oral regression undoubtedly played an important role in this fantasy, and that the good prognosis of her patients resulted from the fact that up until the phallic phase their psychological development had been relatively healthy, whereupon a failure to identify with the father led to a homosexual object choice.

696   FREUD, ANNA. "Some Clinical Remarks Concerning the Treatment of Cases of Male Homosexuality." *International Journal of Psycho-Analysis* 30 (3, 1949): 195.

The prospects of cure in latent and manifest homosexuality are discussed. Manifest homosexuality is seen as a transitional stage in the treatment of latent cases. Active homosexuality and passive homosexuality are criticized as clinical classification categories on the basis that they are purely descriptive categories. The basis for classification should not be overt sexual practice; instead, the fantasy which accompanies the act should determine the classification. Also included are descriptions of the turning points in the treatment of passive homosexuals and of the transitional phase after the attainment of full object love for women.

697   FREUND, KURT. "Some Problems in the Treatment of Homosexuality." In *Behavior Therapy and the Neuroses,* edited by H. J. Eysenck, pp. 312–326. New York: Pergamon Press, 1960.

Methods of treatment of homosexuality are discussed, distinguishing between traditional biochemical and physical techniques, and psychotherapeutic procedures. A review of the literature indicated that studies which had claimed success with biochemical and/or physical treatments, such as male hormone injection, electroshock, and carbon dioxide inhalation methods, were "useless" due to inaccuracies in the description of behavior before as well as after therapy, and because the findings were not replicated in later studies.

Psychotherapeutic procedures such as hypnosis, suggestion, and Moll's "Assoziations therapie," modified homosexual behavior in a number of replicated studies. These studies indicated that modification of homosexual behavior could be effected by the "encouragement" of heterosexuality and the "discouragement" of homosexual behavior patterns. The use of aversion therapy and conditioned reflex therapy experiments is contrasted with simplified therapeutic treatments using traditional systematic verbal exploration, dynamic exploration, or abreaction.

The method of therapy and the subjects' responses are described and discussed in relation to the "encouragement/discouragement" causal element. As a result of the experiments, it was shown that the efficacy of the simplified treatment did not appear to be very different from that of other types of treatment of a psychotherapeutic nature.

698   GLOVER, BENJAMIN. "Observations on Homosexuality Among University Students." *Journal of Nervous and Mental Disease* 113 (5,

1951): 377–387. Reprinted as "Homosexuality Among University Students." In *The Homosexuals: As Seen by Themselves and Thirty Authorities*, edited by Aron M. Krich, pp. 141–153. New York: Citadel Press, 1954.

Observations were made on the cases of 12 single white male homosexuals from 19 to 42 years old, who were treated by the psychiatric staff of the Wisconsin Student Health Department. These students came for psychiatric help out of fear of being caught and ostracized, but mostly out of a fear of loneliness in old age. Traits and characteristics of the group such as social status, interests, meeting places, techniques, and attitudes toward sex and love were analyzed. In spite of treatment, only one of the 12 showed even a slight improvement.

Etiological theories of homosexuality which hold that homosexual tendencies are inherited are presented as being the currently favored approach.

699   GOLD, S., and NEUFELD, I. L. "A Learning Approach to the Treatment of Homosexuality." *Behaviour Research and Therapy* 2 (3, 1965): 201–204.

Because many psychiatrists have found the use of aversion therapy unacceptable for ethical and practical reasons, a new technique was developed using aversive deconditioning in which the patient first imagines himself in a situation which has a potential for homosexual contact. His inclinations to make contact in such a situation are then reduced through suggestions which make the partner unattractive or the situation dangerous. The patient is then presented with alternatives in the form of a discrimination learning task (i.e., learning to choose a female over a male). The treatment and follow-up therapy of a 16-year-old male is described.

700   HADDEN, SAMUEL B. "Group Psychotherapy for Sexual Maladjustments." *American Journal of Psychiatry* 125 (3, 1968): 327–332.

Group psychotherapy, for homosexuals in particular, is reported in some detail. Although the groups described usually consisted only of male homosexuals working with a male therapist, the work of others (Stone, Schengber, and Seifrid; Mintz; and Resnik and Peters) who used mixed groups and even a heterosexual male and female therapy team is reported. The role of the therapist becomes less representative of authority in group therapy; instead, he represents the father figure, permitting transference of group antagonisms to him. A combination of individual therapy is recommended along with the group sessions.

Peer influence in the group permits the exploration and discussion of experiential interparental influences and the deprivation of peer play in the "scrambling period" provides insight as a result of direct and vicarious catharsis.

"There is a growing body of evidence that a group psychotherapeutic approach to sexual maladjustment is a superior approach and one that psychiatrists are coming to utilize with greater frequency and confidence."

701   HADDEN, SAMUEL B. "Group Psychotherapy of Male Homosexuals." *Current Psychiatric Therapies* 6 (1966): 177–186.

The pessimistic attitude prevalent until recently among psychotherapists toward a change from homosexual to heterosexual behavior has had a negative result on treatment. The belief of homosexuals themselves that their sexual orientation is irreversible is another deterrent. Group therapy of homosexuals who successfully reversed the pattern of behavior in about one-third of the patients is reported.

Initial efforts at group therapy which placed homosexuals in a mixed heterosexual group did not prove to be as successful as group treatment of homosexuals alone, with members carefully chosen for favorable prognosis, similar age, and similar intelligence level. The reliving of early life experiences, acceptance into the group, and increasing insight into the patient's own arrested sexual development, afford catharsis and a reduction of anxiety. The therapist encourages participation by each member and acts as a catalyst in the group interpretation of dreams and fantasies. Preliminary individual therapy sessions are required for an understanding of the patient's ego strength and other traits, along with a basic knowledge of family background and experiences which may provide clues to the development of his homosexuality. The group is especially effective in breaking down the rationalization that homosexuality is a desirable way of life. Repeated emphasis is placed on the possibility of change with reassurance about these changes.

No patients who attended less than 20 sessions are considered to have been treated, and usually 100 or more sessions are necessary for success. Most successfully treated patients have ranged in age from 23 to 35 years, and no success with anyone over age 40 is reported. However, it is suggested that intensive work with the latter age group by combining individual and group psychotherapy offers hope of reversal.

702   HADDEN, SAMUEL B. "Newer Treatment Techniques for Homosexuality." *Archives of Environmental Health: Preventive, Occupational and Aerospace Medicine* 13 (3, 1966): 284–288.

A general psychiatric discussion of homosexuality is presented. Homosexuality is a symptom, a manifestation of an over-all pattern of maladaptation.

Group psychotherapy seems to be more effective than individual psychotherapy, especially when the entire group is made up of homosexuals.

703   HADDEN, SAMUEL B. "The Psychotherapy of Homosexuality, 2. Group Psychotherapy in Homosexuality." *Psychiatric Opinion* 4 (2, 1967): 9–12.

Homosexuality is a symptom of a defective personality organization. Many factors are involved in the organization of personality, but nothing is more important than feeling that one compares adequately with one's same-sex peers. Unless a child is allowed to associate freely with other children of about the same age, such a comparison cannot be made and a derogatory self-image results. Persons who make a homosexual adjustment have usually been prevented from participating in the rough-and-tumble preschool play activity which is so important in the development of a sense of belonging and acceptance, and which allows the child to measure himself against others of the same sex. Because the "verbal jousting" which takes place within a group psychotherapy situation can serve as a substitute for this "scrambling" play experience, group psychotherapy can sometimes be more effective than individual treatment for homosexuality.

When the therapy group is composed entirely of homosexuals the outcome is generally more successful. In such a group, rationalization about the desirability of a homosexual commitment is more difficult, resistance to treatment is more easily broken down, and "ego-strengthening occurs as a result of the acceptance and tolerance of other group members and identification with those who have undergone change."

704   HADDEN, SAMUEL B. "Treatment of Homosexuality by Individual and Group Psychotherapy." *American Journal of Psychiatry* 114 (9, 1958): 810–815.

Experiences of treating 10 male homosexuals are reported. Homosexuals can be treated more effectively by group psychotherapy when the groups are made up exclusively of homosexuals. In such groups the rationalization that homosexuality is a pattern of life they wish to follow is destroyed by their fellow homosexuals. Ego strength is gained by identifying with others who are also seeking socially acceptable goals. Identification with this group banishes the feelings of isolation from which they suffer. Their fellow members help them to reject their homosexual identifications and to identify, instead, with heterosexuals.

705   HADDEN, SAMUEL B. "Treatment of Male Homosexuals in Groups." *International Journal of Group Psychotherapy* 16 (1, 1966): 13–22.

Homosexuality is a treatable condition with reasonable hope for success. The treatment of male homosexuals in groups of four to eight members who meet for weekly sessions has had unusual success. The rationalization of its members that they are content to be homosexuals is broken down by the group, which is supportive during the time of anxiety that ensues. Emphasis is on the nature of homosexuality as a symptom of maladaptation which is experientially produced by the experiences and fantasies of childhood, and there are no limited objectives for the treatment.

Psychotherapists owe it to the homosexual and to the community to devote more attention to the problem of homosexuality. They should enlist the cooperation of organized homosexual groups in the development of treatment measures and treatment centers which will help the homosexual attain a mature psychosexual development.

706 HADFIELD, J. A. "The Cure of Homosexuality." *British Medical Journal* (5083, 1958): 1323–1326.

That homosexuals can lose their propensity for their own sex and develop one for the opposite sex is demonstrated by the cases of five males who either practiced homosexuality or fantasized it during their heterosexual relations. Treated by psychotherapy, the patients were cured of their homosexuality once the condition was traced to its basic causes (infantile experiences). However, not all homosexuals can be so cured. The main benefit derived from treating such cases is the discovery of its causes and the resultant prevention of the disorder.

707 HAGMAIER, GEORGE. "The Pastoral Counselling of the Homosexual." 1958. Reprinted as "Homosexuality." In *Counselling the Catholic,* edited by George Hagmaier and Robert W. Gleason, pp. 94–112. New York: Sheed & Ward, 1959.

One chapter, in a textbook in counseling or practical psychology for the seminarian and a reference book for parish priests, includes a general discussion of the psychological aspects of homosexuality and practical information on how to deal with the problem. It is maintained that the informed parish priest may play an important role through his use of preventive educational techniques in assisting individual deviates, but the reader is warned of the psychiatric complexities involved. It is suggested that the priest stay clear of amateur probing and speculation for which he is not trained. However, the priest should be skilled enough to make an elementary diagnosis of a homosexual problem, since many individuals will speak of such matters only to a priest. The latter should be able to assist such individuals in finding psychiatric treatment.

708   HARMS, ERNEST. "Homo-Anonymous." *Diseases of the Nervous System* 14 (10, 1953): 318–319.

A highly refined homosexual musician suggested to the author that a movement for homosexuals be formed similar to Alcoholics Anonymous. It was envisioned that if the participants could maintain platonic friendships by discussing their relationships their overt behavior could be prevented. The therapist tried this with certain patients and, finding it successful, urged other practitioners to further test this idea.

709   HASTINGS, DONALD W. "Homosexuality." In his *Impotence and Frigidity,* pp. 115–127. Boston: Little, Brown & Co., 1963.

Directed to the general physician, a discussion of homosexuality includes its definition, diagnosis, etiology, and treatment. The 7-point Kinsey Scale is suggested as a convenient aid in the making of a diagnosis which will depend upon the personal communication which is established between the doctor and his patient. Latent homosexuality without overt homosexual behavior must also be considered in the diagnosis which is made. The few reports of treatment and cure are probably based upon case histories in which the patient had a childhood disturbed by parental discord or a broken home. In such cases psychotherapy may very well be successful. The physician should not consider marriage as a recommended treatment for homosexuality.

710   HENRY, GEORGE W. "Pastoral Counseling for Homosexuals." 1951. Reprinted in *Homosexuality: A Cross Cultural Approach,* edited by Donald Webster Cory, pp. 384–393. New York: Julian Press, 1956.

Ministers, along with psychiatrists, can be helpful in their treatment of homosexuals. The ministerial function is twofold: to direct the patient toward realistic psychotherapy, and to rid him of his guilt. The minister must accept the patient as a person, for what he is, and must neither condemn nor condone. He must assure him that there is a place for him in the Kingdom of God, and that he can be a socially useful person. The counselor must work toward increasing the homosexual's emotional maturity.

711   HIRSH, HERMAN. "The Homosexual and the Family Doctor." *GP* [*General Practice*] 26 (5, 1962): 103–107.

It is important for the general practitioner to be able to identify homosexuality. Regardless of his moral or religious feelings, the doctor should try to help the patient. The teen-aged latent homosexual, a "worried" adolescent, can be aided by encouragement and reassurance. An older (17 to 25 years old) overt homosexual may seek medical treatment for vague somatic complaints or underlying anxiety, and if the doctor can gain his confidence, it will be possible to refer him to a psychiatrist. The long-term confirmed overt homosexual may profit little from therapy, but can be helped with antidepressants or nighttime sedation if there is anxiety present. In the case of homosexual panic, the patient should be given a tranquilizer and perhaps hospitalized.

712   JAMES, B. "Behaviour Therapy Applied to Homosexuality." *New Zealand Medical Journal* 66 (423, 1967): 752–754.

Behavior therapy is the name given to a system of therapeutic techniques which are directly based on the principles of learning theory. Behaviorists see homosexuality as a symptom, a biologically and socially maladaptive response, learned by reinforcement of homosexual behavior. There is a reduction in sex drive by an avoidance of the heterosexual object which results in reduction in anxiety. As a result, behavior therapy has two phases: the extinction of the homosexual response and the extinction of avoidance responses with the encouragement of approach responses toward an opposite sex object.

In order to extinguish the homosexual response, aversive therapy techniques are used. These techniques are varied, but generally employ either chemical and emetic agents or electric shock to replace the patient's customary pleasurable sexual response to homosexual objects with distinctly unpleasant responses such as feelings of nausea or electric shock.

The extinction of avoidance responses and the encouragement of approach responses to opposite sex objects is a more complicated matter. Behavior therapists employ a process known as desensitization by reciprocal inhibition. A reaction which will reinforce a heterosexual response while inhibiting the old anxiety response is sought by determining the situations, thoughts, and behavior which cause the patient anxiety and attempting to inhibit the anxiety response to each specific stimulus. The therapist establishes a stimulus hierarchy and works up from the least anxiety-producing to the most anxiety-producing stimuli, and helps the patient learn to respond appropriately to each stimulus.

713   JAMES, BASIL. "Case of Homosexuality Treated by Aversion Therapy." *British Medical Journal* (5280, 1962): 768–770.

The treatment by aversion therapy of a 40-year-old patient with an exclusive homosexual commitment is described. Two modifications of the aversion therapy technique were introduced: the patient was given two ounces of brandy with each apomorphine injection; a tape recording, composed according to the patient's personal history and explaining his homosexual attraction and the consequences of his practices, was played. The alcohol was given because it was part of the patient's behavior pattern associated with homosexuality, and it increased the emetic effect of the apomorphine. The treatment described was termed successful because the patient's heterosexual interest was increasing at the time of writing, and he had lost all attraction toward his own sex. The treatment was brief, in no way analytical, and succeeded where other methods had previously failed.

714 JAMES, BASIL, and EARLY, DONALD F. "Aversion Therapy for Homosexuals." *British Medical Journal* (5329, 1963): 538.

Inquiries about sexual drive, family relationships, work record, and mood were made during a follow-up study of a male homosexual who had received aversion therapy treatment 18 months earlier. The report indicated that the patient had established a satisfactory heterosexual relationship with his girl friend, that his family relationships were very good, that he was about to be promoted in his job, and that he had apparently been able to maintain a mood of confidence since the treatment. It appeared that he had become a sexually normal person and that his social adjustment was better than at any previous time.

715 JOHNSON, ROSWELL H. "Counseling the Homosexual Client." *Family Life* 15 (9, 1955): 5–6.

The types of homosexual clients encountered in counseling include the young boy drifting in the wrong direction, the older homosexual who really does not want to change, but who may desire to marry for social reasons, the ambisexual who is not yet exclusively homosexual, and the homosexual referred by legal authorities. The older homosexual and the homosexual referred by the courts are the hardest to help or to reeducate toward heterosexuality. The young boy is the best prospect for counseling.

716 KARPMAN, BENJAMIN. "Mediate Psychotherapy and the Acute Homosexual Panic (Kempf's Disease)." *Journal of Nervous and Mental Disease* 98 (5, 1943): 493–506.

"Mediate" psychotherapy was used in treating a 34-year-old married male who was suffering from homosexual panic. Although the patient was completely uncooperative with the staff, he was meek and submissive during visits with his wife. It was decided, therefore, to attempt therapy through the wife. She was coached by the therapist about questions she should discuss with her husband and met with the therapist to discuss his replies.

The factors which had led to the patient's psychosis are described. After five months of treatment the patient was discharged, despite doubts about his recovery by the ward physicians. After seven years the patient had no recurrence and appeared to be doing well.

717   KIRKENDALL, LESTER A. "Does Homosexuality Threaten My Child?" 1960. Reprinted in *The Third Sex,* edited by Isadore Rubin, pp. 100–101. New York: New Book Co., 1961.

Mild homosexual contact is normal during adolescence and should not alarm parents. If the child seems to have emotional problems, professional help should be sought.

718   KNOX, STUART C. "Another Look at Homosexuality." *Journal of the American Medical Association* 193 (10, 1965): 831.

Homosexuality is one of the "symptom patterns" exhibited by an individual who can neither adjust to nor cope with the responsibilities of adulthood in society. Despite the research, scientific study, and attempts to determine specific causal factors, homosexual behavior will probably never be accepted as "normal."

Legislation and social mores reflect the attitude of rejection which the homosexual encounters when he seeks help. Prevention is an important aspect of therapy, but prevention requires a complete understanding of the homosexual problem, an expanded effort toward the development of improved social awareness, and an informed medical leadership.

719   KOLB, LAWRENCE C. "Therapy of Homosexuality." *Current Psychiatric Therapies* 3 (1963): 131–137.

Etiological factors which establish various types of homosexual adaptation are not at all similar. Therefore, it is necessary to try various techniques in the treatment of the overt male homosexual or bisexual. One must consider the personality structure and the balance of satisfaction obtained through homosexual and heterosexual activity in the bisexual as against the castration anxieties and fears in certain men troubled by their sexual deviations. Overt homosexual behavior probably represents a single expression of a wide variety of psychogenetic forces.

720   KRAFT, TOM. "A Case of Homosexuality Treated by Systematic Desensitization." *American Journal of Psychotherapy* 21 (4, 1967): 815–821.

When a patient is desensitized from anxiety relating to normal sexual intercourse, he loses his homosexual desires even though no treatment is directed toward his homosexuality. An illustration of this is given in the case of a male homosexual. Wolpe's method of systematic desensitization and relaxation was induced by Methohexital Sodium (Brevital). The patient made a complete recovery (i.e., he lost his desire for homosexual activities and could enjoy heterosexual intercourse).

721 LAIDLAW, ROBERT W. "A Clinical Approach to Homosexuality." *Marriage and Family Living* 14 (1, 1952): 39–45.

An "informal presentation" discusses the subject of the rationale of a therapeutic approach to the problem of homosexuality. Kinsey's findings with regard to male homosexuality are reviewed, and hypotheses regarding lesbianism, the causes of homosexuality ("we just don't know . . . we require a multiplicity of causes to account for the multiplicity of homosexual phenomena"), clinical types, and societal treatment of homosexuality are given.

In therapy, many psychiatrists believe that not all homosexuals can be cured, i.e., that some can only be helped to accept themselves. To see if a patient can be cured, the therapist must look at the patient's longitudinal history to find what type of homosexual the person is (with special regard to the fantasy life). The degree of desire for change, as well as the meaningfulness of the patient's homosexual experience in his past must be considered. People "deeply homosexual" cannot be cured; bisexuals have a "fair" chance; and "sporadic" homosexuals have good prospects for cure. Hence, some can be cured, and those who cannot should be helped to accept themselves.

722 LAMBERT, CARL. "Homosexuals." *Medical Press* 232 (1954): 523–526.

The etiology and treatment of homosexuality are discussed. The determinants of homosexuality are nearly always a combination of genetic and environmental factors. There is a large homosexual population not in need of any psychological treatment, and even those who do need it can find little help from psychoanalysis or hormone therapy. Vocational guidance is the most constructive therapeutic approach which can be made in helping homosexuals to improve their social adjustment.

723 LEITSCH, DICK. "In Reply: The Psychotherapy of Homosexuality. Let's Forget Jocasta and Her Little Boy." *Psychiatric Opinion* 4 (3, 1967): 28–35.

The author, president of the Mattachine Society, Inc., of New York, answers articles by John R. Cavanagh, Samuel B. Hadden, and Toby Bieber on the psychotherapy of homosexuality.

Those who define homosexuality as a sickness, a disease, or mental illness are making religious and social standards serve as criteria for measuring mental health. It is contended that homosexuality is neither a disease, nor is it a psychological problem. Instead it is a sociological problem which has its roots in relations between the majority-heterosexual-group and the minority-homosexual-group. Treatment, whether by psychoanalysis or psychotherapy, should not attempt to "cure" homosexuality by changing sexual orientation, but should be aimed at helping the person deal with the social pressures he meets as a result of his homosexual commitment.

724 LEVIN, S. M.; HIRSCH, L. S.; SHUGAR, G.; and KAPCHE, R. "Treatment of Homosexuality and Heterosexual Anxiety with Avoidance Conditioning and Systematic Desensitization: Data and Case Report." *Psychotherapy: Theory, Research and Practice* 5 (3, 1968): 160–168.

A description is provided of the therapy used in treating the homosexuality and accompanying anxiety of a white male in his middle twenties. The three-part therapeutic program included initial interviewing (ten one-hour sessions conducted to explain the therapy to the patient and to assemble material about him), systematic desensitization, and avoidance conditioning. The systematic desensitization therapy and avoidance conditioning are described in detail.

Results of psychological tests given before and after the therapy are discussed. Five months after completion of the treatment the patient returned because of a recurrence of homosexual feelings. Therapy was resumed for a two-month period. A follow-up seven months later indicated that he was continuing to make a good adjustment.

725 LIEBERMAN, DANIEL, and SIEGEL, BENJAMIN A. "A Program for 'Sexual Psychopaths' in a State Mental Hospital." *American Journal of Psychiatry* 113 (March, 1957): 801–807.

A two-year program for sex offenders at a state hospital in California is examined, and California laws governing the determination of "sexual psychopathy," jurisdiction, court medical examination, disposition of the sex offender, and release procedure are described.

Commitment for a 90-day observation period is the first phase in the California "sexual psychopathy" program. The second phase is commitment for an indeterminate period of treatment. The sex offender becomes a treatment patient if he qualifies and if he is likely to benefit from treatment.

Sex offenses involving children under 14 years of age accounted for over 50 percent of the 284 patients studied. Forty-six of the 148 cases of pedophiliac activity involved boys. Sodomy accounted for 4 percent of the kinds of offenses in which the 284 patients were involved. "Other homosexuality" accounted for 12 percent of the offenses.

An outline of the treatment program is given. The results indicate that intensive psychiatric treatment of the sex offender is justified on the basis of the increase in the number of patients discharged following a period of intensive treatment.

726 LIEBMAN, SAMUEL. "Homosexuality, Transvestism, and Psychosis: Study of a Case Treated with Electroshock." *Journal of Nervous and Mental Disease* 99 (6, 1944): 945–958.

The relationship between homosexuality and psychosis is illustrated in the case of a 23-year-old Negro male homosexual and transvestite, who was treated with electroshock therapy at the Norwich State Hospital. As a result of electroshock therapy, he recovered from his psychosis and transvestism, although he remained overtly homosexual.

727 LITMAN, ROBERT E. "Psychotherapy of a Homosexual Man in a Heterosexual Group." *International Journal of Group Psychotherapy* 11 (4, 1961): 440–448.

Although overt homosexuality is listed as a counter-indication for group therapy, the successful treatment is reported of a homosexual man in a group made up of four heterosexual females and three heterosexual males. The interaction between the former and other members of the group facilitated the working through of his use of homosexuality as his only mode of human relationship. The group as a whole progressed at the average rate. The feminine reactions of two of the women served especially to buffer the rest of the group against excessive anxiety about male homosexuality. The homosexual patient finally left the group because of a promotion and a transfer elsewhere. He achieved success in his profession and reported an idyllic love affair with a young European woman.

728 LORAND, SANDOR. "The Therapy of Perversions." In *Perversions: Psychodynamics and Therapy,* edited by Sandor Lorand and Michael Balint, pp. 290–307. New York: Random House, 1956.

In a general consideration of the psychoanalytical therapy of sexual perversion with a special consideration of homosexuality, it is emphasized that perversions have a wide variety of etiological roots and require many different therapeutic approaches. The usual aim should be to reduce anxiety resulting from castration fear. The problem in male homosexuality involves an identification with the mother. The strength of oral desires, wherein the penis unconsciously symbolizes the breast of the mother, is also mentioned.

729 MacCulloch, M. J.; Feldman, M. P.; and Pinshoff, J. M. "The Application of Anticipatory Avoidance Learning to the Treatment of Homosexuality, II. Avoidance Response Latencies and Pulse Rate Changes." *Behaviour Research and Therapy* 3 (1, 1965): 21–43.

As part of a program on the use of anticipatory avoidance learning in the treatment of homosexuality, recordings of avoidance response latencies and pulse rate changes in response to the male photographs used as conditioned stimuli were made. Data on response latencies for four patients and on pulse rate changes in two of them are presented.

Response latencies display a regular learning curve in patients who improve with treatment, but not in those who relapse or fail to improve. Pulse rate changes in response to the stimuli were conditioned in one patient who improved with treatment, but not in another who did not improve. The results suggest an association between pronounced pulse rate changes and successful avoidance learning, and conversely between an absence of pulse rate changes and poor avoidance learning. This finding parallels results obtained in animal studies and appears to have a predictive value for behavior during follow-up. More comprehensive studies are planned.

See also Feldman, M. P., and MacCulloch, M. J. (no. 687). See also Feldman, M. P.; MacCulloch, M. J.; Mellor, Valerie; and Pinschoff, J. M. (no. 688).

730 MacCulloch, M. J., and Feldman, M. P. "Aversion Therapy in Management of 43 Homosexuals." *British Medical Journal* (5552, 1967): 594–597.

To test the use of aversion therapy in the treatment of homosexuality, a study was made of 43 male homosexuals who were either ordered into treatment by the court or who had come willingly. The patients were treated by anticipatory avoidance learning, using an electrical aversive stimulus. Of the 36 patients who completed treatment, 25 were significantly improved. Those who failed to respond to treatment had high Kinsey ratings, were over 30 years old, and had a personality disorder other than the self-insecure type. One of the major variables prognostic of success in the treatment of homosexual males is a history of heterosexual interest and practice at some time in the patient's life.

731 MacCulloch, M. J., and Feldman, M. P. "Personality and the Treatment of Homosexuality." *Acta Psychiatrica Scandinavica* 43 (3, 1967): 300–317.

Reports of treatment of homosexuals by aversion therapy, psychotherapy, and psychoanalysis are reviewed with regard to determining personality factors which might be used as indicators of probable success in treatment. Noting that in these studies personality as a factor in treatment has been either ignored or treated inconsistently, it is contended that no conclusions are possible.

The treatment of 32 male homosexuals by anticipatory avoidance learning (aversion therapy) is described. The personalities of the patients were evaluated according to three clinical types: self-insecure personality abnormality, attention-seeking personality abnormality, and weak-willed personality abnormality. The pre- and post-treatment Kinsey ratings of the patients are given and discussed.

Results indicated that age and personality are important prognostic factors in treatment. The self-secure abnormalities group seemed to do best in treatment.

732 McGUIRE, R. J., and VALLANCE, M. "Aversion Therapy by Electric Shock: A Simple Technique." *British Medical Journal* (5376, 1964): 151–153.

A simple electric shock aversion therapy apparatus which the patient can use at home is described. A diagram and instructions for building the apparatus are included. It is suggested that this machine should be helpful to patients with sexual deviations such as homosexuality.

733 MARKS, I. M. "Aversion Therapy." *British Journal of Medical Psychology* 41 (1, 1968): 47–52.

A description of aversion therapy and a discussion of how it may be properly used in the treatment of sexual deviations mentions the possibility that homosexuality may be successfully treated in this way. The advantage of aversion therapy in the treatment of sexual deviation is that specific deviant symptoms can be made unattractive to the patient without causing a revulsion against socially acceptable sexual activity such as heterosexual intercourse.

734 MASON, STEPHEN C.; JACOB, JOSEPH S.; HIMLER, LEONARD E.; GOULD, STUART M.; and BIRD, H. WALDO. "Homosexuality: A Medico-Legal Problem." *Journal of the Michigan State Medical Society* 60 (5, 1961): 635–638.

There are four roles which psychiatry has to play in the community as regards the problem of homosexuality: cure for those who desire change; differentiation between the practicing homosexual and the psychotic who needs institutionalized treatment; aid for the homosexuals in their adjustment in society; educating the public, ultimately to prevent homosexuality. Several recommendations are made for legal change, one being that homosexual behavior in private by adults should not be illegal.

735   MATHER, NORTHAGE J. de V. "The Treatment of Homosexuality by Aversion Therapy." *Medicine, Science, and the Law* 6 (4, 1966): 200–205.

In a pilot study conducted in an English hospital, aversion therapy was used to treat 36 male homosexuals. Using findings from laboratory research, aversion therapy makes use of classical conditioning and anticipatory avoidance technique. In this particular study, electric shock and slides of clothed and unclothed males and females were used.

The patients were interviewed and tested before treatment, midway through treatment, and five times after treatment was completed. Based upon changes in their Kinsey ratings, 25 cases were considered improved.

Some of the advantages of aversion therapy in treating homosexuality are that it employs laboratory-evolved principles; it is of shorter duration than psychotherapy; it may be more easily administered; and the patient can usually understand the method.

736   MAYERSON, PETER, and LIEF, HAROLD I. "Psychotherapy of Homosexuals: A Follow-Up Study of Nineteen Cases." In *Sexual Inversion: The Multiple Roots of Homosexuality,* edited by Judd Marmor, pp. 302–344. New York: Basic Books, 1965.

To estimate the success of psychotherapy in homosexuality and the factors associated with therapeutic success or failure, a follow-up study of 19 patients (14 males and five females) with homosexual problems was conducted. The method used was modeled after that of Miles, employing the "approach of evaluating the individual patient from the point of view of psychodynamics as well as of descriptive behavioral changes and analyzing holistic character modifications rather than concentrating exclusively on changes in one area of a patient's personality."

The mean duration of therapy for the patients was 1.7 years, and the mean interval between end of therapy and the follow-up was 4.5 years.

A protocol form was devised and used as a general guideline for evaluating each patient's presenting illness and adjustment in the areas of psychic and psychosomatic symptoms, social relationships, sexual relationships, and depth of insight. The charts were reviewed by two psychiatrists and joint follow-up interviews were then conducted and separate evaluations made. Four case histories typical of the three groups of therapeutic evaluation at follow-up are presented. Appendices reproduce the protocol form used in the study and describe the methodology in detail.

At the time of the follow-up, 47.3 percent of the patients were "apparently recovered" or "much improved," and 26.3 percent were "improved" in comparison to their status at the beginning of therapy. In the majority of patients, the follow-up revealed progress in all behavioral areas since the end of treatment.

737　MENDELSOHN, FRED, and ROSS, MATHEW. "An Analysis of 133 Homosexuals Seen at a University Health Service." *Diseases of the Nervous System* 20 (6, 1959): 246–250.

Data used in this study of 109 male homosexuals and 24 female homosexuals seen in the psychiatric section of the Student Health Service at the University of California at Los Angeles included admission histories, periodic progress notes of the therapy sessions, and some psychological test batteries. A smaller percentage of the male homosexuals were in graduate work than was true for the rest of the University population. The male homosexuals tended to be in applied arts, especially theater arts, in greater percentages than the rest of the student body. The academic performance of the undergraduate homosexuals was comparable to the University undergraduate population, except that the academic performance of the undergraduate female homosexuals was decidedly better than that of other undergraduate females. A smaller percentage of male homosexuals were married than were nonhomosexual male psychiatric patients. In a comparison of a group of 20 (15 overt males and five overt females) of the 133 homosexuals and 20 nonhomosexuals (15 men and five women) with similar numbers of hours in therapy, indicated no difference in the therapeutic results of homosexuals (male and female) and heterosexuals (male and female). Young age of the homosexual and little overt homosexual behavior are good prognostic signs for therapy with overt male homosexuals. High scholastic standing may also be a good sign. Those patients who showed considerable improvement were generally the homosexuals and nonhomosexuals who had received the greatest number of hours of therapy. The non-acting-out male homosexual patients in comparison to the overt homosexuals were younger, more often came from nonbroken homes, and engaged in less prepubertal homosexual and heterosexual handling of the genitals.

738　MEYER, ADOLF-ERNST. "Psychoanalytic Versus Behavior Therapy of Male Homosexuals: A Statistical Evaluation of Clinical Outcome." *Comprehensive Psychiatry* 7 (2, 1966): 110–117.

A comparison is made of two studies which used different approaches to the treatment of male homosexuals. Irving Bieber, et al., studied inverts treated by psychoanalysis, and Kurt Freund reported the treatment of male homosexuals by a combination of aversion therapy and positive conditioning. The samples, criteria for success, treatment variables, and results of the studies are compared. The results of treatment were found to be significantly better for the group which underwent psychoanalysis. See Bieber, Irving (no. 314). Freund, Kurt (no. 697).

739 MILLER, MICHAEL M. "Hypnotic-Aversion Treatment of Homosexuality." *Journal of the National Medical Association* 55 (5, 1963): 411–415, 436.

The fairly widespread tendency to deprecate the use of hypnosis in the treatment of homosexuality is criticized. These observations are based upon hypnotic treatment given to four male homosexuals, aged 26 to 38 years. The use of hypnosis rests on the premise that the homosexual patient must come to feel disgust and aversion for his deviant practices. Although hypnosis is not a "cure-all" and should be accompanied by longer-term psychotherapy, it offers the advantage of allowing the disgust and aversion reaction to be prolonged and intensified. It was found that not only could a strong aversion to the male body be induced through hypnotic suggestion, but it was also possible to relieve anxiety and horror reactions toward the female body. It is indicated on the basis of one case that this technique should work equally well for females.

740 MILLER, PETER M.; BRADLEY, JOHN B.; GROSS, RICHARD S.; and WOOD, GENE. "Review of Homosexuality Research (1960–1966) and Some Implications for Treatment." *Psychotherapy: Theory, Research and Practice* 5 (1, 1968): 3–6.

Two schools of thought are found in a review of the research on homosexuality in journals of psychology and psychiatry. One focuses upon the replacement of homosexual behavior with heterosexual behavior. The three major findings which have emerged from this type of research are: certain variables are associated with such a change—the patient's motivation, age, experience of some heterosexual behavior, and whose father is at least not fiercely withdrawn from the subject; group therapy involving homosexual and heterosexual males and females can provide a stimulus for change; behavior therapy, using avoidance or other techniques, has shown "promising" results. The other main approach has as its goal the elimination of anxiety and discomfort in the homosexual, but not of his homosexual behavior per se. For this therapeutic approach to be successful, it is suggested that identification with the normal heterosexual male should be sought.

741 MINTZ, ELIZABETH E. "Overt Male Homosexuality in Combined Group and Individual Treatment." *Journal of Consulting Psychology* 30 (3, 1966): 193–198.

The advantages of combined therapy (both individual treatment and group therapy) became apparent during the use of such therapy with 10 homosexual men. The subjects were self-referred patients who were intellectually above average and who remained in psychotherapy for two or more years.

The once-a-week group therapy included women and heterosexual men. The individual sessions were regularly scheduled from one to three times a week and were psychoanalytically oriented. All the patients reported an improved general adjustment; three of them reported satisfactory heterosexual adjustment; three more hoped to achieve it eventually.

The advantages of the combined group and individual therapy were the dissolution of rationalizations about homosexuality, the development of a stronger sense of personal identity through contact with women and heterosexual men, the emergence of hitherto unconscious anxieties related to their heterosexual drives, and corrective emotional experiences which often resulted in an enhanced self-esteem.

742 MOHR, JOHANN W., and TURNER, R. E. "Sexual Deviations." *Applied Therapeutics* 9 (1, 1967): 78–81; 9 (2, 1967): 165–168.

Sexual deviation must be defined with reference to statistical, social, cultural, and legal norms. In clinical practice, however, it seems more helpful to approach sexual problems in terms of the nature of the act, who is involved, in what situation and with what frequency, rather than in terms of definitions involving clinical categories. In considering referral for treatment, the physician should take into account the degree of impairment a deviation represents and whether the patient has sufficient motivation for change, either from personal unhappiness or because of social pressure.

Homosexuality is the most common sexual deviation; thus the literature about it is usually overgeneralized. Its etiology is unclear; many different phenomena are grouped under the same term. Treatment (psychotherapy or behavior therapy) is possible, at the very least in terms of an amelioration of problem situations. However, treatment will be unsuccessful if the patient is not motivated to change.

743 MONROE, RUSSELL R., and ENELOW, MORTON L. "The Therapeutic Motivation in Male Homosexuals: An Adaptational Analysis." *American Journal of Psychotherapy* 14 (3, 1960): 474–490.

In the hope of clarifying the motivating forces operating in successfully treated homosexuals, an investigation of homosexuals who sought help and showed a sustained interest in psychiatric therapy was conducted. The subjects were seven male patients, two of whom were in complete analysis, and five of whom were in "analytically oriented" brief psychotherapy. Four of the patients were followed for at least five years after treatment. Data were obtained through free association.

Although current literature mentions the competition for dominance between alimentary and orgastic strivings, there was no mention of this by the patients. That is, they did not mention the incompatibility of object choices for these two strivings, although this was common to all the patients. Most of the patients were subjected to parental attitudes which were discordant with regard to sexual and alimentary behavior. These attitudes were conveyed to the child and led to conflict in all adult interpersonal relationships where both alimentary and orgastic behavior were important aspects. This disparity must be dealt with first in therapy. Since partners must meet these two behavioral needs equally but cannot, long-term attachments are impossible. The resulting fears of desertion precipitate anxiety and depression, both of which appear to be primary motivating forces (although not the only motivation) in those homosexuals who seriously seek psychiatric care. Homosexuals who are coerced into treatment do not respond to it.

744   MOORE, KENNETH B., and QUERY, WILLIAM T. "Group Psycho-
       therapy as a Means of Approaching Homosexual Behavior among
       Hospitalized Psychiatric Patients." *Journal of the Kentucky State
       Medical Association* 61 (5, 1963): 403–407.

Group psychotherapy was used in an attempt to deal with homosexual behavior among the patients on a psychiatric ward in the Veterans Administration Hospital in Lexington, Kentucky. A group of 13 patients was formed in response to the negative reactions to this sexual activity on the part of the ward staff, and its original purpose was ward management.

As a means of ward management the group therapy approach was successful. Possibly because they were fearful that members of the group would be labeled "queer," the patients carefully avoided homosexual contacts. The fact that the group existed seems to have brought about an almost total cessation of homosexual activity among other ward patients as well.

Although little basic personality change was apparent, the attention from the psychiatric staff which this group of patients received was instrumental in bringing about marked social improvement in the members' daily lives. In addition, three of the patients were able to make better life adjustments.

By the end of the six months, two members of the group were able to leave the hospital.

745 MUNZER, JEAN. "Treatment of the Homosexual in Group Psychotherapy." *Topical Problems in Psychotherapy* 5 (1965): 164–169.

A homosexual patient is defined as one who identifies himself as a homosexual and whose self-identification has been accepted by one or more other persons before entering therapy. A questionnaire was administered to 47 patients in mixed psychotherapy groups including 10 homosexuals. The questions concerned the sexual orientation of the patient (including a 5-point self-rating scale), his identification of other members of his group as homosexual or heterosexual, and his attitude toward mixing hetero- and homosexuals in the same groups. The responses of the patients to the questions are discussed. In general, it is felt that the problems of self-labeled homosexuals can be dealt with effectively in mixed groups.

746 NAIMAN, JAMES. "Short Term Effects as Indicators of the Role of Interpretations in Psychoanalysis." *International Journal of Psycho-Analysis* 49 (2–3, 1968): 353–357.

There has been a recent emphasis on curative factors rather than dream interpretations in psychoanalysis. Specifically, identification with the analyst is often cited as being important or necessary for therapeutic results. A clinical example of an overt homosexual in which the effect of a particular interpretation resulted in a distinct change on the part of the patient from homosexuality toward heterosexuality is presented. An interpretation of a dream about his sister enabled the patient to better understand why he rejected women. Subsequently, changes in his behavior, his affect, and his dream content were noted. It is suggested that similar observations could provide evidence to support the traditional role of interpretations and insight in psychoanalysis.

Comments by Rudolph M. Lowenstein are included.

747 NEDOMA, KAREL. "Homosexuality in Sexological Practice." *International Journal of Sexology* 4 (4, 1951): 219–224.

The majority of homosexuals do not feel their sexual aberration is a disease, but wish to be recognized by society as a third sex. Often they do not seek help until they are brought to court, and many come for psychiatric help only to receive an assurance that homosexuality is a natural, inherent state which is not changeable. Sometimes relatives and friends bring homosexuals for treatment. Sometimes homosexuals do not have sufficient courage to share their problems with anyone else. Homosexuals who do not wish to be treated outnumber those who sincerely wish to undergo treatment.

748   NEUSTATTER, W. LINDESAY. "Homosexuality from the Psychiatric
       Viewpoint." *Man and Society* 1 (1, 1961): 33–34.

It is suggested that part of the homosexual problem is the interaction
between homosexuals and those prejudiced against them; therefore both
should be studied psychologically. Various views of homosexuality are
reviewed, and it is concluded that often the psychiatrist can only offer
understanding to help the homosexual adjust. Since homosexuality is not
an illnesss, it is unlikely to benefit from therapeutic measures.

749   NEUSTATTER, W. LINDESAY. "Sexual Abnormalities and the Sex-
       ual Offender." *Medico-Legal Journal* 29 (4, 1961): 190–199.

Deviation is often found in otherwise normal individuals, but may be a facet
of psychopathy. Treatment is only rarely effective, dependent upon the
amount of normal heterosexuality present. But treatment can assist self-
control and teach the paraphiliac to live with his handicap—something
punishment cannot do. Prejudice toward these people must be overcome,
and it must be determined if an act is truly socially dangerous. Society can
better protect itself by indefinite nonpunitive detention than by finite punitive measures.

750   OLLENDORFF, ROBERT H. V. *The Juvenile Homosexual Experience
       and Its Effect on Adult Sexuality.* New York: Julian Press, 1966, 245
       pp.

In an anthropological and psychological study, homosexuality is said to
appear only in "sex-negating" societies, as opposed to sex-permissive ones.
Early conditioning by sex taboos fosters neurotic illness. Homosexuality
itself is a neurosis and is found frequently among psychopaths, since any
pleasurable conditioning is greedily accepted by the psychopath. The treatment of homosexuality should be the same as that of other neuroses. The
homosexual must achieve awareness and self-acceptance. Vegetotherapy is
recommended as a major aid. This is a technique that combines self-expression and character analysis with an examination of the muscular system,
facial expression, breathing, digestion, and the sexual functions.

751   ORGEL, SAMUEL ZACHARY. "A Case of Male Homosexuality."
       Samiksa 17 (1, 1963): 43–61.

A person who has made a homosexual commitment is one who has found
a method of dealing with deep-seated anxieties which yields pleasure rather
than pain. Unless he is also neurotic, or unless he has an abnormally bad
conscience which is causing great concern, such a person can rarely be
helped through psychoanalysis. Because analysis not only threatens to de-

stroy the pleasure, but also to stir up all the anxieties and conflicts which have been avoided by choosing a homosexual orientation, the patient will often terminate treatment prematurely.

The difficulty of treating such a person is illustrated by a detailed case study of a 23-year-old male whose analysis took four years (and four different analysts).

752   OVESEY, LIONEL, and GAYLIN, WILLARD M. "Psychotherapy of Male Homosexuality: Prognosis, Selection of Patients, Technique." *American Journal of Psychotherapy* 19 (3, 1965): 382–396.

Prognosis, selection of patients for treatment, and special problems of therapeutic technique for male homosexuals are considered. Since homosexuality is a multidetermined symptom of a neurosis, psychotherapy must be based upon an understanding of the unconscious motivations which impel the individual to flee from women and to seek contact with men. Significant indicators for prognosis are discussed. Selection of homosexuals as patients actually lies in the homosexuals' hands—those who come in for help desire change. Various techniques used in solving many of the problems of homosexuals are described.

753   OWENSBY, NEWDIGATE M. "The Correction of Homosexuality." *Urologic and Cutaneous Review* 45 (8, 1941): 494–496.

Fifteen case histories of homosexuals treated by pharmacologic shock therapy were reported, with one case given in detail. For 13 of the patients who were treated over a period of three years, treatment proved successful, i.e., they did not resume their former practices. The relapses of the other two patients were believed due to an insufficient period of time to complete the psychiatric methods believed essential to success.

It was stressed that most homosexuals shun affectations in behavior and dress and desire only a normal, full life. However, paradoxically, no homosexual who desired to change his sexual habits was found.

754   PAUL, R. "Problems of Psycho-Sexual Orientation." *Guy's Hospital Reports* 114 (3, 1965): 333–336.

Anxiety over psychosexual orientation is a relatively common problem among young adults coming to psychiatric outpatient clinics. Often the therapist, as well as the patient, fears that the condition of homosexuality is innate and cannot be treated. Six patients are discussed, five of whom were greatly improved after therapy.

Homosexuality "represents an adolescent hypochondriacal preoccupation about sexual function and role. Therapy is aimed at the allaying of this anxiety, which has effectively prevented psychosexual maturation."

755   PHILIPP, E. "Homosexuality as Seen in a New Zealand City Practice." *New Zealand Medical Journal* 67 (430, 1968): 397–401.

A group of 47 homosexuals, including three women, seen by a general practitioner is analyzed and compared to the group in Schofield's study, *The Sociological Aspects of Homosexuality,* which was done in Britain. This group and the Schofield study are briefly compared in terms of: occupational status, marriage, age, number of times seen, methods of referral, venereal disease, duration of homosexual relationships, bisexual contact, sexual activity, family history, and religious affiliation. It is concluded that most types of treatment, including psychiatric and aversion therapy, have been unsuccessful in changing the sexual orientation of homosexuals. Most homosexuals would benefit more from the help a general practitioner could provide in helping them to adjust to their situation.

756   POE, JOHN S. "The Successful Treatment of a 40-Year-Old Passive Homosexual Based on an Adaptational View of Sexual Behavior." *Psychoanalytic Review* 39 (1, 1952): 23–33.

In the case of a single white male homosexual, aged 39 years, who underwent psychodynamically directed psychotherapy, it became evident that homosexuality is an adaptation and can therefore be approached in therapy with some hope. The treatment of the case was successful; the patient ceased his homosexual behavior and married.

757   PRINCE, G. STEWART. "The Therapeutic Function of the Homosexual Transference." *Journal of Analytical Psychology* 4 (2, 1959): 117–124.

The case history of a latent homosexual is presented. The subject was a male in his late twenties who underwent psychoanalysis for neurotic symptoms. The latent homosexual orientation of the patient was a very significant factor in his symptom-formation, in its influence upon the homosexual transference, and in particular, in the part it played in the therapeutic process.

758   RAPPAPORT, ERNEST A. "A Case of Facultative Sexual Identity." *Chicago Medical School Quarterly* 26 (3, 1966): 145–151.

The case study of a 32-year-old male social worker whose homosexuality had been latent since adolescence is provided. The female genital structure both attracted him and terrified him. His mother's genitalia had been severely torn at the time of his birth, and he was afraid she would retaliate by castrating him. The fact that the mother, under the guise of obsessive cleanliness, examined and handled the patient's penis every day reinforced this fear. The patient's attitude toward his own sexuality and his sexual identity was also influenced by the severely disturbed family situation during his childhood. Both parents were "ambulatory schizophrenics," alternately hostile and loving. Family bathing and sleeping arrangements were bizarre. The patient was forced to bathe in the same tub with his sister; he slept with his father until he was eight when the father put him out, whereupon he slept with his mother until he was 11.

The patient was not cured during analysis, but after a period of overt homosexual behavior, he was able to make a bisexual adjustment which allowed him to develop a heterosexual relationship which led to marriage. No follow-up was undertaken after treatment was terminated.

759   REIDER, NORMAN. "Problems of Homosexuality." *California Medicine* 86 (6, 1957): 381–384.

Homosexuals have been subjected to excessively punitive laws as a result of the confusion between sin and crime. Homosexuality is essentially a biological and psychological phenomenon and only secondarily a social one. Just as it is more widespread than is commonly believed, it is also less harmful to society. Although constitutional and hereditary factors cannot be ruled out in its etiology, much evidence points to developmental factors, especially those connected with masculine or feminine identification, as being of prime importance. Hormonal treatment only increases the sexual drive without changing its direction. Psychiatric and psychoanalytical treatment seem to hold the only promise of success. The general practitioner should approach the problem with caution and with no more bias than he would have in the treatment of any other medical condition. He should readily refer homosexual patients with a real problem to a psychiatrist for evaluation and for a consideration of the means of treatment.

760   ROMAN, M. "The Treatment of the Homosexual in the Group." *Topical Problems in Psychotherapy* 5 (1965): 170–175.

Clinical material is used to illustrate views about group therapy: neurotic conflicts cannot be resolved in groups; group psychotherapy is effective primarily as a means of correcting certain ego malfunctions; and the effectiveness of the group situation depends upon the extent to which a patient can establish a narcissistic tie with the group as an entity or with some member other than the therapist.

The relations of one of the patients, a female latent homosexual, with the other group members are discussed. After she told one of her dreams, the other patients labeled her as "sick," and this intensified her feelings of guilt and inferiority. Although the patient could not resolve her homosexual feelings within the group, she did develop insight into her problem.

Heterosexual improvement within the group is seen as being due to narcissistic satisfactions, inherent in the situation.

761 ROPER, PETER. "The Effects of Hypnotherapy on Homosexuality." *Canadian Medical Association Journal* 96 (6, 1967): 319–327.

Fifteen homosexual patients with no detectable organic or psychotic illness were treated by hypnosis. While each patient was in a trance, suggestions were made about attraction to women and aversion to men, and an explanation of the onset of his homosexual behavior was given. Results were assessed according to the patients' subsequent behaviors and subjective feelings toward homosexuality. Eight patients showed "marked improvement," four showed "mild improvement," and three showed "no improvement." A significant correlation was found between the depth of hypnosis achieved and the success of the therapy. This led to the conclusion that those homosexuals able to become deeply hypnotized have a greater chance of improvement.

762 ROSEN, ISMOND, ed. *The Pathology and Treatment of Sexual Deviation: A Methodological Approach.* London: Oxford University Press, 1964, 510 pp.

A collection of articles is presented with the intention of meeting the demand of professional and lay readers for a greater knowledge of the range of techniques and current modes of thinking in the understanding and treatment of sexual deviation. Clinical problems and descriptions of technique and results, as well as extensive reviews of the theoretical literature and full bibliographies, receive equal emphasis. Sections on biology, general psychiatry, psychopathology, psychology, and sociology are included. Although homosexuality is so central a theme that it is touched on by nearly all of the contributors, it receives special emphasis in several of the chapters. See Brown, W. Paterson (no. 662). Carstairs, G. Morris (no. 962). Coates, Stephen (no. 671). Ginsberg, Morris (no. 1166). James, T. E. (no. 1191). Khan, M. Masud R. (no. 279). Robinson, Kenneth (no. 1228). Rubinstein, L. H. (no. 237). Scott, Peter D. (no. 557). Stafford-Clark, D. (no. 61).

763 ROTTERSMAN, WILLIAM. "Homosexuality." *Journal of the Medical Association, Georgia* 50 (5, 1961): 245–246.

A physician discusses homosexuality as a biological, medical, and social problem. While physical and constitutional factors may be contributory, homosexuality is primarily a psychological disorder. Although psychoanalysis may prove valuable to selected patients, "most homosexuals are seriously maladjusted individuals for whom at present no treatment offers the prospect of cure."

764 ROWE, WILLIAM S. "The Treatment of Homosexuality and Associated Perversions by Psychotherapy and Aversion Therapy." *Medical Journal of Australia* 2 (14, 1967): 637–639.

Hope of readjustment for homosexuals is better if two factors are present: an internal motivation for change, and some evidence of a heterosexual component in the personality.

Aversion therapy, because it provides only temporary help and does not change the personality disorder of which homosexuality is a symptom, is unsuccessful in treating homosexuality. Psychotherapy—group or individual—and deconditioning based on learning theory are effective in treatment. Because they reduce the sexual drive, estrogens can be effective to some extent in treating homosexuals with a strong homosexual drive but no heterosexual interest.

765 RUBIN, ISADORE. "The Possibility of 'Cure.'" 1959. Reprinted in *The Third Sex,* edited by Isadore Rubin, pp. 73–77. New York: New Book Co., 1961.

The "curing" of homosexuality means the loss of sexual desires for one's own sex and the direction of sexual interests exclusively toward the opposite sex. There are very few cases in the literature which indicate this "cure," and the question of whether or not such a "cure" is possible remains unanswered. Though the exclusive homosexual possibly cannot be cured, many of the nonexclusive homosexuals can be given considerable help in therapy. Treatment will probably be most effective when it is not directed solely toward attempting to change the sexual orientation of the homosexual, but aims at helping him in his adjustment to society.

766 RUBINSTEIN, L. H. "Psychotherapeutic Aspects of Male Homosexuality." *British Journal of Medical Psychology* 31 (1, 1958): 14–18.

Psychoanalytically oriented psychotherapy can help many, but not all, homosexuals. At best, it can clear the way for adequate spontaneous sublimation by strengthening the ego and by diminishing inhibitions and repressions which bar creative expression and genuine love.

767 SERBAN, GEORGE. "The Existential Therapeutic Approach to Homosexuality." *American Journal of Psychotherapy* 22 (3, 1968): 491–501.

A new therapeutic concept based upon the phenomenological interpretation of the homosexual condition is presented. Selecting a single case from a series of 25 homosexuals treated according to this concept, a detailed analysis of the case with the essential aspects of therapeutic interest is given.

This approach attempts to reduce homosexuality to its essential meaning, that is, "an existential mode of seeing and being seen in a sexual situation." The patient's inability to identify his body, sexually or otherwise, with his own sex, led him to an obsessive pursuit of masculinity to relieve the anxiety of nonbeing itself. His distorted logic led him to be a homosexual—the antithesis of maleness. The therapeutic approach analyzed this distortion of thinking and uncovered methodically his formulation of a body concept in the totality of his metalogical *Weltanschauung.* Finally, his erotic perception was reoriented in terms of the opposite sex.

768   "Sexual Issues on the Campus." In *Sex and the College Student,* edited by Group for the Advancement of Psychiatry, pp. 38–79. Report No. 60. New York: Group for the Advancement of Psychiatry, 1965.

Part of this chapter, included in a volume of guidelines for administrative policy and understanding of sexual issues on college campuses, concerns the problems of male and female homosexuality. A general discussion and case examples are included. A distinction must be made between incidental homosexuality in late adolescence and deeply ingrained patterns of overt homosexual behavior, and labeling must be carefully avoided. The wide variety of manifestations of homosexual feelings and the complexity of causes are indicated. Wherever possible, psychoanalysis or intensive psychotherapy should be recommended to students with severe problems due to homosexuality.

769   SILBERGER, JULIUS. "Homosexual Patients in Psychotherapy: A Different Experience." Case Reports of the Massachusetts Mental Health Center, VII. *Psychiatric Opinion* 5 (2, 1968): 34–41.

When homosexuals seek therapy, they usually say they want to overcome their homosexuality because they feel they are expected to say that. However, help is often sought because of some impasse in their life situations.

Three clinical examples point out that the motivations for psychotherapeutic treatment are varied. Since this is the case, it is not useful to discuss one particular type of ontogenesis or treatment for homosexuality. The individual problems of a patient should provide the basis for the type of treatment which is initiated.

770 SINGER, MELVIN, and FISCHER, RUTH. "Group Psychotherapy of Male Homosexuals by a Male and Female Co-Therapy Team." *International Journal of Group Psychotherapy* 17 (1, 1967): 44–52.

An unusual experience by a co-therapy team involving a year's treatment of a homosexual group is recounted. The group had already undergone a year's treatment with two male therapists before they were replaced by the new male and female therapists. Although the female therapist assumed a minor role, making few comments and spending most of the time in note-taking, her presence brought about an immediate change in the group which reacted with explosive animosity and antagonism, carrying on violent verbal debates, and deliberately attacking and distorting any comment made by the male therapist. This continued unabated for six months, when the hostility began to subside and the group began to take the male therapist more into account.

It is maintained that the "male and female co-therapy team was a concrete representation of the parental dyad and that this allowed the development of remarkable transference distortions which were projected onto the corresponding parental surrogate." They consider that an exclusively homosexual group is a valuable modality for promoting emotional growth and maturity, providing a supportive, protective setting in which the patient can express his feelings, attitudes, and ideas. The use of male and female co-therapists not only permitted the projection of transference distortions, but also supplied a natural and safe experience of a heterosexual relationship.

771 SLATER, MANNING R. *Sex Offenders in Group Therapy.* As told to George Bishop. Los Angeles: Sherbourne Press, 1964, 159 pp.

Group therapy is the best method by which to free sex offenders from all types of fears and repressions that underlie their conditions. Most of the text is a verbatim transcript of the discussions of the group which was made up of one homosexual, two exhibitionists, and a child molester.

772 SMITH, ALEXANDER B., and BASSIN, ALEXANDER. "Group Therapy with Homosexuals." *Journal of Social Therapy* 5 (3, 1959): 225–232.

The BARO Civic Center Clinic in Brooklyn, New York, is a private mental hygiene clinic devoted exclusively to the psychiatric treatment of adult offenders. The Clinic's group therapy program obtained encouraging results in the treatment of homosexuals when they were organized into homogeneous groups. In a homogeneous group the homosexual patients usually discussed their sexual and social maladjustments more openly, and most remained with the therapy group for a longer period of time than their original referral. Individual cases are discussed. The ability of the homosexual offender to accept greater social conformity after therapy was the standard for improvement.

773 SOLYOM, LESLIE, and MILLER, S. "A Differential Conditioning Procedure as the Initial Phase of the Behaviour Therapy of Homosexuality." *Behaviour Research and Therapy* 3 (3, 1965): 147–160.

The treatment of six male homosexuals using a double (differential) conditioning technique is described. In order to develop negative conditioning, the patients were given an electric shock when the picture of a seminude male was projected on a screen. Positive reinforcement was accomplished through the termination of continuous electric shock when the patient was shown the photograph of a female. No change was found in autonomic functions, as measured by galvanic skin response and plethysmograph response, but there appeared to be an increase in responses to pictures of females as a result of treatment. Abstention from homosexual activity was the main result of the therapy.

774 SPRAGUE, GEORGE S. "Varieties of Homosexual Manifestations." With discussion by Karl A. Menninger, Isador H. Coriat, Charles I. Lambert, Ernest M. Poate, and S. W. Hartwell. 1935. Reprinted in *The Homosexuals: As Seen by Themselves and Thirty Authorities,* edited by Aron M. Krich, pp. 174–187. New York: Citadel Press, 1954.

A discussion of the forms that homosexuality can take stresses the multiformity of its expression. Homosexuality may be either psychological-structural, or instinctive-psychological with the tendency to produce conduct. Recognition of the varying individual patterns it follows is necessary for successful psychiatric treatment.

The recognition of both conscious and unconscious homosexuality, of both constitutional and environmental factors, and of the bisexuality of man, is urged in the discussion which follows the author's presentation.

775 SRNEC, J., and FREUND, KURT. "Treatment of Male Homosexuality through Conditioning." *International Journal of Sexology* 7 (2, 1953): 92–93.

An author's abstract of a treatise reports endeavors to discover whether it is possible to use a method of conditioned reflexes for effecting a change in sexual desire. The experimental procedure consists of two phases. First, the homosexual is given coffee or tea with emetine. Ten minutes later a subcutaneous injection is given of a mixture of emetine, apomorphine, pilocarpine and ephedrine. He is then shown films and slides of men dressed up, sportsmen in bathing suits and men in the nude. Approximately 5–10 minutes after the beginning of the session the patient begins to vomit as a result of the administered drugs.

In the second phase films are shown in which women appear in situations that would rouse sexual desire in heterosexual men. The films are shown in the evening before bedtime after the patient received an injection of 50 mgs. testosterone the same morning.

Experimentally it was found that by the above method it was possible to effect a considerable change in the sexual desire in 10 out of 25 exclusively or almost exclusively homosexual men who underwent the procedure. It was also found that it is easier to bring about sexual desire for the body of a woman and a desire for heterosexual intercourse than an appreciation of the personalities of women.

It is anticipated that the above procedure would amount to no more than a short-term shift of desire in a heterosexual direction; uncontrolled factors would determine to what extent this method could be used by the patient for further reinforcement of his experimental heterosexuality. (It is pointed out that psychotherapy would have to be introduced in order to create a more permanent change.)

776   STANLEY-JONES, D. "Sexual Inversion: The Problem of Treatment." *Medical Press* 218 (1947): 212–215.

The types of homosexuals and the value of treatment for them are discussed. The pseudo homosexual (acquired type) offers the greatest threat to society, yet can be helped through psychotherapy. The "true invert" gives society little to worry about, and successful treatment for him is questionable.

777   STEKEL, HILDA. "Short-Term Psychotherapy of a Case of Conversion Hysteria." *American Journal of Psychotherapy* 7 (2, 1953): 302–309.

A case of conversion hysteria was presented as an illustration of how "good results can be achieved with a limited number of sessions." An "active" method of psychoanalysis was applied in the treatment. The patient, a 34-year-old single male, considered himself a homosexual because he had not had a girl friend since the age of 14 and he had often masturbated with homosexual fantasies in which he visualized himself assaulting boys. The patient complained of attacks of dyspnea, claustrophobia, and difficulties in swallowing.

It is suggested that the patient's dyspnea was provoked by an identification with his dying father, who had experienced difficulty in breathing, and it also represented defenses against his homosexual fantasies. Anxiety and matters with which the patient could not cope were expressed in the "symbolic language of his throat symptoms."

After the elimination of the manifest symptoms, treatment was not continued. The patient's fixation upon his mother and his unconscious fantasies which were associated with the patient's brothers were not explained to him because of his low level of intelligence and his desire to remain "faithful" to his mother.

778   STEVENSON, IAN, and WOLPE, JOSEPH. "Recovery from Sexual Deviations Through Overcoming Non-Sexual Neurotic Responses." *American Journal of Psychiatry* 116 (8, 1960): 737–742.

Three cases of sexual deviation are reported in which a return to normal heterosexual behavior followed the development of assertive behavior on the part of the patients. It is suggested that the following are untenable as generalizations: a requirement of recovery from psychoneurosis is the recall of repressed memories of early traumatic experiences; such recovery can only occur as a result of the uncovering and modification of specific sexual conflicts; the removal of symptoms or the alteration of behavior without modification of such conflicts must inevitably lead to the outbreak of other symptoms, if not the recurrence of the old. The concept of "repressed emotion" has hindered recovery from neurosis with and without psychotherapy.

779   STONE, MAYER B. "Homosexuality in a Borderline Mental Defective: Rehabilitation Through Hypnosis and Re-education." *Pennsylvania Psychiatric Quarterly* 4 (1964): 42–53.

The case of a 23-year-old male with an I.Q. of 67 and a history of homosexuality and pedophilia is discussed. Treatment involved two major goals: "The removal of blocks to personality development redirecting immature strivings expressed through sexual perversion" and "the strengthening of the ego in terms of helping the subject think energetically of woman in any sexual excitement so that woman be substituted for man." The approach emphasized motivation and schooling in the control of sexual impulses and utilized much support and guidance. Hypnosis was used extensively throughout treatment. A follow-up study two years later revealed no regressions except for two minor instances, neither of which involved genital manipulation.

780   TARAIL, MARK. "New Treatments for the Homosexual." 1961. Reprinted in *The Third Sex,* edited by Isadore Rubin, pp. 63–66. New York: New Book Co., 1961.

Homosexuals can be changed. What is learned can be unlearned in a three-step process: "reconditioning therapy, physical and environmental withdrawal, psychotherapy and motivation therapy."

781   TAYLOR, F. H. "Homosexual Offences and Their Relation to Psychotherapy." *British Medical Journal* (4526, 1947): 525–529.

Ninety-six persons charged with homosexual offenses and received into Brixton Prison are described. A tabulation of the date of offense, age, and previous convictions is presented with brief comments. The prisoners are divided into four groups: pseudo homosexuals, bisexuals, prostitutes, and true inverts. The first three groups are examined, and selected case histories are included. The true invert group is discussed in greater detail with particular attention given to the effects which psychotherapy had on their behavior. Of the seven who had previous treatment none experienced any change, and only one of the 13 in the true invert group is considered likely to benefit from future treatment. The legal aspects of homosexuality are briefly discussed, and the role the psychiatrist can play in dealing with homosexual offenders is commented upon.

782   THOMPSON, GEORGE N. "Electroshock and Other Therapeutic Considerations in Sexual Psychopathy." *Journal of Nervous and Mental Disease* 109 (6, 1949): 531–539.

The notion that shock therapy can be effective in psychopathic states was tested by the administration of Metrazol shock treatments to six white males from 20 to 40 years old. All were patients at Camarillo State Hospital, and all had had a considerable amount of homosexual behavior in their past. It was concluded that sexual psychopathy is not altered by convulsive shock therapy, since none of the six subjects was helped by this means.

783   THORPE, J. G.; SCHMIDT, ELSA; BROWN, PAUL T.; and CASTELL, D. "Aversion-Relief Therapy: A New Method for General Application." *Behaviour Research and Therapy* 2 (1, 1964): 71–82.

An "aversion-relief therapy" technique has been developed to deal with general problems connected with the use of aversion therapy. These problems include the fact that the use of aversion therapy is not considered appropriate for anxious people, that it is difficult to reproduce the actual behavior which the aversion therapy is designed to treat, and that it is difficult to find a method which will extinguish a particular behavior and also facilitate the acquisition of new behavior.

Aversion-relief therapy consists of aversive conditioning followed by relief. The treatment of eight patients, six males and two females with problems including latent and overt homosexuality, cross-dressing, various phobias and fetishes, with this therapeutic technique is described. Patients were positioned in a darkened room and instructed to read aloud from a screen selected antonyms of words usually associated with the patient's problem. After each vocalization a shock was delivered through specially prepared shoes which the subject wore. A more intense shock was given if the patient failed to repeat a word. An appropriate word was chosen for each patient to correspond to the individual's problem, "heterosexual" for those with problems of homosexuality, or "normal dressing" for transvestites. Presentation of the word signaled the end of the electroshock therapy. Treatment of six of the eight patients was considered to have been successful in changing behavior. Symptom changes appeared in the two patients who discontinued treatment.

Although the patients treated had high anxiety scores on several tests, no exacerbation of symptoms was observed. Therapeutic results suggest that the use of words rather than actual behavior will lead to behavioral change.

784   THORPE, J. G.; SCHMIDT, ELSA; and CASTELL, D. "A Comparison of Positive and Negative (Aversive) Conditioning in the Treatment of Homosexuality." *Behaviour Research and Therapy* 1 (4, 1963): 357–362.

The treatment of a male homosexual with the use of faradic aversion conditioning is described. The subject was a 35-year-old male homosexual, who had voluntarily sought help from Banstead Hospital in Surrey.

Three main techniques were used, the first two being positive conditioning and the third being a combination of positive and negative conditioning. The positive methods involved showing a nude female picture to the subject when ejaculating from masturbation and showing the same picture at intervals during masturbation. The positive and negative method involved showing male and female pictures during masturbation and included the use of electric shocks.

The results indicated that the aversion techniques had some part in changing the patient's behavior and that they were more effective than nonaversion techniques.

785   THORPE, J. G., and SCHMIDT, ELSA. "Therapeutic Failure in a Case of Aversion Therapy." *Behaviour Research and Therapy* 1 (4, 1964): 293–296.

The relationship between personality parameters and the therapeutic outcome of aversion therapy is considered.

Two patients, with complaints of homosexuality and with similar psychometric scores on the Maudsley Personality Inventory and the Taylor

Manifest Anxiety Scale, were treated with shock aversion therapy. One patient responded well; the second patient withdrew from the treatment. It is suggested that the second patient discontinued therapy not because of the amount of anxiety present, but rather because he feared the electric shock would cause cancer.

Aversion therapy programs should include precautionary inquiries before actual treatment is begun to insure that patients will not leave the program before therapy is completed.

786 "Treatment for Homosexuality." *British Medical Journal* (4442, 1946): 300.

Although all persons sentenced to prison for homosexual offenses are not suitable subjects for psychological treatment, this type of treatment should be available in all cases where there is a reasonable prospect that it will have beneficial results.

787 "Treatment of Homosexual Tendencies." *British Medical Journal* (4821, 1953): 1234.

In a question and answer section, a query about treatment of an 18-year-old male patient with homosexual tendencies is answered with the suggestion that the patient be referred to a psychiatrist.

788 "Treatment of Homosexuality." *British Medical Journal* (5083, 1958): 1347.

The success of treatment of homosexuality is hard to assess for several reasons. Homosexuals differ greatly, especially in their degree of bisexuality. Reports on treatment often fail to precisely describe the psychosexual status of the individual before and after therapy, or else vague ratings of improvement are used. Claims for successful treatment of homosexuality by chemical substances remain unsubstantiated. Treatment focuses mainly on psychotherapy and social work, although mixed results are noted in these areas as well. A general therapeutic pessimism prevails. Most psychiatrists believe that no cure can be offered to the exclusive homosexual (one who rates a 6 on the Kinsey Scale), but that relief can be given to only some homosexuals.

789 TRIPP, C. A. "Who Is a Homosexual?" *Social Progress: A Journal of Church and Society* 58 (2, 1967): 13–21.

Since man lacks the tight physiologic controls of lower animals, he must learn all of his behavioral techniques. Because of early experimental sexual activities or later opportune situations, it is as easy to learn homosexual preferences as it is to learn heterosexual ones.

In treatment a therapist must distinguish between the sexual and the social nature of the homosexual's complaints. The therapist then has a choice of three positions: he can side with the religious and social mores, he can remain neutral, or he can side with the patient's right to be himself. This last position helps the patient to reduce his guilt and anxiety feelings, and yet it also allows the therapist to be critical if the patient gets into direct conflict with societal norms.

790   UJHELY, VALENTINE A. "An Unusual Case of Renifleurism." *American Journal of Psychotherapy* 7 (1, 1953): 68–71.

A case of olfactory-secual fixation and compulsive paraphiliac behavior is reported, with the suggestion that renifleurism is a substitute for homosexuality. The patient, a middle-aged male, attempted to establish contact between his nose and a female's buttocks for sexual satisfaction. An analysis regarding the situational and historic roots of the compulsion is presented. While A.W.O.L. during World War II, the patient spent five weeks at a French farmhouse. He was apprehended and put into the stockade, where the constant company of other men led him to believe that he had some homosexual tendencies. He sought relief in fantasies of a French girl, especially with regard to her buttocks. While in prison, the patient was unable to have an erection unless he recalled the olfactory impression (perfume, body odor) of the French girl.

In therapy, the patient's attitudes were reset through evoking a chain of sexual images, and a sarcastic, self-confident attitude toward the impulse. Anti-compulsory emergency techniques (unnoticed smelling of a jar of "solid" perfume) and long-range defenses (participation in his veterans service organization and the development of interests with his wife) are described. The patient was readjusted and had no recurrence of the behavior in over three years.

791   VANDERVELDT, JAMES HERMAN, and ODENWALD, ROBERT P. *Psychiatry and Catholicism.* 2d ed. New York: McGraw-Hill Book Co., 1957, 474 pp.

The etiology and therapy of homosexuality are discussed. Pastoral counseling attempts to harmonize homosexuality with Christian ethics as proposed by the Catholic Church. The pastoral counselor should make the homosexual realize that, despite his "perverse passion," he has good qualities and should therefore sublimate his sexual tendencies by the sincere practice of his religious duties and through the development of his desirable traits.

792   WAHL, CHARLES WILLIAM. "The Evaluation and Treatment of the Homosexual Patient." In *Sexual Problems: Diagnosis and Treatment*

in Medical Practice, edited by Charles William Wahl, pp. 192–204. New York: Free Press, 1967.

The development of homosexuality is reviewed from the psychoanalytic point of view, as are the factors to be considered in the diagnosis and prognosis of homosexuality. Psychiatric treatment is eminently worthwhile for all homosexual patients. For those homosexual patients who are not motivated toward a heterosexual adjustment, it is recommended that the progenitive neurosis which is always present with homosexuality can and should be treated. For those homosexual patients in whom the factors affecting prognosis are favorable, psychiatric treatment should cure the homosexuality by the patient's achievement of a permanent heterosexual adjustment.

793　WAHL, CHARLES WILLIAM, ed. *Sexual Problems: Diagnosis and Treatment in Medical Practice.* New York: Free Press, 1967, 300 pp.

An indication of the severe neglect in medical education of the treatment of sexual problems is the fact that only three medical schools in the United States have courses in sex education. In an attempt to meet this need, a collection of brief papers which emphasize the treatment and management of sexual problems, as well as their diagnosis, is presented.

The papers were prepared with the nonpsychiatrically trained physician in mind. The book had its origin in a postgraduate course given in 1963 at the UCLA Center for Health Sciences on "Sexual Problems in Medical Practice." See Arieti, Silvano (no. 291). Casady, Richard R. (no. 343). Golden, Joshua S. (no. 804). Pumpian-Mindlin, Eugene (no. 1109). Wahl, Charles William (no. 591), (no. 792). Willis, Stanley E. (no. 796).

794　WASSERMAN, SIDNEY. "Casework Treatment of a Homosexual Acting-Out Adolescent in a Treatment Center." *Mental Hygiene* 44 (1, 1960): 18–29.

The case history of an adolescent boy whose acting out included homosexual behavior is related. The subject, a male in good health with an I.Q. of 121, had been institutionalized from age 14 to 19 years. He was the eldest child with male and female siblings. The report is based on psychiatric consultation by the caseworker, casework, and casework supervision.

The case was successfully treated through a process of ego support for the boy and by taking a firm, nonpunitive stand against homosexual acting out. The subject is now heterosexually adjusted and living and working in the larger community. The caseworker, rather than interpreting fantasies and fears for the boy, chose to support him by displaying empathy and acceptance. It is interesting to note that the case showed the Bieber familial pattern of a close-binding mother and a withdrawn-hostile father.

795   WHITENER, R. W., and NIKELLY, ARTHUR. "Sexual Deviation in
      College Students." *American Journal of Orthopsychiatry* 34 (3,
      1964): 486–492.

Thirty-nine college student sex deviates who were patients at a university
health center were studied. Thirty of these students were homosexuals, and
the remainder consisted of exhibitionists, transvestites, and one voyeur. The
sexually deviant patients came to the health division both through administrative referral and self-referral. The convenient diagnostic categories were
not adequate for the wide range of individual variation presented by the
students. The dynamic etiology of homosexuality indicated that emphasis
should be placed on sociological and cultural factors, as well as the interpersonal relationships which exist within the family. "Treatment of homosexuality in a student can be a rewarding experience if careful consideration is
given to prognostic signs." Specific difficulties arise concerning administrative referrals, long-range treatment, and the therapist's optimism concerning such cases.

796   WILLIS, STANLEY E. "A Philosophy of Helping the Sexual Devi-
      ate." In *Sexual Problems: Diagnosis and Treatment in Medical Prac-
      tice,* edited by Charles William Wahl, pp. 205–220. New York: Free
      Press, 1967.

Although it is impossible to generalize about the preferred therapeutic
application of theory to the individual patient, a few suggestions are given
to the physician who encounters homosexuality in his patients. Sexual
deviation is often due to the retainment of an infantile, dependent position
and is often an attempt to ward off or reduce anxiety and fear. The patient
should be made to understand that his condition is not caused by hormonal,
constitutional, or genetic factors, and that it is therefore subject to cure. The
elimination of homosexual behavior should not be the primary aim of
effective psychotherapy; rather it should be to "free the patient from the
tyranny of his own unconscious" so that he may make a rational choice and
continue in human relationships characterized by fidelity and by an ability
to give and receive love and care.

797   WOODWARD, L. T. "Homosexual Panic." 1958. In *The Third Sex,*
      edited by Isadore Rubin, pp. 96–99. New York: New Book Co.,
      1961.

A medical counselor argues that adolescents should be counseled not to
panic or to leap to unwarranted conclusions as a result of early homosexual
experiences which are so commonplace.

798 WOODWARD, MARY. "The Diagnosis and Treatment of Homosexual Offenders: A Clinical Survey." *British Journal of Delinquency* 9 (1, 1958): 44–59.

A statistical survey of the diagnostic and treatment records of 113 overt homosexual males referred to the Portman Clinic (London) for treatment during 1952–1953 is presented. Figures are given on the group's age, education, Kinsey rating, incidence of mental disorders, type of partner and technique, prognosis, and the results of treatment.

Some of the results indicate that treatment is most likely to be successful with bisexual men under 30 years of age who had not had overt homosexual experience until their late teens. Older men with a short history of homosexuality who want to change may also be successfully treated. Those with a long homosexual history combined with a psychopathic personality, heavy drinking, or a lack of desire to change are least amenable to treatment.

799 YALOM, IRVIN D. "Group Therapy of Incarcerated Sexual Deviants." *Journal of Nervous and Mental Disease* 132 (2, 1961): 158–170.

Group therapy was carried out with a group of eight inmates convicted of various sex offenses and imprisoned at Patuxent Institution in Jessup, Maryland. Four of the group members had histories of seducing and/or forcing young boys to participate with them in homosexual activities. This report, made after the group had met for an hour and a half every week for nearly two years, indicates some limited success with this form of treatment. Most of the group members had come to accept some personal responsibility for their sexually deviant behavior rather than placing the blame for their actions on outside factors such as alcohol, a delinquent neighborhood environment, a bad family situation, or poverty.

Greater use of group therapy with persons imprisoned for sex offenses is recommended as one way in which psychiatrists can "continue to develop techniques of treatment which provide lasting results in large numbers of patients with the greatest possible conservation of professional manpower."

CROSS-REFERENCES

Allen, Clifford. "The Homosexual." *Medical World* 78 (2, 1953): 144–148. No. 88.
Allen, Clifford. *Homosexuality: Its Nature, Causation and Treatment.* London: Staples Press, 1958, 143 pp. No. 89.
Allen, Clifford. "The Meaning of Homosexuality." *Medical World* 80 (1, 1954): 9–16. Reprinted in *International Journal of Sexology* 7 (4, 1954): 207–212. No. 90.

Allen, Clifford. "When Homosexuals Marry." 1957. Reprinted in *The Third Sex,* edited by Isadore Rubin, pp. 58–62. New York: New Book Co., 1961. No. 94.

Bakwin, Harry, and Bakwin, Ruth M. "Homosexual Behavior in Children." *Journal of Pediatrics* 43 (1, 1953): 108–111. No. 97.

Beggs, Keith Siddons. "Some Legal, Social and Psychiatric Aspects of Homosexual Behavior: A Guide for the Social Worker in the Sex Clinic." Master's thesis, University of Wisconsin, 1950, 298 pp. No. 955.

Benda, Clemens E. "Existential Psychotherapy of Homosexuality." *Review of Existential Psychology and Psychiatry* 3 (1963): 133–152. No. 100.

Bender, Lauretta, and Grugett, Alvin E., Jr. "A Follow-Up Report on Children Who Had Atypical Sexual Experience." *American Journal of Orthopsychiatry* 22 (Oct., 1952): 825–837. No. 303.

Bender, Lauretta, and Paster, Samuel. "Homosexual Trends in Children." *American Journal of Orthopsychiatry* 11 (1941): 730–743. No. 101.

Berg, Charles, and Allen, Clifford. *The Problem of Homosexuality.* New York: Citadel Press, 1958, 221 pp. No. 103.

Bergler, Edmund. *Homosexuality: Disease or Way of Life?* New York: Hill & Wang, 1956, 302 pp. No. 309.

Beukenkamp, Cornelius. "Phantom Patricide." *Archives of General Psychiatry* 3 (3, 1960): 282–288. No. 104.

Bieber, Irving. "Advising the Homosexual." *Medical Aspects of Human Sexuality* 2 (3, 1968): 34–39. No. 105.

Bieber, Irving. "Clinical Aspects of Male Homosexuality." In *Sexual Inversion: The Multiple Roots of Homosexuality,* edited by Judd Marmor, pp. 248–267. New York: Basic Books, 1965. No. 106.

Bieber, Irving, et al. *Homosexuality: A Psychoanalytic Study.* New York: Basic Books, 1962, 358 pp. No. 314.

Bowman, Karl M., and Engle, Bernice. "The Problem of Homosexuality." *Journal of Social Hygiene* 39 (1, 1953): 2–16. No. 109.

Bozarth, René, and Gross, Alfred A. "Homosexuality: Sin or Sickness? A Dialogue." *Pastoral Psychology* 13 (129, 1962): 35–42. No. 322.

Braaten, Leif Johan, and Darling, C. Douglas. "Overt and Covert Homosexual Problems among Male College Students." *Genetic Psychology Monographs* 71 (2, 1965): 269–310. No. 323.

Brown, James H. "Homosexuality as an Adaptation in Handling Aggression." *Journal of the Louisiana State Medical Society* 115 (9, 1963): 304–311. No. 113.

Carstairs, G. Morris, and Grygier, Tadeusz G. "Anthropological, Psychometric, and Psychotherapeutic Aspects of Homosexuality." *Bulletin of the British Psychological Society* 32 (1957): 46–47. No. 964.

Chesser, Eustace. *Odd Man Out: Homosexuality in Men and Women.* London: Victor Gollancz, 1959, 192 pp. No. 1065.

Chesser, Eustace. "Society and the Homosexual." *International Journal of Sexology* 7 (4, 1954): 213–216. No. 1146.

Church of England Moral Welfare Council. *The Problem of Homosexuality: An Interim Report by a Group of Anglican Clergy and Doctors.* Westminster: Church Information Board, n.d., 27 pp. No. 1147.

Cory, Donald Webster. *The Homosexual in America: A Subjective Approach.* New York: Greenberg, 1951, 326 pp. No. 826.

Cory, Donald Webster. "Homosexuality." In *The Encyclopedia of Sexual Behavior,* edited by Albert Ellis and Albert Abarbanel, pp. 485–493. 2d rev. ed. New York: Hawthorn Books, 1967. No. 123.

Curran, Desmond, and Parr, Denis. "Homosexuality: An Analysis of 100 Male Cases Seen in Private Practice." *British Medical Journal* (5022, 1957): 797–801. No. 355.

Demaria, Laura Achard de. "Homosexual Acting Out." *International Journal of Psycho-Analysis* 49 (2–3, 1968): 219–220. No. 366.

Ellis, Albert, and Allen, Clifford. "On the Cure of Homosexuality." *International Journal of Sexology* 5 (3, 1952): 135–142. No. 381.

Freund, Kurt. "On the Problem of Male Homosexuality." *Review of Czechoslovak Medicine* 11 (1, 1965): 11–17. No. 10.

Gerber, Israel Joshua. *Man on a Pendulum: A Case History of an Invert.* New York: American Press, 1955, 320 pp. No. 847.

Gilbert, S. F. "Homosexuality and Hypnotherapy." *British Journal of Medical Hypnotism* 5 (3, 1954): 2–7. No. 415.

Glover, Benjamin. "Control of the Sex Deviate." *Federal Probation* 24 (3, 1960): 38–45. No. 1166.

Glover, Edward, ed. *The Problem of Homosexuality.* London: Institute for the Study and Treatment of Delinquency, 1957, 40 pp. No. 1076.

Glover, Edward. "Sexual Disorders and Offences, I. The Social and Legal Aspects of Sexual Abnormality. [1956. Reprinted.] II. The Problem of Male Homosexuality." In his *The Roots of Crime,* pp. 173–243. New York: International Universities Press, 1960. No. 153.

Glover, Edward. "The Social and Legal Aspects of Sexual Abnormality." *Medico-Legal and Criminological Review* 13 (3, 1945): 133–148. No. 419.

Green, Eugene W., and Johnson, L. G. "Homosexuality." *Journal of Criminal Psychopathology* 5 (3, 1944): 467–480. No. 155.

Hadden, Samuel B. "Attitude toward and Approaches to the Problem of Homosexuality." *Pennsylvania Medical Journal* 6 (9, 1957): 1195–1198. No. 1080.

Hadden, Samuel B. "Etiologic Factors in Male Homosexuality." In *Proceedings of the IV World Congress of Psychiatry,* Madrid, Sept. 5–11, 1966, pp. 3067–3069. International Congress Series no. 150. New York: Excerpta Medica, 1967–68. No. 161.

Hadden, Samuel B. "Male Homosexuality." *Pennsylvania Medicine* 70 (Feb., 1967): 78–80. No. 162.

Hampson, John L. "Deviant Sexual Behavior: Homosexuality, Transvestism." In *Human Reproduction and Sexual Behavior,* edited by Charles W. Lloyd, pp. 498–510. Philadelphia: Lea & Febiger, 1964. No. 166.

Harper, Robert Allan. "Can Homosexuals Be Changed?" 1960. Reprinted in *The Third Sex,* edited by Isadore Rubin, pp. 67–72. New York: New Book Co., 1961. No. 434.

Heersema, Philip H. "Homosexuality and the Physician." *Journal of the American Medical Association* 193 (10, 1965): 815–817. No. 441.

Heilbrun, Gert. "Psychoanalysis of Yesterday, Today, and Tomorrow." *Archives of General Psychiatry* 4 (4, 1961): 321–330. No. 16.

Henry, George W., and Gross, Alfred A. "The Homosexual Delinquent." *Mental Hygiene* 25 (3, 1941): 420–442. No. 170.

Hirschfeld, Magnus. *Sexual Anomalies: The Origins, Nature, and Treatment of Sexual Disorders.* Rev. ed. New York: Emerson Books, 1948, 538 pp. No. 20.

Homosexuality and Prostitution: A Memorandum of Evidence Prepared by a Special Committee of the Council of the British Medical Association for Submission to the Departmental Committee on Homosexuality and Prostitution. London: British Medical Association, 1955, 94 pp. No. 21.

Hooker, Evelyn. "Homosexuality: Summary of Studies." In *Sex Ways in Fact and Faith: Bases for Christian Family Policy,* edited by Evelyn M. Duvall and Sylvanus M. Duvall, pp. 166–183. New York: Association Press, 1961. No. 1260.

Jones, H. Kimball. *Toward a Christian Understanding of the Homosexual.* New York: Association Press, 1966, 160 pp. No. 1086.

Kaplan, Eugene A. "Homosexuality: A Search for the Ego-Ideal." *Archives of General Psychiatry* 16 (3, 1967): 355–358. No. 180.

Karpman, Benjamin. *The Sexual Offender and His Offenses: Etiology, Pathology, Psychodynamics and Treatment.* New York: Julian Press, 1954, 744 pp. No. 182.

Kempe, G. Th. "The Homosexual in Society." *British Journal of Delinquency* 5 (1, 1954): 4–20. Also printed in abridged form as "The Homophiles in Society." *International Journal of Sexology* 7 (4, 1954): 217–219. No. 868.

Koenig, Karl P. "The Differentiation of Hetero- or Homoerotic Interests in the Male: Some Comments on Articles by Brown and Freund." *Behaviour Research and Therapy* 2 (Apr., 1965): 305–307. No. 478.

Kolb, Lawrence C., and Johnson, Adelaide M. "Etiology and Therapy of Overt Homosexuality." *Psychoanalytic Quarterly* 24 (4, 1955): 506–515. No. 187.

Krich, Aron M., ed. *The Homosexuals: As Seen by Themselves and Thirty Authorities.* New York: Citadel Press, 1954, 346 pp. Also published as *Homosexuality: A Subjective and Objective Investigation,* edited by Charles Berg. London: Allen & Unwin, 1958, 416 pp. No. 188.

Lagache, Daniel. "From Homosexuality to Jealousy." *International Journal of Psycho-Analysis* 30 (3, 1949): 195. No. 484.

Laycock, S. R. "Homosexuality—A Mental Hygiene Problem." *Canadian Medical Association Journal* 63 (Sept., 1950): 245–250. No. 191.

Litin, Edward M.; Giffin, Mary E.; and Johnson, Adelaide M. "Parental Influence in Unusual Sexual Behavior in Children." *Psychoanalytic Quarterly* 25 (1, 1956): 37–55. No. 196.

Lorand, Sandor, and Balint, Michael, eds. *Perversions: Psychodynamics and Therapy.* New York: Random House, 1956, 307 pp. No. 198.

McLeish, John. "The Homosexual." *Medical World* 93 (8, 1960): 237–239. No. 201.

Magee, Bryan. *One in Twenty: A Study of Homosexuality in Men and Women.* London: Secker & Warburg, 1966, 192 pp. No. 878.

"Male Homosexuality." *Lancet* 2 (7111, 1959): 1077–1080. No. 879.

Margetts, E. L. "Sex Deviations." *McGill Medical Journal* 19 (1, 1950): 49–63. No. 505.

Marmor, Judd, ed. *Sexual Inversion: The Multiple Roots of Homosexuality.* New York: Basic Books, 1965, 358 pp. No. 206.

Miller, Milton L. "The Relation Between Submission and Aggression in Male Homosexuality." In *Perversions: Psychodynamics and Therapy,* edited by Sandor Lorand and Michael Balint, pp. 160–179. New York: Random House, 1956. No. 510.

Monchy, René de. "A Clinical Type of Male Homosexuality." *International Journal of Psycho-Analysis* 46 (2, 1965): 218–225. No. 212.

Moore, Thomas V. "The Pathogenesis and Treatment of Homosexual Disorders: A Digest of Some Pertinent Evidence." *Journal of Personality* 14 (1945): 47–83. No. 213.

Morse, Benjamin. *The Homosexual: A Frank Study of Abnormal Sex Life among Males.* Derby, Conn.: Monarch Press, 1962, 158 pp. No. 884.

Nacht, S.; Diatkine, R.; and Favreau, J. "The Ego in Perverse Relationships." *International Journal of Psycho-Analysis* 37 (4, 1956): 404–413. No. 514.

Neustatter, W. Lindesay. "Homosexuality: The Medical Aspect." *Practitioner* 172 (Apr., 1954): 364–373. No. 41.

Neustatter, W. Lindesay. "Homosexuality: The Medical Aspects." In *They Stand Apart: A Critical Survey of the Problems of Homosexuality,* edited by John Tudor Rees and Harley V. Usill, pp. 67–139. London: William Heinemann, 1955. No. 42.

Neustatter, W. Lindesay. "Sex and Its Problems, XI. The Medical Aspects of Homosexuality." *Practitioner* 199 (1193, 1967): 704–710. No. 516.

Orgel, Samuel Zachary. "The Development of a Perversion: Homosexuality and Associated Transvestitism." *Journal of the Hillside Hospital* 17 (4, 1968): 405–409. No. 219.

"Origins of Homosexuality." *British Medical Journal* (5470, 1965): 1077–1078. No. 220.

"Psychopathology and Treatment of Sexual Deviation: The Male Homosexual." *British Medical Journal* (5208, 1960): 304. No. 535.

Ramsay, R. W., and Velzen, V. van. "Behaviour Therapy for Sexual Perversions." *Behaviour Research and Therapy* 6 (2, 1968): 233. No. 537.

Regardie, Francis I. "Analysis of a Homosexual." *Psychiatric Quarterly* 23 (3, 1949): 548–566. No. 231.

"Report of the Departmental Committee on Homosexual Offences and Prostitution." *British Medical Journal* (5045, 1957): 639–640. No. 896.

Rom, Paul. "The Problem of 'Distance' in Sex Behavior." *International Journal of Social Psychiatry* 3 (2, 1957): 145–151. No. 234.

Royal Society of Medicine. "Discussion on the Social Aspects of Homosexuality [Summary]." *Proceedings* 40 (10, 1947): 585–592. Also reported in *British Medical Journal* (4506, 1947): 691–692. No. 900.

Rubin, Isadore, ed. *The Third Sex.* New York: New Book Co., 1961, 112 pp. Also printed as his *Homosexuals Today.* New York: Health Publications, 1965, 112 pp. No. 236.

Schur, Edwin M. *Crimes without Victims—Deviant Behavior and Public Policy: Abortion, Homosexuality, and Drug Addiction.* Englewood Cliffs, N. J.: Prentice-Hall, 1965, 180 pp. No. 907.

Scott, Peter D. "Definition, Classification, Prognosis and Treatment." In *The Pathology and Treatment of Sexual Deviation: A Methodological Approach,* edited by Ismond Rosen, pp. 87–119. London: Oxford University Press, 1964. No. 557.

"Sex Today and Tomorrow." *Medical Press* 241 (21, 1959): 459–460. No. 243.

Socarides, Charles W. *The Overt Homosexual.* New York: Grune & Stratton, 1968, 245 pp. No. 571.

Socarides, Charles W. "Theoretical and Clinical Aspects of Overt Male Homosexuality." *Journal of the American Psychoanalytic Association* 8 (3, 1960): 552–566. No. 572.

Solyom, Leslie, and Beck, Philip R. "GSR Assessment of Aberrant Sexual Behavior." *International Journal of Neuropsychiatry* 3 (1, 1967): 52–59. No. 573.

Stafford-Clark, D. "Essentials of the Clinical Approach." In *The Pathology and Treatment of Sexual Deviation: A Methodological Approach,* edited by Ismond Rosen, pp. 57–86. London: Oxford University Press, 1964. No. 61.

Stanley-Jones, D. "Sexual Inversion: An Ethical Study." *Lancet* 252 (6447, 1947): 366–369. No. 250.

Sterling, David Lyn. *Sex in the Basic Personality.* Wichita, Kan.: Hubbard Dianetic Foundation, 1952, 180 pp. No. 1115.

Storr, Anthony. *Sexual Deviation.* Baltimore: Penguin Books, 1964, 139 pp. No. 251.

Tufo, Gustave F. "The Genesis of Homosexuality." *Journal of American Institute of Homeopathy* 57 (3–4, 1964): 33–34. No. 589.

West, D. J. *Homosexuality.* Chicago: Aldine Publishing Co., 1968, 304 pp. No. 922.

West, D. J. "Homosexuality: A Social Problem." *Sexology* 23 (1, 1956): 22–28. No. 923.

West, D. J. *The Other Man: A Study of the Social, Legal and Clinical Aspects of Homosexuality.* New York: Whiteside and William Morrow & Co., 1955, 224 pp. No. 924.

Willis, Stanley E. *Understanding and Counseling the Male Homosexual.* Boston: Little, Brown & Co., 1967, 225 pp. No. 602.

Wolman, Benjamin B. "Interactional Treatment of Homosexuality." *Psychotherapy and Psychosomatics* 15 (1, 1967): 70. No. 607.

Wulff, Moshe. "A Case of Male Homosexuality." 1942. Reprinted in *The Homosexuals: As Seen by Themselves and Thirty Authorities,* edited by Aron M. Krich, pp. 324–342. New York: Citadel Press, 1954. No. 264.

FEMALE

800 ASCHAFFENBURG, HELGA. "Relationship Therapy with a Homosexual: A Case History." *Pastoral Counselor* 4 (1, 1966): 4–12.

The changes in a female homosexual's attitudes toward religion and homosexuality are described. The patient was diagnosed as suffering from borderline schizophrenia and acute depression. Limited results were expected from the therapy, and it was agreed among those who interviewed her that an acceptance of her homosexual adaptation might be all that could be accomplished. After several months of therapy the patient became active in her church. She worked at establishing new interpersonal contacts, and her homosexual activities were, at least temporarily, discontinued.

801   BERNSTEIN, IRVING C. "Homosexuality in Gynecologic Practice." *South Dakota Journal of Medicine* 21 (Mar., 1968): 33–39.

Although gynecologists seldom encounter the classic homosexual, there are certain areas in which a homosexual problem may be present. These include infertility, frigidity, nonconsummation of marriage, impotency, and dysmenorrhea. Representative cases and general principles of management are discussed. The majority of patients consulting the gynecologist or general practitioner with problems basically homosexual in nature are not recognized as such, but the physician should always consider such a possibility. In order to make his diagnosis, the physician must determine what the particular symptom means to the patient and what its basic etiology is. Following this, decisions must be made which vary from deciding to discontinue infertility investigations to immediate referral of the patient to a psychiatrist.

802   BRODY, MORRIS WOLF. "An Analysis of the Psychosexual Development of a Female: With Special Reference to Homosexuality." *Psychoanalytic Review* 30 (1, 1943): 47–58. Reprinted as "Psychosexual Development of a Female." In *The Homosexuals: As Seen by Themselves and Thirty Authorities,* edited by Aron M. Krich, pp. 312–324. New York: Citadel Press, 1954.

The psychosexual development of a female who had never had heterosexual experiences and who had been a passive partner in homosexual relations is studied and traced in reference to those factors which lead to homosexual maladjustment. The psychoanalysis of this patient revealed that difficulties during the Oedipal stage, rivalry with the mother, and the predominance of castration feelings, may lead to homosexuality.

803   GLUCKMAN, L. K. "Lesbianism: A Clinical Approach." *New Zealand Medical Journal* 65 (407, 1966): 443–449.

Homosexuality in women is discussed, and several brief case histories are cited. Since little has been written about female homosexuals, professionals who treat them have little to fall back upon regarding the etiology of lesbianism and the forms the treatment should take. Certain characteristics of lesbians are described. It is recommended that when physicians treat lesbians they should remain physicians and not assume a moralistic attitude.

804   GOLDEN, JOSHUA S. "Varieties of Sexual Problems in Obstetrical and Gynecological Practice." In *Sexual Problems: Diagnosis and Treatment in Medical Practice,* edited by Charles William Wahl, pp. 53–61. New York: Free Press, 1967.

Many adolescent female homosexuals could benefit from psychiatric help, and yet the gynecologist rarely becomes aware of homosexuality when it exists as a sexual difficulty for a patient. To remedy this situation, it is suggested that the gynecologist should routinely direct part of his interest to the sexual lives and adjustment of all his patients by taking a complete sexual history.

805   KEMPH, JOHN P., and SCHWERIN, ERNA. "Increased Latent Homosexuality in a Woman During Group Therapy." *International Journal of Group Psychotherapy* 16 (2, 1966): 217–224.

The difficulty of developing proper sexual identification in a single-sexed group was illustrated in the case of a married woman, who underwent group psychotherapy. The Wechsler-Bellevue Intelligence Quotient Scale and Rorschach were used. The patient became latently more homosexual than she had been prior to therapy—partially as a result of the uniform sexuality of the group (all women with a male psychiatrist).

806   ROBERTIELLO, RICHARD C. *Voyage from Lesbos: The Psychoanalysis of a Female Homosexual.* New York: Citadel Press, 1959, 253 pp.

A complete report of the psychoanalysis of a single female homosexual is recounted. The patient suffered from an unsuccessful resolution of the Oedipus complex and had strong unconscious heterosexual wishes that were blocked by fears of incest. Through analysis, including free association and dream interpretation, the patient was made aware of her unconscious motivations, and her Oedipus complex was successfully resolved. Two years after the last session the patient had not returned to homosexual practices.

807   SOCARIDES, CHARLES W. "Female Homosexuality." In *Sexual Behavior and the Law,* edited by Ralph Slovenko, pp. 462–477. Springfield, Ill.: Charles C. Thomas, 1965.

Homosexual behavior among women constitutes as serious a psychosocial problem as it does among males. A homosexual woman can be effectively treated, her suffering alleviated, and benefit society from her improvement. The homosexual woman has at an earlier time endured a sense of danger which can be revived during the course of treatment, and the anxiety can be shown to be an anachronistic fear of childhood.

808　STONE, WALTER N.; SCHENGBER, JOHN; and SEIFRIED, F. STAN-
　　　LEY. "The Treatment of a Homosexual Woman in a Mixed Group."
　　　International Journal of Group Psychotherapy 16 (4, 1966): 425–433.

The treatment of a homosexual woman in a heterogeneous group during psychotherapy is described. The subject, a 21-year-old woman, requested referral to group therapy from her individual therapist. Weekly group therapy sessions of 90 minutes' duration, involving young adults from 19 to 25 years old, were held. The group included four men, three women, two therapists and a physician who remained silent but who kept a record of what went on during the session.

The patient learned that the revelation of her homosexuality to group members did not lead to rejection. She became increasingly heterosexual during the first eight-months period. It was concluded that "homosexual patients can be treated in mixed groups in selected situations."

CROSS-REFERENCES

Aldrich, Ann. *We Walk Alone.* New York: Fawcett Publications, 1955, 143 pp. No. 931.

Caprio, Frank S. "Female Homosexuality." *Sexology* 21 (8, 1955): 494–499. No. 625.

Caprio, Frank S. *Female Homosexuality: A Psychodynamic Study of Lesbianism.* New York: Citadel Press, 1954, 334 pp. Chapter 16. "Therapeutic Management: Preventive Measures," pp. 285–298. Reprinted as "Preventive Measures." In *Carol in a Thousand Cities,* edited by Ann Aldrich, pp. 153–166. Greenwich, Conn.: Fawcett Publications, 1960. No. 626.

Cavanagh, John R. "The Psychotherapy of Homosexuality, 1. Some Thoughts on Individual Therapy." *Psychiatric Opinion* 4 (2, 1967): 4–8. No. 669.

Chesser, Eustace. *Odd Man Out: Homosexuality in Men and Women.* London: Victor Gollancz, 1959, 192 pp. No. 1065.

Ellis, Albert. "The Effectiveness of Psychotherapy with Individuals Who Have Severe Homosexual Problems." 1956. Reprinted in *The Problem of Homosexuality in Modern Society,* edited by Hendrik M. Ruitenbeek, pp. 175–182. New York: E. P. Dutton & Co., 1963. No. 678.

Kaye, Harvey E., et al. "Homosexuality in Women." *Archives of General Psychiatry* 17 (Nov., 1967): 626–634. No. 276.

Kenyon, F. E. "Studies in Female Homosexuality, IV. Social and Psychiatric Aspects. V. Sexual Development, Attitudes and Experiences." *British Journal of Psychiatry* 114 (Nov., 1968): 1337–1350. No. 278.

Magee, Bryan. *One in Twenty: A Study of Homosexuality in Men and Women.* London: Secker & Warburg, 1966, 192 pp. No. 878.

Mendelsohn, Fred, and Ross, Mathew. "An Analysis of 133 Homosexuals Seen at a University Health Service." *Diseases of the Nervous System* 20 (6, 1959): 246–250. No. 737.

Miller, Michael M. "Hypnotic-Aversion Treatment of Homosexuality." *Journal of the National Medical Association* 55 (5, 1963): 411–415, 436. No. 739.

Mozes, Eugene B. "The Lesbian." *Sexology* 18 (5, 1951): 294–299; 18 (6, 1952): 384–389. No. 281.

Robertiello, Richard C. "Clinical Notes: Results of Separation from Iposexual Parents During the Oedipal Period, [and] A Female Homosexual Panic." *Psychoanalytic Review* 51 (4, 1964–65): 670–672. No. 232.

Schur, Edwin M. *Crimes without Victims—Deviant Behavior and Public Policy: Abortion, Homosexuality, and Drug Addiction.* Englewood Cliffs, N. J.: Prentice-Hall, 1965, 180 pp. No. 907.

Storr, Anthony. *Sexual Deviation.* Baltimore: Penguin Books, 1964, 139 pp. No. 251.

Wade, Carlson. *The Troubled Sex.* New York: Universal Publishing and Distribution Corp., 1961, 192 pp. No. 950.

Wilbur, Cornelia B. "Clinical Aspects of Female Homosexuality." In *Sexual Inversion: The Multiple Roots of Homosexuality,* edited by Judd Marmor, pp. 268–281. New York: Basic Books, 1965. No. 285.

SOCIOLOGICAL
CONSIDERATIONS

The Homosexual Community: Social and Demographic Aspects

GENERAL, MALE

809   ACHILLES, NANCY. "The Development of the Homosexual Bar as an Institution." In *Sexual Deviance,* edited by John H. Gagnon and William Simon, pp. 228–244. New York: Harper & Row, 1967.

Findings reported in an unpublished 1964 thesis at the University of Chicago are briefly summarized in this article.

Arising to meet the specialized social and sexual needs of the homosexual and to preserve the identity of his community, bars lend organization and respectability to homosexual activities and in large cities different kinds of bars can specialize in such a way that they serve more specific functions. Owner-managed bars present fewer opportunities for exploitation, and they tend to discourage overt sexual activity.

Facing the difficulties of underworld control and police corruption, the community and the bar owners find cohesion in their reaction to police hostility. The character of the bar and its clientele is determined by certain ecological factors and often by the personality of the bartender.

810   ALLEN, CLIFFORD. "The Aging Homosexual." 1959. Reprinted in *The Third Sex,* edited by Isadore Rubin, pp. 91–95. New York: New Book Co., 1961.

Homosexual affairs tend to be much more fleeting than heterosexual ones since the homosexual has a more limited field in which to operate and faces much greater competition. Jealousy is a stronger element in homosexual than in heterosexual affairs, sometimes resulting in violence. In general, however, homosexuals are no more likely than heterosexuals to be involved in crimes. Many homosexuals, unable to find partners, resort to alcohol which, when it is used in this way, is merely a substitute for sex. The keynote

340

of old age and homosexuality is loneliness. It is easier for the female homosexual to find someone to live with than it is for the male homosexual. Aging homosexual men sometimes become mentally senile and become involved with children.

811   BEIER, ERNST G. "Homosexuality: Toward a Cultural Definition— A Survey Report." Mimeographed. Salt Lake City, Utah: University of Utah, 1961, 26 pp.

A cross-cultural study examined cultural influences on homosexual behavior. With the help of the Mattachine Society, One, Inc., and "Vennen" (a Danish homophile organization), questionnaires were mailed to 300 (200 in the United States and 100 in Scandinavia) subscribers of journals dealing with homosexual problems. Responses were obtained from 80 male homosexuals in the United States and from 65 male homosexuals in Denmark.

Detailed survey data are presented in the form of percentage tables and the results of a few tests of statistical significance are included. However, no validity is claimed for the results of the research because the samples were not representative, and because the questionnaires—due to difficulties in translation—were not identical.

While the research did not solve the problems it set out to solve, it can be seen as a valuable stimulus to further research.

812   BENJAMIN, HARRY, and MASTERS, R. E. L. "Homosexual Prostitution." In their *Prostitution and Morality,* pp. 286–337. New York: Julian Press, 1964.

Homosexual prostitution is generally reviewed with an emphasis upon the Western World, particularly the United States. A report of male prostitution on the west coast of the United States by Harold Call, president of the Mattachine Society, is also included.

The history of homosexual prostitution from ancient civilizations to the situation in the 1950's is reviewed. Findings by Jens Jersild of Denmark, as well as studies from Germany and the United States, are used to describe conditions as they may exist at the present time in the Western World. Since female homosexual prostitution is viewed as relatively rare the male homosexual prostitute is dealt with more extensively. A conclusion reached on the basis of conjecture is that the majority of male homosexual prostitutes have a homosexual component in their psychological make-up.

Other areas reviewed briefly are lesbian brothels, homosexual transvestite prostitutes, and homosexual prostitution and venereal disease. Several case studies of male homosexual prostitutes are also presented.

813   Bradley, Matt. *Third Sex.* London: G. Gold & Sons, 1963, 159 pp.

An investigation of homosexual society through a survey of the "gay world" in Hollywood is reported. Conversations with male and female homosexuals took place in homosexual bars, clubs, organizations, and movies. Although there are many more homosexuals than people believe, they are not taking over the world. However, they are affecting the life of the general population by influencing fashions, tastes in food and drinks, entertainment, music, books, motion pictures, and television, and even our manner of speech.

814   BRAFF, ERWIN H. "Venereal Disease, Sex Positions, and Homosexuality." *British Journal of Venereal Diseases* 38 (3, 1962): 165–166.

Reviewing the statistics of the incidence of syphilis in the United States and in many European countries, it is noted that the incidence of early infectious syphilis is increasing, with some centers reporting that the homosexual contributes 80 to 85 percent of the total.

Suggestions are given to health workers on how to interview homosexuals. There should be a close interrogation of the patient. A comfortable and competent medical atmosphere is essential. At the time that it has been determined that the disease has reached the infectious stage, epidemiological information must be secured, but many homosexuals find it quite difficult to admit that their contacts are of the same sex. By stressing the value of such epidemiological information and pointing out how discreetly and confidentially it is handled, it is possible to get most patients to cooperate in this type of history-taking. However, questioning homosexuals about sex position adds little to the value of syphilis diagnosis; it can even be misleading and thus defeat syphilis control.

815   BRANSON, HELEN P. *Gay Bar.* San Francisco: Pan-Graphic Press, 1957, 89 pp.

The owner of a bar with an exclusively homosexual (mostly male) clientele recites the stories told to her. She reports on the problems of her clientele, the types of people she meets, and her general impressions of her homosexual patrons.

816   BUTTS, WILLIAM MARLIN. "Boy Prostitutes of the Metropolis." *Journal of Clinical Psychopathology* 8 (4, 1947): 673–681.

Interviews conducted over a period of nine months with male homosexual prostitutes are reported. Of 121 individuals observed soliciting as male prostitutes in a central city area, 38 were interviewed and 26 of these gave

enough information to be included in the study. In the unstructured interviews conducted in restaurants over dinner, biographical information was
usually volunteered.

It was learned that 16 of the 26 lived alone and took customers to their
rooms. Only five were born in the city where the interviews took place. The
prices they charged ranged from two to fifty dollars. Prostitution was the
sole employment of only four. Five were classified as effeminate in manner.
Giving money as the primary motive for their behavior, few (four out of 26)
admitted enjoying homosexual relations. Their home life was generally
remembered as an unhappy experience. Ten of the cases are described in
detail.

817   CALLEJA, M. A. "Homosexual Behavior in Older Men." *Sexology*
      34 (1, 1967): 46–48.

That homosexuality is more common among older men than is ordinarily
supposed was verified by means of 1,737 personal interviews conducted in
Europe and the Americas, but mostly in Spain. The average age of the men
interviewed was 64; they were white, in good health, and of diverse occupations. Eighty-nine percent of the men were married.

The interviews indicated that 38.8 percent of the respondents had experienced a homosexual act at some time in their lives; 31.8 percent had this
experience several times; and 23.3 percent had homosexual experiences with
high frequency. For 6.1 percent of the respondents homosexual activity had
occurred after 60 years of age; most of these had been married and had not
experienced homosexuality between adolescence and age 60. These men
preferred older, mature men who did not display feminine traits, and also
preferred mostly oral-genital acts. These were normal men who were
competent in their occupational and social roles. They sought masculine
affection as the possibility of sexual satisfaction with women decreased.

818   CANTOR, DONALD J. "The Homosexual Revolution: A Status Re-
      port." 1967. Reprinted in *Social Progress* 58 (2, 1967): 5–12.

After a brief historical summary, the present status of the homosexual
revolution is discussed. Freud's comments on the Oedipal complex, Kinsey's studies of sexual behavior, and the Wolfenden Report were instrumental in changing public, legal, and religious attitudes toward homosexuality.
The following current trends are noted: homophile organizations are
becoming more vocal and militant and are actively trying to change commonly held stereotypes of homosexuals; legal actions are becoming more
lenient; church leaders are criticizing legal sanctions against homosexual
acts between consenting adults. Much yet remains to be accomplished
before homosexuals achieve equality with heterosexuals.

819   CAVAN, SHERRI. "Interaction in Home Territories." *Berkeley Journal of Sociology* 8 (1963): 17–32.

"Home territory" may be thought of as an area of restricted entrance providing sufficient freedom of behavior and sense of intimacy to allow the inhabitants relative freedom from proprieties of public deportment and standards of public morals. When a group adopts a public place as home territory, ways must be worked out to regulate the entrance of outsiders and to control their behavior when they are present. A description of the interaction between regular customers (indigenous population) and casual drop-in customers (outsiders) in a San Francisco homosexual bar is given as an illustration of how this is done.

The strategy used by the bar's homosexual clientele and by many of the employees as well is designed to make the outsider appear out of place and feel uncomfortable. The outsider's expectation that he will be inconspicuous is not fulfilled, and his claims to being a respectable person are rejected. An outsider's challenge to the use of these methods in a public place is difficult to sustain because of the united front presented by the indigenous population. As a result the outsider generally behaves in a manner which either explicitly or implicitly supports the homosexual population's definition of the bar as home territory.

820   CAVAN, SHERRI. *Liquor License: An Ethnography of Bar Behavior.* Chicago: Aldine Publishing Co., 1966, 246 pp.

The characteristic features of behavior in public drinking places and the types of public drinking places generated when a particular kind of activity is accented, e.g., homosexual pickups, are considered in a study of behavior in bars. Attention is given to seating and spatial distribution, internal movement, and face-to-face interaction.

References to homosexual behavior in bars are made throughout the book. Some of the topics discussed include the acceptability of displays of affection, milling, homosexual pickup bars, and sexual activity (defined as "a form of play") in home territory bars. The discussion of homosexual behavior usually includes a comparison with similar heterosexual behavior. Explanations of differences in the way homosexual and heterosexual behaviors are handled are also given. Heterosexual displays of affection, for example, are generally permitted while homosexual displays of affection are discouraged because the sex of those involved provides legal grounds for the revocation of the establishment's license.

821   COBURN, VINCENT P. "Homosexuality and the Invalidation of Marriage." *Jurist* 20 (4, 1960): 441–459.

In a review of a number of theories of homosexuality, it is concluded that: genuine homosexuality is increasing in incidence as a marital problem; the effects of homosexuality are more definitely determined, though its causes remain undetermined to a great extent; marriage does not cure the invert; homosexuality does not involve impotence, though many homosexuals are probably impotent; homosexuality can destroy consent, as does insanity; error in reference to homosexuality would not form grounds for an annulment; conditions present and future, concerning homosexuality, could form grounds for annulment; and the intention to practice homosexuality does not invalidate marriage. From the medical viewpoint, a reliable survey suggests that half of the genuine homosexuals are canonically impotent, and that one-third of this same group are incapable of giving free consent to marriage.

822   *Confessions of a Male Prostitute.* As told to John O'Day, with psychological evaluations by Leonard A. Lowag. Los Angeles: Sherbourne Press, 1964, 136 pp.

A male prostitute, who services both women and men, recounts his adventures and the outstanding episodes of his career. Each episode is followed by a "psychologist evaluation." It is concluded that prostitution and deviation will always remain; that there is no such thing as true love or true hate; and that man is destined to become a vegetable unless something stops his "progress."

823   COON, EARL O. "Homosexuality in the News." *Archives of Criminal Psychodynamics* 2 (4, 1957): 843–865.

An attempt is made to demonstrate how a knowledge of abnormal social processes can be used to read between the lines of news stories to see homosexual situations that are not directly mentioned in the news article.

824   CORY, DONALD WEBSTER. "Can Homosexuals Be Recognized?" *One* 1 (9, 1953): 7–11.

When people say they can recognize homosexuals they usually refer only to those who, by definition, are apparent to anyone—the very effeminate homosexuals. Perhaps only 5 to 10 percent of the total homosexual population is flagrantly effeminate, however, and most members of the homosexual community remain undetected. Astute observers can sometimes recognize secretive masculine-appearing homosexuals, but in general such men excel in concealing their sexual orientation, and as a result, exhibit a certain amount of hostility toward stereotyped (effeminate) homosexuals.
    Nevertheless, most homosexuals are quite recognizable to other homo-

sexuals. This mutual recognition has nothing to do with effeminacy; it comes about when people who intermingle with each other extensively and see persons unlike themselves infrequently unconsciously imitate each other, causing a set of common mannerisms to develop. In addition, there is a conscious effort to develop signs of recognition, such as methods of dressing, type of haircut, method of speech (tonal modulation), manner of walk, eye contact or stare, way of shaking hands, et cetera, which will lead homosexuals to each other without exposing them to the outside world.

A homosexual does not usually base his recognition of another on one of these signs alone; other traits will tend to confirm or deny the suspicion. It is the masculine secret group of homosexuals that develop these traits— traits which are neither masculine nor feminine, but specifically and peculiarly homosexual.

825   CORY, DONALD WEBSTER. "Homosexual Attitudes and Heterosexual Prejudices." 1952. Reprinted in *Homosexuality: A Cross Cultural Approach,* edited by Donald Webster Cory, pp. 420–426. New York: Julian Press, 1956.

This discussion of "Homosexual Attitudes and Heterosexual Prejudices" was first published in the *International Journal of Sexology* as an answer to an article by Albert Ellis published earlier in the same journal. Ellis had asserted that most homosexuals are enormously influenced by the heterosexual culture in which they are reared, and that homosexuals accept without question beliefs and actions of the heterosexual culture such as opposition to sexual promiscuity, a superromantic basis for sexual relations, and monogamic fidelity.

The reply states that the homosexual does take over some heterosexual prejudices and that these may play a significant role in aiding the homosexual to make a satisfactory adjustment. The monogamous romantic attachment, for example, is beneficial in solving the homosexual's problem of loneliness and frustration as old age approaches. However, the homosexual also rejects certain prejudices of heterosexual society because some purpose is not served by that prejudice.

Homosexuals do not fear nudity and physical exposure in the same way that heterosexuals do, since prejudice against nudity plays no constructive role either in the homosexual's relations with society or in his struggle with himself. It is suggested that the world in which the homosexual lives is not so much heterosexual as antisexual, and that the homosexual can only make a satisfactory adjustment when he is prepared to completely accept himself and his way of life without regrets, misgivings, shame, or unconscious defense. Such self-acceptance will be facilitated as puritanical prejudices are rejected by all groups in society.

826 CORY, DONALD WEBSTER. *The Homosexual in America: A Subjective Approach.* New York: Greenberg, 1951, 326 pp.

A homosexual views homosexuality in society, covering theories with regard to its causation, the need for legal reform, homosexual society and its characteristics, the treatment of homosexuals, and the relationship between the homosexual and society at large. The worst effect of discrimination against homosexuals is making them doubt themselves and share in others' contempt for sexual inverts. Homosexuals are forced to "carry a mask" and pretend to be something they are not. Homosexuals create a special argot to keep secret from the out-group that which is clear to the in-group. Their reason for participating in the gay life is the need for identification—acceptance. Homosexuals should enter therapy for self-acceptance and in order to become better adjusted to society. The root of their difficulty is that they live not in a heterosexual world, but in an antisexual world.

827 CORY, DONALD WEBSTER. "The Language of the Homosexual." *Sexology* 32 (3, 1965): 163–165.

Homosexual slang has a twofold purpose; it is used by outsiders to refer to homosexuals, and is also used by homosexuals themselves as an "inside" language. To homosexuals, the slang becomes an identifying factor and it imparts a feeling of belonging as well.

An increasing number of these words and phrases are finding their way into our language and literature. A short glossary is included.

828 CORY, DONALD WEBSTER, and LEROY, JOHN P. *The Homosexual and His Society: A View from Within.* New York: Citadel Press, 1963, 276 pp.

An "inside" view of homosexuality, covering patterns of adjustment and maladjustment, social life, common problems, and the value and contributions of homosexuals, poses the question, "Is homosexuality harmful?" The answer is that it can be, but that it can also be beneficial. It may cause individual misery or it may help a person make creative contributions to his culture.

829 CORY, DONALD WEBSTER, and LEROY, JOHN P. "Homosexual Marriage." *Sexology* 29 (10, 1963): 660–662.

The problems of homosexual marriage and its varying types are discussed. These marriages are only temporary since they are not legally sanctioned. Economic hardship is responsible for the role of the "kept" boy. Roommates provide security, but they are not, nor do they call themselves, married.

830   CRAFT, MICHAEL. "Boy Prostitutes and Their Fate." *British Journal of Psychiatry* 112 (492, 1966): 1111–1114.

Several observations emerged from a study of the life histories of 33 apprehended and treated boy prostitutes who were under 16 years old and who had repeatedly performed sexual acts with males for reward. Sixteen of the boys were in the community and 17 were in an institution (their place of activity), although they had not been convicted of such an act. The study was limited to those with behavior disorders. Interviews and follow-up studies were conducted.

It is noted that prostitution which uses the movie house as its locale was found to be fashionable, with the experience viewed somewhat like masturbation, that parental attitudes are conducive to bad conduct in the child, and that homosexual prostitution increases with institutionalization.

831   CUTLER, MARVIN, ed. *Homosexuals Today: A Handbook of Organizations and Publications.* Los Angeles: Publications Division of One, Inc., 1956, 188 pp.

This reference book describes homosexual organizations, their publications, and their activities in the United States, France, Germany, Holland, Italy, Scandinavia, and Switzerland. The publications, which are listed by their parent organizations, are estimated to have a circulation of not less than 20,000 per month, reaching at least 75,000 persons per month.

832   "DOB Questionnaire Reveals Some Comparisons Between Male and Female Homosexuals." *Ladder* 4 (12, 1960): 4–25.

This study is not representative of homosexuals in general since it was carried out by volunteer mail questionnaire. Comparisons thus may not be valid. There were also ambiguities in the questions. Both male and female homosexuals shared a high educational level, professional status, and urban background. Both groups had a fairly stable mode of living. Their interests were similar, as was their occupational choice. Ninety percent of both sexes among the respondents judged themselves to be predominantly homosexual by the Kinsey Scale; 63 percent rated themselves exclusively homosexual.

Homosexual men did not show as great an income superiority as expected, and they had experienced more frequent conflicts with the law. Their family background was more stable, their families were larger, but adjustment appeared to be more difficult for them. More male homosexuals than female homosexuals frequented "gay" bars, but they were not heavy drinkers. Men had more frequent and earlier homosexual experiences, but fewer of them had had heterosexual experiences.

833 DEAN, ROBERT B. "Some Considerations on Promiscuity in Male Homosexuals." Mimeographed. N.p., Apr., 1967.

The concepts of "homosexuality" and "promiscuity" are defined and clarified through the use of "model" cases, "contrary" cases, "related" cases, and "borderline" cases. Sufficient criterion for the identification of an adult homosexual is that he have a preferential erotic attraction to members of his own sex whether or not he engages in overt sexual relations with them.

Homosexual promiscuity is overestimated and does not exist to the extent that many suppose. It is fostered by such institutions as gay bars and other "free markets" for sexual exchange.

Thus, homosexuals are not inherently or compulsively promiscuous as the stereotype maintains, but are more or less promiscuous, depending upon cultural factors and the social milieu.

834 EGLINTON, J. Z. *Greek Love.* New York: Oliver Layton Press, 1964, 504 pp.

A lengthy and scholarly treatise on the subject of Greek love may be considered either as polemic or serious study, according to one's point of view. A postscript by Albert Ellis is included as well as a rebuttal which defends the thesis: an older male has the right to have social-sexual relations with a young boy. Not even homosexual publications such as *One,* the *Mattachine Review,* or the *Ladder* sanction boy love and pedophilia without reservation.

The comprehensive treatise is divided into two parts: theory and practice, and history and literature. The former includes answers to some common objections, describes Greek love as both a social problem and as a solution to a social problem, the theory and practice of love (an attempt at an "orthopsychology" of love in which Greek love can be seen in context as one legitimate manifestation among many others), the sexual aspects of Greek love, and presents some uncomplicated as well as some difficult Greek love affairs.

835 ELLIS, ALBERT. "The Influence of Heterosexual Culture on the Attitudes of Homosexuals." *International Journal of Sexology* 5 (2, 1951): 77–79. Also reprinted as "The Influence of Heterosexual Culture." In *Homosexuality: A Cross Cultural Approach,* edited by Donald Webster Cory, pp. 415–419. New York: Julian Press, 1956.

Most homosexuals are influenced to a great extent by the heterosexual culture in which they were reared. Since such things as opposition to sexual promiscuity, the placing of sexual relations on a superromantic basis, and monogamic fidelity are common to both homosexual and heterosexual society, it is concluded that the average homosexual in our society is, quite unconsciously, for the most part, deeply enmeshed in beliefs and actions which are the inevitable result of living in a society with distinctly heterosexual mores and philosophies.

836   FEIGEN, GERALD MASON. "Proctologic Disorders in Sex Deviates: A Study of Sixty-eight Cases of Sodomy." *California Medicine* 81 (2, 1954): 79–83.

Sixty-eight homosexual patients, 50 of them inmates in two California penal institutions, and 18 patients observed in private practice, were interviewed and given proctologic examinations in a study of the total proctologic problem resulting from the practice of sodomy. They were arbitrarily grouped as to type of homosexual (whether activity was occasional, bisexual, or exclusively homosexual, or whether they were transvestite), and information was sought with regard to appearance, age at onset, frequency of practice, techniques, and proctologic history and disorders. Although no unqualified conclusions could be drawn, apparently sodomy is more prevalent than is ordinarily believed. Most of the individuals practicing passive sodomy will require proctologic attention and are subject to anorectal and venereal disease. The physician's responsibility is one of diagnosis and treatment, and alteration of the degree of homosexuality should be left to the psychiatrist.

837   FINGER, FRANK W. "Sex Beliefs and Practices among Male College Students." *Journal of Abnormal and Social Psychology* 42 (1, 1947): 57–67.

In order to obtain satisfactory figures pertaining to the sexual behavior of college students and also to develop a frank and objective questionnaire for obtaining such figures, a study was made of 111 college students whose average age was 19.4 years. All but 10 were premedical students, and all were enrolled in advanced psychology courses. A questionnaire insuring anonymity was administered to each subject. As a reliability check, it was readministered to some of them. A summary table for purposes of comparison is included.

Twenty-seven percent of the students had had at least one overt homosexual episode leading to orgasm, the mean age of their first experience being 12.2 years. These episodes lasted over a short span of years. This group believed that more than half the male population have had similar experiences, while the nonexperienced students estimated the figure to be 21.5 percent. The reliability of responses was satisfactorily high. Data and beliefs on masturbation and heterosexual intercourse are also presented.

838   FITZGERALD, THOMAS K. "A Theoretical Typology of Homosexuality in the United States." *Corrective Psychiatry and Journal of Social Therapy* 9 (1, 1963): 28–35.

Recognizing that homosexuality is primarily a social phenomenon, the relation between a homosexual's set of values and his role expectations is examined. Three types of possible adjustment (positive, negative, or marginal) are described. In the first instance he may identify with the homosexual culture. In the second, he may reinterpret dominant values, trying to fit undetected into heterosexual society. Marginal adjustment would try to bridge the frustrations of adjustment, perhaps by unrealistic hopes for social acceptance and integration in the near future. The type of adjustment the homosexual accepts is seen as "always being based on some free decision."

839   FLUKER, J. L. "Recent Trends in Homosexuality in West London." *British Journal of Venereal Diseases* 42 (1, 1966): 48–49.

Efforts to encourage homosexuals with venereal disease to attend the West London Luke Clinic are described. The increasing percentage of homosexual cases in males afflicted with venereal disease is noted. The importance of the medical and nursing staff's obtaining the cooperation of homosexual patients is pointed out.

840   FREYHAN, F. A. "Homosexual Prostitution: A Case Report." *Delaware State Medical Journal* 19 (5, 1947): 92–94.

The case history of a young homosexual prostitute is reported. The subject was a 19-year-old white male being treated for homosexuality in the Delaware State Hospital after his arrest for prostitution and for wearing a naval uniform. He was diagnosed as a psychopathic personality and was not helped by therapy. The increase of homosexual prostitution is commented upon.

841   GAGNON, JOHN H., and SIMON, WILLIAM, eds. *Sexual Deviance.* New York: Harper & Row, 1967, 310 pp.

With a single exception, this is a collection of articles reprinted from other sources. Part One contains an "overview" on sexuality and sexual learning in the child; sex offenses, the marginal status of the adolescent; and sex offenses, a sociological critique. Part Two contains three articles on female prostitution. Parts Three and Four contain articles on male and female homosexuality respectively; these are abstracted separately. See Achilles, Nancy (no. 809). Hooker, Evelyn (no. 859). Leznoff, Maurice, and Westley, William A. (no. 874). Reiss, Albert J. (no. 895). Simon, William, and Gagnon, John H. (no. 842).

842   GAGNON, JOHN H., and SIMON, WILLIAM. "Sexual Deviance in Contemporary America." *Annals of the American Academy of Political and Social Science* 376 (Mar., 1968): 106–122.

In an attempt to analyze deviant behavior in its relation to societal norms, a heuristic model is set up using three variables of sexual deviance: incidence of behavior, the existence of a specialized social structure to support it, and the intenseness of sanction applied against behavior.

Male homosexuality and female homosexuality have "high to moderate" incidence and both possess "specialized (supporting) social structures." The level of invoked sanctions against female homosexuality is weak while the level is strong against male homosexuality. Of all forms of deviance included in the model, only male homosexuality has both high incidence and strong sanctions against it. Gagnon and Simon feel that even if legal sanctions are removed, this will not necessarily result in an increase in tolerance of homosexuality.

843   GAGNON, JOHN H., and SIMON, WILLIAM. "The Sociological Perspective on Homosexuality." *Dublin Review* 512 (Summer, 1967): 96–114.

Research efforts in the field of psychology and sociology have been inadequate and simplistic in their efforts to explain homosexuality. The homosexual should be considered through an analysis of the homosexual community and the larger heterosexual community in which he must function. Questions of etiology, so difficult to determine, have received too much attention, leading to the neglect of such areas as patterns of homosexuality observed in a society and in the life cycle of the homosexual.

844   GEBHARD, PAUL H. "Homosexual Socialization." *Excerpta Medica International Congress Series* 150 (Sept., 1966): 1028–1031.

A report on the socialization of homosexuals in the United States was presented in a paper given at the Fourth World Congress of Psychiatry. Questions of etiology should be deferred until the nature of the phenomenon is better understood. A picture of the homosexual community, the roles and careers of the homosexual, and the homosexual's relation to the larger society are sketched.

845 GEBHARD, PAUL H. "Incidence of Overt Homosexuality in the United States and Western Europe." Working Paper Prepared for the National Institute of Mental Health Task Force on Homosexuality. Mimeographed. Bloomington, Ind.: Indiana University, n.d., 22 pp.

Surveys on the incidence of homosexuality in the United States and Great Britain are listed and commented upon. Most of these surveys took place after World War II, with emphasis upon upper-middle-class or upper-class individuals, and upon the better educated. Three empirical turn-of-the-century surveys, those of Römer, Chelenov, and Hirschfeld, are cited. Later Western European studies mentioned include those of Friedelburg, Spencer, Schofield, Giese, and Hertoft, all taking place since 1949. Research studies on the incidence of homosexuality in the United States include those of Davis, Hamilton, Dickinson, Terman, Bromley, Landis, Ramsey, Hohman and Schaffner, Finger, Kinsey, Gilbert, Ross and Mendelsohn, Gebhard, and Simon, occurring from 1929 on.

The formulation of a workable definition of homosexuality and standardization of measurements is urged. Age-specific incidence should be included in studies on sexuality. He draws certain generalizations on incidence from a comparison of the above-mentioned studies, while indicating the need for more surveys using directly comparable methodology and terminology and more representative samples of the population. Future studies are also needed on the incidence of homosexuality among ethnic groups.

846 GEBHARD, PAUL H.; GAGNON, JOHN H.; POMEROY, WARDELL B.; and CHRISTENSEN, CORNELIA V. Sex Offenders: An Analysis of Types. New York: Harper & Row, 1965, 923 pp.

This comparative study of 14 types of convicted sex offenders includes three types of homosexual offenders: offenders against children aged 12 or under (96 men), against minors aged 12 to 15 (136 men), and against adults aged 16 and over (199 men). Data were gathered by interviewing.

All homosexual offenders were characterized by a poor relationship during childhood with their parents, especially with the father. They also had more prepubertal sex play than other sex offenders and the majority of the play was homosexual. Relatively large proportions (one-fifth to one-quarter) while prepubescent had had some sexual experience with adult males. Heterosexual activity in postpubertal life tended to be late in development and low in frequency, and relatively few married. Divorce rates were high. Self-masturbation was always an important source of sexual outlet. Homosexual offenders only very rarely used physical force in obtaining sexual gratification and did not appear to be dangerous or antisocial.

The degree of homosexual commitment varied between the three types, the offenders against children being the least homosexual (47 percent had extensive homosexual activity) and the offenders against adults the most (nearly 90 percent having extensive homosexual experience).

847   GERBER, ISRAEL J. *Man on a Pendulum: A Case History of an Invert.* New York: American Press, 1955, 320 pp.

Mostly autobiographical, this extensive case history and biography of a male homosexual also includes an account of the counseling he received from a rabbi.

848   GINSBURG, KENNETH N. "The 'Meat-Rack': A Study of the Male Homosexual Prostitute." *American Journal of Psychotherapy* 21 (2, 1967): 170–185.

A psychological theory regarding factors relating to homosexual prostitution is put forth in a study based on the personal observations of one who had temporarily been a part of the hustler "community." The theory is that the family constellation of the homosexual prostitute (who may not be homosexual himself) is viewed as the progenitor of a pathologic state characterized by an unstable self-identity, an inadequate self-evaluation, and little learned interaction possibilities or alternatives for action. Such a person relates with his own body and not with people.

849   GREENZWEIG, CHARLES JEROME. "Society Within Society: A Descriptive and Analytical Presentation of Homosexuality as a Social Problem." Master's thesis, Brooklyn College, 1954, 142 pp.

Homosexuality is not only a problem involving undesirable and unacceptable behavior; it also involves public opinion and social prejudice which can operate to accentuate and aggravate this problem. Heterosexual prejudices fostered by stereotypic notions of homosexuality produce great pressure on homosexuals. In response to this, a homosexual community develops where counterstereotypic images of homosexuality are produced. Among these counterimages may be found beliefs that inversion has a hereditary base, that it is natural and cannot be cured, or that homosexuals have special positive qualities such as unusual creative ability.

850   GROSS, ALFRED A. "The Persistent Problem of the Homosexual: A Social Approach." *Psychological Service Center Journal* 9 (1956): 25–36.

A paper originally read before the Charlotte (North Carolina) Mental Hygiene Society in January, 1956, concerns the social factors involved in the problem of homosexuality. The relative merit of the plethora of works on sexual deviations are briefly assessed and those which are more serious and more easily understood are indicated. Oversimplification about sexual orientation is warned against, using the Kinsey 7-point scale as an example. Although the problem of homosexuality in our society is everyone's concern, the natural leaders in research and in the counseling of the homosexual are the psychiatrist and the clergyman.

851   GUNNISON, FOSTER, JR. *An Introduction to the Homophile Movement.* Hartford, Conn.: Institute of Social Ethics, 1967, 37 pp.

A short history and description of the present extent of homophile and homosexual organizations is presented. Various aspects of the general movement are noted, including descriptions of the homophile organizations, the planning conferences, the inner- and outer-directed activities of the organizations, the involvement of the church in the movement, and its short- and long-range goals. Appendices include a list of organizations as well as their publications.

852   HANSEN, EDWARD; BIRD, FRED; and FORRESTER, MARK. *The Tenderloin Ghetto: Youth and Young Adults in the Tenderloin Area of Downtown San Francisco.* Mimeographed. San Francisco: Council on Religion and the Homosexual, [1965?], 29 pp.

A preliminary study of the problems of people living in the Tenderloin area of downtown San Francisco is reported. This ghetto area, a community of some 50,000 people, includes a large group of youth and young adults between the ages of 12 and 25 years. Among their many problems is sexual identification, and homosexual behavior is predominant. In proposing a program for the rehabilitation of and assistance to inhabitants of this area, the authors stress the importance of recognizing that a majority of them are homosexuals who either will not or cannot change their sexual orientation; this must not become a barrier to a helping relationship. These people are also in need of assistance in decisions regarding military duty and employment which have legal implications because of their homosexual behavior.

853   HAUSER, RICHARD. *The Homosexual Society.* London: The Bodley Head, 1962, 167 pp.

Homosexual communities in England are examined from a sociological point of view. Homosexuals are classified into numerous types; included among these types are the bisexual, the married man, the self-isolated homosexual, the fully sublimated homosexual, prostitutes (with five subtypes), "sugar daddies," prison "queers," pub and club types, pedophiliacs, psychopaths, voyeurs, and transvestites. Aspects of homosexual society which receive attention are the family, social and economic setting, rejection of male role, homosexual marriages, and various subcultures. An attempt is made to provide a method for the homosexual reader to view himself in regard to the various types and stages of relationships which are described. Stress is placed upon educating the public, including homosexuals, with regard to homosexuality.

854   HEGELER, INGE, and HEGELER, STEN. "Homosexual, Homosexuality." In their *An ABZ of Love*, pp. 121–131. Translated by David Hohnen. Copenhagen: Chr. Erichsen's Forlag, 1962.

A brief general discussion of homosexuality suggests a classification scheme which divides all persons into nine somewhat overlapping groups according to type and form of sexual behavior. Homosexuals are not to be blamed for their different sex life which can only rarely be cured or changed. They constitute a minority group which is subject to legal and moral injustices even in liberal Denmark. However, such Danish magazines as *Vennen* and *Eos* and certain social organizations at least afford them more opportunity of getting together in peace than is true in other countries.

855   HOFFMAN, MARTIN. *The Gay World: Male Homosexuality and the Social Creation of Evil.* New York: Basic Books, 1968, 212 pp.

Various theories of homosexuality and the important literature in the area are reviewed. It is concluded that the heterogeneity existing among homosexuals makes it impossible to speak of an "etiology" of homosexuality. Certain aspects of homosexual life are described in a discussion of public places, their social characteristics, and the ways in which sex is negotiated and carried out by persons who meet in these places. Considering promiscuity and the problem of intimacy, the argument is advanced that society generates the homosexual's promiscuity by creating anxieties which inhibit stable relationships. Legal statutes, enforcement practices, law reform, et cetera, are discussed in their relationship to homosexuality. It is believed that social attitudes cause whatever psychological manifestations of "illness" are to be found in homosexuals.

856   HOHMAN, LESLIE B., and SCHAFFNER, BERTRAM. "The Sex Lives of Unmarried Men." *American Journal of Sociology* 52 (6, 1947): 501–507.

The results of a study of the sex histories of single, American males made during the course of working with the Selective Service in the Fall of 1941 are reported. Several aspects of sexual activity are surveyed, including homosexuality. The percentage of male homosexuals was lower than that reported by previous investigators. Only 15 homosexuals were found among 4,100 men.

857   "Homosexual Practices and Venereal Diseases." *Lancet* 1 (7331, 1964): 481–482.

Homosexuals are a "problem group" for those concerned with the control of venereal disease because homosexuals tend to be promiscuous. The rate of venereal disease among homosexuals is increasing, gonorrhea being more prevalent than syphilis. There are more dangers from homosexual promiscuity than heterosexual promiscuity since homosexuals are less aware of the symptoms.

858   HOOKER, EVELYN. "An Empirical Study of Some Relations Between Sexual Patterns and Gender Identity in Male Homosexuals." In *Sex Research: New Developments,* edited by John Money, pp. 24–52. New York: Holt, Rinehart and Winston, 1965.

The identity of male homosexuals has for too long a time been assumed to follow one of two paths, usually described as tending to be more masculine or more feminine. This approach is believed to be in error. Interviews and psychological tests were administered over an eight-year period (from 1954 to 1962) to 30 overt homosexual males selected through contacts with friends and homosexual groups. The present report is based on the findings of this research as previously presented in Hooker 1957, 1958, 1961, and 1963.
    Current concepts of sex role and gender identity of male homosexuals are inadequate. This refers to such gross dichotomies as inserter-insertee, active-passive, anal intercourse versus oral intercourse, feminine-masculine, et cetera. A differentiation of role and gender is found to be highly variable. It is suggested that in long-term affairs between homosexuals these distinctions tend to become difficult, if not impossible, to determine.

859   HOOKER, EVELYN. "The Homosexual Community." 1961. Reprinted in *Sexual Deviance,* edited by John H. Gagnon and William Simon, pp. 167–184. New York: Harper & Row, 1967.

The term community is used to refer to a group of persons who share certain interests, activities, and social-psychological characteristics. The ecological features and public institutions of the homosexual community are examined, particularly the role of the gay bar. Gay bars serve several functions in the community: they are sexual marketplaces where the exchange of sexual services may be arranged without obligation or commitment; they are centers of communication and social activity; they serve as induction, training, and integration centers for new members of the community. Homosexual networks and behavior outside the bars are briefly described, and a description of "camping" is included.

860   HOOKER, EVELYN. "Male Homosexuality." In *Taboo Topics*, edited by Norman L. Farberow, pp. 44–55. New York: Atherton Press, 1963.

Among some of the difficulties in researching male homosexuality are the reluctance of homosexuals to be interviewed, the difficulty of drawing a representative sample, the establishment of confidence and trust, and determining the degree of their homosexual activity. These difficulties are not unique to this topic, arising also in scientific investigations of other areas of human behavior; only the specific content is different.

861   HOOKER, EVELYN. "Male Homosexuals and Their 'Worlds.' " In *Sexual Inversion: The Multiple Roots of Homosexuality*, edited by Judd Marmor, pp. 83–107. New York: Basic Books, 1965.

Regularities of behavior that must be in part functions of cultural, structural, social system, or situational variables and appear despite variability in personality, are studied using an ethnographic approach.

Homosexual public meeting places, patterns of public encounter and interaction, communication and socialization are described on the basis of observation of and limited participation in the male homosexual community of Los Angeles. The "gay bar," described as a free market for sexual contacts, is considered to be one of the most important interactional settings.

862   HOOKER, EVELYN. "A Preliminary Analysis of Group Behavior of Homosexuals." *Journal of Psychology* 42 (1956): 217–225.

A study of the relation between individual personality dynamics and group dynamics in determining patterns of behavior on the part of the overt male homosexual is proposed as a problem for research.

As a minority group member, the homosexual exhibits certain traits, including obsessive concern with his homosexuality as a defense against heterosexuality; withdrawal and passivity as an ego defense against victimization (passivity and dependence are among the most characteristic attitudes of a large group of homosexuals); strengthening of in-group ties; protective clowning; and identification with the dominant group and hatred of himself and his own group. Topics of conversation are shared by most homosexual groups throughout the country.

Homosexual group pathology is characterized by mutual overexcitation and the absence of sufficient release of tension (the constant search for sexual partners), and efforts by the group to force members to fulfill expectations with regard to certain types (the feminine or "swish" male). A group may be pathological if its individual members' selective perceptions which are distorted have no possibility of being corrected by the group.

It appears probable that homosexual groups, as well as individuals, contain components of both pathology and health.

863   HUMPHREYS, R. A. LAUD. "The Tearoom Trade: Impersonal Sex in Public Places." Ph.D. dissertation, Washington University, 1968, 293 pp.

By passing as homosexual, the researcher engaged in systematic observation of homosexual acts in public restrooms ("tearooms"). These restrooms were accessible to and easily recognizable by those who wished to engage in anonymous sexual encounters. A group of males who participated in these homosexual encounters (identified through automobile license records) agreed to in-depth interviews about themselves as part of an apparent public health survey. Data about general background, marital and family situations, attitudes toward politics and social issues, health history, religious background, and sexual history and attitudes are compared with data gained through interviews with a matched control group. The result is a composite profile of the individuals involved in "tearoom" sexual activity.

In addition, a sociological analysis of this type of sexual activity is presented as part of a game metaphor; roles are delineated and the strategies employed as the participant moves from "positioning" to "payoff" are outlined.

Several full transcripts of interviews and a copy of the interview schedule are included.

A revised version of this dissertation has recently been published by the Aldine Publishing Company.

864   HUMPHREYS, R. A. LAUD. "They Meet in Tearooms: A Preliminary Study of Participants in Impersonal Homosexual Encounters." Master's thesis, Washington University, 1967, 18 pp.

Since homosexual sex in public restrooms is illegal, carrying out such activity requires the presence of a sexually uninvolved "lookout" who can warn the participants of the approach of park guards or policemen. The researcher in this study assumed this "lookout" role and as a result was able to observe the activity at first hand without unduly influencing the dynamics of these encounters. In addition, the researcher was able to trace, through car licenses, a number of the persons participating in such activity and thus to draw some conclusions about their marital status, social class, and occupation.

Homosexual encounters in public restrooms (usually called "tearooms" by those who frequent them) are extremely impersonal; they are characterized by a pervading atmosphere of fear of discovery, and are carried out in total silence. Sexual contact is almost entirely restricted to fellatio and masturbation. While the oral copulation of one man is taking place, others in the room may watch as they masturbate themselves. Racial and social distinctions are of no consequence, but age is an important factor. Fellation is almost always a service performed by the older partner. If a stranger or a teen-ager enters the restroom, sexual activity is immediately suspended. The roads around the "tearoom" are also used for contact, contract, and, occasionally, for sexual liaison.

Of the 90 participants who were traced and studied, 62 percent were married; one person was classified as upper-class; 17 percent, upper-middle-class; 64 percent, lower-middle-class; 17 percent, working or upper-lower-class, and one person, lower-lower-class. The men who meet in "tearooms" are thus mainly members of the middle-class. "They are the 'average guys' of our society, maintaining nice homes and cars, supporting families, holding good jobs." They can be described as "part-time deviates living otherwise normal lives."

The danger inherent in public sex is seen as an important ingredient of sexual encounters carried on in public places; it adds to the high level of suspense, and thus to the reward the participant receives for engaging in the activity.

865   JACKSON, C. COLIN. "Syphilis: The Role of the Homosexual."
       Medical Services Journal of Canada 19 (Sept., 1963): 631–638.

According to U.S. public health statistics the number of persons discovered to have syphilis tripled between 1957 and 1961. A large number of the syphilitic persons were homosexual. The secrecy with which homosexuals must live and their sexual promiscuity make them particularly prone to venereal disease. Doctors are urged to be alert to the possibility of homosexuality when syphilis is diagnosed. They should also consider the possibility of syphilis when dealing with lesions in the anorectal area.

866   JEFFERISS, F. J. G. "Venereal Disease and the Homosexual." *British Journal of Venereal Diseases* 32 (1, 1956): 17–20.

A significant proportion of male venereal disease patients are homosexuals, and only a few of these are prostitutes. Homosexuals themselves reported that because of a fear of the law, they dared not be known to have male friends. Having no other means of finding partners, they had to resort to picking up strangers and/or male prostitutes and so encouraged the spread of venereal disease.

867   KANEE, B., and HUNT, C. L. "Homosexuality as a Source of Vene-real Disease." *Canadian Medical Association Journal* 65 (2, 1951): 138–140.

Although venereal disease seems to be decreasing in British Columbia, homosexuality seems to be an increasing source of reported cases. Eleven of 19 cases of syphilis in one year were acquired as a result of homosexual practices. Homosexuality is assuming an alarming importance in the dis-semination of venereal diasease, a fact which should be brought to general notice.

868   KEMPE, G. TH. "The Homosexual in Society." *British Journal of Delinquency* 5 (1, 1954): 4–20. Also printed in abridged form as "The Homophiles in Society." *International Journal of Sexology* 7 (4, 1954): 217–219.

Homosexuals are studied sociologically as a minority rather than as a mass or as a community. Dividing the group into the two categories, centrifugals (dissimulants) and centripetals (nondissimulants), the structure and psy-chological problems of the group as a whole and the manner in which persons in both categories deal with these problems are considered. The lack of openness or a point of contact between the group and the heterosexual majority has intensified the problems of the homosexual who seeks not only acceptance but recognition as a person. Cautiously optimistic about the future, it is noted that the advent of the phenomenological or daseins-analytical psychiatry and existentialist philosophy which have brought about a reorientation in the fields of psychology and psychiatry may pro-mote a mutual openness and contact which may bridge the gulf between heterophile and homophile.

869   KINSEY, ALFRED C.; POMEROY, WARDELL B.; and MARTIN, CLYDE E. *Sexual Behavior in the Human Male.* Philadelphia: W. B. Saunders Co., 1948, 804 pp.

Data secured by the Institute for Sex Research through interviews with 5,300 white males provide information on sexual outlets and the factors affecting the differential frequency of these various outlets.

Numerous references to the incidence and frequency of overt homosexual contacts appear throughout the report in tables, charts, and discussions, with one chapter dealing specifically with homosexual outlets. Previous estimates of the incidence of homosexuality are compared with incidence data provided by this study. Frequencies, the heterosexual-homosexual balance and the 0 to 6 scale of heterosexual-homosexual orientation, bisexuality, and the scientific and social implications of homosexuality are considered in detail.

870 KLING, SAMUEL G. "Homosexual Behavior." In his *Sexual Behavior and the Law,* pp. 97–128. New York: Bernard Geis Associates, 1965.

Included in a volume on various aspects of sexual behavior and the law, covering 16 topics such as abortion, adultery and fornication, illegitimacy, and sexual deviations, this discussion follows the question and answer format, and is directed toward the intelligent layman. General information on homosexuality includes definition of the term, types of sexual activity, famous homosexual individuals from the past, the incidence of homosexuality in the United States today (especially in the Armed Forces), society's current attitude, and brief individual summaries of the laws relating to homosexuality in the United States and in the countries of Western Europe.

871 KRONHAUSEN, EBERHARD, and KRONHAUSEN, PHYLLIS. *Sex Histories of American College Men.* New York: Ballantine Books, 1960, 313 pp.

A popularized account of the varieties of sexual behaviors and histories of American college males based upon the personal histories of about 200 students at an all-male college is presented. Although material on homosexuality occurs throughout the text, there is one main chapter on homosexuality. Most attention is given to comparison of these findings with those of Kinsey et al. (indicating a close correspondence). The varieties of homosexual experience are illustrated with numerous autobiographical reports from the students. It was concluded that with regard to homosexuality, as well as other sexual behavior and attitudes investigated, the findings of this study fully supported those of the Kinsey study.

872 LEGG, W. DORR. "Blackmailing the Homosexual." *Sexology* 33 (8, 1967): 554–556.

The blackmail of homosexuals is discussed, mentioning the effect of laws and experiences of homosexuals in dealing with blackmail threats. *The Sexual Offender and His Offenses* by Karpman and the Wolfenden Report are quoted. The experiences of two men against whom blackmail has been attempted are reported.

Inadequate legal codes and social mores provide a screen behind which the blackmailer can operate with impunity, threatening not only the confirmed homosexual but also those who have casual or unique experiences of a homosexual nature.

873   LEZNOFF, MAURICE. "Interviewing Homosexuals." *American Journal of Sociology* 62 (2, 1956): 202–204.

Personal interviews with more than 60 overt and covert homosexuals who were over 40 years old were conducted. The overt homosexuals lived almost exclusively in the deviant culture, were known as homosexuals where they worked, and made little effort to conceal the fact from "normals." They were very cooperative and welcomed the interviews. As they willingly revealed intimate details about their own lives and readily betrayed the secrets of their friends and acquaintances, personal rivalries and animosities were bared and the interviewer had problems of remaining aloof from the quarrels which ensued.

It was difficult to find covert homosexuals who were willing to be interviewed. They were of higher socioeconomic status and when they agreed to be interviewed it caused considerable dissension within the deviant world. Many were severely criticized for their breach of the code of secrecy and some friendships were even ruptured. Feeling insecure about the study, they sought assurance by meeting the interviewer personally. Since these covert homosexuals were linked together by bonds of friendship, they served as sponsors for further interviews. It was found that they had developed two personalities, one for dealing with heterosexuals and the other with homosexuals.

Since interviewing the covert homosexuals proved to be so time-consuming and produced such meager information, a different procedure for these interviews was worked out. At the beginning of each interview the respondent was told his help was needed in the compilation of a glossary of homosexual terms. It was found that by using this procedure communication was facilitated and that the respondent gained confidence in describing his life.

874   LEZNOFF, MAURICE, and WESTLEY, WILLIAM A. "The Homosexual Community." 1956. Reprinted in *The Problem of Homosexuality in Modern Society,* edited by Hendrik M. Ruitenbeek, pp. 162–174. New York: E. P. Dutton & Co., 1963. Also reprinted in *Sexual Deviance,* edited by John H. Gagnon and William Simon, pp. 167–184. New York: Harper & Row, 1967.

An investigation of a homosexual community in a large Canadian city indicates that such a community is made up of a number of distinct homosexual groups whose members are bound together through relatively strong and enduring friendship ties. The homosexual group provides a social context wherein the members find collective support and social acceptance. Sexual partners are not sought among the group members; intragroup sexual activity appears to be prohibited in a manner suggestive of the incest taboo. The search for sexual partners forces the homosexual to move beyond his own group with the result that loose bonds of association grow up between the homosexual groups in the community.

While a tenuous connection between the groups is maintained, a certain amount of distrust and hostility exists between them. This situation is mainly due to the fact that two distinct types of homosexual groups—secret and overt—are present in the homosexual community. The nature of each group is determined by the extent to which identification as a homosexual poses a status threat to group members.

Overt groups are generally made up of persons employed in such occupations as art, interior decorating, hairdressing, or in certain lower-status jobs where becoming known as a homosexual is not necessarily problematic. Secret groups are usually composed of individuals employed in higher-status occupations, especially those in managerial positions or in the professions, where identification as a homosexual could prove to be problematic. The very existence of overt groups is threatening to secret homosexuals, yet interaction between the groups is necessary in order to facilitate sexual liaisons. The consequent stress explains the reciprocal hostility between the various groups in the homosexual community.

875   LINDNER, ROBERT. "Homosexuality and the Contemporary Scene." 1956. Reprinted in *The Problem of Homosexuality in Modern Society,* edited by Hendrik M. Ruitenbeek, pp. 52–79. New York: E. P. Dutton & Co., 1963.

An increased tolerance toward homosexuality is cited by some as evidence of the existence of a "sexual revolution," characterized by liberalized sexual behavior and attitudes. The reality of such a revolution is doubted. In fact, it is believed that in our society the sexual drive is "the object of every conceivable repressive force." Homosexuality is adopted by some as an attempt to resolve the conflict between the urgency of their sexual needs and the repressiveness of the accepted morality.

The extent of homosexuality in the United States (4 to 6 percent of the male population over 16 years of age) and some of the conditions which contribute to its development are discussed. Mention is made of the growth of the homophile movement in Europe and the United States and several organizations which are a part of it are listed. It is believed that these organizations will fail in any attempt to bring about an acceptance of homosexuality, since the fundamental attitudes of our society toward it include hostility and contempt.

876   McIntosh, Mary. "The Homosexual Role." *Social Problems* 16
       (2, 1968): 182–192.

The "homosexual role" is not a constant in all cultures. It exists only in
certain societies, and only emerged in England toward the end of the 17th
century. In modern societies where this separate homosexual role is recognized, the expectation on behalf of those who play the role, and of others,
is that a homosexual will be exclusively or very predominantly homosexual
in his feelings and behavior. Other facets of this role are the expectations
that the homosexual will be effeminate in manner, personality, or preferred
sexual activity, that sexuality will play a part of some kind in all his relations
with other men, and that he will be attracted to boys and very young men
and that he is probably willing to seduce them. In modern America the
existence of the role appears to have some effect upon the distribution of
homosexual behavior, but the role is also sometimes played by persons
whose sexual orientation is not exclusively homosexual.

877   MacNamara, Donal E. J. "Male Prostitution in an American
       City: A Pathological or Socio-Economic Phenomenon?" Paper read
       at American Orthopsychiatric Association Meeting, 18 March 1965,
       in New York City, Mimeographed, 8 pp. Reported in *American
       Journal of Orthopsychiatry* 35 (2, 1965): 204.

Preliminary data on a study of male homosexual prostitutes in New York
City are presented.
    A male homosexual prostitute is defined as a male person who confers
"sexual favors . . . on another [male] for a monetary consideration . . . as
a regular means of full subsistence or as supplementary income" over a long
period of time. A technique called "roping" which is used by the criminal
investigator was employed. Disguising himself, the investigator worked his
way into the confidence of male prostitutes, corroborating information
through school authorities, military records, and prison records. Thirty-
seven male prostitutes were studied. Their ages ranged from 15 to 31 years.
Eight were Spanish, eight Black, seven Irish-American, five Italian-Ameri-
can, three Jewish, one French-Canadian, one Midwestern American, one
Georgia-born (raised in South Carolina as white Protestant), one Polish
immigrant, one New Englander, and one orphanage alumnus of unknown
origin. Twenty-two of the 37 subjects were Roman Catholics. Their education ranged from six to 12 plus years. Nine had been in the United States
Army, only one of whom was discharged for homosexuality. One was
married, and his wife was aware, even if not approving, of his means of
employment. Sixteen of the subjects had served time in jail, but only one
had been arrested for homosexual prostitution. Thirty-one could be clas-

sified as effeminate in dress and manner. Five were "hoodlum types," and one was the "All-American-boy" type. Work attitudes of all 37 subjects were negative. Generally, they exhibited hostility and aggression toward the public and especially toward those in authority. Three of them had been in psychoanalysis. Six of them were from broken homes. None were alcoholics or addicts.

878   MAGEE, BRYAN. *One in Twenty: A Study of Homosexuality in Men and Women.* London: Secker & Warburg, 1966, 192 pp.

Based on reading and interviewing, a journalistic account of male and female homosexuality in Great Britain includes a discussion of the causes of homosexuality, social attitudes toward homosexuals, homosexual attitudes toward society, sexual patterns of male and female homosexuals, the social life of homosexuals, and legal reactions to homosexual behavior. Homosexuality is believed to be based upon early childhood experiences. It can be changed mainly through psychotherapy. The incidence of homosexuality is estimated at one in 20. Homosexuals cannot be distinguished from other people by observation, since concealment is the basic element of their life style. Social attitudes are fraught with stereotypes and prejudices; homosexuals, in turn, feel persecuted. Homosexuality has the advantages of freedom and sexual informality, and the disadvantage of insecurity.

The situation in Holland, where homosexuality between consenting adults is legal, is compared with Great Britain, where this was not the case. In the villages and small towns there was the same fear of discovery as in Britain, but the social life in large cities, particularly in homosexual nightclubs, was somewhat more free. Although no one wanted to be filmed, the behaviors of the clientele were much like what was found in heterosexual nightclubs.

879   "Male Homsexuality." *Lancet* 2 (7111, 1959): 1077–1080.

Sixteen brief case histories are used to illustrate different types of male homosexuals. The following general conclusions are drawn: the cause of homosexuality is still unknown since neither heredity, genetics, nor endocrinology can account for it; explanations advanced by psychiatrists are unconvincing and are not applicable to other societies; total "cures" are doubtful; it is possible that 10 percent of adult men fall into the Kinsey ratings of 4, 5, and 6.

880   MARLOWE, KENNETH. "The Life of the Homosexual Prostitute." *Sexology* 31 (1, 1964): 24–26.

A homosexual prostitute and procurer writes autobiographically of his life, describing the causes of homosexuality as well as the practice of homosexual prostitution. Unlike most homosexuals, the male prostitute cannot adjust to the normal world; he is sick and needs "medical help."

881   MARLOWE, KENNETH. *The Male Homosexual.* Los Angeles: Sherbourne Press, 1965, 158 pp.

A self-proclaimed lifelong homosexual writes a journalistic exposé of homosexuality from the standpoint of intimate personal experience. Discussing sexual practices and social activities in detail, he describes methods of cruising, the pickup, gay bar patterns, beach behavior, prostitution, and homosexual marriage.

882   MARLOWE, KENNETH. *Mr. Madam: Confessions of a Male Madam.* Los Angeles: Sherbourne Press, 1964, 246 pp.

A homosexual, transvestite operator of a male prostitution ring in Hollywood writes autobiographically of his experiences. As a child, he gained friends by submitting sexually, until he found he could do it for money; and as a teen-ager he was "kept" by a "sugar daddy." He later became a stripper in Calumet City and a hairdresser and stylist. At various times he also served in the Army (where he was raped by 14 men), studied to be a missionary, and worked as a B-girl. He describes at length the operation of a call-boy service.

883   MONEY, JOHN, and HOSTA, GEOFFREY. "Negro Folklore of Male Pregnancy." *Journal of Sex Research* 4 (1, 1968): 34–50.

A folklore belief related to male rectal pregnancy and the delivery of a "blood baby" is reported. Information obtained from five subjects (four more were later added) indicated that the belief is current among Negro homosexuals, is passed down at the time of initiation into the homosexual segment of their society, and is not restricted to a specific subtype of homosexual. Psychodynamically, the story of blood babies represents an envy of pregnancy. The origin of the story may lie in the mother-centered and often father-absent structure of the Negro family in the United States today. Tables summarizing the data on variables are included.

884   MORSE, BENJAMIN. *The Homosexual: A Frank Study of Abnormal Sex Life Among Males.* Derby, Conn.: Monarch Press, 1962, 158 pp.

A psychiatric study of "abnormal" sex life among males cites numerous case histories. Some of the homosexual types included are the mama's boy, the convict, the muscle builder, the queen, the male prostitute, and the married homosexual. The basis of this neurotic behavior and attempts to establish guidelines to combat it are discussed. Psychiatrists should not strive to change the homosexual, but to help him adjust to his life. The laws relating to homosexual behavior should be changed for offenses not involving minors or the use of force. Homosexuality is increasing because of the removal of social restraints and the increase of cultural disorganization.

885 MORTON, R. S. *Venereal Diseases.* Baltimore, Md.: Penguin Books, 1966, 185 pp.

Venereal diseases are considered from medical and sociological viewpoints. Their prevalence in the past and today, their medical nature, the types of venereal diseases and the ways they are transmitted are discussed. Rectal gonorrhea, or gonococcal proctitis, and syphilis are found to occur in passive homosexuals while gonococcal urethritis and syphilis occur in their active partners. Sores due to syphilis may occur on the lips or in the mouth as a result of kissing and fellatio. Since venereal diseases are increasing among homosexuals, homosexuality is increasingly contributing to the total incidence of venereal diseases in all men.

886 NICOL, CLAUDE. "Homosexuality and Venereal Disease." *Practitioner* 184 (1101, 1960): 345–349.

Homosexuality is adding to the increase in venereal diseases. The proportion of homosexuals with venereal disease attending clinics is increasing. The diagnosis of the passive homosexual with anal infection is difficult if his sexual activities are not known. Health authorities should inform the public that venereal disease is not an uncommon result of homosexual practices.

887 NORTON, HOWARD. *The Third Sex.* Portland, Ore.: Facts Publishing Co., 1949, 112 pp.

A discourse on homosexuality for laymen presents, in the author's words, "astonishing facts" that are "truly shocking and unbelievable." These facts refer to male and female homosexuality, transvestism, masochism, sadism, fetishism, sodomy, exhibitionism, homosexual clubs, "weddings," and laws on homosexuality. Much of the material is presented as case histories.

888 "The Other Side: Living with Homosexuality." *Canadian Medical Association Journal* 86 (May 12, 1962): 875–878.

A 30-year-old male homosexual describes his views of and experiences with homosexuality. After considering various theories of the etiology of homosexuality, he concludes it to be of psychological origin, but an extremely complex phenomenon. He describes his life and the attitudes against homosexuality which he has encountered, particularly in the Air Force. He feels three choices are open to the homosexual: getting psychiatric help, which is expensive and often useless; forgoing any sexual relations, which seems absurd if there is no good reason; and defying the law and living as a homosexual, which is lonely and dangerous. He urges general enlightenment through education as well as changes in existing laws.

889   PAINE, MARCUS. "Views of a Hidden Homosexual." *Social Progress: A Journal of Church and Society* 58 (2, 1967): 22–25.

A homosexual male in his late forties discusses his views about his own homosexual life. He has overcome being ashamed of it, but is not especially proud of it, either. Distinguishing between casual and serious relationships, he is fairly secure because of having had three long-term love relationships. In none of these did either partner take on a "husband" or "wife" role. He is not attracted by children or teen-agers. While he has many close heterosexual friends and is well accepted in his church, very few know of his homosexuality since this might lead to ostracism. Although his homosexuality is considered a sin by the church, he takes comfort in the belief that we are all sinners.

890   PLUMMER, DOUGLAS. *Queer People: The Truth about Homosexuals.* London: W. H. Allen, 1963, 122 pp.

In a personal survey of homosexuality in Britain today, Plummer describes how he feels as a homosexual, what various kinds of homosexuals are like, where they meet, and what they do. He also criticizes legal reactions to homosexuality, saying they contribute to blackmail and suicide. He calls for greater public tolerance and for law reform.

891   POPKESS, ATHELSTAN. "Some Criminal Aspects of Abnormalities of Sex." *Practitioner* 172 (1030, 1954): 446–450.

The author, the Chief Constable of Nottingham, stresses the rapid increase of homosexuality in England. In the past two decades, homosexuality, "like a cancer," has begun "to eat into the very vitals of the nation." Especially nefarious is the "pollution" of the young by homosexuals. Overt lesbianism, a by-product of World War II, is depicted as considerably less dangerous and more ephemeral. Manifestations of lesbianism, such as male dress and heterosexual types of greetings, may or may not represent true sexual inversion.

892   RAMSEY, GLENN V. "The Sexual Development of Boys." *American Journal of Psychology* 56 (2, 1943): 217–233.

The sexual development, physical and behavioral, of preadolescent and adolescent boys is described. Personal interviews were conducted with 291 boys (286 white, five Negro), aged 12 to 16 years, from a large urban center, and of the middle- and upper-middle-classes. Homosexual experiences were reported by 38 percent of the boys. In 81 percent of the cases, the relationships were restricted to three or fewer companions, with a frequency of 25 or fewer times. Homosexual approaches by adults were reported by 30 boys; eight had had homosexual relations with an adult.

893 RAVEN, SIMON. "Boys Will Be Boys: The Male Prostitute in London." 1960. Reprinted in *The Problem of Homosexuality in Modern Society*, edited by Hendrik M. Ruitenbeek, pp. 279–290. New York: E. P. Dutton & Co., 1963.

How the men and boys are procured in response to the demand for the services of the male prostitute, where they come from, in what manner and in what places they carry on their business, whether they prosper and for how long, and what fate finally overtakes them are all questions which are answered in simple, concrete terms, without considering homosexuality as a "problem."

Five categories of male prostitutes are found in London: men in the armed services, men who wish to improve their incomes, men of low intelligence and low town background without job prospects, men who consider that the only money worth making is that from shady enterprises, and the full-time professional male prostitutes with no other source of income. All these types come from homes in which they are unwanted. Their physical attractiveness and youth fade quickly, whereupon they may return to heterosexual life, go to prison, content themselves with other employment, or drift among the shadier bars and scrape along on earnings or savings.

894 REEVY, WILLIAM R. "Adolescent Sexuality." In *The Encyclopedia of Sexual Behavior*, edited by Albert Ellis and Albert Abarbanel, pp. 52–68. 2d rev. ed. New York: Hawthorn Books, 1967.

A brief discussion of homosexuality is included in a general treatment of adolescent sexuality. Few adolescents of either sex are involved in actual homosexual activities. By the end of adolescence about 20 percent of the males and about 3 percent of the females have engaged in homosexual activity resulting in orgasm. Though adolescent homosexual contacts are of social significance and though the legal, social, and moral restrictions against it are severe, homosexual activity is much less significant in adolescence than is masturbation, heterosexual petting, coitus, or nocturnal sex dreams.

895 REISS, ALBERT J., JR. "The Social Integration of Queers and Peers." 1961. Reprinted in *The Problem of Homosexuality in Modern So-*

ciety, edited by Hendrik M. Ruitenbeek, pp. 249–278. New York: E. P. Dutton & Co., 1963. Also reprinted in *Sexual Deviance,* edited by John H. Gagnon and William Simon, pp. 197–228. New York: Harper & Row, 1967. Also reprinted in *Deviance: The Interactionist Perspective,* edited by Earl Rubington and Martin S. Weinberg, pp. 371–381. New York: Macmillan, 1968.

The deviant identification of boys who receive money from male fellators was reported, following interviews with the boys (peers). There are norms governing the transaction between "queers" and peers: from the point of view of the boys, the relationship must be to make money and not for sexual gratification. The sexual transaction must be limited to fellatio only and must be performed by the man. Both "queers" and the boys must remain neutral in their affective response to each other. Violence will not be used so long as the relationship conforms to these expectations.

The peer hustler develops no conception of himself either as prostitute or as homosexual, and the fellator risks violence if he threatens the boy's self-conception. The boy's peers define one as homosexual not on the basis of homosexual behavior but on the basis of participation in the homosexual role.

896 "Report of the Departmental Committee on Homosexual Offenses and Prostitution." *British Medical Journal* (5045, 1957): 639–640.

A review of the Wolfenden Report focusing on its medical aspects discusses the questions of whether homosexuality is a disease, how widespread it is in Britain, what the patterns of homosexual behavior are, what treatment can be effectively employed in prison, and what therapeutic measures can best be used with homosexual patients.

The conclusions contained in the Wolfenden Report are briefly presented.

897 ROSS, H. LAURENCE. "The 'Hustler' in Chicago." *Journal of Student Research* 1 (1, 1959): 13–19.

These observations are based on formal and informal interviews with and observation of a woman who was a professional model, a well-educated client of male hustlers, and seven male hustlers.

The hustling role has two aspects, that of the whore as a provider of sex, and that of the "con-man" and thief as exploiters of sex. The hustler as a whore types himself according to his most frequent method of operation within the vice area. The three main types are the bar hustler, male or female, who usually visits a certain few bars on a steady basis; the street hustler, usually a teen-aged boy who "turns tricks" with older men;

and the call-boy or call-girl, who does not solicit in public, and who enjoys the highest respect among hustlers.

In considering the hustler as "con-man" and thief, four important reasons are found for patronizing prostitutes: immediate sexual gratification is provided; the client's attractiveness or adeptness is not involved in securing gratification; prostitutes offer their services without emotional involvement; prostitutes are expected to be close-mouthed, and to protect the identity of the client and his deviance.

Hustlers divide into bar cliques which are both male and female and street corner cliques which are almost always male. Within these cliques, competition for clients is restrained by the rule that once a hustler has a client, other hustlers will make no approaches to him. The cliques also have control over the informal minimum price scale for "tricks." Members of the clique settle grievances between hustlers and mutually assist each other in crises. Hustlers are tolerant of other groups of deviants; they romanticize their irresponsibility and their isolation from conventional mores; they make use of vocabularies of adjustment (language which enables them to look upon their actions as essentially noncriminal—as justified); and they perceive themselves as practicing frankly what the rest of the world practices hypocritically.

898   Ross, Mathew, and Mendelsohn, Fred. "Homosexuality in College: A Preliminary Report of Data Obtained from One Hundred Thirty-three Students Seen in a University Student Health Service and a Review of Pertinent Literature." *Archives of Neurology and Psychiatry* 80 (2, 1958): 253–263.

To determine the characteristics of homosexuals in a college population and to determine the results of psychiatric treatment, the case histories of 133 homosexuals seen at the University of California at Los Angeles Student Health Center were studied and psychotherapy was given. The subjects were 111 males and 22 females; 81 percent of them were undergraduates; and the mean age for the males was 23.5 years.

Homosexuals do not differ very markedly from other university students in academic characteristics except in some of the following ways: a smaller percentage of male homosexuals went into graduate work; male homosexuals tended to major in applied arts (especially theater arts); undergraduate female homosexuals have decidedly better academic performance than other females; twice as many female homosexuals as is typical for the university graduate. The male homosexuals engaged in less heterosexual activity than did the female homosexuals. In treating homosexuality, results were the same as for other psychiatric disorders of a nonhomosexual nature. The best results of treatment obtained in the group were with young, intelligent, overt homosexuals with little homosexual experience, for whom the greatest number of therapeutic hours were available. Surprisingly, those homosexuals who benefited from therapy were not strongly motivated for change.

899   ROSS, ROBERT T. "Measures of the Sex Behavior of College Males Compared with Kinsey's Results." *Journal of Abnormal and Social Psychology* 45 (4, 1950): 753–755.

Kinsey's results are compared with those found through questionnaires given by R. T. Ross (1950) and F. W. Finger (1947). A table compares the results of the three surveys with regard to masturbation, homosexuality, and premarital or extra-marital sexual relationships. The comparisons indicate that Kinsey's interviewing technique yields results which are quantitatively the same as those obtained by the older and "heretofore accepted" methods of the anonymous mailed questionnaire and the anonymous group questionnaire.

900   ROYAL SOCIETY OF MEDICINE. "Discussion on the Social Aspects of Homosexuality [Summary]." *Proceedings* 40 (10, 1947): 585–592. Also reported in *British Medical Journal* (4506, 1947): 691–692.

The social aspects of homosexuality were discussed at a symposium held by the Section of Psychiatry at a 1947 meeting of the Royal Society of Medicine. The participants were E. A. Bennet, H. Mannheim, D. Stanley-Jones, John C. Mackwood and Norwood East.

Some of the subjects included in the discussion were the difficulty of drawing conclusions concerning homosexuality because of the lack of knowledge about it, the need for a systematic sociological inquiry to determine how many homosexuals there are and what kinds of persons become homosexual, the relationship between homosexuality and criminology, the classification of homosexuals according to etiology and to overt behavior, and the difficulty of treating homosexuals with psychotherapy while they are in prison.

901   RUBIN, ISADORE. "A Homosexual Doctor's Story." 1960. Reprinted in *The Third Sex,* edited by Isadore Rubin, pp. 44–47. New York: New Book Co., 1961.

An article published anonymously in *Lancet,* a leading British medical publication, in 1959, is reported and commented upon. The author of the article, a homosexual physician, recounted 16 cases of homosexuality among men he had encountered informally. Many, although not all, of the cases described were happy and contented. None could find any reason for their homosexuality, and all agreed that youthful seduction by older persons was not the cause. Psychiatric theories of the cause of homosexuality are not convincing.

Earlier comments of Kenneth Soddy published in the same journal are summarized and it is suggested that it is time to apply scientific methods to the problem.

902   RUBIN, ISADORE. "Secret Homosexual Society." 1958. Reprinted in *The Third Sex,* edited by Isadore Rubin, pp. 78–81. New York: New Book Co., 1961.

What is a "secret homosexual society" and why does it exist? This particular discussion is based on Leznoff and Westley's article, "The Homosexual Community." There is a strong need for homosexuals to get psychological support by associating with a group which will share, or at least accept, their deviant sexual tendencies. Many homosexuals openly admit their homosexuality and do not have to fear loss of their jobs; as a result, they often join open homosexual groups. However, most homosexuals are not in such a position and consequently join small secret cliques. These cliques serve social rather than sexual needs. To satisfy his sexual needs the covert homosexual frequents the meeting places of the more overt homosexuals.

903   SAGARIN, EDWARD. "Structure and Ideology in an Association of Deviants." Ph.D. dissertation, New York University, 1966, 206 pp.

The Mattachine Society, Inc., of New York (MSNY) was studied regarding what it is, who belongs to it, how it functions, its aims and aspirations, and other aspects of its existence which are of significance in a sociological analysis. The study examined, among other things, the society's membership and its periphery, the group as a voluntary association of deviants, and the group as a functioning organization.

As determined from 192 questionnaires, the membership was small, educated, and largely middle-class. The members were contrasted and compared with 25 ex-members, 88 subscribers, and 34 friends of the organization.

As an organization MSNY was found to be overwhelmingly instrumental on the manifest level, while latently almost entirely expressive. As a voluntary association it functions in a weak and ineffective manner as a mediatory agency between the power structure of the community and the mass of individual homosexuals. Instead of working side by side, the formal structure is evaded, despite a board of directors and against its own will, in favor of one man and his coterie. The membership is factional between single and multigoal orientations, which is reflected in the ideologies of the members by subgroups, factions, and struggles for control.

Sociologically, MSNY is compared to other voluntary associations of deviants. Sociological propositions are derived for various organizations using as examples MSNY, Alcoholics Anonymous, and the National Foundation (for Infantile Paralysis).

904   SCHOFIELD, MICHAEL GEORGE. "Early Experiences, Section C. Homosexuality." In his *The Sexual Behavior of Young People,* pp. 57–59. Boston: Little, Brown & Co., 1965.

In research primarily designed to find out about heterosexual experience, 934 boys aged 15 to 19 were interviewed. It was found that 21 percent knew of homosexual activities among their friends; 5 percent admitted taking part in such activities; nearly 2 percent admitted having participated in homosexual practices with adults. On the other hand, 47 percent of the boys agreed that homosexuals should be severely punished.

A similar trend was found among the 939 girls in the sample, although the percentages were smaller.

905   SCHOFIELD, MICHAEL GEORGE. "Social Aspects of Homosexuality." *British Journal of Venereal Diseases* 40 (2, 1964): 129–134.

Not all homosexuals are promiscuous and not all prefer anal intercourse; therefore some of them are not a risk (in communicating venereal disease). Practicing homosexuals are lawbreakers and often fearful of being discovered. Thus, many will not cooperate in tracing the source of venereal infection because they distrust the authorities. This is not necessarily due to a flaw in the homosexual personality, but is caused by the homosexual's social and legal setting. Those who mix in homosexual groups tend to be more promiscuous and the infection can sometimes spread quickly. The incidence of venereal disease among homosexuals can be reduced by obtaining more information on homosexuals, giving them more information on venereal disease, and developing a more enlightened legal and social attitude to the problem.

906   SCHOFIELD, MICHAEL GEORGE. *Sociological Aspects of Homosexuality: A Comparative Study of Three Types of Homosexuals.* Boston: Little, Brown & Co., 1965, 244 pp.

One hundred and fifty male homosexuals were divided into three groups of 50: those in prison, those currently under treatment, and those who had never been in prison or under treatment. These groups were matched with comparison groups made up of 50 men convicted of sexual offenses with boys under 16, 50 nonhomosexual males in psychiatric treatment, and 50 homosexual men who were selected randomly from among the men included in a 1960 study reported in Gordon Westwood's *A Minority.*

Each subject was interviewed with respect to his family background, his social behavior, and his sexual activities. A verbal reasoning test and a personality inventory were also administered. Comparisons made between the homosexual and nonhomosexual groups indicated that the differences between the homosexual and nonhomosexual groups were small, while the differences between homosexual groups were large. It is concluded from this that male homosexuals are different from male heterosexuals mainly in their choice of sex object.

907 SCHUR, EDWIN M. *Crimes without Victims—Deviant Behavior and Public Policy: Abortion, Homosexuality, and Drug Addiction.* Englewood Cliffs, N.J.: Prentice-Hall, 1965, 180 pp.

A sociological analysis of the homosexual community includes causal theories, psychological assessments, psychological treatments, and the impact of unrealistic laws on deviant behavior. Since homosexuality involves the willing exchange between consenting individuals of a desired product or service, the need for reforming the laws prohibiting such behavior is very important. Because the laws are unenforceable due to the lack of a complaining victim, they often give rise to secondary offenses such as blackmail and police corruption.

908 SCOTT, MARVIN B., and LYMAN, STANFORD. "Paranoia, Homosexuality and Game Theory." *Journal of Health and Social Behavior* 9 (3, 1968): 179–187.

Paranoid and homosexual behavior may be understood using a game-theory model in which the subjects are seen as living in a problematic environment for which plans must be made. A game is "underway when at least one actor in an encounter perceives a situation as problematic, estimates his own and others' construction of self and situation, and undertakes a line of action designed to achieve a goal or goals with respect to the situation."

Homosexuals inhabit a problematic environment as long as they live in a "heterosexually oriented society." A game-theory model can identify the elements of homosexual behavior as the actor seeks to protect his identity in a hostile environment. "Passing" for a homosexual involves not only strategy for protection, but there exists an "information game" whereby he tries to communicate his homsexuality to a suspected homosexual. While conveying signs about his homosexuality, he must at the same time protect himself if his suspicions prove to be unwarranted. Because the homosexual inhabits a problematic environment almost continually, he becomes more aware—more "situation conscious."

It is suggested that other categories of persons, such as minority groups and the disabled, may be profitably studied using game-theory models.

909 SIMON, WILLIAM, and GAGNON, JOHN H. "Homosexuality: The Formulation of a Sociological Perspective." *Journal of Health and Social Behavior* 8 (3, 1967): 177–185.

The conceptual framework of homosexuality is considered suggesting that the past emphasis on etiological factors has created a distorted view of the homosexual. The discussion is based on a theoretical consideration of existing reports in the literature.

Knowledge of how a person becomes homosexual may have to wait for an adequate explanation of the etiology of heterosexuality. Also, etiology is not seen as being all-important to an understanding of the role-behavior of an adult homosexual in society. The sexual factor of homosexuality has been stressed too much, to the exclusion of the possibility of normative responses on the part of the homosexual. In sum, it is proposed that the homosexual be studied in terms of the broader responses that he must make to society, including occupational choices, residence patterns, and relations with kin, among other individual and situational factors.

910 SONENSCHEIN, DAVID. "Aspects of Male Homosexual Friendships." Paper Read at the Meeting of the Southern Anthropological Society, 29 February–2 March 1968, at Gainesville, Florida. Mimeographed. 9 pp.

The formation of friendship seems to be largely a function of the specific environment in which male homosexuals first meet. Problems of maintenance present themselves in terms of a succession of an enactment of rights and obligations. A rejection of sexual interests sometimes allows other interests to develop; expectations then differ, too. The dissolution of friendships comes as the result of pairing off with a lover into a more substantial affair, or disinterest, or disappointment, or sex itself.

It is noted that friendship is one of the main coping mechanisms by which homosexuals move through daily life. Contrary to popular belief, homosexuals carry on a meaningful set of purely social friendships that allow them to exist and function in a wide variety of areas of life.

911 SONENSCHEIN, DAVID. "The Ethnography of Male Homosexual Relations." *Journal of Sex Research* 4 (2, 1968): 69–83.

During an anthropological and sociological study of a homosexual subculture in the Southwestern United States, a typology of male homosexual relations within the homosexual group was developed. The study concentrated on the "lower status" homosexuals (i.e., the middle- and lower-classes, students, and military men). Although the total homosexual community in the city was unknown, observed groups ranged from three to 100 members. The subjects of the study were from 16 to 57 years old, the modal age falling in the mid-twenties.

A six-celled table was developed to systematically identify dyadic relationships within the homosexual group. The two main variables were duration of relationship and sexuality. Two aspects of duration were identified as permanent and nonpermanent relationships. The three aspects of sexuality were social, sexual, and sociosexual. From these variables emerged six types of dyadic relationships: first order friendships (best and closest friends), second order friendships (good friends), extended sexual encounters (being kept), brief sexual encounters (one-night stand and affairs lasting up to a year), mateship (a permanent partner), and circumstantial encounters (friendships which may or may not have a sexual content).

912   SONENSCHEIN, DAVID. "Patterns of Homosexual Friendships." Master's thesis, Indiana University, 1968, 125 pp.

In 1967 the Institute for Sex Research made a detailed study of the personal adjustment of 458 homosexual males living in the Chicago area. Friendship relations reported in the data were analyzed with particular reference as to how the patterns of friendship which homosexual men develop may be related to certain aspects of their psychosocial adjustment.

Almost 20 percent of the sample had no more than two close friends, a little over half had between three and five close friends, and nearly 30 percent had six or more such friends. An overwhelming majority, around 80 percent of those considered to be close friends, were male; of these male friends, a high proportion, around 70 percent, were homosexual. Female close friends were much more likely to be heterosexual. From this and the analysis of other friendship variables, it was concluded that the homosexual subculture is a male subculture, and that it is strongly homosocial as well as homosexual.

With regard to the way overt sexual activity is involved in homosexual friendship relations, on the basis of the available statistical data as well as information gained in informal ethnographic interviews, it was suggested that sex plays a role in the initial development of such relationships, but that sexual activity is often discontinued between the two friends if the relationship becomes deeper and more personal.

913   STEARN, JESS. The Sixth Man. Garden City, N.Y.: Doubleday & Co., 1961, 286 pp.

Indicating that every sixth man is a homosexual, a journalist reports on various aspects of the homosexual world. Homosexual hangouts, professional interests, the manner in which contacts are made, problems with the police, blackmail, means of communication, and special homosexual communities are described. Other topics included are homosexual weddings, the aging homosexual, and the clubs and organizations established by and for homosexuals. Different types of homosexuals are typified, from the boy who appears in "drag" to the sedate businessman who keeps his personal life to himself.

914   STEINER, LUCIUS B. *Sex Behavior of the Homosexual.* Hollywood, Calif.: Genell Corp., 1964, 160 pp.

Male homosexuality is the subject of a popularized discussion. Through the medium of case histories, such topics as masculinity among homosexuals, Bohemian sex cults, sexual blackmail, transsexuality, phallic worship, homosexuality in prison, homosexual prostitution, and promiscuity are considered.

One conclusion is that two out of 10 men are homosexuals and that the rate is "increasing with alarming rapidity."

915   SWEET, ROXANNA BERYL THAYER. "Political and Social Action in Homophile Organizations." Ph.D. dissertation, University of California at Berkeley, 1968, 256 pp.

The law and its function in the area of sexual deviance, police rationale, and homosexual response in relation to the law are examined. Law enforcement methods applied to homosexuals are reviewed, and it is concluded that these methods reflect the general societal attitudes toward homosexuality. The societal viewpoint concerning homosexuality is discussed with emphasis upon the hostility and prejudices which the homosexual must face. The homosexual's response to these law enforcement methods and societal attitudes has been one of militancy, leading to the formation of organizations whose purpose is to effect those changes in society as deemed desirable by homosexuals. Organizations of this nature which exist in San Francisco are discussed from the standpoint of their history and organization.

Homosexuals as a group are compared with other minority groups in order to demonstrate their similarity and also to show that homosexuals display characteristics similar to those of members of other minority groups.

916   TARR, JOHN D. F. "The Male Homosexual and Venereal Disease." *GP* [*General Practitioner*] 25 (June, 1962): 91–97.

A marked increase in infectious syphilis is noted in several major American cities. In certain areas this is due largely to transmission by infected homosexual males. This mode of spreading the disease poses unusual problems and means that the general practitioner has a major responsibility in venereal disease control.

917 TARR, JOHN D. F., and LUGAR, ROBERT R. "Early Infectious Syphilis: Male Homosexual Relations as a Mode of Spread." *California Medicine* 93 (1, 1960): 35–37.

Homosexual relations play a large part in the spread of infectious syphilis. A study was made of 194 persons with primary or secondary syphilis as reported in Los Angeles County in 1959 (170 were males). Medical treatment, case records, and interviews were included in the study. Of the 170 males with syphilis, 159 identified their sexual partners—89 (56 percent) named only male sexual contacts; 21 (13.2 percent) named male and female contacts; and 49 (30.8 percent) named only female partners. There was no report of females contracting syphilis from homosexual relatins.

918 "THE Theater and the Homosexual." *Journal of the American Medical Association* 198 (9, 1966): 1027–1028.

Contemporary playwrights, by examining the subject frankly and inviting society to do the same, have become the vanguard of current social change regarding homosexuality. The source of this liberalism is seen as being, perhaps, simply the number of homosexuals in the theater. The question of whether or not homosexuals possess special theatrical talent is raised. Green and Money's "Stage-Acting, Role-Taking, and Effeminate Impersonation During Boyhood" is cited as supporting evidence for the conclusion that personality characteristics responsible for homosexuality may be responsible for the development of acting talent, and that the prevalence of homosexuality in the theater is not great simply because it offers the homosexual a social sanctuary.

919 TRICE, E. RANDOLPH. "Homosexual Transmission of Venereal Diseases." *Medical Times* 88 (11, 1960): 1286–1288.

The incidence of syphilis has been increasing, and a high proportion of the increase has been due to homosexual practices. Physicians, when handling cases of venereal disease, should be suspicious of homosexual acquisition, should take a complete case history, and should be as understanding as possible regarding such behavior.

920 TRICE, E. RANDOLPH, and CLARK, FREDERICK A., JR. "Transmission of Venereal Disease through Homosexual Practices." *Southern Medical Journal* 54 (1, 1961): 76–79.

The transmission of venereal diseases through homosexual practices is a problem of increasing importance and is more common than formerly thought. Its control requires intensive contact interviewing and investigation.

921   TRICE, E. RANDOLPH; GAYLE, SETH, JR.; and CLARK, FREDERICK
       A., JR. "The Transmission of Early Infectious Syphilis through
       Homosexual Practices." *Virginia Medical Monthly* 87 (3, 1960):
       132–134.

As noted in many parts of the nation, homosexual practices have increasingly transmitted early infectious syphilis. Homosexuals with venereal diseases are more promiscuous than their heterosexual counterparts. Control of venereal diseases in homosexuals requires intensive contact interviewing and investigation by skilled and specially trained personnel.

922   WEST, D. J. *Homosexuality.* Chicago: Aldine Publishing Co., 1968,
       304 pp.

Exploring the social and legal aspects of homosexuality in England, an attempt is made to summarize the known factual data and theories on homosexuality, to draw practical conclusions wherever possible, and to indicate areas of prevailing ignorance.

Brief attention is given to the incidence of homosexual behavior in historical times and among primitive peoples. Emphasizing the widespread contemporary occurrence of homosexuality, social and legal problems, homosexual types, and hereditary factors are discussed. Theorizing that heterosexuality is an acquired trait requiring the repression of certain homosexual tendencies natural to the human being, it is maintained that although physical and hereditary factors play a large part in governing the strength of sexual urges, psychological factors are more decisive in determining their direction.

Summarizing current methods of treatment and prevention by medical, psychoanalytic, psychological, and legal means, the inadequacies of each are pointed out. A more tolerant public attitude toward homosexuality in general is urged.

923   WEST, D. J. "Homosexuality: A Social Problem." *Sexology* 23 (1,
       1956): 22–28.

Homosexuality has always been present and in many present-day societies is socially acceptable. Homosexual behavior is not limited to man but occurs commonly in animals as well. There is no such thing as a characteristic homosexual type of physique or temperament, yet there are common traits among homosexuals (feelings of guilt and shame). Treatment which is directed toward "curing" homosexuals is very doubtful, but help in adjustment is possible. Laws prohibiting homosexual behavior should be changed.

924 WEST, D. J. *The Other Man: A Study of the Social, Legal and Clinical Aspects of Homosexuality.* New York: Whiteside and William Morrow & Co., 1955, 224 pp.

The results of research concerned with the social, legal, and clinical aspects of homosexuality (primarily male homosexuality) are presented in nontechnical language. The incidence of homosexuality, characteristics of the homosexual and the homosexual community, legal and social problems, and the causes, treatment, and prevention of homosexuality are the major topics of concern.

925 WESTWOOD, GORDON. *A Minority: A Report on the Life of the Male Homosexual in Great Britain.* London: Longmans, Green, 1960, 216 pp.

One hundred twenty-seven male homosexuals in Great Britain were interviewed to find factual information about them, including early homosexual experiences, their attempts to combat homosexuality, heterosexual interests, sexual adjustment, contacts with the law, and work and leisure activities. From the information gathered, some of the following conclusions were made: many subjects came from unsatisfactory homes; promiscuity is widespread among two-thirds of the subjects and correlates closely with other social maladjustments; the indirect effects of the law produce feelings of insecurity and a tendency to adopt unorthodox and antisocial attitudes. Homosexuals were found in every occupation, and most subjects led useful and productive lives and were reasonably well integrated with the community.

926 WESTWOOD, GORDON. "Problems of Research into Sexual Deviations." *Man and Society* 1 (1, 1961): 29–32.

Problems that a social researcher can expect in studying sexuality are described. For example, administrative difficulties can arise when organizations sponsoring research are ideologically motivated and the research finds either evidence counter to their objectives, or irrelevant evidence, or no evidence at all. Cooperation with other individuals and agencies often becomes problematic in research dealing with sexual deviation. Methodological difficulties arise concerning sampling, questionnaire construction, level of information elicited, interviewer effect and bias, and interpretation of the data.

927   YANKOWSKI, JOHN S., and WOLFF, HERMANN K. *The Tortured Sex.* Los Angeles: Holloway House Publishing Co., 1965, 224 pp.

In a work designed to "unmask" overt male homosexual behavior ". . . in the light of startling current knowledge," and under the guise of sociopsychological discussion, three case histories of homosexual males are presented, as well as chapters dealing with theories of etiology, homosexuality in history, and the gay underground.

Only the case studies and the material found in the chapter entitled "Gay Underground," are presented in a detailed fashion. The narrative accounts of the histories of individual homosexuals contain lengthy descriptions of the subjects' sexual encounters. With regard to the homosexual social community, careful descriptions are given of how "cruising" is carried on and how "pickups" are accomplished. Street addresses of parks, hotels and bars where homosexual activity is common, in such places as Los Angeles, Miami, and New York, are included.

CROSS-REFERENCES

Albany Trust. *Some Questions and Answers about Homosexuality.* London: Albany Trust, n.d., 16 pp. No. 1129.

Allen, Clifford. "The Heterosexual and Homosexual Perversions." In *A Textbook of Psychosexual Disorders,* pp. 165–204. New York: Oxford University Press, 1962. No. 288.

Fitch, J. H. "Men Convicted of Sexual Offenses Against Children: A Descriptive Follow-Up Study." *British Journal of Criminology* 3 (1, 1962): 18–37. No. 1160.

Gross, Alfred A. "Understanding the Homosexual." *National Probation and Parole Association Journal* 1 (2, 1955): 140–147. No. 1079.

"Homosexuality and Prostitution." *British Medical Journal* (4954, 1955): 1492–1493, and *British Medical Journal Supplement* (2656, 1955): 165–170. No. 452.

Hooker, Evelyn. "Homosexuality." In *International Encyclopedia of the Social Sciences,* pp. 222–233. New York: Macmillan Co., 1968. No. 172.

Jersild, Jens. *Boy Prostitution.* Translated by Oscar Bojesen. Copenhagen: G. E. C. Gad, 1956, 101 pp. No. 176.

Masters, R. E. L. *The Homosexual Revolution: A Challenging Exposé of the Social and Political Directions of a Minority Group.* New York: Julian Press, 1962, 230 pp. No. 1205.

Reiss, Albert J., Jr. "Sex Offenses: The Marginal Status of the Adolescent." *Law and Contemporary Problems* 25 (Spring, 1960): 309–333. No. 1223.

Rubin, Isadore. "Homosexuality: Conflicting Theories." 1960. Reprinted in *The Third Sex,* edited by Isadore Rubin, pp. 13–22. New York: New Book Co., 1961. No. 53.

Sonenschein, David. "Homosexuality as a Subject of Anthropological Inquiry." *Anthropological Quarterly* 39 (2, 1966): 73–82. No. 1022.

Spencer, J. C. "Contributions to the Symposium on Sexual Deviation." *Canadian Journal of Corrections* 3 (1961): 481–484. No. 574.

Ullerstam, Lars. *The Erotic Minorities.* New York: Grove Press, 1966, 172 pp. No. 1249.

Westwood, Gordon. *Society and the Homosexual.* New York: E. P. Dutton & Co., 1952, 191 pp. No. 256.

Winterstein-Lambert, E. "Observations on Homosexuals." *Bulletin de la Faculté de Médecine de Istanbul* 12 (3, 1949): 216–220. No. 604.

FEMALE

928   ALDRICH, ANN. *Carol in a Thousand Cities.* Greenwich, Conn.: Fawcett Publications, 1960, 256 pp.

A collection of essays on lesbianism is divided into three parts: lesbianism as seen in fiction, seen through the eyes of the psychoanalyst, and seen autobiographically. The first part consists of fictional accounts of lesbians by Françoise Mallet, N. Martin Kramer, Guy de Maupassant, Rose Kenmore, and Claire Morgan. The second part contains articles by four authorities presenting the psychiatric and psychoanalytic point of view. The third part presents biographical and autobiographical accounts by Ann Aldrich and an anonymous author, as well as an article on the magazine, *The Ladder.* The final article, "Please Listen to Me," contains excerpts from letters to Ann Aldrich by lesbians.

See Aldrich, Ann (no. 929), (no. 930). Beauvoir, Simone de (no. 268). Caprio, Frank S. (no. 626). Freud, Sigmund (no. 273). Thompson, Clara (no. 584).

929   ALDRICH, ANN. "A Girl Comes Out." In *Carol in a Thousand Cities,* edited by Ann Aldrich, pp. 211–224. Greenwich, Conn.: Fawcett Publications, 1960.

The first lesbian experiences of three different lesbians in three different Manhattan cliques are described.

930   ALDRICH, ANN. "The Ladder, Rung by Rung." In *Carol in a Thousand Cities,* edited by Ann Aldrich, pp. 237–247. Greenwich, Conn.: Fawcett Publications, 1960.

An analysis is given of one year's issues of *The Ladder,* a monthly publication of the Daughters of Bilitis, a female homosexual organization. The magazine's contents for the year are abstracted month by month.

931 ALDRICH, ANN. *We Walk Alone*. New York: Fawcett Publications, 1955, 143 pp.

A general discussion of female homosexuality is based on 15 years of personal experience as a lesbian and on conversations with other homosexuals and professional people interested in the subject. The lesbian is "many women," with a wide range of backgrounds and psychological characteristics. The condition is often a result of arrested normal sexual development, but is not necessarily coupled with a fear of men. Types and stereotypes, social life, and the common problems of lesbians are discussed. Bisexuality and unconscious homosexuality are considered separately. Homosexuality can be cured, but only with an active desire for cure on the part of the homosexual. Attempts at marriage as a way out of homosexuality are regarded as generally futile.

932 ALLISON, RUTH. *Lesbianism: Its Secrets and Practices*. Los Angeles: Medico Books, 1967, 167 pp.

A short introduction, which attempts to correct misconceptions and explode myths about lesbianism, is followed by a series of chapters on types of homosexual women. Fictionalized case histories are used to describe the "butch," the "fem," the "fence straddler," the "fag hag," and the "diesel dyke." A discussion of "made" lesbians and descriptions of "a truly bisexual woman," and a "lesbian by choice" are also included.

933 BASS-HASS, RITA. "The Lesbian Dyad." *Journal of Sex Research* 4 (2, 1968): 108–126.

This study describes the characteristics of lesbians, the milieu which creates and maintains lesbianism, and the role expectations of white versus non-white lesbians. Interviews and a questionnaire were given to 195 lesbians, 120 of whom were white and 75 nonwhite. None had been arrested or treated by a psychiatrist and none were institutionalized. The interviews were conducted by the researcher and one other person (a nonwhite lesbian).

Findings in three important areas of the study are reported. There was a difference in the age at which white and nonwhite lesbians entered the gay life. The whites began between the ages of 17 to 22 and the nonwhites between the ages of 23 to 30. White lesbians were unsatisfied whereas nonwhites were satisfied with their "lot in life." The attitude toward previous homosexual and heterosexual experiences before a "marriage" differed in whites and nonwhites. The latter tended to view their past sex life as more gratifying than the present and the white lesbians tended to see it as about the same as the present.

934   CORY, DONALD WEBSTER. *The Lesbian in America.* New York: Citadel Press, 1964, 288 pp.

An ethnographic study of lesbianism by a sympathetic spokesman for their male counterparts reviews causal theories (both physiological and psychological) and concludes that lesbianism is a learned condition, established when experimentation proves to be sufficiently pleasurable. Also discussed are lesbian attitudes toward males, the incidence of lesbianism, "butch" and "femme" styles, bisexuality, needs for love, family relations, "passing," the lesbian as prostitute, gay bars, the lesbian and the law, treatment for lesbianism, and organizations for lesbians.

935   "DOB Questionnaire Reveals Some Facts About Lesbians." *Ladder* 3 (12, 1959): 4–26.

This study is based upon 157 female respondents to a mailed questionnaire, and is limited by the sample size, absence of a control group, ambiguity of several of the questions, and the nonrandom nature of the sample. The group studied was quite different from those usually studied by doctors or criminologists. On the average the respondents, all of whom were members of the Daughters of Bilitis organization, were well-educated, earning above average incomes, overrespresented in the professions, and living a "stable" life. Their family backgrounds appeared to be fairly conventional. The questionnaire data showed little of the family disturbance thought to be associated with deviant personality development, although the validity of this finding is questionable. Ninety-one percent of the group judged themselves to be more homosexual than heterosexual, with 64 percent claiming to be exclusively homosexual. The majority occasionally frequented "gay bars" but they were not heavy drinkers. The first homosexual experience typically fell between the ages of 16 and 20, and 72 percent were currently engaged in a homosexual relationship. The average relationship lasted between four and five years.

936   DANIEL, SUZAN. "The Homosexual Woman in Present Day Society." *International Journal of Sexology* 7 (4, 1954): 223–224.

Lesbianism is an essential sign of our bisexuality, the adult sexual pattern becoming established according to the accidents of life or individual choice. The behavior of the homosexual woman is viewed with a certain amount of tolerance: the very nature of female homosexual relations is seen as of little importance and of only superficial pleasure; it is seen as a form of self-assertion; her love affairs are more discreet than those of male homosexuals; lesbian love affairs seldom appear in court; lesbians are very rarely attracted to young girls as male homosexuals are to young boys; and female homosexuality is probably less frequent than male homosexuality because of the security which a woman can find in marriage.

937   ELLIS, ALBERT. "The Truth about Lesbians." *Sexology* 30 (10, 1964): 652–655.

Commonly accepted myths about lesbians are refuted. It is not true that the "right man" can change a lesbian. Only a minority of lesbians are mannish-looking. They do not look for as many sexual relationships as possible, searching instead for more permanent relationships than male homosexuals are apt to seek. The lesbian is not born homosexual. It is only partly true that her knowledge of sexual techniques is greater than that of the average man. Most lesbians do not become homosexual because of an overattachment to their fathers. Most call girls are not lesbians, although some are. The "career girl" is not a suppressed lesbian. Probably more of the feminine-type lesbians become heterosexual than those of the masculine-type. Girls do not go through "lesbian phases"; whatever "crushes" they experience are not of a sexual nature.

938   "A Happy Life, a Constructive Life." In *Carol in a Thousand Cities,* edited by Ann Aldrich, pp. 225–236. Greenwich, Conn.: Fawcett Publications, 1960.

A 27-year-old female homosexual, who describes herself as a lifelong lesbian, suggests that homosexual persons may lead normal happy lives. The author is a registered nurse, "married" to a female pediatrician. She does not participate in the metropolitan gay life.

939   "Homosexuality." *Lancet* 257 (6568, 1949): 128–129.

The autobiographical sketch of a female homosexual describes an unhappy childhood during which her parents were separated, her mother was alcoholic, and her father had committed suicide. Becoming a nurse, she had many homosexual affairs throughout her life. She tried to become a heterosexual but it did not work, even though she learned to enjoy men both physically and emotionally. Afterwards, she became self-accepting and remained a homosexual.

940   KINSEY, ALFRED C.; POMEROY, WARDELL B.; MARTIN, CLYDE E.; and GEBHARD, PAUL H. *Sexual Behavior in the Human Female.* Philadelphia: W. B. Saunders & Co., 1953, 842 pp.

Case histories of 5,940 white females gathered over a 15-year period serve as the major source of data for a fact-finding survey conducted by the Institute for Sex Research.

One chapter is devoted exclusively to female homosexuality: its physiologic and psychologic bases; its mammalian and anthropologic backgrounds; its relation to age, marital status, educational level, parental occupation, and decade of birth; and its relation to rural-urban and religious backgrounds. The techniques which are used in homosexual contacts and the social significance of homosexuality are also considered.

In addition to reporting findings on female homosexual behavior, the data for females are compared with data about the human male which had been published previously.

941   MacKinnon, Jane. "The Homosexual Woman." *American Journal of Psychiatry* 103 (5, 1947): 661–664.

In this self-report, a female homosexual notes that lesbianism is easier to conceal than male homosexuality. The life of a lesbian is lonely, and homosexuals seldom like each other. The active homosexual woman initiates the relationship with the other, possibly heterosexual, woman. Realization that one is a homosexual comes slowly and painfully. Active relationships with men are for friendship only. The search for a perfect man is part of the psychology of lesbians who marry, but this only brings misery to both marriage partners.

This autobiographical account includes a brief discussion of how this lesbian has dealt with her problem through travel, and through outings with underprivileged children which appear to answer her need to have someone dependent upon her.

942   Morse, Benjamin. *The Lesbian: A Frank, Revealing Study of Women Who Turn to Their Own Sex for Love.* Derby, Conn.: Monarch Books, 1961, 142 pp.

Cases of lesbianism are presented by a psychiatrist in narrative form, as interviews, or as brief summaries. He concludes with an appeal for public education, understanding, and a revision of sex laws.

943   Querlin, Marise. *Women Without Men.* Translated by Malcolm McGraw. New York: Dell Publishing Co., 1965, 174 pp.

A journalistic study of lesbianism consisting of "documented" case histories and personal interviews is presented in a series of vignettes. Also included are short notes on medical explanations of lesbianism, physical types, lesbianism in prison, lesbian marriages in different cultures, and lesbians involved in prostitution.

944   RANCOURT, RÉJANE, and LIMOGES, THÉRÈSE. "Homosexuality Among Women." *Canadian Nurse* 63 (12, 1967): 42–44.

A general discussion of lesbianism includes its nature, incidence, varying forms, etiology, and treatment. Three forms of female homosexuality are described: a counterfeit mother-daughter relationship, a sister-sister type relationship and a pseudo man-woman relationship. The incidence of lesbianism is difficult to determine, but it may be greater than that of homosexuality among men. One of the reasons that homosexuality among females is less well known than among males may be that the indulgent social reaction toward such relationships means that fewer lesbians have guilt reactions and thus fewer lesbians seek psychiatric help. The main causes of homosexuality appear to be psychological, and psychotherapy is the successful form of treatment.

945   SAWYER, ETHEL. "A Study of a Public Lesbian Community." Master's thesis, Washington University, 1965, 46 pp.

An interacting set of Negro female overt homosexuals was subjected to a sociological and ethnological study conducted by means of participant observation, by focused and structured interviews, and by the use of informants and discussion groups. Of the many changes in homosexual patterns or roles observed throughout the study, the main one appeared to be from "fish" (feminine role) to "stud" (masculine role) or vice versa. Although "studs" have higher status as the ultimate in female homosexuality, most of the women started as "fish." A comparison of "fish" and "studs" through a questionnaire of likes and dislikes indicated that "fish" are less completely homosexual and less committed to the life. Though mate stability is highly valued, instability is the general rule. Some of the reasons for this are the public nature of the group, the surplus and/or low commitment of "fish," and the bisexuality of many in the group.

946   SIMON, WILLIAM, and GAGNON, JOHN H. "Femininity in the Lesbian Community." *Social Problems* 15 (2, 1967): 212–221.

An effort is made to bring together an organizing perspective on aspects of both the sexual and nonsexual adaptation of lesbians in terms of general female patterns, which will form a basis for systematic research.

In most cases, the female homosexual follows conventional feminine patterns in developing her commitment to sexuality and in conducting a sexual career. For most lesbians, as for most women, training in love precedes training in sexuality, and often the two cannot later be separated. Repression of sexuality is part of being a female in our society, learned by both heterosexual and homosexual women alike.

For both male and female homosexuals, one may speak of the existence of a community, although the proportion of lesbians involved in the gay world is markedly smaller. Camp behavior (that is, behavior both outraging and outrageous) is a product of the male homosexual; the lesbian is far less likely to display this behavior.

947 SIMON, WILLIAM, and GAGNON, JOHN H. "The Lesbians: A Preliminary Overview." In *Sexual Deviance,* edited by John H. Gagnon and William Simon, pp. 247–282. New York: Harper & Row, 1967.

Whereas previous studies have concentrated on the sexual aspects of lesbianism, this particular study focuses on its social aspects. Female homosexuality results from a great diversity of contingencies. A small number of subjects were interviewed at length. Excerpts from these interviews are presented to illustrate the variety of female homosexual experiences. About half of the subjects came from broken homes, and almost all of them had a strong preference for one of the parents over the other. This preference was almost equally divided between the male and the female parent. This factor, however, did not seem sufficient by itself to produce homosexuality as opposed to some other form of deviance.

A homosexual community exists for females as well as for males, providing social support, identity, and sexual contacts for its participants. Females can do without the community more easily than males, possibly because they can mask their homosexuality more easily. Few lesbians become committed to a masculine role though many may experiment with it for a time.

Common problems of homosexual females involve relations with families, earning a living, finding and keeping friends, finding an enduring love relationship, and self-acceptance. The problem of self-acceptance is heightened by a lack of positive confirmation of their private identities from the majority of people with whom they interact.

948 SPRAGUE, W. D. *The Lesbian in Our Society.* New York: Tower Publications, 1962, 189 pp.

This psychoanalytical discussion of lesbianism includes historical material, major and specialized types of lesbians, and special problems relating to lesbianism. Most of the material is presented in the form of case histories. The typical homosexual woman is described as young, tending toward promiscuity, urban, comparatively well-educated, feminine, unhappy, lonely, and insecure.

949 STEARN, JESS. *The Grapevine.* New York: Macfadden-Bartell Books, 1965, 320 pp.

Types of lesbians, their private and social lives, their marriages, organizations, and other topics relating to lesbianism are treated in a journalistic study. The material is presented mainly as informal, natural-setting interviews. It is asserted that homosexuality is increasing, probably as a result of the continuing drive of women for equality and competition with men.

950   WADE, CARLSON. *The Troubled Sex.* New York: Universal Publishing and Distribution Corp., 1961, 192 pp.

Chapters on lesbianism and how to recognize lesbians and discussions on suggested help for lesbians (such as consultation with clergy or psychiatrist) are interspersed among possibly fictionalized case histories.

951   WINNER, ALBERTINE L. "Homosexuality in Women." *Medical Press* 217 (1947): 219–220.

Notes derived from a nonpsychiatric clinical practice and from Service experience are presented by a woman physician. A little recognized characteristic of lesbianism is that the great majority of homosexual relations among women are not associated with anything that could be described as sexual intercourse. Two antisocial activities practiced by male homosexuals which are almost unknown among women are the "Choir-boy Syndrome" (little girls do not attract their own sex as little boys do) and prostitution.

There is a paucity of information on the subject of lesbianism, and further research and investigation is urged, especially research which is conducted by women.

CROSS–REFERENCES

Allen, Clifford. "The Aging Homosexual." 1959. Reprinted in *The Third Sex,* edited by Isadore Rubin, pp. 91–95. New York: New Book Co., 1961. No. 810.
Benjamin, Harry, and Masters, R. E. L. "Homosexual Prostitution." In their *Prostitution and Morality,* pp. 286–337. New York: Julian Press, 1964. No. 812.
"DOB Questionnaire Reveals Some Comparisons Between Male and Female Homosexuals." *Ladder* 4 (12, 1960): 4–25. No. 832.
Gagnon, John H., and Simon, William, eds. *Sexual Deviance.* New York: Harper & Row, 1967, 310 pp. No. 841.
Gagnon, John H., and Simon, William. "Sexual Deviance in Contemporary America." *Annals of the American Academy of Political and Social Science* 376 (Mar., 1968): 106–122. No. 842.
Kenyon, F. E. "Studies in Female Homosexuality, IV. Social and Psychiatric Aspects. V. Sexual Development, Attitudes and Experiences." *British Journal of Psychiatry* 114 (Nov., 1968): 1337–1350. No. 278.

Magee, Bryan. *One in Twenty: A Study of Homosexuality in Men and Women.* London: Secker & Warburg, 1966, 192 pp. No. 878.

Norton, Howard. *The Third Sex.* Portland, Ore.: Facts Publishing Co., 1949, 112 pp. No. 887.

Popkess, Athelstan. "Some Criminal Aspects of Abnormalities of Sex." *Practitioner* 172 (1030, 1954): 446–450. No. 891.

Reiss, Albert J., Jr. "Sex Offenses: The Marginal Status of the Adolescent." *Law and Contemporary Problems* 25 (Spring, 1960): 309–333. No. 1223.

Ross, Mathew, and Mendelsohn, Fred. "Homosexuality in College: A Preliminary Report of Data Obtained from One Hundred Thirty-three Students Seen in a University Student Health Service and a Review of Pertinent Literature." *Archives of Neurology and Psychiatry* 80 (2, 1958): 253–263. No. 898.

Schofield, Michael George. "Early Experiences, Section C. Homosexuality." In his *The Sexual Behavior of Young People,* pp. 57–59. Boston: Little, Brown & Co., 1965. No. 904.

Schur, Edwin M. *Crimes without Victims—Deviant Behavior and Public Policy: Abortion, Homosexuality, and Drug Addiction.* Englewood Cliffs, N. J.: Prentice-Hall, 1965, 180 pp. No. 907.

Tarr, John D. F., and Lugar, Robert R. "Early Infectious Syphilis: Male Homosexual Relations as a Mode of Spread." *California Medicine* 93 (1, 1960): 35–37. No. 917.

Homosexuality in History, Non-Western Societies, and Special Settings

GENERAL, MALE

952 ANDERSON, CHARLES. "On Certain Conscious and Unconscious Homosexual Responses to Warfare." *British Journal of Medical Psychology* 20 (2, 1944): 161–174.

Of 5,000 patients admitted to a neurosis center, 209 were conscious homosexuals. Homosexual tendencies, overt and latent, were determining factors in the production of neurotic disorders in 8 percent of the cases. Of the 5,000 neurotics, 4 percent were unstable conscious homosexuals, and 4 percent were latent homosexuals. Experience of active warfare can lead to the reactivation of homosexual sado-masochistic trends.

953 *The Armed Services and Homosexuality. Essays on Homosexuality, No. 1.* San Francisco: Society for Individual Rights, 1968 [12 pp.].

The homosexual who faces probable or actual service in the armed forces and active duty personnel who may be accused of homosexuality need certain information to insure that their rights are protected. In order to provide this information, the official policy of the armed services toward homosexuals, and the sequence of events and the procedure followed in cases in which a serviceman has been charged with committing homosexual acts or is suspected of possessing homosexual tendencies is described. Suggestions and recommendations are made concerning the actions that should and should not be taken by individuals accused of homosexuality in the armed services.

954   BALOGH, J. K. "Conjugal Visitations in Prisons: A Sociological Perspective." *Federal Probation* 28 (3, 1964): 52–58.

Out of 52 prison wardens contacted, 13.4 percent favored and 56 percent were opposed to conjugal visitations. Many of those in favor of conjugal visitations saw it as the lesser of two evils—homosexual relations versus heterosexual relations. However, several of the wardens who were opposed felt that conjugal visitations might, in fact, increase homosexual acts since the inmates would be more sexually stimulated after a visit.

955   BEGGS, KEITH SIDDONS. "Some Legal, Social and Psychiatric Aspects of Homosexual Behavior: A Guide for the Social Worker in the Sex Clinic." Master's thesis, University of Wisconsin, 1950, 298 pp.

Chapter one provides definitions of the terms used in this discussion. Homosexuality is seen as "the desire for or the actual sexual contact between two people of the same sex," and can be either overt or latent. Kinsey's 7-point sexuality scale is discussed in relation to the classification of homosexuals. In chapter two the historical and anthropological aspects of homosexuality are considered. Homosexuality in Ancient Greece and the Roman Empire is discussed along with certain early Judeo-Christian concepts. The anthropological account of homosexuality includes examples of present-day cultural groups that accept homosexuality. Chapter three includes a general discussion of the legal aspects of homosexuality and specifically focuses on sodomy laws, sexual psychopath laws, and the courts' interpretations of these laws. Chapter four is an examination of "one-sex communities." Homosexuality practiced in closed one-sex communities (e.g., prisons, reformatories) and open one-sex communities (e.g., armed forces, noncoed schools) are discussed. In chapter five various theories of causation are presented. The theories discussed include: the theory of inheritance, the hormone–endocrine theory, psychoanalytic theories, the psychotic theory, and the symbiotic behaviorism theory. Chapter six concerns itself with the therapy and cure of homosexuality. The works and findings of prominent researchers are discussed. Concluding statements stress the need for a "social cure," the understanding and social acceptance of homosexuality, as well as an individual cure.

956   BLOCH, HERBERT A. "Social Pressures of Confinement Toward Sexual Deviation." *Journal of Social Therapy* 1 (3, 1955): 112–125.

The process of "prisonization" and the factors which play an important part in the completion of the process, as well as the group relationships which develop among prisoners, are described.

The prison environment has an effect upon the development of various forms of sexual deviation. The structure of the prison community is analyzed, together with various significant features of the community which may cause a predisposition toward sexual deviation. The manifest functions and latent elements of the prison structure are defined. The rules for the maintenance and custody of the inmates, the legally defined relationships between official staff and inmates, and the regulatory procedures intended to safeguard the public and maintain control within the institution are all examples of the manifest functions. The latent functions consist of the spontaneous relationships which come into being within the official framework, and the ways in which the inmates use the official framework to satisfy their needs. The degree to which a man becomes "prisonized" is crucial in determining his inclination toward sexual deviation.

957   BLUESTONE, HARVEY; O'MALLEY, EDWARD P.; and CONNELL, SYDNEY. "Homosexuals in Prison." *Corrective Psychiatry and Journal of Social Therapy* 12 (1, 1966): 13–24.

A psychiatric and social study of homosexuals who were in prison gives individual demographic and personal data for 31 exhibitionistic, adolescent homosexuals from Rikers Island Prison, New York City. In institutions for males homosexuality is a relatively less frequent condition than in institutions for women. No correlation was found to exist between homosexuality and crime. Homosexuals in prison have higher educational levels, better work histories, and less drug addiction than do other prisoners.

958   "The Borstal Puzzle." *Lancet* 260 (6670, 1951): 1399–1400.

Borstals (institutions for young offenders between 16 and 21) are discussed in the light of a report compiled by a special committee appointed by the Secretary of State, which had been assigned the task of reviewing punishment in prisons, borstals, approved schools and remand homes. Of the 175 offenses which occurred in four of the borstals during 1947–1949, only five involved homosexual behavior. The committee advised that this "small percentage of untreatable practising homosexuals" should be removed from the borstals and placed in prisons.

Neither this recommendation nor others dealing with various types of punishment and discipline in institutions for young offenders is supported by the author of the present article.

959 BRANHAM, VERNON C. "Behavior Disorders in Prison." *Journal of Criminal Psychopathology* 1 (3, 1940): 234–246.

A classificatory scheme for analyzing the motivation behind violations of rules by prison inmates is sought through a study of guards' reports on inmates. Since individuals tend to repeat offenses, it is thought that some sort of classification should be possible.

In a Freudian approach the offenders are divided into three categories based on the two variables of time and tension: the sustained tension group, the rhythmically recurring tension group, and the unpredictable tension group. Homosexuals are in the sustained tension group which includes individuals whose affective tone and drive to overt behavior never subside to normal levels.

The main cause of homosexuality is the fixation of the libido at the level in which the male identifies with the father in an avoidance of incest with the mother. However, identification with the mother and hostility toward the father may take place, causing hostility as well as homosexuality.

960 BROWN, JULIA S. "A Comparative Study of Deviations from Sexual Mores." *American Sociological Review* 17 (2, 1952): 135–146.

The study focused upon the forms of sexual behavior most generally forbidden and the severity with which they were punished. The sample consisted of 110 societies on which sufficient information on their sexual mores could be obtained from the Human Relations Area File. The findings included: a high positive correlation was found between the frequency with which a given type of behavior was taboo and the severity of the punishment; incest, abduction, and rape were most frequently taboo and most severely punished; the sexual mores of any given society tended to be integrated; punishment tended to be more severe for those deviations which involved greater numbers of individuals, which transgressed marital bonds, and which contained elements of aggression; and in the great majority of cases the sexual mores were actively upheld by human agents and in some cases supplemented by supernatural sanctions.

Male homosexuality was punished by 68 percent of the 44 societies in which it was reported to occur. Female homosexuality was punished in four of the 12 societies in which it was reported. The severity of punishment, rated on a 4-point scale, with regard to homosexuality was relatively low.

Most societies interpreted homosexual acts as affecting only the participants or members of their immediate families.

961 BURTON, RICHARD. "Terminal Essay: The Book of the Thousand Nights and a Night." 1886. Reprinted in *Homosexuality: A Cross Cultural Approach,* edited by Donald Webster Cory, pp. 207–247. New York: Julian Press, 1956.

In a literary and anthropological study of homosexuality among the Arabs, it is argued that homosexuality and related practices, like pederasty, are climatic and geographical, thriving in what is called the "Sotadic Zone" (Asia Minor and Mesopotamia). The material was gathered from the author's travels and from literary sources.

962 CARSTAIRS, G. MORRIS. "Cultural Differences in Sexual Deviation." In *The Pathology and Treatment of Sexual Deviation: A Methodological Approach,* edited by Ismond Rosen, pp. 419–434. London: Oxford University Press, 1964.

In an anthropological survey of cultural variations of sexual deviance, one section, in which various studies are reviewed, is devoted to homosexuality. One of these studies found that 64 percent of the societies which are included in the Human Relations Area Files considered homosexual activities of one sort or another normal and socially acceptable for certain members of the community. It is argued that the evidence "supports the contention that all human beings are capable of learning to respond in homosexual relationships; this potentiality is realized in all the members of some societies, but in only a few members of others."

963 CARSTAIRS, G. MORRIS. "Hinjra and Jiryan: Two Derivatives of Hindu Attitudes to Sexuality." *British Journal of Medical Psychology* 29 (2, 1956): 128–138.

The attitudes of high-caste Hindus in a northern Indian village toward homosexuality and spermatorrhea are reported. Although homosexuality is repudiated. and openly denounced, it is practiced secretly.

964 CARSTAIRS, G. MORRIS, and GRYGIER, TADEUSZ G. "Anthropological, Psychometric, and Psychotherapeutic Aspects of Homosexuality." *Bulletin of the British Psychological Society* 32 (1957): 46–47.

In the first of two papers read at a symposium held by the British Psychological Society in November, 1956, the anthropological aspects of homosexuality are discussed. Particular instances of the wide range of cultural attitudes toward homosexuality are cited with examples from various tribes and countries. The factors which determine the quality of such attitudes are whether sexual relations in general are repressed or easygoing, and whether there is an overemphasis on the domination of the male in socioeconomic roles. The variety of social manifestations of homosexual behavior indicates that it is due more to social conditioning than to constitutional determinants. Anthropological studies confirm that homosexuality is a greater problem among men than among women.

In the second paper the difficulties of research into the genesis and treatment of homosexuality are discussed, the existing psychological tests are surveyed, and their efficiency in this field is evaluated.

965   COOKE, R. A., and RODRIGUE, R. B. "Amoebic Balanitis." *Medical Journal of Australia* 51 (4, 1964): 114–116.

Amoebic balanitis, a disease causing rupture of the prepuce and—if unchecked—erosion of the shaft of the penis, is a condition which is widespread throughout New Guinea and has been reported from other tropical and nontropical countries. The condition, which must be distinguished from other forms of balanitis and from carcinoma, responds rapidly and dramatically to emetine treatment and can also be cured by circumcision.

Detailed descriptions of eight cases of amoebic balanitis in natives of Australian New Guinea are given. Since examinations of the wives of the patients revealed no evidence of amoebic vaginitis, and since it is known that sodomy is common among the inhabitants of this area, it is thought that the most likely method of infection in these cases is through homosexual contact.

966   CORY, DONALD WEBSTER. "Homosexuality in Prison." *Journal of Social Therapy* 1 (3, 1955): 137–140.

Prison officials should legalize heterosexual contacts in prison or home visits by prisoners, and homosexual behavior in prison should not be punished unless force is involved. There are four classes or groups of individuals in prison: exclusive heterosexuals who never engage in homosexual activity, exclusive homosexuals who continue their homosexual activities in prison, those whose only homosexual experience is while they are inside the prison, and those who had homosexual contacts prior to their entrance into prison but who are primarily heterosexual in their arousal and behavior.

967   DAVENPORT, WILLIAM. "Sexual Patterns and Their Regulation in a Society of the Southwest Pacific." In *Sex and Behavior,* edited by Frank A. Beach, pp. 164–207. New York: John Wiley & Sons, 1965.

Verbal reports and attitudes about sexual behavior were used to study some of the regulatory norms by means of which sexual behavior is evaluated and presumably patterned in a group of Melanesian Islands.

Male homosexuality is a socially approved substitute for heterosexual intercourse; in fact, it is an activity that is engaged in extensively by nearly every male. There are two types of homosexuality, that between young single males of similar age and that between older men and young boys. In the relationship between the young men the participants are usually good friends or relatives accommodating one another or fulfilling obligations. In the relationship between the older men and the young boys, the older male takes the active role and is obligated to give the boy presents in return.

968   DAVIS, ALAN J. "Report on Sexual Assaults in the Philadelphia Prison System and Sheriff's Vans." Mimeographed, [1968], 103 pp.

An investigation conducted jointly by the Philadelphia District Attorney's Office and Police Department reports "intolerable" prison conditions leading to an estimated 2,000 sexual assaults (among 60,000 prisoners) during the period from June, 1966, through July, 1968. Truly consensual homosexual acts were excluded from the definition of the term "sexual assault." Data were obtained by interviewing a sample of 5 percent of the inmates and by reviewing all reports prepared by the prison system since June, 1966, of investigations and internal disciplinary actions relating to homosexual assaults or narcotics.

In the Philadelphia system sexual assaults are epidemic. Virtually every slightly-built young man is sexually approached within hours of his admission to prison. Forcible sexual assaults are a major cause of "consensual" homosexuality. Homosexual favors can be purchased. Aggressors tend to be older, larger, and more serious offenders than victims. Sexual assaults are not primarily caused by sexual deprivation, but are expressions of anger, frustration, and racial tensions (over 80 percent of the prison population is Negro, 56 percent of the documented sexual assaults involved Negro aggressors and white victims and none involved white aggressors and Negro victims) which are intensified by imprisonment.

The two major causes of the assaults are inadequate guard supervision and idleness due to gross underprograming. Contributory causes are inadequate diagnostic and classification procedures, ineffective disciplinary and investigatory procedures, and defects in prison structural designs. The sheriff's vans employed for transporting prisoners to court were inadequate for the purpose and permitted sexual assaults and violence without observation by the drivers.

A detailed proposal for controlling the assaults by supervision and constructive outlets for frustration and aggression is presented.

969   DEVEREUX, GEORGE. "Institutionalized Homosexuality of the Mohave Indians." 1937. Reprinted in *The Problem of Homosexuality in Modern America,* edited by Hendrik M. Ruitenbeek, pp. 183–226. New York: E. P. Dutton & Co., 1963.

Two types of homosexuality accepted among the Mohave Indians are described. Males who dress as women and take on a completely female role are known as *alyhā.* Female homosexuals who assume male roles are called *hwamē.* In each case their acceptance by others is complete, with the homosexual always referred to by the assumed sex, unless the intent is to insult.

The data were obtained in three field trips to Needles, California, and Parker, Arizona. The ceremony of initiation, the physiological and psychological patterns assumed by homosexuals, courtship, and social aspects of their role, as well as case histories, are described. Interviews with persons who knew individuals who had accepted homosexual roles are quoted extensively.

970   DEVEREUX, GEORGE, and MOOS, MALCOLM C. "The Social Structure of Prisons, and the Organic Tensions." *Journal of Criminal Psychopathology* 4 (2, 1942): 306–324.

Data gathered during a study of the penal system of Alabama are given a theoretical interpretation. The case histories of a pair of imprisoned male homosexuals are presented. The existential, theoretical, and practical difficulties involved in the study of prison homosexuality are indicated. Existing interpretations of prison homosexuality are unsatisfactory because it is not a universal phenomenon and does not occur simply as a result of the unavailability of heterosexual outlets. Segregation under atypical conditions is only one of the factors responsible for homosexual behavior in prison. Other factors include social segregation, defense against isolation, the problem of regression and infantilism, social stratification, social negativism, the gesture ("Prison homosexuality is the sport of the kings of prison, glamorous and hateful to the casual criminal."), and short-range planning (in response to proximate rather than remote stimuli). In sum, it is the prison system rather than "human" or "criminal nature" that causes prison homosexuality.

971   DINGWALL, ERIC J. "Homosexuality through the Ages." *Sexology* 25 (9, 1959): 584–589; (11, 1959): 710–715. Reprinted in *The Third Sex,* edited by Isadore Rubin, pp. 28–39. New York: New Book Co., 1961.

This historical account of the prevalence of homosexuality refers especially to its occurrence in Greece and Rome. Although homosexual activities have been carried on in nearly every part of the world at different times, in general they have never aroused the horror and disgust with which the Western world has regarded them since the rise of Christianity. Religious, social, and legal punishments (famous examples are given) have never been able to eliminate homosexuality.

972　DRUSS, RICHARD G. "Cases of Suspected Homosexuality Seen at an Army Mental Hygiene Consultation Service." *Psychiatric Quarterly* 41 (1, 1967): 62–70.

Procedures for processing apprehended homosexuals in the United States military services are discussed. A diagnostic evaluation based on the commanding officer's report, a medical report, and the report of the apprehending personnel or the individual himself is used to determine homosexuality. Treatment is limited because immediate separation from the service is thought advisable in all cases except those of the most immature young soldiers for whom curative results are possible.

Most of the cases (40 men sent to an Army Mental Hygiene Consultation Service to be diagnosed) were involuntary and the few self-referred homosexuals were usually there as the result of seeking treatment for some other mental disorder. Whether or not to report an admitted homosexual to his superior officer is an ethical dilemma for the physician in the military services. On the one hand, this violates the normal standard of patient-doctor confidence; on the other, it is a direct violation of military law. It is believed that immediate separation from duty with no punitive measures is the best solution to this problem. Also, an effort should be made to guide the discharged soldier to a counseling service in his home community.

973　EDWARDES, ALLEN. *The Jewel in the Lotus.* New York: Julian Press, 1959, 293 pp.

An historical survey of the sexual culture of the East emphasizes variations of relationships and techniques and social reaction to these variations. Homosexuality and other variations from heterosexuality have mainly been regarded as a matter of taste, tolerated to a high degree in Eastern cultures.

974　EDWARDES, ALLEN, and MASTERS, R. E. L. *The Cradle of Erotica.* New York: Julian Press, 1962, 362 pp.

This historical survey of Afro-Asian sexual expression from the closing decades of the nineteenth century into the twentieth century, indicates differences between East and West in freedom of sexual expression. Homosexual practices and techniques are described, principally in relation to anal intercourse, masturbation, and oral intercourse.

975 EDWARDS, J. O., and HAY, J. W. "How Can the Correction Officer Prevent Acts of Sex Perversion in a Penal Institution?" *Prison World: American Journal of Corrections* 14 (3, 1952): 10–12.

Two correctional officers give specific practical advice on controlling homosexuality in prison. Early recognition is stressed, along with provision of creative channels of activity. Segregation of inmates according to sexual orientation is de-emphasized.

976 EVERHARD, JOHN A. "Problems Involving the Disposition of Homosexuals in the Service." *United States Air Force Judge Advocate General's Bulletin* 2 (6, 1960): 20–23.

The rights and privileges of an alleged homosexual and the desirability of elimination from the service of homosexual cases which fall under Air Force Regulations 35–36 are discussed. An individual who is branded as a homosexual becomes a liability to a military organization by lowering the moral fiber of the military community. Service regulations divide homosexuality into three classes: unwilling participation, willing participation, and preservice acts or the presence of established homosexual tendencies. Military procedures dealing with homosexuality and the difficulties inherent in hearings regarding this problem are described.

977 FISHER, SAUL H. "A Note on Male Homosexuality and the Role of Women in Ancient Greece." In *Sexual Inversion: The Multiple Roots of Homosexuality,* edited by Judd Marmor, pp. 165–172. New York: Basic Books, 1965.

The conditions which gave rise to homosexuality in ancient Greece are briefly considered. Homosexuality was not always prevalent in Greece, but flourished in the form of pederasty, or love of boys, principally from the sixth century B.C. on, coinciding with the development of a monetary, commercial, and slave form of society. Pederasty also coincided with the degraded status of women, suggesting that today social factors must be taken into account in approaching the problem of homosexuality.

978 FLACELIÈRE, ROBERT. "Homosexuality." In *Love in Ancient Greece,* pp. 49–85. Translated by James Cleugh. London: F. Muller, 1962.

Pederasty flourished in Greece during the classical period from the sixth to the fourth centuries B.C. While it often assumed a "platonic" form, there is much evidence from surviving Greek literature of its existence in physical form as well. Encouraged by abnormal social conditions, such as life in military camps or purely masculine communities, it was also an integral part of the tutorial method of secondary education, and was practiced especially in the gymnasia. Although carnal practices between men and youths were proscribed by law, such practices were common and fashionable among the upper classes.

Although arguments are presented for both sides, the allegations attributing the practice of lesbianism to Sappho are considered as dubious. There is at least the possibility that her school for girls and others of its kind may have fostered sexual inversion among its pupils.

979   FORD, CLELLAN S., and BEACH, FRANK A. *Patterns of Sexual Behavior.* New York: Harper & Brothers, 1951, 307 pp.

A psychoanalytical and anthropological investigation of sexual behavior cross-culturally and cross-species includes a chapter on homosexual behavior. The general introduction on homosexuality and its setting in antiquity is followed by discussion of attitudes toward and the frequency of homosexual behavior among men and women in the United States. Attitudes toward homosexuality in 76 other human cultures are also considered; in most of the societies (49 out of 76) it is found to be tolerated and even encouraged.

The conclusion is reached that human homosexual tendencies have a definite biological basis and appear to exist in a large majority of both sexes, although these tendencies may never be recognized and although no overt homosexual behavior may ever occur.

980   GAGNON, John H., and SIMON, WILLIAM. "The Social Meaning of Prison Homosexuality." *Federal Probation* 32 (1, 1968): 23–29.

Homosexuality in prisons serves to meet the basic needs of affection and security; it does not serve principally as an outlet for sexual desire. This observation is based on data obtained from secondary source material.

Homosexuality serves quite different functions for male prisoners than it does for women prisoners. Three basic causes of homosexuality among male prisoners are the need for affection, the validation of their masculinity, and a way of coping with prison life. Female prisoners, on the other hand, tend to establish pseudo families of which the homosexual partner is only a part. Other than allowing periodic visits home, no other way to control homosexual activity is suggested.

981   GARDE, NOEL I. *Jonathan to Gide: The Homosexual in History.* New York: Vantage Press, 1964, 751 pp.

A chronological list of biographies, each followed by one or more citations to the work containing the allegation of homosexuality, is followed by a list of subjects arranged by nationality, and by professions and occupations. An alphabetical index of the subjects is also provided. Magnus Hirschfeld and Richard Burton were major sources used for the allegations. With the exception of Nijinsky and Gide, those living or those dead less than a generation are excluded. The Kinsey 7-point scale was expanded to include repressed, latent, or sublimated homosexuals who were chaste or celibate. Certain subjects with admittedly dubious allegations of homosexuality are included: Jesus, Richard the Lion-Hearted, George Washington, Wild Bill Hickok and Magnus Hirschfeld.

982   GIOSCIA, NICOLAI. "The Gag Reflex and Fellatio." *American Journal of Psychiatry* 107 (5, 1950): 380.

A study of 1,404 soldiers, admitted to military hospitals for psychiatric evaluation and routine physical examinations, was conducted in 1944 to test for the presence or absence of the gag reflex. Twelve percent of the subjects showed no gag reflex. The uvula, soft palate, and pharyngeal vault were desensitized due to conditioning brought about by the control of the reflex during the act of fellatio.

As a result of these findings, the use of the gag reflex test was extended to civilian hospitals and was found to be a definite aid in screening individuals for military service and "positions where the sexual deviant must be eliminated."

983   GRAHAM, JAMES. *The Homosexual Kings of England.* London: Tandem, 1968, 92 pp.

Popularized accounts of homosexual aspects of the lives of six kings of England include speculations on the degree to which deviancy affected the manner and event of their deaths. The kings whose names are linked with homosexuality are William Rufus, Richard I, Edward II, Richard II, James I, and William III.

984   GRECO, MARSHALL C., and WRIGHT, JAMES C. "The Correctional Institution in the Etiology of Chronic Homosexuality." *American Journal of Orthopsychiatry* 14 (2, 1944): 295–307.

To discover the relationship between incarceration and the development of perverted sexual practices in reform school inmates, 10 chronic homosexuals and a control group of 10 heterosexuals incarcerated at the Pennsylvania Industrial School were studied. Personal interviews with the authors, case histories compiled by the institution, and a "write your own story" technique were used as methods of data collection.

Some inmates succumbed to homosexual practices under the same set of influences (erotic talk, solicitation by older inmates, and witnessing perverted acts) that others did not succumb to, due to conditioning which occurred while they were very young and sexually immature.

The psychological mechanisms that enable experiences occurring early in life to condition one to react in a particular way years later are: experiences occurring in highly emotional settings; later life channels developing as a consequence of the conscious and unconscious influence of individuals to whom a person has reacted emotionally; and an emotional conditioning much stronger and more influential than a mere intellectual one.

Therapeutic techniques in an institution should include a thorough and personal case history to determine whether the individual has been violated or is predisposed to serious sexual aberration. Once detected, he should be provided with adequate employment and recreational outlets which would help sublimate his sexual drives.

985   HAHN, MILTON E., and ATKINSON, BYRON H. "The Sexually Deviate Student." *School and Society* 82 (2068, 1955): 85–87.

A concern with students whose sexual behavior places them in conflict with the educational institutions they are attending (homosexuality is used as an example) led to the development of procedures designed to protect the reputation of the institution. At the same time, however, these procedures are designed to protect the individual by discriminating among types and classes of deviates.

986   HAINES, WILLIAM H. "Homosexuality." *Journal of Social Therapy* 1 (3, 1955): 132–136.

A description of homosexuality in prison lists three types of homosexuals found there. These are the frank homosexual—the prison "wolf" or the obvious feminine inmates; the feeble-minded, mentally ill, or insane inmates who do not know what they are doing but who are just used sexually by others; and the occasional or situational homosexual. Homosexuality should not be allowed in prison and those who are caught behaving homosexually should be given psychotherapy.

987   HAINES, WILLIAM H., and MCLAUGHLIN, JOHN J. "Treatment of the Homosexual in Prison." *Diseases of the Nervous System* 13 (3, 1952): 85–87.

Psychiatry has not provided any answers for handling sexual deviates in prison or for their rehabilitation. Homosexuals in prison should not be allowed to "run wild," and, if need be, should be segregated from others.

988   HAMBLY, WILFRID D. "Primitive Homosexuality." *Sexology* 22 (3, 1955): 158–163.

A survey of the literature in anthropology shows that homosexuality has existed and still exists among primitive peoples, although it is not nearly so common as in our own society. Homosexuality is a form of sexual expression which has a long and ancient history in all civilizations.

989   HARRISON, SAUL I., and KLAPMAN, HOWARD J. "Relationships Between Social Forces and Homosexual Behavior Observed in a Children's Psychiatric Hospital." *Journal of the American Academy of Child Psychiatry* 5 (1, 1966): 105–110.

The observation in a children's psychiatric hospital of a natural experiment in which a youngster's overt homosexual behavior seemed to be partly a consequence of a change in his immediate social environment is described. This afforded an opportunity to study current environmental circumstances or immediate precipitating factors which are so infrequently referred to in the literature.

990   HOFFMAN, MARTIN. "The Problem of Male Homosexuality in Classical Antiquity: A Prolegomenon." Working Paper prepared for the National Institute of Mental Health Task Force on Homosexuality. Mimeographed. San Francisco, n.d., 6 pp.

It is concluded that a great deal of scholarly research remains to be done on the character of homosexuality in ancient Greece and Rome if more is to be known about this topic. An experienced classicist with a firm grasp of ancient Greek and Latin, knowledge of the social history of everyday ancient life, and knowledge of psychiatry and social science (or collaboration with someone who has that knowledge), should examine primary rather than secondary sources. At present, secondary sources are contradictory and inadequate, tending to be colored by the authors' own personal attitudes.

991   HUFFMAN, ARTHUR V. "Problems Precipitated by Homosexual Approaches of Youthful First Offenders." *Journal of Social Therapy* 7 (4, 1961): 216–222.

It is hypothesized that the existing environment of correctional institutions favors the development of sexual abnormalities. The cases of 62 youthful first offenders who underwent psychiatric observation following incidents of sexual involvement are cited. Twenty-seven were found to be in need of mental treatment. The 27 in need of mental treatment were cases of situational reactions to homosexual advances, which had caused them extreme anxiety, confusion, and tension. It is believed that if a controlled study of these cases were pursued following their release from prison the hypothesis would be supported.

992   HUFFMAN, ARTHUR V. "Sex Deviation in a Prison Community." *Journal of Social Therapy* 6 (3, 1960): 170–181.

The patterns of sexual outlet in an all-male prison are reported. There are differences between Negro and white homosexual behavior. Unlike the whites, Negroes practice homosexuality in a primitive way, according to stimulus and response, and without emotion. The true homosexuals participate very rarely in prison homosexuality, as they are generally segregated by the prison personnel.

993   JAMES, ANATOLE. "Homosexuality and 'Artistic' Professions." *International Journal of Sexology* 8 (1, 1954): 24–25.

In modern times new concepts of masculinity have emerged. Masculine good looks have been stressed, primarily due to the influence of the cinema and the idolizing of the "hero" or "Adonis." The Diaghilev Russian Ballet was even more important in changing the ordinary person's ideas about male homosexuality and the "arts." Its effect upon homosexuals themselves is discussed. Reference is made to the increasing importance to men of clothes and personal appearance.

994   KARPMAN, BENJAMIN. "Sex Life in Prison." *Journal of Criminal Law and Criminology* 38 (5, 1948): 475–486.

The physical arrangements and psychological aspects of prison favor the development of abnormal sexual behavior. Although at first prisoners try to avoid aberrant sexual practices, sublimation is almost impossible since a prisoner has no other outlets for his energy. Therefore, he turns to masturbation and homosexuality. These practices tend to have long-range effects, lasting past the prison term. Prison authorities could correct this by condoning "immorality" and allowing prostitution, or, even better, could recognize the prisoners as psychically sick persons and have them treated in hospitals.

995   KIRKHAM, GEORGE LESTER. "Homosexuality and Its Alternatives in a Prison Setting." Master's thesis, San Jose State College, 1966, 246 pp.

Research on sexuality in a prison setting conducted at the Soledad, California, Correctional Training Facility is reported. A questionnaire developed after a three-month period of observation was administered to a "stratified and randomized sampling" of the prison population. The schedule of questions included inquiries about sexual abstinence, masturbation, and homosexuality, as well as questions pertaining to the phenomenon of "sex pressuring" (i.e., coercive procurement of homosexual relations), and questions which would provide a comparison of the respondents' attitudes toward masturbation and homosexuality when practiced inside the prison community as opposed to attitudes toward these same behaviors when carried out in conventional society.

The conclusions were that inmates perceive the deprivation of sexual and social relations with women as a severely frustrating aspect of incarceration; that abstinence is not regarded as an acceptable or desirable response to heterosexual deprivation; that masturbation, on the other hand, is viewed as a legitimate response and that it represents the modal adaptation to the prison sexual situation; and that homosexual activity is not regarded as a probable or legitimate response to heterosexual deprivation, although status distinctions are made on the basis of homosexual "role." Sex "pressuring" is condemned, and "the inmate community's attitude toward abstinence, masturbation, and homosexuality in free society is quite congruous with its attitude toward these same phenomena within the institution." Data are analyzed according to race and ethnic group membership, marital status, age, type of offense, and length of sentence of respondents. A sample questionnaire is contained in an appendix.

.An elaborate typology of homosexually involved prisoners based on Sykes' tripartite typology of "wolf," "punk," and "queen" is presented, and the homosexual subculture is described in some detail. Suggestions for attenuating and containing homosexuality within the prison setting are included, and a glossary of prison sexual jargon is provided.

996   LANDES, RUTH. "A Cult Matriarchate and Male Homosexuality." *Journal of Abnormal and Social Psychology* 35 (3, 1940): 386–397.

An anthropological investigation was made of the extent to which male homosexuality becomes a social problem in different cultures.

The extent varies with the attitudes taken toward homosexuality by the different cultures. One of the special attitudes is that which distinguishes sharply between the active and the passive homosexual, with the latter usually protected and even encouraged.

997   LAYARD, JOHN. "Homo-eroticism in Primitive Society as a Function of the Self." *Journal of Analytical Psychology* 4 (2, 1959): 101–115.

A long-term study of the organization of primitive society as an externalized form of the self and its homoerotic aspect is summarized. Through the arrangement of marriages, primitive societies in Australia and elsewhere in Oceania are externally endogamous and internally exogamous. Society is divided into four "kinship sections" which resemble the basic four functions of the self. The method of arranging marriages in brother-sister pairs in such a way that both matrilineal and patrilineal rules of exogamy are observed is viewed as contributing to the development of homoeroticism. Evidence regarding the homosexual act as an incest-substitute is indicated.

998 LEGMAN, GERSHON; LEA, HENRY CHARLES; WRIGHT, THOMAS; WITT, GEORGE H.; TENNENT, JAMES; and DUGDALE, WILLIAM. *The Guilt of the Templars.* New York: Basic Books, 1966, 308 pp.

A series of essays describes the suppression of the Knights Templars in the 1300's on accusations of heresy and other offenses, including homosexuality —though the real reason may have been their political power and wealth. According to the essay by G. Legman, many of the accusations, including those of homosexuality, were true. Confessions and other evidence of homosexual practices are cited, and tortures, punishments, and executions that the Templars underwent are described. An essay by Henry Charles Lea, on the other hand, argues the innocence of the Templars, asserting that the confessions were manufactured and extorted under torture, and that the secret rites were actually a farce, not completely performed or believed in.

999 LEWINSOHN, RICHARD. *A History of Sexual Customs.* New York: Harper & Brothers, 1958, 424 pp.

Past and present sexual practices and customs in all parts of the world are described. Homosexuality in Babylon, Greece, Rome, Germany, the United States, and elsewhere is discussed. Famous cases of homosexuality, including those of Count Eulenberg and Oscar Wilde, are reported.

1000 LICHT, HANS. "Male Homosexuality in Ancient Greece." 1932. Reprinted in *Homosexuality: A Cross Cultural Approach,* edited by Donald Webster Cory, pp. 267–349. New York: Julian Press, 1956.

An historical and literary study of homosexuality in ancient Greece covers the Greek ideals of beauty and boyhood, homosexuality in Greek poetry, and homosexuality in Greek mythology. Greek terminology relevant to homosexuality is discussed, and it is pointed out that the Greek ideal of love of boys referred only to sexually mature youths with punishment for the seduction of those who were younger. Exaltation of boyish beauty in literature and art is extensively reviewed. The eyes, cheeks, and hair were particularly admired. The role of male prostitution is traced, and the ethics and pros and cons of the love of boys are surveyed from the literary viewpoint. A dozen poets are examined individually for their treatments of the subject.

1001 LINDNER, ROBERT. "Sex in Prison." *Complex* 6 (Fall, 1951): 5–20.

Maintaining that sexual behavior is largely unstudied and unknown, an attempt is made to remedy this shortcoming with several "inside observations" based on ideas "formulated over a decade of intimate contact with prisoners in thousands of hours of psychotherapy."

Sexual deviants are not created by the prison situation. Instead, latent tendencies are exposed by the institutional setting. Most deviants in the unisexual environment of the prison are not homosexual, which denotes a life style. Rather a large number of heterosexuals are forced to seek a homoerotic sexual outlet for a period of time. The pressures of erotic desire, active homosexual prisoners, and psychopathic prisoners seeking a sex outlet with a threat of violence usually result in mild forms of mental breakdown in every prisoner. Some examples of prisoner "love" notes are appended.

1002 LIPTON, HARRY R. "Stress in Correctional Institutions." *Journal of Social Therapy* 6 (4, 1960): 216–223.

In a study of anxiety among prisoners, homosexuality is discussed as a frequent source for acute anxiety states. Those prisoners who are homosexually predisposed or sexually fixated at an early stage are often victims of anxiety. Their stress can be caused either by internal struggles over homosexual activities or impulses or by a fear of punishment for homosexual acts. Other homosexuals—insecure by nature—often experience anxiety shortly before release. Once paroled, they occasionally will commit an antisocial act in order to be reunited with a fellow homosexual prisoner. The preferred treatment for homosexual anxieties is isolation in a private room for several days, followed by supervised contact with inmates. No stimulating environment (the presence of effeminate prisoners) should be allowed.

1003 LOESER, LEWIS H. "The Sexual Psychopath in the Military Service: A Study of 270 Cases." *American Journal of Psychiatry* 102 (Jul., 1945): 92–101.

The case records of 270 sexual offenders discharged from the 36th Station Hospital (NP) were studied to find the general characteristics of sexual offenders in the military service.

The problem of sexual psychopathy in the military service is essentially that of homosexuality. There has been a lack of uniformity in medico-legal handling of these cases. There is less reported homosexuality among black troops than among white. The sexual psychopath is largely derived from urban areas, and broken homes form the background of 41 percent. They are predominantly skilled and semiskilled workers. Their intelligence and education are higher than that of other Army personnel. They have higher rankings than the average member of the Army.

1004 MacDONALD, JOHN M. "Homosexuality in Ex-Prisoners." *Journal of the American Medical Association* 175 (9, 1961): 834.

The report of an experiment with rats indicates that when rats are sexually segregated, they will commence homosexual behavior. If the segregation is terminated, heterosexual behavior is resumed. The length of time before heterosexual behavior is resumed depends upon the length of the period of segregation.

While this rule appears to hold true for other animals, it is not certain whether it holds true for human beings or not, and therefore no inference can be drawn about whether sexual segregation and participation in homosexual activities in prison will inhibit a return to heterosexual activity upon release.

1005 MACKWOOD, JOHN CHARSLEY. "A Note on the Psychotherapeutic Treatment of Homosexuality in Prison." *Medical Press* 217 (Sept. 3, 1947): 217–219.

Prison facilities need improvement so as not to impede whatever therapeutic work is being conducted. Group therapy can be effected for homosexuals in prison.

1006 MANTEGAZZA, PAOLO. "The Perversions of Love." 1932. Reprinted in *Homosexuality: A Cross Cultural Approach,* edited by Donald Webster Cory, pp. 248–266. New York: Julian Press, 1956.

"Perverted" sexual behavior, including homoscxuality, among a variety of cultures is described in the manner of early "naturalists." Examples based upon personal travels, documents, and literature are given.

1007 MARTIN, JOHN BARTLOW. *Break Down the Walls.* New York: Ballantine Books, 1953, 310 pp.

In a history and description of modern American prisons, with an emphasis upon riots and the general ineffectiveness of prisons, homosexuality is cited as one factor contributing to the riots. Homosexuality is described as the most difficult problem a warden faces, since it causes more quarrels, fights, and punishment in prison than any other single problem. On release from prison many men either become homosexuals or else return guilt-ridden to their wives. The greatest individual damage is done to adolescents. Conjugal visiting is recommended.

1008   MASTERS, R. E. L. *Forbidden Sexual Behavior and Morality: An Objective Re-examination of Perverse Sex Practices in Different Cultures.* New York: Julian Press, 1962, 431 pp.

One section of this work entitled "Homosexual Acts" presents an examination of sex practices in different cultures where sodomy, fellation, tribadism, cunnilingus, and masturbation are considered to be homosexual acts.

A more sane and sensible sex code based on scientific data is called for. It is urged that a distinction be made between sexual behavior that is genuinely dangerous and harmful to individuals and to society and behavior that does not have these consequences but which is forbidden because it seemed undesirable to ancient Hebrew and Christian lawmakers.

1009   MEAD, MARGARET. *Male and Female: A Study of the Sexes in a Changing World.* New York: William Morrow & Co., 1949, 477 pp.

Sexual development, sex customs, and attitudes toward various forms of sexual behavior in different cultures of the world are studied from the anthropological viewpoint. Among certain cultures, particularly the American Plains Indians, homosexuality and transvestism may result from failures to meet intense pressures and demands for masculinity. In other cultures, homosexual activity may simpy be accepted as a natural occurrence, at least in certain circumstances or at certain ages.

1010   MELIKIAN, LEVON H. "Social Change and Sexual Behavior of Arab University Students." *Journal of Social Psychology* 73 (Dec., 1967): 169–175.

Ninety-six Arab students were given a questionnaire on sexual behavior in 1963. The same questionnaire had been administered in 1952 to a similar group. In general, no change in the incidence of nocturnal emissions, masturbation, heterosexual or homosexual intercourse was reported. However, it is interesting to note that for both groups the mean age at which the first homosexual experience is reported to have occurred is lower than the means for the other three categories. Even though homosexuality appeared to be the first introduction to sex for 43 percent of the subjects, only three subjects in each group reported any homosexual practices during the 12 months preceding the study.

1011   MELIKIAN, LEVON H., and PROTHRO, E. TERRY. "Sexual Behavior of University Students in the Arab Near East." *Journal of Abnormal and Social Psychology* 49 (1, 1954): 59–64.

In order to obtain data on sex practices and beliefs of male university students in the Arab Near East, and to compare them with data from American universities, a questionnaire was administered to 113 students at the American University of Beirut. Conditions were designed to insure anonymity and cooperation.

The mean age for first experience with homosexual intercourse was 13.2 for the Arab students, as compared with 12.2 for the American students. More Arab students than American students had positive histories of both homosexual and heterosexual intercourse. Persons with a positive history of each kind of sex behavior estimated the number of persons in their own community who engaged in such behavior to be higher than those with negative histories.

1012 NICE, RICHARD W. "The Problem of Homosexuality in Corrections." *American Journal of Corrections* 28 (3, 1966): 30–32.

The difficulties of determining the extent of institutional homosexuality are assessed, and the traditional methods of dealing with the problem (identification and isolation) are described. Other approaches more in keeping with the rehabilitative aims of corrections are proposed, including conjugal visits. A program of therapy and redirection would also do much to reduce sexual tension in the prison environment.

1013 OPLER, MARVIN K. "Anthropological and Cross-Cultural Aspects of Homosexuality." In *Sexual Inversion: The Multiple Roots of Homosexuality,* edited by Judd Marmor, pp. 108–123. New York: Basic Books, 1965.

The Freudian notion of normal psychosexual development is refuted; and the extreme cultural diversity of sexual customs is illustrated with a potpourri of examples from around the world.

1014 PARTRIDGE, BURGO. *A History of Orgies.* London: Anthony Blond, 1958, 247 pp.

Orgies from ancient Greece to the early 20th century are described. Most of these were heterosexual, but several, particularly those in Greece, were at least partly homosexual. Although details are not given, the festival of Aphrodite Anosia in Thessaly was totally lesbian.

1015 PATTERSON, HAYWOOD, and CONRAD, EARL. "Shifting Sex Roles." In *The Sociology of Punishment and Correction,* edited by Norman Johnston, Leonard Savitz, and Marvin E. Wolfgang, pp. 140–143. New York: John Wiley & Sons, 1962.

The seduction and coercion of young boys and men into playing a female or "gal-boy" role for homosexuals in prisons is described.

1016   PEARCE, JOHN D. W. "Clinical Aspects of Psychiatric Problems in the Army." *Practitioner* 154 (919, 1945): 33–38.

In a survey of psychiatric problems in the Army, the brief section on homosexuality indicates that many homosexuals in the service are initially referred to psychiatrists for headaches. Those soldiers who allege homosexuality to obtain a discharge can be easily detected by competent psychiatrists.

1017   PEARCE, JOHN D. W. "Problems of Sex in the Services." *Practitioner* 172 (1030, 1954): 436–439.

It is asserted that sexual problems in the military are largely analogous to the civilian milieu. It is doubtful that homosexuality, especially during peacetime, is any more prevalent in the services than in any other sector of society. Most homosexual activity among military personnel is the product of expediency and the lack of heterosexual opportunity. Many homosexuals in the service do exercise sexual restraint when they are on duty; the only "dangerous" homosexuals are male prostitutes and noncommissioned officers who may sexually coerce their juniors.

1018   SEGARD, CHRISTIAN P. "Male Sexual Relations: Deviations from the Normal." *Postgraduate Medicine* 7 (1, 1950): 36–39.

In the vast majority of what are considered to be sex perversions the individual is neither a sex pervert nor a sexual psychopath. Whenever males are isolated, many abnormal sex perversions can be eliminated by proper vocational and recreational activities and by sex education.

1019   SINES, JACOB O., and PITTMAN, DAVID J. "Male Homosexuality: The Relevance of Cross-Species Studies of Sexual Behavior." In *Determinants of Human Sexual Behavior,* edited by George Winokur, pp. 189–192. Springfield, Ill.: Charles C. Thomas, 1963.

Suggestions are made for the cross-species study of male homosexuality. This is seen as providing a parallel set of coordinates to the cross-cultural study of human sexual behavior.

1020   SMITH, CHARLES E. "Prison Pornography." *Journal of Social Therapy* 1 (3, 1955): 126–128.

The relationship of homosexuality to prison pornography is briefly reviewed. All forms of sexual activity can be found in prison pornography; homosexual pornography includes drawing, literature, and "letters of endearment." Some pornographic material reveals overt homosexual trends. Others indicate latent homosexuality. It is suggested that identification of the authors of homosexual materials might better equip penal administrators to deal with homosexuality in prison. It is possible that the circulation of pornography in prison fosters homosexual activity as a means of sexual release.

1021 SMITH, CHARLES E. "Some Problems in Dealing with Homosexuals in the Prison Situation." *Journal of Social Therapy* 2 (1, 1956): 37–45.

The attitudes of imprisoned homosexuals toward their own conditions and toward the institutional program afforded them were assessed through a questionnaire administered to 61 male homosexual prisoners (21 Negro and 41 white with ages ranging from 17 to 59.) The prisoners appeared content with their deviation and showed little desire to change. It is doubtful whether homosexuals can be classified as active or passive, but effeminacy (professed disinterest or even antipathy toward pornography) may prove useful for diagnosis. The homosexual prisoners felt they were treated with prejudice by both the courts and the parole boards.

1022 SONENSCHEIN, DAVID. "Homosexuality as a Subject of Anthropological Inquiry." *Anthropological Quarterly* 39 (2, 1966): 73–82.

A plea is made to anthropologists to study homosexuality. It is maintained that anthropologists can further the knowledge of homosexuality as a social problem through their studies of primitives, especially in connection with the shaman and the berdache, and also through the study of homosexuality as a subculture, as well as through the study of its causes.

1023 STILLER, RICHARD. "Sex Practices in Prison." 1960. Reprinted in *The Third Sex,* edited by Isadore Rubin, pp. 82–85. New York: New Book Co., 1961.

A brief general discussion of homosexuality in prison indicates that although the majority of inmates are not homosexual, homosexuality is a major cause of discipline problems. Conjugal visiting is recommended.

1024 SUTHERLAND, ALISTAIR, and ANDERSON, PATRICK, eds. *Eros: An Anthology of Friendship.* London: Anthony Blond, 1961, 133 pp.

A collection of short miscellaneous selections from literary works, mainly western European, English, and American, illustrates various homosexual themes. The text is divided into chronological periods, beginning with "The Great Originals," which contains examples of homosexuality from the Bible and mythology, and continuing from the ancient Greeks up to the present time. In addition, a chapter entitled "Exotic Encounters," deals with experiences occurring in the Near East, and another, entitled "The School Story," contains literary descriptions of homosexuality in the English public schools. Introductory material is given at the beginning of each chapter, and in some cases explanatory narrative is continued between the literary selections in the chapter.

1025 SYKES, GRESHAM M. *The Society of Captives: A Study of a Maximum Security Prison.* Princeton, N. J.: Princeton University Press, 1958, 144 pp.

In this description of the operation of a maximum security prison for males in Trenton, New Jersey, the relationship between the prison and its location in the larger society, its custodial function, the problems of power within the prison, the organization of the inmates, and the question of crisis and equilibrium within the prison and between it and the community are examined.

Some of the difficulties of the inmates are the deprivation of liberty, goods and services, heterosexual relationships, autonomy, and security. The prisoners develop argot terms to describe the different forms of adaptation to imprisonment. Of relevance to homosexuality are the roles of "wolves," "punks," and "fags." The "wolf" is characterized by an active aggressive masculinity in homosexual relationships. The "punk" merely submits to the importunities of the "wolf," whereas the "fag" takes on the role of a woman in his submission, and both are characterized by the forfeiture of their claims to masculinity. The "punk" loses his masculinity, and the "fag" not only loses his but deliberately takes on the guise of femininity.

1026 TAYLOR, F. KRÄUPL. "Experimental Investigation of Collective Social and Libidinal Motivations in Therapeutic Groups." *British Journal of Medical Psychology* 22 (3–4, 1949): 169–182.

The results of a group experiment designed to test the hypothesis that latent homosexual trends are present in therapeutic groups consisting of only one sex are reported. Two groups, one male and one female, were amalgamated after 10 and seven months of treatment respectively. The purpose was to alter and intensify the libidinal group climate. Prolonged stimulation of homosexual motivations was the most conspicuous collective response. This response is regarded as supporting the original hypothesis.

1027 TAYLOR, GORDON RATTRAY. "Historical and Mythological Aspects of Homosexuality." In *Sexual Inversion: The Multiple Roots of Homosexuality,* edited by Judd Marmor, pp. 140–164. New York: Basic Books, 1965.

A short account of the history of homosexuality in Western culture is given. Significant features of the Mediterranean cultures from which Western culture arose are then outlined, and available data on homosexuality are presented against this background.

Source materials in the form of diaries and travel books are available only from the seventeenth century on. Much of the information on homosexuality in earlier times has been wrongly interpreted in the light of our present culture. Generally, it is in societies which conceive of their deities as father figures that homosexuality is regarded as the overwhelming danger. Gender role changes in the ancient world and in Europe, Greek homoerotism, and Greek bisexuality are discussed. The scarcity of information on other cultures leads to the conclusion that "there is probably no culture from which homosexuality has not been reported."

1028 VEDDER, CLYDE B., and KING, PATRICIA G. *Problems of Homosexuality in Corrections.* Springfield, Ill.: Charles C. Thomas, 1967, 63 pp.

The incidence of homosexuality in prisons, the factors which promote it, and the circumstances under which such behavior takes place, are discussed. Total deprivation of heterosexual activity inevitably increases preoccupation with sexual topics among inmates, forcing them to seek other sexual outlets. Homosexuality among male inmates in some ways presents fewer problems than among female inmates. Prison structural relationships among females are often based on homosexual activity. The practice of granting conjugal visitation or home furloughs in an effort to maintain existing family relationships and diminish the problem of homosexuality is prevalent in several Latin American countries and occurs in many European countries.

In the United States, Mississippi is the only state to have permitted these practices, but since the passage of P.L. 89–176, the Prisoner Rehabilitation Act, in September, 1965, selected inmates of Federal institutions have been permitted unescorted furloughs home for assorted reasons, such as illness or death of relatives, and have also been given releases for work or study in the community during the day. Reporting the results of a 1965 attitude survey of prison administrators, it was found the majority were opposed to conjugal visitation. It was concluded nonetheless that a system of conjugal visitation and home furloughs for selected convicts as a step in rehabilitation warrants at least a trial in the United States.

1029   VOLTAIRE. "The Love Called 'Socrates.'" From Voltaire's *Philosophical Dictionary*. Translated by Donald Webster Cory. In *Homosexuality: A Cross Cultural Approach*, edited by Donald Webster Cory, pp. 350–353. New York: Julian Press, 1956.

Societies welcome the attraction of the two sexes for one another. This attraction is stronger in men than in women and in those instances where the natural object of the men's choice is not available, a young boy who physically resembles a girl will often be chosen. When the boy's age has made this resemblance vanish, then he is no longer considered a reasonable alternative.

It is stated that it is impossible that pederasty was ever condoned by the law because "it is not human nature to make a law that contradicts and outrages Nature, a law that would make the human race disappear if it were followed to the letter."

1030   WALKER, KENNETH. "The Making of a Homosexual." *Sexology* 30 (1, 1963): 8–9.

The experiences are described of one boy who had been "destroyed for good" because of the callous treatment he received from the police, law courts, and penal authorities. Arrested for a homosexual offense as a young man, he was imprisoned for four years; there his homosexuality was irrevocably reinforced.

1031   WARD, JACK L. "Homosexual Behavior of the Institutionalized Delinquent." *Psychiatric Quarterly Supplement* 32 (2, 1958): 301–314.

The homosexual behavior of institutionalized delinquents may stem from: normal adolescent development (curiosity and experimentation), the realization of latent homosexual components (where normal sexual expression is unobtainable, the strength of latent homosexual tendencies may be expressed), and problems of dependency and power (submission and domination—which is the most important basis for the homosexual behavior in institutions). Much of the homosexual behavior of the institutionalized delinquent represents the symbolic acting out of problems of dependency and power. The institutionalized delinquent has great dependency needs and is afraid to trust or depend on adults. Bullying and aggressive homosexual behavior are equated with manliness, and dependence and submission are reflected in passive homosexual behavior. Delinquent adolescents typically act out their problems rather than internalize them.

1032   WEISS, ISIDORE I. "Homosexuality: With Special Reference to Military Prisoners." *Psychiatric Quarterly* 20 (3, 1946): 485–523.

The role of the homosexual in an armed forces rehabilitation center is discussed. It is claimed that a small number of homosexuals act on the other inmates to increase the numbers involved in homosexual acts. An improvement is seen in the treatment process in Army discharge procedure. Now mental defectives can be discharged early to seek treatment on the outside. It is suggested that this practice be extended to homosexuals, thus easing the burden of the institution and providing the patient with an atmosphere conducive to beneficial therapy on the outside. Early release of homosexuals from Army life is seen as the best over-all procedure for both the men and the institution. Some of the findings in the field of homosexuality are reviewed, especially endocrine and experimental studies.

1033   WEST, LOUIS JOLYON; DOIDGE, WILLIAM THOMAS; and WILLIAMS, ROBERT L. "An Approach to the Problem of Homosexuality in Military Services." *American Journal of Psychiatry* 115 (5, 1958): 392–401.

Armed forces regulations and methods of dealing with homosexuals are described and a number of criticisms are made. It is pointed out that present methods fail to distinguish the "true" from the "incidental" homosexual, valuable personnel may be unnecessarily lost to the Services, safeguards for accused individuals are insufficient, there is a lack of consistency of treatment and insufficient consideration of medical factors, and the prolonged investigations are stressful and expensive. Suggestions are made which, it is hoped, will provide the basis of a new approach. It is urged that punitive attitudes of officials be modified. Investigations should be as brief as possible. Separations must be based upon the primary disorder. The special stigma of a discharge because of homosexuality should be eliminated. The trauma of the investigation should be lessened, and the retention of homosexuals in the Services under certain circumstances should be attempted.

1034   WESTERMARCK, EDWARD. "Homosexual Love." 1906. Reprinted in *Homosexuality: A Cross Cultural Approach,* edited by Donald Webster Cory, pp. 101–138. New York: Julian Press, 1956.

An early and extensive anthropological study documented the attitudes of different peoples in different ages toward homosexuality. These attitudes ranged from complete acceptance to those that called for stoning or death.

Homosexuality is viewed as congenital, but the absence of women is stressed as a "very important cause." It is argued that modern attitudes should take into account the "nonvolitional" nature of inversion.

1035 WITTELS, FRITZ. "Collective Defense Mechanisms against Homosexuality." *Psychoanalytic Review* 31 (1, 1944): 19–33.

Covenants of men—religious, military, and small groups—operate as a defense against homosexuality by sublimating or desexualizing it. As long as the covenant remains strong in its aims and practices it succeeds in its sublimation. If it is weakened as a result of a clash with inimical social forces, the homosexual drive breaks through all the more strongly, since the specific energy of the drive was continuously fed in the group.

1036 WOOD, ROBERT. "Homosexuality on the Modern Stage." 1959. Reprinted in *The Third Sex,* edited by Isadore Rubin, pp. 86–90. New York: New Book Co., 1961.

Various modern dramas, especially British and American, have used homosexuality as a literary theme. In this movement toward a serious dramatic treatment of the subject, the old taboo has broken down, affording increasingly frank commentary.

1037 YAKER, HENRI M. "The Black Muslims in the Correctional Institution." *Welfare Reporter* 13 (Oct., 1962): 158–165.

The intrinsic isolation and loneliness of prison creates deep-seated needs for personality defenses. If such defenses fail, anxiety is produced and "agitated depression" ensues. The failure to erect personality defenses is commonly seen among inmates with a deep-seated need to act aggressively to compensate for feelings of psychosexual inadequacy and loss of masculine identity. Whether personality defenses fail, or whether such defenses are not built up, the result is exposure of "the more covert layers of the homosexual level of personality." Anxiety and an even greater need for aggression follow, causing a state commonly described as "homosexual panic."

As a group, white prisoners begin to think that they are being persecuted and develop fears that the Negro inmates are plotting to kill them or conspiring to attack them sexually. Negroes as a group also develop this type of paranoid fear, but among the black inmates, the psychosis takes a more diffuse cultural pattern. Projection of the conflict at the psychosexual level in terms of the satanic provides an ego-defense for those who subscribe to Black Muslim doctrine.

1038 ZUCKERMAN, STANLEY B. "Sex in Prison." *Journal of Social Therapy* 1 (3, 1955): 129–131.

Although most prison pornography is heterosexual in orientation, homosexual subplots are often introduced to add "spice" to the story. An interesting category of homosexual prison pornography is the "daily mail"—love-letters written by "established" homosexual prisoners.

CROSS-REFERENCES

Benjamin, Harry, and Masters, R. E. L. "Homosexual Prostitution." In their *Prostitution and Morality,* pp. 286–337. New York: Julian Press, 1964. No. 812.

Boone, Joel T. "The Sexual Aspects of Military Personnel." *Journal of Social Hygiene* 27 (3, 1941): 113–124. No. 1058.

Croft-Cooke, Rupert. *The Verdict of You All.* London: Secker & Warburg, 1955, 245 pp. No. 1154.

Glover, Edward. "The Social and Legal Aspects of Sexual Abnormality." *Medico-Legal and Criminological Review* 13 (3, 1945): 133–148. No. 419.

Karpman, Benjamin. *The Sexual Offender and His Offenses: Etiology, Pathology, Psychodynamics and Treatment.* New York: Julian Press, 1954, 744 pp. No. 182.

Kling, Samuel G. "Homosexual Behavior." In his *Sexual Behavior and the Law,* pp. 97–128. New York: Bernard Geis Associates, 1965. No. 870.

Litkey, L. J., and Feniczy, Pongrac. "An Approach to the Control of Homosexual Practices." *International Journal of Neuropsychiatry* 3 (1, 1967): 20–23. No. 75.

McIntosh, Mary. "The Homosexual Role." *Social Problems* 16 (2, 1968): 182–192. No. 876.

"Report of the Departmental Committee on Homosexual Offences and Prostitution." *British Medical Journal* (5045, 1957): 639–640. No. 896.

"Sexual Issues on the Campus." In *Sex and the College Student,* edited by Group for the Advancement of Psychiatry, pp. 38–79. Report no. 60. New York: Group for the Advancement of Psychiatry, 1965. No. 768.

Steiner, Lucius B. *Sex Behavior of the Homosexual.* Hollywood, Calif.: Genell Corp., 1964, 160 pp. No. 914.

Tappan, Paul W. "Some Myths about the Sex Offender." *Federal Probation* 19 (2, 1955): 7–12. No. 1248.

Taylor, Gordon Rattray. *Sex in History.* New York: Vanguard Press, 1954, 336 pp. No. 1116.

Ullerstam, Lars. *The Erotic Minorities.* New York: Grove Press, 1966, 172 pp. No. 1249.

Van den Haag, Ernest. "Notes on Homosexuality and Its Cultural Setting." Reprinted in *The Problem of Homosexuality in Modern Society,* edited by Hendrik M. Ruitenbeek, pp. 291–302. New York: E. P. Dutton & Co., 1963. No. 1119.

West, D. J. *Homosexuality.* Chicago: Aldine Publishing Co., 1968, 304 pp. No. 922.

West, Louis Jolyon, and Glass, Albert J. "Sexual Behavior and the Military Law." In *Sexual Behavior and the Law,* edited by Ralph Slovenko, pp. 250–272. Springfield, Ill.: Charles C. Thomas, 1965. No. 1122.

Winokur, George, ed. *Determinants of Human Sexual Behavior.* Springfield, Ill.: Charles C. Thomas, 1963, 230 pp. No. 65.

Yankowski, John S., and Wolff, Hermann K. *The Tortured Sex.* Los Angeles: Holloway House Publishing Co., 1965, 224 pp. No. 927.

FEMALE

1039 ATIA, ISAAD MOHAMMED, and MUFTIC, MAHMOUD KAMAL. "Hypnosis in the Psychosomatic Investigation of Female Homosexuality." *British Journal of Medical Hypnotism* 9 (1, 1957): 41–46.

A review of somatic and psychic approaches to the etiology of homosexuality is followed by a description of a psychosomatic test developed at the King Faisal Hospital (Nasiriyah, Iraq) to diagnose female homosexuality.

After undergoing a physical examination with special emphasis on genitals and secondary sex characteristics, and a laboratory examination which investigated genetic sex, each patient was subjected to hypnoanalysis and psychosomatic tests. The results of these testing procedures were transferred to master sheets and a diagnosis regarding the sexual orientation of the patients was made.

The psychosomatic test, designed to study the subjects' behavior under medium hypnosis, was concerned with whether the patients' reaction to suggestions about homo- and heterosexual behavior would be pleasure or aversion. The conclusion of the study was that many women have a history of homosexual activity and that the homosexual deviation can develop in a variety of ways among females.

It is interesting to note that one of the most important factors leading to the development of homosexuality among Moslem women seems to be the status of the female in Moslem society. Women are despised, mistreated, segregated in harems, and are considered objects rather than personalities. Females are forbidden to develop spontaneous emotional relationships with males, and as a result homosexual liaisons flourish. A correlation between the rigidity and strictness of religion and the rate of homosexual activity among females is suggested.

1040 CORY, DONALD WEBSTER, and LEROY, JOHN P. "The Lesbian in Literature." *Sexology* 30 (2, 1963): 132–135.

The recurrence of the theme of lesbianism in literature from the time of Sappho in ancient Greece to the present (1963) is reviewed. The censorship and prejudice which surrounded such works in the Anglo-Saxon world during the late 19th century and in the 20th century are seen as extant today; despite this fact, lesbianism continues to serve as a literary theme.

1041 GIALLOMBARDO, ROSE. "Social Roles in a Prison for Women." *Social Problems* 13 (3, 1966): 268–288.

Comparisons were made with the relevant literature on social roles assumed by male prisoners, and the social structure inside the prison was viewed in relation to the external environment. Over 650 female inmates in a "progressive" women's prison were observed, administered questionnaires, and interviewed for one to three hours.

The culture that is formed within the prison by females and males is a response to the deprivations of prison life, but the nature of that response is influenced by "the differential participation of males and females in the external culture." The prison culture reflects the external social structure, modified by prison deprivations. Thus, one cannot understand prison cultures by treating them apart from the larger society.

1042 GIALLOMBARDO, ROSE. *Society of Women: A Study of a Women's Prison.* New York: Wiley & Sons, 1966, 244 pp.

This is an exploratory study of a women's prison relating its internal structure to the structure of the community. Relationships between inmates and staff, the organizational goals, and the nature of the prison experience are described. Social relations are set in a milieu characterized by extreme isolation and by the inevitability of concrete objectified time, and adjustments often take the form of a "marriage." The particular marriage unit is a homosexual alliance, and integration occurs through various kinship ties.

1043 GROSS, LEONARD H. "Lesbians in Prison." *Sexology* 34 (7, 1968): 478–481.

This is a short review of findings reported in *Society of Women* by sociologist Dr. Rose Giallombardo and *Women's Prison* by sociologists Ward and Kassebaum. Most prison lesbians are heterosexual in the outside world. They respond to lesbian advances because they are cut off from their families, and in order to make a better adjustment to the restrictions of prison life.

1044 HALLECK, SEYMOUR L., and HERSKO, MARVIN. "Homosexual Behavior in a Correctional Institution for Adolescent Girls." *American Journal of Orthopsychiatry* 32 (5, 1962): 911–917.

The psychological and social determinants of homosexual behavior in a correctional institution for adolescent girls are described. The subjects were 180 girls, aged 12 to 18 years, in a state institution. The average length of stay in the institution was 10 months. Milieu programing, psychotherapy, diagnostic evaluations, and questionnaire studies were used.

The majority of girls were drawn into "homosexually tinged relationships," with different degrees of emotional involvement (usually superficial and short-lived). Nothing showed the girls to be emotionally disturbed (sexually perverted). Most had had poor relationships with men and had found that homosexual involvement provided a chance to be loved and accepted. The training school fosters homosexual behavior by putting similar girls in group living and by preventing contact with the opposite sex. The staff should disapprove of such behavior but should approve of friendship and affection between the girls.

1045 HAMMER, MAX. "Homosexuality in a Women's Reformatory." *Corrective Psychiatry and Journal of Social Therapy* 11 (3, 1965): 168–169.

Homosexuality in a women's institution is given a psychological appraisal. Homosexual contacts appear to be of the mother-daughter love object variety, i.e., the relationships are essentially asexual; love, protection, and security are sought, rather than genital gratification.

1046 KATES, ELIZABETH M. "Sexual Problems in Women's Institutions." *Journal of Social Therapy* 1 (4, 1955): 187–191.

Homosexuality is perhaps the greatest sexual problem in women's prisons. Rather than a homosexual prisoner being discovered after an offense has been committed, it is recommended that a "sexualmetric scale" be developed to identify potential homosexuals. The Terman-Miles M-F tests are suggested as the best index of "the degree of inversion of the sex temperament." Homosexuals allegedly represent the "extremes of the masculinity-femininity problem." If the M-F tests are administered to all incoming prisoners, "passive and potentially passive homosexuals" as well as those women with excessively maculine scores can be identified, isolated from the other inmates, and be helped to "advance to a normal state of living." Most homosexuality in prisons is a substitution for marriage or prostitution; such situational inversion terminates upon the prisoner's release. Those prisoners who are "apparently homosexual either respond to treatment or return to society as a menace." Adequate housing, work, counseling, and supervision will minimize homosexual proclivities within the prison environment.

1047 WARD, DAVID A., and KASSEBAUM, GENE G. "Homosexuality: A Mode of Adaptation in a Prison for Women." *Social Problems* 12 (2, 1964): 159–177.

Part of a larger study published as *Women's Prison: Sex and Social Structure* (1965), the article focuses on the role of female homosexuality as a mode of adjustment to prison role. The prison records of 832 inmates were studied, interviews were conducted with 45 of the inmates, and a questionnaire was given to a random sample representing 45 percent of the inmate population. The prison sample consisted of 293 inmates. The questionnaire was also given to the prison staff.

In an attempt to differentiate between male and female prisoners' sex roles, it was discovered that female prisoners rebel less often, have less of a tendency to resort to smuggling and gambling, and need more emotional support. The questionnaire on attitudes given to the 293 inmates revealed that female prisoners tend to have the most difficulty adjusting to the absence from home and family. Women who were first arrested after age 25 tend to support the "inmate-code" less than those arrested at an earlier age. The official estimate of prison homosexuality is 19 percent of the population. The prison staff expressed estimates from 30 percent to 70 percent for institutional homosexuality (defined as a woman having at least one sexual affair with another woman in prison). Inmate estimates ran as high as 90 percent and were never below 50 percent. The two main types of homosexuals among the inmates were identified as the "jailhouse turn-out" who had her first homosexual experience in prison and reverted to heterosexuality on the outside, being either "butch" or "femme," and the "true homosexual" who was homosexual before and after her prison experience. It was believed that the true homosexual was usually the "butch" type.

1048 WARD, DAVID A., and KASSEBAUM, GENE G. "Lesbian Liaisons." *Trans-Action* 1 (2, 1964): 28–32.

There is more homosexual activity among female prisoners, apparently involving no coercion, than among male prisoners. Most of the women involved are "jailhouse-turnouts," women who are not homosexual on the outside. The temporary turn to homosexuality is seen as a response to and compensation for the pains of imprisonment—a way of adapting to prison life. Since only five of 293 women reported that homosexual behavior was due to a lack of sexual contact with men, the cause of such behavior is probably not primarily sexual. Instead, it reflects an emotional deprivation due especially to being separated from family and friends which, for women, represents the most severe deprivation of confinement.

1049 WARD, DAVID A., and KASSEBAUM, GENE G. *Women's Prison: Sex and Social Structure.* Chicago: Aldine Publishing Co., 1965, 269 pp.

An effort is made to delineate the culture and social structure of the female prisoner community. It was found that homosexuality is the major adaptation employed by women in a prison setting. The most salient distinction to be made among inmates was between those who were and those who were not engaged in homosexual behavior and, of those who were involved, between the incumbents of "masculine" and "feminine" roles. Characteristics of the homosexual population that differentiate it from the non-homosexual group are reported, as well as findings pertaining to the reactions of inmates to the deprivations of prison life, the extent of homosexual behavior in the prison, the principal roles of homosexuals and the functions these roles serve, the dynamics of prison homosexuality, and the implications of the homosexual adaptation for prison staff.

CROSS-REFERENCES

Bluestone, Harvey; O'Malley, Edward P.; and Connell, Sydney. "Homosexuals in Prison." *Corrective Psychiatry and Journal of Social Therapy* 12 (1, 1966): 13–24. No. 957.
Caprio, Frank S. *Female Homosexuality: A Psychodynamic Study of Lesbianism.* New York: Citadel Press, 1954, 334 pp. Chapter 16. "Therapeutic Management: Preventive Measures," pp. 285–298. Reprinted as "Preventive Measures." In *Carol in a Thousand Cities,* edited by Ann Aldrich, pp. 153–166. Greenwich, Conn.: Fawcett Publications, 1960. No. 626.
Devereux, George. "Institutionalized Homosexuality of the Mohave Indians." 1937. Reprinted in *The Problem of Homosexuality in Modern America,* edited by Hendrik M. Ruitenbeek, pp. 183–226. New York: E. P. Dutton & Co., 1963. No. 969.
Flacelière, Robert. "Homosexuality." In *Love in Ancient Greece,* pp. 49–85. Translated by James Cleugh. London: F. Muller, 1962. No. 978.
Ford, Clellan S., and Beach, Frank A. *Patterns of Sexual Behavior.* New York: Harper & Brothers, 1951, 307 pp. No. 979.
Miller, William G., and Hannum, Thomas E. "Characteristics of Homosexually Involved Incarcerated Females." *Journal of Consulting Psychology* 27 (3, 1963): 277. No. 641.
Partridge, Burgo. *A History of Orgies.* London: Anthony Blond, 1958, 247 pp. No. 1014.
Querlin, Marise. *Women without Men.* Translated by Malcom McGraw. New York: Dell Publishing Co., 1965, 174 pp. No. 943.
Vedder, Clyde B., and King, Patricia G. *Problems of Homosexuality in Corrections.* Springfield, Ill.: Charles C. Thomas, 1967, 63 pp. No. 1028.

Societal Attitudes Toward Homosexuality

GENERAL, MALE

1050 BAILEY, DERRICK SHERWIN. "Homosexuality and Christian Morals." In *They Stand Apart: A Critical Survey of the Problems of Homosexuality,* edited by J. Tudor Rees and Harley V. Usill, pp. 36–63. London: William Heinemann, 1955.

A theological statement of the moral issues involved and the Christian attitude toward homosexuality is given. Homosexuality is seen as a part of the broader problem of sexual immorality in general. Legal and strong social reactions have made a scapegoat out of what is merely a symptom, while neglecting the disease, i.e., a general laxity of moral standards. A critical estimate is made of the historical and Biblical factors that have contributed to the development of Western attitudes in this area of human life.

1051 BAILEY, DERRICK SHERWIN. *Homosexuality and the Western Christian Tradition.* London: Longmans, Green, 1955, 181 pp.

A homosexual interpretation of the story of Sodom and Gomorrah is given, and Biblical references to homosexuality are traced. The status of homosexuality in pre-Justinian Roman law is examined. The legislation, teaching, and opinions of the early Christian Church on the subject are described, and medieval reactions are discussed. Recent and present laws in England with respect to homosexuality are outlined.

1052 BAILEY, DERRICK SHERWIN. *Sexual Offenders and Social Punishment.* Westminster: The Church Information Board, 1956, 120 pp.

Material gathered from priests, doctors, psychologists, social workers, lawyers, and homosexuals is used as a basis for judgments made by the Church of England Moral Welfare Council on the subject of "the homosexual, the law, and society." Areas of concern are the homosexual condition, the patterns of sexual behavior, the causes and cures of homosexuality, the homosexual and society, and the legal, moral, and religious aspects of homosexual practice. The appendices include essays entitled "The Homosexual and Christian Morals," and "The Pastor and the Homosexual," as well as a review of statutes relating to homosexual offenses in Great Britain.

1053 BALSER, BEN; BERCHENKO, FRANK; FARNHAM, MARYNIA; and KREMER, MALVINA W. "Panel on 'Homosexuality in the Male Adolescent.'" *International Mental Health Research Newsletter* 4 (1962): 7–10.

A panel discussion of the problems related to the definition of "homosexuality" is presented. Homosexuality is considered an illness. Most of the panel members would render a diagnosis of homosexuality in an adolescent only if it were accompanied by clear-cut overt behavior. Homosexuality is seen as a continuum from "black" to "white" with a "gray" middle area.

1054   BARNES, KENNETH C., et al. *Towards a Quaker View of Sex: An Essay by a Group of Friends.* Rev. ed. London: Friends Home Service Committee, 1964, 84 pp.

Several aspects of sexuality, including homosexuality, are dealt with in this monograph. Homosexuality, the state of loving one's own sex, is seen as one orientation to sex found among adolescents. With increasing age it continues and becomes a way of life for some, while others totally reject it. Homosexuality in Britain, homosexuality and the law, and female homosexuality are discussed. Female homosexuality is distinguished from male homosexuality with reference to the relative advantages and disadvantages inherent in its qualitative differences. Finally, the Christian attitude and the quality of homosexual relationships are considered.

This is a revised edition of the 1963 "Essay by a Group of Friends." See Heron Alastair (no. 1082).

1055   BECKER, RAYMOND DE. *The Other Face of Love.* Translated by Margaret Crosland and Alan Daventry. London: Spearman, 1967, 203 pp.

Reference is made to the universality of homosexuality throughout history; the latent homosexual structure of Christianity is examined; and contemporary attitudes, both literary and scientific, toward homosexuality are presented.

Western civilization remains antisexual and particularly antihomosexual. This tradition has persisted because people have imagined it represented a point of view which the whole world shared. An investigation of primitive and non-Western societies reveals, however, quite different attitudes toward homosexuality, more often regarded as a commonplace occurrence.

In the 20th century two movements connected with homosexuality have begun—one literary-philosophical and the other, medical-scientific. These movements have resulted in homosexuals being seen as having a role in the world and a need to define themselves, and the necessity for society to revise its attitudes toward this phenomenon.

1056   BENNET, E. A. "The Social Aspects of Homosexuality." *Medical Press* 217 (Sept. 3, 1947): 207–210.

In a discussion of the social distinctness of the adult homosexual, particular attention is given to how little is known about certain aspects of male and female homosexuality, and the advantages which might be expected to follow increased knowledge. Facts are needed with regard to the incidence of homosexuality, the significance of constitutional and hereditary factors, the effects of environmental influence in schools and elsewhere, the results of psychiatric treatment, and the consequences of punitive measures upon homosexual and bisexual persons of both sexes. The chief need is for facts on which to base medical, educational, legal, and ethical conceptions of the problem.

It is urged that a fact-finding investigation of the social problem of homosexuality be undertaken by a representative committee.

1057 BENSON, R. O. D. *In Defense of Homosexuality, Male and Female: A Rational Evaluation of Social Prejudice.* New York: Julian Press, 1965, 239 pp.

Several arguments which have been used to equate "homosexual" with "abnormal" are considered. They include the "nature" argument, as well as the religious, psychological, nonrational, and philosophical arguments. It is contended that exclusive heterosexuality is not the norm for sexual behavior, that all people have the right to create their own destinies, and that homosexuals have the right to find their own happiness in their own way.

1058 BOONE, JOEL T. "The Sexual Aspects of Military Personnel." *Journal of Social Hygiene* 27 (3, 1941): 113–124.

Homosexuality is looked upon with loathing and contempt by the vast majority of men in the United States Navy. These men promptly report the presence of "one who is not a male in the healthy sense of the word," and the accused is taken to one of the naval psychiatric institutions for treatment.

1059 BREGER, LOUIS, and LIVERANT, SHEPHARD. "Homosexual Prejudice and Perceptual Defense." *Journal of Consulting Psychology* 25 (5, 1961): 459.

An attempt was made to determine if persons scoring high on a measure of homosexual prejudice show greater indices of threat in response to homosexual words encountered in a perceptual defense situation. A scale of manifest attitudes toward homosexuality was constructed and administered to 68 subjects to determine high, medium, and low levels of prejudice. Subjects were then placed in a perceptual threat situation in which they were asked to identity four homosexual, four sexual, and eight neutral words. A measure of threat was obtained for all subjects.

The results of this study consistently failed to support the major hypothesis. Although perceptual defense of the avoidance type was found for the homosexual and sexual words, a significant difference between homosexual and sexual words was not found. Differential reaction times by the high, medium, and low homosexual scale scorers to the three groups of words indicated that group differences in defensiveness to homosexual words were not manifested.

1060 BUCKLEY, MICHAEL J. *Morality and the Homosexual: A Catholic Approach to a Moral Problem.* Westminster, Md.: Newman Press, 1960, 214 pp.

A theological treatise examines the nature and causes of homosexuality and the problems of moral and religious guidance which homosexuality poses for the church. Principles for evaluating individual responsibility are set down, and the relationship that should obtain between the homosexual, the priest, and the doctor or psychiatrist is discussed.

1061 CALDER, W. "The Sexual Offender: A Prison Medical Officer's Viewpoint." *British Journal of Delinquency* 6 (1, 1956): 26–40.

The relation of a prison medical officer to sex offenders is discussed in a section on homosexuality. It is emphatically stated that homosexuals are abnormal and a threat to human decency. The main cause of concern over nonincarcerated homosexuals is that they are overly prone to seducing young boys. It is suggested that the motivation of homosexual acts performed in the public rest rooms is that the odor stimulates the homosexuals. Imprisonment is the first necessity for homosexual offenders, and then psychiatric treatment should be administered if possible.

1062 CARPENTER, EDWARD. "The Intermediate Sex: A Study of Some Transitional Types of Men and Women." 1908. Reprinted in *Homosexuality: A Cross Cultural Approach,* edited by Donald Webster Cory, pp. 139–206. New York: Julian Press, 1956.

An attempt is made to construct a system of ethics which would allow the homosexual to function within the moral climate of the Victorian era. "Base" sexual acts, both heterosexual and homosexual, are condemned, while "true" homosexuality, i.e., a love relationship between persons of the same sex which does not include acts for the gratification of the sexual appetite, is glorified for its "purity."

1063 CARSON, LAURA E. "Are We Hiding Behind a Word?" *Mental Hygiene* 42 (3, 1958): 558–561.

Generations of conditioning have evoked a "semantic aversion" to the word "homosexual" in many individuals who otherwise consider themselves modern and realistic. Contrary to popular belief, homosexuality is not physiologically determined in an individual, but is created by external psychological and emotional conditioning. Sexually deviant behavior is becoming institutionalized in America. Homosexuals are being encouraged to band together against a society which punishes them for "crimes against nature" instead of treating their deviancy as a "mental infirmity."

There are two inadequacies in our social structure concerning the needed rehabilitation of homosexuals: the law is "antipathetic" to the help of professional psychologists in this area; and there are, at present, no facilities in mental hospitals for the therapeutic treatment of the homosexual.

Programs of education, directed by state officials and committees, are advised to encourage the public to consider the field of psychology for help in solving the problem of homosexuality in the community.

1064 [CHAVASSE, C. M.] BISHOP OF ROCHESTER. "The Church and Sex." *Practitioner* 172 (1030, 1954): 350–354.

Within the context of human sexuality, homosexuality is briefly discussed and differentiated into temperament and practice. Homosexual temperament, "like kleptomania," should be sympathetically understood and restrained; homosexual practice—"unnatural" and "defective sexual intercourse"—must always be suppressed.

1065 CHESSER, EUSTACE. *Odd Man Out: Homosexuality in Men and Women.* London: Victor Gollancz, 1959, 192 pp.

The special problems encountered by the homosexual because he does not conform to the pattern of life imposed by society are discussed. Typical case histories of both male and female homosexuals are presented to illustrate the etiology, treatment, and prevention of homosexuality. The principal etiological factor is assumed to be a faulty child-parent relationship, but the responsibility is that of society as a whole since society has created the problem through the repression of sex by stringent taboos against any behavior which differs from what is considered "normal." Efforts to eliminate homosexuality have failed because it has been taken out of a wider context with only the superficial symptoms rather than the roots being treated.

The Kinsey 7-point scale is cited to demonstrate that sexual behavior is a continuum rather than entirely heterosexual or homosexual in nature. An unsuspected homosexual component exists in all men. Successful treatment may be found mainly in psychoanalysis which is unfortunately unavailable to the majority due to the excessive time and expense involved. In the future, psychosomatic medicine with its concept of treating the mind-body and consideration of the personality factor in disease may make a distinct contribution to the treatment of homosexuality. The main hope of prevention lies in a change of society's attitude toward deviancy, the removal of legal sanctions against consensual homosexual acts between adults in private, and improved sex education in the school and the home.

1066 COLE, WILLIAM G. "Homosexuality in the Bible." In his *Sex and Love in the Bible,* pp. 342–372. New York: Association Press, 1960.

A chapter is devoted to a discussion of stories with homosexual themes. Most of them appear to condemn homosexuality as unnatural and as a sin against God. An attempt is made to link Biblical concepts of homosexuality with today's normative standards regarding homosexuality. Christian clergy and Christians in general are urged to stop being moralistic and to try to understand the sexual deviant as a sick person, not as unnatural.

1067 COMFORT, ALEX. "A Matter of Science and Ethics: Reflections on the B.M.A. Committee's Report on Homosexuality and Prostitution." *Lancet* 270 (6908, 1956): 147–149.

The British Medical Association's report on homosexuality and prostitution is discussed. The report stated that homosexuals should be treated, not punished, yet no recommendations for legal reform are made. The report became caught up in the use of such words as "perverted," "insidious," "corruption," et cetera, with the result that scientific views became superseded by emotion and fear.

1068 CORY, DONALD WEBSTER. "Changing Attitudes Toward Homosexuals." An Address Delivered to the International Committee for Sex Equality at the University of Frankfort, September, 1952. In *Homosexuality: A Cross Cultural Approach,* edited by Donald Webster Cory, pp. 427–440. New York: Julian Press, 1956.

Attitudes toward homosexuals are contrasted with attitudes toward ethnic minorities in this study. It is believed attitudes have already changed from the time when the very word "homosexual" was unspeakable to the point where discussion is at least open, if not enlightened. Some leaders and defenders are emerging from the ranks of the intellectuals, but potential leaders in the task of changing public attitudes face great risks of negative public reaction. There is thus a dilemma wherein increased leadership is needed if society's attitudes are to be changed, but until such change occurs, leaders will not emerge.

1069 CORY, DONALD WEBSTER, ed. *Homosexuality: A Cross Cultural Approach.* New York: Julian Press, 1956, 440 pp.

Outstanding articles from the past are reprinted to afford a broader understanding of the changing attitudes of society toward homosexuals and of homosexuals toward themselves. Selected modern articles are also included "to continue the approach of the various cultural groups by bringing forth the viewpoints of psychoanalysts, psychologists, jurists, and others." Short editorial comments on each article are included. See Burton, Richard (no. 961). Carpenter, Edward (no. 1062). Cory, Donald Webster (no. 825), (no. 1068). Ellis, Albert (no. 377), (no. 835). Hamilton, Gilbert Van Tassel (no. 164). Henry, George W. (no. 710). Kinsey, Alfred C. (no. 25). Licht, Hans (no. 1000). Mantegazza, Paolo (no. 1006). Ploscowe, Morris (no. 1214). Symonds, John Addington (no. 1247). Voltaire (no. 1029). Westermarck, Edward (no. 1034).

1070 EAST, W. NORWOOD; MACKWOOD, JOHN CHARSLEY; FAIRFIELD, LETITIA; and ROBERTS, G. D. "The Sociological Aspects of Homosexuality." *Medico-Legal Journal* 15 (1, 1947): 11–23.

Four authors contribute to a symposium devoted to a consideration of homosexuality. Homosexuality is believed to be an unfortunate condition, and psychotherapeutic treatment is needed. At the same time, the moral needs of society to protect its young must be met, advisedly, through the imprisonment of homosexual offenders. The female homosexual presents no problem for society since females often form lasting friendships with members of their own sex, and young girls are seldom involved.

1071 ELLIS, ALBERT. "How Homosexuals Can Combat Anti-Homosexualism." *One* 5 (2, 1957): 7–9.

There are two main ways in which homosexuals may combat antihomosexualism—a palliative method and a curative one. The palliative approach, which assumes that sociosexual conditions in this country will continue to exist pretty much as they are now, is designed to help the homosexual blend in and become an accepted member of present-day society. The curative approach, on the other hand, is designed to alter society's basic attitudes toward homosexuality.

The palliative program is aimed at individual homosexuals who should do their best to remain law-abiding, responsible citizens, setting good examples for the heterosexual residents of their communities. Attempts to set themselves apart, by cross-dressing, using opposite sex mannerisms, being clannish, et cetera, should be carefully avoided by all homosexuals, who should try to be as open-minded and undogmatic as possible about their views of homosexuality, and should try to keep up with recent scientific and clinical findings regarding homosexuality, and be able to accept facts contrary to their own pro-homosexual prejudices.

The curative method, however, would revise sex attitudes and behavior on the part of the entire American populace. To use this method, homosexuals must begin to combat puritanism and antisexuality of all types. They must accept and promulgate scientific knowledge and attitudes in general and scientific sex viewpoints in particular; and encourage and sponsor sex research. Finally, they must attack their own unscientific attitudes toward their exclusive inversion, accepting the fact that they are not born homosexual but that they have *learned* to become sexually fixated by some combination of circumstances, and thus, that they are, to some degree, emotionally disturbed and could be cured of their exclusive homosexuality.

1072   EPSTEIN, LOUIS M. "Natural and Unnatural Sex Conduct." In *Sex Laws and Customs in Judaism,* pp. 132–147. New York: KTAV Publishing House, 1967.

The Jewish standards of sex conduct which exist outside of marriage are presented. In the first part of this chapter attitudes found in the Bible and the Talmud toward homosexuality are described and discussed as the foundation of the Jewish sexual conduct standards regarding homosexuality. The influence on Jewish worship of the heathen practice of employing *Kadesh* (male sacred prostitutes) in their worship is also discussed.

1073   FARINA, AMERIGO; ALLEN, JON G.; and SAUL, B. BRIGID B. "The Role of the Stigmatized Person in Affecting Social Relationships." *Journal of Personality* 36 (2, 1968): 169–182.

In a study concerned with the role of the blemished individual, an attempt was made to determine the effect of stigmata on social relationships. Two social stigmata, homosexuality and mental illness, were used in an experiment with undergraduate students.

The subjects were divided into an "A" group and a "B" group and then further subdivided into pairs, each pair composed of one person from the "A" group and one from the "B" group. All the persons in the "B" group were told that information about them had been given to their partners in the "A" group, some were led to believe that their partners from the "A" group had been told that they were homosexual, some believed that their partners had been told they were mentally ill, and some were told that their partners believed they were normal. In reality, however, all the members of the "A" group were told that their partners were completely normal.

It was found that the mere belief of the "B" partner that he was stigmatized influenced the performance of the pair on an assigned task and also influenced their conversation. It is suggested that the stigmatized person attempts to dispel the unfavorable impression he believes he has created and consequently his behavior is affected in such a manner as to cause another person with whom he is interacting to reject him.

1074   GERASSI, JOHN. *The Boys of Boise: Furor, Vice, and Folly in an American City.* New York: Macmillan, 1966, 328 pp.

A journalistic account of the homosexual underworld of Boise, Idaho, and of the community's reaction when the underworld was uncovered and widely publicized is given. The arrest and prosecution of many members of the community, including prominent citizens, is described. The scandal was an example of legalized prejudice, involving politics and personal vendettas.

1075   GILBERT, G. M. "Crime and Punishment: An Exploratory Comparison of Public, Criminal, and Penological Attitudes." *Mental Hygiene* 42 (4, 1958): 550–557.

A questionnaire asking respondents to rank 19 felonies in order of seriousness and to recommend length of prison sentence for each was administered to a public sample of 234, a convict sample of 201, and a social science student sample of 134.

The sex offenses included in the list of 19 felonies were assaultive rape of a child, statutory rape, rape, sex perversion (homosexuality, sodomy), and adultery.

Mean rank-orders, standard deviations and modal sentences revealed a fairly high degree of agreement between and within the three groups regarding assaultive rape of a child, rape, and adultery. (Assaultive rape of a child ranked just below murder as the most serious offense, and adultery was consistently ranked least serious of the 19 felonies). There were, however, marked differences in attitudes toward statutory rape and "sex perversion": prisoner attitudes were found to reflect a self-righteous contempt for sex offenders, while social science students more often take a mental hygiene attitude suggesting treatment rather than lengthy prison sentences for statutory rapists and homosexuals.

1076   GLOVER, EDWARD, ed. *The Problem of Homosexuality.* London: Institute for the Study and Treatment of Delinquency, 1957, 40 pp.

Homosexuality is examined briefly from the standpoints of the law, clinical psychology, religion and morals, and public prejudice. The differences in these viewpoints are outlined. Recommendations are made concerning the laws on homosexuality: homosexuality between consenting adults should not be regarded as a crime, but homosexual acts, whether of adults or minors, should be regarded as offenses if they involve a breach of public decency, violence or rape, or seduction. Concerning treatment and prognosis, it is concluded that under present circumstances treatment should not be looked on as the answer, although this does not imply that penal measures are the only alternative. Variables are specified which, when controlled, may lead to better treatment. A statistical study of 113 offenders, their court records, type of treatment, and prognosis is reported in the appendix.

1077   GROSS, ALFRED A. *Strangers in Our Midst.* Washington: Public Affairs Press, 1962, 182 pp.

Formulating a guide to clergymen for the understanding of homosexuality and the counseling of homosexuals, the climate of opinion and social reactions that homosexuals face and the responsibility of the church in helping them face it are discussed. Legislative reform and the education of the public through the dissemination of more accurate information are called for.

1078   GROSS, ALFRED A. "The Troublesome Homosexual." *Focus* 32 (1, 1953): 13–16.

The homosexual is troublesome to society. Using a case history as illustration, it is asserted that society must rid itself of those homosexuals who are public nuisances, as well as ferret out those (but only those) who are security risks in sensitive posts, whether or not they are homosexuals. The homosexual presents a social problem to which society has no valid answer, but it is possible to aid those who desire a more adequate social adjustment.

1079   GROSS, ALFRED A. "Understanding the Homosexual." *National Probation and Parole Association Journal* 1 (2, 1955): 140–147.

A general review of homosexuality includes its incidence, its biological and legal definitions, differences in individual homosexuals, the homosexual's situation in society, society's treatment of homosexuals, and social attitudes concerning homosexuals.

1080   HADDEN, SAMUEL B. "Attitude Toward and Approaches to the Problem of Homosexuality." *Pennsylvania Medical Journal* 6 (9, 1957): 1195–1198.

Attitudes toward homosexuality found among the homosexuals themselves, psychiatrists, the public, and the legal profession are briefly discussed. Group psychotherapy is recommended as treatment.

1081   HARPER, DANA. "What Do Homosexuals Want?" *Sexology* 16 (7, 1950): 426–433; 16 (8, 1950): 510–516.

Homosexuals seek recognition from others that homosexuality is not a disease and that most homosexuals do not want to be "cured," but only left alone. They believe the stigma and disgrace attached to homosexuality need to be removed. The truth about homosexuality needs to be reported so that understanding can take place.

1082   HERON, ALASTAIR, ed. *Towards a Quaker View of Sex: An Essay by a Group of Friends.* London: Friends Home Service Committee, 1963, 75 pp.

To provide guidance for counselors several English members of the Religious Society of Friends evaluate homosexuality in the light of present knowledge and the Friends' philosophy. The course of normal sexual development is traced with citations from the literature, followed by an analysis of male and female homosexuality and social and legal reactions to it. The universality of homosexual experiences in adolescence is noted, as is the devastating effect of fear of public discovery and censure. The Christian moral view of homosexuality should be the same as that of sexuality in general; it should be that homosexuality is not inherently wrong but depends upon the quality of the individual relationship.

A revised edition of this work was published in 1964. See Barnes, Kenneth, C., et al. (no. 1054).

1083   "Homosexual Scandals: Some Misconceptions." *Corrective Psychiatry and Journal of Social Therapy* 11 (1, 1965): 1–2.

The problems of homosexuality are only dimly comprehended and are generally misunderstood by the public at large. Scandals involving homosexuality are usually based upon the conviction that sexual deviation is a moral lapse calling for public censure and even punishment. The truth is that homosexuality is a long-term state originating in a person's early years which had only been concealed or suppressed by the individual prior to its detection.

1084   "Homosexuality and Moral Welfare." *Lancet* 266 (6810, 1954): 505–506.

The summary of an interim report prepared for the Church of England Moral Welfare Council defines homosexuality, discusses psychological causes (overprotective mother, absent or cruel father), and looks at the religious aspects of homosexuality. While sympathy for the homosexual is expressed, the only suggestions that can be made are that the homosexual either seek a cure or else accept his homosexuality. In either case he should seek divine help through the Church in controlling his sexual desires. The summary points out the legal anomalies in the different legal policies which prevail toward male and female homosexuals.

1085   "Homosexuality and Prostitution." *British Journal of Delinquency*
6 (4, 1956): 315–317.

A descriptive review of the memorandum prepared by a special committee of the British Medical Association for submission to the Departmental Committee on Homosexuality and Prostitution questions the validity of the memorandum's classification of homosexuality as "essential" and "acquired." (Homosexuals in the essential group derive their homosexual tendencies from physiological sources and from early environmental factors, while those in the acquired group develop homosexual tendencies later in life.) The proposition that homosexuals may be treated by their family doctors is also questioned.

It is pointed out that the language of the report betrays a bias against homosexuals—that it is moralistic and emotional rather than objective and scientific.

1086   JONES, H. KIMBALL. *Toward a Christian Understanding of the Homosexual.* New York: Association Press, 1966, 160 pp.

An analysis of present-day knowledge and information about homosexuality and its implications for understanding and action on the part of the church is given, including a typology of homosexuals and figures on incidence. A consideration of theories of causation, views of homosexuality as a disease or nondisease, and problems of therapy provides a background for the discussion. Against this background the past and possible reactions of the church are then discussed. In the past the homosexual has found little understanding or sympathy within the Judeo-Christian tradition. An attempt is made to arrive at a "responsible Christian ethic" with regard to homosexuality. Asserting that homosexuals cannot achieve complete sexual fulfillment, the basic question is not whether the homosexual is in a state of sin (since we are all in a state of sin), but how can he make the best of a given (in many cases an unchangeable) situation.

1087   JUZWIAK, MARIJO. "Understanding the Homosexual Patient." *RN*
[*Registered Nurse*] 27 (4, 1964): 53–59, 118.

A verbatim account of an interview with Judd Marmor, a recognized authority on the subject, is presented to help nurses understand homosexuality and to suggest ways in which homosexual patients should be treated.

In a general way the questions cover such areas as types of homosexuals, homosexual etiology, problems of overt homosexual approaches, and/or activity among patients, and handling nurses' attitudes against or fears about homosexuality.

1088   KAMENY, FRANKLIN E. "Federal Government and Homosexuals." *Concern* 8 (Apr. 15, 1966): 10–11, 14.

Discrimination of the United States Civil Service Commission against employing homosexuals is claimed. Unfounded prejudice and a sense of "morals" is viewed as the cause of this discrimination in employment.

1089   KATZ, ROBERT L. "Church History, Attitudes, and Laws." Unedited Working Paper prepared for the National Institute of Mental Health Task Force on Homosexuality. Mimeographed. Cincinnati, O.: Hebrew Union College, Nov. 25–26, 1967, 15 pp.

The works of D. S. Bailey are used as a source for summarizing the historical religious attitude proscribing homosexuality since Biblical times. While Bailey attempts to exonerate the church of blame for this attitude, the author disagrees, giving examples from basic religious sources.

Although recent and contemporary attitudes tend to be more liberal, it is impossible to identify the representative church attitude. Instead, one finds a variety of attitudes expressed by individual clergymen and theologians. In many church circles today "considerable psychological and sociological sophistication can be found coexisting, as it were, with unbroken commitment to traditional theology." It is not predicted that formal church groups will abruptly surrender their historic attitude, but that gradually they may yield to the force of social change.

1090   KITSUSE, JOHN I. "Societal Reaction to Deviant Behavior: Problems of Theory and Method." *Social Problems* 9 (3, 1962): 247–256.

Homosexual behavior and the reactions to it are examined through interviews with 700 undergraduates. A homosexual population is produced sociologically when individuals are identified by others as homosexual and treated in a manner appropriate to that identification. The findings suggest that the conceptions of persons in everyday life concerning "sex-appropriate" and "sex-inappropriate" behavior may lead them to interpret a variety of behavioral forms as indications of homosexuality. The data suggest that the critical feature of the deviant-defining process is the interpretations others make of the individual's behavior, whatever this behavior may be. The process by which persons come to be defined as homosexual was found to be contingent upon the retrospective and prospective interpretations of their behavior by others. The sanctions imposed, and the treatment they are accorded as a consequence of being defined as homosexual, were found to vary widely among members of various groups.

1091   KUHN, DONALD, ed. *The Church and the Homosexual.* San Francisco: Glide Urban Center, 1964, 32 pp.

Ths is a report on a conference attended by members of churches and members of homophile organizations on the relations between the Church and homosexuals. One representative of a homophile organization summarized results of a questionnaire answered by 40 homosexually inclined persons whose answers indicated that they felt rejected and misunderstood by the Church. Another representative offered a series of aphorisms intended to "demolish four-walled thinking" on homosexuality and the Church. Other discussions were held on legal reactions, biblical and theological bases for a Church position on homosexuality, and a statement of goals and purposes for a newly created Council on Religion and the Homosexual.

1092   LEAROYD, C. G. "The Problem of Homosexuality." *Practitioner* 172 (1030, 1954): 355–363.

A general discussion of the types of homosexuals and their treatment is presented. Male homosexuality can be divided into an adolescent, exploratory phase; emotional immaturity; and regression. The retention of the laws against homosexuality is urged since the most important part of the treatment of homosexuals is prevention—punish them so that they will not be able to seduce others. Hostile public opinion is the best preventive.

1093   LEVITT, EUGENE E., and BRADY, JOHN PAUL. "Sexual Preferences in Young Adult Males and Some Correlates," *Journal of Clinical Psychology* 21 (4, 1965): 347–354.

Sixty-eight male graduate students indicated their preferences for 19 different sexual themes by rating photographs. Some of the results pertained to homosexuality. Photographs of female homosexuality were rated higher (more stimulating) than those depicting themes of male homosexuality, which were rated very low. Subjects reared in less populous communities reacted more strongly to the male homosexual themes.

1094   LUCAS, DONALD S. "The Homosexual and the Church." Mimeographed. San Francisco: Mattachine Society, [ca. 1965], 43 pp.

Forty homosexuals completed a questionnaire on their attitudes toward and experiences with the Church. They were asked about their religion, whether they felt the Church was letting them down, how the Church could change, and what it could do. In general they felt that the Church was letting down the homosexual and that there should be a change in Church dogma, although apparently only a few participants were aware of the content of the present dogmas.

1095   LUDOVICI, ANTHONY. "Homosexuality, the Law and Public Senti-
        ment." With a commentary by Clifford Allen. *International Journal
        of Sexology* 5 (3, 1951–1952): 143–150.

Attitudes of the public toward the apprehension and conviction of homosexuals are discussed. It is at least reasonable to demand laws for protecting
the young from defilement. The higher the social standing of the apprehended homosexual the greater is his crime, for not only has he broken
the law, but he has also betrayed his class and has acted against his position
of leadership in the society.

A commentary, given in response to the author's contentions, calls for
the treatment of homosexual offenders rather than imprisonment. The belief
is expressed that assaults on children by homosexuals are not as damaging
as others claim. Sex offenders are divided into three categories: nuisances
(frication, exhibitionism are examples), who need treatment and supervision; potentially dangerous (homosexual, sadist, pederast), for whom treatment in a hospital and supervision after discharge are required; and
menaces (dangerous sadist), who should be imprisoned for life.

1096   M. M. "A Sociologist Looks at Homosexuality: A Criticism of the
        Current Sociological Text, *Sociology of Deviant Behavior* by Mar-
        shall B. Clinard." *Homophile Studies* 1 (2, 1958): 48–49, 64.

Although Clinard defines deviation from social and cultural norms in almost exclusively negative terms, deviation actually refers to any variation
from the norms, positive as well as negative. Homosexual behavior has not
always, for example in ancient Greece, been considered deviant. There is
no recognition of the innate qualities of persons in the development of
deviance; instead it is stated that human nature is determined by social
experiences rather than by a biological inheritance. Clinard is criticized for
placing homosexuality under the "sex offender" classification. It is suggested that if there is reason to do so, the reason should be stated and an
explanation of how it fits in should be given. His failure to indicate any
of the constructive aspects of homosexuality or bisexuality is also criticized.

1097   MCHENRY, F. A. "A Note on Homosexuality, Crime and the News-
        papers." *Journal of Criminal Psychopathology* 2 (4, 1941): 533–548.

The presence of homosexuality as a factor in reported crime has long been
discreetly presented by our newspapers. However, recently the journals

have become more outspoken, although they need still fuller reporting of such instances in order to better serve the community.

1098   "Male Homosexuality." *Medical Journal of Australia* 2 (14, 1967): 651–652.

It is acknowledged that although much is being learned about homosexuality, little is actually being done about it. Four related areas are briefly discussed: further scientific and clinical study and research, further education of medical practitioners, prevention of the disorder, and special community leadership.

1099   MARNEY, CARLYLE. "The Christian Community and the Homosexual." 1966. Reprinted in *Social Progress: A Journal of Church and Society* 58 (2, 1967): 31–40.

For illogical reasons Christian ethics deny that sex can be expressed between those of the same sex. Also, Christian ethics puts much blame on the homosexual while excusing other overt and covert immorality. These problems must be overcome before the Christian community is to become one of compassion and accepting of homosexuals.

1100   MATHEWS, ARTHUR GUY. *Is Homosexuality a Menace?* New York: Robert M. McBride Co., 1957, 302 pp.

Homosexuality is considered not as congenital but as a conditioned moral deterioration that can be cured by psychiatric treatment if the homosexual is sufficiently cooperative. The daily activities of homosexuals, their seduction of the young, and their infiltration into the arts, teaching, and medicine are depicted. It is concluded that homosexuality is, indeed, a menace.

1101   MAZUR, RONALD M. *Commonsense Sex.* Boston: Beacon Press, 1968, 109 pp.

In one chapter, which discusses homosexuality, the conviction is expressed that the persecution of homosexuals is reinforced by religious prejudices but that the main cause of this persecution is not the religious beliefs which are prevalent in our society but the male's image of manhood and his relentless efforts to preserve this image. It is advocated that homosexuality not be viewed as a threat to the stability of the social order. If homosexuality is an emotional illness, it should then be viewed with compassion; if it is a preferred way of life for some people, then these people should be granted the right to their way of life.

1102 MORSE, BENJAMIN. *The Sexual Revolution.* Derby, Conn.: Monarch Books, 1962, 157 pp.

A popularized discussion of the "revolution" in sexual mores and behavior considers many of its aspects, including prostitution, teen-age promiscuity, wife-swapping, and homosexuality. In one chapter entitled "The Rising Tide of Homosexuality," it is asserted that a tremendous and virtually unprecedented increase in both male and female homosexuality is one of the great characteristics of the contemporary sexual revolution.

1103 NEEDHAM, MERRILL A., and SCHUR, EDWIN M. "Student Punitiveness Toward Sexual Deviation." *Marriage and Family Living* 25 (2, 1963): 227–229.

Ninety students at a small private university were asked to respond to 15 items describing sexual behavior. They were given a choice of the degree of punitive action that should be taken for each behavior. Only 16 percent of the students felt that severe punitive action should be taken against "two unmarried adults engaging, by mutual consent and in private, in homosexual acts."

1104 NEW YORK ACADEMY OF MEDICINE, COMMITTEE ON PUBLIC HEALTH. "Homosexuality: Report." *Bulletin of the New York Academy of Medicine* 2d Ser. 40 (7, 1964): 576–580.

The conclusions of this report are as follows: the Committee on Public Health, as a medical body, should state clearly its position on homosexuality; homosexuality is an illness; some cases may be successfully treated; prevention is the easier and more effective course of action; sex education in this country should be realistically examined.

1105 O'GRADY, GERALD B., JR., et al. "Should Homosexual Behavior between Consenting Adults Be Considered a Crime?" Viewpoints: A Special Feature Presenting a Wide Range of Divergent Opinions on Controversial Issues Relating to Sexuality. *Medical Aspects of Human Sexuality* 1 (2, 1967): 39–50.

Clergymen, doctors, and lawyers discuss the moral and legal aspects of the question of homosexual behavior between consenting adults. The general consensus is that such behavior should be considered neither immoral nor illegal.

1106 PARLOUR, RICHARD R. "In Reply: Morality and Homosexuality." *Psychiatric Opinion* 4 (4, 1967): 33–35.

In "Group Psychotherapy and Homosexuality," Samuel B. Hadden had observed that homosexuality "is a problem for psychological medicine and not a basic moral problem." Such is not the case, however. Since sexual conduct has always been a primary moral concern in every society, it follows logically that homosexuality is a moral problem.

Psychologists and psychiatrists see homosexuality as a problem for psychological medicine because their judgments are based upon the patients they see rather than upon "homosexual persons who demonstrate a keen sense of responsibility, moral concern and social awareness, as well as personal proficiency and equanimity."

Like most other problems in psychiatry, homosexuality is a matter of moral concern, and psychiatrists could give more help to their homosexual patients if they were to admit this.

1107   PITTENGER, NORMAN. *Time for Consent: A Christian's Approach to Homosexuality.* London: S.C.M. Press, 1967, 64 pp.

Homosexual acts between persons intending to maintain a permanent union and who are in love are neither criminal nor sinful. Support for this argument is developed through a consideration of the nature of man, the meaning of sin, the homosexual condition, and the morality of homosexual acts.

1108   "A Psychosexual Deviation: The Homosexual." *Police* 3 (Jul.–Aug., 1959): 39.

Law enforcement officials at a conference deplored the lack of therapeutic care available to homosexuals and other sexual deviates and urged a greater effort in the finding of new techniques which would provide proper psychiatric treatment.

1109   PUMPIAN-MINDLIN, EUGENE. "Nymphomania and Satyriasis." In *Sexual Problems: Diagnosis and Treatment in Medical Practice,* edited by Charles William Wahl, pp. 163–171. New York: Free Press, 1967.

Social attitudes toward hyperheterosexuality and toward homosexuality are contrasted. In our society, hyperheterosexuality is condoned and, in the case of satyriasis, even glorified as a proof of masculinity, while homosexuality is viewed with far less tolerance and judged on a moral rather than a medical basis.

1110   ROBERTS, AYMER. *Judge Not.* London: Linden Press, 1957, 195 pp.

An initial section of the present volume contains an autobiographical account of homosexuality designed to promote understanding and empathy.

In addition there is a lengthy theological discussion of Christianity and a description of its development. A memorandum sent to the Departmental Committee of the Home Office with reference to homosexuality and the law is included.

1111 ROCHE, PHILIP Q. "Sexual Deviations." *Federal Probation* 14 (3, 1950): 3–11.

Sexual perversions and sex offenses should not be treated as criminal offenses, but rather as forms of mental illness which call for treatment rather than detention. A brief summary is given of the Freudian view of psychosexual development through the oral, anal, genital, latent, adolescent, and adult heterosexual stage. Sexual perversions arise from an individual's failure to progress past the latent stage. It is pointed out that, though the behavior of the pervert may be unaesthetic or a nuisance, it is not necessarily dangerous. The role of the psychologist and psychiatrist is that of advising the courts on the need for the retention of a convicted offender or for his release with treatment as a condition of parole. Male and female homosexuality are briefly discussed; it is explained how both forms arise out of a genital fear which develops in childhood. Female homosexuality is more basic since the early fixation of a female child to her mother is homosexual. No judgment is made as to the danger of homosexuals to society nor to the criminality of homosexual acts.

1112 ROONEY, ELIZABETH A., and GIBBONS, DON C. "Social Reactions to 'Crimes Without Victims.'" *Social Problems* 13 (4, 1966): 400–410.

Views of policies toward and misconceptions about homosexuality, abortion, and drug addiction were gathered from 353 respondents in the San Francisco area. Over half the respondents felt that homosexuality between consenting adults should be legal, but that homosexuals should not be allowed to organize for their civil liberties. Over 80 percent felt homosexuals are psychologically disturbed and should seek help to adjust to a normal heterosexual life, and almost 70 percent felt homosexuals are dangerous because they try to seduce young boys. Feelings toward homosexuals tended to be based on one's accurate knowledge of homosexuality as well as on one's religion and education.

1113 RUBIN, ISADORE. *Homosexuality.* SIECUS Discussion Guide, no. 2. New York: Sex Information and Education Council of the U.S., 1965, 7 pp. Also published as SIECUS Study Guide, no. 2, 20 pp.

A brief summary of the current problem of homosexuality follows a question and answer format. Intended primarily for use by discussion leaders, its aim is "to substitute understanding based on the best scientific evidence available for condemnation based on ignorance and fear." The 14 questions which are included range from "What is homosexuality?" to "How can homosexuality be prevented?" A selected bibliography is included.

1114   SAGARIN, EDWARD. "Ideology as a Factor in the Consideration of Deviance." *Journal of Sex Research* 4 (2, 1968): 84–94.

In an article dealing with the ideology of scientists as it influences their perception of deviance, it is contended that much of what passes for scientific thought and findings has been influenced by the findings scientists wish to substantiate. In other words, behavioral scientists have allowed their own values to color their attitudes toward deviants—out of sympathy for the deviant they have attempted to picture him as normal and not able to change. While it is not necessary that the scientist be value-free, there is a need for science to be value-free.

1115   STERLING, DAVID LYN. *Sex in the Basic Personality.* Wichita, Kan.: Hubbard Dianetic Foundation, 1952, 180 pp.

An examination of sex and sexual irregularities, particularly homosexuality, is presented from the standpoint of dianetics. Dianetics is devoted to the elimination of insanity, crime, and war, and to increasing the individuals' "survival potentials." The second of the Eight Dynamics, or "subdivisions of survival potential" is "potential survival through the family unit," which is the topic discussed here. Homosexuality endangers this "potential." A "tone scale" is presented for measuring "homosexual potential." The hope of cure is offered through dianetic processing.

1116   TAYLOR, GORDON RATTRAY. *Sex in History.* New York: Vanguard Press, 1954, 336 pp.

An attempt is made to define the place of sex in the European cultural tradition. Adopting a scheme in which society can be defined at different times as either "matrist" or "patrist," it is suggested that it is possible to determine the type of a given society by examining that society's attitude toward sex. If a society, for example, has a somewhat permissive attitude toward homosexuality, this indicates that the society is a "matrist" one, characterized by a dislike of authority, a high respect for women intellectually, and a general liberal attitude toward sexual indulgence. On the other hand, if a society seems to consider homosexuality the greatest sin, the society is a "patrist" one, characterized by authoritarian attitudes and definite restrictions on all forms of sexual activity.

The basic scheme presented is a variation on the matriarchy/patriarchy concepts, based upon a study of attitudes rather than institutions. Several introductory chapters set forth the thesis of the study, and the remainder is made up of descriptions of the main chronological periods in European history, identifying these periods as either "matrist" or "patrist" by describing their attitudes toward sex.

1117 THIELICKE, HELMUT. *The Ethics of Sex.* Translated by John W. Doberstein. New York: Harper & Row, 1964, 338 pp.

In a book which represents an attempt to reevaluate the German Protestant theological position regarding sexuality, one particular chapter is entitled, "The Problem of Homosexuality."

A discussion of the traditional Protestant theological position toward homosexuality is followed by a closely reasoned argument, based upon theological grounds, which concludes that homosexuality, in and of itself, is not necessarily sinful. It is placed instead on the same level with abnormal personality structure, with the conclusion that "theologically one dare not put an endogenous homosexuality, which is a kind of symptomatic participation in the fate of the fallen world, on the same level with concrete acts of libidinous excess. . . ."

Some advice for pastors regarding the counseling of homosexuals, and an argument that the question is an ethical rather than a legal one, conclude the chapter.

1118 UNITED STATES, CONGRESS, SENATE, COMMITTEE ON EXPENDITURES IN THE EXECUTIVE DEPARTMENTS. *Employment of Homosexuals and Other Sex Perverts in Government: Interim Report Submitted to the Committee on Expenditures in the Executive Departments by Its Subcommittee on Investigations Pursuant to S. Res. 280.* 81st Cong., 2d sess., 15 December 1950, Senate Document 241, 26 pp.

The findings of a United States Senate Committee on the employment of homosexuals and other sex perverts are given. The committee concluded that homosexuals are not suitable for government employment because they are immoral and because they are a security risk. It was found that the existing rules on dismissing sex perverts from government service were being ignored. Because of the work of the committee, the branches of the government were made more aware of the dangers of sexual perversion. Ample review and appeal procedures should be established for efficient and fair treatment of the problem. The government must become more alert to the problems of sexual perversion. Further reviews were planned by the committee.

Senator John L. McClellan of Arkansas was chairman of the committee, which included Senator Joseph R. McCarthy of Wisconsin.

1119   VAN DEN HAAG, ERNEST. "Notes on Homosexuality and Its Cultural Setting." Reprinted in *The Problem of Homosexuality in Modern Society*, edited by Hendrik M. Ruitenbeek, pp. 291–302. New York: E. P. Dutton & Co., 1963.

A homosexual is defined as "a person who finds his exclusive or main sexual gratification in . . . sexual relations with persons of his own sex." The beliefs of cultures disapproving of homosexuality are categorized as beliefs that it is contrary to the laws of God, nature, or morality; or beliefs that it is detrimental to the health and welfare of society or detrimental to homosexuals themselves.

Although homosexual behavior, like certain forms of heterosexual behavior, often is a symptom or part of illness; it is doubtful that it is a disease. The fear of homosexuality may lead to an insistence on virility and to hostility toward homosexuality. The actual effects of legal prohibition are an "unmitigated evil," creating occasions for blackmail and worsening the situation psychologically. Homosexuality in the United States is attributed to restrictions on sexual behavior and to the lack of a proper parental model.

1120   WARING, PAUL, and BRYCE, DEAN TRAVIS. *Homosexual Freedom*. N.p.: The Authors, 1961, 26 pp.

Homosexual conduct is perceived as an abomination and as an unnatural practice contrary to the natural order of the venereal act of the human race. Education of the public is advocated to counteract the effectiveness of groups which exist to achieve the removal of legal barriers to homosexual practice and the acceptance of the homosexual by society.

1121   WEAVER, HERBERT B., and ARKOFF, ABE. "Measurement of Attitudes Concerning Sexual Permissiveness." *Social Science* 40 (3, 1965): 163–170.

An attempt is made to construct a scale indicating attitudes toward a very wide range of sexuality: premarital dating behavior, marital and extramarital sexual behavior, and homosexuality. The researchers contrived 142 statements which were to be rated from 1 to 5, disagree to agree, by 176 subjects, including 89 female and 87 male college students, both undergraduates and graduates, and both married and single.

The distribution was bimodal, with a high or liberal group and a low or conservative group. The high group had a 2.5 male:female ratio while the low group had a 2.7 male:female ratio. Married and single proportions were evenly distributed except that low group females tended to be single. The mean response on each statement for the groups was determined, and the difference between the two means reported. Two sets of 30 statements each were selected as being significant in determining attitude differences (mean responses differed by 2.0 or more). Statements on homosexuality with the difference of means between the two groups were as follows: homosexuality is universally wrong (2.97); homosexual acts performed by consenting adults in private are all right (3.10); there should be rigid laws against homosexuality (2.35); homosexuality is unnatural (2.13).

The scale is believed to provide an accurate measurement of sexual permissiveness.

1122 WEST, LOUIS JOLYON, and GLASS, ALBERT J. "Sexual Behavior and the Military Law." In *Sexual Behavior and the Law,* edited by Ralph Slovenko, pp. 250–272. Springfield, Ill.: Charles C. Thomas, 1965.

Homosexuality is the principal area of sexual behavior that is of concern to the military. The primary objective of the military should be the prompt elimination of known or habitual homosexuals or persons with well-defined conscious homosexual tendencies, rather than harsh management or punitive discharge. Homosexuals need not be given punitive-type dishonorable discharges; if they have not committed any known offense while on active duty, they should be sent home promptly and without dishonor.

1123 WHEELER, STANTON. "Sex Offenses: A Sociological Critique." *Law and Contemporary Problems* 25 (2, 1960): 258–278.

A brief review of three problems in the area of adult sex offender legislation is presented. The first problem concerns the types of sex relationships which should be subject to legal restraint; the second problem is related to social attitudes toward various forms of sex conduct between consenting partners; and the third area deals with problems posed by more serious sex offenders with special attention directed to psychopath statutes and to possible sociogenic factors in the development of sex offenders. With reference to social attitudes toward sex conduct between consenting partners, the degree of public tolerance for homosexuals is not known. It is suggested, however, that an increasing body of research indicates that tolerance toward nonconforming behavior may be on the increase.

1124 WHITELEY, C. H., and WHITELEY, WINIFRED M. "Unfruitful Sex." In their *Sex & Morals,* pp. 79–100. New York: Basic Books, 1967.

Homosexuality is discussed within the general context of sexual "perversion" which is defined as any sexual activity which cannot result in procreation. The traditional religious argument against homosexuality as an unnatural activity is presented and answered with the contention that if it were followed to its logical conclusion all sexual activity would be unnatural except that which occurs between a male and a female of childbearing age at a time when the female is capable of conceiving.

It is suggested that homosexuality arouses moral indignation in patriarchial societies because it upsets traditional divisions of sex roles which, in turn, poses a strong threat to male supremacy. The male homosexual is the object of more hostility and indignation because he is seen as rejecting the notion that his duty lies in founding a family and playing out the traditional role of husband and father.

Since groups of homosexuals reject traditional life patterns as set forth in the Old and New Testaments, their existence can be perceived as a threat to the traditions of family life with its emphasis upon male leadership and female subservience. In the fight for male supremacy, male homosexuals are seen as traitors to their sex. Lesbian activity is not regarded with such great indignation and moral condemnation, perhaps because the existence of lesbian groups does not threaten the masculine establishment.

While the religious arguments against homosexuality do not hold up logically, it is possible to argue that the practice is not psychologically desirable since a homosexual life pattern does not include the incentives and opportunities for the taking of family responsibility and for the development of full personal relationships that marriage provides. In addition, as long as family life forms the standard pattern of our society, the homosexual will always be considered something of a misfit.

It is, however, absurd and unjust to punish a person for his choice of sexual partner unless that partner is too young to give his full consent.

1125 WILLIAMS, DANIEL DAY. "Three Studies of Homosexuality in Relation to the Christian Faith." *Social Action* 34 (4, 1967): 30–37.

The Ethics of Sex by Helmut Thielicke, *Toward a Christian Understanding of Homosexuality* by H. Kimball Jones, and *Christ and the Homosexual* by Robert W. Wood are discussed in relation to the issues posed for the church by homosexuality. It is noted that all three books agree on the point that the church has much to learn about homosexuality and about the perspective of the Christian faith upon this aspect of life.

1126 WOLFENDEN, JOHN. "Evolution of British Attitudes toward Homosexuality." *American Journal of Psychiatry* 125 (6, 1968): 792–797.

In 1953 a committee of laymen was organized to advise the government of Great Britain on homosexuality and prostitution. That part of the committee's report which concerned the nature of crime is discussed. The committee suggested that there is no form of behavior which is in itself criminal;

an action is criminal only if so designated by one empowered to do so. Some forms of sexual behavior were regarded as deserving moral condemnation, but not needing to be placed under the jurisdiction of the law.

The committee came to accept the view that the function of the criminal law in the area of sexual behavior is to safeguard public order and decency and to protect those who, for whatever reason, are properly regarded as the weak and, therefore, deserve society's protection. As a result it was held that private sexual behavior of adults is no concern of the criminal law; a position from which it follows that homosexual behavior carried out in private between consenting adults should not be illegal, while solicitation by prostitutes in public places should.

1127 WOOD, ROBERT WATSON. *Christ and the Homosexual: Some Observations.* New York: Vantage Press, 1960, 221 pp.

The homosexual community is seen as a vast complex segment of society which has both influenced and been influenced by events since World War II. The main thesis is that homosexuals are misguided in some of their behavior but that they are not necessarily sinning. The Church's opposition to Christ's teaching concerning homosexuality is documented, and it is suggested that the Church should immediately implement its message of love by positive acts of concern for the homosexual.

CROSS-REFERENCES

Albany Trust. *Some Questions and Answers about Homosexuality.* London: Albany Trust, n.d., 16 pp. No. 1129.

Beggs, Keith Siddons. "Some Legal, Social and Psychiatric Aspects of Homosexual Behavior: A Guide for the Social Worker in the Sex Clinic." Master's thesis, University of Wisconsin, 1950, 298 pp. No. 955.

Benjamin, Harry. "Must the Homosexual Be Rejected?" 1958. Reprinted in *The Third Sex,* edited by Isadore Rubin, pp. 7–12. New York: New Book Co., 1961. No. 1132.

Bozarth, René, and Gross, Alfred A. "Homosexuality: Sin or Sickness? A Dialogue." *Pastoral Psychology* 13 (129, 1962): 35–42. No. 322.

Cantor, Donald J. "The Homosexual Revolution: A Status Report." 1967. Reprinted in *Social Progress* 58 (2, 1967): 5–12. No. 818.

Caprio, Frank S., and Brenner, Donald R. *Sexual Behavior: Psycho-Legal Aspects.* New York: Citadel Press, 1961, 384 pp. No. 1141.

Carstairs, G. Morris. "Hinjra and Jiryan: Two Derivatives of Hindu Attitudes to Sexuality." *British Journal of Medical Psychology* 29 (2, 1956): 128–138. No. 963.

The Challenge and Progress of Homosexual Law Reform. Essays on Homosexuality, no. 2. San Francisco: Council on Religion and the Homosexual, Daughters of

Bilitis, Society for Individual Rights, Tavern Guild of San Francisco, 1968, 72 pp. No. 1144.

Churchill, Wainwright. *Homosexual Behavior Among Males: A Cross-Cultural and Cross-Species Investigation.* New York: Hawthorn Books, 1967, 340 pp. No. 122.

Cory, Donald Webster. *The Homosexual in America: A Subjective Approach.* New York: Greenberg, 1951, 326 pp. No. 826.

Ford, Clellan S., and Beach, Frank A. *Patterns of Sexual Behavior.* New York: Harper & Brothers, 1951, 307 pp. No. 979.

Frey, Egon C. "Dreams of Male Homosexuals and the Attitude of Society." *Journal of Individual Psychology* 18 (1, 1962): 26–34. No. 400.

Gagnon, John H., and Simon, William. "Sexual Deviance in Contemporary America." *Annals of the American Academy of Political and Social Science* 376 (Mar., 1968): 106–122. No. 842.

Ginsberg, Morris. "The Enforcement of Morals." *British Journal of Sociology* 12 (1, 1961): 65–68. No. 1164.

Glover, Edward. "Homosexuality and Prostitution: A Review." *British Journal of Delinquency* 6 (4, 1956): 315–317. No. 1167.

Jepson, N. A. "Homosexuality, Capital Punishment, and the Law: Two Questionnaires," *British Journal of Delinquency* 9 (4, 1959): 246–257. No. 1191.

"Homosexuality." *GP [General Practitioner]* 16 (4, 1957): 132. No. 450.

Hoffman, Martin. *The Gay World: Male Homosexuality and the Social Creation of Evil.* New York: Basic Books, 1968, 212 pp. No. 855.

Greenzweig, Charles Jerome. "Society Within Society: A Descriptive and Analytical Presentation of Homosexuality as a Social Problem." Master's thesis, Brooklyn College, 1954, 142 pp. No. 849.

Karpman, Benjamin. "Considerations Bearing on the Problems of Sexual Offenses." *Journal of Criminal Law, Criminology, and Police Science* 43 (1, 1952): 13–28. No. 1192.

Kling, Samuel G. "Homosexual Behavior." In his *Sexual Behavior and the Law,* pp. 97–128. New York: Bernard Geis Associates, 1965. No. 870.

Knox, Stuart C. "Another Look at Homosexuality." *Journal of the American Medical Association* 193 (10, 1965): 831. No. 718.

Landes, Ruth. "A Cult Matriarchate and Male Homosexuality." *Journal of Abnormal and Social Psychology* 35 (3, 1940): 386–397. No. 996.

Lindner, Robert. "Homosexuality and the Contemporary Scene." 1956. Reprinted in *The Problem of Homosexuality in Modern Society,* edited by Hendrik M. Ruitenbeek, pp. 52–79. New York: E. P. Dutton & Co., 1963. No. 875.

McCreary, John K. "Psychopathia Homosexualis." *Canadian Journal of Psychology* 4 (1950): 63–74. No. 500.

McIntosh, Mary. "The Homosexual Role." *Social Problems* 16 (2, 1968): 182–192. No. 876.

Magee, Bryan. *One in Twenty: A Study of Homosexuality in Men and Women.* London: Secker & Warburg, 1966, 192 pp. No. 878.

Masters, R. E. L. *Forbidden Sexual Behavior and Morality: An Objective Re-Exami-

nation of Perverse Sex Practices in Different Cultures. New York: Julian Press, 1962, 431 pp. No. 1008.

Mead, Margaret. *Male and Female: A Study of the Sexes in a Changing World.* New York: William Morrow & Co., 1949, 477 pp. No. 1009.

"Origins of Homosexuality." *British Medical Journal* (5470, 1965): 1077–1078. No. 220.

"The Other Side: Living with Homosexuality." *Canadian Medical Association Journal* 86 (May 12, 1962): 875–878. No. 888.

Popkess, Athelstan. "Some Criminal Aspects of Abnormalities of Sex." *Practitioner* 172 (1030, 1954): 446–450. No. 891.

Roeburt, John. *Sex Life and the Criminal Law.* New York: Belmont Books, 1963, 157 pp. No. 1227.

Schofield, Michael George. "Early Experiences, Section C. Homosexuality." In his *The Sexual Behavior of Young People,* pp. 57–59. Boston: Little, Brown & Co., 1965. No. 904.

Simpson, George. *People in Families.* New York: Thomas Y. Crowell Co., 1960, 554 pp. No. 245.

Slovenko, Ralph. "Homosexuality and the Law." *Medical Aspects of Human Sexuality* 1 (1, 1967): 35–38. No. 1239.

Sweet, Roxanna Beryl Thayer. "Political and Social Action in Homophile Organizations." Ph.D. dissertation, University of California at Berkeley, 1968, 256 pp. No. 915.

Tappan, Paul W. "Some Myths about the Sex Offender." *Federal Probation* 19 (2, 1955): 7–12. No. 1248.

Ullerstam, Lars. *The Erotic Minorities.* New York: Grove Press, 1966, 172 pp. No. 1249.

West, D. J. *Homosexuality.* Chicago: Aldine Publishing Co., 1968, 304 pp. No. 922.

Westermarck, Edward. "Homosexual Love." 1906. Reprinted in *Homosexuality: A Cross Cultural Approach,* edited by Donald Webster Cory, pp. 101–138. New York: Julian Press, 1956. No. 1034.

FEMALE

1128 POMEROY, WARDELL B. "Why We Tolerate Lesbians." *Sexology* 31 (10, 1965): 652–655.

There are historical reasons which account for the toleration of lesbians. Early Judeo-Christian culture expressed no concern about female sexuality. Homosexuality has traditionally been identified with anal intercourse. There are also other reasons for the tolerance which is found. The female homosexual "butch" role is rare. There is no female homosexual prostitution. The public is unclear as to what constitutes female homosexuality. Female homosexuality does not threaten men or women. Child molestations by homosexual females are rare.

CROSS-REFERENCES

Caprio, Frank S. *Female Homosexuality: A Psychodynamic Study of Lesbianism.* New York: Citadel Press, 1954, 334 pp. Chapter 16. "Therapeutic Management: Preventive Measures," pp. 285–298. Reprinted as "Preventive Measures." In *Carol in a Thousand Cities,* edited by Ann Aldrich, pp. 153–166. Greenwich, Conn.: Fawcett Publications, 1960. No. 626.

Carpenter, Edward. "The Intermediate Sex: A Study of Some Transitional Types of Men and Women." 1908. Reprinted in *Homsexuality: A Cross Cultural Approach,* edited by Donald Webster Cory, pp. 139–206. New York: Julian Press, 1956. No. 1062.

Barnes, Kenneth C., et al. *Towards a Quaker View of Sex: An Essay by a Group of Friends.* Rev. ed. London: Friends Home Service Committee, 1964, 84 pp. No. 1045.

Bennet, E. A. "The Social Aspects of Homosexuality." *Medical Press* 217 (Sept. 3, 1947): 207–210. No. 1056.

Benson, R.O. D. *In Defense of Homosexuality, Male and Female: A Rational Evaluation of Social Prejudice.* New York: Julian Press, 1965, 239 pp. No. 1057.

East, W. Norwood; Mackwood, John Charsley; Fairfield, Letitia; and Roberts, G. D. "The Sociological Aspects of Homosexuality." *Medico-Legal Journal* 15 (1, 1947): 11–23. No. 1070.

Ford, Clellan S., and Beach, Frank A. *Patterns of Sexual Behavior.* New York: Harper & Brothers, 1951, 307 pp. No. 979.

Gagnon, John H., and Simon, William. "Sexual Deviance in Contemporary America." *Annals of the American Academy of Political and Social Science* 376 (Mar., 1968): 106–122. No. 842.

Glover, Edward. *"Homosexuality and Prostitution: A Review." British Journal of Delinquency* 6 (4, 1956): 315–317. No. 1167.

Heron, Alastair, ed. *Towards a Quaker View of Sex: An Essay by a Group of Friends.* London: Friends Home Service Committee, 1963, 75 pp. No. 1082.

Levitt, Eugene E., and Brady, John Paul. "Sexual Preferences in Young Adult Males and Some Correlates." *Journal of Clinical Psychology* 21 (4, 1965): 347–354. No. 1093.

Magee, Bryan. *One in Twenty: A Study of Homosexuality in Men and Women.* London: Secker & Warburg, 1966, 192 pp. No. 878.

Popkess, Athelstan. "Some Criminal Aspects of Abnormalities of Sex." *Practitioner* 172 (1030, 1954): 446–450. No. 891.

Rancourt, Réjane, and Limoges, Thérèse. "Homosexuality among Women." *Canadian Nurse* 63 (12, 1967): 42–44. No. 944.

Schofield, Michael George. "Early Experiences, Section C. Homosexuality." In his *The Sexual Behavior of Young People,* pp. 57–59. Boston: Little, Brown & Co., 1965. No. 904.

Whiteley, C. H., and Whiteley, Winifred M. "Unfruitful Sex." In their *Sex & Morals,* pp. 79–100. New York: Basic Books, 1967. No. 1124.

Homosexuality and the Law

GENERAL, MALE

1129 ALBANY TRUST. *Some Questions and Answers about Homosexuality.*
London: Albany Trust, n.d., 16 pp.

This pamphlet provides information for the public in question and answer
form concerning the nature and extent of homosexuality in Great Britain
and solicits the reader's opinion concerning the Wolfenden Committee's
proposal to change laws relating to homosexual behavior.

1130 ANDENAES, JOHS. "Recent Trends in the Criminal Law and Penal
System in Norway: I. Criminal Law." *British Journal of Delinquency*
5 (1, 1954): 21–26.

A brief description of the laws concerning homosexuality is included in this
general survey of trends in Norwegian criminal law. Homosexual intercourse between males is punishable, but in practice the offense is prosecuted
only when an adult has been involved with a person under 16. The activities
of homosexual clubs and societies are under legal proscription and homophile publications are prohibited.

1131 AYER, A. J. "Homosexuals and the Law." *Mattachine Review* 5 (6,
1959): 5–11.

Changes in English law following the Wolfenden recommendations are
urged since it is believed that the public interest is not threatened by the
measures advocated by the Committee. Young people are protected from
seduction by homosexuals by fixing the age of consent at 21. Homosexuality
is not unnatural nor uncommon and has none of the attributes of a crime.
The present legal sanctions against homosexuality are not an effective deterrent; they are only an encouragement to blackmail. With the growth of
understanding fewer prosecutions against homosexuals may be undertaken
and juries may refuse to convict, so the recommendations of the Wolfenden
Committee will be adopted in practice even if they are rejected in principle.

1132 BENJAMIN, HARRY. "Must the Homosexual Be Rejected?" 1958.
Reprinted in *The Third Sex,* edited by Isadore Rubin, pp. 7–12. New
York: New Book Co., 1961.

Homosexuality is a disease which may have many causes. It should not be considered as "unnatural" or as a crime. The individual homosexual should not be subjected to social rejection and legal harassment.

1133 BERG, CHARLES. "The Wolfenden Report on Homosexual Offences." In his *Fear, Punishment, Anxiety and the Wolfenden Report,* pp. 11–50. London: George Allen & Unwin, 1959.

It is argued that although the Wolfenden Report may be ahead of public opinion in its major legal recommendation, it can be considered scientifically reactionary. It is believed that the Committee was incapable of understanding homosexuality because it was unaware of the psychopathology and etiology of attitudes, defensive mechanisms, and biases. The Committee did not go far enough in separating the realm of law from the realm of private morality nor in extending to homosexuals the full rights and protections of the law enjoyed by heterosexuals.

1134 BOWMAN, KARL M., and ENGLE, BERNICE. "A Psychiatric Evaluation of Laws of Homosexuality." *American Journal of Psychiatry* 112 (Feb., 1956): 577–583.

In an evaluation of the laws against homosexuality it is found that legal phraseology and legal terms referring to homosexual practices, especially those pertaining to sodomy, are enshrouded in confusion, prudery, and rigid tradition.

Several recommendations are made with regard to legal reform: a revision of the penal code; a national commission which would study the entire problem of sex offenses in order to solve the problem of how to achieve greater statutory harmony; a gradual modification of sex laws, starting with those pertaining to heterosexuals in general and married couples specifically; legal procedures which would call for a definite, precise account of a given act with an emphasis upon more reliable testimony and determination of circumstantial evidence; a strict enforcement of these laws; and a refusal to ask for or to use catchall laws.

1135 BOWMAN, KARL M., and ENGLE, BERNICE. "Sex Offenses: The Medical and Legal Implications of Sex Variations." *Law and Contemporary Problems* 25 (2, 1960): 292–308.

In a general medical and legal discussion of sex offenses, specifically homosexuality, the Kinsey data on homosexuality are summarized and certain pertinent facts are pointed out: the treatment of homosexuality with hormones is ineffectual; its causes are unknown; the solution to the problem of homosexuality lies in applying the same standards for determining criminal deviation to both homosexuals and heterosexuals. There should be sanctions against the use of force and the corruption of the young, and public decency should be protected.

1136   BOWMAN, KARL M., and ENGLE, BERNICE. "Sexual Psychopath Laws." In *Sexual Behavior and the Law,* edited by Ralph Slovenko, pp. 757–778. Springfield, Ill.: Charles C. Thomas, 1965.

The sexual psychopath statutes of Iowa and California are used as examples of the 31 jurisdictions of the United States that have laws pertaining to sexual offenders. In general these laws can be divided into pre- and post-conviction laws depending on when special proceedings are instituted in a given case. They have been objected to on various legal grounds, including: the restriction of due process, equal protection, the right to counsel, the right to a jury trial, and the right to appeal, and cross-examination. The medical objections discussed include problems of diagnosis, limitation of criminal responsibility, ineffectiveness of treatment, and inadequate statistics.

Revisions in the legal proceedings are recommended, and among other suggestions a long-term follow-up study is proposed.

1137   BRANCALE, RALPH; ELLIS, ALBERT; and DOORBAR, RUTH R. "Psychiatric and Psychological Investigations of Convicted Sex Offenders: A Summary Report." *American Journal of Psychiatry* 109 (Jul., 1952): 17–21.

A summary of a series of studies of 300 persons convicted of minor or major sex crimes in the state of New Jersey following the New Jersey Sex Offender Act of 1949 indicates that "major" offenses (serious sexual assault, forcible rape, noncoital sex relations and homosexual activity) accounted for 42 percent of the convictions. The exact number of persons convicted of homosexual acts is not given. Relatively high rates of commitment for psychiatric deviation to mental institutions rather than penal institutions were recommended for offenders convicted of noncoital sex relations with a minor or of homosexual relations.

Offenders convicted of sexually deviant acts (noncoital sex with minors, exhibitory acts, homosexual acts, and bestiality) differed from offenders convicted of nondeviational acts in that they generally were older, had histories of previous sex offenses, had committed their offenses "without extenuating circumstances," displayed disturbed behavior, and were thought to have poor prognosis.

The 300 sex offenders were classified into four major groupings: "normal" sex offenders, sexually deviated but psychiatrically nondeviated offenders, sexually deviated and psychiatrically deviated offenders, and sexually nondeviated but psychiatrically deviated offenders. Homosexual offenders generally fall into the second group which is described as being made up of "individuals who regularly or frequently engage in 'abnormal' sex acts . . . but who remain sufficiently well-integrated and emotionally stable to pursue their aberrant behavior without getting into trouble with society or themselves." Homosexual offenders are also classified as compulsive neurotics rather than schizoid or borderline psychotic types.

The psychological-psychiatric examination provided for in the New Jersey Sex Offender Act is seen as a vital and necessary step toward the prevention of sexual offenses and toward the treatment of sex offenders.

1138   CAMPBELL, GEORGE E. "Criminal Law—Sodomy: The Crime and the Penalty." *Arkansas Law Review* 8 (4, 1954): 497–500.

A legalistic description of the sodomy law in Arkansas is presented. Although sodomy specifically refers to anal intercourse, the laws relating to it usually consider it a general category which includes such acts as fellatio and cunnilingus.

1139   Cantor, Donald J. "Deviation and the Criminal Law." *Journal of Criminal Law, Criminology and Police Science* 55 (4, 1964): 441–453.

Laws regulating sexual behavior are ineffective, serving neither a deterrent, preventive, nor a rehabilitative function. They represent the enforcement of a code of morals for their own sake which is a grave misuse of criminal law. Morals and their inculcation are not the province of the state and consensual acts of adults in private are beyond the proper scope of the criminal law. In order to alter these present laws, the organized bar must speak up for the enactment of laws serving a valid social and not a moral purpose. The churches must support this endeavor by stating that homosexual acts pose moral questions within the province of ethics and religion. The medical profession must define the nature of homosexuality and educate the public.

1140   CAPORALE, DOMENICO, and HAMANN, DERYL F. "Sexual Psychopathy: A Legal Labyrinth of Medicine, Morals and Mythology." *Nebraska Law Review* 36 (2, 1957): 320–353.

The impact of the 1949 Nebraska Sexual Psychopath Statute is assessed to determine if it is meeting those problems which it set out to solve. It is concluded that the present status of medical and legal knowledge does not provide an adequate basis for departing from traditional legal methods of dealing with individuals whose sexual conduct does not meet with social approval.

1141 CAPRIO, FRANK S., and BRENNER, DONALD R. *Sexual Behavior: Psycho-Legal Aspects.* New York: Citadel Press, 1961, 384 pp.

A psycho-legal investigation into all forms of sexual behavior, which includes a chapter entitled "The Homosexual Problem," traces the history of legal regulations, and summarizes those laws of the United States and foreign countries which restrict homosexual behavior.

In a discussion of the causes of homosexuality the point is made that homosexuality cannot be attributed to any single factor. The legalization of homosexual behavior between consenting adults in private is recommended. Homosexuals should not be sent to prison. It is observed that both society's attitude toward homosexuality and homosexuals' attitude toward society are unenlightened and prejudiced.

1142 "Castration of a Male Homosexual." *British Medical Journal* (4903, 1954): 1562.

A legal opinion regarding the castration of a male homosexual states that such an operation is undoubtedly against British law unless the Court could be satisfied that the operation genuinely benefited the patient's health.

1143 CAVANAGH, JOHN R. "Sexual Anomalies and the Law." *Catholic Lawyer* 9 (1, 1963): 4–31.

A brief outline of the classification and basic psychopathology of sexual anomalies includes homosexual acts under the heading of "Sexual acts which are 'Contra Naturum,' " along with fellatio, cunnilingus, sodomy (buggery), masturbation, bestiality, pedophilia, and artificial birth control. It is suggested that "sexual anomaly" be used as a substitute for sexual perversion because it is more meaningful. Furthermore, consenting sexual acts between competent adults should be legalized, thus bringing the law into conformity with modern knowledge of sex. Most sexual offenders are nuisances rather than dangers to the community, and the rate of recidivism is low in offenses involving physical contact but high in noncontact offenses. It is concluded that communication between the law and psychiatry should be facilitated.

1144 *The Challenge and Progress of Homosexual Law Reform.* Essays on Homosexuality, no. 2. San Francisco: Council on Religion and the Homosexual, Daughters of Bilitis, Society for Individual Rights, Tavern Guild of San Francisco, 1968, 72 pp.

This extensively documented essay examines the law in the United States as it applies to homosexuality, discusses some proposed legal changes, and presents arguments for and against such changes. A short historical survey and a comparison between English and American attitudes toward homosexual acts in the U.S. and the law is included.

The interpretation and methods of enforcement of existing laws in this country allow the harassment and exploitation of homosexuals. Removal of laws prohibiting private consensual adult homosexual acts—laws which are already dead letter in many jurisdictions—would protect the homosexual not only from legal action, but probably from many of the discriminatory practices our society employs against him as well.

1145 CHESSER, EUSTACE. *Live and Let Live: The Moral of the Wolfenden Report.* London: William Heinemann, 1958, 125 pp.

The moral implications of the Wolfenden Report are considered with respect to homosexuality and prostitution. Historical and cultural variations in the reaction to homosexuality are surveyed, and present English law is outlined. The moral drawn from the Wolfenden Report recommends tolerance in actions as well as in attitudes.

1146 CHESSER, EUSTACE. "Society and the Homosexual." *International Journal of Sexology* 7 (4, 1954): 213–216.

A distinction must be made between the "genuine" homosexual and the heterosexual who adopts and practices homosexuality. Whether the cause of the inversion is genetic or environmental, the true homosexual cannot be changed into a heterosexual. Because change is not possible, the laws which are prejudiced against homosexual behavior should be altered. As in the case of heterosexual conduct, society should intervene only when homosexual behaviors overstep the bounds of decency and propriety.

1147 CHURCH OF ENGLAND MORAL WELFARE COUNCIL. *The Problem of Homosexuality: An Interim Report by a Group of Anglican Clergy and Doctors.* Westminster: Church Information Board, n.d., 27 pp.

Etiology, morality, religion, and the law are discussed with reference to homosexuality. Predisposing causes of inversion are faulty familial relationships—a broken or otherwise unsatisfactory parental relationship (a boy molding his personality upon that of his mother, a "clinging" mother, or a mother who undermines her son's affection and respect for his father). Some of the precipitating factors include the lack of opportunity of mixing with women, homosexual experiences in school, or seduction of the boy by an adult homosexual.

Justice and humanitarian reasons call for the change of the legal prohibitions regarding homosexual behavior. Some of the deleterious effects of these prohibitions are the possibility of suicide by men charged with committing homosexual acts, opportunities for blackmail, possible harm to children who are sought as partners to avoid the threat of blackmail, the prevention of friendships between homosexuals and heterosexuals, the prevention of better diagnosis and more effective treatment, the fostering of moral deterioration, the encouragement of unsavory types of police action, and the breeding of dissatisfaction and ferment.

1148 "Clandestine Police Surveillance of Public Toilet Booth Held To Be Unreasonable Search." *Columbia Law Review* 63 (5, 1963): 955–961.

Clandestine police surveillance of the interior of an enclosed booth in a public rest room, even with the consent of the owner of the premises, has been ruled unreasonable search if there is not probable cause to believe that a particular illegal act is being committed at the time. Such surveillance without probable cause is prohibited by both the Federal and California constitutions.

The decision was based on the assumption that in such investigations the police spy on the innocent and guilty alike with no ground for suspecting illegal activity by any particular individual. General exploratory searches are condemned as unreasonable, and a standard for search is suggested involving the following criteria: the gravity of the offense should be considered; the more police conduct tends to offend normal sensibilities of the public, the more compelling should be its justification; and the weaker the foundations for reasonable suspicion, the more proper it would be to condemn the search as "exploratory."

1149 CLIFFORD, W. "Homosexuality by Consent." *Justice of the Peace and Local Government Review* 129 (37, 1965): 357, 597–598.

The amending of the homosexuality law in England is discussed. On legal and logical bases it is suggested that homosexuality in private does not imperil the Queen's peace or threaten to injure the public. Care must be taken to set age limits for consent.

It is pointed out that blackmail would still be possible even if risk of prosecution were withdrawn. This is because there may not be social acceptance of homosexuality.

1150 "Committee on Homosexuality." *Lancet* 266 (6819, 1954): 986.

The preliminary discussion in the House of Commons that led to the appointment by the Home Secretary and the Secretary of State for Scotland of a committee to examine homosexual offenses is reported. The validity of outmoded laws, the prevalence of homosexual offenses, and various types of treatment for homosexual offenders were the subjects included in the

House discussion. Figures given for the number of convictions and the age of victims or accomplices indicated that 89 percent of the convictions for homosexual offenses involved cases where the victim or accomplices had been under 21 years old.

1151 "The Consenting Adult Homosexual and the Law: An Empirical Study of Enforcement and Administration in Los Angeles County." *UCLA Law Review* 13 (3, 1966): 643–832.

The statutory provisions of Los Angeles County pertaining to homosexual behavior are outlined. Enforcement techniques, the interval between arrest and trial, trial, and disposition are considered with recommendations for change.

Techniques of enforcement include the use of police decoys, observation, routine patrol and harassment, and abatement and licensing controls over establishments frequented by homosexuals. Patterns of police discretion are described. The availability of Public Defender's services, bail provisions, problems of evidence and its admissibility, and trial strategy are considered, with the presentation of statistics on disposition.

It is concluded that adult consensual homosexuality should be of legal concern only in the case of public displays, and then only because it involves an element of public outrage and is an offensive nuisance. A recommendation that the statutes be changed to that end is made. The elimination of registration requirements for offenders convicted of a consensual adult homosexual act is also recommended. Fines and probation are considered the single best disposition category, rather than imprisonment or commitment to mental institutions.

1152 COUNCIL ON RELIGION AND THE HOMOSEXUAL, INC., BOARD OF TRUSTEES. *A Brief of Injustices: An Indictment of Our Society in Its Treatment of the Homosexual.* San Francisco: The Council, 1965, 12 pp.

A number of injustices that have been encountered in San Francisco with reference to homosexuality are listed. Among the injustices cited are: prejudicial treatment by the legal process, social ostracism, entrapment, victimization, and the intimidation and sanctioning of those who aid and publicly serve homosexuals.

1153 "Criminal Factors in Homosexuality." *Corrective Psychiatry and Journal of Social Therapy* 13 (4, 1967): 181–183.

The relationship between homosexuality and crime is stressed in an editorial. Briefly mentioned are incidents of blackmail, assault, murder, and

other forms of criminal victimization of homosexuals as well as the "pathological strains of homosexuality" which may result in criminal acts and
mental disorders.

1154   CROFT-COOKE, RUPERT. *The Verdict of You All.* London: Secker
       & Warburg, 1955, 254 pp.

A personal account of an arrest and subsequent imprisonment for homosexuality is given. Life in prison is fully described. The "witch-hunt" and the
prison treatment of alleged homosexuals are condemned.

1155   DEAN, MICHAEL. "Similar Facts and Homosexual Offences: The
       Resurrection of Sims." *Criminal Law Review* (Nov., 1967): 633–644.

A discussion of legal concerns involved in several cases of homosexuality
is presented. The courts have never solved the problem of the prosecution's
adducing evidence which tends to suggest that a person accused of homosexual offenses has manifested a homosexual propensity quite apart from
the incident resulting in the charge. The procedure needs to be reviewed,
and a ruling should be given with regard to its legality.

1156   DEVLIN, PATRICK. "The Enforcement of Morals." London: Oxford
       University Press, 1959, 25 pp.

In a jurisprudential lecture, the relationship of the Wolfenden Report to the
enforcement of morals is considered. Three questions are posed: Does society have the right to pass judgment on moral matters? If it has this right,
does it have the right to use the law to enforce its judgment? If so, should
it use legal enforcement in all cases or only in some? It is the widespread
abhorrence of and intolerance toward homosexuality which leads to its legal
prohibition, and the limits of tolerance are constantly shifting. It is concluded that the law must be based on Christian morals and must enforce
these morals since the law will fail without the help of Christian teaching.
It is on this basis that the Wolfenden Report, in its liberalization of the law
to legalize homosexual acts between consenting adults in private, is criticized.

1157   DONNELLY, RICHARD C.; GOLDSTEIN, JOSEPH; and SCHWARTZ,
       RICHARD D. *Criminal Law.* New York: Free Press of Glencoe,
       1962, 249 pp.

The first of the three parts of this text for law students pertains to homosexuality. Chapter (or Part) One, entitled "The Case of Dr. Martin," contains
documents supplemented by materials from other disciplines. Court decisions, trial transcripts, legislative committee hearings and reports, probation records, prison records, and parole records and reports are used to

present problems with which decision makers of the criminal law are confronted or with which they may expect to be confronted.

Homosexuality is a focal point for much of this material and one incident is used as the basis for an extensive case study. The case involves a doctor of medicine accused of committing an "indecent assault" upon a child who was his patient at the time. Questions are presented for the student's consideration.

1158 EAST COAST HOMOPHILE ORGANIZATIONS. *Homosexuality: Civil Liberties and Social Rights.* Transcript of Addresses delivered at the E.C.H.O. Conference, October 9th, 10th, and 11th, 1964, Sheraton-Park Hotel, Washington, D. C. Mimeographed. New York: East Coast Homophile Organizations, 1965, 144 pp.

Based on the transcripts of speeches, debates, and panel discussions on the subject of civil liberties and social rights for homosexuals the following topics are considered: the role of politics in achieving the homosexual's aims, the role of government with regard to the regulation of sexual behavior, the Miller Act, criminal sanctions and homosexual behavior, and the alienation of the homosexual from the religious community.

1159 EDDY, J. P. "The Law and Homosexuality." *Criminal Law Review* (1956): 22–25.

Arguments against the revision of the English law are presented on the grounds that successful medical treatment of homosexuals requires that they remain amenable to the law.

1160 FITCH, J. H. "Men Convicted of Sexual Offences Against Children: A Descriptive Follow-Up Study." *British Journal of Criminology* 3 (1, 1962): 18–37.

To ascertain the differences between heterosexual and homosexual offenders and recidivists and nonrecidivists, a study was made of 139 men incarcerated in H. M. Prison in Bristol for sexual offenses against children (under 16 years of age). Seventy-seven of the men were convicted for heterosexual offenses and 62 for homosexual offenses. The case records from the prison and police files were studied. The homosexual offenders had higher status occupations, were single, and were given longer prison sentences than the heterosexual offenders.

1161 FLORIDA LEGISLATIVE INVESTIGATION COMMITTEE. *Homosexuality and Citizenship in Florida: A Report.* Tallahassee, Fla.: The Committee, 1964, 48 pp.

A review of the scope and nature of homosexuality was made in order to understand and to deal more effectively with the growing problem of homosexuality in Florida. The recommendations included: the retention of qualified personnel to be assigned to the Teacher Certification Division of the State Department of Education for the purpose of dealing with allegations of homosexuality involving teachers in the public schools; the formulation of legislation providing for a homosexual practices control act for Florida; provisions for psychiatric treatment of homosexual offenders; centralized confidential administrative records of homosexuals and their activity; and placing sole jurisdiction of a second homosexual offense in a felony court.

The appendix includes a section of Florida laws on sex offenses, a glossary of homosexual terms and deviate acts, and a bibliography on sexual deviations.

1162 FREED, LOUIS F. "Homosexuality and the Bill." In "Correspondance." *South African Medical Journal* 42 (22, 1968): 567.

Specific laws are not needed that apply only to homosexual acts, since this implies that homosexuality is an independent disease entity, which it is not. The incidence of homosexuality is not a menace to society, but rather is a measure of its state of mental ill-health. Legislation will suppress only the symptom, not the disease, and its effects could lead to other more dangerous behavior.

1163 GILES, JOHN W. "Divorce and Homosexuality." *Sexology* 29 (4, 1962): 262–264.

A number of divorce suits involving homosexuality are briefly described. Legally, marriage is a heterosexual institution, and the homosexuality of one of the partners is usually considered grounds for divorce. Since the entire subject of homosexuality is under review by scientists and attorneys, perhaps its relationship to marriage should also be re-examined.

1164 GINSBERG, MORRIS. "The Enforcement of Morals." *British Journal of Sociology* 12 (1, 1961): 65–68.

Whether or not the criminal law ought to be based on ethical principles is the subject of discussion. While the law must keep in touch with the wishes of the community, it is also recognized that the law can play a very important part in shaping the moral sense of the community as well.

As moral ideas change, so do religious views. In the case of homosexuality, however, civil authorities have been harsher than the church in their dealings with homosexuals. Laws can determine for a community a sense of right and wrong. The community should be educated to distinguish between the facts and the law. The legislature, for example, should be provided with relevant facts so that it can distinguish clearly between the facts and whatever moral issues may be involved.

1165 GINSBERG, MORRIS. "Morality, Law and the Climate of Opinion." In *The Pathology and Treatment of Sexual Deviation: A Methodological Approach,* edited by Ismond Rosen, pp. 435–450. London: Oxford University Press, 1964.

In a jurisprudential discussion of the relation between law and morals with special reference to homosexuality and the Wolfenden Report, it is argued that although the law must keep close to the moral sense of the community, it is not completely bound by it but may play an educative role. Public opinion should not be the sole criterion for ethical judgments which the law must make. The Wolfenden Committee is also criticized for failing to explicate the moral philosophy underlying its recommendations. A distinction between questions of fact and value is urged, and some major questions are posed. Three general questions for determining when human liberty may be restricted are: Is force necessary to attain the end? Will the furtherance of liberty in one sphere interfere with equally or more important liberties in other spheres? Can the end in question be attained by compulsion or docs its value depend upon its being freely or spontaneously pursued?

1166 GLOVER, BENJAMIN. "Control of the Sex Deviate." *Federal Probation* 24 (3, 1960): 38–45.

Wisconsin is one of 23 states to produce a functional sex deviate law. The structure of the present law combines medical and legal administrations (the law became effective July, 1951), and is quite simple in make-up. It is composed of two divisions of crimes and two categories of treatment.

The first part of the law deals with such assaultive offenses as rape and sexual intercourse without consent. The second portion of the law deals with the less violent group. It includes fellatio, sodomy, and homosexuality.

This report is primarily concerned with the sex deviate. If the offender is dealt with under the Sex Deviate Law, he is given a presentence evaluation and is treated with psychotherapy while he is on probation, or he is taken to the Waupun State Prison to join in the total program which also includes psychotherapy.

No single school of therapy at the state prison is emphasized, nor is therapy required. But the sex deviate group has many people who are unable to comprehend any deep or intensive therapy, and some of the problems of psychotherapy are examined in this review.

Therapy of sex deviates is subjected to a great deal of criticism because there is no substantial evidence that sex offenders are better after treatment. This is illustrated by the fact that when it comes to the treatment of homosexuals, therapists tend to promote discretion and nonviolent behavior rather than endeavoring to change the total behavior of the patient.

1167   GLOVER, EDWARD. *"Homosexuality and Prostitution:* A Review." *British Journal of Delinquency* 6 (4, 1956): 315–317.

In a mildly critical review of *Homosexuality and Prostitution,* a report by a subcommittee of the British Medical Association, it is asserted that there are no statistical data in the report, merely professional opinions. Although the report does distinguish between the large number of homosexuals who are not in conflict with the law or who are seeking psychiatric help and those who are in conflict with the law or who have received psychiatric treatment, it is lacking in any recommendation for changing those statutes prohibiting private, consensual acts between homosexual adults. That homosexuality is a moral offense is clearly indicated by the committee's report. The report states that female homosexuality is not a problem, which may be due to the lack of laws against it. The portion of the report on prostitution is "noncommittal."

1168   GRAD, FRANK P. "The A.L.I. Model Penal Code." *NPPA Journal* 4 (2, 1958): 127–138.

A model penal code developed over a five-year period by the American Law Institute is presented. The code represents an ideal not bound by any hope of immediate enactment. Of the many sections in the code, the one pertaining directly to homosexuality is labeled "Deviate Intercourse." The code proposes that private, consensual sexual acts between adults no longer be considered a crime. One other section of interest suggests that acts of sexual assault by female homosexuals carry the same penalties as those by male homosexuals.

1169   GREAT BRITAIN, COMMITTEE ON HOMOSEXUAL OFFENCES AND PROSTITUTION. *The Wolfenden Report.* New York: Lancer Books, 1964, 286 pp.

A British governmental committee evaluates the legal provisions regarding homosexuality and prostitution and the administration of these laws in Great Britain. The committee rejects the concept of homosexuality as a disease, thus leaving it liable to legal sanctions. The major recommendation is that homosexual behavior between consenting adults in private should no longer be a criminal offense. The statutory provisions regarding homosexual behavior of an adult with a minor under 16 are not criticized, and public display of offensive behavior is thought to remain an outrage to public decency, as are many heterosexual acts. The present policy of imprisonment is held to be inadequate, and wide disparities in sentencing are noted. However, the committee does not feel that homosexuality is presently "curable" by medical or psychiatric treatment and suggests only better self-control and adaptation to life in general as goals of treatment. Castration is criticized, but the use of estrogens at the request of the offender is recommended.

Reservations by five members of the committee are included. Only one disagrees with the main recommendation of the report, arguing that it will weaken the moral fabric of social life by allowing improper examples to exist under the approval of the law. Other objections by dissenting members are to the distinction between buggery and other homosexual offenses and to the recommended maximum penalties for homosexual offenses.

1170 GUTTMACHER, MANFRED S. "The Homosexual in Court." *American Journal of Psychiatry* 112 (Feb., 1956): 591–598.

In a survey of decisions handed down to homosexual offenders in the Court of General Sessions of New York, the cases of 26 homosexual offenders seen by the court from 1952 to 1954 were reviewed. Homosexual offenses involving only adults were treated with leniency except where one was a professional prostitute or when the acts occurred in public. Probation was given to about one-third of the homosexual offenders and to nearly one-half of the heterosexual sex offenders. Nearly a seventh of them were committed to a state hospital or to an institution for mental defectives. Courts have come to see sex offenders as people who should be referred for psychiatric treatment. Sexual offenses entered into willingly by two adults are viewed benignly.

1171 GUTTMACHER, MANFRED S., and WEIHOFEN, HENRY. *Psychiatry and the Law.* New York: W. W. Norton & Co., 1952, 476 pp.

A psychiatric-legalistic report deals with various subjects and their relationships to psychiatry and the law. One chapter, "Sex Offenders," includes a discussion of the emotional basis on which sex laws are founded and outlines the history of the "sexual psychopath laws" under which laws regulating homosexual behavior fall. These laws are based on the fallacious premise that all types of sex offenders are a distinct type of criminal who is more recidivistic, and that these criminals can be treated by special techniques. Yet the laws make no special provision for treatment, nor has it been determined how and where to deal with these offenders. It is noted that when legal agencies attempt to control homosexual relations between adults, the situation often degenerates into blackmail and police corruption.

1172   HAILSHAM, QUINTIN MCGAREL HOGG, 2d Viscount. "Homosexu-
       ality and Society." In *They Stand Apart: A Critical Survey of the
       Problems of Homosexuality,* edited by John Tudor Rees and Harley
       V. Usill, pp. 21–35. London: William Heinemann, 1955.

Continued legal sanctions against homosexual behavior are favored. It is
noted that the rate of homosexual acts known to the police is "between four
and five times that of 1938." Its potential antisocial consequences, particularly its proselytizing nature among the young, make homosexual behavior
a danger justifiably combated by law. Promiscuity, blackmail, the breakup
of family life, as well as other problems are mentioned.

1173   HAINES, WILLIAM H.; HOFFMAN, HARRY R.; and ESSER, ROBERT
       A. "Commitments under the Criminal Sexual Psychopath Law in
       the Criminal Court of Cook County, Illinois." *American Journal of
       Psychiatry* 105 (6, 1948): 420–425.

A criminal sexual psychopathic act was enacted in Illinois in 1938 for the
commitment of sexual psychopaths to mental hospitals. In 1947 another bill
was enacted making it mandatory for the penitentiary system to have
inmates who were incarcerated on charges of rape, incest, crimes against
nature, or taking indecent liberties with a child, examined before being
released at the expiration of their sentences. Under these acts, a criminal
sexual psychopath is not defined. The Illinois Criminal Sexual Statute states
that anyone "participating in fornication, prostitution, homosexuality, fetishism, exhibitionism, peeping Tom, et cetera, for a period of not less than
one year, may be committed to a state hospital until such time as he is
totally and permanently cured of his psychopathy."

1174   HALL WILLIAMS, J. E. "The Wolfenden Report: An Appraisal."
       Political Quarterly 29 (2, 1958): 132–143.

The findings in the Wolfenden Report on homosexuality and prostitution
are reviewed. The report is considered a major step forward in the progress
of English law. Minor criticism is directed at the liberality of the report in
its recommendation permitting homosexual acts between consenting adults
in private. It is surmised that perhaps the public is not ready for such
freedom. Historically, the law has forbidden certain types of acts between
consenting adults for reasons of protecting both the actors and the public.
Reference is made to laws forbidding abortion, suicide pacts, sterilization,
and so on. Homosexuality is both vulgar and wrong, and means should be
available to prosecute persons for this offense. However, in agreement with
the committee, enforcement should be uniform, not a vendetta by police,

and a distinction should be made between assault and consenting acts, the latter carrying a much lighter sentence.

1175   HAMMELMANN, H. A. "Homosexuality and the Law in Other Countries." In *They Stand Apart: A Critical Survey of the Problems of Homosexuality,* edited by John Tudor Rees and Harley V. Usill, pp. 143–183. London: William Heinemann, 1955.

In a summary of information about the law in countries of Western Europe, including France, Belgium, Holland, Spain, Italy, Switzerland, West Germany, Norway, Denmark, and Sweden, provisions regarding abuse of the young and immature, abuse of the weak by exploitation of a position of authority or dependence, force and fraud, public indecency, and soliciting or importuning are compared. Under each heading, the relevant statutes of each country are quoted, cited, or summarized.

1176   HAMMELMANN, H. A. "Reports of Committees: Committee on Homosexual Offences and Prostitution." *Modern Law Review* 21 (1, 1958): 68–73.

The Wolfenden Report is reviewed from a legal perspective. The report is welcomed as a sensible piece of work, but various aspects of it are criticized, particularly those chapters dealing with the treatment of homosexual offenders and with preventive measures.

1177   HARRIS, ROBERT N. "Private Consensual Adult Behavior: The Requirement of Harm to Others in the Enforcement of Morality." *UCLA Law Review* 14 (1966–1967): 581–603.

Morality is considered in terms of two perspectives: criminal harm to others and one's freedom of choice. The views of Lord Devlin, who argues that even murder would be legal among consenting adults if the philosophy of the Wolfenden Report were valid, are contrasted with the views of John Stuart Mill and H. L. A. Hart, who argue that only behavior involving actual harm to others should be restrained.

Society is seen as having a "condemn or condone syndrome" regarding the legal reform of sex proscriptions. In addition, the fact that legislators may misinterpret the true moral feelings of their constitutents or may defer to long-existing statutes, makes it difficult to legalize private sexual behavior between consenting adults.

There is no criminal harm in homosexual behavior in private between consenting adults, as long as there is no underlying need to increase the population rate. There are three measures by which private consensual behavior may be immune from prosecution by the judiciary: the doctrine of separation of church and state, rejection of the substantive due process clause, and the right to privacy.

1178 "Homosexual Laws in History." *Times* (London), Jan. 14, 1958. Reprinted in *Mattachine Review* 4 (3, 1958): 16–18.

A brief historical account of English laws concerning homosexuality traces their progress from the Middle Ages through the 19th century. Penalties ranging from burning offenders like heretics and apostates to hanging and life imprisonment were once common, but by 1861 the maximum penalty became life imprisonment and the minimum 10 years.

The law cited most frequently today dates from 1885. It punishes any act of "gross indecency" between two men, whether in public or in private. Its maximum penalty is two years.

Although it is felt that the recommendations of the Wolfenden Committee should be followed, British reluctance to even appear to "condone sin" will probably cause delay in the recommendations being accepted.

1179 "Homosexual Offences." *British Medical Journal* (5353, 1963): 393.

This report indicates that there were 3,278 indictable homosexual offenses against boys under 16 known to the police in England and Wales in 1962. Of these cases, 2,245 were dealt with by prosecution. The number of persons involved was 1,303 which indicates that many persons were accused of more than one such offense. In addition, 164 persons were prosecuted in 1962 under the Indecency with Children Act which applies if the victim is under 14.

1180 "Homosexual Offences and Prostitution." *Lancet* 273 (6994, 1957): 527–529.

The findings of the Wolfenden Committee on Homosexual Offences and Prostitution are reviewed, and a general approval of the Committee's work is expressed. Some of the specific recommendations in the report are discussed.

Most of the members of the Committee agreed on several points concerning homosexuality, including the recognition of the existence of transient homosexuality wherein a propensity toward homosexuality occurs at different points in the lives of many people. This agreement was the basis of a recommendation that privately carried out homosexual behavior between consenting adults should not be considered a criminal offense. This recommendation is specifically endorsed.

The report is criticized on several points; for example, homosexual behavior between two boys under 21 years of age is considered a criminal act, while similar behavior between two girls is blameless.

1181   "Homosexuality." *Lancet* 269 (6903, 1955): 1288.

Conclusions from a memorandum prepared by the council of the British Medical Association are presented. Homosexual practices have increased, according to the memorandum, because of a "weakening of the sense of personal responsibility with regard to social and national welfare in a significant proportion of the population." It is not recommended that offenders be imprisoned unless efforts are made to ensure that they do not engage in homosexual activity during the period of their detention. Laws should only be relaxed if persons under 21 are sufficiently protected.

1182   "Homosexuality." *Practitioner* 179 (1072, 1957): 349.

The recommendation of the Committee on Homosexual Offences and Prostitution (Wolfenden Report) that homosexual activity between consenting adults in private be legalized is briefly criticized. The lack of witnesses from the teaching professions and other fields involving the administration and supervision of young people is disturbing. The paramount issue to be resolved is the effect of homosexuality on the "rising generation." The article advises against any immediate change of the homosexual statutes.

1183   "Homosexuality: A New Ground for Annulment?" *Catholic Lawyer* 11 (2, 1965): 158–162.

In New York a marriage can presently be annulled on the grounds of misrepresentation if one partner is homosexual. If this is not applicable, another approach is suggested: since annulment will presently be granted in New York if one can show that the purpose of the marriage relation has been defeated, it may be possible to show that one partner considers the homosexual activities of the other so revolting that the purpose of the marriage relationship is defeated.

1184   "Homosexuality and the Bill." *South African Medical Journal* 42 (19, 1968): 457–458.

Editorial comments are made on a bill which was introduced to amend the Immorality Act of 1957 by making homosexuality an illegal offense. The bill is criticized on the grounds that homosexuality is a psychological disorder which cannot be corrected by punishment and legislation, but, instead, requires help and understanding. Society's ignorance, and not homosexuality, is viewed as the actual menace.

1185   "Homosexuality and the Law." *Lancet* 2 (7119, 1959): 1071.

Homosexual activity, between consenting adults, should not be treated as a crime. The law is not capable of being applied to this area of human behavior. Many homosexuals are able to escape detection or cannot be brought to trial. Punishment by confinement is more of a hindrance than a help, in that prison could be a proving ground for developing young homosexuals. Doctors should attempt to help the public understand the need for legal reform in this area.

1186   "Homosexuality as a Crime." *Lancet* 1 (7396, 1965): 1151–1152.

Parliament is criticized for not having acted on the homosexual aspects of the Wolfenden Report. Arguments proposed by those against homosexual law reform are criticized and disproved. It is hoped that a bill which is being introduced in the House of Commons, similar to Lord Arran's bill with regard to implementing the suggestions of the Wolfenden Report, will be approved.

1187   "Homosexuality in Society." *British Medical Journal* (5045, 1957): 631–632.

The parts of the Wolfenden Report concerned with homosexuality are considered. The committee's recommendation that private consensual homosexual acts no longer be considered criminal are described as the most far-reaching of any of the recommendations made. The question is raised as to whether the present law or better education and the "strengthening of individual responsibility" would be more effective in diminishing homosexual activity. The appointment of government committees to study such questions is seen as being of debatable utility, especially since the effectiveness of the committee's recommendations are often defeated by the inactivity of the government.

1188   HUGHES, GRAHAM. "Consent in Sexual Offences." *Modern Law Review* 25 (6, 1962): 672–686.

The laws regarding sexual intercourse with girls under 16 were created with the express policy of protecting young girls against themselves and against men, but no such policy can be found for the sodomy laws. Attempting to examine rationally the present criminal law with respect to sexual offenses, it is suggested that the law provide that generally no boy or girl under age 16 may be convicted for sodomy as a consenting partner, unless the prosecution can prove that the boy or girl understood the nature and implications of the act and freely consented.

1189 JACOBS, HAROLD. "Decoy Enforcement of Homosexual Laws." *University of Pennsylvania Law Review* 112 (2, 1963): 259–284.

In a discussion of problems which may result when decoys are used in the enforcement of homosexual laws, particular attention is given to the defenses the accused may raise because of the decoy's behavior, and to the problems of proof which arise.

Although no conclusions are reached, it is suggested that the courts continue to allow the accused to use legitimate defenses so as not to "expand the statutes to condemn homosexual tendencies," while also allowing the use of decoys, since they are the only practicable means of enforcement. There is a danger that "if unfounded defenses based on the activity of decoys become increasingly successful, the statutes themselves will become ineffective."

1190 JAMES, T. E. "Law and the Sexual Offender." In *The Pathology and Treatment of Sexual Deviation: A Methodological Approach,* edited by Ismond Rosen, pp. 461–492. London: Oxford University Press, 1964.

A review of the legal reaction in Britain to various sex offenses, (including homosexual) names three basic homosexual offenses: sodomy, with punishments up to life imprisonment; indecent assault, punishable by up to 10 years' imprisonment; and gross indecency or procurement therefor, punishable by up to two years' imprisonment. Gross indecency usually means mutual masturbation, intercrural contact, or oral-genital contact. In addition, there are numerous bylaws relating to such behavior as acts of indecency or annoyance which carry a small fine.

1191 JEPSON, N. A. "Homosexuality, Capital Punishment, and the Law: Two Questionnaires." *British Journal of Delinquency* 9 (4, 1959): 246–257.

A questionnaire was distributed among adult students at Leeds University to determine their reaction to the recommendation made in Part II of the Wolfenden Committee Report, "that homosexual behaviour between consenting adults in private be no longer a criminal offence." In addition to questions on the controversial recommendation and the source of the respondent's information on the Wolfenden Report, two questions on the abolition of capital punishment were included. About 1,300 questionnaires were distributed and 816 were returned. The responses are analyzed in terms of the sex, source of information, age, and occupation of the respondent.

1192 KARPMAN, BENJAMIN. "Considerations Bearing on the Problems of Sexual Offenses." *Journal of Criminal Law, Criminology, and Police Science* 43 (1, 1952): 13–28.

Medico-legal inadequacies in regard to sex offenses are discussed. Whereas law is arbitrarily concerned with crime and punishment, psychiatry is concerned with the offender's motivations and how he may be prevented from committing offenses again. Laws, particularly in respect to sodomy, are archaic, and take little cognizance of mental disorder. Misconceptions and preconceptions are prevalent regarding the relationships between various paraphilias, and a wide variety of charges are used to describe the same offenses.

Deploring the "witch hunts" directed against the homosexual, it is maintained that they happen because the whole problem of homosexuality is confused with social prejudices that have little or no relation to scientific facts. Homosexuality is a condition for which the individual is no more responsible than he would be for tuberculosis or high blood pressure.

1193 KYLER, CLARE W. "Camera Surveillance of Sex Deviates." *Law and Order* 11 (11, 1963): 16–18, 20.

Police investigated the activities taking place in a public men's rest room. Suspicious activities were photographed with a hidden motion picture camera for a two-week period. Sixty-five men were shown committing indecent acts and 37 of the 65 were arrested on charges of sodomy. A 16 mm sound movie concerning the investigation is available.

1194 LAFITTE, FRANÇOIS. "Homosexuality and the Law: The Wolfenden Report in Historical Perspective." *British Journal of Delinquency* 9 (1, 1958): 8–19.

In the early part of the 20th century Britain's attitude toward homosexuality was characterized by a reaction of suppression to cases involving homosexuality, such as those of Oscar Wilde, Havelock Ellis, and Radclyffe Hall. By the middle of the 20th century the intellectual climate had become somewhat more free. Nevertheless, the Wolfenden Committee report probably would have been more effective had it taken further account of the historical, sociological, and legal implications of homosexuality, which might have given the report a more welcome initial reception.

The history of the penal code is discussed with reference to its medieval background, Tudor legislation, Georgian practices, and the Victorian aftermath. Among the questions raised is one concerned with whether the main resistance to law reform comes from a stereotyped hostile response, which has become conventional owing to the mere fact of the law's antiquity. By neglecting history and sociology, the Wolfenden Committee was limited in the questions to which it could address itself. Even so, now that the report has been written, the subject of homosexuality will never again be as shocking as it was before the publication of the report.

1195 LANDIS, JUDSON T. "Experiences of 500 Children with Adult Sexual Deviation." *Psychiatric Quarterly Supplement* 30 (1, 1956): 91–109.

A study of the victims in sex crimes involved 1,800 male and female college students. They were broken down into a control group of 450 and an experimental group of 500 who had had experiences with sexual deviates. A questionnaire was administered.

Thirty percent of the men and 35 percent of the women reported at least one experience with a sexual deviate. Four out of five of the experiences of boys had been with homosexuals; over half of the experiences of girls had been with exhibitionists, and one-fourth with adults who had fondled them sexually. The great majority of the victims seemed to recover quickly and to acquire few permanently negative attitudes from the experience.

1196 LEITCH, A. "Male Homosexuality as a Medico-Legal and Sociological Problem in the United Kingdom." *International Journal of Social Psychiatry* 5 (2, 1959): 98–106.

Homosexuality is no less a medical and legal problem than a social problem. Treating homosexuals wrongly can produce much unhappiness, with repercussions involving their medical and physical health. The medical profession has put great pressure on the legal position for years, attempting to bring the harsh laws of some countries (the United States, Britain, and West Germany, specifically) more into conformity with such enlightened countries as Sweden. The recommendations of the Wolfenden Committee are cited to show that legal reforms, making adult consensual behavior legal, are necessary and will shortly be put into effect.

1197 LEITSCH, DICK. "A New Frontier for Freedom." *Social Action* 34 (4, 1967): 21–29.

The trial and subsequent imprisonment of Oscar Wilde, Walter Jenkin's exile from Washington, McCarthy's association of homosexuality with communism, and the "Kinsey Reports" are all seen as influences contributing to the growing social consciousness of the homosexual group. The Mattachine Society is one manifestation of this growing social consciousness. The Mattachine Society of New York (MSNY) has spearheaded the attack on discriminatory laws and unequal protection in New York City. The efforts of the MSNY have resulted in the termination of police "solicitation," liberalized tavern licensing practices, and liberalized employment practices. Despite these inroads, agencies such as the Immigration and Naturalization Service and the Armed Forces still continue to abuse the rights of homosexuals. Group identification and an increased interest in politics may lead homosexuals to be "the next group to win its freedom."

1198 LEWIS, GLENN M., JR., AND ROWE, CLARENCE J. "The Sexual Offender as Seen in a Municipal Court." *Minnesota Medicine* 45 (11, 1962): 1113–1116.

A summary of findings about 54 convicted sex offenders who were seen by the psychiatric consultant to the Saint Paul Municipal Court over a two-year (1958–1959) period indicates that the average age of the total group was 31.9, that only one of the 54 was female, and that only 15 of the 54 were single.

The most common offense was exhibitionism, closely followed by homosexuality and then voyeurism.

All 10 homosexual offenders were males who had, for the most part, been apprehended in men's rest rooms. Although in one or two cases the indictable offense seems to have been an isolated homosexual act, a majority had a long-term history of sex deviation. The level of education was higher in the homosexual group than in any other group of offenders. None of the group was psychotic, and only one was thought to be a suitable candidate for psychotherapy.

1199 MCKEE, WILLIAM F. "Camera Surveillance of Sex Deviates: Evidentiary Problems." *Law and Order* 12 (8, 1964): 72–74.

In Mansfield, Ohio, colored films were taken of unlawful behavior in a public men's rest room as a part of the extensive investigation of sex deviates. Two legal problems were anticipated: the question of unlawful search and seizure and the general evidence questions as to the admissibility of the film. The Mansfield Police Department was aware of these problems and attempted to conduct the camera surveillance in a manner that would be legally upheld in the courts.

Indictments were returned in every case where positive identification of those involved could be made. The argument that the evidence in these cases had been obtained illegally was used as a basis for proceedings which sought injunctions and writs of prohibition, first to stop the State from presenting the evidence to a grand jury and, afterward, to stop the presentation of the evidence to a trial jury. Appeals based on the same argument were instituted in the Ohio Supreme Court after convictions for violations of the Ohio sodomy laws had been handed down.

The appeal had not been decided when this article was written. [More recent ephemeral material indicates that the convictions were upheld.]

1200 MacKenzie, D. F. "Homosexuality and the Justice Department." *New Zealand Medical Journal* 66 (423, 1967): 745–748.

Homosexual acts by males are punishable in New Zealand by imprisonment for up to 10 years if the victim is under age 16, and up to five years if the partner is over 16. Women over 21 who participate in homosexual acts with girls under 16 are liable to imprisonment for a term up to six years, but consenting adult women cannot be prosecuted for homosexuality. From 1920 to 1952 those men committed for homosexual offenses were segregated in New Plymouth Prison, but since 1952 there has been no attempt to segregate homosexuals, either by assigning them to a separate prison or by segregation within ordinary prisons. Three percent of the total number of prisoners in New Zealand are persons who have been convicted for homosexual acts.

The question of whether homosexual acts done in private between consenting adult males should be made legal (corresponding to what obtains for females) is examined from both the legal and social points of view. Legislation to abolish criminal penalties for private adult homosexual activity could be passed fairly easily, but it is thought that if such legislation were passed prematurely, it could stir up resistance and prejudice among the general population of New Zealand.

1201 Maddocks, Lewis I. "The Homosexual and the Law." *Social Action* 34 (4, 1967): 5–20.

Legal attitudes toward homosexuality in the United States are examined with special reference to sexual conduct, employment, and military service. A plea is made for "equal justice under law, not only in what the law provides, but in the manner of its enforcements."

Statutes concerning sexual conduct vary widely according to the different areas of the U.S., and police enforcement of these statutes is far from uniform. Adoption of the sexual conduct provisions of the American Law Institute's Model Penal Code is recommended. This would include the repeal of laws making homosexual acts between consenting adults in private a crime, as well as the passage of new legislation regarding sexual conduct.

1202 "Male and Female Homosexuality." *British Medical Journal* (4442, 1946): 748.

The reason for the discrepancy in how the law regards homosexual activities of men and women is discussed. It is suggested that the harsh attitude toward sodomy can be explained by the scriptural proscription of the practice, whereas homosexual relations between women are not specifically prohibited by holy scripture. In addition, the discrepancy may be explained by the fact that the laws are made by men who are conscious of the "evil of male aberrations," but who are not aware of similar practices by women.

1203 MANNHEIM, HERMANN. "Sexual Offences, Especially Homosexuality." In his *Criminal Justice and Social Reconstruction,* pp. 60–74. New York: Oxford University Press, 1946.

The basic values of society are reviewed and examined to determine whether criminal law treats these values in harmony with their function in society. Laws penalizing sexual behavior are viewed as being justified only when they are needed for the welfare of society. Present laws dealing with homosexuality are not justified on this basis, and it is likely that new laws will be applied. According to the prevailing views on the need for a penal sentence, either a limited penal detention or an unlimited nonpenal detention are likely to be applied in the future.

1204 MANNHEIM, HERMANN. "Some Criminological Aspects of Homosexuality." *Medical Press* 218 (26, 1947): 210–212.

The need for legal and prison reforms regarding homosexuality is pointed out.

1205 MASTERS, R. E. L. *The Homosexual Revolution: A Challenging Exposé of the Social and Political Directions of a Minority Group.* New York: Julian Press, 1962, 230 pp.

A layman views homosexuality as a social concern of increasing magnitude. The minority status of homosexuals brings them together in social areas (bars, organizations, areas of a city, et cetera) where no other ties exist. Police practices of harassment (entrapment) and legal statutes need reform and revision. The homophile movement represents an effort to win equal rights for inverts, and to end unfair social discrimination. Homosexuals specifically desire acceptance on the basis of their worth as individuals, and wish to be regarded as ordinary citizens who differ only in terms of their sex object choice. Police persecution binds the inverts together with a single purpose and resentment.

1206 MAUDE, JOHN. "Homosexuality and the Criminal Law." *Practitioner* 172 (1030, 1954): 378–380.

A cursory and moralistic review of the laws relating to male homosexuality in England (in 1954) is presented. Laws against sodomy, indecent assault, and importuning are summarized.

1207 MERCER, JESSIE DECAMARRON. *They Walk in Shadow: A Study of Sexual Variations with Emphasis on the Ambisexual and Homosexual Components and Our Contemporary Sex Laws.* New York: Comet Press Books, 1959, 573 pp.

An analytical inquiry into certain biological, psychological, medical, sociomoral and legal aspects of sex, ambisexuality, and homosexuality is addressed primarily to psychologists, psychiatrists, physicians, and social workers. This study is also specially devised for the use of legislators, civil and military jurists, attorneys, government executives, penologists, and law enforcement officers. Theories of causation are analyzed; and the general literature on homosexuality, historical and literary references, the Kinsey Report, the Wolfenden Report, and sex laws are reviewed. Concluding from this review of the literature that homosexual practices are not abnormal or degenerate, but are universal, normal, and natural expressions of the libido, a change to the use of less vague and derogatory terminology with reference to homosexuality is urged.

In a discussion of legal reactions to homosexuality the history of sex laws is reviewed and examples are given which indicate the need for a revision of laws in this area. It is noted that many sex laws prohibit practices recommended by counselors, and that over 90 percent of the population "walk in the shadow" of these laws. The Wolfenden Report is strongly commended.

1208 NEUSTATTER, W. LINDESAY. "The Homosexual Offender." *Justice of the Peace and Local Government Review* 123 (30, 1959): 480–481.

In a question and answer format, a brief outline of homosexuality is presented. Homosexuals are not considered criminals or psychopaths, and should not be incarcerated, nor should complete cures be expected from enforced psychotherapy. It is urged that the recommendations of the Wolfenden Committee Report should be followed.

1209 PARR, DENIS. "Psychiatric Aspects of the Wolfenden Report, II." *British Journal of Delinquency* 9 (1, 1958): 33–43.

A discussion of the Wolfenden Committee Report summarizes the viewpoint of that report and then relates it to clinical experiences and to existing literature in the field. It is concluded there is no reason why homosexual acts between consenting adults in private should be punished and that police forces would be better off if they decreased their efforts to prosecute for public acts since they are usually unobtrusive, often unknown, and unpreventable. Any effort to apprehend and/or treat homosexuals should be aimed at those who direct their attentions to prepubertal boys. See also Scott, Peter D. (no. 1235).

1210 PASCOE, HERBERT. "Deviant Sexual Behavior and the Sex Criminal." *Canadian Medical Association Journal* 84 (Jan. 28, 1961): 206–211.

Men accused of sex crimes, including homosexuals, often exhibit feelings of inadequacy regarding their masculinity. A fear of castration as a consequence of heterosexual intercourse leads them to seek substitute sex objects; some approach children or adolescents, others choose persons of the same sex as sexual partners. A disturbed emotional relationship with a spouse is often an important factor in the commission of a sex crime.

Several case histories are presented as examples of types of persons convicted for sex crimes.

1211 PEBERDY, G. R. "Homosexuality and the Law." *Medico-Legal Journal* 33 (1, 1965): 29–34.

English law involving homosexual offenses is outlined, and the history of its enactment is traced. In 1885 the law was expanded from buggery to "gross indecency." This produced more official incidents, which resulted in wider public indignation and resistance to changes in the law. The legal restrictions against homosexual conduct are based upon emotional grounds. There is need to repeal these laws in order to permit homosexual behavior in private between consenting parties.

1212 PLOSCOWE, MORRIS. "Homosexuality, Sodomy and Crimes against Nature." 1951. Reprinted in *Homosexuality: A Cross Cultural Approach*, edited by Donald Webster Cory, pp. 394–406. New York: Julian Press, 1956.

The legal restrictions against homosexual acts between consenting adults should be eliminated, although it is necessary to maintain two other restrictions. Relations between adults and minors should be proscribed since adolescent exposure may be the precipitating factor in much adult homosexuality. The restriction against homosexual prostitution should also be retained, since it is a major source of crime, disorder, and disease.

1213 PLOSCOWE, MORRIS. "Report to the Hague: Suggested Revisions of Penal Law Relating to Sex Crimes and Crimes Against the Family." *Cornell Law Quarterly* 50 (3, 1965): 425–445.

The recommendations presented in this article were developed at a congress in Bellagio, Italy, in 1963, and were presented to the Hague Congress in

1964. The meetings were concerned with the policy regarding when and how penal law should be applied to certain kinds of sexual behavior and behavior which affects the family. The topics presented included adultery and fornication, incest, dissemination of birth control information, abortion, artificial insemination, homosexual behavior, and the problem of non-support. With reference to homosexuality the Hague Congress resolved that the criminal law should prohibit homosexual behavior under the following circumstances: the use of force to compel deviant or homosexual behavior, homosexual behavior involving a minor with an adult, the use of a position of trust by an individual to involve his subordinate or ward in homosexual behavior, open homosexual behavior which instigates others to perversion, and behavior which instigates homosexual proxenetism (pimping, prostitution, or commercialization).

1214 PLOSCOWE, MORRIS. *Sex and the Law*. Rev. ed. New York: Ace Books, 1962, 288 pp.

A chapter on homosexuality is included in this legalistic treatment of every conceivable variety of sexual conduct (and misconduct).

Modern judges and legislators have labored under the false impression that the forms of sexual behavior usually associated with homosexuality—fellatio, for example—are rare and not indulged in by ordinary individuals. Because these activities are not confined to homosexuals, but are also indulged in by heterosexuals, laws prohibiting such behavior are practically unenforcible. Since homosexuality is not a matter of choice, but of development, the laws against it should be eliminated.

1215 "Points from Parliament." *British Medical Journal* (5487, 1966): 621.

It is reported that between August 1, 1964, and December 31, 1965, some 85 cases relating to homosexual offenses had been referred to the Director of Public Prosecutions, and that 81 of these cases were alleged to have taken place in private between consenting adult males.

1216 "Private Consensual Homosexual Behavior: The Crime and Its Enforcement." *Yale Law Journal* 70 (4, 1961): 623–635.

Consensual homosexual acts in private and the common-law background and statutory history of laws against homosexuality are discussed in connection with the case of a homosexual who was lured by a police officer into committing a homosexual act in private. Some common arguments for criminal sanctions against consensual homosexual conduct are critically examined and arguments for the abolishment of such sanctions are put forth. Police techniques in enforcing existing laws against consensual homosexuality should not include inducement or entrapment.

1217 "Psychiatric Treatment for Prisoners." *Lancet* 256 (6554, 1949): 632.

A question was asked regarding the type of psychiatric treatment being received by prison inmates serving sentences for homosexual offenses. It was reported that six part-time psychiatrists were employed, but no full-time psychiatrists were currently on British prison service staffs; in addition, five prison medical officers had received special psychiatric training. Forty of 412 prisoners serving time for homosexual offenses received psychiatric treatment during the six months prior to the time of the report. An additional 35 cases received psychiatric examination and guidance.

1218 PUXON, MARGARET. " 'Not as Other Men.' " *Solicitors' Journal* 101 (39, 1957): 735–737.

The recommendations of the Wolfenden Report are reviewed and approved. One particular weak point is noted. The Committee should have made stronger recommendations in the area of psychiatric counseling for homosexuals who have been apprehended by the police.

1219 RADZINOWICZ, L., ed. *Sexual Offences: A Report of the Cambridge Department of Criminal Science.* English Studies in Criminal Science, vol. 9. London: Macmillan & Co., 1957, 553 pp.

A statistical analysis of about one-quarter of the sex crimes known to the police during one year from a cross-section of the districts in England and Wales is given. The variables include age, occupation, marital status, and previous record. An analysis of offenders tried, but not convicted, is also given and an estimate is made of the proportions of undetected offenders in each category. Also studied are judicial dispositions, medical evidence on offenders, and follow-ups of released offenders. A comprehensive survey of the law is made, and proposals for amendment are examined. Material on homosexual offenses is found throughout the text, and frequently offender characteristics are contrasted for homosexual and heterosexual offenses. One appendix consists of a summary of certain data relating to homosexual offenses (accounting for almost half of the convictions) drawn from the main body of the report.

1220 REES, JOHN TUDOR. "Homosexuality and the Law." In *They Stand Apart: A Critical Survey of the Problems of Homosexuality,* edited by

John Tudor Rees and Harley V. Usill, pp. 3–20. London: William Heinemann, 1955.

A summary of British law in 1955 indicates wide variations of punishment and an almost total lack of measures providing for treatment.

The age of consent is an inadequate reason for the removal of legal sanctions, since if homosexual practices are wrong at 20, they are equally wrong at age 21.

1221 REES, JOHN TUDOR, and USILL, HARLEY V., eds. *They Stand Apart: A Critical Survey of the Problems of Homosexuality.* London: William Heinemann, 1955, 220 pp.

In a collection of articles designed to shed light on the jurisprudential questions surrounding homosexuality, the nature of homosexuality, the extent to which it is harmful, its moral status, and the current legal reaction to the problem are considered. The aim of the book is exploratory; it does not recommend a definite line of action. Part Four includes a summary of statistics regarding homosexuality in Great Britain. These statistics include figures on the number and types of offenses, conviction records, number of trials, ages of offenders, action taken by the courts, and psychiatric treatment of imprisoned homosexuals. Also included in Part Four are appendices containing abstracts of the debate on homosexuality in the House of Lords on May 19, 1954, and in the House of Commons on April 28, 1954; and extracts from a report of the Joint Committee on Psychiatry and Law, including some recommendations to the courts for general procedures in dealing with sexual offenses. See Bailey, Derrick Sherwin (no. 1050). Hailsham, Quintin McGarel Hogg, 2d Viscount (no. 1173). Hammelmann, H. A. (no. 1176). Neustatter, W. Lindesay (no. 42). Rees, John Tudor (no. 1223).

1222 REINHARDT, JAMES MELVIN. "A Critical Analysis of the Wolfenden Report." *Federal Probation* 23 (3, 1959): 36–41.

A legalistic discussion of the Wolfenden Report's recommendations regarding homosexual behavior and prostitution is given. The laws prohibiting homosexual behavior between consenting adults in private should be repealed. The further recommendation that a research body be established to study the etiology of homosexuality should be followed.

1223 REISS, ALBERT J., JR. "Sex Offenses: The Marginal Status of the Adolescent." *Law and Contemporary Problems* 25 (Spring, 1960): 309–333.

The failure to accord adolescence a distinct status position has several important implications in our society concerning the sanctioning of sexual conduct of adolescents. Juvenile courts often ignore homosexual conduct among adolescent boys of the same age as long as consent is involved, but at the same time tend to regard these boys as mentally ill. Homosexual behavior among adolescent girls is almost totally ignored. The one instance in which the court regards the problem of homosexuality as serious is where a boy or girl is involved with an adult. The most common cases involve lower-status boys and adult males. The social definition of the sexual relationship between an adult male and adolescent boy is often erroneous. Usually the adult male is defined as a homosexual exploiting the juvenile. However, in most cases the relation is a prostitute-client one, with the boy being the prostitute. Lower-status delinquent boys are often involved in this relationship and actively seek out older males on whom they perform fellatio for money. In such cases, the adolescent does not consider himself a homosexual.

1224 RITTY, CHARLES J. "Possible Invalidity of Marriage by Reason of Sexual Anomalies." *Jurist* 23 (4, 1963): 394–422.

No one will deny that those afflicted with sexual anomalies or psychopathic defects should not enter into marriage. The problem arises because such persons do enter marriage and then are unable or unwilling to accept the responsibilities of such a stable union, which eventually leads to desertion and a termination of the marriage. Therefore, the legal question concerns the possibility of canonical relief for those who enter marriage with one afflicted with sexual anomalies such as homosexuality or nymphomania. Depending on the merits and the circumstances of the cases, the judges at present may follow not only the traditional Rotal treatment of such cases based on defects of intellect and will, but also the recent approach based upon the personal incapacity of the subjects to make a contract which they cannot fulfill.

1225 ROBERTS, AYMER. *Forbidden Freedom.* London: Linden Press, 1960, 112 pp.

An informal discussion of the legal reaction to homosexuality and the Wolfenden Report takes the form of correspondence between two men, one a colonist of Juno, an imaginary planet that is considering what form of legal code to adopt. The recommendations of the Wolfenden Report are adopted.

1226 ROBINSON, KENNETH. "Parliamentary and Public Attitudes." In *The Pathology and Treatment of Sexual Deviation: A Methodological*

Approach, edited by Ismond Rosen, pp. 451–460. London: Oxford University Press, 1964.

The initial reaction of the British Parliament to the Wolfenden Committee Report was one of fear about enacting legislation which did not coincide with public opinion. As a result the document was shelved and action was postponed.

1227   ROEBURT, JOHN. *Sex Life and the Criminal Law.* New York: Belmont Books, 1963, 157 pp.

Journalistic case histories are presented on adultery, fornication, miscegenation, incest, prostitution, rape, sadism, lust, murder, criminal psychopathy, homosexuality, sodomy, exhibitionism, voyeurism, fetishism, pedophilia, necrophilia, nymphomania, abortion, and birth control. The legal reaction to these phenomena is discussed.

In the chapter on homosexuality, the hostile reaction of society and the law is explained as an overreaction to repressed instinctual urges. The origin of the taboo is traced to biblical teachings. Homosexual organizations are discussed; the Wolfenden Report is praised; and arguments for and against the homosexual are summarized.

1228   RUBIN, ISADORE. "Our Outmoded Sex Laws." 1960. Reprinted in *The Third Sex,* edited by Isadore Rubin, pp. 102–106. New York: New Book Co., 1961.

Present laws on homosexuality are criticized as too broad and indiscriminate, as invading what should be the realm of private morality, and as punishing what should be treated instead. A report is given on a forum on "Law, Social Change, and the Sexual Psychopath," conducted by the Association of the Bar of the City of New York.

1229   RYLANDER, GOSTA. "Treatment of Mentally Abnormal Offenders in Sweden." *British Journal of Delinquency* 5 (4, 1955): 262–268.

A description of the treatment of all types of mentally abnormal offenders in Sweden includes a section on the treatment of homosexuals. Homosexual acts between adults are no longer a crime, but severe punishment is meted out to a homosexual who approaches children or adolescents.

In and of itself, sexual abnormality is not considered a reason for exemption from punishment. When it is combined with an abnormal state such as schizophrenia, imbecility, or severe anxiety neurosis, however, the offender is handed over to the medical authorities rather than to the prison system.

Voluntary castration of sex offenders is legal, and it may be a more humane solution for a sexually abnormal person than being forced to spend years in prison tortured by abnormal sexual drives.

1230 SADOFF, ROBERT L. "Sexually Deviated Offenders." *Temple Law Quarterly* 40 (3–4, 1967): 305–315.

A psychiatric and legal review of the labels given to the sexually deviated offender shows that there are inconsistencies among the legal definitions of the sexual psychopath, and that various sexual deviations do not fall within the criminal code. There is great need for a more adequate classification of sex offenders and sex deviates; in this regard psychiatrists and lawyers should work together in an attempt to understand each offender as an individual.

1231 ST. JOHN-STEVAS, NORMAN. *Life, Death and the Law: Law and Christian Morals in England and the United States.* Bloomington, Ind.: Indiana University Press, 1961, 375 pp.

A jurisprudential, moral, philosophical, and theological discussion of the relationship between law and morality refers particularly to laws on birth control, homosexuality, sterilization, euthanasia, artificial insemination, and suicide. The necessity of distinguishing between the realms of law and morality is recognized, but the argument is that ultimately the law is rooted in morality. It is the collective conscience of the community on those issues which cannot be left to individual choice, and thus it has moral authority. Injury to the common good, rather than immorality, is proposed as the criterion for legal sanctions. The chapter on homosexuality reviews English and American laws, traces their history and the influence of Judeo-Christian doctrines, and evaluates factual knowledge about homosexuality. Christian and other moral views, treatment, and suggested changes in the law are discussed. Imprisonment is criticized as being "as futile as hoping to rehabilitate a chronic alcoholic by giving him occupational therapy in a brewery."

1232 SCHWARTZ, LOUIS B. "Morals Offenses and the Model Penal Code." *Columbia Law Review* 63 (3, 1963): 669–686.

In a general discussion of morals offenses and the Model Penal Code, it is shown that the absence of any provision for the punishment of private consensual homosexual relations is based upon the idea that the legislation of morality is an inappropriate concern of government, and that there are inherent difficulties in enforcing such legislation.

If the state legislatures do not adopt attitudes exempting morality from the realm of law, the issue will ultimately be put to a constitutional test, the crucial question being whether or not there is a public "consensus" against homosexuality.

1233 SCOTT, PETER D. "Psychiatric Aspects of the Wolfenden Report, I." *British Journal of Delinquency* 9 (1, 1958): 20–32.

The work of the Wolfenden Committee on homosexual offenses is reviewed. The perspective from which the Committee prepared its report is presented and some specific questions are considered.

It is pointed out that the Committee was dealing primarily with the relationship between public opinion, the law, and the need to protect citizens from abuse by sexual offenders. Its task was to recommend reforms in penal codes based upon the present state of knowledge without offending the public to the point where the recommendations of the Committee would be found unacceptable.

The primary finding by the Committee was that it should not be a criminal offense for consenting adults to engage in homosexual behavior in private. However, such a finding is based on an admittedly inadequate store of information on homosexuality. Though agreeing with this finding by the Committee, the reader is warned that the report can in no way serve as a substitute for a complete scientific study of the causes of homosexuality and the connection between homosexuality and psychopathology. See also Parr, Denis (no. 1211).

1234 SHERWIN, ROBERT VEIT. "The Law and Sexual Relationships." *Journal of Social Issues* 22 (2, 1966): 109–122.

A survey of the literature and a consideration of legal cases bearing on the law and sexual relationships indicate that there is a severe lag between revision of criminal codes and changes in public opinion regarding sexual "crimes."

The fact that few women have ever been convicted for homosexual activity is included in the discussion of the laws concerning homosexuality. It is also stated that male homosexuals are often entrapped by police officers, and that this may operate as a masochistic device for the guilt-ridden male homosexual. The elimination of all unenforcible laws and the legalization of relationships between consenting adults in private is suggested.

1235 SHERWIN, ROBERT VEIT. "Laws on Sex Crimes." In *The Encyclopedia of Sexual Behavior,* edited by Albert Ellis and Albert Abarbanel, pp. 620–630. 2d rev. ed. New York: Hawthorn Books, 1967.

A short section on laws regarding homosexuality states that although homosexuality itself is not against the law, some of the sex acts engaged in by homosexuals are illegal. Sexual activity between persons of the same sex often violates sex laws which refer to either homosexual or heterosexual behavior: sodomy, mutual masturbation, "crimes against nature," et cetera. These laws, however, are more efficiently applied in connection with homosexuality.

1236   SHERWIN, ROBERT VEIT. "Sodomy." In *Sexual Behavior and the Law,* edited by Ralph Slovenko, pp. 425–433. Springfield, Ill.: Charles C. Thomas, 1965.

Contrary to other laws, the sex laws of the United States tend to punish a person's sexual desires rather than the methods used to fulfill these desires. Thus, they may actually be considered to be antisexual. An instance of this is that although being a homosexual is not a crime, anything the homosexual may do to express his sexual predilections is a crime in every state except Illinois.

The definition of sodomy in most states is very broad: for example, pederasty, bestiality, buggery, fellatio, and cunnilingus may be combined into one statute. Although the practice of entrapment is illegal in most states, it is condoned by many courts. In effect, sodomy laws tend to encourage extortion and abuse between married couples, are contrary to what is found recommended in most marriage manuals, and serve only to aggravate the problems of homosexuals.

1237   SHERWIN, ROBERT VEIT. "Some Legal Aspects of Homosexuality." *International Journal of Sexology* 4 (1, 1950): 22–25.

Although there are no statutes in any of the states which make being a homosexual a crime, the means of sexual expression which are characteristic of the homosexual are considered criminal: *per anum, per os,* mutual masturbation, and cunnilingus between women. The problems of the homosexual are hardly solved by imprisonment. It is maintained that a person does not force a homosexual relationship on someone not so inclined, and if he does not seduce minors, nor consummate his relationship in public, there is no purpose in imprisoning him. The laws should be changed, and the homosexual should be given psychiatric treatment.

1238   SIMON, CARLETON. "Homosexualists and Sex Crimes." Presented before the International Association of Chiefs of Police at Duluth, Minnesota, September 21–25, 1947, 8 pp.

Although arrests of sexual offenders have greatly increased, society has done little to eradicate the evils described in biblical times. The causes of sexual deviation, primarily homosexuality, are traced to two sources:

hereditary, the most important cause and one which makes it possible for a person to possess the organs of one sex and the mind of the other, and early emotional conflicts or trauma, which can be cured. Various sexual perversions are discussed in relation to crime.

The California law on sexual crimes is highly recommended. It classifies three types of criminals and their appropriate treatment: the psychopath, who is sent to prison; the sexual psychopath, who is sent to an insane asylum; and the psychopathic delinquent, who is sent to an institution for mental defectives.

1239   SLOVENKO, RALPH. "Homosexuality and the Law." *Medical Aspects of Human Sexuality* 1 (1, 1967): 35–38.

Law enforcement is more lenient than public opinion on the question of homosexuality. It is reported that one poll shows two out of three Americans viewing homosexuality with disgust. The present laws are very old and only two states do not consider homosexuality a crime. But in the main, enforcement of homosexual statutes is lenient, concerning itself with public displays. Usually the offender is fined and not sent to jail, which has not proved effective as a deterrent. More and more district attorneys are referring homosexuals to psychiatrists and mental health clinics, instead of charging and prosecuting them.

1240   SLOVENKO, RALPH, ed. *Sexual Behavior and the Law.* Springfield, Ill.: Charles C. Thomas, 1965, 886 pp.

Stressing the legal codes which apply to specific types of sexual deviance, this collection of articles represents the legal and psychiatric approach to sexual behavior. It covers such topics as the psychoanalytic theory of sexuality, morality, race, military law, abortion, homosexuality, pornography, victims, prostitution, et cetera. The conclusion is that the law is ambiguous and vacillating simply because it reflects our attitudes toward sex.

See Bowman, Karl M., and Engle, Bernice (no. 1136). Knight, Edward H. (no. 186). Sherwin, Robert Veit (no. 1238). Socarides, Charles W. (no. 807). West, Louis Jolyon, and Glass, Albert J. (no. 1122).

1241   SÖDDY, KENNETH. "Homosexuality." *Lancet* 267 (6837, 1954): 541–546.

Society needs to learn to distinguish between socially useful and socially harmful forms of homosexuality. It also needs to make improvements in the area of mental hygiene, especially in regard to sexual problems, and to take action to prevent the corruption of susceptible parties. There is little hope for treating homosexuals, but they should not be imprisoned. Laws against homosexual behavior should be repealed, except for acts performed in public.

1242   STANLEY-JONES, D. "Justice and the Homosexual." *Medical Press* 229 (1, 1953): 7–9.

The treatment which homosexuals receive in the courts is often inconsistent and unreasonable. The application of the law varies in different parts of Great Britain, as do the attitudes of judges toward homosexuals. Very severe penalties are often imposed upon men who have been useful, responsible citizens of their communities for years, while persons whose acts indicate a violent, psychotic personality are sometimes shown remarkable leniency. The correction of this situation will come about when the public is educated to the facts concerning homosexuality and the judicial system.

1243   STÜRUP, GEORG K. "Correctional Treatment and the Criminal Sexual Offender." *Canadian Journal of Corrections* 3 (1961): 250–265.

Statistics about recidivism rates are presented in this discussion of the treatment of sexual offenders in a correctional institution. On the basis of a criminological investigation of Danish sexual offenders convicted for sexual offenses from 1929–1939, it was found that of the 2,934 cases included in the investigation, 2,280 had received no further sentence, 10 percent had been sentenced for new sexual offenses, and 14.5 percent had been sentenced for other offenses only.

Different types of sex offenders have different recidivist rates. It seems to be highest for persons who have committed indecent acts against boys and for exhibitionists. First offenders of the homosexual group have a recidivist rate of 12.9 percent and the percentage rises to 17 percent for former recidivists. Comparable statistics for exhibitionists are 12.4 percent for first offenders and 31.2 percent for former recidivists.

1244   STÜRUP, GEORG K. "Sex Offenses: The Scandinavian Experience." *Law and Contemporary Problems* 25 (2, 1960): 361–375.

A legalistic discussion of sex offenses in Scandinavia is presented. Homosexuality there is punishable only when one of the parties is under 18 years of age, and even then punishment may be dispensed with, if both parties are of the same age.

1245   SYMONDS, JOHN ADDINGTON. "A Problem in Modern Ethics." 1896. Reprinted in *Homosexuality: A Cross Cultural Approach*, edited by Donald Webster Cory, pp. 3–100. New York: Julian Press, 1956.

In one of the early considerations of the ethics of homosexuality, it is argued that "abnormal inclinations" (homosexuality) are often congenital, natural, and ineradicable, that legislation neither suppresses nor increases homosexuality, that legal penalties encourage blackmail, and that for these reasons England should reconsider the laws restricting adult freedom with respect to homosexuality.

1246 SZASZ, THOMAS S. *Law, Liberty, and Psychiatry: An Inquiry into the Social Uses of Mental Health Practices.* New York: Macmillan, 1963, 281 pp.

Attention centers upon the issue of promoting and enforcing mental health and the controls under which psychiatric power should operate to preserve moral values and personal liberty. The legal status of homosexual practice as an "unnatural" act, illegal even between consenting adults, is presented as evidence that contemporary American mental health legislation, which seeks to supervise closely people's personal conduct, is moving away from the ethic of personal autonomy and responsibility.

1247 SZASZ, THOMAS S. "Legal and Moral Aspects of Homosexuality." In *Sexual Inversion: The Multiple Roots of Homosexuality,* edited by Judd Marmor, pp. 124–139. New York: Basic Books, 1965.

Homosexuality must not be written off as a medical problem, but must be faced as a moral and legal problem as well. It is a democratic dilemma— a question of how much diversity will be allowed. Just as intellectual self-discipline can be achieved only through intellectual freedom, sexual self-discipline cannot be promoted by the present methods of "heterosexual titillation with dread and prohibition of specific sexual acts."

1248 TAPPAN, PAUL W. "Some Myths about the Sex Offender." *Federal Probation* 19 (2, 1955): 7–12.

Eleven popular but erroneous views about the sex offender are discussed. It is pointed out that the public has been deceived into thinking that murder is commonly committed by "sex fiends." Actually the great majority of the sex deviates are minor offenders; many such offenses never come to official attention at all. It is estimated, for instance, that there are three million homosexual acts performed in the United States for every conviction for homosexuality in our courts.

It is a gross exaggeration to suggest that the person who has been sexually attacked shall be "ruined for life." Much harm is done by the attitudes of public officials and the relatives and friends of the victim. Studies made in other societies reveal that incest, rape, and homosexuality do not produce the effects that are experienced in our country. Furthermore, in many preliterate societies these acts are considered typical events.

It is believed that sex offenders tend to fall back into prior habits, but this study reveals that sex offenders have one of the lowest rates as "repeaters" of all types of crime. Those who do relapse are minor offenders, such as voyeurs, exhibitionists, and homosexuals.

It is important to realize that most of the sex deviates treated under the law are undersexed and are not, contrary to popular belief, oversexed individuals. Sexual deficiency, for example, is characteristic of exhibitionists, voyeurs, and passive homosexuals.

1249   ULLERSTAM, LARS. *The Erotic Minorities.* New York: Grove Press, 1966, 172 pp.

The current situation in Sweden is emphasized in a plea for better social and legal treatment of persons whose sexual lives deviate from the norm. Some reference to the United States is also made.

The chapter on homosexuality emphasizes the legal situation and includes a discussion of various theories of the etiology of homosexuality, physiological treatments, a cross-cultural comparison of attitudes toward homosexuality, and an estimation of the extent of overt homosexual practice.

1250   UNGER, H. R. "Some Aspects of Criminal Homosexuals in New Zealand." Essay presented in partial requirement for the Diploma of Social Science, University of New Zealand, [1954], 31 pp.

On October 20, 1954, the current case records in the New Zealand prison system were examined, and the files of 55 inmates incarcerated for homosexuality were studied. In general, prisoners convicted of homosexual activity with preadolescents or adolescents as partners were unskilled laborers who were more apt to have been under the influence of alcohol when the offense was committed, and were more likely to have been convicted previously for a similar offense. Twenty-seven of the 55 prisoners were reared in homes where at least one of the parents was absent; 23 had been married; 31 were prison repeaters. Four case studies are given.

1251   WALKER, KENNETH. "Homosexual Law Reform." 1960. Reprinted in *The Third Sex,* edited by Isadore Rubin, pp. 107–111. New York: New Book Co., 1961.

An account of the establishment in Great Britain of the Homosexual Law Reform Society is given by its first chairman. The Society was initiated to assist in the implementation of the Wolfenden Report. Very little beyond stimulating debate has been accomplished.

1252 WILDEBLOOD, PETER. *Against the Law.* London: Weidenfeld & Nicolson, 1955, 189 pp.

The author, a diplomatic correspondent of the London *Daily Mail,* was one of the central figures in the "Montagu Case," the homosexual scandal which was one of the factors in the British government's decision to set up a committee to investigate the problem of homosexuality and the English law. The author gives an account of his life, of the circumstances surrounding the trial in the Montagu Case, his imprisonment, and his return to freedom. It is a simple straightforward account pleading throughout for legal reform with regard to the treatment of homosexuals.

1253 ZARRILLI, CANIO LOUIS. "A Critical Analysis of the Royal Commission Report on Homosexuality and Prostitution." In *Crime in America: Controversial Issues in Twentieth Century Criminology,* edited by Herbert A. Bloch, pp. 258–281. New York: Philosophical Library, 1961.

The report of the Departmental Committee on Homosexual Offenses and Prostitution (also known as the Wolfenden Committee) is analyzed in regard to methodology, findings, and salient recommendations from the viewpoint of the basic principles which underlie legislation in the field of homosexuality; the relationship of science, medicine, and psychiatry to law; and the problem of legislation concerning homosexuality and the problems which arise in the attempt to formulate specific laws dealing with homosexuality. The Report is seen as opening up a variety of fields of exploration and as an example of the sociological and scientific approach to the problem of legislation and justice. Proposals based upon the findings of the Wolfenden Committee Report are made with respect to their possible application to the United States.

CROSS–REFERENCES

Allen, Clifford. "The Aging Homosexual." 1959. Reprinted in *The Third Sex,* edited by Isadore Rubin, pp. 91–95. New York: New Book Co., 1961. No. 810.

The Armed Services and Homosexuality. Essays on Homosexuality, No. 1. San Francisco: Society for Individual Rights, 1968 [12 pp.]. No. 953.

Auerback, A. "Understanding Sexual Deviations, 2. Homosexuality." *Postgraduate Medicine* 43 (Mar., 1968): 169–173. No. 96.

Bailey, Derrick Sherwin. *Homosexuality and the Western Christian Tradition.* London: Longmans, Green, 1955, 181 pp. No. 1051.

Beggs, Keith Siddons. "Some Legal, Social and Psychiatric Aspects of Homosexual Behavior: A Guide for the Social Worker in the Sex Clinic." Master's thesis, University of Wisconsin, 1950, 298 pp. No. 955.

Bennet, E. A. "The Social Aspects of Homosexuality." *Medical Press* 217 (Sept. 3, 1947): 207–210. No. 1056.

Berg, Charles. "The Problem of Homosexuality." *American Journal of Psychotherapy* 10 (4, 1956): 696–708; 11 (1, 1957): 65–79. No. 305.

Berg, Charles, and Allen, Clifford. *The Problem of Homosexuality.* New York: Citadel Press, 1958, 221 pp. No. 103.

Bluestone, Harvey; O'Malley, Edward P.; and Connell, Sydney. "Homosexuals in Prison." *Corrective Psychiatry and Journal of Social Therapy* 12 (1, 1966): 13–24. No. 957.

Bouchal, M., and Bártová, D. "The Attitude of Homosexuals after the Change in the Criminal Code." *Activitas Nervosa Superior* 6 (1964): 100–101. No. 660.

Byrne, Thomas R., Jr., and Mulligan, Francis M. " 'Psychopathic Personality' and 'Sexual Deviation': Medical Terms or Legal Catch-Alls—Analysis of the Status of the Homosexual Alien." *Temple Law Quarterly* 40 (4, 1967): 328–347. No. 340.

Candidus. *The Nature of Man: The Problem of Homosexuality.* Cambridge: Deighton, Bell, 1954, 7 pp. No. 342.

Cantor, Donald J. "The Homosexual Revolution: A Status Report." 1967. Reprinted in *Social Progress* 58 (2, 1967): 5–12. No. 818.

Cavan, Sherri. *Liquor License: An Ethnography of Bar Behavior.* Chicago: Aldine Publishing Co., 1966, 246 pp. No. 820.

Churchill, Wainwright. *Homosexual Behavior Among Males: A Cross-Cultural and Cross-Species Investigation.* New York: Hawthorn Books, 1967, 340 pp. No. 122.

Coburn, Vincent P. "Homosexuality and the Invalidation of Marriage." *Jurist* 20 (4, 1960): 441–459. No. 821.

Craft, Michael. "Boy Prostitutes and Their Fate." *British Journal of Psychiatry* 112 (492, 1966): 1111–1114. No. 830.

East, W. Norwood. "Homosexuality." *Medical Press* 217 (Sept. 3, 1947): 215–217. No. 130.

East, W. Norwood; Mackwood, John Charsley; Fairfield, Letitia; and Roberts, G. D. "The Sociological Aspects of Homosexuality." *Medico-Legal Journal* 15 (1, 1947): 11–23. No. 1070.

Eglinton, J. Z. *Greek Love.* New York: Oliver Layton Press, 1964, 504 pp. No. 834.

Foxe, Arthur N. "Psychoanalysis of a Sodomist." *American Journal of Orthopsychiatry* 11 (1, 1941): 133–142. No. 693.

Frey, Egon C. "Dreams of Male Homosexuals and the Attitude of Society." *Journal of Individual Psychology* 18 (1, 1962): 26–34. No. 400.

Gerassi, John. *The Boys of Boise: Furor, Vice, and Folly in an American City.* New York: Macmillan, 1966, 328 pp. No. 1074.

Giese, Hans. "Differences in the Homosexual Relations of Man and Woman." *International Journal of Sexology* 7 (4, 1954): 225–227. No. 414.

Gilbert, G. M. "Crime and Punishment: An Exploratory Comparison of Public,

Criminal, and Penological Attitudes." *Mental Hygiene* 42 (4, 1958): 550–557. No. 1075.

Gilbert, S. F. "Homosexuality and Hypnotherapy." *British Journal of Medical Hypnotism* 5 (3, 1954): 2–7. No. 415.

Glover, Edward, ed. *The Problem of Homosexuality.* London: Institute for the Study and Treatment of Delinquency, 1957, 40 pp. No. 1076.

Glover, Edward. "Sexual Disorders and Offenses, I. The Social and Legal Aspects of Sexual Abnormality. [1956. Reprinted.] II. The Problem of Male Homosexuality." In his *The Roots of Crime.* pp. 173–243. New York: International Universities Press, 1960. No. 153.

Glover, Edward. "The Social and Legal Aspects of Sexual Abnormality." *Medico-Legal and Criminological Review* 13 (3, 1945): 133–148. No. 419.

Glueck, Bernard C., Jr. "An Evaluation of the Homosexual Offender." *Minnesota Law Review* 41 (2, 1957): 187–210. No. 420.

Gross, Alfred A. *Strangers in Our Midst.* Washington: Public Affairs Press, 1962, 182 pp. No. 1077.

Gross, Alfred A. "Understanding the Homosexual." *National Probation and Parole Association Journal* 1 (2, 1955): 140–147. No. 1079.

Group for the Advancement of Psychiatry. Committee on Cooperation with Governmental Agencies. "Report on Homosexuality with Particular Emphasis on This Problem in Governmental Agencies." *Report of the Group for the Advancement of Psychiatry* 30 (1955): 1–7. No. 158.

Hegeler, Inge, and Hegeler, Sten. "Homosexual, Homosexuality." In their *An ABZ of Love,* pp. 121–131. Translated by David Hohnen. Copenhagen: Chr. Erichsen's Forlag, 1962. No. 854.

Hoffman, Martin. *The Gay World: Male Homosexuality and the Social Creation of Evil.* New York: Basic Books, 1968, 212 pp. No. 855.

"Homosexuality and Moral Welfare." *Lancet* 266 (6810, 1954): 505–506. No. 1084.

"Homosexuality and Prostitution." *British Medical Journal* (4954, 1955): 1492–1493, and *British Medical Journal Supplement* (2656, 1955): 165–170. No. 452.

Homosexuality and Prostitution: A Memorandum of Evidence Prepared by a Special Committee of the Council of the British Medical Association for Submission to the Departmental Committee on Homosexuality and Prostitution. London: British Medical Association, 1955, 94 pp. No. 21.

Hooker, Evelyn. "Homosexuality: Summary of Studies." In *Sex Ways in Fact and Faith: Bases for Christian Family Policy,* edited by Evelyn M. Duvall and Sylvanus M. Duvall, pp. 166–183. New York: Association Press, 1961. No. 1260.

Kling, Samuel G. "Homosexual Behavior." In his *Sexual Behavior and the Law,* pp. 97–128. New York: Bernard Geis Associates, 1965. No. 870.

Knight, Edward H. "Overt Male Homosexuality." In *Sexual Behavior and the Law,* edited by Ralph Slovenko, pp. 434–461. Springfield, Ill.: Charles C. Thomas, 1965. No. 186.

Learoyd, C. G. "The Problem of Homosexuality." *Practitioner* 172 (1030, 1954): 355–363. No. 1092.

Legman, Gershon; Lea, Henry Charles; Wright, Thomas; Witt, George H.; Tennent, James; and Dugdale, William. *The Guilt of the Templars.* New York: Basic Books, 1966, 308 pp. No. 998.

Legg, W. Dorr. "Blackmailing the Homosexual." *Sexology* 33 (8, 1967): 554–556. No. 872.

Lieberman, Daniel, and Siegel, Benjamin A. "A Program for 'Sexual Psychopaths' in a State Mental Hospital." *American Journal of Psychiatry* 113 (Mar., 1957): 801–807. No. 725.

Lindner, Robert. *Must You Conform?* New York: Rinehart & Co., 1956, 210 pp. No. 491.

Ludovici, Anthony. "Homosexuality, the Law and Public Sentiment." With a commentary by Clifford Allen. *International Journal of Sexology* 5 (3, 1951–1952): 143–150. No. 1095.

Magee, Bryan. *One in Twenty: A Study of Homosexuality in Men and Women.* London: Secker & Warburg, 1966, 192 pp. No. 878.

"Male Homosexuality." *Lancet* 269 (6884, 1955): 291–293. No. 203.

Marks, Ben. "Homosexuality." *Harper Hospital Bulletin* 26 (5, 1968): 242–247. No. 204.

Marmor, Judd. "Homosexuality." *Student Personnel Newsletter, State University College, Buffalo* 1 (3, 1967): 15–34. No. 205.

Marmor, Judd, ed. *Sexual Inversion: The Multiple Roots of Homosexuality.* New York: Basic Books, 1965, 358 pp. No. 206.

Mason, Stephen C.; Jacob, Joseph S.; Himler, Leonard E.; Gould, Stuart M.; and Bird, H. Waldo. "Homosexuality: A Medico-Legal Problem." *Journal of the Michigan State Medical Society* 60 (5, 1961): 635–638. No. 734.

Masters, R. E. L. *Forbidden Sexual Behavior and Morality: An Objective Re-examination of Perverse Sex Practices in Different Cultures.* New York: Julian Press, 1962, 431 pp. No. 1008.

Mazur, Ronald M. *Commonsense Sex.* Boston: Beacon Press, 1968, 109 pp. No. 1101.

Moore, Thomas V. "The Pathogenesis and Treatment of Homosexual Disorders: A Digest of Some Pertinent Evidence." *Journal of Personality* 14 (1945): 47–83. No. 213.

Morse, Benjamin. *The Homosexual: A Frank Study of Abnormal Sex Life Among Males.* Derby, Conn.: Monarch Press, 1962, 158 pp. No. 884.

Needham, Merrill A., and Schur, Edwin M. "Student Punitiveness toward Sexual Deviation." *Marriage and Family Living* 25 (2, 1963): 227–229. No. 1103.

Neustatter, W. Lindesay. "Sex and Its Problems, XI. The Medical Aspects of Homosexuality." *Practitioner* 199 (1193, 1967): 704–710. No. 516.

Neustatter, W. Lindesay. "Sexual Abnormalities and the Sexual Offender." *Medico-Legal Journal* 29 (4, 1961): 190–199. No. 749.

Norton, Howard. *The Third Sex.* Portland, Ore.: Facts Publishing Co., 1949, 112 pp. No. 887.

"Notes on Homosexuality: Excerpts from a Consultation." *Social Progress: A Journal of Church and Society* 58 (2, 1967): 26–30. No. 521.

O'Grady, Gerald B., Jr., et al. "Should Homosexual Behavior between Consenting Adults Be Considered a Crime?" Viewpoints: A Special Feature Presenting a

Wide Range of Divergent Opinions on Controversial Issues Relating to Sexuality. *Medical Aspects of Human Sexuality* 1 (2, 1967): 39–50. No. 1105.

"Origins of Homosexuality." *British Medical Journal* (5470, 1965): 1077–1078. No. 220.

"The Other Side: Living with Homosexuality." *Canadian Medical Association Journal* 86 (May 12, 1962): 875–878. No. 888.

Plummer, Douglas. *Queer People: The Truth about Homosexuals.* London: W. H. Allen, 1963, 122 pp. No. 890.

Roberts, Aymer. *Judge Not.* London: Linden Press, 1957, 195 pp. No. 1110.

Roche, Philip Q. "Sexual Deviations." *Federal Probation* 14 (3, 1950): 3–11. No. 1111.

Rooney, Elizabeth A., and Gibbons, Don C. "Social Reactions to 'Crimes without Victims.'" *Social Problems* 13 (4, 1966): 400–410. No. 1112.

R[ubin], I[sadore], ed. "Sex Society Forum on Homosexuality." *Sexology* 26 (3, 1959): 169. No. 541.

Savitsch, Eugene de. *Homosexuality, Transvestism, and Change of Sex.* Springfield, Ill.: Charles C. Thomas, 1958, 120 pp. No. 55.

Schofield, Michael George. "Social Aspects of Homosexuality." *British Journal of Venereal Diseases* 40 (2, 1964): 129–134. No. 905.

Schur, Edwin M. *Crimes Without Victims—Deviant Behavior and Public Policy: Abortion, Homosexuality, and Drug Addiction.* Englewood Cliffs, N. J.: Prentice-Hall, 1965, 180 pp. No. 907.

Spencer, J. C. "Contributions to the Symposium on Sexual Deviation." *Canadian Journal of Corrections* 3 (1961): 481–484. No. 574.

Stearn, Jess. *The Sixth Man.* Garden City, N. Y.: Doubleday & Co., 1961, 286 pp. No. 913.

Taylor, F. H. "Homosexual Offences and Their Relation to Psychotherapy." *British Medical Journal* (4526, 1947): 525–529. No. 781.

Van den Haag, Ernest. "Notes on Homosexuality and Its Cultural Setting." Reprinted in *The Problem of Homosexuality in Modern Society,* edited by Hendrik M. Ruitenbeek, pp. 291–302. New York: E. P. Dutton & Co., 1963. No. 1119.

Voltaire. "The Love Called 'Socrates.'" From Voltaire's *Philosophical Dictionary.* Translated by Donald Webster Cory. In *Homosexuality: A Cross Cultural Approach,* edited by Donald Webster Cory, pp. 350–353. New York: Julian Press, 1956. No. 1029.

Walker, Kenneth. "The Making of a Homosexual." *Sexology* 30 (1, 1963): 8–9. No. 1030.

Waring, Paul, and Bryce, Dean Travis. *Homosexual Freedom.* N.p.: The Authors, 1961, 26 pp. No. 1120.

West, D. J. *Homosexuality.* Chicago: Aldine Publishing Co., 1968, 304 pp. No. 922.

West, D. J. "Homosexuality: A Social Problem." *Sexology* 23 (1, 1956): 22–28. No. 923.

West, D. J. *The Other Man: A Study of the Social, Legal and Clinical Aspects of Homosexuality.* New York: Whiteside and William Morrow & Co., 1955, 224 pp. No. 924.

West, Louis Jolyon; Doidge, William Thomas; and Williams, Robert L. "An Approach to the Problem of Homosexuality in Military Services." *American Journal of Psychiatry* 115 (5, 1958): 392–401. No. 1033.

West, Louis Jolyon, and Glass, Albert J. "Sexual Behavior and the Military Law." In *Sexual Behavior and the Law,* edited by Ralph Slovenko, pp. 250–272. Springfield, Ill.: Charles C. Thomas, 1965. No. 1122.

Westwood, Gordon. *A Minority: A Report on the Life of the Male Homosexual in Great Britain.* London: Longmans, Green, 1960, 216 pp. No. 925.

Wheeler, Stanton. "Sex Offenses: A Sociological Critique." *Law and Contemporary Problems* 25 (2, 1960): 258–278. No. 1123.

Wolfenden, John. "Evolution of British Attitudes toward Homosexuality." *American Journal of Psychiatry* 125 (6, 1968): 792–797. No. 1126.

Wolfson, William. "Factors Associated with the Adjustment on Probation of One Hundred Sex Deviates." Master's thesis, College of the City of New York, 1948, 105 pp. No. 606.

Yalom, Irvin D. "Group Therapy of Incarcerated Sexual Deviants." *Journal of Nervous and Mental Disease* 132 (2, 1961): 158–170. No. 799.

FEMALE

1254   "Lesbianism as Cruelty." *British Medical Journal* (4524, 1947): 472.

A British legal action is reported (*Gardner* v. *Gardner,* 1947 1 ALL E.R. 630) in which the flagrant practice of lesbianism was accepted as sufficient grounds for divorce. The case set a precedent since prior to this lesbian acts were not considered sufficient grounds for the legal dissolution of a marriage.

CROSS–REFERENCES

Allen, Clifford. "The Aging Homosexual." 1959. Reprinted in *The Third Sex,* edited by Isadore Rubin, pp. 91–95. New York: New Book Co., 1961. No. 810.

Auerback, A. "Understanding Sexual Deviations, 2. Homosexuality." *Postgraduate Medicine* 43 (Mar., 1968): 169–173. No. 96.

Bennet, E. A. "The Social Aspects of Homosexuality." *Medical Press* 217 (Sept. 3, 1947): 207–210. No. 1056.

Caprio, Frank S. *Female Homosexuality: A Psychodynamic Study of Lesbianism.* New York: Citadel Press, 1954, 334 pp. Chapter 16. "Therapeutic Management: Preventive Measures," pp. 285–298. Reprinted as "Preventive Measures." In *Carol in a Thousand Cities,* edited by Ann Aldrich, pp. 153–166. Greenwich, Conn.: Fawcett Publications, 1960. No. 626.

Cory, Donald Webster. *The Lesbian in America.* New York: Citadel Press, 1964, 288 pp. No. 934.

Daniel, Suzan. "The Homosexual Woman in Present Day Society." *International Journal of Sexology* 7 (4, 1954): 223–224. No. 936.

East, W. Norwood; Mackwood, John Charsley; Fairfield, Letitia; and Roberts, G.

D. "The Sociological Aspects of Homosexuality." *Medico-Legal Journal* 15 (1, 1947): 11–23. No. 1070.

Glover, Edward. *"Homosexuality and Prostitution:* A Review." *British Journal of Delinquency* 6 (4, 1956): 315–317. No. 1167.

Grad, Frank P. "The A.L.I. Model Penal Code." *NPPA Journal* 4 (2, 1958): 127–138. No. 1168.

"Homosexuality and Moral Welfare." *Lancet* 266 (6810, 1954): 505–506. No. 1084.

Hughes, Graham. "Consent in Sexual Offences." *Modern Law Review* 25 (6, 1962): 672–686. No. 1188.

MacKenzie, D. F. "Homosexuality and the Justice Department." *New Zealand Medical Journal* 66 (423, 1967): 745–748. No. 1200.

Magee, Bryan. *One in Twenty: A Study of Homosexuality in Men and Women.* London: Secker & Warburg, 1966, 192 pp. No. 878.

"Male and Female Homosexuality." *British Medical Journal* (4442, 1946): 748. No. 1202.

Morse, Benjamin. *The Lesbian: A Frank, Revealing Study of Women Who Turn to Their Own Sex for Love.* Derby, Conn.: Monarch Books, 1961, 142 pp. No. 942.

Norton, Howard. *The Third Sex.* Portland, Ore.: Facts Publishing Co., 1949, 112 pp. No. 887.

Reiss, Albert J., Jr. "Sex Offenses: The Marginal Status of the Adolescent." *Law and Contemporary Problems* 25 (Spring, 1960): 309–333. No. 1223.

Schur, Edwin M. *Crimes Without Victims—Deviant Behavior and Public Policy: Abortion, Homosexuality, and Drug Addiction.* Englewood Cliffs, N. J.: Prentice-Hall, 1965, 180 pp. No. 907.

Sherwin, Robert Veit. "The Law and Sexual Relationships." *Journal of Social Issues* 22 (2, 1966): 109–122. No. 1234.

Sherwin, Robert Veit. "Some Legal Aspects of Homosexuality." *International Journal of Sexology* 4 (1, 1950): 22–25. No. 1237.

OTHER BIBLIOGRAPHIES
AND DICTIONARIES

1255 BLAU, SIDNEY. *Male Homosexuality: A Topical Annotated Bibliography, 1955–60.* Mimeographed. 1961, 57 pp.

In a selected bibliography of 108 articles and books concerned with male homosexuality, items are drawn from the fields of religion, law, psychiatry, psychology, and social work. The items are classified under 12 major divisions with cross-references. The annotations are brief and objective, reflecting the language and outlook of the individual authors. There is no table of contents, but an author index which includes the full citation is provided.

1256 DAMON, GENE, and STUART, LEE, eds. *The Lesbian in Literature: A Bibliography.* San Francisco: Daughters of Bilitis, 1967, 79 pp.

"An alphabetical listing by author of all known books in the English language, in the general field of literature, concerned with lesbianism, or having lesbian characters. . . . includes novels, short stories, short novels, poems, drama and fictionalized biography." A simple coding system is used in the bibliography to indicate the amount and type of lesbian material included, as well as the quality of the lesbian content in the works. Works which are still available and in print, including those printed through 1966, are included. Supplements to be published at two-year intervals are anticipated. The editors have tried to avoid personal prejudices and value judgments. Full imprint information is included for each item.

1257 FOSTER, JEANNETTE HOWARD. *Sex Variant Women in Literature: A Historical and Quantitative Survey.* New York: Vantage Press, 1956, 412 pp.

The aim of this bibliographical survey is "to trace historically the quantity and temper of imaginative writing on its chosen subject from earliest times to the present day, on the assumption that what has been written and read for pleasure is a fair index of popular interest and social attitude from one century to another." The emphasis is on belles-lettres, mainly poetry, drama, and fiction, with a limited inclusion of biography and memoirs. Coverage extends from ancient times, beginning with Sappho, through the 20th century, and includes works written in English, French, or German. For each variant woman, the following points are noted wherever possible: physical appearance and temperament, emotional history, social reactions to her as expressed or implied within her milieu, and her own personal attitude. A subject index and three-part bibliography are included.

1258   GARDE, NOEL I. *The Homosexual in Literature: A Chronological Bibliography Circa 700 B.C.–1958.* New York: Village Press, 1959, 32 pp.

"This bibliography provides a chronological listing of all known books in the English language, in the general field of fiction, concerned with male homosexuality, or having homosexual characters. It includes novels, short stories, short novels, poems, drama and fictionalized biography, plus a few other minor categories." The list contains two sections, primary and other than primary, according to the predominance of homosexual material included in the work, as well as a simple coding system which refers to the amount of homosexual material found in a given work. The order of arrangement is chronological by years, alphabetical by author's surname within the same year, and numbered consecutively. Imprint information includes place, publisher, and date. In the case of reprints, the original publication date is given, as well as full imprint information on the reprint edition. Five special indexes are by national locales; special locales; professions and special occupations; special roles, types, situations, and relationships of interest; and well-known authors.

1259   *The Guild Dictionary of Homosexual Terms.* Washington, D. C.: Guild Press, 1965, 51 pp.

Including terms found in fiction, scientific works, and in the literature of the homophile movement, the dictionary is intended for current usage. Although the theme of homosexuality is widely found in novels, short stories, plays, newspaper articles, and radio and TV programs, the average reader does not understand and may misinterpret the language. The editor's aim is to produce "a handy reference work," which will be revised every two years, for the use of the contemporary reader.

1260   HOOKER, EVELYN. "Homosexuality: Summary of Studies." In *Sex Ways in Fact and Faith: Bases for Christian Family Policy,* edited by

Evelyn M. Duvall and Sylvanus M. Duvall, pp. 166–183. New York: Association Press, 1961.

A brief summary of studies and an annotated bibliography are presented as an introductory guide for further reading. Problems of definition, prevalence, theories of causation, legal aspects, and prevention and treatment are covered. Various causal theories are presented. Conflicting opinions as to whether or not homosexuality is a psychiatric abnormality and illness are reviewed.

1261 *The Lavender Lexicon: Dictionary of Gay Words and Phrases.* San Francisco: Strait & Associates, 1964 [20 pp.].

Most of the words included in this particular book are taken from the gay society, having been collected from those who frequent the gay bars, coffee shops, and other gathering places. They may therefore be unknown to the isolated homosexual. "Gay" is defined as "that element of society, predominantly homosexually oriented, who make up a 'night life' or a society of some continuity based on common acceptance of each other's sexual expressions." A brief introduction also defines the term "homosexual" and comments on the sexual laws of the United States. Words which may have regular usage in ordinary society are defined according to their particular usage among the gay society. A brief addendum of technical terms is included.

1262 LEGG, W. DORR, and UNDERWOOD, J. M. *An Annotated Bibliography of Homosexuality.* Los Angeles, Calif.: Institute for the Study of Human Resources, 1967 [issued serially].

A bibliography made up of annotations of books and pamphlets employs a classification scheme which divides the items into two categories: those in which homosexuality is dealt with directly, and those in which homosexuality receives secondary treatment among other sex phenomena. The entries—classified under 11 broad headings such as biography, law, zoology, sexology, and philosophy—include author, title, place, date, and pagination. Appendices, indexes, and other bibliographies not yet completed are also indicated.

1263 PARKER, WILLIAM. *Homosexuality: Selected Abstracts and Bibliography.* San Francisco: Society for Individual Rights, 1966, 107 pp.

In a collection of abstracts of various books, articles, court cases, and documents dealing with homosexuality, a bibliographical list of additional materials pertaining to homosexuality is also included.

CROSS-REFERENCES

Cutler, Marvin, ed. *Homosexuals Today: A Handbook of Organizations and Publications.* Los Angeles: Publications Division of One, Inc., 1956, 188 pp. No. 831.
Wiedeman, George H. "Survey of Psychoanalytic Literature on Overt Male Homosexuality." *Journal of the American Psychoanalytic Association* 10 (2, 1962): 386 409. No. 601.

Author Index

Subject Index

The Index refers to annotation numbers.

Mother *(cont'd)*
    225, 244, 252, 254,
    255, 271, 314, 389
  erotic stimulation by, 219
  feared, 239
  fixation, 20, 89, 110, 151,
    195, 202, 248, 260,
    268, 489, 571, 676
  gender identity and, 147,
    149
  hostility toward, 67, 89,
    91–3, 232, 239, 269,
    288, 389
  as ideal, 109
  identification with, 132,
    140–2, 151, 208, 237,
    347, 403, 728
  instrumentality and ex-
    pressiveness, 208
  intimacy, inappropriate,
    105, 156
  Ishmael complex and, 159
  maternal age, 12, 23, 60
  neurotic, 88
  Oedipal and pre-Oedipal
    attachments *(see also*
    Oedipus complex),
    93, 95, 116, 140, 231,
    253, 259, 308, 312
  overprotective, 102, 135,
    213, 219, 1084
  penis envy of, 151
  preferred, 145, 177
  punitive, 132, 261
  regression to attachment
    to, 140, 248
  rejection by, 203
  seductive and/or posses-
    sive, 100, 127, 165,
    187, 454
  sex preference of, 145
  symbiosis, 127, 133, 149
  twins, preference for one
    of, 229
"Mother Complex in Literature, The" (Daly),
  543
Motivation, sexual, 257
Motivation therapy, 780
Movements, homophile *(see
  also* Organizations,
  homophile and
  homosexual), 1055
Mowrer, H., 157
Mutrux, S., 9
Myerson, A., 56
Myocardial infarction, 405

Mythology *(see also* Literature), 1027
  Greek, 1000, 1024

Narcissism, 116, 118, 127,
    180, 209, 337, 339,
    372, 429, 583, 605,
    695
  artistic, 507
  compulsive homosexual-
    ity, 149
  ego and, 115
  female homosexual, 268,
    626, 646
  group therapy, 760
  paranoid, 424, 540
Nationalism, as cultural
    homosexuality, 289
Near East *(see also place
    names),* 961, 1010,
    1011
  homosexuality, female,
    1039
  literature of, 1024
Nebraska, 1140
Negroes, *see* Blacks
Neurocognition, 33
Neurosis *(see also* Mental ill-
    ness; Psychological
    factors; Psychother-
    apy),* 15, 35, 42, 79,
    174, 194, 195, 235,
    247, 248, 309, 334,
    346, 355, 381, 466,
    500, 522, 528, 541,
    584, 586, 604, 656,
    952
  adult and infantile, corre-
    lation of, 419
  anxiety and, 174, 460
  castration anxiety, 140,
    165
  children, 101, 534
  concern, obsessive, with
    homosexuality, 614
  "counterfeit sex," 307
  creativity and, 543
  delinquents, 411, 534
  distance creation and, 234
  effeminacy, 446
  family relationships, 117,
    119, 174
  female homosexuality,
    118, 139, 140, 281,
    619, 625–8, 636, 637
  frustration and, 227
  group therapy, 760

  hysteria, 495
  identification, 480
  inadequacy, heterosexual,
    and, 227
  insecurity and, 139
  latent homosexuality, 457,
    952
  law and, 1229
  maternal, 88, 201
  Oedipal conflict and, 165
  paraphilias, 182
  parent relationships and,
    132
  passive-feminine man, 308
  personality, 429, 460
  perversion and, 15, 377,
    417, 514, 520
  psychoanalysis, 751
  psychotherapy, 88, 166,
    760, 778, 792
  sadism, 539
  sexual development and,
    118
  therapy, 123, 234, 514
Neustadt, R., 56
Neutrality, psychosexual, 33
New Guinea, 965
New York, 1183
New Zealand, 1200, 1250
Newspaper reporting, 823,
    1097
Nicotinic acid, 84
Nonwhites
  female homosexual, 933,
    945
  prison homosexuality, 992
Norms ("normality"), 126,
    675, 967, 1208
  growth and development
    and, 500, 675
  of heterosexuality ques-
    tioned, 1057
  morality and, 184
  sex deviations and, 126,
    184, 320, 349, 354,
    551, 718, 742, 842,
    1068, 1096
Norway, 1130, 1175
Nose, symbolism of, 549
Nudity, attitude toward,
    385, 625
Nuisances, public, 1078
Nurses, treatment and, 1087
Nymphomania, 1224, 1227

Obesity, 405
  covert sensitization, 667

72 73 74 75 10 9 8 7 6 5 4 3 2 1